MODERN BRITISH POETRY

New and Enlarged Edition

NEW AND ENLARGED EDITION

Modern British Poetry

EDITED BY *Louis Untermeyer*

HARCOURT, BRACE & WORLD, INC.
NEW YORK • BURLINGAME

Printed in the United States of America

Library of Congress Catalog Card Number: 62-12184

Four Seas Company for the selections from *War and Love* by Richard Aldington and *The Mountainy Singer* by Seasamh MacCathmhaoil (Joseph Campbell).

Laurence J. Gomme for the selections from *Verses,* copyright, 1916, by Hilaire Belloc.

Grove Press, Inc. for "In Love for Long," "The Animals," "The Good Man in Hell," "The Labyrinth," "The Combat," and "The Horses" from *Collected Poems of Edwin Muir,* published by Grove Press, Inc., copyright © 1957 by Edwin Muir.

Harcourt, Brace & World, Inc. for the selections from *Secrets,* copyright 1924, and *Selected Poems* by W. H. Davies; *The Contemplutive Quarry,* copyright 1921, by Anna Wickham; *The Unknown Goddess,* copyright 1925, by Humbert Wolfe; and *Awake! And Other Wartime Poems,* copyright 1942, by W. R. Rodgers; "Missing Dates," "This Last Pain," "Rolling the Lawn," "Just a Smack at Auden," and "Homage to the British Museum" from *Collected Poems,* copyright, 1935, 1940, 1949, by William Empson; "Naming of Parts," "Chard Whitlow," and "Sailor's Harbor" from *A Map of Verona and Other Poems,* copyright, 1947 by Henry Reed. All these poems reprinted by permission of Harcourt, Brace & World, Inc.

Harper & Brothers for the selections from *Hawthorn and Lavender* by W. E. Henley.

Harper's Magazine for "Under Which Lyre" by W. H. Auden.

William Heinemann for the selections from *Poems* by Isaac Rosenberg.

The Hogarth Press for the selections from *New Signatures* by W. H. Auden, and *A Time to Dance* by C. Day Lewis.

Henry Holt and Company for the selections from *Wild Earth,* copyright 1916, by Padraic Colum; *Peacock Pie,* copyright 1914, *The Listeners,* copyright 1916, *The Veil,* copyright 1922 and *Collected Poems,* copyright 1941, by Walter De la Mare; *A Shropshire Lad* and *Last Poems* by A. E. Housman; and *Poems,* copyright 1917, by Edward Thomas. Reprinted by permission of Henry Holt and Company.

Alfred A. Knopf, Inc. for the selections from *The Collected Poems of William H. Davies,* copyright 1916; *Cautionary Tales for Children* by Hilaire Belloc, *The Bad Child's Book of Beasts* by Hilaire Belloc; *The Waggoner* by Edmund Blunden; *Fairies and Fusiliers* by Robert Graves; *Argonaut and Juggernaut* by Osbert Sitwell; *Rustic Elegies* by Edith Sitwell, and *The Sleeping Beauty* by Edith Sitwell.

The Liveright Company for the selections from *Dublin Days,* copyright 1923, by L. A. G. Strong.

Longmans, Green & Co., Ltd. for "Canal Bank Walk," "The Self-Slaved," "The One," "Question to Life," and "Intimate Parnassus" from *Come Dance With Kitty Stobling and Other Poems,* copyright © 1960 by Patrick Kavanagh. Reprinted by permission of Patrick Kavanagh and the publishers.

The Macmillan Company for the selections from *Selected Poems* by "Æ" (George W. Russell), copyright 1935; *Creatures* by Padraic Colum, copyright 1927; *Fires* by Wilfrid Wilson Gibson, copyright 1912, and *Borderlands and Thoroughfares,* copyright 1915, by Wilfrid Wilson Gibson; *Collected Poems* by Thomas Hardy; *Poems* by Ralph Hodgson; *Good Friday and Other Poems,* copyright 1916, and *Salt-Water Ballads* by John Masefield; the passage (in this volume entitled "Rounding the Horn") from "Dauber" and two poems from *The Story of a Round-House* copyright 1913; and *Collected Poems,* copyright 1918, 1925, by John Masefield; *Saturday Market* by Charlotte Mew; *A Trophy of Arms,* copyright 1936, by Ruth Pitter, *A Mad Lady's Garland,* copyright 1935, by Ruth Pitter, *The Spirit Watches,* copyright 1940, by Ruth Pitter; *Collected Poems* by James Stephens, copyright 1926; *Poems* by William Butler Yeats, *Later Poems,* copyright 1924, by William Butler Yeats, *The Tower,* copyright 1928, by William Butler Yeats, and *Collected Poems,* copyright 1932, by William Butler Yeats. "The Second Coming" from *The Collected Poems of W. B. Yeats: Definitive Edition,* copyright 1924 by The Macmillan Company, renewed 1952 by Bertha Georgie Yeats. "Byzantium" and "A Dialogue of Self and Soul" from *The Collected Poems of W. B. Yeats: Definitive Edition,* copyright 1933 by The Macmillan Company and used with their permission. All these poems reprinted by permission of the publishers, The Macmillan Company.

Macmillan and Co., Ltd. (London) for the selections from *Collected Poems* by Thomas Hardy and *Late Lyrics and Earlier* by Thomas Hardy.

The Marvell Press for "Coming," "Next Please," "No Road," "Spring," "Arrivals," "Departures," and "Church Going" from *The Less Deceived* by Philip Larkin, copyright 1955, 1958 by The Marvell Press and reprinted by permission of The Marvell Press, Hessle, Yorkshire, England.

Elkin Matthews for the poem from *Chambers of Imagery* by Gordon Bottomley.

John Murray for "Inevitable," "Slough," "Arrest of Oscar Wilde," "Remorse," and "The Cottage Hospital" from *John Betjeman's Collected Poems,* copyright © John Betjeman 1958, published in the United States by Houghton Mifflin Company. Reprinted by permission of John Murray. For the selections from *Poetical Works* by Robert Bridges.

New Directions for the selections from *The World I Breathe,* copyright 1939, by Dylan Thomas, and *New Poems,* copyright 1943, by Dylan Thomas; *New Directions in Prose and Poetry: 1940; The New British Poets,* edited by Kenneth Rexroth; and *Sacred and Secular Elegies,* copyright 1943, by George Barker; for the selections from *Poems* by Wilfred Owen. "Do Not Go Gentle Into That Good Night" and "A Refusal to Mourn the Death by Fire of a Child in London" from *Collected Poems of Dylan Thomas.* Copyright 1939, 1942, 1946 by New Directions. Copyright 1952, 1953 by Dylan Thomas, © 1957 by New Directions. Reprinted by permission of New Directions.

Ivan Obolensky, Inc. for "The Crane," "The Jam Trap," and "In Defense of Metaphysics" from *Seeing Is Believing* by Charles Tomlinson, © 1958 by Charles Tomlinson. Reprinted by permission of the author and the publisher.

Oxford University Press for the selections from *The Poems of Gerard Manley Hopkins,* copyright 1918, 1930. Reprinted by permission of the Oxford University Press and the poet's family. Also for the selections from *Short Is the Time,* copyright 1940, 1943, by C. Day Lewis.

James B. Pinker for the selections from *Whipperginny* and for other poems by Robert Graves.

The Poetry Bookshop (London) for the selections from *Spring Morning* and *Autumn Midnight* by Frances Cornford; *The Farmer's Bride* and *The Rambling Sailor* by Charlotte Mew; *Strange Meetings, Children of Love,* and *Real Property* by Harold Monro. Also for the poems reprinted, with the authors' permissions, from the volumes of *Georgian Poetry.*

Random House, Inc. for the selections from *Poems,* copyright 1934, by W. H. Auden, *On This Island,* copyright 1937, by W. H. Auden, *Another Time,* copyright 1940, by W. H. Auden, *For the Time Being,* copyright 1944, by W. H. Auden, *The Collected Poetry of W. H. Auden,* copyright 1945; *Collected Poems,* copyright 1935, by C. Day Lewis; *Poems: 1925-1940,* copyright 1937, 1940, by Louis MacNeice, *Springboard,* copyright 1945, by Louis MacNeice; *Poems,* copyright 1934, by Stephen Spender; *The Still Centre,* copyright 1939, by Stephen Spender; *Ruins and Visions,* copyright 1942, by Stephen Spender; *Poems of Dedication,* copyright 1947, by Stephen Spender; *The Edge of Being,* copyright 1949, by Stephen Spender; and *The Complete Works of J. M. Synge.* Reprinted by permission of, and by special arrangement with, Random House, Inc.

Henry Reed for "The Auction Sale" from *Encounter.*

Grant Richards for the selections from *The Hundred and One Harlequins* by Sacheverell Sitwell.

Routledge & Kegan Paul Ltd. for "Greenwich Observatory," "William Yeats in Limbo," "Early Spring," "Neutrality," and "The Gardener" from *The Collected Poems of Sydney Keyes.* Copyright 1945, 1951. Reprinted by permission of the publisher.

Siegfried Sassoon for the selections from his *Selected Poems, Recreations,* and *Vigils.*

Charles Scribner's Sons for the selections from the *Collected Poems of Alice Meynell, Poems* by William Ernest Henley, and the works of Robert Louis Stevenson.

Martin Secker for the selections from *Collected Poems* by James Elroy Flecker.

Sidgwick and Jackson, Ltd. for the selections from *The Waggoner,* copyright 1920, by Edmund Blunden, and *The Dark Fire,* copyright 1918, by W. J. Turner.

Frederick A. Stokes Company for the selections from *Collected Poems by Alfred Noyes,* copyright 1906 by Alfred Noyes, copyright 1913, by Frederick A. Stokes Company.

The Vanguard Press for the selections from *The Song of the Cold,* copyright 1948, by Edith Sitwell.

The Viking Press, Inc. for the selections from *The Song of Lazarus* by Alex Comfort, copyright 1945 by Alex Comfort; *Chamber Music* by James Joyce, copyright 1918 by B. W. Huebsch, 1946 by Nora Joyce; *Amores* by D. H. Lawrence, copyright 1916 by David Herbert Lawrence, 1944 by Frieda Lawrence; *New Poems* by D. H. Lawrence, copyright 1920 by B. W. Huebsch, Inc., 1948 by Frieda Lawrence; *Look! We Have Come Through!* by D. H. Lawrence; *Collected Poems* by Siegfried Sassoon; *The Espalier* by Sylvia Townsend Warner, and *Time Importuned* by Sylvia Townsend Warner. "The Ship of Death" from *Last Poems* by D. H. Lawrence. Copyright 1933 by Frieda Lawrence. Reprinted by permission of The Viking Press, Inc.

Ann Watkins, Inc. for "Still Falls the Rain" from *Street Song,* copyright 1942, by Edith Sitwell, "Dirge for the New Sunrise" and "Song: Now That Fate Is Dead and Gone" from *The Song of the Cold,* copyright 1948 by Edith Sitwell.

A. P. Watt & Son for "To Bring the Dead to Life," "The White Goddess," "Cry Faugh!" and "To Juan at the Winter Solstice" from *Collected Poems 1955* by Robert Graves. © 1955 Roturman S. A. and published by Doubleday & Co., Inc.

Three of the posthumous poems of Thomas Hardy are reprinted by permission of Mrs. Hardy and Mr. Sidney Cockerell, his executors. The poems of James Elroy Flecker are reprinted by permission of his executors. The poems of Alice Meynell are reprinted with the consent of her husband, Wilfred Meynell. The poems of Harold Monro are reprinted with his consent and that of his widow, Alida Klemantaski, Mrs. Harold Monro. The poems of Charlotte Mew are reprinted with her consent and her executors'.

Foreword
to the New and Enlarged Edition

Since the first edition of this anthology was printed more than forty years ago, two world wars have shattered the security of mankind. The final results are still unpredictable. Instead of establishing peace, they created new battlefronts, quickened "cold" as well as fierce colonial wars, and intensified the spreading conflict of opposed ideologies throughout the world.

It is against this background that the new edition of *Modern British Poetry* has been prepared. As before, the editor aims to show the range of English poetry over a century which includes highly experimental as well as accomplished traditional writing. The emphasis is on reappraisal, so that the work is not only inclusive but critical. To accomplish this, it has been necessary to omit several interesting poets. The editor regrets the omissions, but comforts himself with the thought that even a work of encyclopedic dimensions would not be inclusive enough to satisfy every reader. Researchers and students of the period may find the omitted poets in earlier editions of this collection.

This edition has been revised still further. The biographical and bibliographical notes have been brought sharply up-to-date. The preface has been amplified. Recent innovations which attempt to extend the domain of poetry have been recorded. More than ever, the volume hopes to reflect the variety of experience and vision, the sense of discovery which is the essential power of poetry.

Although the editor believes he has favored no group, movement, or tendency at the expense of any other, he admits that he is less impressed by the repetition of accepted subjects and generally approved poetic formulas, however skillful, than by a distinctive inflection, even though it may lead to oddity, as in the case of Hopkins. This personal idiom, this "difference," may be difficult to define but it is impossible to mistake.

The choice of poems may seem willful to some, but the selection has not been arbitrary. The editor cannot pretend that he has infallibly chosen only the best, but he maintains that he has included nothing that does not represent some phase of the period and does not reveal some aspect of the poet. To achieve this he has mingled the well-known with the unfamiliar. A good poem remains a good poem no matter how often it has been reprinted, but its presence in anthologies is not necessarily a proof of its goodness. New blood is needed not only to quicken the life stream of culture but to keep it fresh and powerful.

It must be repeated that this collection is anything but a complete summary. Since the end of the Victorian era the work of the poets of England and Ireland has been so voluminous, the departures in form and subject matter have been so varied, that no editor would dare claim finality for his labors. Perhaps it is just as well; it might be asserted that finality, even if attainable, is undesirable. The duty of the anthologist, as one anthologist sees it, is to stimulate, not to satisfy, to whet the reader's appetite, not to surfeit it.

Such a collection as this, if its purpose is achieved, should excite the reader's curiosity and rouse him to a closer reading of the poet's own volumes. The following pages are, as already implied, little more than a guide, a critical introduction, to characteristic figures and leading poetic tendencies.

This anthology begins with Thomas Hardy, born in 1840; and the editor acknowledges a special indebtedness to that great figure not only for his general austere example, but for personal advice in the preparation of the early editions of this volume. Thanks must also be given to most of the living poets, too many to list, who have furnished invaluable data, helped in the final choice of selections, and in several instances have supplied new poems in manuscript.

Contents

MODERN BRITISH POETRY

New and Enlarged Edition

Preface

☙ To say this is a collection of modern poetry calls at once for a definition of the term, and it is doubtful whether there is a less exact and more abused adjective in the language than "modern." In the case of this compilation the limits of the term are determined if not defined by the dates 1840-1960, or from the advent of Thomas Hardy in the midst of Victorianism to the emergence of the "post-war" poets who reflect the impasse and precarious balance of the world today.

One line of the arbitrary boundary—a deadline by which any poet born before 1840 is excluded—has been chosen for three reasons. First, it permits the other end to round out something more than a full century of poetic accomplishment, so that the book acts as a comparison as well as a companion to *Modern American Poetry*. Second, it begins with Thomas Hardy, a pioneer in candor, one of the first to express the scientific thought of the times in a poetry at once vigorous, uncompromising, and austere—a poetry which anticipated the direct speech of the contemporary generation. Third, the division brings us close to the end of four-square, Victorian conservatism and the beginning of the energetic experimentalism which still engages us.

Most of the great Victorian figures are thus eliminated; reaction takes the place of reflection. Nothing, it has been said, is more permanent than the spirit of change, and we have come a long way since the time when a poet was seriously praised (in 1870) because he held "the proud honor of never uttering one single line which an English mother once would wish unwritten or an English girl would wish unread." The poet was Tennyson who (in *Idylls of the King*) reduced Malory's Round Table to the board of a royal family in the best suburban manner, proving that no laureate could have been more appropriate to the era. But if Tennyson, as G. K. Chesterton dryly remarked, "did hold a great many of the same views as Queen Victoria, though he was gifted with a more fortunate literary style," it was his style even more than his views from which his successors revolted. He presented a conventionalized tightness of sentiment; Swinburne offered an equally conventionalized looseness of rhetoric. Taste tired of both. They suggested the extremes which Yeats defined in another connection, "Sentimentality is deceiving one's self; rhetoric is deceiving other people." Artificial emotions were waning. The inversions, the elaborate diction, the strained affections were doomed by the demand for truth.

This was not achieved overnight. Within the larger curve traced in this volume, there are the records of conflicting tendencies. In general—if I may be permitted an arbitrary grouping—these smaller movements may be classified as (1) The end of Victorianism and the growth of a purely decorative art, (2) The Pre-Raphaelites and Swinburne, (3) The rise and decline of the esthetic philosophy, (4) The muscular influence of Henley, (5) William Butler Yeats and the Celtic revival in Ireland, (6) Rudyard Kipling and the ascendancy of mechanism in art, (7) John Masefield and the return of the rhymed narrative, (8) The war and its effects upon the Georgians, (9) The aftermath and the new bucolic poetry, (10) The "literature of nerves," and (11) The "post-war" group. It may be interesting to follow these developments in somewhat closer detail.

THE END OF VICTORIANISM

The age commonly called Victorian came to an end in England about 1880. It was an age distinguished by many true idealists and many false ideals. It was, in spite of its notable artists, on an entirely different level from the epoch preceding. Its poetry was, in the main, not universal but parochial; its romanticism was gilt and tinsel; its realism was kin to its showy glass pendants, red plush, parlor chromos and antimacassars. The period was full of a pessimistic resignation (the note popularized by Fitzgerald's Omar Khayyám) and a kind of negation which, refusing to see any glamor in the present world, turned to the Middle Ages, to King Arthur, to the legend of Troy—to the suave surroundings of a dream-world instead of the hard contours of actual experience.

At its worst, it was a period of smugness, of placid and pious sentimentality, epitomized by the rhymed sermons of Martin Farquhar Tupper, whose *Proverbial Philosophy* was devoured, with all its cloying and indigestible sweetmeats, by tens of thousands. The same tendency is apparent, though a little less objectionably, in the moralizing lays of Lord Thomas Macaulay, in the theatrically emotionalized verses of Robert Buchanan, Edwin Arnold and Sir Lewis Morris, even in the lesser work of Alfred Lord Tennyson.

The poets of a generation before this time were fired with such ideas as freedom, an adoration of nature, an insatiable hunger for truth in all its forms and manifestations. The characteristic poets of the Victorian Era, says Max Plowman, "wrote under the dominance of churchliness, of 'sweetness and light,' and a thousand lesser theories that have not truth but comfort for their end."

The revolt against the tawdriness of the period had already begun; the best of Victorianism can be found not in men who were typically Victorian, but in pioneers like Browning and insurrectionary spirits like Swinburne, Rossetti, William Morris, who were completely out of sympathy with their time.

THE PRE-RAPHAELITES AND SWINBURNE

That band of painters and poets who called themselves quaintly The Pre-Raphaelite Brotherhood hurried the demise of Victorianism. Their work was a continual denial of its forms; their poems aspired to be paintings, their paintings poems. Under the leadership of William Morris The Pre-Raphaelites enlisted the coöperation of Burne-Jones, the Rossettis, and the insecure loyalty of Swinburne. Morris, the most practical member of the group, sought to make over an entire culture; he designed everything from chintzes to stained-glass windows, created furniture, wrought iron, printed books, manufactured glass, needlework, tapestries, tools—all as a protest against the rapid commercialism of a period whose prosperity was essentially shoddy. Morris was a consistent protestant in his poetry and his politics. In the rôle of poet he rebuked the smallness of his times with epics like *The Earthly Paradise;* in the rôle of propagandist he answered narrow individualism with *News from Nowhere,* picturing an ideal England in which the principles of communism had triumphed. Here Morris, dreaming of a medieval Utopia, confused the future with the past. With a simplicity surpassed only by his energy, he turned back to passion in suits of antique armor and to gallants whose heroism was suspiciously like heroics.

Morris failed, partly because the trend toward standardized production was too sweeping to take account of his theories, partly because he himself was not so much concerned with humanity as with things. He advocated a knightly Socialism not because it would make a more beautiful race but more decorative objects. His sagas show that his preoccupation was with literature instead of life; and, by an ungrateful paradox, a literature that is preferred to life has a swift mortality.

Swinburne suffered from a similar defect. Flying from the prim domesticity sanctified by Tennyson, Swinburne rushed to the unholy (and purely literary) arms of Dolores, Faustine, Félise, Fragoletta, to the neo-paganism of *Atalanta in Calydon,* to the lush intransigence of *Songs Before Sunrise,* to Gautier and Hugo and Baudelaire, to a quick succession of enthusiasms and influences. But it was neither Swinburne's political convictions nor his vaguely revolutionary tendencies which made the young men of his day go about "chanting to one another these new, astonishing melodies." It was his mastery of the lightning phrase, cutting through murky philosophizing and wave-like rhythms arising and crashing on startled shores; it was his headlong fervor coming immediately after a decade of cautious hesitancy. Most of all, from a literary-historical point of view, it was his technique which affected the entire conception of English metrics. English poetry had been slavishly devoted to its norm, the *iamb;* Swinburne, by a lavish use of the dactyl, the choriambus and the anapest, gave poetry a new motion, a polyphonic freedom, an orchestral sweep and sonority. He enlarged the potentialities of English prosody. "Nor," writes Edmund Gosse, "was his singular vogue due only to this extraordinary metrical ingenuity; the effect of his artistic personality was itself intoxicating, even delirious. He was the poet of youth insurgent against all the restraints of conventionality and custom."

The "purest" poet of the group was one only loosely affiliated with it, the quiet sister of Dante Gabriel, Christina Rossetti. Her delicate reticences have been often portrayed, but it remained for Frances Winwar, in *Poor Splendid Wings: The Rossettis and Their Circle,* to depict the outer softness and the inner sharpness, "protecting, like a coat of armor, something she held above the treasures of the world." Struggling between the desires of her womanhood and a congenital refusal to face life, her philosophy grew more and more ascetic. Denial and loss became her favorite themes, she grew increasingly preoccupied with the thought of death as the undemanding lover, the final appeasement. But the thought of sundering to which she always returned, the tremulous abnegation, stirred the depths of her music and inspired her most memorable poetry.

RISE AND DECLINE OF THE ESTHETIC PHILOSOPHY

A somewhat more fashionable revolt ensued. Oscar Wilde, dilettante *de luxe,* attempted to make the 'Nineties draw up an esthetic declaration of independence; the beauty thus championed, taking a leaf from the French symbolists, was to be "its own excuse for being." Wilde's was, in the most outspoken manner, the first use of estheticism as a slogan; the battle-cry of the group was actually the now outworn but then revolutionary "Art for Art's sake"! And, so sick were people of the pinchbeck ornaments of the immediate past, that the slogan won. At least, temporarily.

The Yellow Book, the organ of the révoltés, appeared (1894-1897), representing a reasoned if limited reaction. The Rhymers' Club was the nucleus, and its members—among them Ernest Dowson, Lionel Johnson, Victor Plarr, John Davidson, Arthur Symons, William Butler Yeats—met at the Cheshire Cheese where, over their cakes and ale, they fondly hoped to restore the spirit of the Elizabethan age. Unfortunately they lacked both the gusto and the initiative of their Mermaid Tavern models. Where the Elizabethans were all for size, the sad young men were all for subtlety; instead of being large and careless, they were cramped and self-conscious, writing with one eye on the British public which they hoped to startle, and the other on the French poets whom they hoped to impress. But, underneath the desire to shock the middle-classes their standards were as prescribed as those they derided. To be mildly heretical was their unwritten orthodoxy; instead of being sentimental about virgins they were sentimental about street-walkers. Prostitutes were "soiled doves" and the street-lamps under which they plied their trade were "the iron lilies of the Strand."

Until its collapse after the trial of Wilde, the Esthetic Movement gathered a show of strength which was, however, weakened by its central fallacy. It tried to drag life down to literature instead of bringing literature up to life. The young men's prophet was Walter Pater; their stronghold the ivory tower; their program a mixture of Anglican intellectuality and Parnassian impressionism. "But," as C. E. Andrews and M. O. Percival point out in *Poetry of the Nineties,* "they left behind the intellectual side of Pater, and the 'gem-like flame' was fed purely by emotions. The esthetes' search for beauty became a search for sensations. They did not face the whole of life . . . but they selected from life its strange colors and its strange experiences. They loved to see in the real world glimpses that *seemed* exotic and remote."

Almost the first act of the "new" men was to rouse and outrage their immediate predecessors. This end-of-the-century desire to shock, which was so strong and natural an impulse, still has a place of its own as an antidote. Mid-Victorian propriety and self-satisfaction crumbled under the swift audacities of rebellious spirits. The old walls fell; the public, once so apathetic to *belles-lettres,* was more than attentive to every phase of literary experimentation. The last decade of the nineteenth century was so tolerant of novelty in art and ideas, that it would seem, says Holbrook Jackson in his penetrative summary, *The Eighteen-Nineties,* "as though the declining century wished to make amends for several decades of artistic monotony. It may indeed be something more than a coincidence that placed this decade at the close of a century, and *fin de siècle* may have been at once a swan song and a death-bed repentance."

Thereafter, the movement (if such it may be called) surfeited with its own excesses fell into the mere poses of revolt; it degenerated into a half-hearted defense of artificialities.

It scarcely needed W. S. Gilbert (in *Patience*) or Robert Hichens (in *The Green Carnation*) to satirize its distorted attitudinizing. It strained itself to death; it became its own burlesque of the bizarre, an extravaganza of extravagance. "The period" (I am again quoting Holbrook Jackson) "was as certainly a period of decadence as it was a period of renaissance. The decadence was to be seen in a perverse and finicking glorification of the fine arts and mere artistic virtuosity on the one hand, and a militant commercial movement on the other. . . . The eroticism which became so prevalent in the verse of many of the younger poets was minor because it was little more than a pose—not because it was erotic. . . . It was a passing mood which gave the poetry of the hour a hothouse fragrance; a perfume faint, yet unmistakable and strange."

But most of the elegant and disillusioned young men overshot their mark. Vulgar health reasserted itself; an inherent though long-repressed vitality sought new channels. Arthur Symons deserted his hectic Muse, Richard Le Gallienne abandoned his preciosity, and the group began to disintegrate. The esthetic philosophy was wearing thin; it had already begun to fray and reveal its essential shabbiness. Wilde, himself, possessed the three things which he said the English would never forgive—youth, power, and enthusiasm. But in trying to make an exclusive cult of beauty, Wilde had also tried to make it evade actuality; he urged that art should not, in any sense, be a part of life but an escape from it. "The proper school to learn art in is not Life—but Art." And in the same essay ("The Decay of Lying") he wrote, "All bad Art comes from returning to Life and Nature, and elevating them into ideals." Elsewhere he declared his motto: "The first duty in life is to be as artificial as possible. What the second duty is no one has discovered."

Such a cynical and, in essence, silly philosophy could not go unchallenged. Its snobbish fastidiousness, its very pretense, was bound to arouse the blood of common reality. This negative attitude received its answer in the work of that determined yea-sayer, W. E. Henley.

WILLIAM ERNEST HENLEY

Henley repudiated languid estheticism; he scorned a mincing art which was out of touch with the world. His was a large and sweeping affirmation. He felt that mere existence was glorious: life was coarse, difficult, often dangerous and dirty, but splendid at the heart. Art, he knew, could not be separated from the dreams and hungers of man; it could not flourish only on its own essences or technical accomplishments. To live, poetry would have to share the fears, angers, hopes and struggles of the prosaic world. So Henley came like a salt breeze blowing through a perfumed, heavily screened studio. He sang loudly (often, indeed, too loudly) of the joy of living and the courage of the "unconquerable soul." He was a powerful influence not only as a poet but as a critic and editor. In the latter capacity he gathered about him such men as Robert Louis Stevenson, Rudyard Kipling, Thomas Hardy, H. G. Wells, William Butler Yeats, T. E. Brown, J. M. Barrie. None of these men were his disciples, some were much older, but none came into contact with him without being influenced in some way by his sharp and positive personality. A pioneer and something of a prophet, he was one of the first to champion the paintings of Whistler and to proclaim the genius of Rodin.

Historically considered, Henley represents another transition; his is the bridge between the loose optimism of Browning and the applied imperialism of Kipling. Both extremes find a voice—and a prolonged one—in his work. "Life! More life!" he shouted with the over-eagerness of one afflicted by physical infirmities. "More life!"—particularly English life which, with the authority of sword and gospel, must be broadcast over both hemispheres—but life, no matter how undisciplined, at any cost. And the more boisterous the better.

Life—give me life until the end,
That at the very top of being,
The battle-spirit shouting in my blood,
Out of the reddest hell of the fight
I may be snatched and flung
Into the everlasting lull,
The immortal, incommunicable dream.

But Henley's verse was not always shrill. When he forgot to be muscular, he fashioned ballades and rondeaus with a dexterity scarcely surpassed by Swinburne, lyrics of surprisingly delicate texture, free verse that anticipated a movement two generations later, and "voluntaries" of the city on the Thames with Whistlerian glamor. Further than that, Henley's noisy periods are redeemed by his passionate enthusiasm for nobility in whatever cause it was joined. He loved the world in all its moods. Bus-drivers, hospital interiors, scrubwomen, a panting train, the mystery and squalor of London's alleys, all found a voice in his lines; his later work contains more than a hint of the delight in science and machinery which was later to be sounded more fully in the work of Rudyard Kipling.

THE CELTIC REVIVAL AND J. M. SYNGE

In 1889, William Butler Yeats published his *Wanderings of Oisin;* in the same year Douglas Hyde, scholar and folk-lorist, brought out his *Book of Gaelic Stories.*

The revival of Gaelic and the renascence of Irish literature may be said to date from the publication of those two books. The fundamental idea of both men and their followers was the same. It was to create a literature which would express the national consciousness of Ireland through a purely national art. They began to reflect the strange background of dreams, politics, hopelessness, and heroism which is proverbially Irish. This community of fellowship and aims is to be found in the varied but allied work of William Butler Yeats,

"Æ" (George W. Russell), Moira O'Neill, Lionel Johnson, Katharine Tynan, Padraic Colum, and others. The first fervor gone, a period of dullness set in. After reanimating the old myths, surcharging the legendary heroes with a new significance, it seemed that the movement was losing itself in a literary mysticism. But there followed an increasing concern with the peasant, the migratory laborer, the tramp; an interest that was a reaction against the influence of Yeats and his then arbitrary, over-symbolized otherworldliness. In 1904, the Celtic Revival reached its height with John Millington Synge, who was not only the greatest dramatist of the Irish Theater, but (to quote such contrary critics as George Moore and Harold Williams) "one of the greatest dramatists who has written in English." Synge's poetry, brusque and all too small in quantity, was a minor occupation with him, yet the quality and power of it is unmistakable. Its content was not great, but the raw vigor in it served as a bold banner—a sort of a brilliant Jolly Roger—for the younger men of a subsequent period.

In the introduction to *The Playboy of the Western World,* Synge declared, "When I was writing *The Shadow of the Glen* some years ago, I got more aid than any learning could have given me from a chink in the floor of the old Wicklow house where I was staying that let me hear what was being said by the servant girls in the kitchen. This matter is, I think, of some importance; for in countries where the imagination of the people and the language they use, is rich and living, it is possible for a writer to be rich and copious in his words—and at the same time to give the reality which is at the root of all poetry, in a natural and comprehensive form." This not only explains Synge's impulse but his idiom, possibly the raciest in modern literature.

Synge's poetic power is unquestionably greatest in his plays. In *The Well of the Saints, The Playboy of the Western World,* and *Riders to the Sea* there is more beauty of form, more richness of language than in any piece of dramatic writing since the Elizabethans. Yeats, when he first heard Synge's early one-act play, *The Shadow of the Glen,* is said to have exclaimed "Euripides." A half year later when Synge read him *Riders to the Sea,* Yeats again confined his enthusiasm to a single word:—"Aeschylus!" Time has shown that Yeats's exaggeration was not wholly a compatriot's *beau geste.*

Although Synge's poetry was not his major concern, numbering only twenty-four original pieces and eighteen translations, it had a surprising effect. It marked a point of departure, a reaction against the too-polished verse of his immediate predecessors as well as the dehumanized mysticism of many of his associates. In that memorable preface to his *Poems* he wrote what was a manifesto and at the same time a classic *credo* for all that called itself the "new" poetry. "I have often thought," it begins, "that at the side of poetic diction, which everyone condemns, modern verse contains a great deal of poetic material, using 'poetic' in the same special sense. The poetry of exaltation will be always the highest, but when men lose their poetic feeling for ordinary life and cannot write poetry of ordinary things, their exalted poetry is likely to lose its strength of exaltation in the way that men cease to build beautiful churches when they have lost happiness in building shops. . . . Even if we grant that exalted poetry can be kept successfully by itself, the strong things of life are needed in poetry also, to show that what is exalted or tender is not made by feeble blood."

WILLIAM BUTLER YEATS

William Butler Yeats began by being part of the Celtic movement; before he was sixty he had inspired a movement of his own. With the publication of his *Collected Poems* in 1933 he was acclaimed Ireland's uncrowned laureate and was considered by many the finest poet of his day. Yeats's early poetry was in the style popularized by the Celtic twilight with all its musing and mistiness. Such volumes as *Crossways* (1889), *The Rose* (1893), *The Wind Among the Reeds* (1899), illustrate his gift for pure song. With *The Green Helmet* (1910) a more colloquial tone entered his verse and in *Responsibilities* (1914) a new articulation manifested itself. Yeats had met Ezra Pound and was greatly impressed with the young American's idiom. His later work grew firmer in thought, more complex in harmony. Common speech mingled wit and wisdom in a way scarcely suggested by his early poetry.

The publication of *Collected Poems,* when Yeats was in his sixty-eighth year, was the signal for an international salute; poets of every school and tendency united to acclaim Yeats's increased power. Charles Powell wrote in the *Manchester Guardian,* "In Mr. Yeats there is, perhaps, the clearest link between the modern and the more traditional. There is no poet writing today, old or new, who gets so surely through to reality or who has so vitally the contemporary consciousness. . . . Now that he has established something like an equipoise between the intellect and the imagination, his poetry has the energy of life that is at once passionate and serene."

Even before Yeats's death in 1939 it was evident that he had helped to make and destroy a movement. He had begun by believing that a new culture would grow with the common man, but he confessed his disillusion. "I could not foresee that a new class would change the nature of the Irish movement. . . Power passed to small shopkeepers, to men who had risen above the traditions of the countryman without learning those of cultivated life and who, because of their poverty, ignorance, and superstitious piety, are much subject to all kinds of fear. Immediate victory, immediate utility, became everything, and we artists, who are the servants not of any cause but of mere naked life . . . became, as elsewhere in Europe, protesting individual voices."

Yeats had hoped to speak to and for the average man, but he had in mind "the divine average." Events destroyed his hopes. He wrote Lady Gregory that "we must accept the baptism of the gutter," yet he defended aristocracy in art as in life. He had championed the ordinary individual, but he revolted from the commercial middle classes who "fumble in the greasy till/ And add the halfpence to the pence." Reluctantly he gave up his early dream of awaking Ireland, and concluded:

> Romantic Ireland's dead and gone,
> It's with O'Leary in the grave.

Faced with the physical terror of revolt he declared scornfully:

Hurrah for revolution! Let the cannon shoot!
The beggar upon horseback lashes the beggar upon foot.

Although Yeats never quite repudiated his "aristocratic" affiliations, he delighted to employ the "vulgar" tone; he discarded the early elaborateness for a final sharpness. He turned away from the poetry of incantation for a plain-speaking verse, from the mystic rose and wild swans to a more personal symbolism, to swords and towers and winding stairs. He borrowed from his juniors, even from those he disliked (Pound and Auden, for example), and he never disdained to learn from them. He did more; he used his experience, his changing taste, and his poetic instinct to surpass them all.

HARDY, HOUSMAN, AND HOPKINS

The nineteenth century ended on a dwindling note, a thin echo of the confident imperialism with which it began. The revolt against Victorianism was anticipated by the skepticism of Darwin and the agnosticism of John Stuart Mill; the end of the century was marked by a resistance to everything which Victoria had established, symbolized, and sanctified. One of the most undaunted questioners of the conventions was Thomas Hardy, a Victorian in everything but spirit. Hardy acknowledged the shifting backgrounds, the increased tempo, and the dictates of modern science, but he accepted them without joy and with little hope. His predecessors and most of his contemporaries regarded Nature not only as the friend of man but as the Great Mother, the Divine Healer. Hardy had no such illusions; he agreed with Matthew Arnold who had written:

Man must begin, know this, where Nature ends;
Nature and man can never be fast friends.

Although Hardy did not believe in the lovingkindness of Nature, he did not conclude, as some of his critics have maintained, that it was evil. Nature was not malevolent, but indifferent. God was equally unconcerned, Hardy added grimly, with man's personal life, even with humanity's "destiny." If He should stop to observe the antics of man, one of his minor creations, He would smile ironically at the distorted human standards presumed to be reflections of eternal "values." Man may "explain" God's labors, but God himself, "sense-sealed," wrought His work without logic, even without suspicion that He had evolved a creature with sufficient consciousness "to ask for reasons why."

This is a far cry from the unflinching certainties and devout standards of the Victorians. Hardy offered little comfort to the smug church-goers who believed themselves "in tune with the Infinite" and the complacent citizens who prided themselves upon living in "the best of all possible worlds." Not that Hardy was hopeless about humanity. On the contrary, he admired its accomplishments in the face of adversity; mankind, he implied, was all the greater when it struggled against overwhelming odds. In its very failures, more than in its occasional triumphs, humanity's stature increased; it became tragic and, hence, noble.

A similar note of stubborn heroism was sounded in the poetry of A. E. Housman. Like Hardy, Housman was a quiet but forceful pessimist. A cloistered Latin scholar and teacher, Housman wrote with detachment about individual betrayal and cosmic grief. Evil is a constant, says Housman—"the troubles of our proud and angry dust are from eternity and shall not fail"—but evil must be borne. Cruelty is natural in this our world, but it can, somehow, be endured.

Therefore, since the world has still
Much good, but much less good than ill,
And while the sun and moon endure
Luck's a chance, but trouble's sure,
I'd face it as a wise man would,
And train for ill and not for good.

This was a startling note, a new expression of the old stoic bitterness. In laconic lines Housman affirmed Hardy's contention that the sense of suffering makes for strength, an immunity against too much pain. His incongruously blithe verse assured the reader that, though man is "a stranger and afraid in the world he never made," there are compensations. For example, there is always enough love, laughter, and liquor to go round—and the latter

. . . does more than Milton can
To justify God's ways to man.

An attitude completely opposed to that of Hardy and Housman was taken by Gerard Manley Hopkins. God's ways to man were justified by His sense of love and, even more generously, by His gift of Beauty—by a world where thrush's eggs look like "little low heavens," where a common horse-shoe becomes a "bright and battering sandal," where the stars are "fire-folk sitting in the air," a world "barbarous in beauty," prodigal in energy "charged with the grandeur of God."

Hopkins, a devout but highly imaginative Jesuit, embodied a religious confidence at a time when skepticism was in favor. In brilliantly original verse he brought a new manner to the old tradition. Almost unknown in his day, neglected by practically all his contemporaries, Hopkins influenced another generation by the richness of his style, the splendor of his vocabulary, and his way of packing every phrase with far-reaching allusions.

RUDYARD KIPLING

New tendencies are contagious. But they also disclose themselves simultaneously in places and people where there has been no point of contact. Even before Synge proclaimed the wild beauty in rude life, Kipling was illuminating the wealth of poetic material in things hitherto regarded as too commonplace for poetry. Before literary England had quite recovered from a surfeit of Victorian priggishness and Pre-Raphaelite preciosity, the young Kipling came out of India with high spirits and a great tide of life, sweeping all before him. An obscure Anglo-Indian journalist, the publication of his *Barrack-room Ballads* in 1892 brought him sudden notice. By 1895, he was internationally famous. Plunging through the past as through a withered underbrush, he sprang into the open field of the present. Its mechanical obstacles did not deter him. Kipling gloried in the material world; he did more—he glorified it. He pierced the tough exteriors of seemingly prosaic things—things like machinery, bridge-building, cockney soldiers, slang, steam, the dirty by-products of science (witness "M'Andrews Hymn" and "The Bell Buoy")—and uncovered their hidden glamor. "Romance is gone," sighed most of his contemporaries, whereupon Kipling countered:

> . . . and all unseen
> Romance brought up the nine-fifteen.

Reality is Kipling's romanticism; he rolls drums and sounds clarions for another "crowded hour of glorious life." He composes marches for soldiers, explorers, mechanics, foot-sloggers—for life in action. Motion itself is apostrophized in his verse. Where the world is going is of no particular concern to Kipling; that it moves as a beneficent Britannia directs is gratifying, but that it moves is sufficient to rouse Kipling's enthusiasm.

Kipling, with his perception of ordinary people in terms of ordinary life, is one of the strongest links between the Wordsworth-Browning era and the apostles of vigor, beginning with Masefield. There are serious defects in Kipling's work, particularly in his more facile poetry. He falls into a journalistic ease with a tendency to jingle; he is fond of a militaristic drum-banging as blatant as the insularity he condemns. His best work vibrates with an intensity that transforms the tawdry, that lifts the vulgar and incidental to the universal—the universal, that is, in terms of the British Empire.

JOHN MASEFIELD

All art is a twofold reviving—a reappraisal of subject and a reanimating of form. Poetry becomes perennially "new" by returning to the old with a different consciousness, a greater awareness. In 1911, when art was again searching for novelty, John Masefield created something startling and new by going back to 1385 and *The Canterbury Tales*. Employing both the Chaucerian model and a form similar to the practically forgotten Byronic stanza, Masefield wrote in rapid succession, *The Everlasting Mercy* (1911), *The Widow in the Bye Street* (1912), *Dauber* (1912), *The Daffodil Fields* (1913)—four long rhymed narratives. Expressive of every rugged phase of life, these poems responded to Synge's proclamation that "the strong things of life are needed in poetry also . . . and it may almost be said that before verse can be human again it must be brutal."

Masefield brought back to poetry a mixture of beauty and brutality which is its most human and enduring quality. He brought back that rich and vulgar vividness which is the life-blood of Chaucer, of Shakespeare, of Burns, of Villon, of Heine. As a purely descriptive poet, he won a place with the masters of seascape and landscape. As an imaginative realist, he showed those who were stumbling from one wild eccentricity to another that humanity itself was wilder, stranger, far more thrilling than anything in the world—or out of it. Few things in contemporary poetry are as powerful as the regeneration of Saul Kane (in *The Everlasting Mercy*) or the story of *Dauber,* the tale of a tragic sea-voyage and a dreamer who wanted to be a painter. The vigorous description of rounding Cape Horn in the latter poem is a masterpiece in itself.

THE WAR AND THE GEORGIANS

In 1914, the line of demarcation between Masefield and the younger men was not sharp. Realism was again in the ascendancy. So definite a style as Masefield's was bound to be imitated. It even attracted W. W. Gibson, who deserted bowery arcades to follow the rude trail Masefield had blazed. Gibson reënforced the interest in actuality by turning from a preoccupation with shining knights, faultless queens, ladies in distress, and all the paraphernalia of hackneyed medieval romances, to write about ferrymen, berry-pickers, stone-cutters, farmers, printers, circus-men, carpenters—dramatizing (and often theatricalizing) the primitive emotions of ordinary people in *Livelihood, Daily Bread,* and *Fires.* Candor had been asking new questions. It found unexpected answers in the war; repressed emotionalism discovered a new and terrible outlet.

The first volume of the biennial *Georgian Poetry* had just appeared when the war caught up the youth of England in a gust of national fervor. Not only the young men but their seniors joined what seemed then to be "the Great Adventure," only to find that it was, as one of them has since called it, "the Late Great Nightmare." After the early flush of romanticism had passed, the voices of bitter disillusion were heard. Not at first, for censorship was omnipresent. But Siegfried Sassoon's fierce satires and burning denunciations could not be stilled; the mocking lines of Robert Graves began to be quoted; Wilfred Owen's posthumous poems painted a picture the very opposite of the journalistic jingo verses which attempted to paint civilization's greatest horror in bright and cheerful colors.

Rupert Brooke, the most popular of his group, remains, in most minds, as the type of romantic warrior, a symbolic figure not uncommon at the beginning of the first World War. But his poetry, as well as his correspondence, contains evidence that, had he survived the first few years of warfare, his verse —had he written at all—would have been akin to the unromanticized passion of those who, like Sassoon and Rosenberg and Owen, saw the horror at close range and at length. Even his comrade, Charles Hamilton Sorley, that marvelous boy killed at twenty, hearing the news of Brooke's enlistment, wrote: "Rupert Brooke is far too obsessed with his own sacrifice, regarding the going to war of himself (and others) as a highly intense, remarkable and sacrificial exploit, whereas it is merely the conduct demanded of him (and others) by the turn of circumstances, where non-compliance with this demand would have made life intolerable. He has clothed his attitude in fine words: but his is, nevertheless, the sentimental attitude."

EFFECTS OF THE WAR

Meanwhile the Georgians had rediscovered the direct speech of Wordsworth; but they relied uncritically upon the spirit of his pastoral lyrics. They echoed his assurances of natural beauty, and extended his confidence in the benign power of the country scene. They avoided the uglier implications of rural life, the losing struggles with the soil, poverty and hunger, the spiritual barrenness, and the economic failures. Theirs was a poetry of happy dawns, song-filled dusks, peace-breathing nights.

The more original poets outgrew the group. The fierce and self-flagellating D. H. Lawrence had little enough in common with his fellows at the beginning; at the end he spoke in a language which most of them preferred not to comprehend. Walter De la Mare, a neo-Gothic romancer lost in the actual present, created a fabulous world of ghosts, of unfulfilled longings and unhappy memories, in which the very landscape was haunted. Ralph Hodgson masked a far-reaching imagination in deceptive simplicities. Charlotte Mew and Anna Wickham, two women never admitted into the Georgian anthologies, combined a searching gravity with fretted energy. James Stephens and Humbert Wolfe mingled whimsical fantasy and impudent versatility.

The effect of the first World War on the established poets was definite and disastrous. The Georgian group issued two more volumes (there were five in all, the last being *Georgian Poetry 1920-1922*), but the spirit had gone out of it. Rupert Brooke and Edward Thomas had been silenced by death. The work of Walter De la Mare grew increasingly somber; John Masefield no longer contributed; D. H. Lawrence—never a Georgian at heart and admitted to the volumes with a few circumspect poems—turned to prose and bitter *pensées;* Lascelles Abercrombie wrote little after 1919; Ralph Hodgson ceased to write at all. Only W. H. Davies, living in a world which, seemingly common-pastoral, was really a world of his own, continued to warble his delighted, thought-free bird-notes. The loss to the group of these men—or the loss of their power—was not compensated by the addition of Martin Armstrong, William Kerr, J. D. C. Pellow, Edward Shanks, Thomas Moult, and other fashioners of what Sassoon called "crocus-crowded lyrics."

AFTERMATH

Peace brought back but few of the younger poets. The most brilliant of them, Charles Hamilton Sorley, was killed on the threshold of an indubitably great future. The career of Isaac Rosenberg, author of an amazing poetic drama, was ended almost before it had begun. Rupert Brooke died in the midst of his singing; so did Edward Thomas, Francis Ledwidge, Cameron Wilson. Wilfred Owen was struck down just as he had found his own full-throated utterance. It is impossible to calculate how much was lost to English poetry by the death of these singers.

One after-effect was particularly noticeable. English literature suffered not only from individual losses but from general shock. This shock affected the writers of every school and diverted where it did not arrest the current of contemporary verse. It threw Masefield back to pontifical sonnets and the classic drama of half a century ago; it silenced such of its War-poets as refused to continue to write about "the collective madness" and yet could think of little else. It created the sharp division between the new group of English pastoral poets and the still younger intellectuals. The reactions of the two contradictory movements are easy to understand. Wishing to escape the mechanistic urban civilization which had scarred Europe with ruins, many of the poets turned hopefully to the traditional curlew-calling, plover-haunted English countryside. The machine is a dead thing spreading death, they cried; only the soil brings forth. "We have had enough of destructive ingenuities; let us go back to creative simplicities." Following, more or less consciously, the example of the naïf poet, W. H. Davies, a small cohort of writers began to sing exclusively about the charms of childhood, sunsets, and rural delights. But where Davies' innocence was natural, the simplicity of most of the Georgians was predetermined. Much of the resulting poetry was inspired by the wish to avoid past memories rather than by a spontaneous affection for the present scene; much of it was a sort of protracted convalescence.

The Georgian group developed a vocabulary built on the colloquial, but it failed to emphasize any conviction behind it. Although it was devoted to real objects, it favored a gentlemanly realism. It was, as L. A. G. Strong has written, "soothing, reassuring. Its outbursts of indignation were directed against precisely the right objects, and were timed for precisely the right moment." The technique was always enviably neat—a finical contrast to the vivid bucolic records of Edward Thomas—and the conceits were properly restrained. Sometimes they reached extremes of insipidity; one of the collections enshrines this *reductio ad absurdum,* in which a literary shepherd composes such unintentionally comic strophes as:

I lingered at a gate and talked
A little with a lonely lamb.
He told me of the great still night,
Of calm starlight,
And of the lady moon, who'd stoop
For a kiss sometimes. . . .
Of how, when sheep grew old,
As their faith told
They went without a pang
To far green fields, where fall
Perpetual streams that call
To deathless nightingales.

THE "LITERATURE OF NERVES"

Opposed to the rustic tendency, a group emerged headed by the three Sitwells, Edith, Osbert, and Sacheverell. Revolting from the false naïveté of the Georgians—particularly that part of it dominated by J. C. Squire of *The London Mercury* and derisively nicknamed the Squirearchy—the expression at first took the form of satire. Sometimes the burlesque was broad, sometimes the allusions were so erudite and private that only the initiate found them intelligible. The Sitwells advertised themselves liberally, even caricatured their offerings as the "queer" products of a disordered age, bellowed their verses through megaphones, and capitalized their well-organized unpopularity. Their poetry was not always compounded of wildness prepense; it was mad only north-north-west, and soon it became evident that what they had to say was of some significance to their times. Their artificial figures began to breathe; their pastiche was humanized. Nostalgia welled up beneath the elegances, reminiscent of the 'Nineties, and (again reminding us of the *fin de siècle* esthetes) this yearning for a happier world clothed itself in foreign symbolism. Differing from the Parnassian poets, they did not depict their objects—or objectives—by direct statement. Like the Symbolists, they relied on the power of elision and suggestion; they compelled readers to participate in the process of creation and made them fill the gaps between thought and figure, between meaning and mystery.

The movement was primarily intellectual and inflexible. It attempted to develop through the senses, but it distrusted the emotions and was bound to a manner. It was conceived in the latest fashion—the fashion of rebellion without responsibility, cynicism without satire—and fashion changes with unfortunate rapidity.

For several years the "anti-Georgians" sent up rockets of esoteric brilliance. Nor did all of these explosions end in a shower of burnt sticks. Whatever their defects, they were faults of excess; their idiom (particularly Edith Sitwell's and Peter Quennell's) was like no other's. Much of it, high-pitched and exacerbated, belongs to the literature of nerves. But it was provocative and never dull.

THE POST-WAR POETS

A more serious group of poets arose in the early nineteen thirties. These youths had seen space shrink with the airplane while radio annihilated all borders. They had watched governments turn more nationalistic and men grow more unneighborly. Part of a world-wide depression, they entered a decade so financially bankrupt and morally insolvent that it was sometimes known as the Threadbare 'Thirties.

The men of the nineteen thirties were not optimistic, but they had hopes; they dreamed of a new society risen from the ashes of the old. As writers they had more than youth and poetry in common; they shared the fear that they were born in one war and doomed to die in another. Their vocabulary, their taste, their technique, most of all their social and political convictions, offered the greatest possible contrasts to those of the Georgians and the Sitwellians. They owed much to two experimental predecessors: Gerard Manley Hopkins, that richly associative and daring poet, and the American T. S. Eliot, who so strongly influenced English poetry at the beginning of the twentieth century. Eliot prepared the way, celebrating and satirizing the end of a cycle, the cultural decay of a period and a system. But Eliot retreated into Anglo-Catholicism and increasingly obscure allegories. Here the younger Englishmen broke with him; they refused to follow his desperate evasions and defeatism. They borowed from Eliot's style but repudiated his thought.

The most important members of the post-war group were W. H. Auden, Stephen Spender, Cecil Day Lewis, and Louis MacNeice. Their volumes appeared almost simultaneously in the early thirties; they shared the same point of view toward art and nature, politics and poetry. Considering their contribution, Alastair Miller in *The Saturday Review of Literature* wrote: "Nature is no longer considered anthropomorphically, nor love religiously. The poet no longer looks out of his windw in the country and, blinding himself to the railway track, sees a beneficent Providence creating the pleasures and necessities of men: he sees electric pylons conveying imprisoned power, telegraph wires defying distance, motor ploughs forcing fertility into the soil. There is no disrespect, as is sometimes maintained, for primroses and budding trees; but they are not accepted as a solution of, or consolation for, human misery." Stephen Spender makes this particularly explicit in his "Landscape near an Aerodrome" which begins:

More beautiful and soft than any moth
With burring furred antennae feeling its huge path
Through dusk, the air-liner with shut-off engines
Glides over suburbs and the sleeves set trailing tall
To point the wind.

In "The Express" Spender pictures "the first powerful plain manifesto, the black statement of pistons," and at the end of one of his sonnets he emphasizes the post-war poet's attitude:

Real were iron lines, and, smashing the grass
The cars in which we ride, and real our compelled time:
Painted on enamel beneath moving glass
Unreal were cows, the wave-winged storks, the line:
These burned in a clear world from which we pass
Like *rose* and *love* in a forgotten rhyme.

C. Day Lewis, in his revealing essay, "A Hope for Poetry," makes plain the salient characteristic of post-war verse technique. "The deliberate insertion into a lyrical context of pieces of slang and 'prosaic' words; the juxtaposition of highly charged 'poetical' images and dull, commonplace images; the use of bathos—all these have been taken over from the Symbolists, largely through the instrumentality of Eliot; and the verse that results offers an uneven, conversational surface shot through with gleams of lyricism, rather thaan a uniformly lyrical texture. . . . The desire for intensity and for freshness of language which leads these poets to syntactical ellipses, produces also that preoccupation with internal rhyme and assonance which may succeed in reestablishing poetry as a delight to the ear."

As Lewis concludes, no amount of technical experiment can of itself produce poetry, but the experimentation was conducted with an energy and optimism that was startling. The poetic art in England received a sudden increase in vitality. It was quickened so exuberantly that those who challenged its philosophy could not dispute its stimulative effect. Quoting some lines of

W. H. Auden, Hugh Walpole wrote, "The Waste Land is, at last, to be cultivated. . . . The real importance comes from the undoubted fact that these poets accept life rather than curse or despise it." Auden, the most forceful if also the least simple, not only inspired Day Lewis and Spender, but seems to have engendered a poetry revival by himself.

THE STREAM OF CONSCIOUSNESS AND SURREALISM

The younger poets were accused of irreverence, lack of standards, and obscurity of aim. They were not without defenders. Writing in *Recent Poetry: 1923-1933,* Alida Monro agreed that the poet who is the product of the twentieth century may not be understood by persons born during the 'Sixties, 'Seventies, and 'Eighties of the last century, but she added: "At no time in the history of man has there been so sudden and violent a change in his environment and circumstances as has taken place in the past twenty-five years. It is far easier, in some ways, to understand the past, even the past of two hundred years ago, than it is to understand our own time, or to try to imagine what life may be like twenty years hence. It is, then, not remarkable that, oppressed by every fresh scientific discovery, with the Great War behind, with the Greater and more horrible War before him, the poet today should be preoccupied with subjects and forms that do not seem to fit into the preconceived notions of what constitutes poetry according to the canons of an age in literature that is now as dead as is the Augustan age."

Caught in a world that was growing increasingly terrifying, a few poets sought to escape reality by avoiding a program of ideas. Life and art had become too demanding for them; they hoped to liberate themselves from everything, even from logic, by letting themselves drift on the erratic stream of consciousness. They substituted intuition for thinking, tension for fluency, and improvisation for form. Much of the poetry produced was so allusive as to seem to move in all directions at once. The first few lines of a cryptogrammatic poem by W. H. Empson illustrate the method:

The god arkitect whose coping with the Flood
Groyned the white stallion arches of the main
  (And miner deeps that in the dome of the brain
  Take Iris' arches' pupillage and Word)
Walked on the bucking water like a bird
And, guard, went round its ramparts and its ball
  (Columbus' egg sat on earth's garden wall
  And held the equitation of his bar;
  Waves beat his bounds until he foamed a star
  And mapped with fire the skyline that he ploughed),
Trod and divined the inwheeling serene cloud—
  (And who knows if Narcissus dumb and bent—)
Shed and fermented to a firmament. . . .

Surrealism was the result, an extreme manifestation of the tendency to discard logic and coherence, to pass literally "beyond realism." Henry Miller, one of the most experimental of American writers, declared that surrealism was a self-defeating movement, "a confession of intellectual and spiritual bankruptcy, a reflection of the death process, a quickening of the foredoomed end of civilization." The beginning of a poem by Dylan Thomas, using the surrealist method at its best, is revealing in its daring technique and verbal ambiguity:

Into her lying down head
His enemies entered bed,
Under the encumbered eyelid,
Through the rippled drum of the hair-buried ear;
And Noah's rekindled now unkind dove
Flew man-bearing there.
Last night in a raping wave
Whales quaked loose from the green grave
In fountains of origin gave up their love,
Along her innocence glided
Juan aflame and savagely young King Lear,
Queen Catherine howling bare
And Samson drowned in his hair—
The colossal intimacies of silent
Once seen strangers or shades on a stair. . . .

One senses the feeling and direction of the images in these lines; the emotion is apparent, although the phrases present a gathering confusion. Perhaps confusion is the purpose, for the intention itself is left vague, ambiguous instead of exact. The surrealists contended that ambiguity was not only more provocative than precision, but a more honest reflection of the times and therefore more rewarding to the reader. But the attempt to picture a chaotic inner world was doomed; it was dwarfed by the greater chaos of the second World War.

"THE AGE OF ANXIETY"

The stream of consciousness never developed into a main current; it wandered haphazardly and finally went underground. Surrealism became a passing curiosity. Extreme stylistic subtlety was followed by a return to simplicity. After attempting to speak publicly in what seemed a private code, the poets clarified their utterance and their intentions. They proclaimed a fresh affirmation; they announced a renewed interest in, and a desire to reach, the common man. Spender, as spokesman, declared that nothing could withstand "the palpable and obvious love of man." Auden echoed: "We must love one another or die." They praised candor instead of complexity, and celebrated those who were visionaries, pioneers, leaders in nobility. Auden, hoping for salvation from within rather than violent upheaval from without, paid tribute to Freud, who attempted to unite "the unequal moieties fractured by our own well-meaning sense of justice," and William Butler Yeats: "In the deserts of the heart/ Let the healing fountain start,/ In the prison of his days/ Teach the free man how to praise." Spender in "I think continually of those who were truly great" exalted those who "left the vivid air signed with their honor."

By the end of the nineteen thirties, the hopes and affirmations were challenged by a universal denial. The total war which began in September, 1939, unleashed unprecedented horrors and threatened contemporary culture. Dictatorships upset the balance of power; the military state—a state of mind as well as a form of misgovernment—violated nations and betrayed humanity.

The feeling of tension increased as the war grew in length and intensity. The arts seemed haunted by ghosts of undefined but devastating guilt. Poetry echoed the mind's despair aand the heart's desolation. A sense of universal shame became an expression of personal apprehension. W. H. Auden characterized his time in a bitter book-length poem entitled *The Age of Anxiety*.

During the 1930s poetry had become confused with politics. Auden and Spender had been prime movers among those who, revolted by the spread of Fascism and the threat of totalitarian victories, looked hopefully toward the promise of Communism and a new social order. Their attacks on the old order were bitter and often persuasive, but their enthusiasm for the new dispensation waned. After the debacle in Spain and the violent extremes in Russian policy, they were forced back upon personal rather than political problems: the difficulties of the disillusioned individual in a disordered world. The spirit, however, remained indomitable and their writing, amplified in scope as well as depth, proved once more that creation, not chaos, was a constant.

THE NEW CRITICISM AND THE NEW POETS

Concomitant with a new note in poetry there arose an antiseptic tone and technique in criticism. It owed much to the taste and practice of Ezra Pound and T. S. Eliot in both their poetry and criticism. I. A. Richards, followed by William Empson and perhaps paralleled in zigzag by F. R. Leavis—and later abetted by the Americans R. P. Blackmur, Cleanth Brooks, Yvor Winters and others to whom John Crowe Ransom devoted a work entitled *The New Criticism*—were largely responsible for the notion that poetry was written not so much for delight as for the covert expression of multiple meanings. Being such, poetry obviously required dissection and thus this school became so busy searching for devious meanings, remote associations, and levels of irony and ambiguity that, in a zeal for *explication de texte,* it took the life out of narratives, dismembered sonnets, and twisted twelve-line lyrics through twenty paragraphs of tortured prose. Its methods are catalogued in a formidable American handbook of the late forties—Rene Wellek and Austin Warren's *Theory of Literature.*

Beginning in the late 1930s a new group of poet-critics supplemented and supplanted the "new criticism." *Auden and After* (1942) announced the change and carried the challenging subtitle, "The Liberation of Poetry"; *The New British Poetry* (1949) disclosed some seventy poets, most of whom were little known; the new edition of *The Chatto Book of Modern Poetry* (1959) presented still more recent names. Among the poets who aroused readers with fresh creative energy were George Barker, Patrick Kavanagh, W. R. Rodgers, Henry Reed, Alex Comfort, Norman Nicholson, Sidney Keyes, Kathleen Raine, and Philip Larkin. The explosive exuberance of Dylan Thomas was overwhelming and overcame even those who could not understand him, while such older poets as Edwin Muir and Robert Graves were rediscovered and acclaimed by a new audience.

The flight from reality had ended; the battle for freedom of expression had been won. New ideas framed in new images gave metaphors a power beyond logic and a speed they had never attained. Intuition strengthened by experience produced a poetry which was dynamic, immediate, and intensified. Once again the poet fulfilled his function. He sharpened the reader's perception, increased his appreciation, and heightened his awareness not only of life's accepted simplicities but also its endless complexities.

Thomas Hardy

Thomas Hardy was born at Upper Bockhampton, near Dorchester, June 2, 1840, of parents in humble circumstances, his father being a stone-mason. His schooling was fitful. When sixteen, he was apprenticed to an ecclesiastical architect. Later, he left his native village and worked in London, where he won the prize offered by the Royal Institute of British Architects. This was in 1863. A few years after, he abandoned architecture and, in 1871, his first novel, *Desperate Remedies,* was published anonymously. It was a failure, little attention being paid to the author until the publication of *Under the Greenwood Tree.* From that time on his success as a writer was assured.

It was not until he was almost sixty—in 1898, to be precise—that Hardy abandoned prose and challenged attention as a poet, verse having been the form of expression with which he began and, as many (including the editor and Hardy himself) believe, the form by which he will be remembered longest. Technically considered, the rhythms of his verse are, at first reading, irritatingly rude; his syntax is often clumsy; his language involved. But, beneath the surface crudities—and many of them are efforts to achieve particular effects—Hardy's poetry is as disciplined as it is original. If its idiom is sometimes overweighted, it corresponds to the large design and complexities of his thought. "It has," says Dorothy Martin, in an essay on Hardy's lyrics, "an elemental power which, in its wide range of emotion, its sense of inner conflict between mind and heart, affords something like a counterpart in poetry to the art of Rodin in sculpture. To the horror of the orthodox, it has outwardly the same challenging roughnesses and acerbities; it has also the same profundity and stimulating power for those who, refusing to be put off by a difficult exterior, push on to the inner spirit of which this exterior is the vigorous, provocative but fitting expression."

As has been said, by Hardy himself, he "was *compelled* to give up verse for prose," but at no time did he prefer the many works of fiction which won him an international reputation. On the contrary, he was bitter that necessity had forced him to discontinue the creation of poetry for the writing of novels, and in private life would refer to the latter as "pot-boilers" and "wretched stuff." Nevertheless, between the ages of thirty-four and fifty-seven, Hardy published eleven novels and three collections of stories, of which *The Return of the Native* and *The Mayor of Casterbridge* are the sharpest in characterization although *Tess of the D'Urbervilles* (1891) and *Jude the Obscure* (1896) caused more comment. The former started a controversy which grew into an attack, chiefly because of the social criticism which had been implicit in his previous work but which was now openly expressed. With greater violence, almost with vituperation, Hardy was called to account for *Jude the Obscure.* This further example of critical stupidity hurt Hardy so deeply that he said it "cured him of all interest in novel-writing."

Two years later he turned definitely and exclusively to poetry, publishing *Wessex Poems* (1898) with his own drawings, and *Poems of the Past and Present* (1902). Both volumes were respectfully but unenthusiastically received. Then, when Hardy was sixty-four years old and critics had decided that his power had waned, he published the first part of *The Dynasts* (1904), that epic which was to spread itself on the largest canvas of his time. By 1908 the work was complete, a huge drama of the Napoleonic Wars in three books, nineteen acts, and one hundred and thirty scenes. This triumph is the apotheosis of the poet. Of it, the *London Times* wrote: "A work which combines as only a work of genius could combine, a poetic philosophy with minute historical knowledge and a shrewd eye for the tragical and comical ways of men and women." Lascelles Abercrombie, a most conservative appraiser, unhesitatingly called it "the biggest and most consistent exhibition of fatalism in literature." Hardy himself liked, so he informed the editor, two or three of the lyrics in *The Dynasts* (particularly "Trafalgár") as well as anything in his *Collected Poems*.

As Hardy grew older, his poems increased, and his powers with them. Explaining the large number of verses written after his sixtieth year, he said that he would merely "go to a drawer and take something out." But, although it is true that he resuscitated and refurbished many lyrics of an earlier period, Hardy continued to create new ones no less knotted, no less characteristically acrid, delicately nostalgic, pungently bitter-sweet, until he was almost ninety. When he was seventy-nine his *Collected Poems* (1919) displayed the range and fecundity but not the end of his gifts. As an octogenarian, he published *Late Lyrics and Earlier* (1922), *Human Shows: Far Phantasies, Songs and Trifles* (1925), and *Winter Words in Various Moods and Metres,* which, though appearing posthumously, had been arranged and selected by Hardy before his death.

Hardy's death in his eighty-eighth year on January 11, 1928, deprived contemporary England of its most honored author. Although his ashes were placed in Westminster Abbey, his heart (as requested in his Will) was buried in the churchyard of his own village, in the soil he loved so faithfully.

His work resists a pat synthesis. Hardy wrote in almost every manner, good and bad, in every meter, old and new, mixing novelty and banality, dropping heavy cacophonies into the lightest melodies, balancing the profound with the trivial, the cosmic with the comic. Most readers prefer him in that curiously lyric-narrative style which he perfected, but his intensities escape category. Each of his collections runs the gamut of life and its reflection in literature, and his style follows the scale. Modern and ancient, his technique is as advanced as the youngest contemporary's, as formal as a poetic ballet-master's. "In the Servants' Quarters" is a splendid instance of Hardy's talk-flavored verse, which ascends from casual speech on a *crescendo* of dramatic effect, to a half-expected yet startling climax. In quite another manner, his *Satires of Circumstance* (reminding an American reader of Masters' *Spoon River Anthology,* which it anticipated by a generation) are epigrammatic vignettes in which he condensed whole domestic dramas. "The Dark-Eyed Gentleman," on the other hand, is as simple-spontaneous as a folk-tune and quite unlike Hardy's other verse.

Hardy's resources are seemingly endless. At one moment he plays the pathetic fanciful as in "The Tree and the Lady," the next moment he strikes the ironically bizarre in "Ah, Are You Digging on My Grave?" "In Time of 'The Breaking of Nations' " packs an epic into twelve quiet-colored lines; "'Snow in the Suburbs" is a purely objective delineation in black and white; "When I Set Out for Lyonnesse" (one of Hardy's favorites among his own poems) is pure song; "The Oxen" turns a superstition to tender humor. And, though each of these is a lyric and all are straightforward in rhythm, each has its own dexterous difference in meter. It has passed unnoted, but Hardy even ventured into the French forms for occasional effects; "The Roman Road" is as neat a rondeau as Austin Dobson ever fashioned; "Winter in Durnover Field" and "Birds at Winter Nightfall" are thoroughly Hardyesque and yet precise if unusual triolets.

Hardy's questioning the beneficence of Nature led to accusations of pessimism, a charge that he continually but ineffectually denied. Actually the poet was an unorthodox moralist whose heart went out to the things, people, and elements he loved. These elements—as he says ironically in "New Year's Eve," affirmatively in "The Subalterns"—are not actuated either by blind hate or blinder chance, but are subject to laws beyond the rules of logic. Hardy denied no God, but sensed design in chaos. Even when he could not rationalize a universe struggling to establish order in imperfection, he praised it, "hoping it might be so."

In the brief note preceding Hardy's contribution in *Great Names* (1926) Siegfried Sassoon wrote, "Without laboring the analogy between poetry and religion, it may be said that sham poetry is as pernicious as sham religion; and that for poets a merely poetical state of mind is as dangerous as a religious belief based on superficial religious emotion. That is why Hardy's poetry of experience is so significant. He records with microscopic exactitude, preserving a flawless artistic integrity. In his short poems he fuses all that he has learned from the past and endured in the present, in a supreme imaginative vision with masterly and original craft in words and subtle ironic sense. He realizes that the true satisfaction of life lies in imaginative conflict. Whatever their ultimate purpose, men are alive only while they struggle. When they grow aware of the futility of their effort, and yet strive to fashion something from it, they become noble and tragic. Such is Hardy; but his despair is mitigated by tenderness and pity for his fellows. . . . With a wistful understanding he surveys the human scene."

No consideration of Hardy could end on a finer coda. Throughout Hardy's work there shines a greater triumph than the technician's: a triumphant personality.

Three excellent studies of Hardy, presenting the novelist and poet from three distinctly different points of view, are those by Lionel Johnson (1894), Lascelles Abercrombie (1912), and Ernest Brennecke (1925).

IN TIME OF "THE BREAKING OF NATIONS"

Only a man harrowing clods
  In a slow silent walk,
With an old horse that stumbles and nods
  Half asleep as they stalk.

Only thin smoke without flame
  From the heaps of couch grass:
Yet this will go onward the same
  Though Dynasties pass.

Yonder a maid and her wight
  Come whispering by;
War's annals will fade into night
  Ere their story die.

THE DARKLING THRUSH

I leaned upon a coppice gate
  When Frost was specter-gray,
And Winter's dregs made desolate
  The weakening eye of day.

The tangled bine-stems scored the sky
  Like strings from broken lyres,
And all mankind that haunted nigh
  Had sought their household fires.

The land's sharp features seemed to be
  The Century's corpse outleant;
His crypt the cloudy canopy,
  The wind his death-lament.
The ancient pulse of germ and birth
  Was shrunken hard and dry,
And every spirit upon earth
  Seemed fervorless as I.

At once a voice burst forth among
  The bleak twigs overhead
In a full-hearted evensong
  Of joy illimited;
An aged thrush, frail, gaunt and small,
  In blast-beruffled plume,
Had chosen thus to fling his soul
  Upon the growing gloom.

So little cause for carolings
  Of such ecstatic sound
Was written on terrestrial things
  Afar or nigh around,
That I could think there trembled through
  His happy good-night air
Some blessed hope, whereof he knew
  And I was unaware.

THE MAN HE KILLED

  "Had he and I but met
  By some old ancient inn,
We should have sat us down to wet
  Right many a nipperkin!

  "But ranged as infantry,
  And staring face to face,
I shot at him as he at me,
  And killed him in his place.

  "I shot him dead because—
  Because he was my foe,
Just so: my foe of course he was;
  That's clear enough; although

  "He thought he'd 'list, perhaps,
  Off-hand-like—just as I—
Was out of work—had sold his traps—
  No other reason why.

  "Yes; quaint and curious war is!
  You shoot a fellow down
You'd treat, if met where any bar is,
  Or help to half-a-crown."

IN THE SERVANTS' QUARTERS

"Man, you too, aren't you, one of these rough followers of the criminal?
All hanging hereabout to gather how he's going to bear
Examination in the hall." She flung disdainful glances on
The shabby figure standing at the fire with others there,
    Who warmed them by its flare.

"No, indeed, my skipping maiden: I know nothing of the trial here,
Or criminal, if so he be.—I chanced to come this way,
And the fire shone out into the dawn, and morning airs are cold now;
I, too, was drawn in part by charms I see before me play,
    That I see not every day."

"Ha, ha!" then laughed the constables who also stood to warm themselves,
The while another maiden scrutinized his features hard,
As the blaze threw into contrast every knot and line that wrinkled them,
Exclaiming, "Why, last night when he was brought in by the guard,
    You were with him in the yard!"

"Nay, nay, you teasing wench, I say! You know you speak mistakenly.
Cannot a tired pedestrian who has legged it long and far
Here on his way from northern parts, engrossed in humble marketings,
Come in and rest awhile, although judicial doings are
Afoot by morning star?"

"'O come, come!" laughed the constables. "Why, man, you speak the dialect
He uses in his answers; you can hear him up the stairs.
So own it. We sha'n't hurt ye. There, he's speaking now! His syllables
Are those you sound yourself when you are talking unawares,
As this pretty girl declares."

"And you shudder when his chain clinks!" she rejoined. "O yes, I noticed it.
And you winced, too, when those cuffs they gave him echoed to us here.
They'll soon be coming down, and you may then have to defend yourself
Unless you hold your tongue, or go away and keep you clear
When he's led to judgment near!"

"No! I'll be damned in hell if I know anything about the man!
No single thing about him more than everybody knows!
Must not I even warm my hands but I am charged with blasphemies?" . . .
—His face convulses as the morning cock that moment crows,
And he droops, and turns, and goes.

NEUTRAL TONES

We stood by a pond that winter day,
And the sun was white, as though chidden of God,
And a few leaves lay on the starving sod;
They had fallen from an ash, and were gray.

Your eyes on me were as eyes that rove
Over tedious riddles solved years ago;
And some words played between us to and fro
On which lost the more by our love.

The smile on your mouth was the deadest thing
Alive enough to have strength to die;
And a grin of bitterness swept thereby
Like an ominous bird a-wing. . . .

Since then, keen lessons that love deceives,
And wrings with wrong, have shaped to me
Your face, and the God-curst sun, and a tree,
And a pond edged with grayish leaves.

NEW YEAR'S EVE

"I have finished another year," said God,
"In gray, green, white and brown;
I have strewn the leaf upon the sod,
Sealed up the worm within the clod,
And let the last sun down."

"And what's the good of it?" I said,
"What reasons made you call
From formless void this earth we tread,
When nine-and-ninety can be read
Why nought should be at all?

"Yea, Sire; why shaped you us, 'who in
This tabernacle groan'—
If ever a joy be found herein,
Such joy no man had wished to win
If he had never known!"

Then he: "My labors—logicless—
You may explain; not I:
Sense-sealed I have wrought, without a guess
That I evolved a Consciousness
To ask for reasons why.

"Strange that ephemeral creatures who
 By my own ordering are,
Should see the shortness of my view,
Use ethic tests I never knew,
 Or made provision for!"

He sank to raptness as of yore,
 And opening New Year's Day
Wove it by rote as theretofore,
And went on working evermore
 In his unweeting way.

THE NIGHT OF TRAFALGÁR

(from "The Dynasts")

In the wild October night-time, when the wind raved round the land,
And the Back-sea met the Front-sea, and our doors were blocked with sand,
And we heard the drub of Dead-man's Bay, where bones of thousands are,
We knew not what the day had done for us at Trafalgár.
 Had done,
 Had done,
 For us at Trafalgár!

"Pull hard, and make the Nothe, or down we go!" one says, says he.
We pulled; and bedtime brought the storm; but snug at home slept we.
Yet all the while our gallants after fighting through the day,
Were beating up and down the dark, sou'-west of Cadiz Bay.
 The dark,
 The dark,
 Sou'-west of Cadiz Bay!

The victors and the vanquished then the storm it tossed and tore,
As hard they strove, those worn-out men, upon that surly shore;
Dead Nelson and his half-dead crew, his foes from near and far,
Were rolled together on the deep that night at Trafalgár!
 The deep,
 The deep,
 That night at Trafalgár!

WEATHERS

This is the weather the cuckoo likes,
 And so do I;
When showers betumble the chestnut spikes,
 And nestlings fly;
And the little brown nightingale bills his best,
And they sit outside the "Traveler's Rest,"
And maids come forth sprig-muslin drest,
And citizens dream of the South and West,
 And so do I.

This is the weather the shepherd shuns,
 And so do I;
When beeches drip in browns and duns,
 And thresh, and ply;
And hill-hid tides throb, throe on throe,
And meadow rivulets overflow,
And drops on gate-bars hang in a row,
And rooks in families homeward go,
 And so do I.

"AH, ARE YOU DIGGING ON MY GRAVE?"

"Ah, are you digging on my grave
 My beloved one?—planting rue?"
—"No: yesterday he went to wed
One of the brightest wealth has bred,
'It cannot hurt her now,' he said,
 'That I should not be true.'"

"Then who is digging on my grave?
  My nearest, dearest kin?"
—"Ah, no: they sit and think, 'What use!
What good will planting flowers produce?
No tendance of her mound can loose
  Her spirit from Death's gin.' "

"But someone digs upon my grave?
  My enemy?—prodding sly?"
—"Nay: when she heard you had passed the
    Gate
That shuts on all flesh soon or late,
She thought you no more worth her hate,
  And cares not where you lie."

"Then, who is digging on my grave?
  Say—since I have not guessed!"
—"O it is I, my mistress dear,
Your little dog, who still lives near,
And much I hope my movements here
  Have not disturbed your rest?"

"Ah, yes! *You* dig upon my grave. . . .
  Why flashed it not on me
That one true heart was left behind!
What feeling do we ever find
To equal among human kind
  A dog's fidelity!"

"Mistress, I dug upon your grave
  To bury a bone, in case
I should be hungry near this spot
When passing on my daily trot.
I am sorry, but I quite forgot
  It was your resting-place."

FIVE "SATIRES OF CIRCUMSTANCE"

In Church

"And now to God the Father," he ends,
And his voice thrills up to the topmost tiles:
Each listener chokes as he bows and bends,
And emotion pervades the crowded aisles.
Then the preacher glides to the vestry-door,
And shuts it, and thinks he is seen no more.

The door swings softly ajar meanwhile,
And a pupil of his in the Bible class,
Who adores him as one without gloss or guile,
Sees her idol stand with a satisfied smile
And reënact at the vestry-glass
Each pulpit gesture in deft dumb-show
That had moved the congregation so.

By Her Aunt's Grave

"Sixpence a week," says the girl to her lover,
"Aunt used to bring me, for she could confide
In me alone, she vowed. It was to cover
The cost of her headstone when she died.
And that was a year ago last June;
I've not yet fixed it. But I must soon."

"And where is the money now, my dear?"
"O, snug in my purse. . . . Aunt was *so* slow
In saving it—eighty weeks, or near.". . .
"Let's spend it," he hints. "For she won't know.
Theres a dance tonight at the *Load of Hay*."
She passively nods. And they go that way.

At the Altar-Rail

"My bride is not coming, alas!" says the groom,
And the telegram shakes in his hand. "I own
It was hurried! We met at a dancing-room
When I went to the Cattle-Show alone,
And then, next night, where the Fountain leaps,
And the Street of the Quarter-Circle sweeps.

"Aye, she won me to ask her to be my wife—
'Twas foolish perhaps!—to forsake the ways
Of the flaring town for a farmer's life.
She agreed. And we fixed it. Now she says:
'It's sweet of you, dear, to prepare me a nest,
But a swift, short, gay life suits me best.
What I really am you have never gleaned;
I had eaten the apple ere you were weaned.' "

In the Restaurant

"But hear. If you stay, and the child be born,
It will pass as your husband's with the rest,
While, if we fly, the teeth of scorn
Will be gleaming at us from east to west;
And the child will come as a life despised.
I feel an elopement is ill-advised!"

"O you realize not what it is, my dear,
To a woman! Daily and hourly alarms
Lest the truth should out. How can I stay here
And nightly take him into my arms!
Come to the child no name or fame,
Let us go, and face it, and bear the shame."

At the Draper's

"I stood at the back of the shop, my dear,
  But you did not perceive me.
Well, when they deliver what you were shown
  I shall know nothing of it, believe me!"

And he coughed and coughed as she paled and said,
  "O, I didn't see you come in there—
Why couldn't you speak?"—"Well, I didn't. I left
  That you should not notice I'd been there.

"You were viewing some lovely things. *'Soon required*
  For a widow, of latest fashion';
And I knew 'twould upset you to meet the man
  Who had to be cold and ashen

"And screwed in a box before they could dress you
  'In the last new note in mourning,'
As they defined it. So, not to distress you,
  I left you to your adorning."

AFTERWARDS

When the Present has latched its postern behind my tremulous stay,
  And the May month flaps its glad green leaves like wings,
Delicate-filmed as new-spun silk, will the neighbors say,
  "He was a man who used to notice such things"?

If it be in the dusk when, like an eyelid's soundless blink,
  The dewfall-hawk comes crossing the shades to alight
Upon the wind-warped upland thorn, a gazer may think,
  "To him this must have been a familiar sight."

If I pass during some nocturnal blackness, mothy and warm,
  When the hedgehog travels furtively over the lawn,
One may say, "He strove that such innocent creatures should come to no harm,
  But he could do little for them; and now he is gone."

If, when hearing that I have been stilled at last, they stand at the door,
  Watching the full-starred heavens that winter sees,
Will this thought rise on those who will meet my face no more,
  "He was one who had an eye for such mysteries"?

And will any say when my bell of quittance is heard in the gloom,
  And a crossing breeze cuts a pause in its outrollings,
Till they rise again, as they were a new bell's boom,
  "He hears it not now, but used to notice such things"?

BIRDS AT WINTER NIGHTFALL

Around the house the flakes fly faster,
And all the berries now are gone
From holly and cotoneaster
Around the house. The flakes fly!—faster
Shutting indoors that crumb-outcaster
We used to see upon the lawn
Around the house. The flakes fly faster,
And all the berries now are gone!

WINTER IN DURNOVER FIELD

SCENE.—*A wide stretch of fallow ground recently sown with wheat, and frozen to iron hardness. Three large birds walking about thereon, and wistfully eyeing the surface. Wind keen from north-east: sky a dull gray.*

Rook: Throughout the field I find no grain;
The cruel frost encrusts the cornland!

Starling: Aye: patient pecking now is vain
Throughout the field, I find . . .

Rook: No grain!

Pigeon: Nor will be, comrade, till it rain,
Or genial thawings loose the lorn land
Throughout the field.

Rook: I find no grain:
The cruel frost encrusts the cornland!

THE ROMAN ROAD

The Roman Road runs straight and bare
As the pale parting-line in hair
Across the heath. And thoughtful men
Contrast its days of Now and Then,
And delve, and measure, and compare;

Visioning on the vacant air
Helmed legionnaires, who proudly rear
The Eagle, as they pace again
The Roman Road.

But no tall brass-helmed legionnaire
Haunts it for me. Uprises there
A mother's form upon my ken,
Guiding my infant steps, as when
We walked that ancient thoroughfare,
The Roman Road.

MY SPIRIT WILL NOT HAUNT THE MOUND

My spirit will not haunt the mound
Above my breast,
But travel, memory-possessed,
To where my tremulous being found
Life largest, best.

My phantom-footed shape will go
When nightfall grays
Hither and thither along the ways
I and another used to know
In backward days.

And there you'll find me, if a jot
You still should care
For me, and for my curious air;
If otherwise, then I shall not,
For you, be there.

WHEN I SET OUT FOR LYONNESSE

When I set out for Lyonnesse,
A hundred miles away,
The rime was on the spray,
And starlight lit my lonesomeness
When I set out for Lyonnesse
A hundred miles away.

What could bechance at Lyonnesse
While I should sojourn there
No prophet durst declare,
Nor did the wisest wizard guess
What would bechance at Lyonnesse
While I should sojourn there.

When I came back from Lyonnesse
With magic in my eyes,
All marked with mute surmise
My radiance rare and fathomless,
When I came back from Lyonnesse
With magic in my eyes.

THE DARK-EYED GENTLEMAN

I pitched my day's leazings[1] in Crimmercrock Lane,
To tie up my garter and jog on again,
When a dear dark-eyed gentleman passed there and said,
In a way that made all o' me color rose-red,
"What do I see—
O pretty knee!"
And he came and he tied up my garter for me.

'Twixt sunset and moonrise it was, I can mind:
Ah, 'tis easy to lose what we nevermore find!—
Of the dear stranger's home, of his name, I knew nought,
But I soon knew his nature and all that it brought.
Then bitterly
Sobbed I that he
Should ever have tied up my garter for me!

[1] "Leazings"; bundles of gleaned corn.

Yet now I've beside me a fine lissom lad,
And my slip's nigh forgot, and my days are not sad;
My own dearest joy is he, comrade, and friend,
He it is who safe-guards me, on him I depend;
No sorrow brings he,
And thankful I be
That his daddy once tied up my garter for me!

THE SUBALTERNS

"Poor wanderer," said the leaden sky,
"I fain would lighten thee,
But there be laws in force on high
Which say it must not be."

"I would not freeze thee, shorn one," cried
The North, "knew I but how
To warm my breath, to slack my stride;
But I am ruled as thou."

"Tomorrow I attack thee, wight,"
Said Sickness. "Yet I swear
I bear thy little ark no spite,
But am bid enter there."

"Come hither, Son," I heard Death say;
"I did not will a grave
Should end thy pilgrimage today,
But I, too, am a slave!"

We smiled upon each other then,
And life to me wore less
Of that fell guise it wore ere when
They owned their passiveness.

THE OXEN

Christmas Eve, and twelve of the clock,
"Now they are all on their knees,"
An elder said as we sat in a flock
By the embers in hearthside ease.

We pictured the meek mild creatures where
They dwelt in their strawy pen,
Nor did it occur to one of us there
To doubt they were kneeling then.

So fair a fancy few would weave
In these years! Yet, I feel,
If someone said on Christmas Eve,
"Come; see the oxen kneel

"In the lonely barton[1] by yonder coomb[2]
Our childhood used to know,"
I should go with him in the gloom,
Hoping it might be so.

THE TREE AND THE LADY

I have done all I could
For that lady I knew! Through the heats I have shaded her,
Drawn to her songsters when summer has jaded her,
Home from the heath or the wood.

At the mirth-time of May,
When my shadow first lured her, I'd donned my new bravery
Of greenth: 'twas my all. Now I shiver in slavery,
Icicles grieving me gray.

Plumed to every twigs end
I could tempt her chair under me. Much did I treasure her
During those days she had nothing to pleasure her;
Mutely she used me as friend.

[1] Barton: farmyard.
[2] Coomb: valley, hollow.

I'm a skeleton now,
And she's gone, craving warmth. The rime sticks like skin to me;
Through me Arcturus peers; Nor'lights shoot into me;
Gone is she, scorning my bough!

SNOW IN THE SUBURBS

Every branch big with it,
Bent every twig with it;
Every fork like a white web-foot;
Every street and pavement mute:
Some flakes have lost their way, and grope back upward, when
Meeting those meandering down they turn and descend again.
The palings are glued together like a wall,
And there is no waft of wind with the fleecy fall.

A sparrow enters the tree
Whereon immediately
A snow-lump thrice his own slight size
Descends on him and showers his head and eyes.
And overturns him,
And near inurns him,
And lights on a nether twig, when its brush
Starts off a volley of other lodging lumps with a rush.

The steps are a blanched slope,
Up which, with feeble hope,
A black cat comes, wide-eyed and thin;
And we take him in.

THE SELF-UNSEEING

Here is the ancient floor,
Footworn and hollowed and thin,
Here was the former door
Where the dead feet walked in.

She sat here in her chair,
Smiling into the fire;
He who played stood there,
Bowing it higher and higher.

Childlike, I danced in a dream;
Blessings emblazoned that day;
Everything glowed with a gleam,
Yet we were looking away!

A PLACID MAN'S EPITAPH

As for my life, I've led it
With fair content and credit:

It said: "Take this." I took it:
Said: "Leave." And I forsook it.
If I had done without it
None would have cared about it,
Or said: "One has refused it
Who might have meetly used it."

WAITING BOTH

A star looks down at me,
And says: "Here I and you
Stand, each in our degree:
What do you mean to do—
  Mean to do?"

I say: "For all I know,
Wait, and let Time go by,
Till my change come."—"Just so,"
The star says: "So mean I—
  So mean I."

HAP

If but some vengeful god would call to me
From up the sky, and laugh: "Thou suffering thing,
Know that thy sorrow is my ecstasy,
That thy love's loss is my hate's profiting!"

Then would I bear it, clench myself, and die,
Steeled by the sense of ire unmerited;
Half-eased in that a Powerfuller than I
Had willed and meted me the tears I shed.

But not so. How arrives it joy lies slain,
And why unblooms the best hope ever sown?
—Crass Casualty obstructs the sun and rain,
And dicing Time for gladness casts a moan. . . .
These purblind Doomsters had as readily strown
Blisses about my pilgrimage as pain.

THE CONVERGENCE OF THE TWAIN

(*Lines on the loss of the "Titanic"*)

I

In a solitude of the sea
Deep from human vanity,
And the Pride of Life that planned her, stilly couches she.

II

Steel chambers, late the pyres
Of her salamandrine fires,
Cold currents thrid, and turn to rhythmic tidal lyres.

III

Over the mirrors meant
To glass the opulent
The sea-worm crawls—grotesque, slimed, dumb, indifferent.

IV

Jewels in joy designed
To ravish the sensuous mind
Lie lightless, all their sparkles bleared and black and blind.

V

Dim moon-eyed fishes near
Gaze at the gilded gear
And query: "What does this vaingloriousness down here?"

VI

Well: while was fashioning
This creature of cleaving wing,
The Immanent Will that stirs and urges everything

VII

Prepared a sinister mate
For her—so gaily great
A Shape of Ice, for the time far and dissociate.

VIII

And as the smart ship grew
In stature, grace, and hue,
In shadowy silent distance grew the Iceberg too.

IX

Alien they seemed to be;
No mortal eye could see
The intimate welding of their later history,

X

Or sign that they were bent
By paths coincident
On being anon twin halves of one august event,

XI

Till the Spinner of the Years
Said "Now!" And each one hears,
And consummation comes, and jars two hemispheres

Gerard Manley Hopkins

Gerard Manley Hopkins was born in Essex, July, 28, 1844, became a Jesuit, and taught Greek and Greek meters at University College in Dublin. He was, in addition, a painter and a musician of no little ability, and his various gifts equipped him to be an innovator in poetic structure. Although he wrote much during an intensely spiritual life, none of his poetry appeared during his lifetime, and it was not until thirty years after his death that his extraordinary verse was collected. Hopkins died in 1889 and the world was not given the *Poems of Gerard Hopkins, Now First Published, with Notes by Robert Bridges* until 1918. Many of the verses in this posthumous volume were deciphered from manuscript by the Poet-Laureate and it is to him that one must be grateful for rescuing the work of a most original mind from oblivion.

A casual reader of Hopkins should expect obstacles; he must be prepared for difficulties that, at first, seem insuperable. He must be willing to accept a series of musical dissonances, compared to which the most cacophonous passages in Browning are limpid and bird-like. He must penetrate obscurities which are cloudy to the point of confusion. But he will be rewarded. Behind the tortured constructions and heaped-up epithets there is magnificence. In spite of the verbal excesses and idiomatic oddities there is an originality of vision which is nothing less than startling. In its intimate fancifulness, the imagery sometimes reminds one of the more controlled extravagances of Emily Dickinson. Like the New England poetess, Hopkins' poetry is sometimes eccentric, but it is always logical, never arbitrary or perverse, and sometimes breathless with ecstasy.

Hopkins himself worked out a curious scheme of prosody (he even invented a system of signs to make plain the effects he wished to achieve) and his lines (as his own preface tells us) are "written in Running Rhythm, the common rhythm in English use, some in Sprung Rhythm (a free beat strongly suggestive of later *vers libre*) and some in a mixture of both." The peculiar beauty in his poems makes it lamentable that Hopkins (to quote his editor) "died when, to judge by his latest work, he was beginning to concentrate the force of all his luxuriant experiments in rhythm and diction, and castigate his art into a more reserved style." Even in the cloudiest of his effects there is a splendor, a rush of rhyme, a cataract of color, attained by scarcely any of his plainer-speaking contemporaries.

The most outspoken admirer of this highly imaginative and highly elliptical poetry must admit its structural awkwardness. Hopkins himself wrote, "No doubt my poetry errs on the side of oddness. I hope in time to have a more balanced and Miltonic style. But as air, melody, is what strikes me most of all in music, and design in painting, so design, pattern, or what I am in the habit of calling *inscape* is what above all I aim at in poetry. Now it is the virtue of design, pattern, or 'inscape' to be distinctive, and it is the vice of distinctiveness to become queer. This vice I cannot have escaped." Yet Dr. Robert Bridges has made too much of Hopkins' mannerisms. If these poems, Bridges comments, "were to be arraigned for errors of what might be called taste, they might be convicted of occasional affectation in metaphor, as where the hills are 'as a stallion stalwart, very-violet-sweet' " . . .

As Robert Graves and Laura Riding inquire in *A Survey of Modernist Poetry,* "Why cannot what Dr. Bridges calls a fault of taste, an affectation, in the description of hills as 'a stallion stalwart, very-violet-sweet' be, with the proper sympathy for Hopkins' enthusiasm, appreciated as a phrase reconciling the two seemingly opposed qualities of mountains, their male, animal-like roughness and strength and, at the same time, their ethereal quality under soft light for which the violet in the gentle eye of the horse makes exactly the proper association?" That Bridges never understood Hopkins is proved by Bridges' other comments in the introduction, and emphasized by Hopkins' letters—Bridges having (significantly, it seems) destroyed his side of the correspondence.

Continually daring, Hopkins' work has never the note of ostentatious bravado. His boldness is instinctive; even such extraordinary departures as "Hurrahing in Harvest" and "Felix Randal" are extensions of the sonnet form but not violations of its spirit.

One of the more enthusiastic disciples (C. Day Lewis) has compared Hopkins to Shakespeare, not only because of Hopkins' continual "re-creation of word and image," but because of the exuberant quality of his images.

> I caught this morning morning's minion, king-
> dom of daylight's Dauphin, dapple-dawn-drawn Falcon, in his riding
> Of the rolling level underneath him steady air.

In such lines Hopkins explores the limbo which divides the ridiculous from the sublime. Here is a riotous alliteration which even the prodigal Swinburne might have hesitated to use, and yet Hopkins lifts the device into grandeur. Here, and almost everywhere in his poetry, is the concealed music, the subtle modulation, which breaks down the current poetic speech and forms it into a new language. "The poetic language of an age," Hopkins wrote, improving on Wordsworth, "should be the current language heightened, to any degree heightened and unlike itself, but not an obsolete one." Such heightening sometimes causes the reader to confess his inability to follow the poet's vision, but, as Day Lewis remarked in *A Hope for Poetry,* "what obscurity we may find is due, not to a clouded imagination or an unsettled intellect, but to his lightning dashes from image to image, so quick that we are unable at first to perceive the points of contact."

Hopkins' epithets may seem erratic but they are actually if oddly precise. As with his punctuation, he could give a rule for everything, even for the frequent and deliberate omission of the relative pronoun which he dropped not only "to crowd out every merely grammatical or toneless element" but to stress the heavy accents of his verse. "The Habit of Perfection," "The Starlight Night," "The Golden Echo," its companion piece, "The Leaden Echo," and "God's Grandeur" will not be shaken out of the mind. If "emphasis seems to oust euphony" in a struggle of intense contractions, his style, pushed by the extremities of his theories, is a triumph of elisions. Far from being a "fascinating failure" (T. Earle Welby's summary), his poetry lifts exact if unfamiliar verity of phrase to a burning beauty.

Hopkins having found an audience thirty-five years after his death, his least fragments were collated and an enlarged edition of his *Poems* was issued in 1930. A year later there appeared *The Letters of Gerard Manley Hopkins to Robert Bridges* (1935) and *The Correspondence of Gerard Manley Hopkins and Richard Watson Dixon* (1935), two volumes rich in delicate humor, insight, and discrimination, possibly the finest criticism written in English. Memorable are his disposals of Dickens, Wordsworth, Tennyson—he called the Idylls "Charades of the Middle Ages"—and Swinburne of the "delirium-tremendous imagination." And who, after once reading his estimate of Browning, can forget that Browning has "a way of talking and making his people talk with the air and spirit of a man bouncing up from table with his mouth full of bread and cheese and saying that he meant to stand no blasted nonsense." A third augmented edition of *Poems* appeared in 1948.

Gerard Manley Hopkins: A Biography (1930) by G. F. Lahey, and *Three Friends,* by Robert Bridges, memoirs of Digby Mackworth Dolben, Richard Watson Dixon and Henry Bradley, shed further light on this rich personality.

One of the most erudite critics and certainly the most inventive poet of his day—such was the man who refused to fight for fame because, as a Jesuit, he had vowed to serve God. Like the things he loved most, he, too, was "counter, original, spare, strange," possibly the most original genius of his generation. Everywhere in his work there is a new extravagance of metaphor. The opulence is not carefully built up; it is reckless, almost agonized, as though the poet could not lay his hands on figures rich and rapid enough to express the speed of his intuitions. To Hopkins everything was happy and magnificent. The world was not merely colorful but prodigal, "barbarous in beauty." Nature was a divine turmoil, and God was an eternal exuberance.

THOU ART INDEED JUST, LORD

Thou art indeed just, Lord, if I contend
With thee; but, sir, so what I plead is just.
Why do sinners' ways prosper? and why must
Disappointment all I endeavour end?
Wert thou my enemy, O thou my friend,
How wouldst thou worse, I wonder, than thou dost
Defeat, thwart me? Oh, the sots and thralls of lust
Do in spare hours more thrive than I that spend,
Sir, life upon thy cause. See, banks and brakes
Now, leavèd how thick! lacèd they are again
With fretty chervil, look, and fresh wind shakes
Them; birds build—but not I build; no, but strain,
Time's eunuch, and not breed one work that wakes.
Mine, O thou lord of life, send my roots rain.

PIED BEAUTY

Glory be to God for dappled things—
For skies of couple-color as a brinded cow;
For rose-moles all in stipple upon trout that swim;
Fresh-firecoal chestnut-falls; finches' wings;
Landscapes plotted and pieced—fold, fallow, and plow;
And all trades, their gear and tackle and trim.
All things counter, original, spare, strange;
Whatever is fickle, freckled (who knows how?)
With swift, slow; sweet, sour; adazzle, dim;
He fathers-forth whose beauty is past change:
Praise Him.

THE HABIT OF PERFECTION

Elected Silence, sing to me
And beat upon my whorlèd ear,
Pipe me to pastures still, and be
The music that I care to hear.

Shape nothing, lips; be lovely-dumb;
It is the shut, the curfew sent
From there where all surrenders come
Which only makes you eloquent.

Be shellèd, eyes, with double dark
And find the uncreated light:
This ruck and reel which you remark
Coils, keeps, and teases simple sight.

Palate, the hutch of tasty lust,
Desire not to be rinsed with wine:
The can must be so sweet, the crust
So fresh that come in fasts divine!

Nostrils, your careless breath that spend
Upon the stir and keep of pride,
What relish shall the censers send
Along the sanctuary side!

O feel-of-primrose hands, O feet
That want the yield of plushy sward,
But you shall walk the golden street
And you unhouse and house the Lord.

And, Poverty, be thou the bride
And now the marriage feast begun,
And lily-colored clothes provide
Your spouse, not labored-at nor spun.

THE LEADEN ECHO

How to keep—is there any, any, is there none such, nowhere known, some bow or
brooch or braid or brace, lace, latch or catch or key to keep
Back beauty, keep it, beauty, beauty, beauty, . . . from vanishing away?
Oh, is there no frowning of these wrinkles, ranked wrinkles deep,
Down? no waving-off of these most mournful messengers, still messengers, sad and
stealing messengers of gray?
No, there's none, there's none—oh, no, there's none!
Nor can you long be, what you now are, called fair—
Do what you may do, do what you may,
And wisdom is early to despair:

Be beginning; since, no, nothing can be done
To keep at bay
Age and age's evils—hoar hair,
Ruck and wrinkle, drooping, dying, death's worst, winding sheets, tombs and worms, and tumbling to decay;
So be beginning, be beginning to despair.
Oh, there's none—no, no, no, there's none:
Be beginning to despair, to despair,
Despair, despair, despair, despair.

THE GOLDEN ECHO

Spare!
There is one, yes, I have one (Hush there!);
Only not within seeing of the sun,
Not within the singeing of the strong sun,
Tall sun's tingeing, or treacherous the tainting of the earth's air,
Somewhere elsewhere there is ah, well, where! one,
One. Yes, I can tell such a key, I do know such a place,
Where whatever's prized and passed of us, everything that's fresh and fast-flying of us, seems to us sweet of us and swiftly away with, done away with, undone,
Undone, done with, soon done with, and yet dearly and dangerously sweet
Of us, the wimpled-water-dimpled, not-by-morning-matchèd face,
The flower of beauty, fleece of beauty, too too apt to, ah! to fleet,
Never fleets more, fastened with the tenderest truth
To its own best being and its loveliness of youth: it is an everlastingness of, O it is an all youth!
Come then, your ways and airs and looks, locks, maiden gear, gallantry and gayety and grace,
Winning ways, airs innocent, maiden manners, sweet looks, loose locks, long locks, lovelocks, gaygear, going gallant, girlgrace—
Resign them, sign them, seal them, send them, motion them with breath,
And with sighs soaring, soaring sighs deliver
Them; beauty-in-the-ghost, deliver it, early now, long before death
Give beauty back, beauty, beauty, beauty, back to God, beauty's self and beauty's giver.
See; not a hair is, not an eyelash, not the least lash lost; every hair
Is, hair of the head, numbered.
Nay, what we had lighthanded left in surely the mere mold
Will have waked and have waxed and have walked with the wind whatwhile we slept,
This side, that side hurling a heavyheaded hundredfold
What while we, while we slumbered.
O then, weary then why should we tread? O why are we so haggard at the heart, so care-coiled, care-killed, so fagged, so fashed, so cogged, so cumbered,
When the thing we freely forfeit is kept with fonder a care,
Fonder a care kept than we could have kept it, kept
Far with fonder a care (and we, we should have lost it) finer, fonder
A care kept.—Where kept? Do but tell us where kept, where.—
Yonder.—What high as that! We follow, now we follow.—Yonder, yes, yonder, yonder,
Yonder.

GOD'S GRANDEUR

The world is charged with the grandeur of God.
  It will flame out, like shining from shook foil;
  It gathers to a greatness, like the ooze of oil
Crushed. Why do men then now not reck his rod?
Generations have trod, have trod, have trod;
  And all is seared with trade; bleared, smeared with toil;
  And wears man's smudge and shares man's smell: the soil
Is bare now, nor can foot feel, being shod.

And for all this, nature is never spent;
  There lives the dearest freshness deep down things;
And though the last lights off the black West went
  Oh, morning, at the brown brink eastward, springs—
Because the Holy Ghost over the bent
  World broods with warm breast and with ah! bright wings.

THE STARLIGHT NIGHT

Look at the stars! look, look up at the skies!
  O look at all the fire-folk sitting in the air!
  The bright boroughs, the circle-citadels there!
Down in dim woods the diamond delves! the elves'-eyes!
The gray lawns cold where gold, where quickgold lies!
  Wind-beat whitebeam! airy abeles set on a flare!
  Flake-doves sent floating forth at a farmyard scare!
Ah, well! it is all a purchase, all is a prize.
Buy then! bid then!—What?—Prayer, patience, alms, vows.
Look, look: a May-mess, like on orchard boughs!
  Look! March-bloom, like on mealed-with-yellow sallows!
These are indeed the barn; withindoors house
The shocks. This piece-bright paling shuts the spouse
  Christ home, Christ and his mother and all his hallows.

SPRING

Nothing is so beautiful as spring—
  When weeds, in wheels, shoot long and lovely and lush;
  Thrush's eggs look little low heavens, and thrush
Through the echoing timber does so rinse and wring
The ear, it strikes like lightning to hear him sing;
  The glassy peartree leaves and blooms, they brush
  The descending blue; that blue is all in a rush
With richness; the racing lambs too have fair their fling.

What is all this juice and all this joy?
  A strain of the earth's sweet being in the beginning
In Eden garden.—Have, get, before it cloy,
  Before it cloud, Christ, lord, and sour with sinning,
Innocent mind and Mayday in girl and boy,
  Most, O maid's child, thy choice and worthy the winning.

HURRAHING IN HARVEST

Summer ends now; now, barbarous in beauty, the stooks
  Around; up above, what wind-walks! what lovely behav
  Of silk-sack clouds! has wilder, willful-wavier
Meal-drift molded ever and melted across skies?

I walk, I lift up, I lift up heart, eyes,
  Down all that glory in the heavens to glean our Saviour;
  And, eyes, heart, what looks, what lips yet gave you a
Rapturous love's greeting of realer, of rounder replies?

And the azurous hung hills are his world-wielding shoulder
  Majestic—as a stallion stalwart, very-violet-sweet!—
These things, these things were here and but the beholder
  Wanting; which two when they once meet,
The heart rears wings bold and bolder
   And hurls for him, O half hurls earth for him off under his feet.

THE CAGED SKYLARK

As a dare-gale skylark scanted in a dull cage
  Man's mounting spirit in his bone-house, mean house, dwells—
  That bird beyond the remembering his free fells;
This in drudgery, day-laboring-out life's age.

Though aloft on turf or perch or poor low stage,
  Both sing sometimes the sweetest, sweetest spells,
  Yet both droop deadly sometimes in their cells
Or wring their barriers in bursts of fear or rage.

Not that the sweet-fowl, song-fowl, needs no rest—
Why, hear him, hear him babble and drop down to his nest,
  But his own nest, wild nest, no prison.

Man's spirit will be flesh-bound when found at best,
But uncumbered: meadow-down is not distressed
  For a rainbow footing it nor he for his bones risen.

MOONRISE

I awoke in the Midsummer not to call night, in the white and the walk of the
    morning:
The moon, dwindled and thinned to the fringe of a finger-nail held to the candle,
Or paring of paradisaïcal fruit, lovely in waning but lusterless,
Stepped from the stool, drew back from the barrow, of dark Maenefa the mountain;
A cusp still clasped him, a fluke yet fanged him, entangled him, not quit utterly.
This was the prized, the desirable sight, unsought, presented so easily,
Parted me leaf and leaf, divided me, eyelid and eyelid of slumber.

GERARD MANLEY HOPKINS

FELIX RANDAL

Felix Randal the farrier, O he is dead then? my duty all ended,
Who have watched his mold of man, big-boned and hardy-handsome
Pining, pining, till time when reason rambled in it and some
Fatal four disorders, fleshed there, all contended?

Sickness broke him. Impatient he cursed at first, but mended
Being anointed and all; though a heavenlier heart began some
Months earlier, since I had our sweet reprieve and ransom
Tendered to him. Ah, well, God rest him all road ever he offended!

This seeing the sick endears them to us, us too it endears.
My tongue had taught the comfort, touch had quenched thy tears,
Thy tears that touched my heart, child, Felix, poor Felix Randal;

How far from then forethought of, all thy more boisterous years,
When thou at the random grim forge, powerful amidst peers,
Didst fettle for the great gray drayhorse his bright and battering sandal!

TO HIS WATCH

(unfinished)

Mortal my mate, bearing my rock-a-heart
Warm beat with cold beat company, shall I
Earlier or you fail at our force, and lie
The ruins of, rifled, once a world of art?
The telling time our task is; time's some part,
Not all, but we were framed to fail and die—
One spell and well that one. There, ah, thereby
Is comfort's carol of all or woe's worst smart.

Field-flown the departed day no morning brings
Saying "This was yours" with her, but new one, worse,
And then that last and shortest . . .

THE CUCKOO

Repeat that, repeat,
Cuckoo, bird, and open ear wells, heart-springs, delightfully sweet,
With a ballad, with a ballad, a rebound
Off trundled timber and scoops of the hillside ground, hollow hollow hollow ground:
The whole landscape flushes on a sudden at a sound.

HEAVEN-HAVEN

A Nun Takes the Veil

I have desired to go
  Where springs not fail,
To fields where flies no sharp and sided hail,
  And a few lilies blow.

And I have asked to be
  Where no storms come,
Where the green swell is in the havens dumb
  And out of the swing of the sea.

THE WINDHOVER

To Christ Our Lord

I caught this morning morning's minion, king-
  dom of daylight's dauphin, dapple-dawn-drawn Falcon, in his riding
  Of the rolling level underneath him steady air, and striding
High there, how he rung upon the rein of a wimpling wing
In his ecstasy! then off, off forth on swing,
  As a skate's heel sweeps smooth on a bow-bend: the hurl and gliding
  Rebuffed the big wind. My heart in hiding
Stirred for a bird,—the achieve of, the mastery of the thing!

Brute beauty and valor and act, oh, air, pride, plume, here
  Buckle! AND the fire that breaks from thee then, a billion
Times told lovelier, more dangerous, O my chevalier!

  No wonder of it: sheer plod makes plough down sillion
Shine, and blue-bleak embers, ah my dear,
  Fall, gall themselves, and gash gold-vermilion.

INVERSNAID

This darksome burn, horseback brown,
His rollrock highroad roaring down,
In coop and in comb the fleece of his foam
Flutes and low to the lake falls home.

A windpuff-bonnet of fawn-froth
Turns and twindles over the broth
Of a pool so pitchblack, fell-frowning,
It rounds and rounds Despair to drowning.

Degged with dew, dappled with dew
Are the groins of the braes that the brook treads through,
Wiry heathpacks, flitches of fern,
And the beadbonny ash that sits over the burn.

What would the world be, once bereft
Of wet and of wildness? Let them be left,
O let them be left, wildness and wet;
Long live the weeds and the wilderness yet.

WHAT I DO IS ME

As kingfishers catch fire, dragonflies draw flame;
As tumbled over rim in roundy wells
Stones ring; like each tucked string tells, each hung bell's
Bow swung finds tongue to fling out broad its name;
Each mortal thing does one thing and the same:
Deals out that being indoors each one dwells;

Selves—goes itself; *myself* it speaks and spells,
Crying *What I do is me: for that I came.*

I say more: the just man justices;
Keeps grace: that keeps all his goings graces;
Acts in God's eye what in God's eye he is—
Christ—for Christ plays in ten thousand places,
Lovely in limbs, and lovely in eyes not his
To the Father through the features of men's faces.

NO WORST, THERE IS NONE

No worst, there is none. Pitched past pitch of grief,
More pangs will, schooled at forepangs, wilder wring.
Comforter, where, where is your comforting?
Mary, mother of us, where is your relief?
My cries heave, herds-long; huddle in a main, a chief
Woe, world-sorrow; on an age-old anvil wince and sing—
Then lull, then leave off. Fury had shrieked "No ling-
ering! Let me be fell: force I must be brief."

O the mind, mind has mountains; cliffs of fall
Frightful, sheer, no-man-fathomed. Hold them cheap
May who ne'er hung there. Nor does long our small
Durance deal with that steep or deep. Here! creep,
Wretch, under a comfort serves in a whirlwind: all
Life death does end and each day dies with sleep.

MY OWN HEART

My own heart let me more have pity on; let
Me live to my sad self hereafter kind,
Charitable; not live this tormented mind
With this tormented mind tormenting yet.
I cast for comfort I can no more get
By groping round my comfortless, than blind
Eyes in their dark can day or thirst can find
Thirst's all-in-all in all a world of wet.

Soul, self; come, poor Jackself, I do advise
You, jaded, let be; call off thoughts awhile
Elsewhere; leave comfort root-room; let joy size
At God knows when to God knows what; whose smile
's not wrung, see you; unforseen times rather—as skies
Betweenpie mountains—lights a lovely mile.

Robert Bridges

Robert (Seymour) Bridges was born October 23, 1844. He was educated at Eton and Corpus Christi, Oxford, and, after having traveled, studied medicine, taking the post of Casualty Surgeon at St. Bartholomew's Hospital, London. He retired from the medical profession in 1882 to devote himself entirely to literature. Although many more prominent poets were suggested for the office, the classic restraint of his verse won him the highest official honor: he became Poet Laureate in 1913. So often has the Laureateship been nothing more than a political prize that is gratifying to observe that the award went to one distinguished for nothing more zealous than his art. As essayist, he wrote considerably for the Society of Pure English which, largely through his efforts, was founded in 1913. His interests were unusually varied and included cricket, hymnology (he collaborated in the editing of a hymnal), spoken English, reformed spelling, the encouragement of fellow poets (Hopkins, for example), and music, especially music for the harpsichord. He died, after a short illness, in his eighty-sixth year, on April 21, 1930.

The subjects of his many volumes are indicative of his expression; a few of the titles are: *Prometheus the Firegiver; Eros and Psyche; Achilles in Scyros; The Feast of Bacchus. Poems* appeared as early as 1873. The distinguishing features of his *Shorter Poems* (1894) are a subtlety of rhythm, a precise command of metrical delicacies. It is, in fact, as a metrician that his work is most interesting; even his most academic lines bear a beauty of pattern. Apart from the skill of versification, there are many delights for the most casual reader in his collected *Poetical Works* (excluding the dramas) which appeared in 1913.

Robert Hillyer, the American poet and teacher, has made a study of Bridges' poems and a particularly delicate analysis of his major work. "Until the publication of *The Testament of Beauty* (1929)," writes Mr. Hillyer, "the genius of Robert Bridges was known to comparatively few. In spite of the prolonged neglect of his earlier works on the part of the large public, most of the poets of England and a few in America recognized him as a master. The *Shorter Poems* were accounted the height of lyric artistry. Some of these, such as 'A Passer-by,' 'London Snow,' and 'Awake, My Heart, to Be Loved,' found a more general audience; but, for the most part, Bridges remained a poet's poet until the publication of *The Testament of Beauty.*

"Both those who admire and those who dislike the poetry of Bridges agree on one point: that technically he was one of the masters of English verse. His experiments within the tradition are bolder and more informed than most of those outside it. His skill has often been cited against him by the school of modern critics who prefer verse to be slip-shod or, as they would express it, 'unacademic.' Starting early with Gerard Manley Hopkins and other friends a systematic study of what could be done in English meters without breaking down the instrument, he explored possibilities which, though not so obviously startling as Hopkins' 'sprung rhythm,' were subtly quite as adventurous. His main impulse came from classical prosody, and his early adaptations of quantity to English metrics have never been equaled. In his later work, notably in the 'loose Alexandrines' of *The Testament of Beauty,* he combined with this strong quantitative influence an element wholly derived from our own ancient verse; that is, great liberty in the number of syllables within the single line.

"Space forbids any detailed analysis of this great work. It has been compared to Wordsworth's *Prelude* and to Lucretius's *De Rerum Natura.* The main theme, based on Christian teleology, is the evolution of the human soul toward perfection, the reunion of all things in God through the growth of spiritual love. The poet shows how in Man the blind instincts of Nature become transformed, through influences such as that of beauty, into spiritual forces. Thus, the indiscriminate mating of lower forms of life rises to love inspired by the beauty of the beloved, and in higher natures becomes completely transmuted, as in Dante's love for Beatrice. The theme is developed by the high logic of poetry, which combines with the philosopher's learning and reasoning, the persuasion of beauty itself."

A PASSER-BY

Whither, O splendid ship, thy white sails crowding,
Leaning across the bosom of the urgent West,
That fearest nor sea rising nor sky clouding,
Whither away, fair rover, and what thy quest?
Ah! soon, when Winter has all our vales opprest,
When skies are cold and misty, and hail is hurling,
Wilt thou glide on the blue Pacific, or rest
In a summer haven asleep, thy white sails furling.

I there before thee, in the country that well thou knowest,
Already arrived am inhaling the odorous air:
I watch thee enter unerringly where thou goest,
And anchor queen of the strange shipping there,
Thy sails for awnings spread, thy masts bare;
Nor is aught from the foaming reef to the snow-capp'd, grandest
Peak, that is over the feathery palms, more fair
Than thou, so upright, so stately, and still thou standest.

And yet, O splendid ship, unhail'd and nameless,
I know not if, aiming a fancy, I rightly divine
That thou hast a purpose joyful, a courage blameless,
Thy port assured in a happier land than mine.
But for all I have given thee, beauty enough is thine,
As thou, aslant with trim tackle and shrouding,
From the proud nostril curve of a prow's line
In the offing scatterest foam, thy white sails crowding.

AWAKE, MY HEART, TO BE LOVED

Awake, my heart, to be loved, awake, awake!
The darkness silvers away, the morn doth break,
It leaps in the sky: unrisen lusters slake
The o'ertaken moon. Awake, O heart, awake!

She too that loveth awaketh and hopes for thee;
Her eyes already have sped the shades that flee,
Already they watch the path thy feet shall take:
Awake, O heart, to be loved, awake, awake!

And if thou tarry from her,—if this could be,—
She cometh herself, O heart, to be loved, to thee;
For thee would unashamèd herself forsake:
Awake to be loved, my heart, awake, awake!

Awake! the land is scattered with light, and see,
Uncanopied sleep is flying from field and tree:
And blossoming boughs of April in laughter shake;
Awake, O heart, to be loved, awake, awake!

Lo all things wake and tarry and look for thee:
She looketh and saith, "O sun, now bring him to me.
Come more adored, O adored, for his coming's sake,
And awake, my heart, to be loved: awake, awake!"

O WEARY PILGRIMS

(from "The Growth of Love")

O weary pilgrims, chanting of your woe,
That turn your eyes to all the peaks that shine,
Hailing in each the citadel divine
The which ye thought to have entered long ago;
Until at length your feeble steps and slow
Falter upon the threshold of the shrine,
And your hearts overburdened doubt in fine
Whether it be Jerusalem or no:
Disheartened pilgrims, I am one of you;
For, having worshiped many a barren face,
I scarce now greet the goal I journeyed to:
I stand a pagan in the holy place;
Beneath the lamp of truth I am found untrue,
And question with the God that I embrace.

THOU DIDST DELIGHT MY EYES

Thou didst delight my eyes:
Yet who am I? nor first
Nor last nor best, that durst
Once dream of thee for prize;
Nor this the only time
Thou shalt set love to rhyme.

Thou didst delight my ear:
Ah! little praise; thy voice
Makes other hearts rejoice,
Makes all ears glad that hear;
And short my joy: but yet,
O song, do not forget.

For what wert thou to me?
How shall I say? The moon,
That poured her midnight noon
Upon his wrecking sea;—
A sail, that for a day
Has cheered the castaway.

WINTER NIGHTFALL

The day begins to droop,—
  Its course is done:
But nothing tells the place
  Of the setting sun.

The hazy darkness deepens,
  And up the lane
You may hear, but cannot see,
  The homing wain.

An engine pants and hums
  In the farm hard by:
Its lowering smoke is lost
  In the lowering sky.

The soaking branches drip,
  And all night through
The drooping will not cease
  In the avenue.

A tall man there in the house
  Must keep his chair:
He knows he will never again
  Breathe the spring air:

His heart is worn with work;
  He is giddy and sick
If he rise to go as far
  As the nearest rick:

He thinks of his morn of life,
  His hale, strong years;
And braves as he may the night
  Of darkness and tears.

LONDON SNOW

When men were all asleep the snow came flying,
In large white flakes falling on the city brown,
Stealthily and perpetually settling and loosely lying,
  Hushing the latest traffic of the drowsy town;
Deadening, muffling, stifling its murmurs failing;
Lazily and incessantly floating down and down;
  Silently sifting and veiling road, roof and railing;
Hiding difference, making unevenness even,
Into angles and crevices softly drifting and sailing.
  All night it fell, and when full inches seven
It lay in the depth of its uncompacted lightness,
The clouds blew off from a high and frosty heaven;
  And all woke earlier for the unaccustomed brightness
Of the winter dawning, the strange unheavenly glare:
The eye marveled—marveled at the dazzling whiteness;
  The ear harkened to the stillness of the solemn air;
No sound of wheel rumbling nor of foot falling,
And the busy morning cries came thin and spare.
  Then boys I heard, as they went to school, calling;
They gathered up the crystal manna to freeze
Their tongues with tasting, their hands with snow-balling;
  Or rioted in a drift, plunging up to the knees;
Or peering up from under the white-mossed wonder,
"O look at the trees!" they cried. "O look at the trees!"
  With lessened load, a few carts creak and blunder,
Following along the white deserted way,
A country company long dispersed asunder:
  When now already the sun, in pale display
Standing by Paul's high dome, spread forth below

His sparkling beams, and awoke the stir of the day.
  For now doors open, and war is waged with the snow;
And trains of somber men, past tale of number,
Tread down brown paths, as toward their toil they go:
  But even for them awhile no cares encumber
Their minds diverted; the daily word is unspoken,
The daily thoughts of labor and sorrow slumber
At the sight of the beauty that greets them, for the charm they
    have broken.

NIGHTINGALES

Beautiful must be the mountains whence ye come,
And bright in the fruitful valleys the streams wherefrom
    Ye learn your song:
Where are those starry woods? O might I wander there,
  Among the flowers, which in that heavenly air
    Bloom the year long!

Nay, barren are those mountains and spent the streams:
Our song is the voice of desire, that haunts our dreams,
    A throe of the heart,
Whose pining visions dim, forbidden hopes profound,
  No dying cadence nor long sigh can sound,
    For all our art.

Alone, aloud in the raptured ear of men
We pour our dark nocturnal secret; and then,
    As night is withdrawn
From these sweet-springing meads and bursting boughs of May,
  Dream, while the innumerable choir of day
    Welcome the dawn.

I HAVE LOVED FLOWERS

I have loved flowers that fade,
Within whose magic tents
Rich hues have marriage made
With sweet unmemoried scents:
A honeymoon delight,—
A joy of love at sight,
That ages in an hour:—
My song be like a flower!

I have loved airs that die
Before their charm is writ
Along a liquid sky
Trembling to welcome it.
Notes that with pulse of fire
Proclaim the spirit's desire,
Then die, and are nowhere:—
My song be like an air!

Die, song, die like a breath,
And wither as a bloom:
Fear not a flowery death,
Dread not an airy tomb!
Fly with delight, fly hence!
'Twas thine love's tender sense
To feast; now on thy bier
Beauty shall shed a tear.

NIMIUM FORTUNATUS

I have lain in the sun,
I have toil'd as I might,
I have thought as I would,
And now it is night.

My bed full of sleep,
My heart of content
For friends that I met
The way that I went.

I welcome fatigue
While frenzy and care
Like thin summer clouds
Go melting in air.

To dream as I may
And awake when I will
With the song of the birds
And the sun on the hill.

Or death—were it death—
To what should I wake
Who loved in my home
All life for its sake?

What good have I wrought?
I laugh to have learned
That joy cannot come
Unless it be earned;

For a happier lot
Than God giveth me
It never hath been
Nor ever shall be.

William Ernest Henley

William Ernest Henley was born August 23, 1849, at Gloucester, and was educated at the Grammar School of Gloucester. From childhood he was afflicted wtih a tuberculous disease which finally necessitated the amputation of a foot. His *Hospital Sketches,* those vivid precursors of free verse, were a record of the time when he was at the infirmary at Edinburgh; they are sharp with the sights, sensations, even the smells, of the sick-room. In spite (or, more probably, because) of his continued poor health, Henley never ceased to worship strength and energy; courage and a triumphant belief shine out of the athletic *London Voluntaries* (1892) and the light lyrics in *Hawthorn and Lavender* (1901).

The buoyancy, rousing at first, becomes wearing; it is too insistent, a little shrill. When Henley ceased to overrate animal energy he was no less himself, and a better poet. When not banging drums and flashing swords, he could distill the essence of a lyric, turn a triolet or ballade with the most expert practitioner of the French forms, paint impressionistic side-lights of intimate London, and, in such pieces as "Madame Life," combine grimness and gay *bizarrerie.*

The mixture of lightness and lustiness dates from his early youth. An infectious idiom, it flowered under his first influence, which was that of his schoolmaster, T. E. Brown, and remained to the end.

The bulk of Henley's poetry is not great in volume. He has himself explained the small quantity of his work in a Preface to his *Poems,* first published in 1888. "A principal reason," he says, "is that, after spending the better part of my life in the pursuit of poetry, I found myself (about 1877) so utterly unmarketable that I had to own myself beaten in art, and to indict myself to journalism for the next ten years." Later on, he began to write again—"old dusty sheaves were dragged to light; the work of selection and correction was begun; I burned much; I found that, after all, the lyrical instinct had slept—not died."

As editor he was fearless, prejudiced, violent in preferences and antipathies, and always sincere. His unflinching candor won over even those who completely disagreed with him. His friendships were many; one of the closest was with Robert Louis Stevenson, with whom he wrote three plays published in 1892. (Henley is only slightly disguised as the characteristic "Burly" in Stevenson's essay, "Talk and Talkers.") He compiled a book of poems for boys, *Lyra Heroica* (1891), and collaborated on a dictionary of English slang. Though continually in conflict, he remained belligerent until 1894; in that year the death of his six-year-old daughter broke the heart of one whose head had been "bloody but unbowed."

In 1901 he published *Hawthorn and Lavender,* releasing a far finer though smaller music than he had ever uttered. His unrhythmed rhythms, reminiscent of Heine's *North Sea* cycles, anticipated in color and accent the subsequent vogue of *vers libre.* Although he was not one of the great poets of his period, his period, as well as ours, would be incomplete without him. After a brilliant and varied career devoted mostly to journalism, Henley died in 1903.

INVICTUS

Out of the night that covers me,
  Black as the Pit from pole to pole,
I thank whatever gods may be
  For my unconquerable soul.

In the fell clutch of circumstance
  I have not winced nor cried aloud.
Under the bludgeonings of chance
  My head is bloody, but unbowed.

Beyond this place of wrath and tears
  Looms but the horror of the shade,
And yet the menace of the years
  Finds, and shall find me, unafraid.

It matters not how strait the gate,
  How charged with punishments the scroll,
I am the master of my fate:
  I am the captain of my soul.

THE BLACKBIRD

The nightingale has a lyre of gold,
  The lark's is a clarion call,
And the blackbird plays but a boxwood flute,
  But I love him best of all.

For his song is all of the joy of life,
  And we in the mad, spring weather,
We two have listened till he sang
  Our hearts and lips together.

A BOWL OF ROSES

It was a bowl of roses:
  There in the light they lay,
Languishing, glorying, glowing
  Their life away.

And the soul of them rose like a presence,
  Into me crept and grew,
And filled me with something—someone—
  O, was it you?

BEFORE

Behold me waiting—waiting for the knife.
A little while, and at a leap I storm
The thick sweet mystery of chloroform,
The drunken dark, the little death-in-life.
The gods are good to me: I have no wife,
No innocent child, to think of as I near
The fateful minute; nothing all-too dear
Unmans me for my bout of passive strife.
Yet I am tremulous and a trifle sick,
And, face to face with chance, I shrink a little:
My hopes are strong, my will is something weak.
Here comes the basket? Thank you. I am ready.
But, gentlemen my porters, life is brittle:
You carry Caesar and his fortunes—Steady!

BALLADE

Made in the Hot Weather

Fountains that frisk and sprinkle
The moss they overspill;
Pools that the breezes crinkle;
The wheel beside the mill,
With its wet, weedy frill;
Wind-shadows in the wheat;
A water-cart in the street;
The fringe of foam that girds
An islet's ferneries;
A green sky's minor thirds—
To live, I think of these!

Of ice and glass the tinkle,
Pellucid, silver-shrill;
Peaches without a wrinkle;
Cherries and snow at will,
From china bowls that fill
The senses with a sweet
Incuriousness of heat;
A melon's dripping sherds;
Cream-clotted strawberries;
Dusk dairies set with curds—
To live, I think of these!

Vale-lily and periwinkle;
Wet stone-crop on the sill;
The look of leaves a-twinkle
With windlets clear and still;
The feel of a forest rill
That wimples fresh and fleet
About one's naked feet;
The muzzles of drinking herds;
Lush flags and bulrushes;
The chirp of rain-bound birds—
To live, I think of these!

Envoy

Dark aisles, new packs of cards,
Mermaidens' tails, cool swards,
Dawn dews and starlit seas,
White marbles, whiter words—
To live, I think of these!

WE'LL GO NO MORE A-ROVING

We'll go no more a-roving by the light of the moon.
November glooms are barren beside the dusk of June.
The summer flowers are faded, the summer thoughts are sere.
We'll go no more a-roving, lest worse befall, my dear.

We'll go no more a-roving by the light of the moon.
The song we sang rings hollow, and heavy runs the tune.
Glad ways and words remembered would shame the wretched year.
We'll go no more a-roving, nor dream we did, my dear.

We'll go no more a-roving by the light of the moon.
If yet we walk together, we need not shun the noon.
No sweet thing left to savor, no sad thing left to fear,
We'll go no more a-roving, but weep at home, my dear

MADAM LIFE

Madam Life's a piece in bloom
Death goes dogging everywhere:
She's the tenant of the room,
He's the ruffian on the stair.

You shall see her as a friend,
You shall bilk him once and twice;
But he'll trap you in the end,
And he'll stick you for her price.

With his kneebones at your chest,
And his knuckles in your throat,
You would reason—plead—protest!
Clutching at her petticoat;

But she's heard it all before,
Well she knows you've had your fun,
Gingerly she gains the door,
And your little job is done.

OUT OF TUNE

The spring, my dear,
Is no longer spring.
Does the blackbird sing
What he sang last year?
Are the skies the old
Immemorial blue?
Or am I, or are you,
Grown cold?

Though life be change,
It is hard to bear
When the old sweet air
Sounds forced and strange,
To be out of tune,
Plain You and I . . .
It were better to die,
And soon!

FALMOUTH[1]

O, Falmouth is a fine town with ships in the bay,
And I wish from my heart it's there I was today;
I wish from my heart I was far away from here,
Sitting in my parlor and talking to my dear.
For it's home, dearie, home—it's home I want to be.
Our topsails are hoisted, and we'll away to sea.
O, the oak and the ash and the bonnie birken tree
They're all growing green in the old countrie.

In Baltimore a-walking a lady I did meet
With her babe on her arm, as she came down the street;
And I thought how I sailed, and the cradle standing ready
For the pretty little babe that has never seen its daddie.
And it's home, dearie, home . . .

O, if it be a lass, she shall wear a golden ring;
And if it be a lad, he shall fight for his king:
With his dirk and his hat and his little jacket blue
He shall walk the quarter-deck as his daddie used to do.
And it's home, dearie, home . . .

[1] The burden and the third stanza are adapted from an old song.

O, there's a wind a-blowing, a-blowing from the west,
And that of all the winds is the one I like the best,
For it blows at our backs, and it shakes our pennon free,
And it soon will blow us home to the old countrie.
For it's home, dearie, home—it's home I want to be.
Our topsails are hoisted, and we'll away to sea.
O, the oak and the ash and the bonnie birken tree
They're all growing green in the old countrie.

ENGLAND, MY ENGLAND

What have I done for you,
England, my England?
What is there that I would not do,
England, my own?
With your glorious eyes austere,
As the Lord were walking near,
Whispering terrible things and dear
As the Song on your bugles blown,
England—
Round the world on your bugles blown!

Where shall the watchful Sun,
England, my England,
Match the master-work you've done,
England, my own?
When shall he rejoice again
Such a breed of mighty men
As come forward, one to ten,
To the Song on your bugles blown,
England—
Down the years on your bugles blown?

Ever the faith endures,
England, my England:—
"Take and break us: we are yours,
"England, my own!
"Life is good, and joy runs high
"Between English earth and sky:
"Death is death; but we shall die
"To the Song on your bugles blown,
"England—
"To the stars on your bugles blown!"

They call you proud and hard,
England, my England:
You with worlds to watch and ward,
England, my own!
You whose mailed hand keeps the keys
Of such teeming destinies
You could know nor dread nor ease
Were the Song on your bugles blown,
England,
Round the Pit on your bugles blown!

Mother of Ships whose might,
England, my England,
Is the fierce old Sea's delight,
England, my own,
Chosen daughter of the Lord,
Spouse-in-Chief of the ancient sword,
There's the menace of the Word
In the Song on your bugles blown,
England—
Out of heaven on your bugles blown!

O GATHER ME THE ROSE

O gather me the rose, the rose,
While yet in flower we find it,
For summer smiles, but summer goes,
And winter waits behind it.

For with the dream foregone, foregone,
The deed forborne for ever,
The worm Regret will canker on,
And time will turn him never.

So were it well to love, my love,
And cheat of any laughter
The fate beneath us and above,
The dark before and after.

The myrtle and the rose, the rose,
The sunshine and the swallow,
The dream that comes, the wish that goes
The memories that follow!

TO ROBERT LOUIS STEVENSON

A child,
Curious and innocent,
Slips from his Nurse, and rejoicing
Loses himself in the Fair.

Thro' the jostle and din
Wandering, he revels,
Dreaming, desiring, possessing;
Till, of a sudden
Tired and afraid, he beholds
The sordid assemblage
Just as it is; and he runs
With a sob to his Nurse
(Lighting at last on him),
And in her motherly bosom
Cries him to sleep.

Thus thro' the World,
Seeing and feeling and knowing,
Goes Man: till at last,
Tired of experience, he turns
To the friendly and comforting breast
Of the old nurse, Death.

MARGARITAE SORORI

A late lark twitters from the quiet skies;
And from the west,
Where the sun, his day's work ended,
Lingers as in content,
There falls on the old, gray city
An influence luminous and serene,
A shining peace.

The smoke ascends
In a rosy-and-golden haze. The spires
Shine, and are changed. In the valley
Shadows rise. The lark sings on. The sun,
Closing his benediction,
Sinks, and the darkening air
Thrills with a sense of the triumphing
night—
Night with her train of stars
And her great gift of sleep.

So be my passing!
My task accomplished and the long day done,
My wages taken, and in my heart
Some late lark singing,
Let me be gathered to the quiet west,
The sundown splendid and serene,
Death.

Robert Louis Stevenson

Robert Louis Stevenson was born at Edinburgh in 1850 and attended the university there. From infancy he was afflicted with illness, nearly dying of gastric fever at the age of eight, a sickness which left him constitutionally weak. The rest of his life was a struggle between his work and a search for health in Switzerland, America, and the South Seas. He was at first trained to be a lighthouse engineer, following the profession of his family. However, he studied law instead, was admitted to the bar in 1875, and abandoned law for literature a few years later. After wandering several years about Europe, he recorded his peregrinations in *An Inland Voyage* (1878) and *Travels with a Donkey* (1879). Although he had written much before his thirtieth year, it was not until the publication of *Treasure Island* (1883) that he became popular. In 1885 he published, with misgivings, *A Child's Garden of Verses;* and again won public favor a year later with that *tour de force, The Strange Case of Dr. Jekyll and Mr. Hyde.*

In 1887, after a prolonged breakdown, he left England never to return. In rapid succession he tried the Adirondacks, New Jersey, California, and, in 1888 sailed, as Sidney Colvin said, "on what was only intended to be an excursion, but turned into a voluntary exile, prolonged until the hour of his death." He lived in Honolulu, Australia, and finally Samoa, where, after a long fight, he succumbed to tuberculosis in 1894.

Though primarily a novelist, Stevenson has left one book which is equally at home in the nursery and the library: *A Child's Garden of Verses* is second only to Mother Goose's own collection in simplicity and universal appeal. With the exception of these favorite verses and a posthumous *New Poems* (1918), *Underwoods* (1887) and *Ballads* (1890) comprise his entire poetic output. As a genial essayist, he is usually ranked with Charles Lamb. As a romancer, his fame rests on *Kidnapped,* the unfinished masterpiece, *Weir of Hermiston,* and that classic of youth, *Treasure Island.*

Stevenson's writing is inseparable from his charm and the personal appeal of his life-story. He is persuasive, not profound, too concerned with his craft, but never dull, and finally winning.

SUMMER SUN

Great is the sun, and wide he goes
Through empty heaven without repose;
And in the blue and glowing days
More thick than rain he showers his rays.

Though closer still the blinds we pull
To keep the shady parlor cool,
Yet he will find a chink or two
To slip his golden fingers through.

The dusty attic, spider-clad,
He, through the keyhole, maketh glad;
And through the broken edge of tiles
Into the laddered hay-loft smiles.

Meantime his golden face around
He bares to all the garden ground,
And sheds a warm and glittering look
Among the ivy's inmost nook.

Above the hills, along the blue,
Round the bright air with footing true,
To please the child, to paint the rose,
The gardener of the World, he goes.

WINTER TIME

Late lies the wintry sun a-bed,
A frosty, fiery sleepy-head;
Blinks but an hour or two; and then,
A blood-red orange, sets again.

Before the stars have left the skies
At morning in the dark I rise;
And, shivering in my nakedness,
By the cold candle, bathe and dress.

Close by the jolly fire I sit
To warm my frozen bones a bit;
Or, with a reindeer-sled, explore
The colder countries round the door.

When to go out, my nurse doth wrap
Me in my comforter and cap;
The cold wind burns my face, and blows
Its frosty pepper up my nose.

Black are my steps on silver sod;
Thick blows my frosty breath abroad;
And tree and house, and hill and lake,
Are frosted like a wedding-cake.

THE CELESTIAL SURGEON

If I have faltered more or less
In my great task of happiness;
If I have moved among my race
And shown no glorious morning face;
If beams from happy human eyes
Have moved me not; if morning skies,
Books, and my food, and summer rain
Knocked on my sullen heart in vain:—
Lord, thy most pointed pleasure take
And stab my spirit broad awake;
Or, Lord, if still too obdurate I,
Choose thou, before that spirit die,
A piercing pain, a killing sin,
And to my dead heart run them in!

ROMANCE

I will make you brooches and toys for your delight
Of bird-song at morning and star-shine at night.
I will make a palace fit for you and me,
Of green days in forests and blue days at sea.

I will make my kitchen, and you shall keep your room,
Where white flows the river and bright blows the broom
And you shall wash your linen and keep your body white
In rainfall at morning and dewfall at night.

And this shall be for music when no one else is near,
The fine song for singing, the rare song to hear!
That only I remember, that only you admire,
Of the broad road that stretches and the roadside fire.

REQUIEM

Under the wide and starry sky
  Dig the grave and let me lie:
Glad did I live and gladly die,
  And I laid me down with a will.

This be the verse you 'grave for me:
  Here he lies where he long'd to be;
Home is the sailor, home from sea,
  And the hunter home from the hill.

GO, LITTLE BOOK

Go, little book, and wish to all
Flowers in the garden, meat in the hall,
A bin of wine, a spice of wit,
A house with lawns enclosing it,
A living river by the door,
A nightingale in the sycamore.

Alice Meynell

Alice (Christiana Thompson) Meynell was born in 1850, educated at home and spent a great part of her early life in Italy. Later, she married Wilfred Meynell, friend, editor, and literary executor of Francis Thompson. For eighteen years she contributed to the *Weekly Register* of which her husband was editor; for twelve years was co-editor with him on *Merrie England;* wrote countless essays, columns for other periodicals, issued several volumes of poetry, took on responsibilities not the least of which was the sponsorship of Francis Thompson which saved him from ruin—all with a huge family growing up about her. There were seven Meynell children, among them being Francis, who became a typographer and poet, Viola, the novelist and essayist, Monica, the critical, and Everard, author of *The Life of Francis Thompson.* As described in the authorized Memoir *Alice Meynell* (1929) by her daughter, Viola, the children, aping their elders, conceived editing as a species of indoor sport and made up papers of their own. In one of these, the youngsters, attempting to answer Mrs. Meynell's critics, unconsciously appraised her:

"Her thought is a thought which very few writers got. It is mystical but excucite. She is a little obscure to readers who are not up in literature sufficiently to understand mystical touches. . . . Hers is a very docile temperament and thoroughly sympathetic. When she is singing a sympathetic song you can tell that she must have some excellent powers in her head."

The child Monica, touched with the family passion for salvation and trying to save her mother from literature, put the case against "ecstasy" in these delightful sentences:

"Dear Mother,—I hope you will in time give up your absurd thoughts about literature. It makes my mind quite feverish when I think of the exhaltation your undergoing. I'm getting quite frightened about calling you 'dear Mother' because you will begin to take it quite seriously. Just because Mr. Henley and those sort of unsencere men say you write well simply because they know if they don't flatter you they'll never get anything for their paper. Now mother take my advise and don't be quite so estatic, you'll get on just as well in the world and much better because you'll be respected. Now just see. MONNIE."

Whatever form Alice Meynell chose, her work was always a reflection of her spirit. She scorned sentimentality, "the facile literary opportunity," despised slovenliness, "the fashion of an animated strut of style," and kept herself aloof from them. Her later years were spent collecting her poems, revising her early prose and publishing the best of it in *Essays.* She died in 1923.

Preludes was published in 1876. Since then, various collections of her poems and essays have appeared at irregular intervals, and, in 1923, Charles Scribner's Sons published *The Poems of Alice Meynell.* From the earliest restrained verses to the later more ornate conceits, one strain is dominant: the music of religious emotion. It is, obviously, emotion controlled, almost intellectualized. Yet the poetry is never dull. The reader is always aware of a nature disciplined, but which, for all its self-imposed strictures, is rich in feeling, exquisite in communication.

Selected Poems of Alice Meynell (1931), with a valuable introductory note by Wilfred Meynell, is a careful winnowing of her best, although one of her finest short lyrics ("Chimes") is omitted. The book begins appropriately with the quietly original and wholly beautiful "A Letter from a Girl to Her Own Old Age" and ends with tributes from Ruskin, Meredith, Coventry Patmore, Chesterton and others.

Dante Gabriel Rossetti considered her "Renouncement" one of the three finest sonnets ever written by women. "Christ in the Universe," "To a Daisy," and "A Thrush Before Dawn," show a literary as well as spiritual kinship with Francis

Thompson; but where Thompson is lavish to the point of gaudiness, Mrs. Meynell's fastidiousness dictates a fine economy.

TO A DAISY

Slight as thou art, thou art enough to hide,
  Like all created things, secrets from me,
  And stand a barrier to eternity.
And I, how can I praise thee well and wide
From where I dwell—upon the hither side?
  Thou little veil for so great mystery,
  When shall I penetrate all things and thee,
And then look back? For this I must abide,
Till thou shalt grow and fold and be unfurled
Literally between me and the world.
  Then I shall drink from in beneath a spring,
And from a poet's side shall read his book.
O daisy mine, what will it be to look
  From God's side even on such a simple thing?

THE SHEPHERDESS

She walks—the lady of my delight—
  A shepherdess of sheep.
Her flocks are thoughts. She keeps them white;
  She guards them from the steep;
She feeds them on the fragrant height,
  And folds them in for sleep.

She roams maternal hills and bright
  Dark valleys safe and deep.
Into that tender breast at night,
  The chastest stars may peep.
She walks—the lady of my delight—
  A shepherdess of sheep.

She holds her little thoughts in sight,
  Though gay they run and leap.
She is so circumspect and right;
  She has her soul to keep.
She walks—the lady of my delight—
  A shepherdess of sheep.

THE WIND IS BLIND

"Eyeless, in Gaza, at the mill, with slaves."
—MILTON'S SAMSON.

  The wind is blind.
The earth sees sun and moon; the height
Is watch-tower to the dawn; the plain

Shines to the summer; visible light
Is scattered in the drops of rain.

The wind is blind.
The flashing billows are aware;
With open eyes the cities see;
Light leaves the ether, everywhere
Known to the homing bird and bee.

The wind is blind,
Is blind alone. How has he hurled
His ignorant lash, his sinless dart,
His eyeless rush upon the world,
Unseeing, to break his unknown heart!

The wind is blind.
And the sail traps him, and the mill
Captures him; and he cannot save
His swiftness and his desperate will
From those blind uses of the slave.

NOVEMBER BLUE

The golden tint of the electric lights seems to give a complementary color to the air in the early evening. —ESSAY ON LONDON.

O heavenly color, London town
Has blurred it from her skies;
And, hooded in an earthly brown,
Unheaven'd the city lies.
No longer, standard-like, this hue
Above the broad road flies;
Nor does the narrow street the blue
Wear, slender pennon-wise.

But when the gold and silver lamps
Color the London dew,
And, misted by the winter damps,
The shops shine bright, anew—
Blue comes to earth, it walks the street,
It dyes the wide air through;
A mimic sky about their feet
The throng go crowned with blue.

CHIMES

Brief, on a flying night
From the shaken tower,
A flock of bells take flight,
And go with the hour.

Like birds from the cote to the gales,
  Abrupt—O hark!
A fleet of bells set sails,
  And go to the dark.

Sudden the cold airs swing,
  Alone, aloud,
A verse of bells takes wing
  And flies with the cloud.

A LETTER FROM A GIRL TO HER OWN OLD AGE

Listen, and when thy hand this paper presses,
O time-worn woman, think of her who blesses
What thy thin fingers touch, with her caresses.

O mother, for the weight of years that break thee!
O daughter, for slow time must yet awake thee,
And from the changes of my heart must make thee!

O fainting traveler, morn is gray in heaven.
Dost thou remember how the clouds were driven?
And are they calm about the fall of even?

Pause near the ending of thy long migration;
For this one sudden hour of desolation
Appeals to one hour of thy meditation.

Suffer, O silent one, that I remind thee
Of the great hills that stormed the sky behind thee,
Of the wild winds of power that have resigned thee.

Know that the mournful plain where thou must wander
Is but a gray and silent world; but ponder
The misty mountains of the morning yonder.

Listen:—the mountain winds with rain were fretting,
And sudden gleams the mountain-tops besetting.
I cannot let thee fade to death, forgetting.

What part of this wild heart of mine I know not
Will follow with thee where the great winds blow not,
And where the young flowers of the mountain grow not.

Yet let my letter with thy lost thoughts in it
Tell what the way was when thou didst begin it,
And win with thee the goal when thou shalt win it.

I have not writ this letter of divining
To make a glory of thy silent pining,
A triumph of thy mute and strange declining.

Only one youth, and the bright life was shrouded;
Only one morning, and the day was clouded;
And one old age with all regrets is crowded.

O hush, O hush! Thy tears my words are steeping.
O hush, hush, hush! So full, the fount of weeping?
Poor eyes, so quickly moved, so near to sleeping?

Pardon the girl; such strange desires beset her.
Poor woman, lay aside the mournful letter
That breaks thy heart; the one who wrote, forget her:

The one who now thy faded features guesses,
With filial fingers thy gray hair caresses,
With morning tears thy mournful twilight blesses.

THE OCTOBER REDBREAST

Autumn is weary, halt, and old;
  Ah, but she owns the song of joy!
Her colors fade, her woods are cold.
  Her singing-bird's a boy, a boy.

In lovely Spring the birds were bent
  On nests, on use, on love, forsooth!
Grown-up were they. This boy's content,
  For his is liberty, his is youth.

The musical stripling sings for play
  Taking no thought, and virgin-glad.
For duty sang those mates in May.
  This singing-bird's a lad, a lad.

A THRUSH BEFORE DAWN

A voice peals in this end of night
  A phrase of notes resembling stars,
Single and spiritual notes of light.
  What call they at my window-bars?
    The South, the past, the day to be,
    An ancient infelicity.

Darkling, deliberate, what sings
  This wonderful one, alone, at peace?
What wilder things than song, what things
  Sweeter than youth, clearer than Greece,
    Dearer than Italy, untold
    Delight, and freshness centuries old?

And first first-loves, a multitude,
  The exaltation of their pain;
Ancestral childhood long renewed;
  And midnights of invisible rain;
    And gardens, gardens, night and day,
    Gardens and childhood all the way.

What Middle Ages passionate,
  O passionless voice! What distant bells
Lodged in the hills, what palace state
  Illyrian! For it speaks, it tells,
    Without desire, without dismay
    Some morrow and some yesterday.

All-natural things! But more—Whence came
  This yet remoter mystery?
How do these starry notes proclaim
  A graver still divinity?
    This hope, this sanctity of fear?
    O innocent throat! O human ear!

RENOUNCEMENT

I must not think of thee; and, tired yet strong,
I shun the thought that lurks in all delight—
The thought of thee—and in the blue Heaven's height,
And in the sweetest passage of a song.

O just beyond the fairest thoughts that throng
This breast, the thought of thee waits hidden yet bright;
But it must never, never come in sight;
I must stop short of thee the whole day long.

But when sleep comes to close each difficult day,
When night gives pause to the long watch I keep,
And all my bonds I needs must loose apart,

Must doff my will as raiment laid away,
With the first dream that comes with the first sleep
I run, I run, I am gathered to thy heart.

CHRIST IN THE UNIVERSE

With this ambiguous earth
His dealings have been told us. These abide:
The signal to a maid, the human birth,
The lesson, and the young Man crucified.

But not a star of all
The innumerable hosts of stars has heard
How He administered this terrestrial ball.
Our race have kept their Lord's entrusted Word.

Of His earth-visiting feet
None knows the secret, cherished, perilous,
The terrible, shamefast, frightened, whispered, sweet,
Heart-shattering secret of His way with us.

No planet knows of this.
Our wayside planet, carrying land and wave,
Love and life multiplied, and pain and bliss,
Bears, as chief treasure, one forsaken grave.

Nor, in our little day,
May His devices with the heavens be guessed;
His pilgrimage to thread the Milky Way,
Or His bestowals there, be manifest.

But, in the eternities,
Doubtless we shall compare together, hear
A million alien Gospels, in what guise
He trod the Pleiades, the Lyre, the Bear.

O be prepared, my soul!
To read the inconceivable, to scan
The million forms of God those stars unroll
When, in our turn, we show to them a Man.

Oscar Wilde

⁂ Oscar (Fingall O'Flahertie) Wilde was born at Dublin, Ireland, October 16, 1856, and even as an undergraduate at Oxford was marked for a brilliant career. When he was scarcely twenty-one years of age, he won the Newdigate Prize with his poem "Ravenna." Devoting himself almost entirely to prose, he speedily became known as a writer of brilliant epigrammatic essays and even more brilliant paradoxical plays, such as *An Ideal Husband* and *The Importance of Being Earnest.* Wilde's aphorisms and flippancies were quoted everywhere; his fame as a wit was only surpassed by his notoriety as an esthete, the scandal of his trial, and the final prison sentence.

Most of his poems in prose (such as "The Happy Prince," "The Birthday of the Infanta," and "The Fisherman and His Soul") are more imaginative and richly colored than his rococo verse which suffers from deliberate decadence. But in one long poem, "The Ballad of Reading Gaol" (1898), he sounded his simplest and most enduring note. Prison was, in some ways, a regeneration for Wilde. It not only produced "The Ballad of Reading Gaol," but made possible his finest piece of writing, "De Profundis," only a small part of which has been published. "Salomé," which has made the author's name a household word, was originally written in French in 1892 and later translated into English by Lord Alfred Douglas, accompanied by the famous illustrations by Aubrey Beardsley. More recently, this heated drama, based on the story of Herod and Herodias, was made into an opera by Richard Strauss and performed in a dozen countries and several languages.

Wilde's society plays, flashing and cynical, were the forerunners of Bernard Shaw's audacious and far more searching ironies. One sees the origin of a whole school of drama in such epigrams as "The history of woman is the history of the worst form of tyranny the world has ever known: the tyranny of the weak over the strong. It is the only tyranny that lasts." Or "There is only one thing in the world worse than being talked about, that is not being talked about."

Wilde's flair for publicity, avowed in the last quotation, was gratified to the full. No man of his time was more talked about. The end of the Esthetic Movement came coincidentally—and ironically—with the trial of Oscar Wilde and his indictment for a social crime. His predilection for extremes caused his artistic ruin: in youth he was ultra-Keatsian; in early manhood, ultra-Rossettian; in maturity, ultra-Wilde—and he pushed preciosity to the limits of the absurd. He believed in nothing, not even himself, except for the passing effect; he was essentially the "Pierrot of the minute"—a Pierrot whose shifting passions and impertinences convinced no one. Even his Pierroticism was a pose.

"Impression du Matin" and "Symphony in Yellow" are among the poems which suggest a verbal Whistler, with whom Wilde waged many an epigrammatic battle, and "Hélas" is an unusually honest fragment of self-analysis.

Wilde borrowed from Swinburne no little of his spirit and as much of his technique as he could master. But Swinburne's rebelliousness, though vague and general, was sincere; Wilde, the antithesis of a rebel by instinct, was a social snob who clung to his insurgence for the entrée it won him in properly breathless gatherings. His success was without dignity, his failure without pathos.

Wilde died at Paris, November 30, 1900, his body being buried in the Cemetery of Bagneux. On July 20, 1909, it was transferred to the great Cemetery of Père Lachaise, where later a striking monument by Epstein was erected to his memory.

REQUIESCAT

Tread lightly, she is near
 Under the snow,
Speak gently, she can hear
 The daisies grow.

All her bright golden hair
 Tarnished with rust,
She that was young and fair
 Fallen to dust.

Lily-like, white as snow,
 She hardly knew
She was a woman, so
 Sweetly she grew.

Coffin-board, heavy stone,
 Lie on her breast;
I vex my heart alone,
 She is at rest.

Peace, peace; she cannot hear
 Lyre or sonnet;
All my life's buried here.
 Heap earth upon it.

IMPRESSION DU MATIN

The Thames nocturne of blue and gold
 Changed to a harmony in gray;
 A barge with ocher-colored hay
Dropt from the wharf: and chill and cold

The yellow fog came creeping down
 The bridges, till the houses' walls
 Seemed changed to shadows, and St. Paul's
Loomed like a bubble o'er the town.

Then suddenly arose the clang
 Of waking life; the streets were stirred
 With country wagons; and a bird
Flew to the glistening roofs and sang.

But one pale woman all alone,
 The daylight kissing her wan hair,
 Loitered beneath the gas lamps' flare,
With lips of flame and heart of stone.

HÉLAS

To drift with every passion till my soul
Is a stringed lute on which all winds can play,
Is it for this that I have given away
Mine ancient wisdom, and austere control?
Methinks my life is a twice-written scroll
Scrawled over on some boyish holiday
With idle songs for pipe and virelay,
Which do but mar the secret of the whole.
Surely there was a time I might have trod
The sunlit heights, and from life's dissonance
Struck one clear chord to reach the ears of
 God:
Is that time dead? lo! with a little rod
I did but touch the honey of romance—
And must I lose a soul's inheritance?

MAGDALEN WALKS

The little white clouds are racing over the sky,
 And the fields are strewn with the gold of the flower of March,
 The daffodil breaks under foot, and the tasseled larch
Sways and swings as the thrush goes hurrying by.

A delicate odor is borne on the wings of the morning breeze,
  The odor of deep wet grass, and of brown new-furrowed earth,
  The birds are singing for joy of the Spring's glad birth,
Hopping from branch to branch on the rocking trees.

And all the woods are alive with the murmur and sound of Spring,
  And the rose-bud breaks into pink on the climbing briar,
  And the crocus-bed is a quivering moon of fire
Girdled round with the belt of an amethyst ring.

And the plane of the pine-tree is whispering some tale of love
  Till it rustles with laughter and tosses its mantle of green,
  And the gloom of the wych-elm's hollow is lit with the iris sheen
Of the burnished rainbow throat and the silver breast of a dove.

See! the lark starts up from his bed in the meadow there,
  Breaking the gossamer threads and the nets of dew,
  And flashing adown the river, a flame of blue!
The kingfisher flies like an arrow, and wounds the air.

And the sense of my life is sweet! though I know that the end is nigh:
  For the ruin and rain of winter will shortly come,
  The lily will lose its gold, and the chestnut-bloom
In billows of red and white on the grass will lie.

And even the light of the sun will fade at the last,
  And the leaves will fall, and the birds will hasten away,
  And I will be left in the snow of a flowerless day
To think on the glories of Spring, and the joys of a youth long past.

Yet be silent, my heart! do not count it a profitless thing
  To have seen the splendor of the sun, and of grass, and of flower!
  To have lived and loved! for I hold that to love for an hour
Is better for man and woman than cycles of blossoming Spring.

E TENEBRIS

Come down, O Christ, and help me! reach thy hand,
  For I am drowning in a stormier sea
  Than Simon on thy lake of Galilee:
The wine of life is spilt upon the sand,
My heart is as some famine-murdered land
  Whence all good things have perished utterly,
  And well I know my soul in Hell must lie
If I this night before God's throne should stand.
"He sleeps perchance, or rideth to the chase,
  Like Baal, when his prophets howled that name
  From morn to noon on Carmel's smitten height."
Nay, peace, I shall behold, before the night,
  The feet of brass, the robe more white than flame,
The wounded hands, the weary human face.

SYMPHONY IN YELLOW

An omnibus across the bridge
  Crawls like a yellow butterfly,
  And, here and there, a passer-by
Shows like a little restless midge.

Big barges full of yellow hay
  Are moved against the shadowy wharf,
  And, like a yellow silken scarf,
The thick fog hangs along the quay.

The yellow leaves begin to fade
  And flutter from the Temple elms,
  And at my feet the pale green Thames
Lies like a rod of rippled jade.

THE HARLOT'S HOUSE

We caught the tread of dancing feet,
We loitered down the moonlit street,
And stopped beneath the harlot's house.

Inside, above the din and fray,
We heard the loud musicians play
The "Treues Liebes Herz" of Strauss.

Like strange mechanical grotesques,
Making fantastic arabesques,
The shadows raced across the blind.

We watched the ghostly dancers spin
To sound of horn and violin,
Like black leaves wheeling in the wind.

Like wire-pulled automatons,
Slim silhouetted skeletons
Went sidling through the slow quadrille.

They took each other by the hand,
And danced a stately saraband;
Their laughter echoed thin and shrill.

Sometimes a clockwork puppet pressed
A phantom lover to her breast,
Sometimes they seemed to try to sing.

Sometimes a horrible marionette
Came out, and smoked its cigarette
Upon the steps like a live thing.

Then, turning to my love, I said,
"The dead are dancing with the dead,
The dust is whirling with the dust."

But she—she heard the violin,
And left my side and entered in:
Love passed into the house of lust.

Then suddenly the tune went false,
The dancers wearied of the waltz,
The shadows ceased to wheel and whirl.

And down the long and silent street,
The dawn, with silver-sandaled feet,
Crept like a frightened girl.

FROM "THE SPHINX"

How subtle-secret is your smile! Did you love none then? Nay, I know
Great Ammon was your bedfellow! He lay with you beside the Nile!

The river-horses in the slime trumpeted when they saw him come
Odorous with Syrian galbanum and smeared with spikenard and with thyme.

He came along the river bank like some tall galley argent-sailed,
He strode across the waters, mailed in beauty, and the waters sank.

He strode across the desert sand: he reached the valley where you lay:
He waited till the dawn of day: then touched your black breasts with his hand.

You kissed his mouth with mouth of flame: you made the hornèd god your own:
You stood behind him on his throne: you called him by his secret name.

You whispered monstrous oracles into the caverns of his ears:
With blood of goats and blood of steers you taught him monstrous miracles.

White Ammon was your bedfellow! Your chamber was the steaming Nile!
And with your curved archaic smile you watched his passion come and go.

FROM "THE BALLAD OF READING GAOL"

He did not wear his scarlet coat,
For blood and wine are red,
And blood and wine were on his hands
When they found him with the dead,
The poor dead woman whom he loved,
And murdered in her bed.

He walked amongst the Trial Men
In a suit of shabby gray;
A cricket cap was on his head,
And his step seemed light and gay;
But I never saw a man who looked
So wistfully at the day.

I never saw a man who looked
With such a wistful eye
Upon that little tent of blue
Which prisoners call the sky,
And at every drifting cloud that went
With sails of silver by.

I walked, with other souls in pain,
Within another ring,
And was wondering if the man had done
A great or little thing,
When a voice behind me whispered low,
"That fellow's got to swing."

Dear Christ! the very prison walls
Suddenly seemed to reel,
And the sky above my head became
Like a casque of scorching steel;
And, though I was a soul in pain,
My pain I could not feel.

I only knew what hunted thought
Quickened his step, and why
He looked upon the garish day
With such a wistful eye:
The man had killed the thing he loved,
And so he had to die.

*

Yet each man kills the thing he loves,
By each let this be heard,
Some do it with a bitter look,
Some with a flattering word,
The coward does it with a kiss,
The brave man with a sword!

Some kill their love when they are young,
And some when they are old;
Some strangle with the hands of Lust,
Some with the hands of Gold:
The kindest use a knife, because
The dead so soon grow cold.

Some love too little, some too long,
Some sell, and others buy;
Some do the deed with many tears,
And some without a sigh:
For each man kills the thing he loves,
Yet each man does not die.

He does not die a death of shame
On a day of dark disgrace,
Nor have a noose about his neck,
Nor a cloth upon his face,
Nor drop feet foremost through the floor
Into an empty space.

He did not wring his hands nor weep,
Nor did he peak or pine,
But he drank the air as though it held
Some healthful anodyne;
With open mouth he drank the sun
As though it had been wine!

And I and all the souls in pain,
Who tramped the other ring,
Forgot if we ourselves had done
A great or little thing,
And watched with gaze of dull amaze
The man who had to swing.

And strange it was to see him pass
With a step so light and gay,

And strange it was to see him look
  So wistfully at the day,
And strange it was to think that he
  Had such a debt to pay.

*

For oak and elm have pleasant leaves
  That in the spring-time shoot:
But grim to see is the gallows-tree
  With its adder-bitten root,
And, green or dry, a man must die
  Before it bears its fruit!

The loftiest place is that seat of grace
  For which all worldlings try:
But who would stand in hempen band
  Upon a scaffold high,
And through a murderer's collar take
  His last look at the sky?

It is sweet to dance to violins
  When Love and Life are fair:
To dance to flutes, to dance to lutes
  Is delicate and rare:
But it is not sweet with nimble feet
  To dance upon the air!

So with curious eyes and sick surmise
  We watched him day by day,
And wondered if each one of us
  Would end the self-same way,
For none can tell to what red Hell
  His sightless soul may stray.

At last the dead man walked no more
  Amongst the Trial Men,
And I knew that he was standing up
  In the black dock's dreadful pen,
And that never would I see his face
  In God's sweet world again.

Like two doomed ships that pass in storm
  We had crossed each other's way:
But we made no sign, we said no word,
  We had no word to say;
For we did not meet in the holy night,
  But in the shameful day.

A prison wall was round us both,
  Two outcast men we were:
The world had thrust us from its heart,
  And God from out His care:
And the iron gin that waits for Sin
  Had caught us in its snare.

John Davidson

John Davidson was born at Barrhead, Renfrewshire, in 1857. His *Ballads and Songs* (1895) and *New Ballads* (1897) attained a sudden but too short-lived popularity; his great promise was quenched by an apathetic public and by his own growing disillusion and despair. Neither the later *Holiday and Other Poems* (1906) nor the ambitious trilogy, *God and Mammon* (the first volume of which appeared in 1907) received anything more than frozen respect. His somber poetry never tired of repeating his favorite theme: "Man is but the Universe grown conscious." Author of some four "testaments," six plays, three novels, and various collections of poems and essays, Davidson died by his own hand at Penzance in 1909.

The theme of "A Ballad of a Nun" is one which has attracted many writers since the Middle Ages, but Davidson has given it a turn which makes the tale sound far fresher than Vollmoeller's employment of it in *The Miracle*. "A Ballad of Hell," Davidson's only "popular" poem, is wholly his own material.

Davidson's work may be divided into three stages. His first phase, announced in *The North Wall* (1885), was conscious cleverness. In the second stage he tried to reach sophisticated audiences, attempting the metropolitan note with sketches, plays, and novels in the manner of the febrile Nineties. It was not until *Ballads and Songs* and *The Last Ballad* (1899) that he struck what for him and his readers was the true note. "A Ballad of Hell" and "A Ballad of a Nun," among others, are infused with the old ballad spirit; they have the traditional reach and vigor, modernized without becoming topical, pointed but not over-personalized.

After 1900 Davidson's work suffered. As his biographer R. M. Wenley puts it, "cosmogonic passion overwhelming him, the artist pales before the prophet in travail." Somberness developed into pessimism, pessimism into self-persecution. He identified himself with the unhappy James Thomson, another maladjusted soul; he became paranoiac, losing himself in "strange passions, outlandish affaires, overstrung rhetoric." Over-emphasizing extremes, his later work was not only neurotic but melodramatic. Hysteria tainted a half-Nietzschean, half-Calvinistic philosophy; his twisted apprehension of the "hero" concept of history (in which he seemed to himself one of the defeated martyrs) was, as Wenley remarks, "like other Neo-Romantics'—from Nietzsche *in excelsis* to D'Annunzio *in inferis*."

But it is only in his last phase that Davidson turned from singing to shrieking. His huge and misshapen trilogies are forgotten; his exaggerated colors have faded; the ballads and a few of the lyrics remain. They have persistent if not permanent stuff.

A BALLAD OF HELL

"A letter from my love today!
  Oh, unexpected, dear appeal!"
She struck a happy tear away,
  And broke the crimson seal.

"My love, there is no help on earth,
  No help in heaven; the dead-man's bell
Must toll our wedding; our first hearth
  Must be the well-paved floor of hell."

The color died from out her face,
  Her eyes like ghostly candles shone;
She cast dread looks about the place,
  Then clenched her teeth and read right on.

"I may not pass the prison door;
  Here must I rot from day to day,
Unless I wed whom I abhor,
  My cousin, Blanche of Valencay.

"At midnight with my dagger keen,
  I'll take my life; it must be so.
Meet me in hell tonight, my queen,
  For weal and woe."

She laughed, although her face was wan,
  She girded on her golden belt,
She took her jeweled ivory fan,
  And at her glowing missal knelt.

Then rose, "And am I mad?" she said:
  She broke her fan, her belt untied;
With leather girt herself instead,
  And stuck a dagger at her side.

She waited, shuddering in her room,
  Till sleep had fallen on all the house.
She never flinched; she faced her doom:
  They two must sin to keep their vows.

Then out into the night she went,
  And, stooping, crept by hedge and tree;
Her rose-bush flung a snare of scent,
  And caught a happy memory.

She fell, and lay a minute's space;
  She tore the sward in her distress;
The dewy grass refreshed her face;
  She rose and ran with lifted dress.

She started like a morn-caught ghost
  Once when the moon came out and stood
To watch; the naked road she crossed,
  And dived into the murmuring wood.

The branches snatched her streaming cloak;
  A live thing shrieked; she made no stay!
She hurried to the trysting-oak—
  Right well she knew the way.

Without a pause she bared her breast,
  And drove her dagger home and fell,
And lay like one that takes her rest,
  And died and wakened up in hell.

She bathed her spirit in the flame,
  And near the center took her post;
From all sides to her ears there came
  The dreary anguish of the lost.

The devil started at her side,
  Comely, and tall, and black as jet.
"I am young Malespina's bride;
  Has he come hither yet?"

"My poppet, welcome to your bed."
  "Is Malespina here?"
"Not he! Tomorrow he must wed
  His cousin Blanche, my dear!"

"You lie, he died with me tonight."
  "Not he! it was a plot" . . . "You lie."
"My dear, I never lie outright."
  "We died at midnight, he and I."

The devil went. Without a groan
  She, gathered up in one fierce prayer,
Took root in hell's midst all alone,
  And waited for him there.

She dared to make herself at home
  Amidst the wail, the uneasy stir.
The blood-stained flame that filled the dome,
  Scentless and silent, shrouded her.

How long she stayed I cannot tell;
  But when she felt his perfidy,
She marched across the floor of hell;
  And all the damned stood up to see.

The devil stopped her at the brink:
  She shook him off; she cried, "Away!"
"My dear, you have gone mad, I think."
  "I was betrayed: I will not stay."

Across the weltering deep she ran;
  A stranger thing was never seen:
The damned stood silent to a man;
  They saw the great gulf set between.

To her it seemed a meadow fair;
  And flowers sprang up about her feet.
She entered heaven; she climbed the stair
  And knelt down at the mercy-seat.

Seraphs and saints with one great voice
  Welcomed that soul that knew not fear.
Amazed to find it could rejoice,
  Hell raised a hoarse, half-human cheer.

IMAGINATION

(from "New Year's Eve")

There is a dish to hold the sea,
  A brazier to contain the sun,
A compass for the galaxy,
  A voice to wake the dead and done!

That minister of ministers,
  Imagination, gathers up
The undiscovered Universe,
  Like jewels in a jasper cup.

Its flame can mingle north and south;
  Its accent with the thunder strive;
The ruddy sentence of its mouth
  Can make the ancient dead alive.

The mart of power, the fount of will,
  The form and mold of every star,
The source and bound of good and ill,
  The key of all the things that are,

Imagination, new and strange
  In every age, can turn the year;
Can shift the poles and lightly change
  The mood of men, the world's career.

THE UNKNOWN

(Villanelle)

To brave and to know the unknown
  Is the high world's motive and mark,
Though the way with snares be strewn.

The earth itself alone
  Wheels through the light and the dark
Onward to meet the unknown.

Each soul, upright or prone,
  While the owl sings or the lark,
Must pass where the bones are strewn.

Power on the loftiest throne
  Can fashion no certain ark
That shall stem and outride the unknown.

Beauty must doff her zone,
  Strength trudge unarmed and stark
Though the way with eyes be strewn.

This only can atone,
  The high world's motive and mark,
To brave and to know the unknown
Though the way with fire be strewn.

A BALLAD OF A NUN

From Eastertide to Eastertide
  For ten long years her patient knees
Engraved the stones—the fittest bride
  Of Christ in all the diocese.

She conquered every earthly lust;
  The abbess loved her more and more;
And, as a mark of perfect trust,
  Made her the keeper of the door.

High on a hill the convent hung,
  Across a duchy looking down,
Where everlasting mountains flung
  Their shadows over tower and town.

The jewels of their lofty snows
  In constellations flashed at night;
Above their crests the moon arose;
  The deep earth shuddered with delight.

Long ere she left her cloudy bed,
  Still dreaming in the orient land,
On many a mountain's happy head
  Dawn lightly laid her rosy hand.

The adventurous sun took heaven by storm;
  Clouds scattered largesses of rain;
The sounding cities, rich and warm,
  Smoldered and glittered in the plain.

Sometimes it was a wandering wind,
  Sometimes the fragrance of the pine,
Sometimes the thought how others sinned,
  That turned her sweet blood into wine.

Sometimes she heard a serenade
  Complaining sweetly far away:
She said, "A young man woos a maid";
  And dreamt of love till break of day.

Then she would ply her knotted scourge
  Until she swooned; but evermore
She had the same red sin to purge,
  Poor, passionate keeper of the door!

For still night's starry scroll unfurled,
  And still the day came like a flood:
It was the greatness of the world
  That made her long to use her blood.

In winter-time when Lent drew nigh,
  And hill and plain were wrapped in snow
She watched beneath the frosty sky
  The nearest city nightly glow.

Like peals of airy bells outworn
  Faint laughter died above her head
In gusts of broken music borne:
  "They keep the Carnival," she said.

Her hungry heart devoured the town:
  "Heaven save me by a miracle!
Unless God sends an angel down,
  Thither I go though it were Hell."

Fillet and veil in strips she tore;
  Her golden tresses floated wide;
The ring and bracelet that she wore
  As Christ's betrothed, she cast aside.

"Life's dearest meaning I shall probe;
  Lo! I shall taste of love at last!
Away!" She doffed her outer robe,
  And sent it sailing down the blast.

Her body seemed to warm the wind;
  With bleeding feet o'er ice she ran:
"I leave the righteous God behind;
  I go to worship sinful man."

She reached the sounding city's gate;
  No question did the warder ask:
He passed her in: "Welcome, wild mate!"
  He thought her some fantastic mask.

Half-naked through the town she went;
Each footstep left a bloody mark;
Crowds followed her with looks intent;
Her bright eyes made the torches dark.

Alone and watching in the street
There stood a grave youth nobly dressed;
To him she knelt and kissed his feet;
Her face her great desire confessed.

Straight to his house the nun he led:
"Strange lady, what would you with me?"
"Your love, your love, sweet lord," she said;
"I bring you my virginity."

He healed her bosom with a kiss;
She gave him all her passion's hoard;
And sobbed and murmured ever, "This
Is life's great meaning, dear, my lord.

"I care not for my broken vows;
Though God should come in thunder soon,
I am sister to the mountains now,
And sister to the sun and moon."

Through all the towns of Belmarie
She made a progress like a queen.
"She is," they said, "whate'er she be,
The strangest woman ever seen.

"From fairyland she must have come,
Or else she is a mermaiden."
Some said she was a ghoul, and some
A heathen goddess born again.

But soon her fire to ashes burned;
Her beauty changed to haggardness;
Her golden hair to silver turned;
The hour came of her last caress.

At midnight from her lonely bed
She rose, and said, "I have had my will."
The old ragged robe she donned, and fled
Back to the convent on the hill.

Half-naked as she went before,
She hurried to the city wall,
Unnoticed in the rush and roar
And splendor of the Carnival.

She ran across the icy plain;
Her worn blood curdled in the blast;
Each footstep left a crimson stain;
The white-faced moon looked on aghast.

She said between her chattering jaws,
"Deep peace is mine, I cease to strive;
Oh, comfortable convent laws,
That bury foolish nuns alive!

"A trowel for my passing-bell,
A little bed within the wall,
A coverlet of stones; how well
I there shall keep the Carnival!"

Like tired bells chiming in their sleep,
The wind faint peals of laughter bore;
She stopped her ears and climbed the steep
And thundered at the convent door.

It opened straight: she entered in,
And at the wardress' feet fell prone:
"I come to purge away my sin;
Bury me, close me up in stone."

The wardress raised her tenderly;
She touched her wet and fast-shut eyes:
"Look, sister; sister, look at me;
Look; can you see through my disguise?"

She looked and saw her own sad face,
And trembled, wondering, "Who art thou?"
"God sent me down to fill your place:
I am the Virgin Mary now."

And with the word, God's mother shone:
The wanderer whispered, "Mary, hail!"
The vision helped her to put on
Bracelet and fillet, ring and veil.

"You are sister to the mountains now,
And sister to the day and night;
Sister to God." And on the brow
She kissed her thrice, and left her sight,

While dreaming in her cloudy bed,
Far in the crimson orient land,
On many a mountain's happy head
Dawn lightly laid her rosy hand.

Francis Thompson

Francis Thompson was born in Ashton in Lancashire in 1859. The son of a doctor, he was intended for the profession and took the medical course at Owens College, Manchester. He had, however, no interest in medicine, but from youth evinced a passion for religion, particularly for the ritual of Catholicism.

His attempts to earn a living were a succession of failures. He was employed as a book-agent, and sold no books; he was apprenticed to the boot trade, and spent many hours of his apprenticeship in public libraries; he enlisted as a soldier, and was discharged as incompetent. He went to London, as Francis Meynell says, "not so much to seek his fortune as to escape his bad fortune. He lost in the gamble, but literature gained. He lived for four years as errand man, seller of matches, holder of horses' heads. Soon he became too shabby to gain admittance into the public libraries, so that when one says that desire of reading was with him a passion, one restores to its literal meaning that abused word. He slept on the Embankment, and 'saw the traffic of Jacob's ladder Pitched betwixt Heaven and Charing Cross.' A woman of the streets took pity on him and kept him alive by her charity—the spirit and the deed. He began to write—now for the first time. His poem, 'Dream Tryst,' written on blue sugar wrapping, found after many months an editorial welcome. Thereafter he was persuaded, though with difficulty, to come off the streets; and even to give up for many years the laudanum he had been taking. For the remaining nineteen years of his life he had an existence at any rate three-quarters protected from the physical tragedies of his starved and homeless young manhood."

Francis Meynell does not name the persons who gave Thompson "an editorial welcome" and who provided him with the shelter which made it possible for him to continue writing and, for that matter, living. These persons were Wilfred Meynell (later to become Thompson's editor and executor) and the poet Alice Meynell (see page 59), who named their son Francis after the genius who became his godfather.

Thompson's first volume, *Poems,* appeared in 1893, disclosing beneath a surface of wild metaphors and violent neologisms an affinity with the august. This volume was followed by *Sister Songs* (1895) and *New Poems* (1897). In these, as well as in the essays on De Quincey and Shelley, there was tropical strangeness. Plenitude is here not only in the large concept but in the small detail. Here are metaphors as bold as

> . . . laden with its lampèd clusters bright
> The fiery-fruited vineyard of this night.

and

> I broke through the doors of sunset,
> Ran before the hooves of sunrise.

The "Anthem of Earth," from which the last quotation is taken, is second only to Thompson's highest achievement. "The Hound of Heaven," which Coventry Patmore declared "one of the very few 'great' odes the language can boast," has captured more readers than any religious poem of this century. In a mystic circle, in which the God-pursuing is the God-pursued, the poem moves with the unhurried majesty of a Bach Chorale, building verse upon fugual verse into an unterrestrial architecture. Recognition of a divine order is celebrated with an almost divine excess. Everything, like Thompson's bright laburnum, spills its "honey of wild flame."

Thompson's poetry was embedded in his philosophy to an unusual degree; he saw all things related and linked by immortal power. It was a super-Berkeley who wrote:

> . . . thou canst not stir a flower
> Without troubling of a star.

Thompson's philosophy, however, exalted though it was, could not maintain him on the heights. Rapture and despair fought within him. "Down the arcane where Night would perish in night," he wandered, lost in "incredible excess"; the heart's cry in "The Dread of Height" sounds the ecstatic reaches and profound depths which his spirit touched. His suspensions were unresolved. But if neither man nor nature granted him final solution, the Church offered him serenity, and no singer has ever put the Catholic creed to more inspired measures.

Influenced at first by the dazzling Crashaw and the conceits of the seventeenth century metaphysicians, Thompson allowed himself the fullest play of purple-pompous tropes. He was as prodigal with strange colors and curious words as a child; the words he applied to characterize Shelley might be used with even greater justice to describe Thompson himself: "To the last, in a degree uncommon even among poets, he retained the idiosyncrasy of childhood, expanded and matured without differentiation. To the last, he was the enchanted child."

Riotous images and extravagant archaisms were Thompson's delight and his defect; he toyed with a style that loved to toss the stars and swing constellations by the hair. His was, not infrequently, a baroque magnificence. He often confused glitter with gold, painting the sublime in terms of the theatrical, falling from the grand manner into the grand-opera manner. At worst, Thompson overdressed his lines with a showy vocabulary; at his best, he attained sublimity. Such poems as "A Fallen Yew," "Ode to the Setting Sun," "Any Saint," "In No Strange Land," and, first and last, "The Hound of Heaven," provide a noble shrine for a noble vision. Here he captured, if only for glowing moments, a glory of which most of his contemporaries were not even aware.

Thompson died, after a fragile and spasmodic life, in St. John's Wood, London, in November, 1907. Since that time, several *Selected Poems* have revealed Thompson's pomp and prodigality to a new generation; an inexpensive *Complete Poetical Works* may be found in The Modern Library.

DAISY

Where the thistle lifts a purple crown
  Six foot out of the turf,
And the harebell shakes on the windy hill—
  O breath of the distant surf!—

The hills look over on the South,
  And southward dreams the sea;
And with the sea-breeze hand in hand
  Came innocence and she.

Where'mid the gorse the raspberry
  Red for the gatherer springs;
Two children did we stray and talk
  Wise, idle, childish things.

She listened with big-lipped surprise,
  Breast-deep 'mid flower and spine:

Her skin was like a grape whose veins
  Run snow instead of wine.

She knew not those sweet words she spake,
  Nor knew her own sweet way;
But there's never a bird, so sweet a song
  Thronged in whose throat all day.

Oh, there were flowers in Storrington
  On the turf and on the spray;
But the sweetest flower on Sussex hills
  Was the Daisy-flower that day!

Her beauty smoothed earth's furrowed face.
  She gave me tokens three:—
A look, a word of her winsome mouth,
  And a wild raspberry.

A berry red, a guileless look,
  A still word,—strings of sand!
And yet they made my wild, wild heart
  Fly down to her little hand.

For standing artless as the air
  And candid as the skies,
She took the berries with her hand
  And the love with her sweet eyes.

The fairest things have fleetest end,
  Their scent survives their close:
But the rose's scent is bitterness
  To him that loved the rose.

She looked a little wistfully,
  Then went her sunshine way:—
The sea's eye had a mist on it,
  And the leaves fell from the day.

She went her unremembering way,
  She went and left in me
The pang of all the partings gone,
  And partings yet to be.

She left me marveling why my soul
  Was sad that she was glad;
At all the sadness in the sweet,
  The sweetness in the sad.

Still, still I seemed to see her, still
  Look up with soft replies,
And take the berries with her hand,
  And the love with her lovely eyes.

Nothing begins, and nothing ends,
  That is not paid with moan,
For we are born in other's pain,
  And perish in our own.

TO A SNOWFLAKE

What heart could have thought you?—
Past our devisal
(O filigree petal!)
Fashioned so purely,
Fragilely, surely,
From what Paradisal
Imagineless metal,
Too costly for cost?
Who hammered you, wrought you,
From argentine vapor?—

"God was my shaper.
Passing surmisal,
He hammered, He wrought me,
From curled silver vapor,
To lust of his mind:—
Thou couldst not have thought me!
So purely, so palely,
Tinily, surely,
Mightily, frailly,
Insculped and embossed,
With His hammer of wind,
And His graver of frost."

AN ARAB LOVE-SONG

The hunchèd camels of the night[1]
Trouble the bright
And silver waters of the moon.
The Maiden of the Morn will soon
Through Heaven stray and sing,
Star gathering.

[1] Cloud-shapes observed by travelers in the East.

Now while the dark about our loves is strewn,
Light of my dark, blood of my heart, O come!
And night will catch her breath up, and be dumb.

Leave thy father, leave thy mother
And thy brother;
Leave the black tents of thy tribe apart!
Am I not thy father and thy brother,
And thy mother?
And thou—what needest with thy tribe's black tents
Who hast the red pavilion of my heart?

ALL'S VAST

O nothing, in this corporal earth of man,
That to the imminent heaven of his high soul
Responds with color and with shadow, can
Lack correlated greatness. If the scroll
Where thoughts lie fast in spell of hieroglyph
Be mighty through its mighty inhabitants;
If God be in His Name; grave potence if
The sounds unbind of hieratic chants;
All's vast that vastness means. Nay, I affirm
Nature is whole in her least things exprest,
Nor know we with what scope God builds the worm.
Our towns are copied fragments from our breast;
And all man's Babylons strive but to impart
The grandeurs of his Babylonian heart.

EPILOGUE

(from "A Judgment in Heaven")

Heaven, which man's generations draws,
Nor deviates into replicas,
Must of as deep diversity
In judgment as creation be.
There is no expeditious road
To pack and label men for God,
And save them by the barrel-load.
Some may perchance, with strange surprise,
Have blundered into Paradise.
In vasty dusk of life abroad,
They fondly thought to err from God,
Nor knew the circle that they trod;
And, wandering all the night about,
Found them at morn where they set out.
Death dawned; Heaven lay in prospect wide:—
Lo! they were standing by His side!

THE POPPY

(*To Monica*)

Summer set lip to earth's bosom bare,
And left the flushed print in a poppy there:
Like a yawn of fire from the grass it came,
And the fanning wind puffed it to flapping flame.

With burnt mouth, red like a lion's, it drank
The blood of the sun as he slaughtered sank,
And dipped its cup in the purpurate shine
When the Eastern conduits ran with wine.

Till it grew lethargied with fierce bliss,
And hot as a swinked gypsy is,
And drowsed in sleepy savageries,
With mouth wide a-pout for a sultry kiss.

A child and man paced side by side,
Treading the skirts of eventide;
But between the clasp of his hand and hers
Lay, felt not, twenty withered years.

She turned, with the rout of her dusk South hair,
And saw the sleeping gypsy there:
And snatched and snapped it in swift child's whim,
With—"Keep it, long as you live!"—to him.

And his smile, as nymphs from their laving meres,
Trembled up from a bath of tears;
And joy, like a mew sea-rocked apart,
Tossed on the waves of his troubled heart.

For *he* saw what she did not see,
That—as kindled by its own fervency—
The verge shriveled inward smolderingly:
And suddenly 'twixt his hand and hers
He knew the twenty withered years—
No flower, but twenty shriveled years.

"Was never such thing until this hour,"
Low to his heart he said; "the flower
Of sleep brings wakening to me,
And of oblivion, memory.

"Was never this thing to me," he said,
"Though with bruisèd poppies my feet are red!"
And again to his own heart very low:
"O child! I love, for I love and know;

"But you, who love nor know at all
The diverse chambers in Love's guest-hall,
Where some rise early, few sit long:
In how differing accents hear the throng
His great Pentecostal tongue;

"Who know not love from amity,
Nor my reported self from me;
A fair fit gift is this, meseems,
You give—this withering flower of dreams.

"O frankly fickle, and fickly true,
Do you know what the days will do to you?
To your love and you what the days will do,
O frankly fickle, and fickly true?

"You have loved me, Fair, three lives—or days:
'Twill pass with the passing of my face.
But where *I* go, your face goes too,
To watch lest I play false to you.

"I am but, my sweet, your foster-lover,
Knowing well when certain years are over
You vanish from me to another;
Yet I know, and love, like the foster-mother.

"So frankly fickle, and fickly true!
For my brief life-while I take from you
This token, fair and fit, meseems,
For me—this withering flower of dreams."

The sleep-flower sways in the wheat its head,
Heavy with dreams, as that with bread:
The goodly grain and the sun-flushed sleeper
The reaper reaps, and Time the reaper.

I hang 'mid men my needless head,
And my fruit is dreams, as theirs is bread:
The goodly men and the sun-hazed sleeper
Time shall reap, but after the reaper
The world shall glean of me, me the sleeper.

Love, love! your flower of withered dream
In leavèd rhyme lies safe, I deem,
Sheltered and shut in a nook of rhyme,
From the reaper man, and his reaper Time.

Love! *I* fall into the claws of Time:
But last within a leavèd rhyme
All that the world of me esteems—
My withered dreams, my withered dreams.

THE SUN

(from "Ode to the Setting Sun")

Who lit the furnace of the mammoth's heart?
Who shagged him like Pilatus' ribbèd flanks?
Who raised the columned ranks
Of that old pre-diluvian forestry,
Which like a continent torn oppressed the sea,
When the ancient heavens did in rains depart,
While the high-dancèd whirls
Of the tossed scud made hiss thy drenchèd curls?
Thou rear'dst the enormous brood;
Who hast with life imbued
The lion maned in tawny majesty,
The tiger velvet-barred,
The stealthy-stepping pard,
And the lithe panther's flexous symmetry?

How came the entombèd tree a light-bearer,
Though sunk in lightless lair?
Friend of the forgers of earth,
Mate of the earthquake and thunders volcanic,
Clasped in the arms of the forces Titanic
Which rock like a cradle the girth
Of the ether-hung world;
Swart son of the swarthy mine,
When flame on the breath of his nostrils feeds
How is his countenance half-divine,
Like thee in thy sanguine weeds?
Thou gavest him his light,
Though sepultured in night
Beneath the dead bones of a perished world;
Over his prostrate form
Though cold, and heat, and storm,
The mountainous wrack of a creation hurled.

Who made the splendid rose
Saturate with purple glows;
Cupped to the marge with beauty; a perfume-press
Whence the wind vintages
Gushes of warmèd fragrance richer far
Than all the flavorous ooze of Cyprus' vats?
Lo, in yon gale which waves her green cymar,
With dusky cheeks burnt red
She sways her heavy head,
Drunk with the must of her own odorousness;
While in a moted trouble the vexed gnats
Maze, and vibrate, and tease the noontide hush.
Who girt dissolvèd lightnings in the grape?
Summered the opal with an Irised flush?
Is it not thou that dost the tulip drape,

And huest the daffodilly,
Yet who hast snowed the lily,
And her frail sister, whom the waters name,
Dost vestal-vesture 'mid the blaze of June,
Cold as the new-sprung girlhood of the moon
Ere Autumn's kiss sultry her cheek with flame?
Thou sway'st thy sceptered beam
O'er all delight and dream,
Beauty is beautiful but in thy glance:
And like a jocund maid
In garland-flowers arrayed,
Before thy ark Earth keeps her sacred dance.

A FALLEN YEW

It seemed corrival of the world's great prime,
Made to un-edge the scythe of Time,
And last with stateliest rhyme.

No tender Dryad ever did indue
That rigid chiton of rough yew,
To fret her white flesh through:

But some god like to those grim Asgard lords,
Who walk the fables of the hordes
From Scandinavian fjords,

Upheaved its stubborn girth, and raised unriven,
Against the whirl-blast and the levin,
Defiant arms to Heaven.

When doom puffed out the stars, we might have said,
It would decline its heavy head,
And see the world to bed.

For this firm yew did from the vassal leas,
And rain and air, its tributaries,
Its revenues increase,

And levy impost on the golden sun,
Take the blind years as they might run,
And no fate seek or shun.

But now our yew is strook, is fallen—yea,
Hacked like dull wood of every day
To this and that, men say.

Never!—To Hades' shadowy shipyards gone,
Dim barge of Dis, down Acheron
It drops, or Lethe wan.

Stirred by its fall—poor destined bark of Dis!—
Along my soul a bruit there is
Of echoing images,

Reverberations of mortality:
  Spelt backward from its death, to me
    Its life reads saddenedly.

Its breast was hollowed as the tooth of eld;
  And boys, there creeping unbeheld,
    A laughing moment dwelled.

Yet they, within its very heart so crept,
  Reached not the heart that courage kept
    With winds and years beswept.

And in its boughs did close and kindly nest
  The birds, as they within its breast,
    By all its leaves caressed.

But bird nor child might touch by any art
  Each other's or the tree's hid heart,
    A whole God's breadth apart;

The breadth of God, the breadth of death and life!
  Even so, even so, in undreamed strife
    With pulseless Law, the wife,—

The sweetest wife on sweetest marriage-day,—
  Their souls at grapple in mid-way,
    Sweet to her sweet may say:

"I take you to my inmost heart, my true!"
  Ah, fool! but there is one heart you
    Shall never take him to!

The hold that falls not when the town is got,
  The heart's heart, whose immurèd plot
    Hath keys yourself keep not!

Its ports you cannot burst—you are withstood—
  For him that to your listening blood
    Sends precepts as he would.

Its gates are deaf to Love, high summoner;
  Yea, love's great warrant runs not there:
    You are your prisoner.

Yourself are with yourself the sole consortress
  In that unleaguerable fortress;
    It knows you not for portress.

Its keys are at the cincture hung of God;
  Its gates are trepidant to His nod;
    By Him its floors are trod.

And if His feet shall rock those floors in wrath,
  Or blest aspersion sleek His path,
    Is only choice it hath.

Yea, in that ultimate heart's occult abode
  To lie as in an oubliette of God,
    Or in a bower untrod,

Built by a secret Lover for His Spouse;—
  Sole choice is this your life allows,
    Sad tree, whose perishing boughs
      So few birds house!

A COUNSEL OF MODERATION

On him the unpetitioned heavens descend,
Who heaven on earth proposes not for end;
The perilous and celestial excess
Taking with peace, lacking with thankfulness.
Bliss in extreme befits thee not until
Thou'rt not extreme in bliss; be equal still:
Sweets to be granted think thyself unmeet
Till thou have learned to hold sweet not too sweet.

This thing not far is he from wise in art
Who teacheth; nor who doth, from wise in heart.

ANY SAINT

(*Condensed*)

His shoulder did I hold
Too high that I, o'erbold
    Weak one,
  Should lean thereon.

But He a little hath
Declined His stately path
    And my
  Feet set more high;

That the slack arm may reach
His shoulder, and faint speech
    Stir
  His unwithering hair.

And bolder now and bolder
I lean upon that shoulder,
    So dear
  He is and near:

And with His aureole
The tresses of my soul
    Are blent
  In wished content.

Yea, this too gentle Lover
Hath flattering words to move her
    To pride
  By his sweet side.

Ah, Love! somewhat let be—
Lest my humility
    Grow weak
  When Thou dost speak.

Rebate Thy tender suit,
Lest to herself impute
    Some worth
  Thy bride of earth!

A maid too easily
Conceits herself to be
    Those things
  Her lover sings;

And being straitly wooed,
Believes herself the Good
    And Fair
  He seeks in her.

Turn something of Thy look,
And fear me with rebuke,
That I
May timorously

Take tremors in Thy arms,
And with contrivèd charms
Allure
A love unsure.

Not to me, not to me,
Builded so flawfully,
O God,
Thy humbling laud!

Not to this man, but Man,—
Universe in a span;
Point
Of the spheres conjoint;

In whom eternally
Thou, Light, dost focus Thee!—
Didst pave
The way o' the wave.

*

Thou meaning, couldst thou see,
Of all which dafteth thee;
So plain,
It mocks thy pain.

Stone of the Law indeed,
Thine own self couldst thou read;
Thy bliss
Within thee is.

Compost of Heaven and mire,
Slow foot and swift desire!
Lo,
To have Yes, choose No;

*

To feel thyself and be
His dear nonentity—
Caught
Beyond human thought

In the thunder-spout of Him,
Until thy being dim,
And be
Dead deathlessly.

Stoop, stoop; for thou dost fear
The nettle's wrathful spear,
So slight
Art thou of might!

Rise; for Heaven hath no frown
When thou to thee pluck'st down,
Strong clod!
The neck of God.

THE HOUND OF HEAVEN

I fled Him, down the nights and down the days;
I fled Him, down the arches of the years;
I fled Him, down the labyrinthine ways
Of my own mind; and in the mist of tears
I hid from Him, and under running laughter.
Up vistaed hopes I sped;
And shot, precipitated,
Adown Titanic glooms of chasmèd fears,
From those strong Feet that followed, followed after.
But with unhurrying chase,
And unperturbèd pace,
Deliberate speed, majestic instancy,
They beat—and a Voice beat
More instant than the Feet—
"All things betray thee, who betrayest Me."

I pleaded, outlaw-wise,
By many a hearted casement, curtained red,
Trellised with intertwining charities
(For, though I knew His love Who followèd,

Yet was I sore adread
Lest, having Him, I must have naught beside);
But, if one little casement parted wide,
The gust of His approach would clash it to:
Fear wist not to evade, as Love wist to pursue.
Across the margent of the world I fled,
And troubled the gold gateways of the stars,
Smiting for shelter on their clangèd bars;
Fretted to dulcet jars
And silvern chatter the pale ports o' the moon.
I said to Dawn: Be sudden—to Eve: Be soon;
With thy young skiey blossoms heap me over
From this tremendous Lover—
Float thy vague veil about me, lest He see!
I tempted all His servitors, but to find
My own betrayal in their constancy,
In faith to Him their fickleness to me,
Their traitorous trueness, and their loyal deceit.
To all swift things for swiftness did I sue;
Clung to the whistling mane of every wind.
But whether they swept, smoothly fleet,
The long savannahs of the blue;
Or whether, Thunder-driven,
They clanged his chariot 'thwart a heaven,
Plashy with flying lightnings round the spurn o' their feet:—
Fear wist not to evade as Love wist to pursue.
Still with unhurrying chase,
And unperturbèd pace,
Deliberate speed, majestic instancy,
Came on the following Feet,
And a Voice above their beat—
"Naught shelters thee, who wilt not shelter Me."

I sought no more that after which I strayed
In face of man or maid;
But still within the little children's eyes
Seems something, something that replies,
They at least are for me, surely for me!
I turned me to them very wistfully;
But just as their young eyes grew sudden fair
With dawning answers there,
Their angel plucked them from me by the hair.
"Come then, ye other children, Nature's—share
With me" (said I) "your delicate fellowship;
Let me greet you lip to lip,
Let me twine with you caresses,
Wantoning
With our Lady-Mother's vagrant tresses.
Banqueting

With her in her wind-walled palace,
Underneath her azured daïs,
Quaffing, as your taintless way is,
From a chalice
Lucent-weeping out of the dayspring."
So it was done:
I in their delicate fellowship was one—
Drew the bolt of Nature's secrecies.
I knew all the swift importings
On the willful face of skies;
I knew how the clouds arise
Spumèd of the wild sea-snortings;
All that's born or dies
Rose and drooped with; made them shapers
Of mine own moods, or wailful or divine;
With them joyed and was bereaven.
I was heavy with the even,
When she lit her glimmering tapers
Round the day's dead sanctities.
I laughed in the morning's eyes.
I triumphed and I saddened with all weather,
Heaven and I wept together,
And its sweet tears were salt with mortal mine;

Against the red throb of its sunset-heart
I laid my own to beat,
And share commingling heat;
But not by that, by that, was eased my human smart.
In vain my tears were wet on Heaven's gray cheek.
For ah! we know not what each other says,
These things and I; in sound *I* speak—
Their sound is but their stir, they speak by silences.
Nature, poor stepdame, cannot slake my drouth;
Let her, if she would owe me,
Drop yon blue bosom-veil of sky, and show me
The breasts o' her tenderness:
Never did any milk of hers once bless
My thirsting mouth.
Nigh and nigh draws the chase,
With unperturbèd pace,
Deliberate speed, majestic instancy;
And past those noisèd Feet
A Voice comes yet more fleet—
"Lo! naught contents thee, who content'st not Me."

'Naked I wait Thy love's uplifted stroke!
My harness piece by piece Thou hast hewn from me,
And smitten me to my knee;
I am defenseless utterly.
I slept, methinks, and woke,

And, slowly gazing, find me stripped in sleep.
In the rash lustihead of my young powers,
        I shook the pillaring hours
And pulled my life upon me; grimed with smears,
I stand amid the dust o' the mounded years—
My mangled youth lies dead beneath the heap.
My days have crackled and gone up in smoke,
Have puffed and burst as sun-starts on a stream.
        Yea, faileth now even dream
The dreamer, and the lute the lutanist;
Even the linked fantasies, in whose blossomy twist
I swung the earth a trinket at my wrist,
Are yielding; cords of all too weak account
For earth with heavy griefs so overplused.
        Ah! is Thy love indeed
A weed, albeit an amaranthine weed,
Suffering no flowers except its own to mount?
        Ah! must—
        Designer infinite!—
Ah! must Thou char the wood ere Thou canst limn with it?
My freshness spent its wavering shower i' the dust;
And now my heart is as a broken fount,
Wherein tear-drippings stagnate, spilt down ever
        From the dank thoughts that shiver
Upon the sighful branches of my mind.
        Such is; what is to be?
The pulp so bitter, how shall taste the rind?
I dimly guess what Time in mists confounds;
Yet ever and anon a trumpet sounds
From the hid battlements of Eternity;
Those shaken mists a space unsettle, then
Round the half-glimpsèd turrets slowly wash again.
        But not ere him who summoneth
        I first have seen, enwound
With glooming robes purpureal, cypress-crowned;
His name I know, and what his trumpet saith.
Whether man's heart or life it be which yields
        Thee harvest, must Thy harvest-fields
        Be dunged with rotten death?

          Now of that long pursuit
          Comes on at hand the bruit;
        That Voice is round me like a bursting sea:
          "And is thy earth so marred,
          Shattered in shard on shard?
        Lo, all things fly thee, for thou fliest Me!
        Strange, piteous, futile thing!
Wherefore should any set thee love apart?
Seeing none but I makes much of naught" (He said),
"And human love needs human meriting:
        How hast thou merited—

Of all man's clotted clay the dingiest clot?
Alack, thou knowest not
How little worthy of any love thou art!
Whom wilt thou find to love ignoble thee
Save Me, save only Me?
All which I took from thee I did but take,
Not for thy harms,
But just that thou might'st seek it in My arms.
All which thy child's mistake
Fancies as lost, I have stored for thee at home:
Rise, clasp My hand, and come!"

Halts by me that footfall:
Is my gloom, after all,
Shade of His hand, outstretched caressingly?
"Ah, fondest, blindest, weakest,
I am He Whom thou seekest!
Thou dravest love from thee, who dravest Me."

FROM "GRACE OF THE WAY"

Now of that vision I, bereaven,
This knowledge keep, that may not dim:
Short arm needs man to reach to Heaven,
So ready is Heaven to stoop to him.

TO OLIVIA

I fear to love thee, Sweet, because
Love's the ambassador of loss;
White flake of childhood, clinging so
To my soiled raiment, thy shy snow
At tenderest touch will shrink and go.
Love me not, delightful child.
My heart, by many snares beguiled,
Has grown timorous and wild.
It would fear thee not at all,
Wert thou not so harmless-small.
Because thy arrows, not yet dire,
Are still unbarbed with destined fire,
I fear thee more than hadst thou stood
Full-panoplied in womanhood.

"IN NO STRANGE LAND"[1]

O world invisible, we view thee,
O world intangible, we touch thee,
O world unknowable, we know thee,
Inapprehensible, we clutch thee!

Does the fish soar to find the ocean,
The eagle plunge to find the air—
That we ask of the stars in motion
If they have rumor of thee there?

Not where the wheeling systems darken,
And our benumbed conceiving soars!—
The drift of pinions, would we hearken,
Beats at our own clay-shuttered doors.

The angels keep their ancient places;
Turn but a stone, and start a wing!
'Tis ye, 'tis your estrangèd faces,
That miss the many-splendored thing.

But, when so sad thou canst not sadder,
Cry;—and upon thy so sore loss
Shall shine the traffic of Jacob's ladder
Pitched betwixt Heaven and Charing Cross.

Yea, in the night, my Soul, my daughter,
Cry,—clinging Heaven by the hems;
And lo, Christ walking on the water
Not of Gennesareth, but Thames!

[1] These verses, unpublished during his lifetime, were found among Francis Thompson's papers after his death.

ENVOY

Go, songs, for ended is our brief, sweet play;
  Go, children of swift joy and tardy sorrow:
And some are sung, and that was yesterday,
  And some unsung, and that may be tomorrow.

Go forth; and if it be o'er stony way,
  Old joy can lend what newer grief must borrow:
And it was sweet, and that was yesterday,
  And sweet is sweet, though purchasèd with sorrow.

Go, songs, and come not back from your far way:
  And if men ask you why ye smile and sorrow,
Tell them ye grieve, for your hearts know Today,
  Tell them ye smile, for your eyes know Tomorrow.

A. E. Housman

A(lfred) E(dward) Housman was born March 26, 1859, and educated at Oxford where he received his M.A. He was a Higher Division Clerk in the British Patent Office for ten years (1882-1892), leaving the office to become a teacher. Professor of Latin at University College, London, from 1892 to 1911, at Cambridge after 1911, one of the great classical scholars of his day, he died April 30, 1936.

In 1895 Housman offered for publication a manuscript entitled *Poems by Terence Hearsay*—a title which accounts for the personal reference in the "Epilogue" on page 100. The poems were rejected. Housman changed the title, and another publisher brought the book out as *A Shropshire Lad*. Only five hundred copies were printed; the publisher refused to print a second edition except at the poet's expense. The critical reception was fair, but sales were sluggish. It was not until 1914, during the war, that their militant masculine spirit made the poems immensely popular.

The extraordinary success of *A Shropshire Lad* is comparable to that of Fitzgerald's *Rubáiyát of Omar Khayyám*. Both works reveal a mood of pessimism and defeat. The philosophy would ordinarily have found little favor, but it was expressed in quotable phrases and captivating music. Fitzgerald and Housman wrote with such skill that they charmed readers who might otherwise have been repelled by the intellectual content of the poetry. The spell was woven less by the meaning than by the sheer charm of the brisk and brilliant measures.

A Shropshire Lad is limited in range and idea. Nature is not kind; lovers are untrue; men cheat and girls betray; lads, though lightfoot, drink and die; an occasional drum calls to a conflict without reason, a struggle without hope. Nevertheless, courage is dominant, declared over and over in such poems as "Réveillé," "When Smoke Stood Up from Ludlow," "The Chestnut Casts His Flambeaux," and Housman's bitter but fearless philosophy reaches the heights in his "Epilogue."

Purely as writing, however, *A Shropshire Lad* is incomparable. Owing nothing to any poet of his own generation and showing few influences other than Heine's, Housman's verse is condensed to the uttermost, stripped of every superfluous ornament, pared and precise. Not the least of his triumph is the mingling of pungent humor and poignance. Possibly the outstanding virtue is the seemingly artless but extraordinarily skillful simplicity of tone. This is song sharpened, acid-flavored, yet always song.

A Shropshire Lad was first published in 1896 when Housman was thirty-seven, although several of the lyrics were written when the poet was younger. After a silence of twenty-six years, there appeared his *Last Poems* (1922). The title is significant, Housman saying, "I publish these poems, few though they are, because it is not likely that I shall ever be impelled to write much more. I can no longer expect to be revisited by the continuous excitement under which in the early months of 1895 I wrote the greater part of my other book, nor indeed could I well sustain it if it came." Most of the second volume belongs to an earlier period, to the years between 1895 and 1910. Here in *Last Poems* the Shropshire lad lives again to pipe his mournful-merry tunes; here again the rose-lipt maiden kisses carelessly as ever, and the heart out of the bosom is given in vain. Here Wenlock Edge is still in trouble, young men shoulder the sky and face the hills whose comfort cannot delay "the beautiful and deathstruck year." The pessimism assumes a half-careless, half-heroic note.

A Shropshire Lad sounded the note of a wry surrender:

> Be still, be still, my soul; it is but for a season:
> Let us endure an hour and see injustice done.
>
> Aye, look, high heaven and earth ail from the prime foundation;
> All thoughts to rive the heart are here, and all in vain:
> Horror and scorn and hate and fear and indignation—
> Oh, why did I awake? When shall I sleep again?

And in *Last Poems* the no less disillusioned spirit cries:

> We of a certainty are not the first
> Have sat in taverns while the tempest hurled
> Their hopeful plans to emptiness, and cursed
> Whatever brute or blackguard made the world.

The rhythms of *Last Poems* are a trifle slower, the cadences somewhat more acrid, but Housman's command of his instrument is still unfaltering. Some critics have pointed out Housman's "echoes" and John Sparrow, in *The Nineteenth Century,* has traced certain general resemblances and a few specific phrases to earlier writers, especially Shakespeare, Heine, and the Greek lyrists. But Housman's touch is so definitely his own, his accent so individualized that the occasional (and usually intentional) allusions are absorbed in the English poet's idiom. Who else could modernize the story of Jesus as concisely as Housman has done in "The Carpenter's Son"; who but he could have turned such simple material as "Loveliest of Trees" to the words and music of possibly the finest lyric in the English language? Each reader will have his favorites, and those admirers who know the two volumes almost by heart will even resent learning that Thomas Hardy considered "Is My Team Ploughing" one of the most dramatic short poems in the language.

A posthumous *More Poems* (1936) was edited by Housman's brother Laurence; this and the preceding volumes were assembled, together with some hitherto unpublished verse, in a comprehensive *Collected Poems* (1940). The introductions to his editions of Manilius, Juvenal, and Lucan reveal Housman's passion for chiseled form and his contempt for careless work. His scholarly papers are edged with sarcasm and bristle with cold contempt; he wrote of a certain teacher, "When X has acquired a scrap of misinformation he cannot rest till he has imparted it." A similar tone, trenchant and controversial, is heard in *The Name and Nature of Poetry* (1933), a lecture which conceals as much about the process of creation as it reveals. For example, when asked to define poetry Housman replied, "I could no more define poetry than a terrier can define a rat, but I thought we both recognized the object by the symptoms which it provokes in us. . . . Experience has taught me, when I am shaving, to keep watch over my thoughts, because if a line of poetry strays into my memory, my skin bristles so that the razor ceases to act." But it is as a poet that Housman will live, and his verse already seems marked for permanence. A dozen or more of his poems have the authority that comes only with age and tradition. They are fastidious; they are small; they are limited in range, restricted in outlook, and sometimes inflexible because of their overdisciplined line. But they haunt the mind, and many of them are as nearly perfect as lyrics can hope to be.

The most informative as well as the most informal account of Housman's life was written by Laurence Housman and entitled *My Brother, A. E. Housman.*

RÉVEILLÉ

Wake: the silver dusk returning
  Up the beach of darkness brims,
And the ship of sunrise burning
  Strands upon the eastern rims.

Wake: the vaulted shadow shatters,
  Trampled to the floor it spanned,
And the tent of night in tatters
  Straws the sky-pavilioned land.

Up, lad, up, 'tis late for lying:
  Hear the drums of morning play;
Hark, the empty highways crying
  "Who'll beyond the hills away?"

Towns and countries woo together,
  Forelands beacon, belfries call;
Never lad that trod on leather
  Lived to feast his heart with all.

Up, lad: thews that lie and cumber
  Sunlit pallets never thrive;
Morns abed and daylight slumber
  Were not meant for man alive.

Clay lies still, but blood's a rover;
Breath's a ware that will not keep.
Up, lad: when the journey's over
There'll be time enough to sleep.

WITH RUE MY HEART IS LADEN

With rue my heart is laden
For golden friends I had,
For many a rose-lipt maiden
And many a lightfoot lad.

By brooks too broad for leaping
The lightfoot boys are laid;
The rose-lipt girls are sleeping
In fields where roses fade.

INTO MY HEART

Into my heart an air that kills
From yon far country blows:
What are those blue remembered hills,
What spires, what farms are those?

That is the land of lost content,
I see it shining plain:
The happy highways where I went
And cannot come again.

WHEN I WAS ONE-AND-TWENTY

When I was one-and-twenty
I heard a wise man say,
"Give crowns and pounds and guineas
But not your heart away;
Give pearls away and rubies
But keep your fancy free."
But I was one-and-twenty,
No use to talk to me.

When I was one-and-twenty
I heard him say again,
"The heart out of the bosom
Was never given in vain;
'Tis paid with sighs a-plenty
And sold for endless rue."
And I am two-and-twenty,
And oh, 'tis true, 'tis true.

TO AN ATHLETE DYING YOUNG

The time you won your town the race
We chaired you through the market-place;
Man and boy stood cheering by,
And home we brought you shoulder-high.

Today, the road all runners come,
Shoulder-high we bring you home,
And set you at your threshold down,
Townsman of a stiller town.

Smart lad, to slip betimes away
From fields where glory does not stay,
And early though the laurel grows
It withers quicker than the rose.

Eyes the shady night has shut
Cannot see the record cut,
And silence sounds no worse than cheers
After earth has stopped the ears:

Now you will not swell the rout
Of lads that wore their honors out,
Runners whom renown outran
And the name died before the man.

So set, before its echoes fade,
The fleet foot on the sill of shade,
And hold to the low lintel up
The still-defended challenge-cup.

And round that early-laureled head
Will flock to gaze the strengthless dead,
And find unwithered on its curls
The garland briefer than a girl's.

LOVELIEST OF TREES

Loveliest of trees, the cherry now
Is hung with bloom along the bough,
And stands about the woodland ride
Wearing white for Eastertide.

Now, of my threescore years and ten,
Twenty will not come again,
And take from seventy springs a score,
It only leaves me fifty more.

And since to look at things in bloom
Fifty springs are little room,
About the woodlands I will go
To see the cherry hung with snow.

IS MY TEAM PLOUGHING

"Is my team ploughing,
That I used to drive
And hear the harness jingle
When I was man alive?"

Aye, the horses trample,
The harness jingles now;
No change though you lie under
The land you used to plough.

"Is football playing
Along the river shore,
With lads to chase the leather,
Now I stand up no more?"

Aye, the ball is flying,
The lads play heart and soul;
The goal stands up, the keeper
Stands up to keep the goal.

"Is my girl happy,
That I thought hard to leave,
And has she tired of weeping
As she lies down at eve?"

Aye, she lies down lightly,
She lies not down to weep:
Your girl is well contented.
Be still, my lad, and sleep.

"Is my friend hearty,
Now I am thin and pine;
And has he found to sleep in
A better bed than mine?"

Aye, lad, I lie easy,
I lie as lads would choose;
I cheer a dead man's sweetheart.
Never ask me whose.

WHEN SMOKE STOOD UP FROM LUDLOW

When smoke stood up from Ludlow,
And mist blew off from Teme,
And blithe afield to ploughing
Against the morning beam
I strode beside my team,

The blackbird in the coppice
Looked out to see me stride,
And hearkened as I whistled
The trampling team beside,
And fluted and replied:

"Lie down, lie down, young yeoman;
What use to rise and rise?
Rise man a thousand mornings
Yet down at last he lies,
And then the man is wise."

I heard the tune he sang me,
And spied his yellow bill;

I picked a stone and aimed it
  And threw it with a will:
  And then the bird was still.

Then my soul within me
  Took up the blackbird's strain,
And still beside the horses
  Along the dewy lane
  It sang the song again:

"Lie down, lie down, young yeoman;
  The sun moves always west;
The road one treads to labor
  Will lead one home to rest,
  And that will be the best."

WHEN I WATCH THE LIVING MEET

When I watch the living meet,
  And the moving pageant file
Warm and breathing through the street
  Where I lodge a little while,

If the heats of hate and lust
  In the house of flesh are strong,
Let me mind the house of dust
  Where my sojourn shall be long.

In the nation that is not
  Nothing stands that stood before;
There revenges are forgot,
  And the hater hates no more;

Lovers lying two and two
  Ask not whom they sleep beside,
And the bridegroom all night through
  Never turns him to the bride.

OH, SEE HOW THICK THE GOLDCUP FLOWERS

Oh, see how thick the goldcup flowers
  Are lying in field and lane,
With dandelions to tell the hours
  That never are told again,
Oh, may I squire you round the meads
  And pick you posies gay?
—'Twill do no harm to take my arm.
  "You may, young man, you may."

Ah, spring was sent for lass and lad,
  'Tis now the blood runs gold,
And man and maid had best be glad
  Before the world is old.
What flowers today may flower tomorrow,
  But never as good as new.
—Suppose I wound my arm right round.
  " 'Tis true, young man, 'tis true."

Some lads there are, 'tis shame to say,
  That only court to thieve,
And once they bear the bloom away
  'Tis little enough they leave.
Then keep your heart for men like me
  And safe from trustless chaps.
My love is true and all for you.
  "Perhaps, young man, perhaps."

Oh, look in my eyes then, can you doubt?
  —Why, 'tis a mile from town.
How green the grass is all about!
  We might as well sit down.
—Ah, life, what is it but a flower?
  Why must true lovers sigh?
Be kind, have pity, my own, my pretty,—
  "Good-by, young man, good-by."

THE LADS IN THEIR HUNDREDS

The lads in their hundreds to Ludlow come in for the fair,
  There's men from the barn and the forge and the mill and the fold,
The lads for the girls and the lads for the liquor are there,
  And there with the rest are the lads that will never be old.

There's chaps from the town and the field and the till and the cart,
  And many to count are the stalwart, and many the brave,
And many the handsome of face and the handsome of heart,
  And few that will carry their looks or their truth to the grave.

I wish one could know them, I wish there were tokens to tell
  The fortunate fellows that now you can never discern;
And then one could talk with them friendly and wish them farewell
  And watch them depart on the way that they will not return.

But now you may stare as you like and there's nothing to scan;
  And brushing your elbow unguessed-at and not to be told
They carry back bright to the coiner the mintage of man,
  The lads that will die in their glory and never be old.

WHEN THE LAD FOR LONGING SIGHS

When the lad for longing sighs,
  Mute and dull of cheer and pale,
If at death's own door he lies,
  Maiden, you can heal his ail.

Lovers' ills are all to buy:
  The wan look, the hollow tone,
The hung head, the sunken eye,
  You can have them for your own.

Buy them, buy them: eve and morn
  Lovers' ills are all to sell.
Then you can lie down forlorn;
  But the lover will be well.

THE IMMORTAL PART

When I meet the morning beam,
Or lay me down at night to dream,
I hear my bones within me say,
"Another night, another day.

"When shall this slough of sense be cast,
This dust of thoughts be laid at last,
The man of flesh and soul be slain
And the man of bone remain?

"This tongue that talks, these lungs that shout,
These thews that hustle us about,
This brain that fills the skull with schemes,
And its humming hive of dreams,—

"These today are proud in power
And lord it in their little hour:
The immortal bones obey control
Of dying flesh and dying soul.

" 'Tis long till eve and morn are gone:
Slow the endless night comes on,
And late to fullness grows the birth
That shall last as long as earth.

"Wanderers eastward, wanderers west,
Know you why you cannot rest?
'Tis that every mother's son
Travails with a skeleton.

"Lie down in the bed of dust;
Bear the fruit that bear you must;
Bring the eternal seed to light,
And morn is all the same as night.

"Rest you so from trouble sore,
Fear the heat o' the sun no more,
Nor the snowing winter wild,
Now you labor not with child.

"Empty vessel, garment cast,
We that wore you long shall last.
—Another night, another day."
  So my bones within me say.

Therefore they shall do my will
Today while I am master still,
And flesh and soul, now both are strong,
Shall hale the sullen slaves along,

Before this fire of sense decay,
This smoke of thought blow clean away,
And leave with ancient night alone
The steadfast and enduring bone.

ON WENLOCK EDGE

On Wenlock Edge the wood's in trouble;
His forest fleece the Wrekin heaves;
The gale, it plies the saplings double,
And thick on Severn snow the leaves.

'Twould blow like this through holt and hangar
When Uricon the city stood:
'Tis the old wind in the old anger,
But then it threshed another wood.

Then, 'twas before my time, the Roman
At yonder heaving hill would stare:
The blood that warms an English yeoman,
The thoughts that hurt him, they were there.

There, like the wind through woods in riot,
Through him the gale of life blew high;
The tree of man was never quiet:
Then 'twas the Roman, now 'tis I.

The gale, it plies the saplings double,
It blows so hard, 'twill soon be gone:
Today the Roman and his trouble
Are ashes under Uricon.

OH, WHEN I WAS IN LOVE WITH YOU

Oh, when I was in love with you,
Then I was clean and brave,
And miles around the wonder grew
How well did I behave.

And now the fancy passes by,
And nothing will remain,
And miles around they'll say that I
Am quite myself again.

ALONG THE FIELD AS WE CAME BY

Along the field as we came by
A year ago, my love and I,
The aspen over stile and stone
Was talking to itself alone.
"Oh, who are these that kiss and pass?
A country lover and his lass;
Two lovers looking to be wed;
And time shall put them both to bed,
But she shall lie with earth above,
And he beside another love."

And sure enough beneath the tree
There walks another love with me,
And overhead the aspen heaves
Its rainy-sounding silver leaves;
And I spell nothing in their stir,
But now perhaps they speak to her,
And plain for her to understand
They talk about a time at hand
When I shall sleep with clover clad,
And she beside another lad.

ON THE IDLE HILL OF SUMMER

On the idle hill of summer,
Sleepy with the flow of streams,
Far I hear the steady drummer
Drumming like a noise in dreams.

Far and near and low and louder
On the roads of earth go by,
Dear to friends and food for powder,
Soldiers marching, all to die.

East and west on fields forgotten
Bleach the bones of comrades slain,
Lovely lads and dead and rotten;
None that go return again.

Far the calling bugles hollo,
High the screaming fife replies,
Gay the files of scarlet follow:
Woman bore me, I will rise.

BREDON HILL

In summertime on Bredon
The bells they sound so clear;
Round both the shires they ring them
In steeples far and near,
A happy noise to hear.

Here of a Sunday morning
My love and I would lie,
And see the colored counties,
And hear the larks so high
About us in the sky.

The bells would ring to call her
In valleys miles away:
"Come all to church, good people;
Good people, come and pray."
But here my love would stay.

And I would turn and answer
Among the springing thyme,
"Oh, peal upon our wedding,

And we will hear the chime,
And come to church in time."

But when the snows at Christmas
On Bredon top were strown,
My love rose up so early
And stole out unbeknown
And went to church alone.

They tolled the one bell only,
Groom there was none to see,
The mourners followed after,
And so to church went she,
And would not wait for me.

The bells they sound on Bredon,
And still the steeples hum.
"Come all to church, good people,—"
Oh, noisy bells, be dumb;
I hear you, I will come.

LANCER

I 'listed at home for a lancer,
Oh who would not sleep with the brave?
I 'listed at home for a lancer
To ride on a horse to my grave.

And over the seas we were bidden
A country to take and to keep;
And far with the brave I have ridden,
And now with the brave I shall sleep.

For round me the men will be lying
That learned me the way to behave,
And showed me my business of dying:
Oh who would not sleep with the brave?

They ask and there is not an answer;
Says I, I will 'list for a lancer,
Oh who would not sleep with the brave?

And I with the brave shall be sleeping
At ease on my mattress of loam,
When back from their taking and keeping
The squadron is riding at home.

The wind with the plumes will be playing,
The girls will stand watching them wave,
And eyeing my comrades and saying
Oh who would not sleep with the brave?

They ask and there is not an answer;
Says you, I will 'list for a lancer,
O who would not sleep with the brave?

THE CHESTNUT CASTS HIS FLAMBEAUX, AND THE FLOWERS

The chestnut casts his flambeaux, and the flowers
Stream from the hawthorn on the wind away,
The doors clap to, the pane is blind with showers.
Pass me the can lad; there's an end of May.

There's one spoilt spring to scant our mortal lot,
One season ruined of our little store.
May will be fine next year as like as not:
Oh, aye, but then we shall be twenty-four.

We for a certainty are not the first
Have sat in taverns while the tempest hurled
Their hopeful plans to emptiness, and cursed
Whatever brute and blackguard made the world.

It is in truth iniquity on high
To cheat our sentenced souls of aught they crave,
And mar the merriment as you and I
Fare on our long fool's errand to the grave.

Iniquity it is; but pass the can.
My lad, no pair of kings our mothers bore;
Our only portion is the estate of man:
We want the moon, but we shall get no more.

If here today the cloud of thunder lours
  Tomorrow it will hie on far behests;
The flesh will grieve on other bones than ours
  Soon, and the soul will mourn in other breasts.

The troubles of our proud and angry dust
  Are from eternity, and shall not fail.
Bear them we can, and if we can we must.
  Shoulder the sky, my lad, and drink your ale.

EIGHT O'CLOCK

He stood, and heard the steeple
  Sprinkle the quarters on the morning town.
One, two, three, four, to market-place and people
  It tossed them down.

Strapped, noosed, nighing his hour,
  He stood and counted them and cursed his luck;
And then the clock collected in the tower
  Its strength, and struck.

EPILOGUE

"Terence, this is stupid stuff;
You eat your victuals fast enough;
There can't be much amiss, 'tis clear,
To see the rate you drink your beer.
But oh, good Lord, the verse you make,
It gives a chap the belly-ache.
The cow, the old cow, she is dead;
It sleeps well, the horned head:
We poor lads, 'tis our turn now
To hear such tunes as killed the cow.
Pretty friendship 'tis to rhyme
Your friends to death before their time
Moping melancholy mad:
Come, pipe a tune to dance to, lad."

Why, if 'tis dancing you would be,
There's brisker pipes than poetry.
Say, for what were hop-yards meant,
Or why was Burton built on Trent?
Oh, many a peer of England brews
Livelier liquor than the Muse,
And malt does more than Milton can
To justify God's ways to man.
Ale, man, ale's the stuff to drink
For fellows whom it hurts to think:
Look into the pewter pot
To see the world as the world's not.
And faith, 'tis pleasant till 'tis past:
The mischief is that 'twill not last.
Oh, I have been to Ludlow fair
And left my necktie God knows where.
And carried half way home, or near,
Pints and quarts of Ludlow beer:
Then the world seemed none so bad,
And I myself a sterling lad;
And down in lovely muck I've lain,
Happy till I woke again.
Then I saw the morning sky:
Heigho, the tale was all a lie;
The world, it was the old world yet,
I was I, my things were wet,
And nothing now remained to do
But begin the game anew.

Therefore, since the world has still
Much good, but much less good than ill,
And while the sun and moon endure
Luck's a chance, but trouble's sure,
I'd face it as a wise man would,
And train for ill and not for good.
'Tis true, the stuff I bring for sale
Is not so brisk a brew as ale:
Out of a stem that scored the hand
I wrung it in a weary land.
But take it: if the smack is sour,
The better for the embittered hour;

It should do good to heart and head
When your soul is in my soul's stead;
And I will friend you, if I may,
In the dark and cloudy day.

There was a king reigned in the East:
There, when kings will sit to feast,
They get their fill before they think
With poisoned meat and poisoned drink.
He gathered all that springs to birth
From the many-venomed earth;
First a little, thence to more,
He sampled all her killing store;
And easy, smiling, seasoned sound,
Sate the king when healths went round.
They put arsenic in his meat
And stared aghast to watch him eat;
They poured strychnine in his cup
And shook to see him drink it up:
They shook, they stared as white's their
shirt:
Them it was their poison hurt.
I tell the tale that I heard told.
Mithridates, he died old.

OTHERS, I AM NOT THE FIRST

Others, I am not the first,
Have willed more mischief than they durst:
If in the breathless night I too
Shiver now, 'tis nothing new.

More than I, if truth were told,
Have stood and sweated hot and cold,
And through their reins in ice and fire
Fear contended with desire.

Agued once like me were they,
But I like them shall win my way
Lastly to the bed of mould
Where there's neither heat nor cold.

But from my grave across my brow
Plays no wind of healing now,
And fire and ice within me fight
Beneath the suffocating night.

THE CARPENTER'S SON

Here the hangman stops his cart:
Now the best of friends must part
Fare you well, for ill fare I:
Live, lads, and I will die.

"Oh, at home had I but stayed
'Prenticed to my father's trade,
Had I stuck to plane and adze,
I had not been lost, my lads.

"Then I might have built perhaps
Gallows-trees for other chaps,
Never dangled on my own,
Had I but left ill alone.

"Now, you see, they hang me high,
And the people passing by
Stop to shake their fists and curse;
So 'tis come from ill to worse.

"Here hang I, and right and left
Two poor fellows hang for theft:
All the same's the luck we prove,
Though the midmost hangs for love.

"Comrades, all, that stand and gaze,
Walk henceforth in other ways;
See my neck and save your own:
Comrades all, leave ill alone.

"Make some day a decent end,
Shrewder fellows than your friend.
Fare you well, for ill fare I:
Live, lads, and I will die."

BE STILL, MY SOUL, BE STILL

Be still, my soul, be still; the arms you bear are brittle,
  Earth and high heaven are fixt of old and founded strong.
Think rather,—call to thought, if now you grieve a little,
  The days when we had rest, O soul, for they were long.

Men loved unkindness then, but lightless in the quarry
  I slept and saw not; tears fell down, I did not mourn;
Sweat ran and blood sprang out and I was never sorry:
  Then it was well with me, in days ere I was born.

Now, and I muse for why and never find the reason,
  I pace the earth, and drink the air, and feel the sun.
Be still, be still, my soul; it is but for a season:
  Let us endure an hour and see injustice done.

Ay, look: high heaven and earth ail from the prime foundation;
  All thoughts to rive the heart are here, and all are vain:
Horror and scorn and hate and fear and indignation—
  Oh, why did I awake? When shall I sleep again?

FROM FAR, FROM EVE

From far, from eve and morning
  And yon twelve-winded sky,
The stuff of life to knit me
  Blew hither: here am I.

Now—for a breath I tarry
  Nor yet disperse apart—
Take my hand quick and tell me,
  What have you in your heart.

Speak now, and I will answer;
  How shall I help you, say;
Ere to the wind's twelve quarters
  I take my endless way.

I HOED AND TRENCHED

I hoed and trenched and weeded,
  And took the flowers to fair:
I brought them home unheeded;
  The hue was not the wear.

So up and down I sow them
  For lads like me to find,
When I shall lie below them,
  A dead man out of mind.

Some seeds the birds devour,
  And some the season mars,
But here and there will flower
  The solitary stars,

And fields will yearly bear them
  As light-leaved spring comes on,
And luckless lads will wear them
  When I am dead and gone.

THE ISLE OF PORTLAND

The star-filled stars are smooth tonight
  From France to England strown;
Black towers above the Portland light
  The felon-quarried stone.

On yonder island, not to rise,
  Never to stir forth free,
Far from his folk a dead lad lies
  That once was friends with me.

Lie you easy, dream you light,
  And sleep you fast for aye;
And luckier may you find the night
  Than ever you found the day.

THE LAWS OF GOD, THE LAWS OF MAN

The laws of God, the laws of man,
He may keep that will and can;
Not I: let God and man decree
Laws for themselves and not for me;
And if my ways are not as theirs
Let them mind their own affairs.
Their deed I judge and much condemn,
Yet when did I make laws for them?
Please yourselves, say I, and they
Need only look the other way.
But no, they will not; they must still
Wrest their neighbour to their will,
And make me dance as they desire
With jail and gallows and hell-fire.
And how am I to face the odds
Of man's bedevilment and God's?
I, a stranger and afraid
In a world I never made.
They will be master, right or wrong;
Though both are foolish, both are strong
And since, my soul, we cannot fly
To Saturn nor to Mercury,
Keep we must, if keep we can,
These foreign laws of God and man.

THE NEW MISTRESS

"Oh, sick I am to see you, will you never let me be?
You may be good for something, but you are not good for me.
Oh, go where you are wanted, for you are not wanted here."
And that was all the farewell when I parted from my dear.

I will go where I am wanted, to a lady born and bred
Who will dress me free for nothing in a uniform of red;
She will not be sick to see me if I only keep it clean:
I will go where I am wanted for a soldier of the Queen.

I will go where I am wanted, for the sergeant does not mind;
He may be sick to see me but he treats me very kind:
He gives me beer and breakfast and a ribbon for my cap,
And I never knew a sweetheart spend her money on a chap.

I will go where I am wanted, where there's room for one or two,
And the men are none too many for the work there is to do;
Where the standing line wears thinner and the dropping dead lie thick;
And the enemies of England, they shall see me and be sick.

FAREWELL

"Farewell to barn and stack and tree,
 Farewell to Severn shore.
Terence, look your last at me,
 For I come home no more.

"The sun burns on the half-mown hill,
 By now the blood is dried;
And Maurice among the hay lies still
 And my knife is in his side.

"My mother thinks us long away;
 'Tis time the field were mown.
She had two sons at rising day,
 To-night she'll be alone.

"And here's a bloody hand to shake,
 And oh, man, here's good-bye;
We'll sweat no more on scythe and rake,
 My bloody hands and I.

"I wish you strength to bring you pride,
 And love to keep you clean,
And I wish you luck, come Lammastide,
 At racing on the green.

"Long for me the rick will wait,
 And long will wait the fold,
And long will stand the empty plate,
 And dinner will be cold."

William Butler Yeats

William Butler Yeats, son of John B. Yeats, the Irish artist, was born at Sandymount, Ireland, June 13, 1865. He studied art for a short time at the Royal Dublin Society, but his childhood was spent in the wild district of Sligo. He was educated at Godolphin School, Hammersmith, and Erasmus Smith School, Dublin. In 1888 he came to London where he lived many years. Later in life he spent much time abroad, in Paris, on the Italian Riviera, always returning to his Ireland as the source of his inspiration. He died, after a brief illness, at Roquebrune, near Nice, January 28, 1939; his body was taken to his native Ireland.

It is not easy to summarize Yeats' contribution, for his activities have been so varied and his work does not divide in fixed periods nor fit into convenient categories. He was folk-lorist, playwright, pamphleteer, editor, experimenter in Spiritualism—and above these rôles, prompting them all, he was a poet.

In the capacity of folk-lorist he prepared the collections of old wives' tales and mythical legends: *Fairy and Folk Tales* (1888) and *Representative Irish Tales* (1891). As essayist he wrote *The Celtic Twilight* (1893); as editor he collaborated with Edwin T. Ellis on an invaluable edition of *The Works of William Blake* (1893); as playwright, he helped organize a native theater and impel the movement known as the Celtic revival.

It was through the "Young Ireland" society that Yeats became identified with an Irish literary theater. He dreamed of a national poetry which would be traditional yet dramatic, written in simple English but spiritually Irish. He founded and edited a paper, the first number appearing in May, 1899, to expound his views. He collaborated with George Moore, with whom he had become associated, wrote his first original play in prose, *Katheleen ni Houlihan* (1902), and became one of the leaders of the movement, his chief associates being J. M. Synge, Douglas Hyde, Moore, and Lady Gregory. He worked incessantly for the cause both as propagandist and playwright; his *Plays for an Irish Theatre* (1913) containing *Where There Is Nothing, The Hour-Glass, Kathleen ni Houlihan, The Pot of Broth, The King's Threshold,* and *On Baile's Strand.*

Others who followed Yeats intensified the Irish drama; they established a closer contact between the peasant and poet. No one, however, had so great a part as Yeats in the actual shaping of modern drama in Ireland. His *Deirdre* (1907), a beautiful retelling of the great Gaelic legend, is far more dramatic than the earlier plays; it is particularly interesting to read as a complement to Synge's more idiomatic play on the same theme, *Deirdre of the Sorrows.*

The poet was already at work—*Mosada: A Poem* was published in 1886, in Yeats' twenty-first year—but he was not yet ready to declare himself definitely. Before his verse marked the rise of a new Irish school he was one of the group contributing to the *fin de siècle* publication *The Yellow Book;* he became the friend of Lionel Johnson and Oscar Wilde, and with them founded the Rhymer's Club; he was represented in both its anthologies. But, as he has told in his autobiographical volumes, *Reveries over Childhood and Youth* (1915) and *The Trembling of the*

Veil (1922), he was forced to walk about London because he could not afford the bus fare, and tea with hospitable friends was not only a social function but a meal that kept him from days of hunger. Accepting his enforced asceticism he turned it into a discipline, and those critics who consider his mysticism a later affectation might well study this period of Yeats' life and trace its essential reality.

It was in London, at the age of twenty-four, that he decided to devote himself to poetry, and it was there that his first representative volume was published in 1889, *The Wanderings of Oisin*. There appeared in rapid succession *The Countess Kathleen and Various Lyrics* (1892), a drama with appended verses; *A Book of Irish Verse* (1895); *The Wind Among the Reeds* (1899), which contains some of Yeats' finest early lyrics; and *The Shadowy Waters* (1900), another poetic play.

By this time Yeats had established himself as a poet of delicate effects and inconclusive loveliness. His was both a vague and personal music—the translation of faery charms and elfin songs into traditionally romantic yet highly individualized lyrics. The very music of the early lyrics—favored by those who prefer sensuousness to depth of feeling—is a limitation. They are almost too musical; they sacrifice strength of thought and utterance to limpidity. In this period Yeats presumably depended on a small set of colorful symbols, symbols which were both arbitrary and facile. It seemed that Yeats had found his métier and that he would continue to sound the charming if restricted gamut of fancy. But the poet revolted against fancifulness; he turned away from the comfort of sheer sentiment and the reliance on rhetoric. "Sentimentality," he said, "is deceiving one's self; rhetoric is deceiving other people."

With *Responsibilities* (1914) and *The Wild Swans at Coole* (1919) a change in tone is immediately apparent. The idiom is sharper, the imagery sparser. The language, no longer richly colored, is almost bare of ornament, the tone pitched on a conversational plane. This contrast to the earlier poetry was emphasized in *Later Poems* (1922), *Michael Robartes and the Dancer* (1923), *The Tower* (1928), and *The Winding Stair* (1932). One likes to believe that it was the later work which won Yeats the Nobel Prize for literature in 1924. In the comprehensive *Collected Poems* of 1933 the complete change is fully revealed not only in the quality of the later work but in the alterations Yeats had made in the earlier poems, often substituting the exact and sometimes harsh word for the smooth and dreamlike one.

In changing the wavering outlines of his poetry to a more rigorous line Yeats did not sacrifice music. On the contrary, the revisions disclose a music which is, at the same time, subtler and more precise. The poet has freed himself from his preoccupations with shadowy waters, Gaelic gods, and the mystic Rose's multiple meanings; he has emerged from his "labyrinth of images." Not that he has discarded symbolism, but his symbols now have a greater value; they are intellectually finer and firmer. Originally influenced by Blake and the French Symbolists, he finally accomplished a "more subtle rhythm, a more organic form."

I made my song a coat
Covered with embroideries
Out of old mythologies
From heel to throat;
But the fools caught it,

Wore it in the world's eyes
As though they'd wrought it.
Song, let them take it,
For there's more enterprise
In walking naked.

Here Yeats says explicitly what so many of the later poems imply. He repudiates his imitators and mocks his own early mythological manner. Instead of the purple patches and the multicolored "cloths of Heaven" Yeats seems less interested in talking to poets and more concerned with the simple people he used to live among. Desire for direct communication must have prompted such a poem as the one which begins

Although I see him still
The freckled man who goes
To a gray place on the hill

and ends

I shall have written him one
Poem maybe as cold
And passionate as the dawn.

"Leda" (a modern poem in spite of its classical subject), "The Wild Swans at Coole," some of the political poems, "Among School Children," and "Sailing to Byzantium" are among the many verses illustrating the deeper contemplative manner with which "the last of the romantics," as Yeats called himself, rose from remote fantasies into immediate experience. More intensely self-searching the poet turns, regretfully but resolutely, to a new set of symbols expressing his adjustment with the actual world. "Sailing to Byzantium" shows the conflict and its solution with particular clarity. Cleanth Brooks, in "A Note on Symbol and Conceit" (in *The American Review* for May, 1934), summarizes it thus: "The poet's own country is a land of natural beauty, beauty of the body. But his own body is old. The soul must, therefore, sing the louder to compensate for the old and dying flesh.

An aged man is but a paltry thing,
A tattered coat upon a stick, unless
Soul clap its hands and sing, and louder sing
For every tatter in its mortal dress.

But there is no singing school for the soul except in studying the works of the soul. 'And therefore' he has sailed to Byzantium, for the artists of Byzantium do not follow the forms of nature but intellectual forms, ideal patterns. He appears to them to

Consume my heart away; sick with desire
And fastened to a dying animal

and by severing him from the dying world of the body, to gather him into what is at least 'the artifice of eternity.'

"A comparison of this clumsy paraphrase with the poem in its entirety illustrates better than anything else why the poet must write as he does—how much we lose by substituting concepts for his richer 'symbols.' Byzantium is, for instance, a very rich symbol. It may be thought a very indefinite one. But richness and complexity are not vagueness, and it will be easy to show that the symbol has its precision. It means many things, but if one misses the connection with intellectual art, one has missed the poem. The whole poem demands, as do the poems of Donne and Marvell, mental agility on the part of the reader."

As Yeats grew old his intellectual power increased. "I am content to follow to its source every event in action or in thought," Yeats wrote in "A Dialogue of Self and Soul," and he concluded the poem with Blake-like divination:

When such as I cast out remorse
So great a sweetness flows into the breast
We must laugh and we must sing,
We are blest by everything,
Everything we look upon is blest.

The Winding Stair (1932), *The King of the Great Clock Tower* (1935), published in Yeats's seventieth year, and the posthumous *Last Poems and Plays* (1940), contain the utterances of a man not afraid to taste unpalatable truths and even less afraid to say that they are bitter. The later poems are weighted with a sense of isolation, with the disillusionments of the age—and of old age—with defeated dreams, with the decay of beauty, with the death of friends, and the degeneration of the contemporary world. Yet, though Yeats voiced his horror and even his disgust in the later work, he did not despair. The ladder of happy fantasy was gone, but, even at the end, he was willing to begin the long ascent again.

"I must lie down where all the ladders start,
In the foul rag-and-bone shop of the heart."

Letters on Poetry from W. B. Yeats to Dorothy Wellesley (1940) posthumously reveal the poet's limitations, prejudices, and persuasions. But the ordinary reader will be fascinated by the mingled wit and profundity. The letters are studded with such epigrams as: "People much occupied with morality always lose heroic ecstasy." "The correction of prose, because it has no fixed laws, is endless; a poem comes right with a click like a closing box." Yeats distrusted change, yet he shifted his point of view as radically as he changed his idiom. He learned to suspect national panaceas and millennial dreams; in "The Second Coming" he wrote:

Mere anarchy is loosed upon the world,
The blood-dimmed tide is loosed, and everywhere
The ceremony of innocence is drowned;
The best lack all conviction, while the worst
Are full of passionate intensity.

Failing to find any certainty in politics, he sought for solutions in occult lore, in spiritualism, even in crystal-gazing. To the last he held that "nature, races, and individual men are unified by an image," and insisted that when men desert one myth they will substitute another. This is proved by his verse. If his symbolism is complicated and questionable, the directness of his best poetry is undeniable.

Yeats's own memories and meditations are in his *Autobiographies* (1926). Joseph Hone wrote the poet's official biography, but the best analyses of his work are in Edmund Wilson's *Axel's Castle* (1931), Stephen Spender's *The Destructive Element* (1935), David Daiches's *Poetry and the Modern World* (1940), and Richard Ellmann's scholarly and intensive study, *Yeats: The Man and the Masks* (1948).

THE LAKE ISLE OF INNISFREE

I will arise and go now, and go to Innisfree,
And a small cabin build there, of clay and wattles made;
Nine bean rows will I have there, a hive for the honey bee,
And live alone in the bee-loud glade.

And I shall have some peace there, for peace comes dropping slow,
Dropping from the veils of the morning to where the cricket sings;
There midnight's all a glimmer, and noon a purple glow,
And evening full of the linnet's wings.

I will arise and go now, for always night and day
I hear lake water lapping with low sounds by the shore;
While I stand on the roadway, or on the pavements gray,
I hear it in the deep heart's core.

AEDH WISHES FOR THE CLOTHS OF HEAVEN

Had I the heavens' embroidered cloths,
Enwrought with golden and silver light,
The blue and the dim and the dark cloths
Of night and light and the half-light,
I would spread the cloths under your feet:
But I, being poor, have only my dreams;
I have spread my dreams under your feet;
Tread softly because you tread on my dreams.

THE SONG OF WANDERING AENGUS

I went out to the hazel wood,
Because a fire was in my head,
And cut and peeled a hazel wand,
And hooked a berry to a thread,
And when white moths were on the wing,
And moth-like stars were flickering out,
I dropped the berry in a stream
And caught a little silver trout.

When I had laid it on the floor
I went to blow the fire a-flame,
But something rustled on the floor,
And someone called me by my name:
It had become a glimmering girl
With apple blossoms in her hair
Who called me by my name and ran
And faded through the brightening air.

Though I am old with wandering
Through hollow lands and hilly lands,

I will find out where she has gone,
And kiss her lips and take her hands;
And walk among long dappled grass,
And pluck till time and times are done,
The silver apples of the moon,
The golden apples of the sun.

AEDH TELLS OF THE ROSE IN HIS HEART

All things uncomely and broken, all things worn out and old,
The cry of a child by the roadway, the creak of a lumbering cart,
The heavy steps of the plowman, splashing the wintry mold,
Are wronging your image that blossoms a rose in the deeps of my heart.

The wrong of unshapely things is a wrong too great to be told;
I hunger to build them anew and sit on a green knoll apart,
With the earth and the sky and the water, remade, like a casket of gold
For my dreams of your image that blossoms a rose in the deeps of my heart.

FAIRY SONG

(*from "The Land of Heart's Desire"*)

The wind blows out of the gates of the day,
The wind blows over the lonely of heart,
And the lonely of heart is withered away,
While the faëries dance in a place apart,
Shaking their milk-white feet in a ring,
Tossing their milk-white arms in the air:
For they hear the wind laugh, and murmur and sing
Of a land where even the old are fair,
And even the wise are merry of tongue;
But I heard a reed of Coolaney say,
"When the wind has laughed and murmured and sung,
The lonely of heart is withered away!"

WHEN YOU ARE OLD

When you are old and gray and full of sleep,
And nodding by the fire, take down this book,
And slowly read, and dream of the soft look
Your eyes had once, and of their shadows deep;

How many loved your moments of glad grace,
And loved your beauty with love false or true;
But one man loved the pilgrim soul in you,
And loved the sorrows of your changing face.

And bending down beside the glowing bars
Murmur, a little sadly, how love fled
And paced upon the mountains overhead
And hid his face amid a crowd of stars.

THE CAP AND BELLS

A Queen was beloved by a jester,
  And once when the owls grew still
He made his soul go upward
  And stand on her window sill.

In a long and straight blue garment,
  It talked before morn was white,
And it had grown wise by thinking
  Of a footfall hushed and light.

But the young queen would not listen;
  She rose in her pale nightgown,
She drew in the brightening casement
  And pushed the brass bolt down.

He bade his heart go to her,
  When the bats cried out no more,
In a red and quivering garment
  It sang to her through the door.

The tongue of it sweet with dreaming
  Of a flutter of flower-like hair,
But she took up her fan from the table
  And waved it off on the air.

"I've cap and bells," he pondered,
  "I will send them to her and die."
And as soon as the morn had whitened
  He left them where she went by.

She laid them upon her bosom,
  Under a cloud of her hair,
And her red lips sang them a love song.
  The stars grew out of the air.

She opened her door and her window,
  And the heart and the soul came through,
To her right hand came the red one,
  To her left hand came the blue.

They set up a noise like crickets,
  A chattering wise and sweet,
And her hair was a folded flower,
  And the quiet of love her feet.

THE INDIAN UPON GOD

I passed along the water's edge below the humid trees,
My spirit rocked in evening light, the rushes round my knees,
My spirit rocked in sleep and sighs; and saw the moorfowl pace
All dripping on a grassy slope, and saw them cease to chase
Each other round in circles, and heard the eldest speak:
Who holds the world between His bill and made us strong or weak
Is an undying moorfowl, and He lives beyond the sky.
The rains are from His dripping wing, the moonbeams from His eye.
I passed a little further on and heard a lotus talk:
Who made the world and ruleth it, He hangeth on a stalk,
For I am in His image made, and all this tinkling tide
Is but a sliding drop of rain between His petals wide.
A little way within the gloom a roebuck raised his eyes
Brimful of starlight, and he said: *The Stamper of the Skies,*
He is a gentle roebuck; for how else, I pray, could He
Conceive a thing so sad and soft, a gentle thing like me?
I passed a little further on and heard a peacock say:
Who made the grass and made the worms and made my feathers gay,
He is a monstrous peacock, and He waveth all the night
His languid tail above us, lit with myriad spots of light.

AN OLD SONG RESUNG[1]

Down by the salley gardens my love and I did meet;
She passed the salley gardens with little snow-white feet.
She bid me take love easy, as the leaves grow on the tree;
But I, being young and foolish, with her would not agree.

In a field by the river my love and I did stand,
And on my leaning shoulder she laid her snow-white hand.
She bid me take life easy, as the grass grows on the weirs;
But I was young and foolish, and now am full of tears.

THE ROSE OF THE WORLD

Who dreamed that beauty passes like a dream?
  For these red lips, with all their mournful pride,
  Mournful that no new wonder may betide,
Troy passed away in one high funeral gleam,
  And Usna's children died.

We and the laboring world are passing by:
  Amid men's souls, that waver and give place,
  Like the pale waters in their wintry race,
Under the passing stars, frame of the sky,
  Lives on this lonely face.

Bow down, archangels, in your dim abode:
Before you were, or any hearts to beat,
  Weary and kind, one lingered by His seat;
He made the world to be a grassy road
  Before her wandering feet.

THE SORROW OF LOVE

The quarrel of the sparrows in the eaves,
The full round moon and the star-laden sky,
And the loud song of the ever-singing leaves,
Has hid away earth's old and weary cry.

And then you came with those red mournful lips,
And with you came the whole of the world's tears,
And all the trouble of her laboring ships,
And all the trouble of her myriad years.

And now the sparrows warring in the eaves,
The curd-pale moon, the white stars in the sky,
And the loud chaunting of the unquiet leaves,
Are shaken with earth's old and weary cry.

[1] "This," Yeats wrote in a footnote in one of the early editions, "is an extension of three lines sung to me by an old woman of Ballisodare."

THE SONG OF THE OLD MOTHER

I rise in the dawn, and I kneel and blow
Till the seed of the fire flicker and glow.
And then I must scrub, and bake, and sweep,
Till stars are beginning to blink and peep;
But the young lie long and dream in their bed
Of the matching of ribbons, the blue and the red,
And their day goes over in idleness,
And they sigh if the wind but lift up a tress.
While I must work, because I am old
And the seed of the fire gets feeble and cold.

THE BALLAD OF FATHER GILLIGAN

The old priest Peter Gilligan
Was weary night and day;
For half his flock were in their beds,
Or under green sods lay.

Once, while he nodded on a chair,
At the moth-hour of eve,
Another poor man sent for him,
And he began to grieve.

"I have no rest, nor joy, nor peace,
"For people die and die";
And after cried he, "God forgive!
"My body spake, not I."

He knelt, and leaning on the chair
He prayed and fell asleep;
And the moth-hour went from the fields,
And stars began to peep.

They slowly into millions grew,
And leaves shook in the wind;
And God covered the world with shade,
And whispered to mankind.

Upon the time of sparrow chirp
When the moths came once more,
The old priest Peter Gilligan
Stood upright on the floor.

"Mavrone, mavrone! the man has died,
"While I slept on the chair";
He roused his horse out of its sleep
And rode with little care.

He rode now as he never rode,
By rocky lane and fen;
The sick man's wife opened the door;
"Father! You come again!"

"And is the poor man dead?" he cried.
"He died an hour ago."
The old priest Peter Gilligan
In grief swayed to and fro.

"When you were gone, he turned and died
"As merry as a bird."
The old priest Peter Gilligan
He knelt him at that word.

"He who hath made the night of stars
"For souls, who tire and bleed,
"Sent one of His great angels down
"To help me in my need.

"He who is wrapped in purple robes,
"With planets in His care,
"Had pity on the least of things
"Asleep upon a chair."

THE WILD SWANS AT COOLE

The trees are in their autumn beauty,
The woodland paths are dry,
Under the October twilight the water
Mirrors a still sky;

Upon the brimming water among the stones
Are nine and fifty swans.

The nineteenth Autumn has come upon me
Since I first made my count;
I saw, before I had well finished,
All suddenly mount
And scatter, wheeling, in great broken rings
Upon their clamorous wings.

I have looked upon those brilliant creatures,
And now my heart is sore.
All's changed since I, hearing at twilight,
The first time on this shore,
The bell-beat of their wings above my head,
Trod with a lighter tread.

Unwearied still, lover by lover,
They paddle in the cold,
Companionable streams or climb the air;
Their hearts have not grown old;
Passion or conquest, wander where they will,
Attend upon them still.

But now they drift on the still water
Mysterious, beautiful;
Among what rushes will they build,
By what lake's edge or pool
Delight men's eyes, when I awake some day
To find they have flown away?

LEDA AND THE SWAN

A sudden blow: the great wings beating still
Above the staggering girl, her thighs caressed
By the dark webs, her nape caught in his bill,
He holds her helpless breast upon his breast.

How can those terrified vague fingers push
The feathered glory from her loosening thighs?
And how can body, laid in that white rush,
But feel the strange heart beating where it lies?

A shudder in the loins engenders there
The broken wall, the burning roof and tower
And Agamemnon dead.
Being so caught up,
So mastered by the brute blood of the air,
Did she put on his knowledge with his power
Before the indifferent beak could let her drop?

SAILING TO BYZANTIUM

I

That is no country for old men. The young
In one another's arms, birds in the trees,
—Those dying generations—at their song,
The salmon-falls, the mackerel-crowded seas,
Fish, flesh, or fowl, commend all summer long
Whatever is begotten, born, and dies.
Caught in that sensual music all neglect
Monuments of unaging intellect.

II

An aged man is but a paltry thing,
A tattered coat upon a stick, unless
Soul clap its hands and sing, and louder sing
For every tatter in its mortal dress,
Nor is there singing school but studying
Monuments of its own magnificence;
And therefore I have sailed the seas and come
To the holy city of Byzantium.

III

O sages standing in God's holy fire
As in the gold mosaic of a wall,
Come from the holy fire, perne [1] in a gyre,
And be the singing-masters of my soul.
Consume my heart away; sick with desire
And fastened to a dying animal
It knows not what it is; and gather me
Into the artifice of eternity.

IV

Once out of nature I shall never take
My bodily form from any natural thing,
But such a form as Grecian goldsmiths make
Of hammered gold and gold enameling
To keep a drowsy Emperor awake;
Or set upon a golden bough to sing
To lords and ladies of Byzantium
Of what is past, or passing, or to come.

AMONG SCHOOL CHILDREN

I

I walk through the long schoolroom questioning;
A kind old nun in a white hood replies;
The children learn to cipher and to sing,
To study reading-books and history,

[1] Perne: Change attitude.

To cut and sew, be neat in everything
In the best modern way—the children's eyes
In momentary wonder stare upon
A sixty-year-old smiling public man.

II

I dream of a Ledaean body, bent
Above a sinking fire, a tale that she
Told of a harsh reproof, or trivial event
That changed some childish day to tragedy—
Told, and it seemed that our two natures blent
Into a sphere from youthful sympathy,
Or else, to alter Plato's parable,
Into the yolk and white of the one shell.

III

And thinking of that fit of grief or rage
I look upon one child or t'other there
And wonder if she stood so at that age—
For even daughters of the swan can share
Something of every paddler's heritage—
And had that color upon cheek or hair,
And thereupon my heart is driven wild:
She stands before me as a living child.

IV

Her present image floats into the mind—
Did Quattrocento finger fashion it
Hollow of a cheek as though it drank the wind
And took a mess of shadows for its meat?
And I though never of Ledaean kind
Had pretty plumage once—enough of that,
Better to smile on all that smile, and show
There is a comfortable kind of scarecrow.

V

What youthful mother, a shape upon her lap
Honey of generation had betrayed,
And that must sleep, shriek, struggle to escape
As recollection or the drug decide,
Would think her son, did she but see that shape
With sixty or more winters on its head,
A compensation for the pang of his birth,
Or the uncertainty of his setting forth?

VI

Plato thought nature but a spume that plays
Upon a ghostly paradigm of things;
Soldier Aristotle played the taws
Upon the bottom of a king of kings;

World-famous golden-thighed Pythagoras
Fingered upon a fiddle-stick or strings
What a star sang and careless Muses heard:
Old clothes upon old sticks to scare a bird.

VII

Both nuns and mothers worship images,
But those the candles light are not as those
That animate a mother's reveries,
But keep a marble or a bronze repose.
And yet they too break hearts—O Presences
That passion, piety or affection knows,
And that all heavenly glory symbolize—
O self-born mockers of man's enterprise;

VIII

Labor is blossoming or dancing where
The body is not bruised to pleasure soul,
Nor beauty born out of its own despair,
Nor blear-eyed wisdom out of midnight oil
O Chestnut tree, great rooted blossomer,
Are you the leaf, the blossom or the bole?
O body swayed to music, O brightening glance,
How can we know the dancer from the dance?

THE LEADERS OF THE CROWD

They must to keep their certainty accuse
All that are different of a base intent;
Pull down established honor; hawk for news
Whatever their loose phantasy invent
And murmur it with bated breath, as though
The abounding gutter had been Helicon
Or calumny a song. How can they know
Truth flourishes where the student's lamp has shone,
And there alone, that have no solitude?
So the crowd come they care not what may come.
They have loud music, hope every day renewed
And heartier loves; that lamp is from the tomb.

AN IRISH AIRMAN FORESEES HIS DEATH

I know that I shall meet my fate
Somewhere among the clouds above;
Those that I fight I do not hate,
Those that I guard I do not love;
My country is Kiltartan Cross,
My countrymen Kiltartan's poor,
No likely end could bring them loss
Or leave them happier than before.
Nor law, nor duty bade me fight,
Nor public men, nor cheering crowds,
A lonely impulse of delight
Drove to this tumult in the clouds;
I balanced all, brought all to mind,
The years to come seemed waste of breath,
A waste of breath the years behind
In balance with this life, this death.

TO A FRIEND WHOSE WORK HAS COME TO NOTHING

Now all the truth is out,
Be secret and take defeat
From any brazen throat,
For how can you compete,
Being honor bred, with one
Who, were it proved he lies,
Were neither shamed in his own
Nor in his neighbors' eyes?
Bred to a harder thing
Than Triumph, turn away
And like a laughing string
Whereon mad fingers play
Amid a place of stone,
Be secret and exult,
Because of all things known
That is most difficult.

THE SECOND COMING

Turning and turning in the widening gyre
The falcon cannot hear the falconer;
Things fall apart; the centre cannot hold;
Mere anarchy is loosed upon the world,
The blood-dimmed tide is loosed, and everywhere
The ceremony of innocence is drowned;
The best lack all conviction, while the worst
Are full of passionate intensity.

Surely some revelation is at hand;
Surely the Second Coming is at hand.
The Second Coming! Hardly are those words out
When a vast image out of *Spiritus Mundi*
Troubles my sight: somewhere in sands of the desert
A shape with lion body and the head of a man,
A gaze blank and pitiless as the sun,
Is moving its slow thighs, while all about it
Reel shadows of the indignant desert birds.
The darkness drops again; but now I know
That twenty centuries of stony sleep
Were vexed to nightmare by a rocking cradle,
And what rough beast, its hour come round at last,
Slouches towards Bethlehem to be born?

BYZANTIUM

The unpurged images of day recede;
The Emperor's drunken soldiery are abed;
Night resonance recedes, night-walkers' song
After great cathedral gong;
A starlit or a moonlit dome disdains
All that man is,
All mere complexities,
The fury and the mire of human veins.

Before me floats an image, man or shade,
Shade more than man, more image than a shade;
For Hades' bobbin bound in mummy-cloth
May unwind the winding path;
A mouth that has no moisture and no breath
Breathless mouths may summon;
I hail the superhuman;
I call it death-in-life and life-in-death.

Miracle, bird or golden handiwork,
More miracle than bird or handiwork,
Planted on the star-lit golden bough,
Can like the cocks of Hades crow,
Or, by the moon embittered, scorn aloud
In glory of changeless metal

Common bird or petal
And all complexities of mire or blood.

At midnight on the Emperor's pavement flit
Flames that no faggot feeds, nor steel has lit,
Nor storm disturbs, flames begotten of flame,
Where blood-begotten spirits come
And all complexities of fury leave,
Dying into a dance,
An agony of trance,
An agony of flame that cannot singe a sleeve.

Astraddle on the dolphin's mire and blood,
Spirit after spirit! The smithies break the flood,
The golden smithies of the Emperor!
Marbles of the dancing floor
Break bitter furies of complexity,
Those images that yet
Fresh images beget,
That dolphin-torn, that gong-tormented sea.

A DIALOGUE OF SELF AND SOUL

I

My Soul. I summon to the winding ancient stair;
Set all your mind upon the steep ascent,
Upon the broken, crumbling battlement,
Upon the breathless starlit air,
Upon the star that marks the hidden pole;
Fix every wandering thought upon
That quarter where all thought is done:
Who can distinguish darkness from the soul?

My Self. The consecrated blade upon my knees
Is Sato's ancient blade, still as it was,
Still razor-keen, still like a looking-glass
Unspotted by the centuries;
That flowering, silken, old embroidery, torn
From some court-lady's dress and round
The wooden scabbard bound and wound,
Can, tattered, still protect, faded adorn.

My Soul. Why should the imagination of a man
Long past his prime remember things that are
Emblematical of love and war?
Think of ancestral night that can,
If but imagination scorn the earth
And intellect its wandering
To this and that and t'other thing,
Deliver from the crime of death and birth.

My Self. Montashigi, third of his family, fashioned it
Five hundred years ago, about it lie

Flowers from I know not what embroidery—
Heart's purple—and all these I set
For emblems of the day against the tower
Emblematical of the night,
And claim as by a soldier's right
A charter to commit the crime once more.

My Soul. Such fullness in that quarter overflows
And falls into the basin of the mind
That man is stricken deaf and dumb and blind,
For intellect no longer knows
Is from the *Ought,* or *Knower* from the *Known*—
That is to say, ascends to Heaven;
Only the dead can be forgiven;
But when I think of that my tongue's a stone.

II

My Self. A living man is blind and drinks his drop.
What matter if the ditches are impure?
What matter if I live it all once more?
Endure that toil of growing up;
The ignominy of boyhood; the distress
Of boyhood changing into man;
The unfinished man and his pain
Brought face to face with his own clumsiness;
The finished man among his enemies?—
How in the name of Heaven can he escape
That defiling and disfigured shape
The mirror of malicious eyes
Casts upon his eyes until at last
He thinks that shape must be his shape?
And what's the good of an escape
If honour find him in the wintry blast?

I am content to live it all again
And yet again, if it be life to pitch
Into the frog-spawn of a blind man's ditch,
A blind man battering blind men;
Or into that most fecund ditch of all,
The folly that man does
Or must suffer, if he woos
A proud woman not kindred of his soul.

I am content to follow to its source,
Every event in action or in thought;
Measure the lot; forgive myself the lot!
When such as I cast out remorse
So great a sweetness flows into the breast
We must laugh and we must sing,
We are blest by everything,
Everything we look upon is blest.

Rudyard Kipling

(Joseph) Rudyard Kipling was born at Bombay, India, December 30, 1865. Both his parents were English; his father, John Lockwood Kipling, was curator of the Lahore Museum and an illustrator of some note. At six young Kipling was taken to Westward Ho, in North Devon, and his experiences at the English school furnished the basis for the grimly amusing *Stalky and Co.* (1899). Returning to India, he engaged in journalism; at seventeen he became sub-editor of the *Lahore Civil and Military Gazette.* At twenty-one Kipling published his first volume, *Departmental Ditties* (1886), a book of light verse. A year later he challenged attention as a story-teller with *Plain Tales from the Hills* (1887). Before he was twenty-four he had brought out six small collections of stories which showed his mastery in the form. They were astonishing in their vigor, accurate observation, and swift inventiveness. A new province was added to fiction: a realistic *Arabian Nights* transplanted to India and cultivated by an Englishman.

With maturity, Kipling's gift grew in power and range. His soldier stories embodied characters which rank with those of Dickens. His stories for children—*The Jungle Books* (1894-95), *Captains Courageous* (1897) and *Just So Stories* (1902)—became contemporary classics. He appealed equally to youth and age with *Kim* (1901), *Puck of Pook's Hill* (1906), *Rewards and Fairies* (1910).

Between his twenty-third and twenty-sixth year Kipling traveled to China, Japan, India, and America. In England he found himself famous at twenty-seven. On a return visit to the United States in 1892 Kipling married an American, Caroline Starr Balestier, sister of Wolcott Balestier, with whom he wrote *The Naulahka,* 1891, and lived for a few years in Brattleboro, Vermont. Here he wrote several of his most popular works, and it seems likely that he would have remained in America if a quarrel with another brother-in-law, Beatty Balestier, and threats of legal action, had not driven him back to England. Sensitive to criticism and increasingly wary of social contacts, Kipling buried himself in a little Sussex village. He had lost a daughter; the death of a son during the World War embittered and almost silenced him. Although he had received the Nobel Prize for literature in 1907, changes in taste caused a reaction against Kipling's militant "imperialism," which had once influenced British sentiment and, to some extent, its policies. Nevertheless, Kipling's work continued to grow in subtlety, if not in quantity, and he was at work on a collection of autobiographical notes when he died a few weeks after his seventieth birthday, January 17, 1936.

Considered solely as a poet, Kipling is one of the most vigorous figures of his time. He shared the experiences of all classes of people, and his verse spoke for civilians as well as soldiers, office-holders and vagabond adventurers. His brisk lines communicate a common joy in the snapping of a banner, the tingle of salt spray, the lurch and rumble of the sea; his poetry is woven of the stuff of myths, but it never loses its hold on actualities. Kipling himself in his poem "The Benefactors" (from *The Years Between* [1919]) writes:

Ah! What avails the classic bent
  And what the cultured word,
Against the undoctored incident
  That actually occurred?

What attracted the average reader to Kipling was this attitude to the world's work. Where others sang of lilies and leisure, Kipling celebrated difficulties, duty, hard labor; where others evoked Greek nymphs, he hailed bridge-builders, engineers, sweating stokers—all those who exulted in the job. If he sometimes lost his head in a general hurrahing, his high spirits carried off specious prophesying and brought sing-song meters to a pitch of excitement. Life was all gusto. *A Choice of Kipling's Verse* (1941) was compiled, surprisingly enough, by T. S. Eliot.

If Kipling's energy is boisterous it is irresistible. His varied poems, ranging from the lustry *Barrack-Room Ballads* to the quieter verse in *The Five Nations, The Seven Seas* and the later work, were collected in a remarkable one-volume *Inclusive Edition* (1885-1918), an indispensable part of any student's library. Subsequent to this collection, a new volume, *The Years Between,* was published in 1919.

The best and worst of Kipling are obvious to the least critical reader. His worst is inherent in a heartiness which is too loud and too prolonged, a vehemence which changes robustiousness into rowdiness. Max Beerbohm excoriated this Kipling in the cartoon showing an irate little man, helmeted and spectacled, blowing a tin trumpet, waving a Union Jack, and dancing himself into a paroxysm of patriotic fury. This Kipling, overcome by the conquering chauvinism of the Colonist, loses his sense of values, belittling the weak to the tune of British imperialism. The tune, one must admit, is an attractive one, and even those who object to its burden of bombast have learned to whistle it by heart. The rhythms are often the beat of journalistic verse, but they communicate to the "average man" something he seeks and which he would not recognize in finer measures. It is indisputable that Kipling too often tries to force beauty in a rape of violence. But there are also those poems in which, as T. Earle Welby says in *A Popular History of English Poetry,* "he has been humbler and more passive, and in which beauty is a voluntary captive. One emotion has never failed to inspire him, the inverted nostalgia of the man returned home and yearning for far and once familiar scenes of exile. It arouses all the poet in him, puts wistfulness into his generally brazen music, clears his style of semi-Biblical claptrap, and sets his extraordinary descriptive talent to work more legitimately than usual." Such a descriptive talent is illustrated by "Mandalay," "Fuzzy Wuzzy," "Chant-Pagan," "The Return," even by such a stanza as:

Rivers at night that cluck an' jeer,
  Plains which the moonshine turns to sea,
Mountains which never let you near,
  An' stars to all eternity;
An' the quick-breathin' dark that fills
  The 'ollows of the wilderness,
When the wind worries through the 'ills—
  These may 'ave taught me more or less.

Such work shows that Kipling, though a poet, is something besides a poet. He is not so much a writer for those who enjoy writing—although his craftsmanship will repay study—as he is the singer of those who have never risen to an understanding of song. After World War I it became the fashion to disparage Kipling's work as well as his philosophy. When his name was mentioned it was accompanied by a deprecatory shrung or a remark about the decline of his fame; in 1935 a New York newspaper referred to him as "the forgotten man of English letters."

Reaction follows reaction, and if Kipling is underpraised today for the very qualities which were overpraised thirty years ago his hour will strike again. Few poems have revealed a richer and more resigned understanding of the soil and those whose live close to it than "The Land"; the wanderlust has never been so poignantly expressed as in "For to Admire." His ballads have not only the swing but the vitality of the ancient Border Ballads, and it is altogether possible that he will outlast most of his contemporaries, and go down to posterity as a people's poet, a balladist whose songs were the popular tunes of one age and the folk-classics of another.

GUNGA DIN

You may talk o' gin an' beer
When you're quartered safe out 'ere,
An' you're sent to penny-fights an' Aldershot it;
But when it comes to slaughter
You will do your work on water,
An' you'll lick the bloomin' boots of 'em that's got it.
Now in Injia's sunny clime,
Where I used to spend my time
A-servin' of 'Er Majesty the Queen,
Of all them black-faced crew
The finest man I knew
Was our regimental *bhisti,*[1] Gunga Din.

It was "Din! Din! Din!
You limping lump o' brick-dust, Gunga Din!
Hi! *slippy hitherao!*
Water, get it! *Panee lao*[2]
You squidgy-nosed old idol, Gunga Din!"

The uniform 'e wore
Was nothin' much before,
An' rather less than 'arf o' that be'ind,
For a twisty piece o' rag
An' a goatskin water-bag
Was all the field-equipment 'e could find.
When the sweatin' troop-train lay
In a sidin' through the day,
Where the 'eat would make your bloomin' eyebrows crawl,
We shouted *"Harry By!"*[3]

[1] The *bhisti,* or water-carrier, attached to regiments in India, is often one of the most devoted of the Queen's servants. He is also appreciated by the men.

[2] Bring water swiftly.

[3] Tommy Atkins' equivalent for "O Brother!"

Till our throats were bricky-dry,
Then we wopped 'im 'cause 'e couldn't serve us all.

It was "Din! Din! Din!
You 'eathen, where the mischief 'ave you been?
You put some *juldee*[1] in it,
Or I'll *marrow*[2] you this minute,
If you don't fill up my helmet, Gunda Din!"

'E would dot an' carry one
Till the longest day was done,
An' 'e didn't seem to know the use o' fear.
If we charged or broke or cut,
You could bet your bloomin' nut,
'E'd be waitin' fifty paces right flank rear.
With 'is *mussick*[3] on is back,
'E would skip with our attack,
An' watch us till the bugles made "Retire."
An' for all 'is dirty 'ide,
'E was white, clear white, inside
When 'e went to tend the wounded under fire!

It was "Din! Din! Din!"
With the bullets kickin' dust-spots on the green.
When the cartridges ran out,
You could 'ear the front-files shout:
"Hi! ammunition-mules an' Gunga Din!"

I sha'n't forgit the night
When I dropped be'ind the fight
With a bullet where my belt-plate should 'a' been.
I was chokin' mad with thirst,
An' the man that spied me first
Was our good old grinnin', gruntin' Gunga Din.
'E lifted up my 'ead,
An' 'e plugged me where I bled,
An' 'e guv me 'arf-a-pint o' water—green;
It was crawlin' an' it stunk,
But of all the drinks I've drunk,
I'm gratefulest to one from Gunga Din.

It was "Din! Din! Din!
'Ere's a beggar with a bullet through 'is spleen;
'E's chawin' up the ground an' 'e's kickin' all around:
For Gawd's sake, git the water, Gunga Din!"

'E carried me away
To where a *dooli* lay,
An' a bullet come an' drilled the beggar clean.
'E put me safe inside,
An' just before 'e died:
"I 'ope you liked your drink," sez Gunga Din.

[1] Speed. [2] Hit you. [3] Water-skin.

So I'll meet 'im later on
In the place where 'e is gone—
Where it's always double drill and no canteen;
'E'll be squattin' on the coals
Givin' drink to pore damned souls,
An' I'll get a swig in Hell from Gunga Din!

Din! Din! Din!
You Lazarushian-leather Gunga Din!
Tho' I've belted you an' flayed you,
By the livin' Gawd that made you,
You're a better man than I am, Gunga Din!

DANNY DEEVER

"What are the bugles blowin' for?" said Files-on-Parade.
"To turn you out, to turn you out," the Color-Sergeant said.
"What makes you look so white, so white?" said Files-on-Parade.
"I'm dreadin' what I've got to watch," the Color-Sergeant said.
For they're hangin' Danny Deever, you can 'ear the Dead March play,
The regiment's in 'ollow square—they're hangin' him today;
They've taken of his buttons off an' cut his stripes away,
An' they're hangin' Danny Deever in the mornin'.

"What makes the rear-rank breathe so 'ard?" said Files-on-Parade.
"It's bitter cold, it's bitter cold," the Color-Sergeant said.
"What makes that front-rank man fall down?" says Files-on-Parade.
"A touch of sun, a touch of sun," the Color-Sergeant said.
They are hangin' Danny Deever, they are marchin' of 'im round.
They 'ave 'alted Danny Deever by 'is coffin on the ground:
An 'e'll swing in 'arf a minute for a sneakin' shootin' hound—
O they're hangin' Danny Deever in the mornin'!

" 'Is cot was right-'and cot to mine," said Files-on-Parade.
" 'E's sleepin' out an' far tonight," the Color-Sergeant said.
"I've drunk 'is beer a score o' times," said Files-on-Parade.
" 'E's drinkin' bitter beer alone," the Color-Sergeant said.
They are hangin' Danny Deever, you must mark 'im to 'is place,
For 'e shot a comrade sleepin'—you must look 'im in the face;
Nine 'undred of 'is county an' the regiment's disgrace,
While they're hangin' Danny Deever in the mornin.'

"What's that so black agin the sun?" said Files-on-Parade.
"It's Danny fightin' 'ard for life," the Color-Sergeant said.
"What's that that whimpers over'ead?" said Files-on-Parade.
"It's Danny's soul that's passin' now," the Color-Sergeant said.
For they're done with Danny Deever, you can 'ear the quickstep play,
The regiment's in column, an' they're marchin' us away;
Ho! the young recruits are shakin', an' they'll want their beer today,
After hangin' Danny Deever in the mornin'.

MANDALAY

By the old Moulmein Pagoda, lookin' eastward to the sea,
There's a Burma girl a-settin', an' I know she thinks o' me;
For the wind is in the palm-trees, an' the temple-bells they say:
"Come you back, you British soldier; come you back to Mandalay!"
    Come you back to Mandalay,
    Where the old Flotilla lay:
    Can't you 'ear their paddles chunkin' from Rangoon to Mandalay?
    On the road to Mandalay,
    Where the flyin'-fishes play,
    An' the dawn comes up like thunder outer China 'crost the Bay!

'Er petticut was yaller an' 'er little cap was green,
An' 'er name was Supi-yaw-let—jes' the same as Theebaw's Queen,
An' I seed her fust a-smokin' of a whackin' white cheroot,
An' a-wastin' Christian kisses on an 'eathen idol's foot:
    Bloomin' idol made o' mud—
    What they called the Great Gawd Budd—
    Plucky lot she cared for idols when I kissed 'er where she stud!
    On the road to Mandalay—

When the mist was on the rice-fields an' the sun was droppin' slow,
She'd git 'er little banjo an' she'd sing *"Kulla-lo-lo!"*
With 'er arm upon my shoulder an' her cheek agin my cheek
We useter watch the steamers an' the *hathis* pilin' teak.
    Elephints a-pilin' teak
    In the sludgy, squdgy creek,
    Where the silence 'ung that 'eavy you was 'arf afraid to speak!
    On the road to Mandalay—

But that's all shove be'ind me—long ago an' fur away,
An' there ain't no 'busses runnin' from the Bank to Mandalay;
An' I'm learnin' 'ere in London what the ten-year sodger tells:
"If you've 'eard the East a-callin', why, you won't 'eed nothin' else."
    No! you wont 'eed nothin' else
    But them spicy garlic smells
    An' the sunshine an' the palm-trees an' the tinkly temple bells!
    On the road to Mandalay—

I am sick o' wastin' leather on these gritty pavin'-stones,
An' the blasted Henglish drizzle wakes the fever in my bones;
Tho' I walks with fifty 'ousemaids outer Chelsea to the Strand,
An' they talks a lot o' lovin', but wot do they understand?
    Beefy face an' grubby 'and—
    Law! wot *do* they understand?
    I've a neater, sweeter maiden in a cleaner, greener land!
    On the road to Mandalay—

Ship me somewheres east of Suez where the best is like the worst,
Where there aren't no Ten Commandments, an' a man can raise a thirst;

For the temple-bells are callin', an' it's there that I would be—
By the old Moulmein Pagoda, lookin' lazy at the sea—
    On the road to Mandalay,
    Where the old Flotilla lay,
    With our sick beneath the awnings when we went to Mandalay!
    Oh, the road to Mandalay,
    Where the flyin'-fishes play,
    An' the dawn comes up like thunder outer China 'crost the Bay!

"FUZZY-WUZZY"

(Soudan Expeditionary Force)

We've fought with many men acrost the seas,
  An' some of 'em was brave an' some was not:
The Paythan an' the Zulu an' Burmese;
  But the Fuzzy was the finest o' the lot.
We never got a ha'porth's change of 'im:
  'E squatted in the scrub an' 'ocked our 'orses,
'E cut our sentries up at Sua*kim,*
  An' 'e played the cat an' banjo with our forces.
    So 'ere's *to* you, Fuzzy-Wuzzy, at your 'ome in the Sowdan;
    You're a pore benighted 'eathen but a first-class fightin' man;
    We gives you your certifikit, an' if you want it signed
    We'll come an' 'ave a romp with you whenever you're inclined.

We took our chanst among the Kyber 'ills,
  The Boers knocked us silly at a mile,
The Burman guv us Irriwaddy chills,
  An' a Zulu *impi* dished us up in style:
But all we ever got from such as they
  Was pop to what the Fuzzy made us swaller;
We 'eld our bloomin' own, the papers say,
  But man for man the Fuzzy knocked us 'oller.
    Then 'ere's *to* you, Fuzzy-Wuzzy, an' the missis and the kid;
    Our orders was to break you, an' of course we went an' did.
    We sloshed you with Martinis, an' it wasn't 'ardly fair;
    But for all the odds agin you, Fuzzy-Wuz, you bruk the square.

'E 'asn't got no papers of 'is own,
  'E 'asn't got no medals nor rewards,
So we must certify the skill 'e's shown
  In usin of 'is long two-'anded swords;
When 'e's 'oppin' in an' out among the bush
  With 'is coffin-'eaded shield an' shovel-spear,
A 'appy day with Fuzzy on the rush
  Will last a 'ealthy Tommy for a year.
    So 'ere's *to* you, Fuzzy-Wuzzy, an' your friends which is no more,
    If we 'adn't lost some messmates we would 'elp you to deplore;
    But give an' take's the gospel, an' we'll call the bargain fair,
    For if you 'ave lost more than us, you crumpled up the square!

'E rushes at the smoke when we let drive,
  An', before we know, 'e's 'ackin' at our 'ead;
'E's all 'ot sand an' ginger when alive,
  An' 'e's generally shammin' when 'e's dead.
'E's a daisy, 'e's a ducky, 'e's a lamb!
  'E's a injia-rubber idiot on the spree,
'E's the on'y thing that doesn't care a damn
  For the Regiment o' British Infantree.
    So 'ere's *to* you, Fuzzy-Wuzzy, at your 'ome in the Sowdan;
    You're a pore benighted 'eathen but a first-class fightin' man;
    An 'ere's *to* you, Fuzzy-Wuzzy, with your 'ayrick 'ead of 'air—
    You big black boundin' beggar—for you bruk a British square.

TOMMY

I went into a public-'ouse to get a pint o' beer,
The publican 'e up an' sez, "We serve no red-coats here."
The girls be'ind the bar they laughed an' giggled fit to die,
I outs into the street again, an' to myself sez I:
  O it's Tommy this, an' Tommy that, an' "Tommy go away";
  But it's "Thank you, Mister Atkins," when the band begins to play,
  The band begins to play, my boys, the band begins to play,
  O it's "Thank you, Mister Atkins," when the band begins to play.

I went into a theater as sober as could be,
They give a drunk civilian room, but 'adn't none for me;
They sent me to the gallery or round the music-'alls,
But when it comes to fightin', Lord! they'll shove me in the stalls.
  For it's Tommy this, an' Tommy that, an' "Tommy wait outside";
  But it's "Special train for Atkins," when the trooper's on the tide,
  The troopship's on the tide, my boys, etc.

O makin' mock o' uniforms that guard you while you sleep
Is cheaper than them uniforms, an' they're starvation cheap;
An' hustlin' drunken sodgers when they're goin' large a bit
Is five times better business than paradin' in full kit.
  Then it's Tommy this, an' Tommy that, an' "Tommy 'ow's yer soul?"
  But it's "Thin red line of 'eroes" when the drums begin to roll,
  The drums begin to roll, my boys, etc.

We aren't no thin red 'eroes, nor we aren't no blackguards too,
But single men in barricks, most remarkable like you;
An' if sometimes our conduck isn't all your fancy paints,
Why, single men in barricks don't grow into plaster saints.
  While it's Tommy this, an' Tommy that, an' "Tommy fall be'ind";
  But it's "Please to walk in front, sir," when there's trouble in the wind,
  There's trouble in the wind, my boys, etc.

You talk o' better food for us an' schools, an' fires, an' all:
We'll wait for extry rations if you treat us rational.
Don't mess about the cook-room slops, but prove it to our face
The Widow's uniform is not the soldier-man's disgrace.

But it's Tommy this, an' Tommy that, an' "Chuck him out, the brute!"
But it's "Savior of 'is country" when the guns begin to shoot;
An' it's Tommy this, an' Tommy that, an' anything you please;
An' Tommy ain't a bloomin' fool—you bet that Tommy sees!

THE LADIES

I've taken my fun where I've found it;
  I've rogued an' I've ranged in my time;
I've 'ad my pickin' o' sweet'earts,
  An' four o' the lot was prime.
One was an 'arf-caste widow,
  One was a woman at Prome,
One was the wife of a *jemadar-sais,*
  An' one is a girl at 'ome.

Now I aren't no 'and with the ladies,
  For, takin' 'em all along,
You never can say till you've tried 'em,
  An' then you are like to be wrong.
There's times when you'll think that you mightn't,
  There's times when you'll know that you might;
But the things you will learn from the Yellow an' Brown,
  They'll 'elp you a lot with the White!

I was a young un at 'Oogli,
  Shy as a girl to begin;
Aggie de Castrer she made me,
  An' Aggie was clever as sin;
Older than me, but my first un—
  More like a mother she were—
Showed me the way to promotion an' pay,
  An' I learned about women from 'er!

Then I was ordered to Burma,
  Actin' in charge o' Bazar,
An' I got me a tiddy live 'eathen
  Through buyin' supplies off 'er pa.
Funny an' yellow an' faithful—
  Doll in a teacup she were,
But we lived on the square, like a true-married pair,
  An' I learned about women from 'er!

Then we was shifted to Neemuch
  (Or I might ha' been keepin' 'er now),
An' I took with a shiny she-devil,
  The wife of a nigger at Mhow;
Taught me the gypsy-folks' *bolee;*
  Kind o' volcano she were,
For she knifed me one night 'cause I wished she was white,
  An' I learned about women from 'er!

Then I come 'ome in the trooper,
  'Long of a kid o' sixteen—
Girl from a convent at Meerut,
  The straightest I ever 'ave seen.
Love at first sight was 'er trouble,
  She didn't know what it were;
An' I wouldn't do such, 'cause I liked 'er too much,
  But—I learned about women from 'er!

I've taken my fun where I've found it,
  An' now I must pay for my fun,
For the more you 'ave known o' the others
  The less you will settle to one;
An' the end of it's sittin' and thinkin',
  An' dreamin' Hell-fires to see;
So be warned by my lot (which I know you will not),
  An' learn about women from me!

What did the Colonel's Lady think?
  Nobody never knew.
Somebody asked the Sergeant's wife,
  An' she told 'em true!
When you get to a man in the case,
  They're like as a row of pins—
For the Colonel's Lady an' Judy O'Grady
  Are sisters under their skins!

BOOTS

(Infantry Columns of the Earlier War)

We're foot—slog—slog—slog—sloggin' over Africa!
Foot—foot—foot—foot—sloggin' over Africa—
(Boots—boots—boots—boots, movin' up an' down again!)
        There's no discharge in the war!

Seven—six—eleven—five—nine-an'-twenty mile today—
Four—eleven—seventeen—thirty-two the day before—
(Boots—boots—boots—boots, movin' up an' down again!)
        There's no discharge in the war!

Don't—don't—don't—don't—look at what's in front of you
(Boots—boots—boots—boots, movin' up an' down again);
Men—men—men—men—men go mad with watchin' 'em,
        An' there's no discharge in the war!

Try—try—try—try—to think o' something different—
Oh—my—God—keep—me from goin' lunatic!
(Boots—boots—boots—boots, movin' up an' down again!)
        There's no discharge in the war!

Count—count—count—count—the bullets in the bandoliers;
If—your—eyes—drop—they will get atop o' you
(Boots—boots—boots—boots, movin' up an' down again)—
There's no discharge in the war!

We—can—stick—out—'unger, thirst, an' weariness,
But—not—not—not—not the chronic sight of 'em—
Boots—boots—boots—boots, movin' up an' down again,
An' there's no discharge in the war!

'Tain't—so—bad—by—day because o' company,
But night—brings—long—strings o' forty thousand million
Boots—boots—boots—boots, movin' up an' down again.
There's no discharge in the war!

I—'ave—marched—six—weeks in 'Ell an' certify
It—is—not—fire—devils, dark or anything
But boots—boots—boots, movin' up an' down again,
An' there's no discharge in the war!

THE RETURN

Peace is declared, and I return
To 'Ackneystadt, but not the same;
Things 'ave transpired which made me learn
The size and meanin' of the game.
I did no more than others did,
I don't know where the change began;
I started as a average kid,
I finished as a thinkin' man.

If England was what England seems
An' not the England of our dreams,
But only putty, brass, an' paint,
'Ow quick we'd drop 'er! But she ain't!

Before my gappin' mouth could speak
I 'eard it in my comrade's tone;
I saw it on my neighbor's cheek
Before I felt it flush my own.
An' last it come to me—not pride,
Nor yet conceit, but on the 'ole
(If such a term may be applied)
The makin's of a bloomin' soul.

Rivers at night that cluck an' jeer,
Plains which the moonshine turns to sea,
Mountains that never let you near,
An' stars to all eternity;

An' the quick-breathin' dark that fills
  The 'ollows of the wilderness,
When the wind worries through the 'ills—
  These may 'ave taught me more or less.

Towns without people, ten times took,
  An' ten times left an' burned at last;
An' starvin' dogs that come to look
  For owners when a column passed;
An' quiet, 'omesick talks between
  Men, met by night, you never knew
Until—'is face—by shellfire seen—
  Once—an' struck off. They taught me, too.

The day's lay-out—the mornin' sun
  Beneath your 'at-brim as you sight;
The dinner-'ush from noon till one,
  An' the full roar that lasts till night;
An' the pore dead that look so old
  An' was so young an hour ago,
An' legs tied down before they're cold—
  These are the things which make you know.

Also Time runnin' into years—
  A thousand Places left be'ind—
An' Men from both two 'emispheres
  Discussin' things of every kind;
So much more near than I 'ad known,
  So much more great than I 'ad guessed—
An' me, like all the rest, alone—
  But reachin' out to all the rest!

So 'ath it come to me—not pride,
  Nor yet conceit, but on the 'ole
(If such a term may be applied)
  The makin's of a bloomin' soul.
But now, discharged, I fall away
  To do with little things again. . . .
Gawd, 'oo knows all I cannot say,
  Look after me in Thamesfontein!

If England was what England seems
  An' not the England of our dreams,
But only putty, brass, an' paint,
  'Ow quick we'd chuck 'er! But she ain't!

THE CONUNDRUM OF THE WORKSHOPS

When the flush of a newborn sun fell first on Eden's green and gold,
Our father Adam sat under the Tree and scratched with a stick in the mold;
And the first rude sketch that the world had seen was joy to his mighty heart,
Till the Devil whispered behind the leaves: "It's pretty, but is it Art?"

Wherefore he called to his wife and fled to fashion his work anew—
The first of his race who cared a fig for the first, most dread review;
And he left his lore to the use of his sons—and that was a glorious gain
When the Devil chuckled: "Is it Art?" in the ear of the branded Cain.

They builded a tower to shiver the sky and wrench the stars apart,
Till the Devil grunted behind the bricks: "It's striking, but is it Art?"
The stone was dropped by the quarry-side, and the idle derrick swung,
While each man talked of the aims of art, and each in an alien tongue.

They fought and they talked in the north and the south, they talked and they fought in the west,
Till the waters rose on the jabbering land, and the poor Red Clay had rest—
Had rest till the dank blank-canvas dawn when the dove was preened to start,
And the Devil bubbled below the keel: "It's human, but is it Art?"

The tale is old as the Eden Tree—as new as the new-cut tooth—
For each man knows ere his lip-thatch grows he is master of Art and Truth;
And each man hears as the twilight nears, to the beat of his dying heart,
The Devil drum on the darkened pane: "You did it, but was it Art?"

We have learned to whittle the Eden Tree to the shape of a surplice-peg,
We have learned to bottle our parents twain in the yolk of an addled egg,
We know that the tail must wag the dog, as the horse is drawn by the cart;
But the Devil whoops, as he whooped of old: "It's clever, but is it Art?"

When the flicker of London's sun falls faint on the club-room's green and gold,
The sons of Adam sit them down and scratch with their pens in the mold—
They scratch with their pens in the mold of their graves, and the ink and the anguish start
When the Devil mutters behind the leaves: "It's pretty, but is it Art?"

Now, if we could win to the Eden Tree where the four great rivers flow,
And the wreath of Eve is red on the turf as she left it long ago,
And if we could come when the sentry slept, and softly scurry through,
By the favor of God we might know as much—as our father Adam knew.

EVARRA AND HIS GODS

Read here,
This is the story of Evarra—man—
Maker of Gods in lands beyond the sea.
Because the city gave him of her gold,
Because the caravans brought turquoises,
Because his life was sheltered by the King,
So that no man should maim him, none should steal,
Or break his rest with babble in the streets
When he was weary after toil, he made
An image of his God in gold and pearl,
With turquoise diadem and human eyes,
A wonder in the sunshine, known afar
And worshiped by the King; but drunk with pride,

Because the city bowed to him for God,
He wrote above the shrine: *"Thus Gods are made,*
And whoso makes them otherwise shall die."
And all the city praised him. . . . Then he died.

Read here the story of Evarra—man—
Maker of Gods in lands beyond the sea.
Because his city had no wealth to give,
Because the caravans were spoiled afar,
Because his life was threatened by the King,
So that all men despised him in the streets,
He hacked the living rock, with sweat and tears,
And reared a God against the morning-gold,
A terror in the sunshine, seen afar,
And worshiped by the King; but, drunk with pride,
Because the city fawned to bring him back,
He carved upon the plinth: *"Thus Gods are made,*
And whoso makes them otherwise shall die."
And all the people praised him. . . . Then he died.

Read here the story of Evarra—man—
Maker of Gods in lands beyond the sea.
Because he lived among the simple folk,
Because his village was between the hills,
Because he smeared his cheeks with blood of ewes,
He cut an idol from a fallen pine,
Smeared blood upon its cheeks, and wedged a shell
Above its brow for eye, and gave it hair
Of trailing moss, and plaited straw for crown.
And all the village praised him for his craft,
And brought him butter, honey, milk, and curds.
Wherefore, because the shoutings drove him mad,
He scratched upon that log: *"Thus Gods are made,*
And whoso makes them otherwise shall die."
And all the people praised him. . . . Then he died.

Read here the story of Evarra—man—
Maker of Gods in lands beyond the sea.
Because his God decreed one clot of blood
Should swerve a hair's-breadth from the pulse's path,
And chafe his brain, Evarra mowed alone,
Rag-wrapped, among the cattle in the fields,
Counting his fingers, jesting with the trees,
And mocking at the mist, until his God
Drove him to labor. Out of dung and horns
Dropped in the mire he made a monstrous God,
Abhorrent, shapeless, crowned with plantain tufts.
And when the cattle lowed at twilight-time,
He dreamed it was the clamor of lost crowds,
And howled among the beasts: *"Thus Gods are made,*
And whoso makes them otherwise shall die."
Thereat the cattle bellowed. . . . . Then he died.

Yet at the last he came to Paradise,
And found his own four Gods, and that he wrote;
And marveled, being very near to God,
What oaf on earth had made his toil God's law,
Till God said, mocking: "Mock not. These be thine."
Then cried Evarra: "I have sinned!"—"Not so.
If thou hadst written otherwise, thy Gods
Had rested in the mountain and the mine,
And I were poorer by four wondrous Gods,
And thy more wondrous law, Evarra. Thine,
Servant of shouting crowds and lowing kine."
Thereat with laughing mouth, but tear-wet eyes,
Evarra cast his Gods from Paradise.

This is the story of Evarra—man—
Maker of Gods in lands beyond the sea.

LA NUIT BLANCHE

A Much-Discerning Public hold
The Singer generally sings
Of personal and private things,
And prints and sells his past for gold.

Whatever I may here disclaim,
The very clever folk I sing to
Will most indubitably cling to
Their pet delusion, just the same.

I had seen, as dawn was breaking
And I staggered to my rest,
Tari Devi softly shaking
From the Cart Road to the crest.
I had seen the spurs of Jakko
Heave and quiver, swell and sink.
Was it Earthquake or tobacco,
Day of Doom or Night of Drink?

In the full, fresh, fragrant morning
I observed a camel crawl,
Laws of gravitation scorning,
On the ceiling and the wall;
Then I watched a fender walking,
And I heard gray leeches sing,
And a red-hot monkey talking
Did not seem the proper thing.

Half the night I watch the Heavens
Fizz like '81 champagne—
Fly to sixes and to sevens,
Wheel and thunder back again;
And when all was peace and order
Save one planet nailed askew,
Much I wept because my warder
Would not let me set it true.

After frenzied hours of waiting,
When the Earth and Skies were dumb,
Pealed an awful voice dictating
An interminable sum,
Changing to a tangled story—
"What she said you said I said—"
Till the Moon arose in glory,
And I found her . . . in my head;

Then a Face came, blind and weeping,
And It couldn't wipe Its eyes,
And It muttered I was keeping
Back the moonlight from the skies;
So I patted it for pity,
But it whistled shrill with wrath,
And a huge black Devil City
Poured its peoples on my path.

So I fled with steps uncertain
On a thousand-year long race,
But the bellying of the curtain
Kept me always in one place;
While the tumult rose and maddened
To the roar of Earth on fire,
Ere it ebbed and sank and saddened
To a whisper tense as wire.

In intolerable stillness
Rose one little, little star,
And it chuckled at my illness,
And it mocked me from afar;
And its brethren came and eyed me,
Called the Universe to aid,
Till I lay, with naught to hide me,
'Neath the Scorn of All Things Made.

Dun and saffron, robed and splendid,
  Broke the solemn, pitying Day,
And I knew my pains were ended,
  And I turned and tried to pray;
But my speech was shattered wholly,
  And I wept as children weep,
Till the dawn-wind, softly, slowly,
  Brought to burning eyelids sleep.

AN ASTROLOGER'S SONG

To the Heavens above us
  Oh, look and behold
The Planets that love us
  All harnessed in gold!
What chariots, what horses
  Against us shall bide
While the Stars in their courses
  Do fight on our side?

All thought, all desires,
  That are under the sun,
Are one with their fires,
  As we also are one:
All matter, all spirit,
  All fashion, all frame,
Receive and inherit
  Their strength from the same.

(Oh, man that deniest
  All power save thine own,
Their power in the highest
  Is mightily shown.
Not less in the lowest
  That power is made clear.
Oh, man, if thou knowest,
  What treasure is here!)

Earth quakes in her throes
  And we wonder for why!
But the blind planet knows
  When her ruler is nigh;
And, attuned since Creation
  To perfect accord,
She thrills in her station
  And yearns to her Lord.

The waters have risen,
  The springs are unbound—
The floods break their prison,
  And ravin around.
No rampart withstands 'em,
  Their fury will last,
Till the Sign that commands 'em
  Sinks low or swings past.

Through abysses unproven
  And gulfs beyond thought,
Our portion is woven,
  Our burden is brought.
Yet They that prepare it,
  Whose Nature we share,
Make us who must bear it
  Well able to bear.

Though terrors o'ertake us
  We'll not be afraid.
No power can unmake us
  Save that which has made.
Nor yet beyond reason
  Or hope shall we fall—
All things have their season,
  And Mercy crowns all!

Then doubt not, ye fearful—
  The Eternal is King—
Up, heart, and be cheerful,
  And lustily sing:—
What chariots, what horses
  Against us shall bide
While the Stars in their courses
  Do fight on our side?

RECESSIONAL

God of our fathers, known of old,
  Lord of our far-flung battle-line,
Beneath whose awful hand we hold
  Dominion over palm and pine—
Lord God of Hosts, be with us yet,
Lest we forget—lest we forget!

The tumult and the shouting dies;
  The captains and the kings depart:
Still stands Thine ancient sacrifice,
  An humble and a contrite heart.
Lord God of Hosts, be with us yet,
Lest we forget—lest we forget!

Far-called, our navies melt away;
  On dune and headland sinks the fire:

Lo, all our pomp of yesterday
  Is one with Nineveh and Tyre!
Judge of the Nations, spare us yet,
  Lest we forget—lest we forget!

If, drunk with sight of power, we loose
  Wild tongues that have not Thee in awe,
Such boastings as the Gentiles use,
  Or lesser breeds without the Law—
Lord God of Hosts, be with us yet,
  Lest we forget—lest we forget!

For heathen heart that puts her trust
  In reeking tube and iron shard,
All valiant dust that builds on dust,
  And, guarding, calls not Thee to guard,
For frantic boast and foolish word—
  Thy Mercy on Thy People, Lord!

THE LAST CHANTEY

"And there was no more sea"

Thus said the Lord in the Vault above the Cherubim,
  Calling to the Angels and the Souls in their degree:
    "Lo! Earth has passed away
    On the smoke of Judgment Day.
  That Our word may be established shall We gather up the sea?"

Loud sang the souls of the jolly, jolly mariners:
  "Plague upon the hurricane that made us furl and flee!
    But the war is done between us,
    In the deep the Lord hath seen us—
  Our bones we'll leave the barracout', and God may sink the sea!"

Then said the soul of Judas that betrayed Him:
  "Lord, hast Thou forgotten Thy covenant with me?
    How once a year I go
    To cool me on the floe?
  And Ye take my day of mercy if Ye take away the sea."

Then said the soul of the Angel of the Off-shore Wind:
  (He that bits the thunder when the bull-mouthed breakers flee):
    "I have watch and ward to keep
    O'er Thy wonders on the deep,
  And Ye take mine honor from me if Ye take away the sea!"

Loud sang the souls of the jolly, jolly mariners:
  "Nay, but we were angry, and a hasty folk are we.
    If we worked the ship together
    Till she foundered in foul weather,
  Are we babes that we should clamor for a vengeance on the sea?"

Then said the souls of the slaves that men threw overboard:
  "Kenneled in the picaroon a weary band were we;
    But Thy arm was strong to save,
    And it touched us on the wave,
  And we drowsed the long tides idle till Thy Trumpets tore the sea."

Then cried the soul of the stout Apostle Paul to God:
  "Once we frapped a ship, and she labored woundily.

There were fourteen score of these,
And they blessed Thee on their knees,
When they learned Thy Grace and Glory under Malta by the sea!"

Loud sang the souls of the jolly, jolly mariners,
Plucking at their harps, and they plucked unhandily:
"Our thumbs are rough and tarred,
And the tune is something hard—
May we lift a Deepsea Chantey such as seamen use at sea?"

Then said the souls of the gentlemen-adventurers—
Fettered wrist to bar all for red iniquity:
"Ho, we revel in our chains
O'er the sorrow that was Spain's;
Heave or sink it, leave or drink it, we were masters of the sea!"

Up spake the soul of a gray Gothavn 'speckshioner—
(He that led the flenching in the fleets of fair Fundee):
"Oh, the ice-blink white and near,
And the bowhead breaching clear!
Will Ye whelm them all for wantonness that wallow in the sea?"

Loud sang the souls of the jolly, jolly mariners,
Crying: "Under Heaven, here is neither lead nor lea!
Must we sing for evermore
On the windless, glassy floor?
Take back your golden fiddles and we'll beat to open sea!"

Then stooped the Lord, and He called the good sea up to Him,
And 'stablished its borders unto all eternity,
That such as have no pleasure
For to praise the Lord by measure,
They may enter into galleons and serve Him on the sea.

Sun, Wind, and Cloud shall fail not from the face of it,
Stinging, ringing spindrift, nor the fulmar flying free;
And the ships shall go abroad
To the Glory of the Lord
Who heard the silly sailor-folk and gave them back their sea!

SESTINA OF THE TRAMP-ROYAL

Speakin' in general, I 'ave tried 'em all—
The 'appy roads that take you o'er the world.
Speakin' in general, I 'ave found them good
For such as cannot use one bed too long,
But must get 'ence, the same as I 'ave done,
An' go observin' matters till they die.

What do it matter where or 'ow we die,
So long as we've our 'ealth to watch it all—
The different ways that different things are done,

An' men an' women lovin' in this world;
Takin' our chances as they come along,
An' when they ain't, pretendin' they are good?

In cash or credit—no, it aren't no good;
You 'ave to 'ave the 'abit or you'd die,
Unless you lived your life but one day long,
Nor didn't prophesy nor fret at all,
But drew your tucker some'ow from the world,
An' never bothered what you might ha' done.

But, Gawd, what things are they I 'aven't done!
I've turned my 'and to most, an' turned it good,
In various situations round the world—
For 'im that doth not work must surely die;
But that's no reason man should labor all
'Is life on one same shift—life's none so long.

Therefore, from job to job I've moved along.
Pay couldn't 'old me when my time was done,
For something in my 'ead upset it all,
Till I 'ad dropped whatever 't was for good,
An' out at sea, be'eld the dock-lights die,
An' met my mate—the wind that tramps the world!

It's like a book, I think, this bloomin' world,
Which you can read and care for just so long,
But presently you feel that you will die
Unless you get the page you're readin' done,
An' turn another—likely not so good;
But what you're after is to turn 'em all.

Gawd bless this world! Whatever she 'ath done—
Excep' when awful long—I've found it good.
So write, before I die, " 'E liked it all!"

THE LAND

When Julius Fabricius, Sub-Prefect of the Weald,
In the days of Diocletian owned our Lower River-field,
He called to him Hobdenius—a Briton of the Clay,
Saying, "What about that River-piece for layin' in to hay?"

And the aged Hobden answered: "I remember as a lad
My father told your father that she wanted dreenin' bad.
An' the more that you neeglect her the less you'll get her clean.
Have it jest *as* you've a mind to, but, if I was you, I'd dreen."

So they drained it long and crossways in the lavish Roman style.
Still we find among the river-drift their flakes of ancient tile,
And in drouthy middle August, when the bones of meadows show,
We can trace the lines they followed sixteen hundred years ago.

Then Julius Fabricius died as even Prefects do,
And after certain centuries, Imperial Rome died too.
Then did robbers enter Britain from across the Northern main
And our Lower River-field was won by Ogier the Dane.

Well could Ogier work his war-boat—well could Ogier wield his brand—
Much he knew of foaming waters—not so much of farming land.
So he called to him a Hobden of the old unaltered blood,
Saying: "What about that River-bit, she doesn't look so good."

And that aged Hobden answered: " 'Tain't for *me* to interfere,
But I've known that bit o' meadow now for five and fifty year.
Have it *jest* as you've a mind to, but I've proved it time on time,
If you want to change her nature you have *got* to give her lime!"

Ogier sent his wains to Lewes, twenty hours' solemn walk,
And drew back great abundance of the cool, gray, healing chalk.
And old Hobden spread it broadcast, never heeding what was in't;
Which is why in cleaning ditches, now and then we find a flint.

Ogier died. His sons grew English. Anglo-Saxon was their name,
Till out of blossomed Normandy another pirate came;
For Duke William conquered England and divided with his men,
And our Lower River-field he gave to William of Warenne.

But the Brook (you know her habit) rose one rainy Autumn night
And tore down sodden flitches of the bank to left and right.
So, said William to his Bailiff as they rode their dripping rounds:
"Hob, what about that River-bit—the Brook's got up no bounds?"

And that aged Hobden answered: "Tain't my business to advise,
But ye might ha' known 'twould happen from the way the valley lies.
When ye can't hold back the water you must try and save the sile.
Hev it jest as you've a *mind* to, but if I was you I'd spile."

They spiled along the water-course with trunks of willow-trees
And planks of elms behind 'em and immortal oaken knees.
And when the spates of Autumn whirl the gravel-beds away
You can see their faithful fragments iron-hard in iron clay.

Georgii Quinti, Anno Sexto, I, who own the River-field,
Am fortified with title-deeds, attested, signed and sealed,
Guaranteeing me, my assigns, my executors and heirs
All sorts of powers and profits which—are neither mine nor theirs.

I have rights of chase and warren, as my dignity requires.
I can fish—but Hobden tickles. I can shoot—but Hobden wires.
I repair, but he reopens, certain gaps which, men allege,
Have been used by every Hobden since a Hobden swapped a hedge.

Shall I dog his morning progress o'er the track-betraying dew?
Demand his dinner-basket into which my pheasant flew?
Confiscate his evening faggot into which the conies ran,
And summons him to judgment? I would sooner summons Pan.

His dead are in the churchyard—thirty generations laid.
Their names went down in Domesday Book when Domesday Book was made.
And the passion and the piety and prowess of his line
Have seeded, rooted, fruited in some land the Law calls mine.

Not for any beast that burrows, nor for any bird that flies,
Would I lose his large sound council, miss his keen amending eyes.
He is bailiff, woodman, wheelwright, field-surveyor, engineer,
And if flagrantly a poacher—'tain't for me to interfere.

"Hob, what about that River-bit?" I turn to him again
With Fabricius and Ogier and William of Warenne.
"Hev it jest as you've a mind to, *but*"—and so he takes command.
For whoever pays the taxes, old Mus' Hobden owns the land.

FOR TO ADMIRE

The Injian Ocean sets an' smiles
  So sof', so bright, so bloomin' blue;
There aren't a wave for miles an' miles
  Excep' the jiggle from the screw.
The ship is swep', the day is done,
  The bugle's gone for smoke and play;
An' black agin' the settin' sun
  The Lascar sings, *"Hum deckty hai!"*[1]

For to admire an' for to see,
  For to be'old this world so wide—
It never done no good to me,
  But I can't drop it if I tried!

I see the sergeants pitchin' quoits,
  I 'ear the women laugh an' talk,
I spy upon the quarter-deck
  The orficers an' lydies walk.
I thinks about the things that was,
  An' leans an' looks acrost the sea,
Till spite of all the crowded ship
  There's no one lef' alive but me.

The things that was which I 'ave seen,
  In barrick, camp, an' action too,
I tells them over by myself,
  An' sometimes wonders if they're true;
For they was odd—most awful odd—
  But all the same now they are o'er,
There must be 'eaps o' plenty such,
  An' if I wait I'll see some more.

Oh, I 'ave come upon the books,
  An' frequent broke a barrick rule,
An' stood beside an' watched myself
  Be'avin like a bloomin' fool.
I paid my price for findin' out,
  Nor never grutched the price I paid,
But sat in Clink without my boots,
  Admirin' 'ow the world was made.

Be'old a crowd upon the beam,
  An' 'umped above the sea appears
Old Aden, like a barrick-stove
  That no one's lit for years an' years!
I passed by that when I began,
  An' I go 'ome the road I came,
A time-expired soldier-man
  With six years' service to 'is name.

My girl she said, "Oh, stay with me!"
  My mother 'eld me to 'er breast.
They've never written none, an' so
  They must 'ave gone with all the rest—
With all the rest which I 'ave seen
  An' found an' known an' met along.
I cannot say the things I feel,
  And so I sing my evenin' song:

For to admire an' for to see,
  For to be'old this world so wide—
It never done no good to me,
  But I can't drop it if I tried!

[1] "I'm looking out."

L'ENVOI

What is the moral? Who rides may read.
When the night is thick and the tracks are blind
A friend at a pinch is a friend indeed,
But a fool to wait for the laggard behind.
Down to Gehenna or up to the Throne,
He travels the fastest who travels alone.

White hands cling to the tightened rein,
Slipping the spur from the booted heel,
Tenderest voices cry "Turn again!"
Red lips tarnish the scabbarded steel.
High hopes faint on a warm hearth stone—
He travels the fastest who travels alone.

One may fall but he falls by himself—
Falls by himself with himself to blame.
One may attain and to him is pelf—
Loot of the city in Gold or Fame.
Plunder of earth shall be all his own
Who travels the fastest and travels alone.

Wherefore the more ye be holpen and stayed,
Stayed by a friend in the hour of toil,
Sing the heretical song I have made—
His be the labour and yours be the spoil.
Win by his aid and the aid disown—
He travels the fastest who travels alone!

"Æ"

George William Russell was born April 10, 1867, in the small town of Lurgan, County Armagh, Ireland. At sixteen he studied painting in the School of Art in Dublin, and became the close friend of W. B. Yeats and, later, James Stephens. While working as an accountant in a draper's establishment, he read much in Oriental mystical literature, becoming the leader of a small theosophical group. At that time he wrote an aricle for *The Irish Theosophist* under the pseudonym "Æon" but the compositor omitted the two last letters and the piece appeared under the diphthong "Æ," a pen-name which Russell adopted.

In 1897 he became active in Irish politics. For several years he devoted himself to establishing coöperative societies, aiding rural communities, editing (in 1904) *The Irish Homestead* and (in 1923) *The Irish Statesman.* There were two distinct, almost opposed, sides to Russell. There was the political and practical side which took him all over Ireland, founding poultry and creamery coöperatives, and made him goad his countrymen out of their ruinously antiquated methods of farming. There was the mystical side which prompted him to join the Theosophists, to see the inanimate earth as a powerfully living organism, and "to run in and out of a house of dream." Russell always maintained he had a double identity, and he kept his two selves clearly separated.

Besides being a public speaker, propagandist, and sociologist, Russell was a painter; his landscapes have the misty-mystical color of his verse, serene and appropriately vague in their otherworldliness. He was the author of several volumes of prose ranging from *Coöperatives and Nationality* (1912) to *The Avatars* (1933). *Song and Its Fountains* (1932) voices his poetic credo.

It was as poet that Russell established himself beyond national borders. The best of his early poetry is in *Homeward: Songs by the Way* (1894) and *The Earth Breath* (1897). Thirteen subsequent volumes revealed, as Yeats wrote, "a kind of scented flame consuming them from within." The choicest of these were collected in *Selected Poems* (1935). The poetry is a curious contradiction of the things for which Russell fought. Completely unconcerned with agrarian issues or, for that matter, any other problems, his poetry maintains that the world is an unreal world, an insubstantial shadow, in which dreams and visions are the only true guides. It is the poetry of one who is drunk with abstract Beauty, devoted to "the Heavenly Brooding" and a sense of the Everlasting.

In spite of a struggle with disease—he was afflicted with cancer—Russell continued working until the end. He died after an operation at Bournemouth, England, July 17, 1935.

SELF-DISCIPLINE

When the soul sought refuge in the place of rest,
Overborne by strife and pain beyond control,
From some secret hollow, whisper soft-confessed,
Came the legend of the soul.

Some bright one of old time laid his sceptre down,
So his heart might learn of sweet and bitter truth;
Going forth bereft of beauty, throne, and crown,
And the sweetness of his youth.

So the old appeal and fierce revolt we make
Through the world's hour dies within our primal will;
And we justify the pain and hearts that break,
And our lofty doom fulfil.

PAIN

Men have made them gods of love,
Sun-gods, givers of the rain,
Deities of hill and grove:
I have made a god of Pain.

Of my god I know this much,
And in singing I repeat,
Though there's anguish in his touch,
Yet his soul within is sweet.

TRUTH

The hero first thought it;
To him 'twas a deed:
To those who retaught it,
A chain on their speed.

The fire that we kindled,
A beacon by night,
When darkness has dwindled
Grows pale in the light.

For life has no glory
Stays long in one dwelling,
And time has no story
That's true twice in telling.

And only the teaching
That never was spoken
Is worthy thy reaching,
The fountain unbroken.

TRAGEDY

A man went forth one day at eve;
The long day's toil for him was done;
The eye that scanned the page could leave
Its task until tomorrow's sun.

Upon the threshold as he stood
Flared on his tired eyes the sight,
Where host on host the multitude
Burned fiercely in the dusky height.

The starry lights at play—at play—
The giant children of the blue
Heaped scorn upon his trembling clay,
And with their laughter pierced him through.

They seemed to say in scorn of him:
"The power we have was once in thee.
King, is thy spirit grown so dim,
That thou art slave and we are free?"

As out of him the power—the power—
The free, the fearless, whirled in play,
He knew himself that bitter hour
The close of all his royal day.

And from the stars' exultant dance
Within the fiery furnace glow,
Exile of all the vast expanse,
He turned him homeward sick and slow.

THE GREAT BREATH

Its edges foamed with amethyst and rose,
Withers once more the old blue flower of day:
There where the ether like a diamond glows,
Its petals fade away.

A shadowy tumult stirs the dusky air;
Sparkle the delicate dews, the distant snows;
The great deep thrills—for through it everywhere
The breath of Beauty blows.

I saw how all the trembling ages past,
Molded to her by deep and deeper breath,
Near'd to the hour when Beauty breathes her last
And knows herself in death.

FROLIC

The children were shouting together
And racing along the sands,
A glimmer of dancing shadows,
A dovelike flutter of hands.

The stars were shouting in heaven,
The sun was chasing the moon:
The game was the same as the children's,
They danced to the self-same tune.

The whole of the world was merry,
One joy from the vale to the height,
Where the blue woods of twilight encircled
The love-lawns of the light.

THE SECRET

One thing in all things have I seen:
One thought has haunted earth and air:
Clangor and silence both have been
Its palace chambers. Everywhere

I saw the mystic vision flow
And live in men and woods and streams,
Until I could no longer know
The dream of life from my own dreams.

Sometimes it rose like fire in me
Within the depths of my own mind,
And spreading to infinity,
It took the voices of the wind:

It scrawled the human mystery—
Dim heraldry—on light and air;
Wavering along the starry sea
I saw the flying vision there.

Each fire that in God's temple lit
Burns fierce before the inner shrine,
Dimmed as my fire grew near to it
And darkened at the light of mine.

At last, at last, the meaning caught—
The Spirit wears its diadem;
It shakes its wondrous plumes of thought
And trails the stars along with them.

THE UNKNOWN GOD

Far up the dim twilight fluttered
   Moth-wings of vapor and flame:
The lights danced over the mountains,
   Star after star they came.

The lights grew thicker unheeded,
   For silent and still were we;
Our hearts were drunk with a beauty
   Our eyes could never see.

CONTINUITY

No sign is made while empires pass,
The flowers and stars are still His care,
The constellations hid in grass,
The golden miracles in air.

Life in an instant will be rent,
Where death is glittering blind and wild—
The Heavenly Brooding is intent
To that last instant on Its child.

It breathes the glow in brain and heart,
Life is made magical. Until
Body and spirit are apart,
The Everlasting works Its will.

In that wild orchid that your feet
In their next falling shall destroy,
Minute and passionate and sweet
The Mighty Master holds His joy.

Though the crushed jewels droop and fade,
The Artist's labors will not cease,
And of the ruins shall be made
Some yet more lovely masterpiece.

EPILOGUE

Well, when all is said and done
Best within my narrow way,
May some angel of the sun
Muse memorial o'er my clay:

"Here was Beauty all betrayed
From the freedom of her state;
From her human uses stayed
On an idle rhyme to wait.

"Ah, what deep despair might move
If the beauty lit a smile,
Or the heart was warm with love
That was pondering the while.

"He has built his monument
With the winds of time at strife,
Who could have, before he went,
Written in the Book of Life.

"To the stars from which he came
Empty-handed he goes home;
He who might have wrought in flame
Only traced upon the foam."

EXILES

The gods have taken alien shapes upon them,
Wild peasants driving swine
In a strange country. Through the swarthy faces
The starry faces shine.

Under grey tattered skies they strain and reel there:
Yet cannot all disguise
The majesty of fallen gods, the beauty,
The fire beneath their eyes.

They huddle at night within low, clay-built cabins;
And, to themselves unknown,
They carry with them diadem and sceptre
And move from throne to throne.

GERMINAL

Call not thy wanderer home as yet
  Though it be late.
Now is his first assailing of
  The invisible gate.
Be still through that light knocking. The hour
  Is thronged with fate.

To that first tapping at the invisible door
  Fate answereth.
What shining image or voice, what sigh
  Or honied breath,
Comes forth, shall be the master of life
  Even to death.

Satyrs may follow after. Seraphs
  On crystal wing
May blaze. But the delicate first comer
  It shall be King.
They shall obey, even the mightiest,
  That gentle thing.

All the strong powers of Dante were bowed
  To a child's mild eyes,
That wrought within him travail
  From depths up to skies,
Inferno, Purgatorio,
  And Paradise.

Amid the soul's grave councillors
  A petulant boy
Laughs under the laurels and purples, the elf
  Who snatched at his joy,
Ordering Caesar's legions to bring him
  The world for his toy.

In ancient shadows and twilights
  Where childhood had strayed,
The world's great sorrows were born
  And its heroes were made.
In the lost boyhood of Judas
  Christ was betrayed.

Let thy young wanderer dream on:
  Call him not home.
A door opens, a breath, a voice
  From the ancient room,
Speaks to him now. Be it dark or bright
  He is knit with his doom.

Ernest Dowson

Ernest Dowson was born at Belmont Hill in Kent, August 2, 1867. His great-uncle was Alfred Domett (Browning's "Waring"), one time Prime Minister of New Zealand. Dowson, practically an invalid all his life, lived intermittently in London, Paris, Normandy, and on the Riviera. He was reckless with himself and, as disease weakened him more and more, hid in miserable surroundings; for almost two years he lived in sordid supper-houses known as "cab-men's shelters."

He formed only one passion but that one was final and devastating. He fell in love with a restaurant-keeper's daughter, paid court to her with the most delicate reserve, and she—impatient alike of his words and his reticences—married a waiter. The shock to Dowson was profound. He grew more and more withdrawn, even his contacts with fellow-members of the Rhymers' Club became slighter. He sank into despondency and dissipation; he literally drank himself to death.

Dowson's delicate and fantastic poetry was an attempt to escape from a reality too brutal for him. It is not only typically *fin de siécle;* it is, as any psychoanalytical critic will recognize, curiously autobiographical. He, himself, was his own pitiful "Pierrot of the Minute," throwing "roses, riotously with the throng"—even though the throng was ignorant of him. His passionate lyric, "I have been faithful to thee, Cynara! in my fashion," a triumph of despair and disillusion, is an outburst in which Dowson epitomized himself. "One of the greatest lyrical poems of our time," writes Arthur Symons; "in it he has for once said everything, and he has said it to an intoxicating and perhaps immortal music."

Yet, in spite of the fact that this familiar poem has been quoted in almost every contemporary collection, several of Dowson's less well-known poems strike a higher and far more resonant note. Among such poems are "Extreme Unction," possibly the finest expression of his Catholicism, and "A Last Word," which expresses his revulsion from the "perverse and aimless band."

Dowson's poems of decadence are no less typical than his religious poems; both, unlike the product of much of his period, are sincere. His mysticism, no less than his idealization of preciosity, is an esthetic one. Unable to find fulfillment in either, he wavered, as C. E. Andrews and M. O. Percival say in *Poetry of the Nineties,* "between heaping garlands upon the altars of Aphrodite and lighting candles to the Blessed Virgin."

Dowson died obscure in 1900, one of the least effectual but one of the most gifted of modern minor poets. His life was a tragedy of a weak nature buffeted by a strong and merciless environment. His poetry, highly special but never specious, survives.

A LAST WORD

Let us go hence: the night is now at hand;
  The day is overworn, the birds all flown;
  And we have reaped the crops the gods have sown;
Despair and death; deep darkness o'er the land,

Broods like an owl; we cannot understand
  Laughter or tears, for we have only known
  Surpassing vanity: vain things alone
Have driven our perverse and aimless band.

Let us go hence, somewhither strange and cold,
  To Hollow Lands where just men and unjust
  Find end of labor, where's rest for the old,
Freedom to all from love and fear and lust.
Twine our torn hands! O pray the earth enfold
Our life-sick hearts and turn them into dust.

NON SUM QUALIS ERAM BONAE SUB REGNO CYNARAE

Last night, ah, yesternight, betwixt her lips and mine
There fell thy shadow, Cynara! thy breath was shed
Upon my soul between the kisses and the wine;
And I was desolate and sick of an old passion,
  Yea, I was desolate and bowed my head:
I have been faithful to thee, Cynara! in my fashion.

All night upon mine heart I felt her warm heart beat,
Night-long within mine arms in love and sleep she lay;
Surely the kisses of her bought red mouth were sweet;
But I was desolate and sick of an old passion,
  When I awoke and found the dawn was gray;
I have been faithful to thee, Cynara! in my fashion.

I have forgot much, Cynara! gone with the wind,
Flung roses, roses riotously with the throng,
Dancing, to put thy pale, lost lilies out of mind;
But I was desolate and sick of an old passion,
  Yea, all the time, because the dance was long:
I have been faithful to thee, Cynara! in my fashion.

I cried for madder music and for stronger wine,
But when the feast is finished and the lamps expire,
Then falls thy shadow, Cynara! the night is thine;
And I am desolate and sick of an old passion,
  Yea, hungry for the lips of my desire:
I have been faithful to thee, Cynara! in my fashion.

SPLEEN

I was not sorrowful, I could not weep,
And all my memories were put to sleep.

I watched the river grow more white and strange,
All day till evening I watched it change.

All day till evening I watched the rain
Beat wearily upon the window-pane.

I was not sorrowful, but only tired
Of everything that ever I desired.

Her lips, her eyes, all day became to me
The shadow of a shadow utterly.
All day mine hunger for her heart became
Oblivion, until the evening came.

And left me sorrowful, inclined to weep,
With all my memories that could not sleep.

TO ONE IN BEDLAM

With delicate, mad hands, behind his sordid bars,
Surely he hath his posies, which they tear and twine;
Those scentless wisps of straw that, miserable, line
His strait, caged universe, whereat the dull world stares,

Pedant and pitiful. O, how his rapt gaze wars
With their stupidity! Know they what dreams divine
Lift his long, laughing reveries like enchanted wine,
And make his melancholy germane to the stars?

O lamentable brother! if those pity thee,
Am I not fain of all thy lone eyes promise me;
Half a fool's kingdom, far from men who sow and reap,
All their days, vanity? Better than mortal flowers,
Thy moon-kissed roses seem: better than love or sleep,
The star-crowned solitude of thine oblivious hours!

EXTREME UNCTION

Upon the eyes, the lips, the feet,
On all the passages of sense,
The atoning oil is spread with sweet
Renewal of lost innocence.

The feet, that lately ran so fast
To meet desire, are soothly sealed;
The eyes that were so often cast
On vanity, are touched and healed.

From troublous sights and sounds set free;
In such a twilight hour of breath
Shall one retrace his life, or see
Through shadows the true face of death?

Vials of mercy! Sacring oils!
I know not where nor when I come,
Nor through what wanderings and toils,
To crave of you Viaticum.

Yet, when the walls of flesh grow weak,
In such an hour, it well may be,
Through mist and darkness, light will break,
And each anointed sense will see!

YOU WOULD HAVE UNDERSTOOD ME

You would have understood me had you waited;
I could have loved you, dear! as well as he:
Had we not been impatient, dear! and fated
Always to disagree.

What is the use of Speech? Silence were fitter:
Lest we should still be wishing things unsaid.
Though all the words we ever spake were bitter,
Shall I reproach you, dead?

Nay, let this earth, your portion, likewise cover
All the old anger, setting us apart:
Always, in all, in truth was I your lover;
Always, I held your heart.

I have met other women who were tender,
As you were cold, dear! with a grace as rare.
Think you, I turned to them, or made surrender,
I who had found you fair?

Had we been patient, dear! ah, had you waited,
I had fought death for you, better than he:
But from the very first, dear! we were fated
Always to disagree.

Late, late, I come to you, now death discloses
Love that in life was not to be our part:
On your low lying mound between the roses,
Sadly I cast my heart.

I would not waken you: nay! this is fitter;
Death and the darkness give you unto me;
Here we who loved so, were so cold and bitter,
Hardly can disagree.

VILLANELLE OF MARGUERITES

"A little, passionately, not at all?"
She casts the snowy petals on the air;
And what care we how many petals fall?

Nay, wherefore seek the seasons to forestall?
It is but playing, and she will not care,
A little, passionately, not at all!

She would not answer us if we should call
Across the years; her visions are too fair;
And what care we how many petals fall!

She knows us not, nor recks if she enthrall
With voice and eyes and fashion of her hair,
A little, passionately, not at all!

Knee-deep she goes in meadow-grasses tall,
Kissed by the daisies that her fingers tear;
And what care we how many petals fall!

We pass and go; but she shall not recall
What men we were, nor all she made us bear;
"A little, passionately, not at all!"
And what care we how many petals fall!

ENVOY

(Vitae summa brevis spem nos vetat incohare longam)

They are not long, the weeping and the laughter,
Love and desire and hate;
I think they have no portion in us after
We pass the gate.

They are not long, the days of wine and roses:
Out of a misty dream
Our path emerges for a while, then closes
Within a dream.

Lionel Johnson

Born in 1867, at Broadstairs in Kent, Lionel (Pigot) Johnson received a classical education at Oxford; his poetry is a reflection of his studies in Greek and Latin literatures. Though he allied himself with the modern Irish poets, his Celtic origin is a literary myth; Johnson, having been converted to Catholicism in 1891, became imbued with Catholic and Irish traditions. Yeats, who became his intimate friend, says it was Johnson's habit to sleep all day and read and write all night, the ordinary world about him having no significance to the recluse. "In my library," Johnson said, "I have all the knowledge I need of the world."

Before any of his poetry was collected in a volume, he published a book on *The Art of Thomas Hardy* (1894) which, though planned before the appearance of *Jude the Obscure* or *The Dynasts,* remains one of the most sensitive studies of Hardy yet written. His verse, published originally among the bizarre novelties of *The Yellow Book,* was curiously cool and removed; he seemed, as one of his associates had said, a young monk surrounded by dancing pagans. "Divine austerity" is the goal to which his verse aspires. While sometimes over-decorated, it is chastely designed, and, like that of the Cavalier poets of the seventeenth century, fiercely devotional. Today, with such poems as "Mystic and Cavalier," "The Precept of Silence," and "The Dark Angel," he seems the most important of his group; his voice has found echoes in recent poetry, particularly in the poems of Yeats.

Johnson was one of the many poets to whom conversion to the Church supplied not only a new color but a new impetus. It is a subject rich in speculation why this period should have yielded so many artists who turned to the Catholic Church for inspiration in their life and work; among the most eminent converts, besides Johnson, were Alice Meynell, Ernest Dowson, Oscar Wilde, and Aubrey Beardsley.

Poems (1895) and *Ireland* (1897) were published during his lifetime; a posthumous collection of essays, *Post Liminium,* appeared in 1911. A collected edition of his poems was brought out in 1915. Johnson died tragically in 1902.

MYSTIC AND CAVALIER

Go from me: I am one of those who fall.
What! hath no cold wind swept your heart at all,
In my sad company? Before the end,
Go from me, dear my friend!

Yours are the victories of light: your feet
Rest from good toil, where rest is brave and sweet:
But after warfare in a mourning gloom,
I rest in clouds of doom.

Have you not read so, looking in these eyes?
Is it the common light of the pure skies
Lights up their shadowy depths? The end is set:
Though the end be not yet.

When gracious music stirs, and all is bright,
And beauty triumphs through a courtly night;
When I too joy, a man like other men:
Yet, am I like them, then?

And in the battle, when the horsemen sweep
Against a thousand deaths, and fall on sleep:
Who ever sought that sudden calm, if I
Sought not? yet could not die!

Seek with thine eyes to pierce this crystal sphere:
Canst read a fate there, prosperous and clear?
Only the mists, only the weeping clouds,
Dimness and airy shrouds.

Beneath, what angels are at work? What powers
Prepare the secret of the fatal hours?
See! the mists tremble, and the clouds are stirred:
When comes the calling word?

The clouds are breaking from the crystal ball,
Breaking and clearing: and I look to fall.
When the cold winds and airs of portent sweep,
My spirit may have sleep.

O rich and sounding voices of the air!
Interpreters and prophets of despair:
Priests of a fearful sacrament! I come
To make with you mine home.

TO MORFYDD

A voice on the winds,
A voice by the waters,
Wanders and cries:
Oh! what are the winds?
And what are the waters?
Mine are your eyes!

Western the winds are,
And western the waters,
Where the light lies:
Oh! what are the winds?
And what are the waters?
Mine are your eyes!

Cold, cold grow the winds,
And wild grow the waters,
Where the sun dies:
Oh! what are the winds?
And what are the waters?
Mine are your eyes!

And down the night winds,
And down the night waters,
The music flies:
Oh! what are the winds?
And what are the waters?
Cold be the winds,
And wild be the waters,
So mine be your eyes!

BY THE STATUE OF KING CHARLES AT CHARING CROSS

Somber and rich, the skies,
Great glooms, and starry plains;
Gently the night wind sighs;
Else a vast silence reigns.

The splendid silence clings
Around me: and around
The saddest of all Kings,
Crown'd, and again discrown'd.

Comely and calm, he rides
Hard by his own Whitehall.
Only the night wind glides:
No crowds, no rebels, brawl.

Gone, too, his Court: and yet,
The stars his courtiers are:
Stars in their stations set;
And every wandering star.

Alone he rides, alone,
The fair and fatal King:
Dark night is all his own,
That strange and solemn thing.

Which are more full of fate:
The stars, or those sad eyes?
Which are more still and great:
Those brows, or the dark skies?

Although his whole heart yearn
In passionate tragedy,
Never was face so stern,
With sweet austerity.

Vanquish'd in life, his death
By beauty made amends:
The passing of his breath
Won his defeated ends.

Brief life and hapless? Nay:
Through death, life grew sublime,
Speak after sentence? Yea:
And to the end of time.

Armor'd he rides, his head
Bare to the stars of doom;
He triumphs now, the dead,
Beholding London's gloom.

Our wearier spirit faints,
Vex'd in the world's employ:
His soul was of the saints;
And art to him was joy.

King, tried in fires of woe!
Men hunger for thy grace:
And through the night I go,
Loving thy mournful face.

Yet, when the city sleeps,
When all the cries are still,
The stars and heavenly deeps
Work out a perfect will.

TO A TRAVELER

The mountains, and the lonely death at last
Upon the lonely mountains: O strong friend!
The wandering over, and the labor passed,
Thou art indeed at rest:
Earth gave thee of her best,
That labor and this end.

Earth was thy mother, and her true son thou:
Earth called thee to a knowledge of her ways,
Upon the great hills, up the great streams: now:
Upon earth's kindly breast
Thou art indeed at rest:
Thou, and thine arduous days.

Fare thee well, O strong heart! The tranquil night
Looks calmly on thee: and the sun pours down
His glory over thee, O heart of might!
Earth gives thee perfect rest:
Earth, whom thy swift feet pressed:
Earth, whom the vast stars crown.

THE DARK ANGEL

Dark Angel, with thine aching lust
To rid the world of penitence:
Malicious Angel, who still dost
My soul such subtile violence!

Because of thee, no thought, no thing,
Abides for me undesecrate:
Dark Angel, ever on the wing,
Who never reachest me too late!

When music sounds, then changest thou
Its silvery to a sultry fire:
Nor will thine envious heart allow
Delight untortured by desire.

Through thee, the gracious Muses turn
To Furies, O mine Enemy!
And all the things of beauty burn
With flames of evil ecstasy.

Because of thee, the land of dreams
Becomes a gathering place of fears.
Until tormented slumber seems
One vehemence of useless tears.

When sunlight glows upon the flowers,
Or ripples down the dancing sea:
Thou, with thy troop of passionate powers,
Beleaguerest, bewilderest, me.

Within the breath of autumn woods,
Within the winter silences:
Thy venomous spirit stirs and broods,
O Master of impieties!

The ardor of red flames is thine,
And thine the steely soul of ice:
Thou poisonest the fair design
Of nature, with unfair device.

Apples of ashes, golden bright;
Waters of bitterness, how sweet!
O banquet of a foul delight,
Prepared by thee, dark Paraclete!

Thou art the whisper in the gloom,
The hinting tone, the haunting laugh:
Thou art the adorner of my tomb,
The minstrel of mine epitaph.

I fight thee, in the Holy Name!
Yet, what thou dost is what God saith:
Tempter! should I escape thy flame,
Thou wilt have helped my soul from Death:

The second Death, that never dies,
That cannot die, when time is dead:
Live Death, wherein the lost soul cries,
Eternally uncomforted.

Dark Angel, with thine aching lust!
Of two defeats, of two despairs;
Less dread, a change to drifting dust,
Than thine eternity of cares.

Do what thou wilt, thou shalt not so,
Dark Angel! triumph over me:
Lonely, unto the Lone I go;
Divine, to the Divinity.

THE PRECEPT OF SILENCE

I know you: solitary griefs,
Desolate passions, aching hours!
I know you: tremulous beliefs,
Agonized hopes, and ashen flowers!

The winds are sometimes sad to me;
The starry spaces, full of fear:
Mine is the sorrow on the sea,
And mine the sigh of places drear.

Some players upon plaintive strings
Publish their wistfulness abroad:
I have not spoken of these things,
Save to one man, and unto God.

Laurence Binyon

(Robert) Laurence Binyon was born at Lancaster, August 10, 1869, son of a clergyman, and a cousin of the poet and playwright, Stephen Phillips. Educated at Trinity College, Oxford, Binyon won the Newdigate Prize in his twenty-first year with the long poem *Persephone*. The publication of this poem was followed by *Primavera* (1890), a collaboration with his cousin and two friends; a tragedy in four acts entitled *Attila;* studies of Dutch etchers of the seventeenth century; and *The Popularization of Art* (1896).

Although Binyon's energy and versatility was apparent, his early poetry showed little distinction until he published *London Visions,* which, in an enlarged edition in 1908, revealed a gift of characterization and a turn of speech in surprising contrast to his previous academic *Lyrical Poems* (1894). His *Odes* (1901) contains his ripest work; two poems in particular, "The Threshold" and "The Bacchanal of Alexander," are glowing and unusually spontaneous.

Binyon's talent continued to grow; age gave his verse a new sharpness. Sixty poems were published in *The Secret* (1920), most of which reflect the poet's dignity with a definiteness which he never before attained. *Selected Poems* (1924) is an excellently arranged sequence which includes Binyon's finest work, with the exception of *The Sirens* (1927), a long, elaborate ode in which the slow-paced rhythms have wide scope.

Binyon's *Collected Poems* (1931), in two volumes, reveal his progress from purely scholarly patterns to flexibility. The later verses are deepened with an unusual power of thought and with a restrained music.

For fifty years—from 1893 until his death in 1943—Binyon was head of the Department of Printed Books in the British Museum. One volume of his critical studies—*English Poetry in its Relation to Painting and the Other Arts* (1919)—is especially rewarding to those interested in the kinship of the arts.

THE LITTLE DANCERS

Lonely, save for a few faint stars, the sky
Dreams; and lonely, below, the little street
Into its gloom retires, secluded and shy.
Scarcely the dumb roar enters this soft retreat;
And all is dark, save where come flooding rays
From a tavern window; there, to the brisk measure
Of an organ that down in an alley merrily plays,
Two children, all alone and no one by,
Holding their tattered frocks, thro' an airy maze
Of motion lightly threaded with nimble feet
Dance sedately; face to face they gaze,
Their eyes shining, grave with a perfect pleasure.

O WORLD, BE NOBLER

O world, be nobler, for her sake!
  If she but knew thee what thou art,
What wrongs are borne, what deeds are done
In thee, beneath thy daily sun,
  Know'st thou not that her tender heart
For pain and very shame would break?
  O World, be nobler, for her sake!

NOTHING IS ENOUGH

Nothing is enough!
No, though our all be spent—

Heart's extremest love,
Spirit's whole intent,
All that nerve can feel,
All that brain invent,—
Still beyond appeal
Will Divine Desire
Yet more excellent
Precious cost require
Of this mortal stuff,—
Never be content
Till ourselves be fire.
Nothing is enough!

BEAUTY

I think of a flower that no eye has ever seen,
  That springs in a solitary air.
Is it no one's joy? It is beautiful as a queen
  Without a kingdom's care.

We have built houses for Beauty, and costly shrines,
  And a throne in all men's view:
But she was far on a hill where the morning shines
  And her steps were lost in the dew.

A SONG

For Mercy, Courage, Kindness, Mirth,
There is no measure upon earth.
Nay, they wither, root and stem,
If an end be set to them.

Overbrim and overflow,
If your own heart you would know;
For the spirit born to bless
Lives but in its own excess.

THE HOUSE THAT WAS

Of the old house, only a few crumbled
  Courses of brick, smothered in nettle and dock,
Or a squared stone, lying mossy where it tumbled.
  Sprawling bramble and saucy thistle mock
What once was firelit floor and private charm
  Whence, seen in a windowed picture, were hills fading
At dusk, and all was memory-colored and warm,
  And voices talked, secure from the wind's invading.

Of the old garden, only a stray shining
  Of daffodil flames amid April's cuckoo-flowers,

Or a cluster of aconite mixt with weeds entwining!
  But, dark and lofty, a royal cedar towers
By homely thorns; and whether the white rain drifts
  Or sun scorches, he holds the downs in ken,
The western vales; his branchy tiers he lifts,
  Older than many a generation of men.

Charlotte Mew

Charlotte (Mary) Mew was born November 15, 1869, the daughter of an architect of distinction, who died when she was an infant. Little is generally known of her life except that it was a long struggle not only with poverty but with adversity and private sorrows that finally overcame her. In her late fifties, through the joint efforts of Hardy, De la Mare, and Masefield, she was granted a Civil List pension. Though she loved the country, she was forced to live almost continually in London, in the very heart of Bloomsbury, becoming more and more of a recluse. One of her few excursions was a week-end at Max Gate, where she was the guest of Thomas Hardy, who considered her the best woman poet of her day. The death of her mother was a blow from which she never recovered; the death of her sister hastened her end. As Sidney C. Cockerell wrote, "Charlotte and Anne Mew had more than a little in them of what made another Charlotte and Anne, and their sister Emily, what they were. They were indeed like two Brontë sisters reincarnate."

Charlotte Mew died by her own hand in a nursing home March 24, 1928.

In the obituary note which Sidney Cockerell wrote for the *London Times* few new facts came to light. It was learned that Charlotte Mew wrote much more than was suspected, but "how much she destroyed at house-movings and during periods of overwhelming depression, we shall never know. There can be no doubt that her fastidious self-criticism proved fatal to much work that was really good, and that the printed poems are far less than a tithe of what she composed. These first appeared in various periodicals. In 1916, seventeen of them were collected into a thin volume which was issued by the Poetry Book Shop for a shilling. In 1921 this volume, named *The Farmer's Bride,* after the opening poem, was re-issued with the addition of 11 new poems, 28 in all. Perhaps not more than another 20 have seen the light. But, although the visible output was so small, the quality was in each case poignant and arresting. These poems are written as though with the life-blood of a noble and passionate heart."

One of Charlotte Mew's first discoverers was Alida Klemantaski (later Mrs. Harold Monro), who was not only responsible for the publication of *The Farmer's Bride,* but for the printing of the posthumous *The Rambling Sailor* (1929) to which she furnished a Memoir. The first book was brought out in America under the title of *Saturday Market* in 1921. Had Miss Mew printed nothing but the original booklet, it would have been sufficient to rank her among the most distinctive and intense of living poets. Hers is the distillation, the essence of emotion, rather than the stirring up of passion. Her most remarkable work is in dramatic projections and monologues (unfortunately too long to quote) like "The Changeling," with its fantastic pathos, and that powerful meditation, "Madeleine in Church." But lyrics as swift as "Sea Love," or as ageless as "Song," with its simple finality, or as hymn-like as "I Have Been Through the Gates" are equally sure of their place in English literature. They are, in common with all of Charlotte Mew's work, disturbing in their direct beauty; full of a speech that is noble and profound without ever becoming pompous. Apart from her other qualities (not the least of which is her control of an unusually long and extraordinarily flexible line) Miss Mew's work is a series of triumphs in condensation.

"To a Child in Death," a strangely premonitory poem, "In the Fields," and "Old Shepherd's Prayer" are among those given in manuscript by Charlotte Mew to the editor shortly before her death. These, with thirty other posthumous poems, appeared in a definitive *Collected Poems* (1954).

IN THE FIELDS

Lord, when I look at lovely things which pass,
  Under old trees the shadow of young leaves
Dancing to please the wind along the grass,
  Or the gold stillness of the August sun on the August sheaves;
Can I believe there is a heavenlier world than this?
  And if there is
Will the strange heart of any everlasting thing
  Bring me these dreams that take my breath away?
They come at evening with the home-flying rooks and the scent of hay,
  Over the fields. They come in Spring.

SEA LOVE

Tide be runnin' the great world over:
  'Twas only last June month I mind that we
Was thinkin' the toss and the call in the breast of the lover
  So everlastin' as the sea.

Here's the same little fishes that sputter and swim,
  Wi' the moon's old glim on the gray, wet sand;
An' him no more to me nor me to him
  Than the wind goin' over my hand.

I HAVE BEEN THROUGH THE GATES

His heart, to me, was a place of palaces and pinnacles and shining towers;
I saw it then as we see things in dreams,—I do not remember how long I slept;
I remember the trees, and the high, white walls, and how the sun was always on the towers;
The walls are standing today, and the gates: I have been through the gates, I have groped, I have crept
Back, back. There is dust in the streets, and blood; they are empty; darkness is over them;

His heart is a place with the lights gone out, forsaken by great winds and the
heavenly rain, unclean and unswept,
Like the heart of the holy city, old, blind, beautiful Jerusalem,
Over which Christ wept.

TO A CHILD IN DEATH

You would have scoffed if we had told you yesterday
Love made us feel—or so it was with me—like some great bird
Trying to hold and shelter you in its strong wing;—
A gay little shadowy smile would have tossed us back such a solemn word,
And it was not for that you were listening
When so quietly you slipped away
With half the music of the world unheard.
What shall we do with this strange Summer, meant for you,—
Dear, if we see the Winter through
What shall be done with Spring—?
This, this is the victory of the grave; here is death's sting.
That it is not strong enough, our strongest wing.

But what of His who like a Father pitieth—?
His Son was also, once, a little thing,
The wistfulest child that ever drew breath,
Chased by a sword from Bethlehem and in the busy house at Nazareth
Playing with little rows of nails, watching the carpenter's hammer swing,
Long years before His hands and feet were tied
And by a hammer and the three great nails He died,
Of youth, of Spring,
Of sorrow, of loneliness, of victory the king,
Under the shadow of that wing.

SONG

Love, Love today, my dear,
Love is not always here;
Wise maids know how soon grows sere
The greenest leaf of Spring;
But no man knoweth
Whither it goeth
When the wind bloweth
So frail a thing.

Love, Love, my dear, today,
If the ship's in the bay,
If the bird has come your way
That sings on summer trees;
When his song faileth
And the ship saileth
No voice availeth
To call back these.

THE FARMER'S BRIDE

Three summers since I chose a maid,
Too young maybe—but more's to do
At harvest-time than bide and woo.
  When us was wed she turned afraid
Of love and me and all things human;
Like the shut of a winter's day.
Her smile went out, and 'twasn't a woman—
  More like a little frightened fay.
    One night, in the Fall, she runned away.

"Out 'mong the sheep, her be," they said,
"Should properly have been abed;
But sure enough she wasn't there
Lying awake with her wide brown stare.
So over seven-acre field and up-along across the down
We chased her, flying like a hare
Before our lanterns. To Church-Town
  All in a shiver and a scare
We caught her, fetched her home at last
  And turned the key upon her, fast.

She does the work about the house
As well as most, but like a mouse:
  Happy enough to chat and play
  With birds and rabbits and such as they,
  So long as men-folk keep away.
"Not near, not near!" her eyes beseech
When one of us comes within reach.
  The women say that beasts in stall
  Look round like children at her call.
  I've hardly heard her speak at all.

Shy as a leveret, swift as he,
Straight and slight as a young larch tree,
Sweet as the first wild violets, she
To her wild self. But what to me?

The short days shorten and the oaks are brown,
  The blue smoke rises to the low gray sky,
One leaf in the still air falls slowly down,
  A magpie's spotted feathers lie
On the black earth spread white with rime,
The berries redden up to Christmas-time.
  What's Christmas-time without there be
  Some other in the house than we!

  She sleeps up in the attic there
  Alone, poor maid. 'Tis but a stair
Betwixt us. Oh! my God! the down,
The soft young down of her, the brown,
The brown of her—her eyes, her hair, her hair . . .

BESIDE THE BED

Someone has shut the shining eyes, straightened and folded
  The wandering hands quietly covering the unquiet breast:
So, smoothed and silenced you lie, like a child, not again to be questioned or scolded:
  But, for you, not one of us believes that this is rest.

Not so to close the windows down can cloud and deaden
  The blue beyond: or to screen the wavering flame subdue its breath:
Why, if I lay my cheek to your cheek, your gray lips, like dawn, would quiver and redden,
  Breaking into the old, odd smile at this fraud of death.

Because all night you have not turned to us or spoken
  It is time for you to wake; your dreams were never very deep:
I, for one, have seen the thin bright, twisted threads of them dimmed suddenly and broken.
  This is only a most piteous pretense of sleep!

FROM "MADELEINE IN CHURCH"

How old was Mary out of whom you cast
So many devils? Was she young or perhaps for years
She had sat staring, with dry eyes, at this and that man going past
Till suddenly she saw You on the steps of Simon's house
And stood and looked at You through tears.
I think she must have known by those
The thing, for what it was that had come to her.
For some of us there is a passion, I suppose,
So far from earthly cares and earthly fears
That in its stillness you can hardly stir
Or in its nearness lift your hand,
So great that you have simply got to stand
Looking at it through tears, through tears.
Then straight from these there broke the kiss.
I think You must have known by this
The thing, for what it was that had come to You:
She did not love You like the rest,
It was in her own way, but at the worst, the best,
She gave you something altogether new.
And through it all, from her, no word,
She scarcely saw You, scarcely heard:
Surely You knew when she so touched You with her hair,
Or by the wet cheek lying there,
And while her perfume clung to You from head to feet all through the day
That You can change the things for which we care,
But even You, unless You kill us, not the way.

This then was peace for her, but passion too.
I wonder was it like a kiss that once I knew,

The only one that I would care to take
Into the grave with me, to which if there were afterwards, to wake
Almost as happy as the carven dead
In some dim chancel lying head to head
We slept with it, but face to face, the whole night through—
One breath, one throbbing quietness, as if the thing behind our lips was endless life,
Lost, as I woke, to hear in the strange earthly dawn, his "Are you there?"
And lie still, listening to the wind outside, among the firs.

So Mary chose the dream of Him for what was left to her of night and day.
It is the only truth: it is the dream in us that neither life nor death nor any other thing can take away:
But if she had not touched Him in the doorway of the dream could she have cared so much?
She was a sinner, we are what we are: the spirit afterwards, but first, the touch.

And He has never shared with me my haunted house beneath the trees
Of Eden and Calvary, with its ghosts that have not any eyes for tears,
And the happier guests, who would not see, or if they did, remember these,
Though they lived here a thousand years.
Outside, too gravely looking at me, He seems to stand,
And looking at Him if my forgotten spirit came
Unwillingly back, what could it claim
Of those calm eyes, that quiet speech,
Breaking like a slow tide upon the beach,
The scarred, not quite human hand?—
Unwillingly back to the burden of old imaginings
When it has learned so long not to think, not to be,
Again, again it would speak as it has spoken to me of things
That I shall not see!

AGAIN

One day, not here, you will find a hand
Stretched out to you as you walk down some heavenly street;
You will see a stranger scarred from head to feet;
But when he speaks to you you will not understand,
Nor yet who wounded him nor why his wounds are sweet.
And saying nothing, letting go his hand,
You will leave him in the heavenly street—
So we shall meet!

OLD SHEPHERD'S PRAYER

Up to bed by the window, where I be lyin',
Comes bells and bleats of the flock wi' they two children's clack.
Over, from under the eaves there's the starlings flyin',
And down in yard, fit to burst his chain, yapping out at Sue I do hear young Mac.

Turning around like a falled-over sack
I can see team plowin' in Whithy-bush field and meal carts startin' up road to
    Church-Town;
Saturday arternoon then men goin' back
And the women from market, trapin' home over the down.

Heavenly Master, I wud like to wake to they same green places
Where I'd be know'd for breakin' dogs and follerin' sheep.
And if I may not walk in th' old ways and look on th' old faces
I wud sooner sleep.

THE TREES ARE DOWN

—and he cried with a loud voice:
Hurt not the earth, neither the sea, nor the trees—
(Revelation.)

They are coming down the great plane-trees at the end of the gardens.
For days there has been the grate of the saw, the swish of the branches as they fall,
The crash of trunks, the rustle of trodden leaves,
With the "Whoops" and the "Whoas," the loud common talk, the loud common
    laughs of the men, above it all.

I remember one evening of a long past Spring
Turning in at a gate, getting out of a cart, and finding a large dead rat in the
    mud of the drive.
I remember thinking: alive or dead, a rat was a god-forsaken thing,
But at least, in May, that even a rat should be alive.

The week's work here is as good as done. There is just one bough
  On the roped bole, in the fine gray rain,
    Green and high
    And lonely against the sky.
      (Down now!—)
    And but for that,
    If an old dead rat
Did once, for a moment, unmake the Spring, I might never have thought of him
    again.

It is not for a moment the Spring is unmade today;
These were great trees, it was in them from root to stem:
When the men with the "Whoops" and the "Whoas" have carted the whole of the
    whispering loveliness away
Half the Spring, for me, will have gone with them.

It is going now, and my heart has been struck with the hearts of the planes;
Half my life it has beat with these, in the sun, in the rains,
    In the March wind, the May breeze,
In the great gales that came over to them across the roofs from the great seas.
    There was only a quiet rain when they were dying;
    They must have heard the sparrows flying,
And the small creeping creatures in the earth where they were lying—
    But I, all day, I heard an angel crying:
      "Hurt not the trees."

HERE LIES A PRISONER

Leave him: he's quiet enough: and what matter
Out of his body or in, you can scatter
The frozen breath of his silenced soul, of his outraged soul to the winds that rave:
Quieter now than he used to be, but listening still to the magpie chatter
Over his grave.

NOT FOR THAT CITY

Not for that city of the level sun,
Its golden streets and glittering gates ablaze—
The shadeless, sleepless city of white days,
White nights, or nights and days that are as one—
We weary, when all is said, all thought, all done.
We strain our eyes beyond this dusk to see
What, from the threshold of eternity,
We shall step into. No, I think we shun
The splendor of that everlasting glare,
The clamor of that never-ending song.
And if for anything we greatly long,
It is for some remote and quiet stair
Which winds to silence and a space of sleep
Too sound for waking and for dreams too deep.

ABSENCE

Sometimes I know the way
You walk, up over the bay;
It is a wind from that far sea
That blows the fragrance of your hair to me.

Or in this garden when the breeze
Touches my trees
To stir their dreaming shadows on the grass
I see you pass.

In sheltered beds, the heart of every rose
Serenely sleeps tonight. As shut as those
Your guarded heart; as safe as they from the beat, beat
Of hooves that tread dropped roses in the street.

Turn never again
On these eyes blind with a wild rain
Your eyes; they were stars to me.
There are things stars may not see.

But call, call, and though Christ stands
Still with scarred hands
Over my mouth, I must answer. So,
I will come—He shall let me go!

ON THE ASYLUM ROAD

Theirs is the house whose windows—every pane—
  Are made of darkly stained or clouded glass:
Sometimes you come upon them in the lane,
  The saddest crowd that you will ever pass.

But still we merry town or village folk
  Throw to their scattered stare a kindly grin,
And think no shame to stop and crack a joke
  With the incarnate wages of man's sin.

None but ourselves in our long gallery we meet,
  The moor-hen stepping from her reeds with dainty feet,
    The hare-bell bowing on his stem,
Dance not with us; their pulses beat
  To fainter music; nor do we to them
    Make their life sweet.

The gayest crowd that they will ever pass
  Are we to brother-shadows in the lane:
Our windows, too, are clouded glass
  To them, yes, every pane!

Hilaire Belloc

(Joseph) Hilaire (Pierre) Belloc, who has been described as "a Frenchman, an Englishman, an Oxford man, a country gentleman, a soldier, a satirist, a democrat, a novelist, and a practical journalist," was born near Paris, July 27, 1870. Four of his great-uncles were generals under Napoleon; his father was an eminent French lawyer; his mother, an Englishwoman, was a leader in the feminist movement which finally secured votes for women. After leaving school Belloc served as a driver in the 8th Regiment of French Artillery at Toul. Later he became a naturalized British subject, finished his education at Balliol College, Oxford, and in 1906 entered the House of Commons as Liberal Member for South Salford. He was a member of Parliament from 1906 to 1910.

Besides his other multifarious activities, he was the author (by 1940) of about one hundred volumes. These books range the gamut of literature: from travel-sketches to essays significantly entitled *On Nothing and Kindred Subjects* (1908), *On Everything* (1909), *On Anything* (1910), and simply *On* (1923); from *A Book of Beasts* (1896) to a *History of England,* three volumes of which were published by 1927. He wrote several books of satirical fiction, one of which, *Mr. Clutterbuck's Election* (1908), exposed British underground politics, and which bristled with affable Bellocosity.

Belloc's *Path to Rome* (1902) is a high-spirited travel book; his historical studies and biographies of *Robespierre* and *Marie Antoinette* (1909) are classics of their kind. His nonsense-rhymes (*Cautionary Tales, The Bad Child's Book of Beasts,* and *More Beasts for Worse Children*) are comparable to Edward Lear's. As a serious poet, Belloc is engaging but somewhat less original. Although his humorous and burlesque stanzas are refreshing, Belloc is most himself when he writes of malt liquor and his beloved Sussex. "The South County" and the "Lines to a Don" in defense of his friend Chesterton are the most persuasive of his earnest poems. "Tarantella," with its internal rhymes and shifting rhythms, is a skilful approximation of the dance which gives the poem its name. His poetic as well as spiritual kinship with that other protagonist of a burly Catholicism, G. K. Chesterton, is obvious. He died of severe burns in his Sussex home, July 16, 1953.

Like Chesterton, Belloc is equally at home in a highly personal prose and in brightly ringing rhyme. He likes to grumble, but he does not groan. He is crotchety, often quarrelsome—in company with Chesterton he violently resents progress—but he is fiercely loyal to his loves in art, religion, and history. His faith is evident in the tributes and epigrams in *Collected Poems* (1923) as well as in the varied papers in *The Silence of the Sea and Other Essays* (1940).

WEST SUSSEX DRINKING SONG

They sell good Beer at Haslemere
And under Guildford Hill.
At Little Cowfold as I've been told
A beggar may drink his fill:
There is a good brew in Amberley too,
And by the bridge also;
But the swipes they take in at Washington Inn
Is the very best Beer I know.

Chorus:

With my here it goes, there it goes,
All the fun's before us:
The Tipple's Aboard and the night is young,
The door's ajar and the Barrel is sprung,
I am singing the best song ever was sung,
And it has a rousing chorus.

If I were what I never can be,
The master or the squire:
If you give me the hundred from here to the sea,
Which is more than I desire:
Then all my crops should be barley and hops,
And did my harvest fail
I'd sell every rood of mine acres, I would,
For a bellyful of good Ale.
[*Chorus*]

TARANTELLA

Do you remember an Inn,
Miranda?
Do you remember an Inn?

And the tedding and the spreading
Of the straw for a bedding,
And the fleas that tease in the High Pyrenees,
And the wine that tasted of the tar?
And the cheers and the jeers of the young muleteers
(Under the vine of the dark verandah)?
Do you remember an Inn, Miranda,
Do you remember an Inn?
And the cheers and the jeers of the young muleteers
Who hadn't got a penny,
And who weren't paying any,
And the hammer at the doors and the din?
And the *hip! hop! hap!*
Of the clap
Of the hands to the twirl and the swirl
Of the girl gone chancing,
Glancing,
Dancing,
Backing and advancing,
Snapping of the clapper to the spin
Out and in—
And the *ting, tong, tang* of the guitar!
Do you remember an Inn,
Miranda?
Do you remember an Inn?

Never more;
Miranda,
Never more.
Only the high peaks hoar:
And Aragon a torrent at the door.
No sound
In the walls of the halls where falls
The tread
Of the feet of the dead to the ground,
No sound:
But the boom
Of the far waterfall like doom.

THE SOUTH COUNTRY

When I am living in the Midlands
  That are sodden and unkind,
I light my lamp in the evening:
  My work is left behind;
And the great hills of the South Country
  Come back into my mind.

The great hills of the South Country
  They stand along the sea;

And it's there walking in the high woods
  That I could wish to be,
And the men that were boys when I was a boy
  Walking along with me.

The men that live in North England
  I saw them for a day:
Their hearts are set upon the waste fells,
  Their skies are fast and gray;
From their castle-walls a man may see
  The mountains far away.

The men that live in West England
  They see the Severn strong,
A-rolling on rough water brown
  Light aspen leaves along.
They have the secret of the rocks,
  And the oldest kind of song.

But the men that live in the South Country
  Are the kindest and most wise,
They get their laughter from the loud surf,
  And the faith in their happy eyes
Comes surely from our Sister the Spring
  When over the sea she flies;
The violets suddenly bloom at her feet,
  She blesses us with surprise.

I never get between the pines
  But I smell the Sussex air;
Nor I never come on a belt of sand
  But my home is there.
And along the sky the line of the Downs
  So noble and so bare.

A lost thing could I never find,
  Nor a broken thing mend:
And I fear I shall be all alone
  When I get towards the end.
Who will there be to comfort me
  Or who will be my friend?

I will gather and carefully make my friends
  Of the men of the Sussex Weald;
They watch the stars from silent folds,
  They stiffly plow the field.
By them and the God of the South Country
  My poor soul shall be healed.

If I ever become a rich man,
  Or if ever I grow to be old,
I will build a house with deep thatch
  To shelter me from the cold,

And there shall the Sussex songs be sung
And the story of Sussex told.

I will hold my house in the high wood
Within a walk of the sea,
And the men that were boys when I was a boy
Shall sit and drink with me.

HA'NACKER MILL

Sally is gone that was so kindly,
Sally is gone from Ha'nacker Hill.
And the Briar grows ever since then so blindly
And ever since then the clapper is still,
And the sweeps have fallen from Ha'nacker Mill.

Ha'nacker Hill is in Desolation:
Ruin a-top and a field unplowed,
And Spirits that call on a fallen nation,
Spirits that loved her calling aloud:
Spirits abroad in a windy cloud.

Spirits that call and no one answers;
Ha'nacker's down and England's done.
Wind and Thistle for pipe and dancers
And never a plowman under the Sun.
Never a plowman. Never a one.

FOUR BEASTS

The Big Baboon

The Big Baboon is found upon
The plains of Cariboo;
He goes about with nothing on
(A shocking thing to do.)
But if he dressed respectably
And let his whiskers grow
How like this Big Baboon would be
To Mister So-and-So!

The Yak

As a friend to the children commend me the Yak;
You will find it exactly the thing:
It will carry and fetch, you can ride on its back,
Or lead it about with a string.

The Tartar who dwells on the plains of Thibet
(A desolate region of snow)
Has for centuries made it a nursery pet,
And surely the Tartar should know!

Then tell your papa where the Yak can be got,
And if he is awfully rich
He will buy you the creature—or else he will not.
(I cannot be positive which.)

The Lion

The Lion, the Lion, he dwells in the waste,
He has a big head and a very small waist;
But his shoulders are stark, and his jaws they are grim,
And a good little child will not play with him.

The Tiger

The Tiger, on the other hand, is kittenish and mild,
He makes a pretty playfellow for any little child;
And mothers of large families (who claim to common sense)
Will find a Tiger well repays the trouble and expense.

LINES TO A DON

Remote and ineffectual Don
That dared attack my Chesterton,
With that poor weapon, half-impelled,
Unlearnt, unsteady, hardly held,
Unworthy for a tilt with men—
Your quavering and corroded pen;
Don poor at Bed and worse at Table,
Don pinched, Don starved, Don miserable;
Don stuttering, Don with roving eyes,
Don nervous, Don of crudities;
Don clerical, Don ordinary,
Don self-absorbed and solitary;
Don here-and-there, Don epileptic;
Don puffed and empty, Don dyspeptic;
Don middle-class, Don sycophantic,
Don dull, Don brutish, Don pedantic;
Don hypocritical, Don bad,
Don furtive, Don three-quarters mad;
Don (since a man must make an end),
Don that shall never be my friend.

*

Don different from those regal Dons!
With hearts of gold and lungs of bronze,
Who shout and bang and roar and bawl
The Absolute across the hall,
Or sail in amply bellowing gown
Enormous through the Sacred Town,
Bearing from College to their homes
Deep cargoes of gigantic tomes;
Dons admirable! Dons of Might!
Uprising on my inward sight
Compact of ancient tales, and port
And sleep—and learning of a sort.
Dons English, worthy of the land;
Dons rooted; Dons that understand.
Good Dons perpetual that remain
A landmark, walling in the plain—
The horizon of my memories—
Like large and comfortable trees.

Don very much apart from these,
Thou scapegoat Don, thou Don devoted,
Don to thine own damnation quoted,
Perplexed to find thy trivial name
Reared in my verse to lasting shame.
Don dreadful, rasping Don and wearing
Repulsive Don—Don past all bearing,
Don of the cold and doubtful breath,
Don despicable, Don of death;
Don nasty, skimpy, silent, level;
Don evil; Don that serves the devil.
Don ugly—that makes fifty lines.
There is a Canon which confines
A Rhymed Octosyllabic Curse
If written in Iambic Verse
To fifty lines. I never cut;
I far prefer to end it—but
Believe me I shall soon return.
My fires are banked, but still they burn
To write some more about the Don
That dared attack my Chesterton.

SONNET

We will not whisper, we have found the place
Of silence and the endless halls of sleep.
Of that which breathes alone throughout the deep
The end and the beginning; and the face
Between the level brows of whose blind eyes
Lie plenary contentment, full surcease
Of violence, and the passionless long peace
Wherein we lose our human lullabies.

Look up and tell the immeasurable height
Betwen the vault of the world and your dear head;
That's death, my little sister, and the night
Which was our Mother beckons us to bed,
Where large oblivion in her house is laid
For us tired children, now our games are played.

SIX EPIGRAMS

On Lady Poltagrue, a Public Peril

The Devil, having nothing else to do,
Went off to tempt My Lady Poltagrue.
My Lady, tempted by a private whim,
To his extreme annoyance, tempted him.

On a Dead Hostess

Of this bad world the loveliest and the best
Has smiled and said "Good Night," and gone to rest.

On Hygiene

Of old when folk lay sick and sorely tried,
The doctors gave them physic, and they died.
But here's a happier age: for now we know
Both how to make men sick and keep them so.

On His Books

When I am dead, I hope it may be said:
"His sins were scarlet, but his books were read."

Epitaph on the Politician

Here, richly, with ridiculous display,
The Politician's corpse was laid away.
While all of his acquaintance sneered and slanged,
I wept: for I had longed to see him hanged.

For False Heart

I said to Heart, "How goes it?" Heart replied:
"Right as a Ribstone Pippin!" But it lied.

W. H. Davies

☙ According to his own biography, W(illiam) H(enry) Davies was born in a public-house called Church House at Newport, in the County of Monmouthshire, April 20, 1870, of Welsh parents. He was, until Bernard Shaw "discovered" him, a cattleman, a berry-picker, a panhandler—in short, a vagabond. In a preface to Davies' *The Autobiography of a Super-Tramp* (1906), Shaw describes how the manuscript came into his hands:

"In the year 1905 I received by post a volume of poems by one William H. Davies, whose address was The Farm House, Kennington, S.E. I was surprised to learn that there was still a farmhouse left in Kennington; for I did not then suspect that The Farm House, like the Shepherdess Walks and Nightingale Lane and Whetstone Parks of Bethnal Green and Holborn, is so called nowadays in irony, and is, in fact, a doss-house, or hostelry, where single men can have a night's lodging, for, at most, sixpence. . . . The author, as far as I could guess, had walked into a printer's or stationer's shop; handed in his manuscript; and ordered his book as he might have ordered a pair of boots. It was marked 'price, half a crown.' An accompanying letter asked me very civilly if I required a half-crown book of verses; and if so, would I please send the author the half-crown: if not, would I return the book. This was attractively simple and sensible. I opened the book, and was more puzzled than ever; for before I had read three lines I perceived that the author was a real poet. His work was not in the least strenuous or modern; there was indeed no sign of his ever having read anything otherwise than as a child reads. . . . Here, I saw, was a genuine innocent, writing odds and ends of verse about odds and ends of things; living quite out of the world in which such things are usually done, and knowing no better (or rather no worse) than to get his book made by the appropriate craftsman and hawk it round like any other ware."

It is more than likely that Davies' first notoriety as a tramp-poet who had ridden the rails in the United States and had had his right foot cut off by a train in Canada, obscured his merit as a singer. Even his early *The Soul's Destroyer* (1907) revealed that simplicity which is as *naïf* as it is unexpected.

Between 1906, when Davies published his first book, and 1935, the poet issued twenty-two volumes, five of autobiography, seventeen of verse. Besides these, there were four different *Collected Poems,* appearing in 1916, 1923, 1929, and 1935. The difficulty of strictly evaluating this verse is the greater since the Welsh-English poet depended on repetitions of a few ideas, and rarely trusted his imagination with any but the most tested themes. *Love Poems* (1935) is a typical mixture of Davies' plain-song sagacities and painful banalities. It needs all one's faith in a poet to forgive him such a stanza as:

The sun has his spots, the moon has her shadows,
  The sea has his wrinkles, the land has her warts;
Sweet faith has her doubts and lovers their quarrels,
  And nothing is perfect in all its parts.

But Davies merits our faith, for his best, like the best of the Caroline poets, moves us not only because of the innocence of vision but because of the adequacy of communicating it. If, in his later work, his thought is confused and tempts Davies out of his depth, his ear remains quick and sensitive as the thrush he celebrates:

That speckled thrush, that stands so still,
  Is listening for the worms to stir;
He hears a worm—what marvelous ears
  That he can live by ear alone,
And save his eyes to guard his fears!

Collected Poems (1935) contains some five hundred poems in which good, indifferent, and bad mingle so inextricably that the reader must accept Davies *en masse* or reject him *in toto*. One can no more imagine Davies self-critical than one can imagine him in the labor of creation, his "labor" being about as arduous as a bird's and his song being no less recreational. The figure is not far-fetched, for no poetry has ever been more obviously bird-like. But, it may be asked with a proper regard for ornithology, what bird? Not the lark, for Davies is no Shelley hurling himself and his cry far above the comfortable altitudes of man. Not the nightingale, for his is not Keats' clear passion nor Swinburne's operatic coloratura. It is the English robin that Davies most resembles or the American goldfinch, whose song, limited in range, is cleanly, sharply pitched. Without the variability of greater singers, his notes are only three or four, but the tones are so cool, the delivery so fresh that we would not exchange the crisp spontaneity even for the versatile brilliance of the hermit-thrush. No less than thirty-three poems begin: "When I in praise of babies speak," "When on a summer morn I wake," "When I came forth this morn I saw," "When I am old," "When I complained," "When . . ."

It is easy enough to deride such naïveté, easy enough to confuse Davies with his compatriots who pipe their placid week-end pastorals. But, although a Georgian in point of time, Davies shakes himself free of "Georgianism," that false simplicity sicklied o'er with the pale cast of thoughtlessness. He does not study his subjects from the outside; it is doubtful if he studies them at all; he is always within his bucolics. Thus his sympathies are as genuine as they are ingenuous. His sense of wonder is as direct, as unmistakable as an untutored child's. He looks at clouds, cowslips, lovely ladies, glow-worms, sheep, dogs, dolls, and daisies, as though they had never existed prior to his observation; and he puts them to rhyme as unselfconsciously as though never before had they been employed in verse. Davies rediscovers the common objects which everyone takes for granted; he regards them with an air of surprise and what is more, communicates his astonished wonder.

Observe the poem entitled "A Great Time" and note what details prompt his adjective. Beauty to Davies is not in the elaboration but in the mere being; greatness is, therefore, implicit in the coming together of a rainbow and a cuckoo. These are his auguries of innocence; for him, also, "a dog starv'd at his master's gate Predicts the ruin of the State." His rapport with lamb and bat and game-cock may lead us to imply a kinship with Blake, but he is, at the best, a Blake in words of one syllable. Where Blake projects apocalypses and flaming images, Davies offers a panorama of quiet pictures; we drop from passionate vision into pleasant reverie.

Davies was planning another volume of homely and spontaneous verse when he died at his home in Gloucestershire, September 26, 1940.

THE HOUR OF MAGIC

This is the hour of magic, when the Moon
  With her bright wand has charmed the tallest tree
To stand stone-still with all his million leaves!
  I feel around me things I cannot see;
I hold my breath, as Nature holds her own.
  And do the mice and birds, the horse and cow,
Sleepless in this deep silence, so intense,
  Believe a miracle has happened now,
And wait to hear a sound they'll recognize,
To prove they still have life with earthly ties?

A GREETING

Good morning, Life—and all
Things glad and beautiful.
My pockets nothing hold,
But he that owns the gold,
The Sun, is my great friend—
His spending has no end.

Hail to the morning sky,
Which bright clouds measure high;
Hail to you birds whose throats
Would number leaves by notes;
Hail to you shady bowers,
And you green fields of flowers.

Hail to you women fair,
That make a show so rare
In cloth as white as milk—
Be't calico or silk:
Good morning, Life—and all
Things glad and beautiful.

DAYS TOO SHORT

When primroses are out in Spring,
  And small, blue violets come between;
  When merry birds sing on boughs green,
And rills, as soon as born, must sing;

  When butterflies will make side-leaps,
  As though escaped from Nature's hand
  Ere perfect quite; and bees will stand
Upon their heads in fragrant deeps;

When small clouds are so silvery white
  Each seems a broken rimmèd moon—
  When such things are, this world too soon,
For me, doth wear the veil of Night.

THE MOON

Thy beauty haunts me heart and soul,
  O thou fair Moon, so close and bright;
Thy beauty makes me like the child
  That cries aloud to own thy light:
The little child that lifts each arm
To press thee to her bosom warm.

Though there are birds that sing this night
  With thy white beams across their throats,
Let my deep silence speak for me
  More than for them their sweetest notes:
Who worships thee till music fails
Is greater than thy nightingales.

THE VILLAIN

While joy gave clouds the light of stars,
  That beamed where'er they looked;
And calves and lambs had tottering knees,
  Excited, while they sucked;
While every bird enjoyed his song,
Without one thought of harm or wrong—
I turned my head and saw the wind,
  Not far from where I stood,
Dragging the corn by her golden hair,
  Into a dark and lonely wood.

THE EXAMPLE

Here's an example from
 A Butterfly;
That on a rough, hard rock
 Happy can lie;
Friendless and all alone
On this unsweetened stone.

Now let my bed be hard,
 No care take I;
I'll make my joy like this
 Small Butterfly,
Whose happy heart has power
To make a stone a flower.

THE TWO STARS

Day has her star, as well as Night,
One star is black, the other white.
I saw a white star burn and pant
 And swirl with such a wildness, once—
That I stood still, and almost stared
 Myself into a trance!

The star of Day, both seen and heard,
Is but a little, English bird:
The Lark, whose wings beat time to his
 Wild rapture, sings, high overhead;
When silence comes, we almost fear
 That Earth receives its dead.

THE DOG

The dog was there, outside her door,
 She gave it food and drink,
She gave it shelter from the cold:
 It was the night young Molly robbed
An old fool of his gold.

"Molly," I said, "you'll go to hell—"
 And yet I half believed
That ugly, famished, tottering cur
 Would bark outside the gates of Heaven,
To open them for Her!

JENNY WREN

Her sight is short, she comes quite near;
A foot to me's a mile to her;
And she is known as Jenny Wren,
The smallest bird in England. When
I heard that litle bird at first,
Methought her frame would surely burst
With earnest song. Oft had I seen
Her running under leaves so green,
 Or in the grass when fresh and wet,
 As though her wings she would forget.
And, seeing this, I said to her—
"My pretty runner, you prefer
To be a thing to run unheard
 Through leaves and grass, and not a bird!"
'Twas then she burst, to prove me wrong,
Into a sudden storm of song;
So very loud and earnest, I
Feared she would break her heart and die,
"Nay, nay," I laughed, "be you no thing
To run unheard, sweet scold, but sing!
O I could hear your voice near me,
Above the din in that oak tree,
When almost all the twigs on top
Had starlings chattering without stop."

AMBITION

I had Ambition, by which sin
 The angels fell;
I climbed and, step by step, O Lord,
 Ascended into Hell.

Returning now to peace and quiet,
 And made more wise,
Let my descent and fall, O Lord,
 Be into Paradise.

THE HERMIT

What moves that lonely man is not the boom
 Of waves that break against the cliff so strong;
Nor roar of thunder, when that traveling voice
 Is caught by rocks that carry far along.

'Tis not the groan of oak tree in its prime,
  When lightning strikes its solid heart to dust.
Nor frozen pond when, melted by the sun,
  It suddenly doth break its sparkling crust.

What moves that man is when the blind bat taps
  His window where he sits alone at night;
Or when the small bird sounds like some great beast
  Among the dead, dry leaves so frail and light;

Or when the moths on his night-pillow beat
  Such heavy blows he fears they'll break his bones;
Or when a mouse inside the papered walls,
  Comes like a tiger crunching through the stones.

WHEN YON FULL MOON

When yon full moon's with her white fleet of stars,
  And but one bird makes music in the grove;
When you and I are breathing side by side,
  Where our two bodies make one shadow, love;

Not for her beauty will I praise the moon,
  But that she lights thy purer face and throat;
The only praise I'll give the nightingale
  Is that she draws from thee a richer note.

For, blinded with thy beauty, I am filled,
  Like Saul of Tarsus, with a greater light;
When he had heard that warning voice in Heaven,
  And lost his eyes to find a deeper sight.

Come, let us sit in that deep silence then,
  Launched on love's rapids, with our passions proud,
That makes all music hollow—though the lark
  Raves in his windy heights above a cloud.

SHEEP

When I was once in Baltimore,
  A man came up to me and cried,
"Come, I have eighteen hundred sheep,
  And we will sail on Tuesday's tide.

"If you will sail with me, young man,
  "I'll pay you fifty shillings down;
These eighteen hundred sheep I take
  From Baltimore to Glasgow town."

He paid me fifty shillings down,
  I sailed with eighteen hundred sheep;
We soon had cleared the harbor's mouth,
  We soon were in the salt sea deep.

The first night we were out at sea
  Those sheep were quiet in their mind;
The second night they cried with fear—
  They smelt no pastures in the wind.

They sniffed, poor things, for their green fields,
  They cried so loud I could not sleep;
For fifty thousand shillings down
  I would not sail again with sheep.

THE MIND'S LIBERTY

The mind, with its own eyes and ears,
  May for these others have no care;
No matter where this body is,
  The mind is free to go elsewhere.
My mind can be a sailor, when
  This body's still confined to land;
And turn these mortals into trees,
  That walk in Fleet Street or the Strand.

So, when I'm passing Charing Cross,
  Where porters work both night and day,
I ofttimes hear sweet Malpas Brook,
  That flows thrice fifty miles away.
And when I'm passing near St. Paul's,
  I see, beyond the dome and crowd,
Twm Barlum, that green pap in Gwent,
  With its dark nipple in a cloud.

A GREAT TIME

Sweet Chance, that led my steps abroad,
  Beyond the town, where wild flowers
      grow—
A rainbow and a cuckoo, Lord!
  How rich and great the times are now!
    Know, all ye sheep
    And cows that keep
On staring that I stand so long
  In grass that's wet from heavy rain—
A rainbow and a cuckoo's song
  May never come together again;
    May never come
    This side the tomb.

THE ELEMENTS

No house of stone
  Was built for me;
When the Sun shines—
  I am a bee.

No sooner comes
  The Rain so warm,
I come to light—
  I am a worm.

When the Winds blow,
  I do not strip,
But set my sails—
  I am a ship.

When Lightning comes,
  It plays with me
And I with it—
  I am a tree.

When drowned men rise
  At Thunder's word,
Sings Nightingale—
  I am a bird.

LEAVES

Peace to these little broken leaves,
  That strew our common ground;
That chase their tails, like silly dogs,
  As they go round and round.

For though in winter boughs are bare,
  Let us not once forget
Their summer glory, when these leaves
  Caught the great Sun in their strong net;
And made him, in the lower air,
Tremble—no bigger than a star!

SONGS OF JOY

Sing out, my Soul, thy songs of joy;
  Such as a happy bird will sing
Beneath a Rainbow's lovely arch
  In early spring.

Think not of Death in thy young days;
  Why shouldst thou that grim tyrant fear,
And fear him not when thou art old,
  And he is near.

Strive not for gold, for greedy fools
  Measure themselves by poor men never;
Their standards still being richer men,
  Makes them poor ever.

Train up thy mind to feel content,
  What matters then how low thy store!
What we enjoy, and not possess,
  Makes rich or poor.

Filled with sweet thought, then happy I
  Take not my state from others' eyes;
What's in my mind—not on my flesh
  Or theirs—I prize.

Sing, happy Soul, thy songs of joy;
  Such as a Brook sings in the wood,
That all night had been strengthened by
  Heaven's purer flood.

TO A LADY FRIEND

Since you have turned unkind,
  Then let the truth be known:
We poets give our praise
  To any weed or stone,
Or sulking bird that in
  The cold, sharp wind is dumb;
To this, or that, or you—
  Whatever's first to come.

You came my way the first,
  When the life-force in my blood—
Coming from none knows where—
  Had reached its highest flood;
A time when anything,
  No matter old or new,
Could bring my song to birth—
  Sticks, bones, or rags, or you!

LEISURE

What is this life if, full of care,
We have no time to stand and stare.

No time to stand beneath the boughs
And stare as long as sheep or cows.

No time to see, when woods we pass,
Where squirrels hide their nuts in grass.

No time to see, in broad daylight,
Streams full of stars, like skies at night.

No time to turn at Beauty's glance,
And watch her feet, how they can dance.

No time to wait till her mouth can
Enrich that smile her eyes began.

A poor life this if, full of care,
We have no time to stand and stare.

J. M. Synge

John M. Synge, the most brilliant star of the Celtic revival, was born at Rathfarnham, near Dublin, in 1871, his maternal grandfather, Robert Traill, being famous for a splendid translation of Josephus. As a child in Wicklow, Synge was already fascinated by the strange idioms and rhythmic speech he heard there, a native utterance which was his delight and which was rare material for his greatest work. He did not use this folk-language merely as he heard it; he was an artist first, and, as an artist, he bent and shaped the rough matter, selecting with fastidiousness, so that in his plays every speech is, as he himself declared all good speech should be, "as fully flavored as a nut or apple." Even in *The Tinker's Wedding* (1907), the least important of his plays, Synge's peculiarly inflected sentences vivify every scene; one is arrested by snatches of illuminated prose like:

"That's a sweet tongue you have, Sarah Casey; but if sleep's a grand thing, it's a grand thing to be waking up a day the like of this, when there's a warm sun in it, and a kind of air, and you'll hear the cuckoos singing and crying out on the top of the hill."

For some time, Synge's career was uncertain. He went to Germany half intending to become a professional musician. There he studied the theory of music, perfecting himself meanwhile in Gaelic and Hebrew, winning prizes in both of these languages. He took up Heine with great interest, familiarized himself with the peasant-dramas of Anzengruber, and was planning to translate the ballads of the old German minnesingers into Anglo-Irish dialect. Then he went to Paris.

Yeats found him in France in 1898 and advised him to go to the Aran Islands, to live there as if he were one of the people. "Express a life," said Yeats, "that has never found expression." Synge went. He became part of the life of Aran, living upon salt fish and eggs, talking Irish for the most part, but listening also to that beautiful English which, to quote Yeats again, "has grown up in Irish-speaking districts and takes its vocabulary from the time of Malory and of the translators of the Bible, but its idiom and vivid metaphor from Irish." The result of this close contact can be seen in five dramas which are like nothing produced in Synge's own time; in them the imagination of the artist is linked with the imaginings of the people.

In *Riders to the Sea* (1903), *The Well of the Saints* (1905), and *The Playboy of the Western World* (1907), there is a richness of imagery, a new language startling in its vigor; a wildness and passion that contrast strangely with the suave mysticism and delicate spirituality of the playwright's associates in the Irish Theatre.

Synge's *Poems and Translations* (1910), a volume which was not issued until after his death, contains not only his few hard and earthy verses, but also the famous preface embodying his theory of poetry. The translations, which have been rendered in a highly intensified prose, are as racy as anything in his plays; his versions of Villon and Petrarch are remarkable for their adherence to the original though they radiate the adapter's own personality.

Synge died of an old illness, just as his reputation had broken down borders, at a private hospital in Dublin, March 24, 1909.

PRELUDE

Still south I went and west and south again,
Through Wicklow from the morning till the night,
And, far from cities and the sights of men,
Lived with the sunshine and the moon's delight.

I knew the stars, the flowers, and the birds,
The gray and wintry sides of many glens,
And did but half remember human words,
In converse with the mountains, moors and fens.

BEG-INNISH

Bring Kateen-beug and Maurya Jude
To dance in Beg-Innish,[1]
And when the lads (they're in Dunquin)
Have sold their crabs and fish,
Wave fawny shawls and call them in,
And call the little girls who spin,
And seven weavers from Dunquin,
To dance in Beg-Innish.

[1] The accent is on the last syllable.

I'll play you jigs, and Maurice Kean,
Where nets are laid to dry,
I've silken strings would draw a dance
From girls are lame or shy;
Four strings I've brought from Spain and France
To make your long men skip and prance,
Till stars look out to see the dance
Where nets are laid to dry.

We'll have no priest or peeler in
To dance in Beg-Innish;
But we'll have drink from M'riarty Jim
Rowed round while gannets fish,
A keg with porter to the brim,
That every lad may have his whim,
Till we up sails with M'riarty Jim
And sail from Beg-Innish.

IN KERRY

We heard the thrushes by the shore and sea,
And saw the golden stars' nativity,
Then round we went the lane by Thomas Flynn,
Across the church where bones lie out and in;
And there I asked beneath a lonely cloud
Of strange delight, with one bird singing loud,
What change you'd wrought in graveyard, rock and sea,
To wake this new wild paradise for me. . . .
Yet knew no more than knew those merry sins
Had built this stack of thigh-bones, jaws and shins.

A QUESTION

I asked if I got sick and died, would you
With my black funeral go walking too,
If you'd stand close to hear them talk or pray
While I'm let down in that steep bank of clay.

And, No, you said, for if you saw a crew
Of living idiots pressing round that new
Oak coffin—they alive, I dead beneath
That board—you'd rave and rend them with your teeth.

ON AN ISLAND

You've plucked a curlew, drawn a hen,
Washed the shirts of seven men,
You've stuffed my pillow, stretched the sheet,
And filled the pan to wash your feet,

You've cooped the pullets, wound the clock,
And rinsed the young men's drinking crock;
And now we'll dance to jigs and reels,
Nailed boots chasing girls' naked heels,
Until your father'll start to snore,
And Jude, now you're married, will stretch on the floor.

DREAD

Beside a chapel I'd a room looked down,
Where all the women from the farms and town
On Holy-days and Sundays used to pass
To marriages, and christenings, and to Mass.

Then I sat lonely watching score and score,
Till I turned jealous of the Lord next door. . . .
Now by this window, where there's none can see,
The Lord God's jealous of yourself and me.

IN MAY

In a nook
That opened south,
You and I
Lay mouth to mouth.

A snowy gull
And sooty daw
Came and looked
With many a caw;

"Such," I said,
"Are I and you,
When you've kissed me
Black and blue!"

A TRANSLATION FROM PETRARCH

(*He is Jealous of the Heavens and the Earth*)

What a grudge I am bearing the earth that has its arms about her, and is holding that face away from me, where I was finding peace from great sadness.

What a grudge I am bearing the Heavens that are after taking her, and shutting her in with greediness, the Heavens that do push their bolt against so many.

What a grudge I am bearing the blessed saints that have got her sweet company, that I am always seeking; and what a grudge I am bearing against Death, that is standing in her two eyes, and will not call me with a word.

A TRANSLATION FROM WALTER VON DER VOGELWEIDE

I never set my two eyes on a head was so fine as your head, but I'd no way to be looking down into your heart.

It's for that I was tricked out and out—that was the thanks I got for being so steady in my love.

I tell you, if I could have laid my hands on the whole set of the stars, the moon and the sun along with it, by Christ I'd have given the lot to her. No place have I set eyes on the like of her; she's bad to her friends, and gay and playful with those she'd have a right to hate. I ask you can that behaviour have a good end come to it?

TWO TRANSLATIONS FROM VILLON

I

(*Prayer of the Old Woman, Villon's Mother*)

Mother of God that's Lady of the Heavens, take myself, the poor sinner, the way I'll be along with them that's chosen.

Let you say to your own Son that He'd have a right to forgive my share of sins, when it's the like He's done, many's the day, with big and famous sinners. I'm a poor aged woman, was never at school, and is no scholar with letters, but I've seen pictures in the chapel with Paradise on one side, and harps and pipes in it, and the place on the other side, where sinners do be boiled in torment; the one gave me great joy, the other a great fright and scaring; let me have the good place, Mother of God, and it's in your faith I'll live always.

It's yourself that bore Jesus, that has no end or death, and He the Lord Almighty, that took our weakness and gave Himself to sorrows, a young and gentle man. It's Himself is our Lord surely, and it's in that faith I'll live always.

2

(*An Old Woman's Lamentations*)

The man I had a love for—a great rascal would kick me in the gutter—is dead thirty years and over it, and it is I am left behind, grey and aged. When I do be minding the good days I had, minding what I was one time, and what it is I'm come to, and when I do look on my own self, poor and dry, and pinched together, it wouldn't be much would set me raging in the streets.

Where is the round forehead I had, and the fine hair, and the two eyebrows, and the eyes with a big gay look out of them would bring folly from a great scholar? Where is my straight, shapely nose, and two ears, and my chin with a valley in it, and my lips were red and open?

Where are the pointed shoulders were on me, and the long arms and nice hands to them? Where is my bosom was as white as any, or my straight rounded sides?

It's the way I am this day—my forehead is gone away into furrows, the hair of my head is grey and whitish, my eyebrows are tumbled from me, and my two eyes have died out within my head—those eyes that would be laughing to the men—my nose has a hook on it, my ears are hanging down, and my lips are sharp and skinny.

That's what's left over from the beauty of a right woman—a bag of bones, and legs the like of two shrivelled sausages going beneath it.

It's of the like of that we old hags do be thinking, of the good times are gone away from us, and we crouching on our hunkers by a little fire of twigs, soon kindled and soon spent, we that were the pick of many.

QUEENS

Seven dog-days we let pass
Naming Queens in Glenmacnass,
All the rare and royal names
Wormy sheepskin yet retains:
Etain, Helen, Maeve, and Fand,
Golden Deirdre's tender hand;
Bert, the big-foot, sung by Villon,
Cassandra, Ronsard found in Lyon.
Queens of Sheba, Meath, and Connaught,
Coifed with crown, or gaudy bonnet;
Queens whose finger once did stir men,
Queens were eaten of fleas and vermin,
Queens men drew like Mona Lisa,
Or slew with drugs in Rome and Pisa.
We named Lucrezia Crivelli,
And Titian's lady with amber belly,
Queens acquainted in learned sin,
Jane of Jewry's slender shin:
Queens who cut the bogs of Glanna,
Judith of Scripture, and Gloriana,
Queens who wasted the East by proxy,
Or drove the ass-cart, a tinker's doxy.
Yet these are rotten—I ask their pardon—
And we've the sun on rock and garden;
These are rotten, so you're the Queen
Of all are living, or have been.

TO THE OAKS OF GLENCREE

My arms are round you, and I lean
Against you, while the lark
Sings over us, and golden lights and green
Shadows are on your bark.

There'll come a season when you'll stretch
Black boards to cover me;
Then in Mount Jerome I will lie, poor wretch,
With worms eternally.

Ralph Hodgson

☙ Ralph Hodgson was born in Yorkshire in 1871. Though he has been most reticent regarding the facts of his life, separating the poet from the casual man by the intimation that "the poet should live in his poetry," this much has been gathered: He lived for a while in America; he worked as a pressman in Fleet Street; he was a professional draughtsman, employed on the pictorial staff of an evening paper; he edited *Fry's Magazine;* he has bred bull terriers and, as a leading authority, has judged them; pugilism is one of his private enthusiasms. In 1924, Hodgson accepted an invitation to visit Japan as lecturer in English literature at Sendai University, about two hundred miles from Tokyo. In 1928 the invitation was renewed and again accepted. In 1940 Hodgson came to America and bought a farm near Canton, Ohio.

Although Hodgson has earned a livelihood in many capacities, he kept his writing severely apart; he refused to stain his pen with hack-work of any sort. He has given only his highest moments to his art, believing with Housman that lyric poetry—and Hodgson is one of the purest lyric poets of his age—is not a casual recreation. Writing little and publishing less, Hodgson was unknown until he was thirty-six; his first book, *The Last Blackbird and Other Lines,* appeared in 1907. In 1913, he went into partnership with Lovat Fraser and Holbrook Jackson to publish broadsides and chapbooks; many of his most famous poems appeared in the exquisite booklets issued by their press and illustrated by Fraser, "The Sign of Flying Fame." *Eve, The Bull, The Song of Honor, The Mystery and Other Poems* (1913-1914) found a wide circle of delighted readers in this format. A collected edition (entitled simply *Poems*) was published in 1917 and reissued in America some months later.

Hodgson's verses, full of the love of all natural things, a love that goes out to

"an idle rainbow
No less than laboring-seas,"

establish, like Davies' and De la Mare's, the wonder of essentially simple objects, or they (as in "Time, You Old Gypsy Man") personify abstractions.

One of the most graceful of word-magicians, Ralph Hodgson will retain his freshness as long as there are lovers of fresh and timeless songs. It is difficult to think of any showing of contemporary English poetry that could omit "Eve," "The Bull," "The Song of Honor," and that memorable snatch of music, "Time, You Old Gypsy Man." One succumbs to the charm of "Eve" at the first reading; here is the oldest of all legends told with a surprising simplicity and still more surprising difference. This Eve is neither the conscious sinner nor the symbolic Mother of men; she is, in Hodgson's candid lines, any young English country girl filling her basket, regarding the world and the serpent itself with a frank and childlike wonder.

Outstanding in Hodgson's work is his sympathy with animal life. This wide humanitarianism is implicit in poems like "The Bull," but it is explicit in his outrage against the slaughter of birds for fine feathers ("Stupidity Street") and the irony of "The Bells of Heaven."

Influences are far to seek in this work, although one scents rather than sees a trace of Christina Rossetti's "Goblin Market" in "Eve" and Christopher Smart's "Song to David" in "The Song of Honor."

At eighty-three Hodgson received the Queen's Gold Medal for Poetry, and at eighty-seven published another slim volume, *The Skylark and Other Poems* (1958).

REASON

Reason has moons, but moons not hers
  Lie mirrored on her sea,
Confusing her astronomers,
  But O! delighting me.

EVE

Eve, with her basket, was
Deep in the bells and grass,
Wading in bells and grass
Up to her knees.
Picking a dish of sweet
Berries and plums to eat,
Down in the bells and grass
Under the trees.

Mute as a mouse in a
Corner the cobra lay,
Curled round a bough of the
Cinnamon tall. . . .
Now to get even and
Humble proud heaven and
Now was the moment or
Never at all.

"Eva!" Each syllable
Light as a flower fell,
"Eva!" he whispered the
Wondering maid,
Soft as a bubble sung
Out of a linnet's lung,
Soft and most silverly
"Eva!" he said.

Picture that orchard sprite;
Eve, with her body white,
Supple and smooth to her
Slim finger tips;
Wondering, listening,
Listening, wondering,
Eve with a berry
Half-way to her lips.

Oh, had our simple Eve
Seen through the make-believe!
Had she but known the
Pretender he was!
Out of the boughs he came,
Whispering still her name,
Tumbling in twenty rings
Into the grass.

Here was the strangest pair
In the world anyhere,
Eve in the bells and grass
Kneeling, and he
Telling his story low. . . .
Singing birds saw them go
Down the dark path to
The Blasphemous Tree.

Oh, what a clatter when
Titmouse and Jenny Wren
Saw him successful and
Taking his leave!
How the birds rated him,
How they all hated him!
How they all pitied
Poor motherless Eve!

Picture her crying
Outside in the lane,
Eve, with no dish of sweet
Berries and plums to eat,
Haunting the gate of the
Orchard in vain. . . .
Picture the lewd delight
Under the hill tonight—
"Eva!" the toast goes round,
"Eva!" again.

TIME, YOU OLD GYPSY MAN

Time, you old gypsy man,
  Will you not stay,
Put up your caravan
  Just for one day?

All things I'll give you
Will you be my guest,
Bells for your jennet
Of silver the best,
Goldsmiths shall beat you
A great golden ring,
Peacocks shall bow to you,
Little boys sing,
Oh, and sweet girls will
Festoon you with may.
Time, you old gypsy,
Why hasten away?

Last week in Babylon,
Last night in Rome,
Morning, and in the crush
Under Paul's dome;
Under Paul's dial
You tighten your rein—
Only a moment,
And off once again;

Off to some city
Now blind in the womb,
Off to another
Ere that's in the tomb.

Time, you old gypsy man,
  Will you not stay,
Put up your caravan
  Just for one day?

THE BIRDCATCHER

When flighting time is on, I go
With clap-net and decoy,
A-fowling after goldfinches
And other birds of joy;

I lurk among the thickets of
The Heart where they are bred,
And catch the twittering beauties as
They fly into my Head.

THE MOOR

The world's gone forward to its latest fair
And dropt an old man done with by the way,
To sit alone among the bats and stare
At miles and miles and miles of moorland bare
Lit only with last shreds of dying day.

Not all the world, not all the world's gone by:
Old man, you're like to meet one traveler still,
A journeyman well kenned for courtesy
To all that walk at odds with life and limb;
If this be he now riding up the hill
Maybe he'll stop and take you up with him. . . .

"But thou art Death?" "Of Heavenly Seraphim
None else to seek thee out and bid thee come."
"I only care that thou are come from Him,
Unbody me—I'm tired—and get me home."

AFTER

"How fared you when you mortal were?
  "What did you see on my peopled star?"
"Oh well enough," I answered her,
  "It went for me where mortals are!

"I saw blue flowers and the merlin's flight
  "And the rime on the wintry tree,
"Blue doves I saw and summer light
  "On the wings of the cinnamon bee."

THE SONG OF HONOR

I climbed the hill as light fell short,
And rooks came home in scramble sort,
And filled the trees and flapped and fought
And sang themselves to sleep;
An owl from nowhere with no sound
Swung by and soon was nowhere found,
I heard him calling half-way round,
Holloing loud and deep;
A pair of stars, faint pins of light,
Then many a star, sailed into sight,
And all the stars, the flower of night,
Were round me at a leap;
To tell how still the valleys lay
I heard the watchdog miles away
And bells of distant sheep.
I heard no more of bird or bell,
The mastiff in a slumber fell,
I stared into the sky,
As wondering men have always done
Since beauty and the stars were one,
Though none so hard as I.

It seemed, so still the valleys were,
As if the whole world knelt at prayer,
Save me and me alone;
So pure and wide that silence was
I feared to bend a blade of grass,
And there I stood like stone.

There, sharp and sudden, there I heard—
Ah! some wild lovesick singing bird
Woke singing in the trees?
The nightingale and babble-wren
Were in the English greenwood then,
And you heard one of these?
The babble-wren and nightingale
Sang in the Abyssinian vale
That season of the year!
Yet, true enough, I heard them plain,
I heard them both again, again,
As sharp and sweet and clear
As if the Abyssinian tree
Had thrust a bough across the sea,
Had thrust a bough across to me
With music for my ear!

I heard them both, and, oh! I heard
The song of every singing bird
That sings beneath the sky,
And with the song of lark and wren
The song of mountains, moths and men
And seas and rainbows vie!

I heard the universal choir,
The Sons of Light exalt their Sire
With universal song,
Earth's lowliest and loudest notes,
Her million times ten million throats
Exalt Him loud and long,
And lips and lungs and tongues of Grace
From every part and every place
Within the shining of His face,
The Universal throng.

I heard the hymn of being sound
From every well of honor found
In human sense and soul:
The song of poets when they write
The testament of Beautysprite
Upon a flying scroll,
The song of painters when they take
A burning brush for Beauty's sake
And limn her features whole—

The song of men divinely wise
Who look and see in starry skies
Not stars so much as robins' eyes,
And when these pale away
Hear flocks of shiny pleiades
Among the plums and apple trees
Sing in the summer day—

The song of all both high and low
To some blest vision true,
The song of beggars when they throw
The crust of pity all men owe
To hungry sparrows in the snow,
Old beggars hungry too—
The song of kings of kingdoms when
They rise above their fortune men,
And crown themselves anew—

The song of courage, heart and will
And gladness in a fight,
Of men who face a hopeless hill
With sparkling and delight,
The bells and bells of song that ring
Round banners of a cause or king
From armies bleeding white—

The song of sailors every one
When monstrous tide and tempest run
At ships like bulls at red,
When stately ships are twirled and spun
Like whipping tops and help there's none
And mighty ships ten thousand ton
Go down like lumps of lead—

And song of fighters stern as they
At odds with fortune night and day,
Crammed up in cities grim and gray
As thick as bees in hives,
Hosannas of a lowly throng
Who sing unconscious of their song,
Whose lips are in their lives—

And song of some at holy war
With spells and ghouls more dread by far
Than deadly seas and cities are,
Or hordes of quarreling kings—
The song of fighters great and small
The song of petty fighters all
And high heroic things—

The song of lovers—who knows how
Twitched up from place and time
Upon a sigh, a blush, a vow,
A curve or hue of cheek or brow,
Borne up and off from here and now
Into the void sublime!

And crying loves and passions still
In every key from soft to shrill
And numbers never done,
Dog-loyalties to faith and friend,
And loves like Ruth's of old no end,
And intermissions none—

And burst on burst for beauty and
For numbers not behind,
From men whose love of motherland
Is like a dog's for one dear hand,
Sole, selfless, boundless, blind—
And song of some with hearts beside
For men and sorrows far and wide,
Who watch the world with pity and pride
And warm to all minkind—

And endless joyous music rise
From children at their play,
And endless soaring lullabies
From happy, happy mothers' eyes,
And answering crows and baby cries,
How many who shall say!
And many a song as wondrous well
With pangs and sweets intolerable
From lonely hearths too gray to tell,
God knows how utter gray!
And song from many a house of care
When pain has forced a footing there
And there's a Darkness on the stair
Will not be turned away—

And song—that song whose singers come
With old kind tales of pity from
The Great Compassion's lips,
That make the bells of Heaven to peal
Round pillows frosty with the feel
Of Death's cold finger tips—

The song of men all sorts and kinds,
As many tempers, moods and minds
As leaves are on a tree,
As many faiths and castes and creeds,
As many human bloods and breeds
As in the world may be;

The song of each and all who gaze
On Beauty in her naked blaze,
Or see her dimly in a haze,
Or get her light in fitful rays
And tiniest needles even,
The song of all not wholly dark,
Not wholly sunk in stupor stark
Too deep for groping Heaven—

And alleluias sweet and clear
And wild with beauty men mishear,
From choirs of song as near and dear
To Paradise as they,
The everlasting pipe and flute
Of wind and sea and bird and brute,
And lips deaf men imagine mute
In wood and stone and clay,
The music of a lion strong
That shakes a hill a whole night long,
A hill as loud as he,
The twitter of a mouse among
Melodious greenery,
The ruby and the night-owl's song,
The nightingale's—all three,

The song of life that wells and flows
From every leopard, lark and rose
And everything that gleams or goes
Lack-luster in the sea.

I heard it all, each, every note
Of every lung and tongue and throat,
Aye, every rhythm and rhyme
Of everything that lives and loves
And upward ever upward moves
From lowly to sublime!
Earth's multitudinous Sons of Light,
I heard them lift their lyric might
With each and every chanting sprite
That lit the sky that wondrous night
As far as eye could climb!

I heard it all, I heard the whole
Harmonious hymn of being roll
Up through the chapel of my soul
And at the altar die,
And in the awful quiet then
Myself I heard, Amen, Amen,
Amen I heard me cry!
I heard it all and then although
I caught my flying senses, oh,
A dizzy man was I!
I stood and stared; the sky was lit,
The sky was stars all over it,
I stood, I knew not why,
Without a wish, without a will,
I stood upon that silent hill
And stared into the sky until
My eyes were blind with stars and still
I stared into the sky.

THE LATE, LAST ROOK

The old gilt vane and spire receive
The last beam eastward striking;
The first shy bat to peep at eve
Has found her to his liking.
The western heaven is dull and gray,
The last red glow has followed day.

The late, last rook is housed and will
With cronies lie till morrow;
If there's a rook loquacious still
In dream he hunts a furrow,
And flaps behind a specter team,
Or ghostly scarecrows walk his dream.

THE BULL

See an old unhappy bull,
Sick in soul and body both,
Slouching in the undergrowth
Of the forest beautiful,
Banished from the herd he led,
Bulls and cows a thousand head.

Cranes and gaudy parrots go
Up and down the burning sky;
Tree-top cats purr drowsily
In the dim-day green below;
And troops of monkeys, nutting some,
All disputing, go and come;
And things abominable sit
Picking offal buck or swine,
On the mess and over it
Burnished flies and beetles shine,
And spiders big as bladders lie
Under hemlocks ten foot high;

And a dotted serpent curled
Round and round and round a tree,
Yellowing its greenery,
Keeps a watch on all the world,
All the world and this old bull
In the forest beautiful.

Bravely by his fall he came:
One he led, a bull of blood
Newly come to lustihood,
Fought and put his prince to shame,
Snuffed and pawed the prostrate head
Tameless even while it bled.

There they left him, every one,
Left him there without a lick,
Left him for the birds to pick,
Left him for the carrion,
Vilely from their bosom cast
Wisdom, worth and love at last.
When the lion left his lair
And roared his beauty through the hills,
And the vultures pecked their quills
And flew into the middle air,
Then this prince no more to reign
Came to life and lived again.
He snuffed the herd in far retreat,
He saw the blood upon the ground,
And snuffed the burning airs around

Still with beevish odors sweet,
While the blood ran down his head
And his mouth ran slaver red.
Pity him, this fallen chief,
All his splendor, all his strength
All his beauty's breadth and length
Dwindled down with shame and grief,
Half the bull he was before,
Bones and leather, nothing more.

See him standing dewlap-deep
In the rushes at the lake,
Surly, stupid, half asleep,
Waiting for his heart to break
And the birds to join the flies
Feasting at his bloodshot eyes,—
Standing with his head hung down
In a stupor, dreaming things:
Green savannas, jungles brown,
Battlefields and bellowings,
Bulls undone and lions dead
And vultures flapping overhead.
Dreaming things: of days he spent
With his mother gaunt and lean
In the valley warm and green,
Full of baby wonderment,
Blinking out of silly eyes
At a hundred mysteries;
Dreaming over once again
How he wandered with a throng
Of bulls and cows a thousand strong,
Wandered on from plain to plain,
Up the hill and down the dale,
Always at his mother's tail;
How he lagged behind the herd,
Lagged and tottered, weak of limb,
And she turned and ran to him
Blaring at the loathly bird
Stationed always in the skies,
Waiting for the flesh that dies.

Dreaming maybe of a day,
When her drained and drying paps
Turned him to the sweets and saps,
Richer fountains by the way,
And she left the bull she bore
And he looked to her no more;
And his little frame grew stout,
And his little legs grew strong,
And the way was not so long;
And his little horns came out,
And he played at butting trees
And bowlder-stones and tortoises,
Joined a game of knobby skulls
With the youngsters of his year,
All the other little bulls,
Learning both to bruise and bear,
Learning how to stand a shock
Like a little bull of rock.

Dreaming of a day less dim,
Dreaming of a time less far,
When the faint but certain star
Of destiny burned clear for him,
And a fierce and wild unrest
Broke the quiet of his breast,
And the gristles of his youth
Hardened in his comely pow,
And he came to fighting growth,
Beat his bull and won his cow,
And flew his tail and trampled off
Past the tallest, vain enough.
And curved about in splendor full
And curved again and snuffed the airs
As who should say, Come out who dares!
And all beheld a bull, a Bull,
And knew that here was surely one
That backed for no bull, fearing none.
And the leader of the herd
Looked and saw, and beat the ground,
And shook the forest with his sound,
Bellowed at the loathly bird
Stationed always in the skies,
Waiting for the flesh that dies.

Dreaming, this old bull forlorn,
Surely dreaming of the hour
When he came to sultan power,
And they owned him master-horn,
Chiefest bull of all among
Bulls and cows a thousand strong,
And in all the trampling herd
Not a bull that barred his way,
Not a cow that said him nay,
Not a bull or cow that erred
In the furnace of his look
Dared a second, worse rebuke;
Not in all the forest wide,
Jungle, thicket, pasture, fen,
Not another dared him then,
Dared him and again defied;

Not a sovereign buck or boar
Came a second time for more.
Not a serpent that survived
Once the terrors of his hoof,
Risked a second time reproof,
Came a second time and lived,
Not a serpent in its skin
Came again for discipline;

Not a leopard bright as flame,
Flashing fingerhooks of steel,
That a wooden tree might feel,
Met his fury once and came
For a second reprimand,
Not a leopard in the land,
Not a lion of them all,
Not a lion of the hills,
Hero of a thousand kills,
Dared a second fight and fall,
Dared that ram terrific twice,
Paid a second time the price....

Pity him, this dupe of dream,
Leader of the herd again
Only in his daft old brain,
Once again the bull supreme
And bull enough to bear the part
Only in his tameless heart.

Pity him that he must wake.
Even now the swarm of flies
Blackening his bloodshot eyes
Bursts and blusters round the lake,
Scattered from the feast half-fed,
By great shadows overhead,
And the dreamer turns away
From his visionary herds
And his splendid yesterday,
Turns to meet the loathly birds
Flocking round him from the skies,
Waiting for the flesh that dies.

THE BELLS OF HEAVEN

'Twould ring the bells of Heaven
The wildest peal for years,
If Parson lost his senses
And people came to theirs,
And he and they together
Knelt down with angry prayers
For tamed and shabby tigers
And dancing dogs and bears,
And wretched, blind pit ponies,
And little hunted hares.

THE HAMMERS

Noise of hammers once I heard
Many hammers, busy hammers,
Beating, shaping night and day,
Shaping, beating dust and clay
To a palace; saw it reared;
Saw the hammers laid away.

And I listened, and I heard
Hammers beating, night and day,
In the palace newly reared,
Beating it to dust and clay:
Other hammers, muffled hammers,
Silent hammers of decay.

STUPIDITY STREET

I saw with open eyes
Singing birds sweet
Sold in the shops
For the people to eat,
Sold in the shops of
Stupidity Street.

I saw in a vision
The worm in the wheat,
And in the shops nothing
For people to eat:
Nothing for sale in
Stupidity Street.

THE MYSTERY

He came and took me by the hand
  Up to a red rose tree,
He kept His meaning to Himself
  But gave a rose to me.

I did not pray Him to lay bare
  The mystery to me,
Enough the rose was Heaven to smell,
  And His own face to see.

THE GIPSY GIRL

"Come, try your skill, kind gentlemen,
A penny for three tries!"
Some threw and lost, some threw and won
A ten-a-penny prize.

She was a tawny gipsy girl,
A girl of twenty years,
I liked her for the lumps of gold
That jingled from her ears;

I liked the flaring yellow scarf
Bound loose about her throat,
I liked her showy purple gown
And flashy velvet coat.

A man came up, too loose of tongue,
And said no good to her;
She did not blush as Saxons do,
Or turn upon the cur;

She fawned and whined, "Sweet gentleman
A penny for three tries!"
—But, oh, the den of wild things in
The darkness of her eyes!

GHOUL CARE

Sour fiend, go home and tell the Pit
For once you met your master,—
A man who carried in his soul
Three charms against disaster,
The Devil and disaster.

Away, away, and tell the tale
And start your whelps a-whining,
Say "In the greenwood of his soul
A lizard's eye was shining,
A little eye kept shining."

Away, away, and salve your sores,
And set your hags a-groaning,
Say "In the greenwood of his soul
A drowsy bee was droning,
A dreamy bee was droning."

Prodigious Bat! Go start the walls
Of Hell with horror ringing,
Say "In the greenwood of his soul
There was a goldfinch singing,
A pretty goldfinch singing."

And then come back, come, if you please,
A fiercer ghoul and ghaster,
With all the glooms and smuts of Hell
Behind you, I'm your master!
You know I'm still your master.

Walter De la Mare

Walter (John) De la Mare was born at Charlton, in Kent, in 1873. He was educated at St. Paul's school in London and was employed for eighteen years in the English branch of The Standard Oil Company of America. Later he retired to the village of Taplow near London. He died in Twickenham on June 22, 1956.

His first volume, *Songs of Childhood* (1902), was published under the pseudonym of "Walter Ramal," an anagram of part of his name. The first volume published under his own name was the novel *Henry Brocken* (1904), a form to which he returned with phenomenal success in *Memoirs of a Midget* (1921), a permanent addition to the world's small stock of philosophic fiction.

By 1929 De la Mare was the author of some twenty-three volumes which seem to fall into four categories: (1) The poetry of metaphysical phantasy. (2) The poems to and of children. (3) The mixture of prose and verse achieved in *Ding Dong Bell* (1924). (4) The introspective prose.

Although not the most important, his most popular verse is that which is centered in the child's sphere. As Harold Williams has written, "De la Mare is the singer of a young and romantic world, understanding and perceiving as a child." This poet paints simple scenes of miniature loveliness; he uses fragments of fairy-like delicacy and, with the least consequential matter, achieves a grace remarkable in its appeal. "In a few words, seemingly artless and unsought" (to quote Williams again) "he can express a pathos or a hope as wide as man's life."

De la Mare is an astonishing joiner of words; in *Peacock Pie* (1913) and *Down-a-Down Derry* (1922) he surprises us again and again by transforming what began as a child's nonsense-rhyme into a thrilling snatch of music. A score of times he takes events as casual as the feeding of chickens, or the swallowing of physic, berry-picking, eating, hair-cutting—and turns them into magic. These poems read like lyrics of William Shakespeare rendered by Mother Goose. The trick of revealing the ordinary in whimsical colors, of catching the commonplace off its guard, as in "Martha" and "The Sleeper," is the first of De la Mare's two chief gifts.

This poet's second gift is his sense of the supernatural, of the fantastic otherworld that lies on the edges of our consciousness. Sometimes, as in "At the Keyhole" and "The Mocking Fairy," the sinister turns into the lightly *macabre;* often the unbelievable, as in "Sam" and "Berries," is more homely-natural than the real. *The Listeners* (1912) is a book that, like all the best of De la Mare, is full of half-heard whispers. Moonlight and mystery seem soaked in the lines, and a cool wind from Nowhere blows over them. That most suggestive of modern verses, "The Listeners," and the brief music of "An Epitaph" are two examples among many. In the first of these poems there is an uncanny splendor. What we have here is the effect, the thrill, the overtones, of a ghost story rather than the narrative itself—the less than half-told adventure of some new Childe Roland heroically challenging a heedless universe. Never have silence and black night been reproduced more creepily, nor has the symbolism of man's courage facing the cryptic riddle of life been more memorably expressed.

De la Mare's chief distinction, however, lies not so much in what he says as in how he says it; he can take outworn words like "thridding," "athwart," "amaranthine" and make them live again in a poetry that is of no time and of all time. He writes, it has been said, as much for antiquity as for posterity; he is a poet who is distinctively in the world and yet not wholly of it.

Motley and Other Poems (1918) was followed by *Collected Poems, 1901-1918,* published in 1920, and *The Veil and Other Poems* (1921). *Come Hither* (1923), a collection apparently designed for children, is actually for mature minds. In all of these—even in the anthology—De la Mare betrays a speculation which is kin to a preoccupation: the paradox of mortality and immortality. Henry Newbolt, in *New Paths on Helicon,* recognizes this pervading quality, but perfers to call it "an inveterate habit of questioning. . . . Even the descriptions in which he excels are of the nature of a search: he attempts, like the Pre-Raphaelite painters, to pierce by intensity of vision through to the reality behind the visible word."

The Fleeting and Other Poems (1934) displays less of De la Mare's technical virtuosity than its forerunners; the awareness of the dream world, so characteristic of De la Mare, is a little strained and the spirit seems tired. But the vocabulary is still supple, the harmonies delicate and often exquisite. *Collected Poems* (1941) displays, more effectively than any of De la Mare's separate volumes, the poet's creation of his own limbo, a fitful region between the natural and the supernatural order of things. *Love* (1946) is a nostalgic garland of prose and verse.

It is a curiously remembering quality which characterizes De la Mare. He is spellbound by the magic of dreams—his *Behold, This Dreamer* (1939) is the largest anthology ever published about dreams "so various in their shocking disregard of our tastes and ideals"—fascinated by the borderland between hallucination and true vision, by the conflict between the outer event and the inner eye, by mystery *as* mystery. It is as if De la Mare, unable to remain a child, so feared adult reality that his whole work becomes a defense against it, a retreat into bitter-sweet remembrances of things past, into a domain (half faery fantasy, half nightmare reality) where everything is veiled in an unearthly loveliness and the impossible is more likely to happen than not.

It is in this hushed and recessive mood that De la Mare triumphs. Whether he is examining the extra-rational, or harking back to irresponsible childhood and irresistible romance, or exploring territories of spectral solitude, his poetry is soaked in a pervasive and musical melancholy. *The Burning Glass* (1945), full of ghostly, wistful romanticism, contains some of his saddest and some of his most serene poems. His "motto" may be found in a verse from the ancient "Tom o' Bedlam":

With a host of furious fancies
Whereof I am commander;
With a burning spear,
And a horse of air,
To the wilderness I wander.

It is as a determined "knight of ghosts" that De la Mare journeys into the terra incognita of time and spaciousness. He is one of the poets who have ventured "ten leagues beyond the wide world's end" and have returned to tell us something incredible yet, somehow, believable about that uncharted and illimitable universe.

THE SONG OF FINIS

At the edge of All the Ages
  A Knight sate on his steed,
His armor red and thin with rust,
  His soul from sorrow freed;
And he lifted up his visor
  From a face of skin and bone,
And his horse turned head and whinnied
  As the twain stood there alone.

No bird above that steep of time
  Sang of a livelong quest;
No wind breathed,
    Rest:
"Lone for an end!" cried Knight to steed,
  Loosed an eager rein—
Charged with his challenge into Space:
  And quiet did quiet remain.

THE LISTENERS

"Is there anybody there?" said the Traveler,
  Knocking on the moonlit door;
And his horse in the silence champed the grasses
  Of the forest's ferny floor.
And a bird flew up out of the turret,
  Above the Traveler's head:
And he smote upon the door again a second time;
  "Is there anybody there?" he said.
But no one descended to the Traveler;
  No head from the leaf-fringed sill
Leaned over and looked into his gray eyes,
  Where he stood perplexed and still.
But only a host of phantom listeners
  That dwelt in the lone house then
Stood listening in the quiet of the moonlight
  To that voice from the world of men:
Stood thronging the faint moonbeams on the dark stair
  That goes down to the empty hall,
Hearkening in an air stirred and shaken
  By the lonely Traveler's call.
And he felt in his heart their strangeness,
  Their stillness answering his cry,

While his horse moved, cropping the dark turf,
  'Neath the starred and leafy sky;
For he suddenly smote on the door, even
  Louder, and lifted his head:—
"Tell them I came, and no one answered,
  That I kept my word," he said.
Never the least stir made the listeners,
  Though every word he spake
Fell echoing through the shadowiness of the still house
  From the one man left awake:
Aye, they heard his foot upon the stirrup,
  And the sound of iron on stone,
And how the silence surged softly backward,
  When the plunging hoofs were gone.

AN EPITAPH

Here lies a most beautiful lady,
Light of step and heart was she;
I think she was the most beautiful lady
That ever was in the West Country.

But beauty vanishes; beauty passes;
However rare—rare it be;
And when I crumble, who will remember
This lady of the West Country?

THE TRUANTS

Ere my heart beats too coldly and faintly
  To remember sad things, yet be gay,
I would sing a brief song of the world's little children
  Magic hath stolen away.

The primroses scattered by April,
  The stars of the wide Milky Way,
Cannot outnumber the hosts of the children
  Magic hath stolen away.

The buttercup green of the meadows,
  The snow of the blossoming may,
Lovelier are not than the legions of children
  Magic hath stolen away.

The waves tossing surf in the moonbeam,
  The albatross lone on the spray,
Alone knew the tears wept in vain for the children
  Magic hath stolen away.

In vain: for at hush of the evening,
  When the stars twinkle into the gray,
Seems to echo the far-away calling of children
  Magic hath stolen away.

OLD SUSAN

When Susan's work was done, she'd sit
With one fat guttering candle lit,
And window opened wide to win
The sweet night air to enter in;
There, with a thumb to keep her place
She'd read, with stern and wrinkled face.
Her mild eyes gliding very slow
Across the letters to and fro,
While wagged the guttering candle flame
In the wind that through the window came.
And sometimes in the silence she
Would mumble a sentence audibly,
Or shake her head as if to say,
"You silly souls, to act this way!"
And never a sound from night I'd hear,
Unless some far-off cock crowed clear;
Or her old shuffling thumb should turn
Another page; and rapt and stern,
Through her great glasses bent on me,
She'd glance into reality;
And shake her round old silvery head,
With—"You!—I thought you was in bed!"—
Only to tilt her book again,
And rooted in Romance remain.

MARTHA

"Once . . . once upon a time . . ."
  Over and over again,
Martha would tell us her stories,
  In the hazel glen.

Hers were those clear gray eyes
  You watch, and the story seems
Told by their beautifulness
  Tranquil as dreams.

She'd sit with her two slim hands
  Clasped round her bended knees;
While we on our elbows lolled,
  And stared at ease.

Her voice and her narrow chin,
  Her grave small lovely head,
Seemed half the meaning
  Of the words she said.

"Once . . . once upon a time . . ."
  Like a dream you dream in the night,
Fairies and gnomes stole out
  In the leaf-green light.

And her beauty far away
  Would fade, as her voice ran on,
Till hazel and summer sun
  And all were gone:—

All fordone and forgot;
  And like clouds in the height of the sky,
Our hearts stood still in the hush
  Of an age gone by.

SOMEONE

Someone came knocking
  At my wee, small door;
Someone came knocking,
  I'm sure—sure—sure;
I listened, I opened,
  I looked to left and right,
But nought there was a-stirring
  In the still dark night;
Only the busy beetle
  Tap-tapping in the wall,
Only from the forest
  The screech-owl's call,
Only the cricket whistling
  While the dewdrops fall,
So I know not who came knocking,
  At all, at all, at all.

THE SLEEPER

As Ann came in one summer's day,
  She felt that she must creep,
So silent was the clear cool house,
  It seemed a house of sleep.
And sure, when she pushed open the door,
  Rapt in the stillness there,
Her mother sat with stooping head,
  Asleep upon a chair;
Fast—fast asleep; her two hands laid
  Loose-folded on her knee,
So that her small unconscious face
  Looked half unreal to be:
So calmly lit with sleep's pale light
  Each feature was; so fair
Her forehead—every trouble was
  Smooth'd out beneath her hair.

But though her mind in dream now moved,
  Still seemed her gaze to rest
From out beneath her fast-sealed lids,
  Above her moving breast,
On Ann, as quite, quite still she stood;
  Yet slumber lay so deep
Even her hands upon her lap
  Seemed saturate with sleep.
And as Ann peeped, a cloudlike dread
  Stole over her, and then,
On stealthy, mouselike feet she trod,
  And tiptoed out again.

THE OLD MEN

Old and alone sit we,
Caged, riddle-rid men;
Lost to earth's "Listen!" and "See!"
Thought's "Wherefore?" and "When?"
Only far memories stray
Of a past once lovely, but now
Wasted and faded away,
Like green leaves from the bough.
Vast broods the silence of night;
And the ruinous moon
Lifts on our faces her light,
Whence all dreaming is gone.
We speak not; trembles each head;
In their sockets our eyes are still;
Desire as cold as the dead,
Without wonder or will.
And one, with a lanthorn, draws near,
At clash with the moon in our eyes:
"Where art thou?" he asks: "I am here!"
One by one we arise.
And none lifts a hand to withhold
A friend from the touch of that foe:
Heart cries unto heart, "Thou art old!"
Yet reluctant we go.

AT THE KEYHOLE

"Grill me some bones," said the Cobbler,
  "Some bones, my pretty Sue;
I'm tired of my lonesome with heels and
    soles,
Springsides and uppers too;
A mouse in the wainscot is nibbling;
A wind in the keyhole drones;
And a sheet webbed over my candle,
    Susie,
  Grill me some bones!"

"Grill me some bones," said the Cobbler,
  "I sat at my tic-tac-to;
And a footstep came to my door and stopped
And a hand groped to and fro;
And I peered up over my boot and last;
And my feet went cold as stones:—
I saw an eye at the keyhole, Susie!—
  Grill me some bones!"

THE MOCKING FAIRY

"Won't you look out of your window, Mrs. Gill?"
  Quoth the Fairy, nidding, nodding in the garden;
"*Can't* you look out of your window, Mrs. Gill?"
  Quoth the Fairy, laughing softly in the garden;
But the air was still, the cherry boughs were still,
And the ivy-tod[1] 'neath the empty sill,
And never from her window looked out Mrs. Gill
  On the Fairy shrilly mocking in the garden.

"What have they done with you, your poor Mrs. Gill?"
  Quoth the Fairy brightly glancing in the garden;
"Where have they hidden you, you poor old Mrs. Gill?"
  Quoth the Fairy dancing lightly in the garden;
But night's faint veil now wrapped the hill,
Stark 'neath the stars stood the dead-still Mill,
And out of her cold cottage never answered Mrs. Gill
  The Fairy mimbling mambling in the garden.

[1] Tod = dense foliage.

SAM

When Sam goes back in memory,
It is to where the sea
Breaks on the shingle, emerald-green,
In white foam, endlessly;
He says—with small brown eye on mine—
"I used to keep awake,
And lean from my window in the moon,
Watching those billows break.
And half a million tiny hands,
And eyes, like sparks of frost,
Would dance and come tumbling into the moon,
On every breaker tossed.
And all across from star to star,
I've seen the watery sea,
With not a single ship in sight,
Just ocean there, and me;
And heard my father snore. And once,
As sure as I'm alive,
Out of those wallowing, moon-flecked waves
I saw a mermaid dive;
Head and shoulders above the wave,
Plain as I now see you,
Combing her hair, now back, now front,
Her two eyes peeping through;
Calling me, 'Sam!'—quietlike—'Sam!' . . .
But me . . . I never went,
Making believe I kind of thought
'Twas someone else she meant . . .
Wonderful lovely there she sat,
Singing the night away,
All in the solitudinous sea
Of that there lonely bay.
P'raps," and he'd smooth his hairless mouth,
"P'raps, if 'twere now, my son,
P'raps, if I heard a voice say, 'Sam!'
Morning would find me gone."

BERRIES

There was an old woman
Went blackberry picking
Along the hedges
From Weep to Wicking.
Half a pottle—
No more she had got,
When out steps a Fairy
From her green grot;
And says, "Well, Jill,
Would 'ee pick 'ee mo?"
And Jill, she curtseys,
And looks just so.
"Be off," says the Fairy,
"As quick as you can,
Over the meadows
To the little green lane,
That dips to the hayfields
Of Farmer Grimes:
I've berried those hedges
A score of times;
Bushel on bushel
I'll promise 'ee, Jill,

This side of supper
  If 'ee pick with a will."
She glints very bright,
  And speaks her fair;
Then lo, and behold!
  She had faded in air.

Be sure Old Goodie
  She trots betimes
Over the meadows
  To Farmer Grimes.
And never was queen
  With jewelry rich
As those same hedges
  From twig to ditch;
Like Dutchmen's coffers,
  Fruit, thorn, and flower—
They shone like William
  And Mary's Bower.
And be sure Old Goodie
  Went back to Weep,
So tired with her basket
  She scarce could creep.

When she comes in the dusk
  To her cottage door,
There's Towser wagging
  As never before,
To see his Missus
  So glad to be
Come from her fruit-picking
  Back to he.
As soon as next morning
  Dawn was gray,
The pot on the hob
  Was simmering away;
And all in a stew
  And a hugger-mugger
Towser and Jill
  A-boiling of sugar,
And the dark clear fruit
  That from Faërie came
For syrup and jelly
  And blackberry jam.

Twelve jolly gallipots
  Jill put by;
And one little teeny one,
  One inch high;
And that she's hidden
  A good thumb deep,
Half way over
  From Wicking to Weep.

ALL BUT BLIND

All but blind
  In his chambered hole
Gropes for worms
  The four-clawed Mole.

All but blind
  In the evening sky,
The hooded Bat
  Twirls softly by.

All but blind
  In the burning day
The Barn-Owl blunders
  On her way.

And blind as are
  These three to me,
So, blind to Someone
  I must be.

SUMMER EVENING

The sandy cat by the Farmer's chair
Mews at his knee for dainty fare;
Old Rover in his moss-greened house
Mumbles a bone, and barks at a mouse.
In the dewy fields the cattle lie
Chewing the cud 'neath a fading sky.
Dobbin at manger pulls his hay:
Gone is another summer's day.

THERE BLOOMS NO BUD IN MAY

There blooms no bud in May
Can for its white compare
With snow at break of day,
On fields forlorn and bare.

For shadow it hath rose,
Azure, and amethyst;
And every air that blows
Dies out in beauteous mist.

It hangs the frozen bough
With flowers on which the night
Wheeling her darkness through
Scatters a starry light.

Fearful of its pale glare
In flocks the starlings rise;
Slide through the frosty air,
And perch with plaintive cries.

Only the inky rook,
Hunched cold in ruffled wings,
Its snowy nest forsook,
Caws of unnumbered Springs.

THE SCARECROW

All winter through I bow my head
  Beneath the driving rain;
The North wind powders me with snow
  And blows me black again;
At midnight 'neath a maze of stars
  I flame with glittering rime,
And stand, above the stubble, stiff
  As mail at morning-prime.
But when that child, called Spring, and all
  His host of children, come,
Scattering their buds and dew upon
  These acres of my home,
Some rapture in my rags awakes;
  I lift void eyes and scan
The skies for crows, those ravening foes
  Of my strange master, Man.
I watch him striding lank behind
  His clashing team, and know
Soon will the wheat swish body high
  Where once lay sterile snow;
Soon shall I gaze across a sea
  Of sun-begotten grain,
Which my unflinching watch hath sealed
  For harvest once again.

THE GHOST

"Who knocks?" "I, who was beautiful,
Beyond all dreams to restore,
I, from the roots of the dark thorn am hither,
And knock on the door."

"Who speaks?" "I—once was my speech
Sweet as the bird's on the air.
When echo lurks by the waters to heed;
'Tis I speak thee fair."

"Dark is the hour!" "Aye, and cold."
"Lone is my house." "Ah, but mine?"
"Sight, touch, lips, eyes yearned in vain."
"Long dead these to thine. . . ."

Silence. Still faint on the porch
Brake the flames of the stars.
In gloom groped a hope-wearied hand
Over keys, bolts, and bars.

A face peered. All the grey night
In chaos of vacancy shone;
Nought but vast sorrow was there—
The sweet cheat gone.

SILVER

Slowly, silently, now the moon
Walks the night in her silver shoon;
This way, and that, she peers, and sees
Silver fruit upon silver trees;
One by one the casements catch
Her beams beneath the silvery thatch;
Couched in his kennel, like a log,
With paws of silver sleeps the dog;
From their shadowy cote the white breasts peep
Of doves in a silver-feathered sleep;
A harvest mouse goes scampering by,
With silver claws and a silver eye;
And moveless fish in the water gleam,
By silver reeds in a silver stream.

THE SONG OF SHADOWS

Sweep thy faint strings, Musician,
  With thy long lean hand;
Downward the starry tapers burn,
  Sinks soft the waning sand;
The old hound whimpers couched in sleep
  The embers smolder low;
Across the walls the shadows
  Come, and go.

Sweep softly thy strings, Musician,
  The minutes mount to hours;
Frost on the windless casement weaves
  A labyrinth of flowers;

Ghosts linger in the darkening air,
  Hearken at the open door;
Music hath called them, dreaming,
  Home once more.

NOD

Softly along the road of evening,
  In a twilight dim with rose,
Wrinkled with age, and drenched with dew
  Old Nod, the shepherd, goes.

His drowsy flock streams on before him,
  Their fleeces charged with gold,
To where the sun's last beam leans low
  On Nod the shepherd's fold.

The hedge is quick and green with briar,
  From their sand the conies creep;
And all the birds that fly in heaven
  Flock singing home to sleep.

His lambs outnumber a noon's roses,
  Yet, when night's shadows fall,
His blind old sheep-dog, Slumber-soon,
  Misses not one of all.

His are the quiet steeps of dreamland,
  The waters of no-more-pain;
His ram's bell rings 'neath an arch of stars,
  "Rest, rest, and rest again."

THE LAST CHAPTER

I am living more alone now than I did;
This life tends inward, as the body ages;
And what is left of its strange book to read
Quickens in interest with the last few pages.

Problems abound. Its authorship? A sequel?
Its hero-villain, whose ways so little mend?
The plot? still dark. The style? a shade unequal.
And what of the denouement? And the end?

No, no, have done! Lay the thumbed thing aside;
Forget its horrors, folly, incitement, lies;
In silence and in solitude abide,
And con what yet may bless your inward eyes.

Pace, still, for pace with you, companion goes,
Though now, through dulled and inattentive ear,
No more—as when a child's—your sick heart knows
His infinite energy and beauty near.

His, too, a World, though viewless save in glimpse;
He, too, a book of imagery bears;
And as your halting foot beside him limps,
Mark you whose badge and livery he wears.

PEACE

Night arches England, and the winds are still;
Jasmine and honeysuckle steep the air;
Softly the stars that are all Europe's fill
Her heaven-wide dark with radiancy fair;
That shadowed moon now waxing in the west,
Stirs not a rumor in her tranquil seas;

Mysterious sleep has lulled her heart to rest,
Deep even as theirs beneath her churchyard trees.

Secure, serene; dumb now the nighthawk's threat;
The gun's low thunder drumming o'er the tide;
The anguish pulsing in her stricken side . . .
All is at peace. Ah, never, heart, forget
For this her youngest, best, and bravest died,
These bright dews once were mixed with blood and sweat.

G. K. Chesterton

That brilliant journalist, novelist, essayist, publicist and lyricist, Gilbert Keith Chesterton, was born at Campden Hill, Kensington, May 29, 1874, and began his literary life by reviewing books on art for various magazines. He is best known as a writer of paradoxical essays on anything and everything, such as *Tremendous Trifles* (1909), *Varied Types* (1905), and *All Things Considered* (1910). But he was also a stimulating critic; a keen appraiser, as shown in his volume *Heretics* (1905) and his analytical studies of Robert Browning, Charles Dickens, and George Bernard Shaw; a writer of strange and grotesque romances like *The Napoleon of Notting Hill* (1906), *The Man Who Was Thursday* (1908), which Chesterton himself has sub-titled "A Nightmare," and that mad extravaganza with songs for a sublimated comic-opera, *The Flying Inn* (1914). This being insufficient to exhaust his creative energy, he was also the author of several books of fantastic short stories, ranging from the whimsical narratives in *The Club of Queer Trades* (1905) to that amazing sequence begun with *The Innocence of Father Brown* (1911), which is a series of religious detective stories.

Besides being the creator of all these, Chesterton found time to be a prolific if sometimes too acrobatic newspaperman, a lay preacher in disguise (witness *Orthodoxy* [1908], *What's Wrong with the World* [1910], *The Ball and the Cross* [1909]) and a pamphleteer. He was also—his admirers say, primarily—a poet. His first volume of verse, *The Wild Knight and Other Poems* (1900), a collection of quaintly flavored affirmative verses, was followed by *The Ballad of the White Horse* (1911), one long poem which, in spite of Chesterton's ever-present sermonizing, is possibly the most stirring creation he ever achieved.

Scarcely less notable is the ringing "Lapanto" from his later, more epigrammatic *Poems* (1915) which, anticipating the clanging verses of Vachel Lindsay's "The Congo," is one of the finest of modern chants. The syllables beat, as though on brass; the armies sing; the feet tramp; the drums snarl; the tides of marching crusaders surge through such lines as

Strong gongs groaning as the guns boom far,
Don John of Austria is going to the war;
Stiff flags straining in the night-blasts cold
In the gloom black-purple, in the glint old-gold;
Torchlight crimson on the copper kettle-drums,
Then the tuckets, then the trumpets, then the cannon, and he comes. . . .

Subsequent volumes established the poet's rollicking reactions. Aware that something was wrong with the economic system, he revolted against both capitalism and socialism, and proclaimed a new order which was curiously like an old disorder: a confused and romanticized medievalism. Here Chesterton revealed his irrational rationalism. He wrote like an adult who lived in a world of childish fantasy, a serious thinker who thought only in terms of paradox, a philosopher who defended the obvious with the zeal of a fanatic crucified for heresy. When Chesterton died on June 14, 1936, he was the author of more than one hundred volumes of fiction, poetry, plays, biographies, criticisms, essays, and studies.

A clue to Chesterton's tricky humor is contained in some of his later titles: *The Unthinkable Theory of Professor Green* (1925), *The Moderate Murderer* (1929), *The Poet and the Lunatics* (1929), *A Defence of Nonsense* (1911), and *The Scandal of Father Brown* (1935). His charm is the charm of gusto, a zest which does not stop to appraise its defects. His criticism of Mrs. Browning's style might well be applied to Chesterton himself: "Whenever her verse is bad, it is bad from some violence of comparison, some kind of debauch of cleverness. Her nonsense never arises from weakness, but from a confusion of powers. . . . She cannot leave anything alone, she cannot write a line, without a conceit. She gives the reader the impression that she never declined a fancy."

ECCLESIASTES

There is one sin: to call a green leaf gray,
  Whereat the sun in heaven shuddereth.
There is one blasphemy: for death to pray,
  For God alone knoweth the praise of death.

There is one creed: 'neath no world-terror's wing
  Apples forget to grow on apple-trees.
There is one thing is needful—everything—
  The rest is vanity of vanities.

LEPANTO

White founts falling in the Courts of the sun,
And the Soldan of Byzantium is smiling as they run;
There is laughter like the fountains in that face of all men feared,
It stirs the forest darkness, the darkness of his beard;
It curls the blood-red crescent, the crescent of his lips;
For the inmost sea of all the earth is shaken with his ships.
They have dared the white republics up the capes of Italy,
They have dashed the Adriatic round the Lion of the Sea,
And the Pope has cast his arms abroad for agony and loss,
And called the kings of Christendom for swords about the Cross.
The cold queen of England is looking in the glass;
The shadow of the Valois is yawning at the Mass;
From evening isles fantastical rings faint the Spanish gun,
And the Lord upon the Golden Horn is laughing in the sun.

Dim drums throbbing, in the hills half heard,
Where only on a nameless throne a crownless prince has stirred,

Where, risen from a doubtful seat and half-attainted stall,
The last knight of Europe takes weapons from the wall,
The last and lingering troubadour to whom the bird has sung,
That once went singing southward when all the world was young.
In that enormous silence, tiny and unafraid,
Comes up along a winding road the noise of the Crusade.
Strong gongs groaning as the guns boom far,
Don John of Austria is going to the war;
Stiff flags straining in the night-blasts cold
In the gloom black-purple, in the glint old-gold,
Torchlight crimson on the copper kettle-drums,
Then the tuckets, then the trumpets, then the cannon, and he comes.
Don John laughing in the brave beard curled,
Spurning of his stirrups like the thrones of all the world,
Holding his head up for a flag of all the free.
Love-light of Spain—hurrah!
Death-light of Africa!
Don John of Austria
Is riding to the sea.

Mahound is in his paradise above the evening star,
(Don John of Austria is going to the war.)
He moves a mighty turban on the timeless houri's knees,
His turban that is woven of the sunsets and the seas.
He shakes the peacock gardens as he rises from his ease,
And he strides among the tree-tops and is taller than the trees;
And his voice through all the garden is a thunder sent to bring
Black Azrael and Ariel and Ammon on the wing.
Giants and the Genii,
Multiplex of wing and eye,
Whose strong obedience broke the sky
When Solomon was king.

They rush in red and purple from the red clouds of the morn,
From the temples where the yellow gods shut up their eyes in scorn;
They rise in green robes roaring from the green hells of the sea
Where fallen skies and evil hues and eyeless creatures be,
On them the sea-valves cluster and the gray sea-forests curl,
Splashed with a splendid sickness, the sickness of the pearl;
They swell in sapphire smoke out of the blue cracks of the ground,—
They gather and they wonder and give worship to Mahound.
And he saith, "Break up the mountains where the hermit-folk can hide,
And sift the red and silver sands lest bone of saint abide,
And chase the Giaours flying night and day, not giving rest,
For that which was our trouble comes again out of the west.
We have set the seal of Solomon on all things under sun,
Of knowledge and of sorrow and endurance of things done.
But a noise is in the mountains, in the mountains; and I know
The voice that shook our palaces—four hundred years ago:
It is he that saith not 'Kismet'; it is he that knows not Fate;
It is Richard, it is Raymond, it is Godfrey at the gate!

It is he whose loss is laughter when he counts the wager worth,
Put down your feet upon him, that our peace be on the earth."
For he heard drums groaning and he heard guns jar,
(*Don John of Austria is going to the war.*)
Sudden and still—hurrah!
Bolt from Iberia!
Don John of Austria
Is gone by Alcalar.

St. Michael's on his Mountain in the sea-roads of the north
(*Don John of Austria is girt and going forth.*)
Where the gray seas glitter and the sharp tides shift
And the sea-folk labor and the red sails lift.
He shakes his lance of iron and he claps his wings of stone;
The noise is gone through Normandy; the noise is gone alone;
The North is full of tangled things and texts and aching eyes,
And dead is all the innocence of anger and surprise,
And Christian killeth Christian in a narrow dusty room,
And Christian dreadeth Christ that hath a newer face of doom,
And Christian hateth Mary that God kissed in Galilee,—
But Don John of Austria is riding to the sea.
Don John calling through the blast and the eclipse,
Crying with the trumpet, with the trumpet to his lips,
Trumpet that sayeth *ha!*
Domino Gloria!
Don John of Austria
Is shouting to the ships.

King Philip's in his closet with the Fleece about his neck
(*Don John of Austria is armed upon the deck.*)
The walls are hung with velvet that is black and soft as sin,
And little dwarfs creep out of it and little dwarfs creep in.
He holds a crystal phial that has colors like the moon,
He touches, and it tingles, and he trembles very soon,
And his face is as a fungus of a leprous white and gray
Like plants in the high houses that are shuttered from the day,
And death is in the phial and the end of noble work,
But Don John of Austria has fired upon the Turk.
Don John's hunting, and his hounds have bayed—
Booms away past Italy the rumor of his raid.
Gun upon gun, ha! ha!
Gun upon gun, hurrah!
Don John of Austria
Has loosed the cannonade.

The Pope was in his chapel before day or battle broke,
(*Don John of Austria is hidden in the smoke.*)
The hidden room in man's house where God sits all the year,
The secret window whence the world looks small and very dear.
He sees as in a mirror on the monstrous twilight sea
The crescent of his cruel ships whose name is mystery;

They fling great shadows foe-wards, making Cross and Castle dark,
They veil the plumèd lions on the galleys of St. Mark;
And above the ships are palaces of brown, black-bearded chiefs,
And below the ships are prisons, where with multitudinous griefs,
Christian captives, sick and sunless, all a laboring race repines
Like a race in sunken cities, like a nation in the mines.
They are lost like slaves that swat, and in the skies of morning hung
The stair-ways of the tallest gods when tyranny was young.
They are countless, voiceless, hopeless as those fallen or fleeing on
Before the high Kings' horses in the granite of Babylon.
And many a one grows witless in his quiet room in hell
Where a yellow face looks inward through the lattice of his cell,
And he finds his God forgotten, and he seeks no more a sign—
(*But Don John of Austria has burst the battle-line!*)
Don John pounding from the slaughter-painted poop,
Purpling all the ocean like a bloody pirate's sloop,
Scarlet running over on the silvers and the golds,
Breaking of the hatches up and bursting of the holds,
Thronging of the thousands up that labor under sea
White for bliss and blind for sun and stunned for liberty.
Vivat Hispania!
Domino Gloria!
Don John of Austria
Has set his people free!

Cervantes on his galley sets the sword back in the sheath
(*Don John of Austria rides homeward with a wreath.*)
And he sees across a weary land a straggling road in Spain,
Up which a lean and foolish knight for ever rides in vain,
And he smiles, but not as Sultans smile, and settles back the blade . . .
(*But Don John of Austria rides home from the Crusade.*)

A PRAYER IN DARKNESS

This much, O heaven—if I should brood or rave,
  Pity me not; but let the world be fed,
  Yea, in my madness if I strike me dead,
Heed you the grass that grows upon my grave.

If I dare snarl between this sun and sod,
  Whimper and clamor, give me grace to own,
  In sun and rain and fruit in season shown,
The shining silence of the scorn of God.

Thank God the stars are set beyond my power,
  If I must travail in a night of wrath;
  Thank God my tears will never vex a moth,
Nor any curse of mine cut down a flower.

Men say the sun was darkened: yet I had
  Thought it beat brightly, even on—Calvary:
  And He that hung upon the Torturing Tree
Heard all the crickets singing, and was glad.

ELEGY IN A COUNTRY CHURCHYARD

The men that worked for England
They have their graves at home;
And bees and birds of England
About the cross can roam.

But they that fought for England,
Following a falling star,
Alas, alas, for England
They have their graves afar.

And they that rule in England
In stately conclave met,
Alas, alas, for England
They have no graves as yet.

THE DONKEY

When fishes flew and forests walked
  And figs grew upon thorn,
Some moment when the moon was blood,
  Then surely I was born;

With monstrous head and sickening cry
  And ears like errant wings,
The devil's walking parody
  On all four-footed things.

The tattered outlaw of the earth,
  Of ancient crooked will;
Starve, scourge, deride me: I am dumb,
  I keep my secret still.

Fools! For I also had my hour;
  One far fierce hour and sweet:
There was a shout about my ears,
  And palms before my feet!

THE PRAISE OF DUST

"What of vile dust?" the preacher said.
  Methought the whole world woke,
The dead stone lived beneath my foot,
  And my whole body spoke.

"You, that play tyrant to the dust,
  And stamp its wrinkled face,
This patient star that flings you not
  Far into homeless space,

"Come down out of your dusty shrine
  The living dust to see,
The flowers that at your sermon's end
  Stand blazing silently.

"Rich white and blood-red blossom; stones,
  Lichens like fire encrust;
A gleam of blue, a glare of gold,
  The vision of the dust.

"Pass them all by: till, as you come
  Where, at a city's edge,
Under a tree—I know it well—
  Under a lattice ledge,

"The sunshine falls on one brown head.
  You, too, O cold of clay,
Eater of stones, may haply hear
  The trumpets of that day.

"When God to all his paladins
  By his own splendor swore
To make a fairer face than heaven,
  Of dust and nothing more."

WINE AND WATER

Old Noah he had an ostrich farm and fowls on the largest scale,
He ate his egg with a ladle in an egg-cup big as a pail,
And the soup he took was Elephant Soup, and the fish he took was Whale,
But they all were small to the cellar he took when he set out to sail,
And Noah he often said to his wife when he sat down to dine,
"I don't care where the water goes if it doesn't get into the wine."

The cataract of the cliff of heaven fell blinding off the brink
As if it would wash the stars away as suds go down a sink,
The seven heavens came roaring down for the throats of hell to drink,
And Noah he cocked his eye and said, "It looks like rain, I think,

The water has drowned the Matterhorn as deep as a Mendip mine,
But I don't care where the water goes if it doesn't get into the wine."

But Noah he sinned, and we have sinned; on tipsy feet we trod,
Till a great big, black teetotaler was sent to us for a rod,
And you can't get wine at a P. S. A., or chapel, or Eisteddfod.
For the Curse of Water has come again because of the wrath of God,
And water is on the Bishop's board and the Higher Thinker's shrine,
But I don't care where the water goes if it doesn't get into the wine.

THE SWORD OF SURPRISE

Sunder me from my bones, O sword of God,
Till they stand stark and strange as do the trees;
That I whose heart goes up with the soaring woods
May marvel as much at these.

Sunder me from my blood that in the dark
I hear that red ancestral river run,
Like branching buried floods that find the sea
But never find the sun.

Give me miraculous eyes to see my eyes,
Those rolling mirrors made alive in me,
Terrible crystal more incredible
Than all the things they see.

Sunder me from my soul, that I may see
The sins like streaming wounds, the life's brave beat
Till I shall save myself, as I would save
A stranger in the street.

THE HOUSE OF CHRISTMAS

There fared a mother driven forth
  Out of an inn to roam;
In the place where she was homeless
  All men are at home.
The crazy stable close at hand,
With shaking timber and shifting sand,
Grew a stronger thing to abide and stand
  Than the square stones of Rome.

For men are homesick in their homes,
  And strangers under the sun,
And they lay their heads in a foreign land
  Whenever the day is done.
Here we have battle and blazing eyes,
And chance and honor and high surprise;
But our homes are under miraculous skies
  Where the yule tale was begun.

A child in a foul stable,
  Where the beasts feed and foam;
Only where He was homeless
  Are you and I at home;
We have hands that fashion and heads that know,
But our hearts we lost—how long ago!
In a place no chart nor ship can show
  Under the sky's dome.

This world is wild as an old wives' tale,
  And strange the plain things are,
The earth is enough and the air is enough
  For our wonder and our war;
But our rest is as far as the fire-drake swings,
And our peace is put in impossible things
Where clashed and thundered unthinkable wings
  Round an incredible star.

To an open house in the evening
  Home shall men come,
To an older place than Eden
  And a taller town than Rome;
To the end of the way of the wandering star,
To the things that cannot be and that are,
To the place where God was homeless
  And all men are at home.

Gordon Bottomley

Gordon Bottomley was born at Keighley in 1874 and educated at the Grammar School. He is best known as a dramatist, his volumes—and there are ten of them dating from 1904—having elicited high praise upon publication. When the dramas were collected in two volumes, *King Lear's Wife and Other Plays* (1920) and *Gruach and Britain's Daughter* (1921), the tributes were still more enthusiastic. Referring to *Gruach,* which is a portrait of the Lady Macbeth at the time of her first meeting with the Thane, Lascelles Abercrombie wrote, "It was remarkable enough that Mr. Bottomley should have proved himself capable of worthily inventing a prelude to 'Lear'; it is astonishing that the success should be repeated in a prelude to 'Macbeth.' But it has become clear now that at no time in the history of English poetry since the seventeenth century has the requisite combination of dramatic and poetic talents existed until now in the person of Mr. Bottomley."

His poetry, collected in *Chambers of Imagery, First Series* (1907), *Second Series* (1912), displays the same command of vivid characterization and imaginative vigor one finds in his poetic dramas. What lends technical, if contemporary, interest to both volumes is that they anticipated the effects of the Imagists long before the group created a movement. A comprehensive collection, *Poems of Thirty Years*

(1925), synthesizes the combination of force and delicacy which is Bottomley's own. "The End of the World" (which should be read in connection with Abercrombie's play of the same title) is typical, simple in language, dramatic in effect, and extraordinarily supple in rhythm. Here, as in his dramas, the fine intricacies of phrase are paralleled by a knit power of thought. Bottomley died in 1948.

THE END OF THE WORLD

The snow had fallen many nights and days;
The sky was come upon the earth at last,
Sifting thinly down as endlessly
As though within the system of blind planets
Something had been forgot or overdriven.
The dawn now seemed neglected in the gray,
Where mountains were unbuilt and shadowless trees
Rootlessly paused or hung upon the air.
There was no wind, but now and then a sigh
Crossed that dry falling dust and rifted it
Through crevices of slate and door and casement.
Perhaps the new moon's time was even past.
Outside, the first white twilights were too void
Until a sheep called once, as to a lamb,
And tenderness crept everywhere from it;
But now the flock must have strayed far away.
The lights across the valley must be veiled,
The smoke lost in the grayness or the dusk.
For more than three days now the snow had thatched
That cow-house roof where it had ever melted
With yellow stains from the beasts' breath inside;
But yet a dog howled there, though not quite lately.
Someone passed down the valley swift and singing,
Yes, with locks spreaded like a son of morning;
But if he seemed too tall to be a man
It was that men had been so long unseen,
Or shapes loom larger through a moving snow.
And he was gone and food had not been given him.
When snow slid from an overweighted leaf
Shaking the tree, it might have been a bird
Slipping in sleep or shelter, whirring wings;
Yet never bird fell out, save once a dead one—
And in two days the snow had covered it.
The dog had howled again—or thus it seemed
Until a lean fox passed and cried no more.
All was so safe indoors where life went on
Glad of the close enfolding snow—O glad
To be so safe and secret at its heart,
Watching the strangeness of familiar things.
They knew not what dim hours went on, went by,
For while they slept the clock stopt newly wound
As the cold hardened. Once they watched the road,
Thinking to be remembered. Once they doubted

If they had kept the sequence of the days,
Because they heard not any sound of bells.
A butterfly, that hid until the Spring
Under a ceiling's shadow, dropt, was dead.
The coldness seemed more nigh, the coldness deepened
As a sound deepens into silences;
It was of earth and came not by the air;
The earth was cooling and drew down the sky.
The air was crumbling. There was no more sky.
Rails of a broken bed charred in the grate,
And when he touched the bars he thought the sting
Came from their heat—he could not feel such cold . . .
She said, "O do not sleep,
Heart, heart of mine, keep near me. No, no; sleep.
I will not lift his fallen, quiet eyelids,
Although I know he would awaken then—
He closed them thus but not of his own will.
He can stay with me while I do not lift them."

DAWN

A thrush is tapping a stone
With a snail-shell in its beak;
A small bird hangs from a cherry
Until the stem shall break.
No waking song has begun,
And yet birds chatter and hurry
And throng in the elm's gloom
Because an owl goes home.

EAGER SPRING

Whirl, snow, on the blackbird's chatter;
You will not hinder his song to come.
East wind, sleepless, you cannot scatter
Quince-bud, almond-bud,
Little grape-hyacinth's
Clustering brood.
Nor unfurl the tips of the plum.
No half-born stalk of a lily stops;
There is sap in the storm-torn bush;
And, ruffled by gusts in a snow-blurred copse,
"Pity to wait" sings a thrush.

Love, there are few Springs left for us;
They go, and the count of them as they go
Makes surer the count that is left for us.
More than the East wind, more than the snow,
I would put back these hours that bring
Buds and bees and are lost;
I would hold the night and the frost,
To save for us one more Spring.

EAGLE SONG

(from "Suilven and the Eagle")

O deep, creating Light,
My energy, my desire,
Receive me into you in the height
And force me to aspire.

Alone I am made for you;
I alone rise and gaze
With lidless eyes, alone pursue
Like spiring flame your ways.

I am that part of life
Which will not live but to dare:
When I must rest from joyful strife
I climb the lonely air,

And climbing strive again.
On fellow life I prey,
Know that immaterial pain
Passes and things remain

In me or outside me,
Which deepen in that fierce way
Life, and by wisdom and cruelty
Continue it for a day.

Out of the fathomless height,
Come, show to me here
This thing I have held in my breast all night,
Desired, devoted, dear.
On strange, small limb and brow
Come, Light, now.

Edward Thomas

Philip Edward Thomas was born in 1878 and educated at Lincoln College, Oxford. Before he turned to verse, Thomas had a large following as author of travel books, biographies, and pot-boilers. Hating his hack-work, yet unable to free himself of it, he had so repressed his creative ability that he had grown doubtful concerning his power. It needed something foreign to animate and release what was native in him. When Robert Frost, the New England poet, went abroad in 1912 for two years and became an intimate of Thomas's, the English critic began to write poetry.

Thomas's verse was first published under the pseudonym "Edward Eastaway." It immediately attracted the attention of a small circle, but (as with his American preceptor) editors were slow to recognize the distinction of the poet's rusticities. Loving, like Frost, the *minutiae* of existence, the quaint and casual turns of ordinary life, Thomas caught the magic of the English countryside in its unpoeticized quietude. Many of his poems are full of a slow, sad contemplation of life and a reflection of its brave futility. It is not exactly disillusion; it is rather an absence of illusion. *Poems* (1917), dedicated to Robert Frost, is full of Thomas's fidelity to little things, things as unglorified as the unfreezing of the "rock-like mud," a child's path, a list of quaint-sounding villages, birds' nests uncovered by the autumn wind, dusty nettles. Thomas somehow manages to combine close observation of the familiar with a sense of strangeness.

Thomas was killed at Arras at an observatory outpost on Easter Monday, 1917. *Last Poems,* published posthumously in 1919, has less of Frost's idiom (apparent in such poems as "Fifty Faggots," "Tall Nettles," "Haymaking") and more of Thomas's darkening concern. Faithful to a beauty unseen or scorned by others, his heart "floats through the window to a tree down in the misting, quiet vale":

> Not like a peewit that returns to wail
> For something it has lost, but like a dove
> That slants unswerving to its home and love.
> There I find my rest, and through the dark air
> Flies what yet lives in me. Beauty is there.

This poetry is a constant search for neglected loveliness: the vortex in an eddy of dead leaves, the dying sun in a fading sunflower, the sedgewarbler's pipe, a music of songlessness. Aldous Huxley characterized it as "a nameless emotion of quiet happiness shot through with melancholy."

Collected Poems, a richly inclusive volume with an introduction by Walter De la Mare, was published in 1922. Thomas must be reckoned among the most natural—and most English—of nature poets. As De la Mare wrote, "When Edward Thomas was killed in Flanders, a mirror of England was shattered of so pure a crystal that a clearer and tenderer reflection can be found no otherwhere than in these poems." Behind the accuracy of observation there is an emotional tensity, a vision of things seen "not with but through the eye."

Thomas's biography has been twice told by his wife, Helen Thomas, in *World Without End* and *As It Was.* The best essay, laudatory but analytical, is to be found in Aldous Huxley's *On the Margin* (1923).

THE NEW HOUSE

Now first, as I shut the door,
  I was alone
In the new house; and the wind
  Began to moan.

Old at once was the house,
  And I was old;
My ears were teased with the dread
  Of what was foretold,

Nights of storm, days of mist, without end;
  Sad days when the sun
Shone in vain: old griefs and griefs
  Not yet begun.

All was foretold me; naught
  Could I foresee;
But I learned how the wind would sound
  After these things should be.

TALL NETTLES

Tall nettles cover up, as they have done
These many springs, the rusty harrow, the plow
Long worn out, and the roller made of stone:
Only the elm butt tops the nettles now.

This corner of the farmyard I like most:
As well as any bloom upon a flower
I like the dust on the nettles, never lost
Except to prove the sweetness of a shower.

IF I SHOULD EVER BY CHANCE

If I should ever by chance grow rich
I'll buy Codham, Cockridden, and Childerditch,
Roses, Pyrgo, and Lapwater,
And let them all to my elder daughter.
The rent I shall ask of her will be only
Each year's first violets, white and lonely,
The first primroses and orchises—
She must find them before I do, that is.
But if she finds a blossom on furze
Without rent they shall all for ever be hers,
Codham, Cockridden, and Childerditch,
Roses, Pyrgo, and Lapwater,—
I shall give them all to my elder daughter.

COCK-CROW

Out of the wood of thoughts that grows by night
To be cut down by the sharp ax of light,—
Out of the night, two cocks together crow,
Cleaving the darkness with a silver blow:

And bright before my eyes twin trumpeters stand,
Heralds of splendor, one at either hand,
Each facing each as in a coat of arms:—
The milkers lace their boots up at the farms.

THE PENNY WHISTLE

The new moon hangs like an ivory bugle
  In the naked frosty blue;
And the ghylls of the forest, already blackened
  By Winter, are blackened anew.

The brooks that cut up and increase the forest,
  As if they had never known
The sun, are roaring with black hollow voices
  Betwixt rage and a moan.

But still the caravan-hut by the hollies
  Like a kingfisher gleams between;
Round the mossed old hearths of the charcoal-burners,
  First primroses ask to be seen.

The charcoal-burners are black, but their linen
  Blows white on the line;
And white the letter the girl is reading
  Under that crescent fine:

And her brother who hides apart in a thicket,
  Slowly and surely playing
On a whistle an olden nursery melody,
  Says far more than I am saying.

THE TRUMPET

Rise up, rise up,
And, as the trumpet blowing
Chases the dreams of men,
As the dawn glowing
The stars that left unlit
The land and water,
Rise up and scatter
The dew that covers
The print of last night's lovers—
Scatter it, scatter it!

While you are listening
To the clear horn,
Forget, men, everything
On this earth newborn,
Except that it is lovelier
Than any mysteries.
Open your eyes to the air
That has washed the eyes of stars
Through all the dewy night:
Up with the light,
To the old wars;
Arise, arise!

DIGGING

Today I think
Only with scents,—scents dead leaves yield,
And bracken and wild carrot's seed,
And the square mustard field;

Odors that rise
When the spade wounds the root of a tree,
Rose, currant, raspberry, or goutweed,
Rhubarb or celery;

The smoke's smell, too,
Flowing from where a bonfire burns
The dead, the waste, the dangerous,
And all to sweetness turns.

It is enough
To smell, to crumble the dark earth,
While the robin sings over again
Sad songs of Autumn mirth.

THAW

Over the land freckled with snow half-thawed
The speculating rooks at their nests cawed,
And saw from elm-tops, delicate as flower of grass,
What we below could not see, Winter pass.

GALLOWS

There was a weasel lived in the sun
With all his family,
Till a keeper shot him with his gun
And hung him up on a tree,
Where he swings in the wind and the rain,
In the sun and in the snow,
Without pleasure, without pain
On the dead oak tree bough.

There was a crow who was no sleeper,
But a thief and a murderer
Till a very late hour; and this keeper
Made him one of the things that were,
To hang and flap in the rain and wind,
In the sun and in the snow.
There are no more sins to be sinned
On the dead oak tree bough.

There was a magpie, too,
Had a long tongue and a long tail;
He could both talk and do—
But what did that avail?
He, too, flaps in the wind and rain
Alongside weasel and crow.
Without pleasure, without pain,
On the dead oak tree bough.

And many other beasts
And birds, skin, bone and feather,
Have been taken from their feasts
And hung up there together,
To swing and have endless leisure
In the sun and in the snow,
Without pain, without pleasure,
On the dead oak tree bough.

FIFTY FAGGOTS

There they stand, on their ends, the fifty faggots
That once were underwood of hazel and ash
In Jenny Pink's copse. Now, by the hedge
Close packed they make a thicket fancy alone
Can creep through with the mouse and wren. Next Spring
A blackbird or a robin will nest there,
Accustomed to them, thinking they will remain
Whatever is forever to a bird:
This Spring it is too late; the swift has come.
'Twas a hot day for carrying them up:
Better they will never warm me, though they must
Light several Winters' fires. Before they are done
The war will have ended, many other things
Have ended, maybe, that I can no more
Foresee or more control than robin and wren.

HAYMAKING

After night's thunder far away had rolled,
The fiery day had a sweet kernel of cold,
And in the perfect blue the clouds uncurled,
Like the first gods before they made the world
And misery, swimming the stormless sea
In beauty and in divine gayety.
The smooth white empty road was lightly strewn
With leaves—the holly's Autumn falls in June—
And fir cones standing stiff up in the heat.
The mill-foot water tumbled white and lit
With tossing crystals, happier than any crowd
Of children pouring out of school aloud.
And in the little thickets where a sleeper
For ever might lie lost, the nettle-creeper
And garden warbler sang unceasingly;
While over them shrill shrieked in his fierce glee
The swift with wings and tail as sharp and narrow
As if the bow had flown off with the arrow.
Only the scent of woodbine and hay new-mown
Traveled the road. In the field sloping down,
Park-like to where its willows showed the brook,
Haymakers rested. The tosser lay forsook
Out in the sun; and the long wagon stood
Without its team, it seemed it never would
Move from the shadow of that single yew.
The team, as still, until their task was due,
Beside the laborers enjoyed the shade
That three squat oaks mid-field together made
Upon a circle of grass and weed uncut,
And on the hollow, once a chalk-pit, but
Now brimmed with nut and elder-flower so clean.
The men leaned on their rakes, about to begin,
But still. And all were silent. All was old,
This morning time, with a great age untold,
Older than Clare and Cobbett, Morland and Crome
Than, at the field's far edge, the farmer's home,
A white house crouched at the foot of a great tree.
Under the heavens that know not what years be
The men, the beasts, the trees, the implements
Uttered even what they will in times far hence—
All of us gone out of the reach of change—
Immortal in a picture of an old grange.

OUT IN THE DARK

Out in the dark over the snow
The fallow fawns invisible go
With the fallow doe;

And the winds blow
Fast as the stars are slow.

Stealthily the dark haunts round
And, when a lamp goes, without sound
At a swifter bound
Than the swiftest hound,
Arrives, and all else is drowned;

And I and star and wind and deer,
Are in the dark together,—near,
Yet far,—and fear
Drums on my ear
In that sage company drear.

How weak and little is the light,
All the universe of sight,
Love and delight,
Before the might,
If you love it not, of night.

John Masefield

John Masefield was born June 1, 1878, in Ledbury, Herefordshire. His father, a lawyer, died while Masefield was still a child; at fourteen the boy was indentured to a merchant ship and became a wanderer for several years. At one time (in 1895, to be exact) he worked for a few months as a sort of third assistant barkeeper in Luke O'Connor's saloon, the Columbia Hotel, on the corner of Sixth and Greenwich Avenues, New York City. Later he worked in a carpet factory in Yonkers, and earned his living at various odd jobs. In 1897, he returned to England where he made friends with Synge in London, living, for a time, in Bloomsbury. Reading Chaucer's *The Parlement of Foules* in 1896 Masefield determined to be a poet. After the death of Robert Bridges in 1930 he was appointed Poet Laureate.

The results of his wanderings showed in his early works, *Salt-Water Ballads* (1902), *Ballads* (1903), frank, often crude, but rightly measured poems of sailors written in their own speech, and *A Mainsail Haul* (1905), a collection of short nautical stories. In these books Masefield occasionally overemphasized passion and brutality, yet, underneath the violence, he captured a highly colored realism.

It was not until he published *The Everlasting Mercy* (1911) that Masefield became famous. Followed quickly by long narrative poems, *The Widow in the Bye Street* (1912), *Dauber* (1912), and *The Daffodil Fields* (1913), these works vibrate with a blend of physical exulting and spiritual exaltation. It is typical of Masefield that the very rudeness is lifted to a plane of religious intensity. The religious undercurrent did not save the volumes from causing a scandal. The combination of profanity and ecstasy, sordid melodrama and spiritual elevation created a sensation;

they overwhelmed the critics as well as ordinary readers. Masefield's sympathy with workers and "common characters" often brought him to the verge of sentimentality —his dramatis personae usually "got religion" and reformed—but Masefield was one of the first to make the Georgian movement seem a movement of innovation, even of protest. Moreover he succeeded (if only temporarily) in bringing narrative verse back to favor. The popularity of his rude and sometimes shocking story-poems was appreciated because of their gusto; they achieved a blend of personal strength and irresponsible vigor. But the World War, which outdid Masefield in intensity, did not stimulate a literature of violence. On the contrary, force lost its power and gave way to a literature of exhaustion.

The exhaustion is apparent in the work which Masefield wrote after the first World War, in which he served with the Red Cross in France and on the Gallipoli Peninsula. After the Armistice, most of the Georgian poets turned from bugle calls to pastorals and exchanged the field of battle for fields of buttercups and daisies. Masefield joined the movement of escape. Logically enough, he wrote classical sonnets, religious verse, and new versions of old myths such as *King Cole* (1921) and *A Tale of Troy* (1932). But in sacrificing the early vigor of epithet and plot he also sacrificed individuality. Critical opinion changed. It began to be suspected that the rebellious Georgian was little more than a roughened Victorian.

Masefield attempted to recapture his high spirits in *Reynard the Fox* (1919) and *Right Royal* (1920). The vigor is there, but a sense of strain pervades the too packed, too rapidly propelled stanzas; influenced by Chaucer, they are marred by excess. "There is," says Middleton Murry, speaking of *Reynard the Fox,* "in Chaucer, a naturalness, a lack of emphasis, a confidence that the object will not fail to make its own impression, beside which Mr. Masefield's demonstration and underlining seem almost *malsain* . . . tainted by the desperate *bergerie* of the Georgian era. Chaucer is at home with his speech and at home with his world; by his side Mr. Masefield seems nervous and uncertain about both." But though the Chaucerian influence is obvious, it is not wholly a handicap to Masefield; it stimulates him to overcome a nostalgia, roused (if overanimated) by the English countryside. It is said that *Reynard the Fox* did more than any other single poem to earn him the Laureateship.

After 1930 Masefield grew less and less self-critical, and his work suffered from prolixity. *Midsummer Night* (1928) still has the narrative sweep of the earlier poems, but *Minnie Maylow's Story and Other Tales and Scenes* (1931) is a sort of British Night's Entertainment neither interesting in idea nor technique. The thirteen "tales and scenes" ranging from the Chaucerian "Adamas and Eva" to the outworn theme of "Tristan and Isolt," will not bear close scrutiny. *A Tale of Troy* (1932) shows Masefield, for no discernible reason, retelling the drama of the Trojan War. *End and Beginning* (1933) is a poem-drama of the last days and execution of Mary, Queen of Scots, the title being from her prophetic remark when notified of her death sentence, "In the end is my beginning." A generous *Collected Poems* was issued in 1923 and enlarged in 1935. The former is the more commendable since it contains the best of his poetry from youth to maturity and does not include the later tedious work. Besides his poetry, Masefield wrote more than a dozen plays (including translations from Racine); a standard work on *Shakespeare* (1911); about twelve volumes of essays and studies, which range from *Sea Life in*

Nelson's Time (1905) through *The Battle of the Somme* (1919) to *Chaucer* (1931); several books for boys, and "adventure" novels which capture the early robustiousness.

In his early sixties Masefield turned to reminiscences and retelling of old tales; an account of his working days in America was entitled *In the Mill* (1941). A later and more comprehensive autobiography, *So Long to Learn* (1952), tries, said Masefield, "to set down what matters have been helpful to me in the finding, framing, and telling of stories in prose and verse, according to the tale and power within me."

A CONSECRATION

Not of the princes and prelates with periwigged charioteers
Riding triumphantly laureled to lap the fat of the years,—
Rather the scorned—the rejected—the men hemmed in with the spears;

The men of the tattered battalion which fights till it dies,
Dazed with the dust of the battle, the din and the cries.
The men with the broken heads and the blood running into their eyes.

Not the be-medaled Commander, beloved of the throne,
Riding cock-horse to parade when the bugles are blown,
But the lads who carried the koppie and cannot be known.

Not the ruler for me, but the ranker, the tramp of the road,
The slave with the sack on his shoulders pricked on with the goad,
The man with too weighty a burden, too weary a load.

The sailor, the stoker of steamers, the man with the clout,
The chantyman bent at the halliards putting a tune to the shout,
The drowsy man at the wheel and the tired look-out.

Others may sing of the wine and the wealth and the mirth,
The portly presence of potentates goodly in girth;—
Mine be the dirt and the dross, the dust and scum of the earth!

Theirs be the music, the color, the glory, the gold;
Mine be a handful of ashes, a mouthful of mold.
Of the maimed, of the halt and the blind in the rain and the cold—
Of these shall my songs be fashioned, my tales be told.

AMEN.

SEA-FEVER

I must down to the seas again, to the lonely sea and the sky,
And all I ask is a tall ship and a star to steer her by,
And the wheel's kick and the wind's song and the white sail's shaking
And a gray mist on the sea's face and a gray dawn breaking.

I must down to the seas again, for the call of the running tide
Is a wild call and a clear call that may not be denied;
And all I ask is a windy day with the white clouds flying,
And the flung spray and the blown spume, and the sea-gulls crying.

I must down to the seas again to the vagrant gypsy life.
To the gull's way and the whale's way where the wind's like a whetted knife;
And all I ask is a merry yarn from a laughing fellow-rover,
And quiet sleep and a sweet dream when the long trick's over.

A WANDERER'S SONG

A wind's in the heart of me, a fire's in my heels,
I am tired of brick and stone and rumbling wagon-wheels;
I hunger for the sea's edge, the limits of the land,
Where the wild old Atlantic is shouting on the sand.

Oh I'll be going, leaving the noises of the street,
To where a lifting foresail-foot is yanking at the sheet;
To a windy, tossing anchorage where yawls and ketches ride,
Oh I'll be going, going, until I meet the tide.

And first I'll hear the sea-wind, the mewing of the gulls,
The clucking, sucking of the sea about the rusty hulls,
The songs at the capstan in the hooker warping out,
And then the heart of me'll know I'm there or thereabout.

Oh I am sick of brick and stone, the heart of me is sick,
For windy green, unquiet sea, the realm of Moby Dick;
And I'll be going, going, from the roaring of the wheels,
For a wind's in the heart of me, a fire's in my heels.

SORROW OF MYDATH

Weary the cry of the wind is, weary the sea,
Weary the heart and the mind and the body of me.
Would I were out of it, done with it, would I could be
    A white gull crying along the desolate sands!

Outcast, derelict soul in a body accurst,
Standing drenched with the spindrift, standing athirst,
For the cool green waves of death to arise and burst
    In a tide of quiet for me on the desolate sands!

Would that the waves and the long white hair of the spray
Would gather in splendid terror and blot me away
To the sunless place of the wrecks where the waters sway
    Gently, dreamily, quietly over desolate sands!

TOMORROW

Oh yesterday the cutting edge drank thirstily and deep,
The upland outlaws ringed us in and herded us as sheep,
They drove us from the stricken field and bayed us into keep;
        But tomorrow,
    By the living God, we'll try the game again!

Oh yesterday our little troop was ridden through and through,
Our swaying, tattered pennons fled, a broken, beaten few,
And all a summer afternoon they hunted us and slew;
        But tomorrow,
    By the living God, we'll try the game again!

And here upon the turret-top the bale-fire glowers red,
The wake-lights burn and drip about our hacked, disfigured dead,
And many a broken heart is here and many a broken head;
        But tomorrow,
    By the living God, we'll try the game again!

THE WEST WIND

It's a warm wind, the west wind, full of birds' cries;
I never hear the west wind but tears are in my eyes.
For it comes from the west lands, the old brown hills,
And April's in the west wind, and daffodils.

It's a fine land, the west land, for hearts as tired as mine,
Apple orchards blossom there, and the air's like wine.
There is cool green grass there, where men may lie at rest,
And the thrushes are in song there, fluting from the nest.

"Will ye not come home, brother? ye have been long away,
It's April, and blossom time, and white is the may;
And bright is the sun, brother, and warm is the rain,—
Will ye not come home, brother, home to us again?

"The young corn is green, brother, where the rabbits run,
It's blue sky, and white clouds, and warm rain and sun.
It's song to a man's soul, brother, fire to a man's brain,
To hear the wild bees and see the merry spring again.

"Larks are singing in the west, brother, above the green wheat,
So will ye not come home, brother, and rest your tired feet?
I've a balm for bruised hearts, brother, sleep for aching eyes,"
Says the warm wind, the west wind, full of birds' cries.

It's the white road westwards is the road I must tread
To the green grass, the cool grass, and rest for heart and head,
To the violets and the warm hearts and the thrushes' song,
In the fine land, the west land, the land where I belong.

ROUNDING THE HORN

(from "Dauber")

Then came the cry of "Call all hands on deck!"
The Dauber knew its meaning; it was come:
Cape Horn, that tramples beauty into wreck,
And crumples steel and smites the strong man dumb.

Down clattered flying kites and staysails; some
Sang out in quick, high calls: the fair-leads skirled,
And from the south-west came the end of the world . . .

"Lay out!" the Bosun yelled. The Dauber laid
Out on the yard, gripping the yard, and feeling
Sick at the mighty space of air displayed
Below his feet, where mewing birds were wheeling.
A giddy fear was on him; he was reeling.
He bit his lip half through, clutching the jack.
A cold sweat glued the shirt upon his back.

The yard was shaking, for a brace was loose.
He felt that he would fall; he clutched, he bent,
Clammy with natural terror to the shoes
While idiotic promptings came and went.
Snow fluttered on a wind-flaw and was spent;
He saw the water darken. Someone yelled,
"Frap it; don't stay to furl! Hold on!" He held.

Darkness came down—half darkness—in a whirl;
The sky went out, the waters disappeared.
He felt a shocking pressure of blowing hurl
The ship upon her side. The darkness speared
At her with wind; she staggered, she careered;
Then down she lay. The Dauber felt her go,
He saw her yard tilt downwards. Then the snow

Whirled all about—dense, multitudinous, cold—
Mixed with the wind's one devilish thrust and shriek,
Which whiffled out men's tears, defeated, took hold,
Flattening the flying drift against the cheek.
The yards buckled and bent, man could not speak.
The ship lay on her broadside; the wind's sound
Had devilish malice at having got her downed.

How long the gale had blown he could not tell,
Only the world had changed, his life had died.
A moment now was everlasting hell.
Nature an onslaught from the weather side,
A withering rush of death, a frost that cried,
Shrieked, till he withered at the heart; a hail
Plastered his oilskins with an icy mail. . . .

"Up!" yelled the Bosun; "up and clear the wreck!"
The Dauber followed where he led; below
He caught one giddy glimpsing of the deck
Filled with white water, as though heaped with snow.
He saw the streamers of the rigging blow
Straight out like pennons from the splintered mast,
Then, all sense dimmed, all was an icy blast.

Roaring from nether hell and filled with ice,
Roaring and crashing on the jerking stage,
An utter bridle given to utter vice,
Limitless power mad with endless rage
Withering the soul; a minute seemed an age.
He clutched and hacked at ropes, at rags of sail,
Thinking that comfort was a fairy tale,

Told long ago—long, long ago—long since
Heard of in other lives—imagined, dreamed—
There where the basest beggar was a prince.
To him in torment where the tempest screamed,
Comfort and warmth and ease no longer seemed
Things that a man could know; soul, body, brain,
Knew nothing but the wind, the cold, the pain.

C. L. M.

In the dark womb where I began
My mother's life made me a man.
Through all the months of human birth
Her beauty fed my common earth.
I cannot see, nor breathe, nor stir,
But through the death of some of her.

Down in the darkness of the grave
She cannot see the life she gave.
For all her love, she cannot tell
Whether I use it ill or well,
Nor knock at dusty doors to find
Her beauty dusty in the mind.

If the grave's gates could be undone,
She would not know her little son,
I am so grown. If we should meet,
She would pass by me in the street,
Unless my soul's face let her see
My sense of what she did for me.

What have I done to keep in mind
My debt to her and womankind?
What woman's happier life repays
Her for those months of wretched days?
For all my mouthless body leech'd
Ere Birth's releasing hell was reach'd?

What have I done, or tried, or said
In thanks to that dear woman dead?
Men triumph over women still,
Men trample women's rights at will,
And man's lust roves the world untamed.

O grave, keep shut lest I be shamed.

CARGOES

Quinquireme of Nineveh from distant Ophir
Rowing home to haven in sunny Palestine,
With a cargo of ivory,
And apes and peacocks,
Sandalwood, cedarwood, and sweet white wine.

Stately Spanish galleon coming from the Isthmus,
Dipping through the Tropics by the palm-green shores,
With a cargo of diamonds,
Emeralds, amethysts,
Topazes, and cinnamon, and gold moidores.

Dirty British coaster with a salt-caked smoke-stack
Butting through the Channel in the mad March days,
With a cargo of Tyne coal,
Road-rail, pig-lead,
Firewood, iron-ware, and cheap tin trays.

CAPTAIN STRATTON'S FANCY

Oh some are fond of red wine, and some are fond of white,
And some are all for dancing in the pale moonlight;
But rum alone's the tipple and the heart's delight
Of the old bold mate of Henry Morgan.

Oh some are fond of Spanish wine, and some are fond of French,
And some'll swallow tay and stuff fit only for a wench;
But I'm for right Jamaica till I roll beneath the bench,
Says the old bold mate of Henry Morgan.

Oh some are for the lily, and some are for the rose,
But I am for the sugar-cane that in Jamaica grows;
For it's that makes the bonny drink to warm my copper nose,
Says the old bold mate of Henry Morgan.

Oh some are fond of fiddles and a song well sung,
And some are all for music for to lilt upon the tongue;
But mouths were made for tankards, and for sucking at the bung,
Says the old bold mate of Henry Morgan.

And some are fond of dancing, and some are fond of dice,
And some are all for red lips and pretty lasses' eyes;
But a right Jamaica puncheon is a finer prize
To the old bold mate of Henry Morgan.

Oh some that's good and godly ones they hold that it's a sin
To troll the jolly bowl around and let the dollars spin;
But I'm for toleration and for drinking at an inn,
Says the old bold mate of Henry Morgan.

Oh some are sad and wretched folk that go in silken suits,
And there's a mort of wicked rogues that live in good reputes;
So I'm for drinking honestly, and dying in my boots,
Like an old bold mate of Henry Morgan.

NIGHT ON THE DOWNLAND

Night is on the downland, on the lonely moorland,
On the hills where the wind goes over sheep-bitten turf,
Where the bent grass beats upon the unplowed poorland
And the pine-woods roar like the surf.

Here the Roman lived on the wind-barren lonely,
Dark now and haunted by the moorland fowl;
None comes here now but the peewit only,
And moth-like death in the owl.

Beauty was here on this beetle-droning downland;
The thought of a Caesar in the purple came
From the palace by the Tiber in the Roman townland
To this wind-swept hill with no name.

Lonely Beauty came here and was here in sadness,
Brave as a thought on the frontier of the mind,
In the camp of the wild upon the march of madness,
The bright-eyed Queen of the Blind.

Now where Beauty was are the wind-withered gorses,
Moaning like old men in the hill-wind's blast;
The flying sky is dark with running horses,
And the night is full of the past.

ON GROWING OLD

Be with me, Beauty, for the fire is dying;
My dog and I are old, too old for roving.
Man, whose young passion sets the spindrift flying,
Is soon too lame to march, too cold for loving.
I take the book and gather to the fire,
Turning old yellow leaves; minute by minute
The clock ticks to my heart. A withered wire,
Moves a thin ghost of music in the spinet.
I cannot sail your seas, I cannot wander
Your cornland, nor your hill-land, nor your valleys
Ever again, nor share the battle yonder
Where the young knight the broken squadron rallies.
Only stay quiet while my mind remembers
The beauty of fire from the beauty of embers.

Beauty, have pity! for the strong have power,
The rich their wealth, the beautiful their grace,
Summer of man its sunlight and its flower.
Spring-time of man all April in a face.
Only, as in the jostling in the Strand,
Where the mob thrusts or loiters or is loud,
The beggar with the saucer in his hand
Asks only a penny from the passing crowd,
So, from this glittering world with all its fashion,
Its fire, and play of men, its stir, its march,
Let me have wisdom, Beauty, wisdom and passion,
Bread to the soul, rain when the summers parch.
Give me but these, and though the darkness close
Even the night will blossom as the rose.

SONNET

Flesh, I have knocked at many a dusty door,
Gone down full many a windy midnight lane,
Probed in old walls and felt along the floor,
Pressed in blind hope the lighted window-pane,
But useless all, though sometimes when the moon
Was full in heaven and the sea was full,
Along my body's alleys came a tune
Played in the tavern by the Beautiful.
Then for an instant I have felt at point
To find and seize her, whosoe'er she be,
Whether some saint whose glory doth anoint
Those whom she loves, or but a part of me,
Or something that the things not understood
Make for their uses out of flesh and blood.

SONNET

Is there a great green commonwealth of Thought
Which ranks the yearly pageant, and decides
How Summer's royal progress shall be wrought,
By secret stir which in each plant abides?
Does rocking daffodil consent that she,
The snowdrop of wet winters, shall be first?
Does spotted cowslip with the grass agree
To hold her pride before the rattle burst?
And in the hedge what quick agreement goes,
When hawthorn blossoms redden to decay,
That Summer's pride shall come, the Summer's rose,
Before the flower be on the bramble spray?
Or is it, as with us, unresting strife,
And each consent a lucky gasp for life?

LAUGH AND BE MERRY

Laugh and be merry, remember, better the world with a song,
Better the world with a blow in the teeth of a wrong.
Laugh, for the time is brief, a thread the length of a span.
Laugh, and be proud to belong to the old proud pageant of man.

Laugh and be merry: remember, in olden time,
God made Heaven and Earth for joy He took in a rhyme,
Made them, and filled them full with the strong red wine of His mirth,
The splendid joy of the stars: the joy of the earth.

So we must laugh and drink from the deep blue cup of the sky,
Join the jubilant song of the great stars sweeping by,
Laugh, and battle, and work, and drink of the wine outpoured
In the dear green earth, the sign of the joy of the Lord.

Laugh and be merry together, like brothers akin,
Guesting awhile in the rooms of a beautiful inn,
Glad till the dancing stops, and the lilt of the music ends.
Laugh till the game is played; and be you merry, my friends.

THE CHOICE

The Kings go by with jeweled crowns;
Their horses gleam, their banners shake, their spears are many.
The sack of many-peopled towns
Is all their dream:
The way they take
Leaves but a ruin in the brake,
And, in the furrow that the plowmen make,
A stampless penny; a tale, a dream.

The Merchants reckon up their gold,
Their letters come, their ships arrive, their freights are glories;
The profits of their treasures sold
They tell and sum;
Their foremen drive
Their servants, starved to half-alive,
Whose labors do but make the earth a hive
Of stinking stories; a tale, a dream.

The Priests are singing in their stalls,
Their singing lifts, their incense burns, their praying clamors;
Yet God is as the sparrow falls,
The ivy drifts;
The votive urns
Are all left void when Fortune turns,
The god is but a marble for the kerns
To break with hammers; a tale, a dream.

O Beauty, let me know again
The green earth cold, the April rain, the quiet waters figuring sky,
The one star risen.
So shall I pass into the feast
Not touched by King, Merchant, or Priest;
Know the red spirit of the beast,
Be the green grain;
Escape from prison.

THE PASSING STRANGE

Out of the earth to rest or range
Perpetual in perpetual change,
The unknown passing through the strange.

Water and saltness held together
To tread the dust and stand the weather,
And plow the field and stretch the tether,

To pass the wine-cup and be witty,
Water the sands and build the city,
Slaughter like devils and have pity,

Be red with rage and pale with lust,
Make beauty come, make peace, make
trust,
Water and saltness mixed with dust;

Drive over earth, swim under sea,
Fly in the eagle's secrecy,
Guess where the hidden comets be;

Know all the deathy seeds that still
Queen Helen's beauty, Caesar's will,
And slay them even as they kill;

Fashion an altar for a rood,
Defile a continent with blood,
And watch a brother starve for food:

Love like a madman, shaking, blind,
Till self is burnt into a kind
Possession of another mind;

Brood upon beauty, till the grace
Of beauty with the holy face
Brings peace into the bitter place;

Probe in the lifeless granites, scan
The stars for hope, for guide, for plan;
Live as a woman or a man;

Fasten to lover or to friend,
Until the heart break at the end
The break of death that cannot mend:

Then to lie useless, helpless, still,
Down in the earth, in dark, to fill
The roots of grass or daffodil.

Down in the earth, in dark, alone,
A mockery of the ghost in bone,
The strangeness, passing the unknown.

Time will go by, that outlasts clocks,
Dawn in the thorps will rouse the cocks,
Sunset be glory on the rocks:

But it, the thing, will never heed
Even the rootling from the seed
Thrusting to suck it for its need.

*

Since moons decay and suns decline,
How else should end this life of mine?
Water and saltness are not wine.

But in the darkest hour of night,
When even the foxes peer for sight,
The byre-cock crows; he feels the light.

So, in this water mixed with dust,
The byre-cock spirit crows from trust
That death will change because it must.

For all things change: the darkness changes,
The wandering spirits change their ranges,
The corn is gathered to the granges.

The corn is sown again, it grows;
The stars burn out, the darkness goes;
The rhythms change, they do not close.

They change, and we, who pass like foam,
Like dust blown through the streets of Rome,
Change ever, too; we have no home,

Only a beauty, only a power,
Sad in the fruit, bright in the flower,
Endlessly erring for its hour,

But gathering as we stray, a sense
Of Life, so lovely and intense,
It lingers when we wander hence,

That those who follow feel behind
Their backs, when all before is blind,
Our joy, a rampart to the mind.

Harold Monro

Harold Monro was born in Brussels in 1879 and educated at Caius College, Cambridge. He described himself as "author, publisher, editor and book-seller." Monro founded The Poetry Bookshop in London in 1912, a unique establishment having as its object a practical relation between poetry and the public: it kept in stock nothing but poetry, the drama, and books connected with the subjects. His quarterly, *Poetry and Drama* (discontinued during the war and revived in 1919 as *The Chapbook*), was in a sense the organ of the younger men; and his shop, in which he lived for the last twenty years of his life except while he was in the army, became a literary center. In spite of changing fashions Monro remained an influence, the "rare Ben Jonson" of a modern Mermaid Tavern, until his death in 1932.

Monro's poetry depicts the play between the world of reality and the limbo of fantasy. *Before Dawn* (1911) has little of his peculiar mysticism, but *Children of Love* (1914), *Trees* (1915) and *Strange Meetings* (1917) present, with indubitable originality, the relation of man, not only to the earth he rose from, but to the inanimate things among which he moves. Even the most whimsical poems disclose an emotional intensity beneath the skillful rhythms. Monro's kettles are as animated as his cats; his machines, domestic furniture, ordinary interiors are both surprising and natural—surprising in the revelation of what might well be their "inner selves," natural in the way their speech is communicated.

Monro has been criticized as being a poet by intention but not a singer by intuition. Defending certain of the more determined "modernist" poets—and, by implication, himself—Monro has written, "It will be no use to say that their poetry 'does not sing.' It is not meant to. The word *Song* has been abandoned and swept out, with *Ode, Sonnet, Quatrain*, and other similar verbal lumber. The test of intellect is more important to them than tests of prosody, or tradition. The passing event and its effect on the mind is everything to them. . . . Thus they think in terms of the whole poem rather than of the single line, and thus they are often unquotable except in *extenso*." While this is interesting (and only partially true) Monro's own poetry is at its best when intellect is subservient to imagination and music.

Real Property (1922) represents a further advance. Although Monro has not lost his whimsical appraisal of "still life," the note is graver, the implications larger. Some of the poems, as Monro states in a prefatory note, are "tainted with slight Georgian affectations." But such verses as the metaphysical "Earthliness" (too long for quotation) and the simpler poems of Part Two, four of which are reprinted in the group below, mark this poet as one of the most original though, undeservedly, one of the least popular creators of the period.

The Earth for Sale (1928) is a continuation and extension of the more somber speculations. Besides his poetry, Monro is the author of *Some Contemporary Poets* (1920), a set of sharply critical estimates.

EVERY THING

Since man has been articulate,
Mechanical, improvidently wise
(Servant of Fate),
He has not understood the little cries
And foreign conversations of the small
Delightful creatures that have followed him
Not far behind;
Has failed to hear the sympathetic call
Of Crockery and Cutlery, those kind
Reposeful Teraphim
Of his domestic happiness; the Stool
He sat on, or the Door he entered through:
He has not thanked them, overbearing fool!
What is he coming to?

But you should listen to the talk of these.
Honest they are, and patient they have kept;
Served him without his Thank you or his Please . . .
I often heard
The gentle Bed, a sigh between each word,
Murmuring, before I slept.
The Candle, as I blew it, cried aloud,
Then bowed,
And in a smoky argument
Into the darkness went.
The Kettle puffed a tentacle of breath:—
"Pooh! I have boiled his water, I don't know
Why; and he always says I boil too slow.
He never calls me 'Sukie, dear,' and oh,
I wonder why I squander my desire
Sitting submissive on his kitchen fire."

Now the old Copper Basin suddenly
Rattled and tumbled from the shelf,
Bumping and crying: "I can fall by myself;
Without a woman's hand
To patronize and coax and flatter me,
I understand
The lean and poise of gravitable land."
It gave a raucous and tumultuous shout,
Twisted itself convulsively about,
Rested upon the floor, and, while I stare,
It stares and grins at me.

The old impetuous Gas above my head
Begins irascibly to flare and fret,
Wheezing into its epileptic jet,
Reminding me I ought to go to bed.

The rafters creak; an Empty-Cupboard door
Swings open; now a wild Plank of the floor

Breaks from its joist, and leaps behind my foot.
Down from the chimney, half a pound of Soot
Tumbles and lies, and shakes itself again.
The Putty cracks against the window-pane.
A piece of Paper in the basket shoves
Another piece, and toward the bottom moves.
My independent Pencil, while I write,
Breaks at the point: the ruminating Clock
Stirs all its body and begins to rock,
Warning the waiting presence of the Night,
Strikes the dead hour, and tumbles to the plain
Ticking of ordinary work again.

You do well to remind me, and I praise
Your strangely individual foreign ways.
You call me from myself to recognize
Companionship in your unselfish eyes.
I want your dear acquaintances, although
I pass you arrogantly over, throw
Your lovely sounds, and squander them along
My busy days. I'll do you no more wrong.

Purr for me, Sukie, like a faithful cat.
You, my well-trampled Boots, and you, my Hat,
Remain my friends: I feel, though I don't speak,
Your touch grow kindlier from week to week.
It well becomes our mutual happiness
To go toward the same end more or less.
There is not much dissimilarity,
Not much to choose, I know it well, in fine,
Between the purposes of you and me,
And your eventual Rubbish Heap, and mine.

FROM "WEEK-END"

I

The train! The twelve o'clock for paradise.
  Hurry, or it will try to creep away.
Out in the country everyone is wise:
  We can be wise only on Saturday.
There you are waiting, little friendly house:
  Those are your chimney-stacks with you between,
Surrounded by old trees and strolling cows,
  Staring through all your windows at the green.
Your homely floor is creaking for our tread;
  The smiling tea-pot with contented spout
Thinks of the boiling water, and the bread
  Longs for the butter. All their hands are out

To greet us, and the gentle blankets seem
Purring and crooning: "Lie in us, and dream."

II

The key will stammer, and the door reply,
  The hall wake, yawn, and smile; the torpid stair
Will grumble at our feet, the table cry:
  "Fetch my belongings for me; I am bare."
A clatter! Something in the attic falls.
  A ghost has lifted up his robes and fled.
The loitering shadows move along the walls;
  Then silence very slowly lifts his head.
The starling with impatient screech has flown
  The chimney, and is watching from the tree.
They thought us gone for ever: mouse alone
  Stops in the middle of the floor to see.
Now all you idle things, resume your toil.
Hearth, put your flames on. Sulky kettle, boil.

THE BIRD AT DAWN

What I saw was just one eye
In the dawn as I was going:
A bird can carry all the sky
In that little button glowing.

Never in my life I went
So deep into the firmament.

He was standing on a tree,
All in blossom overflowing;
And he purposely looked hard at me,
At first, as if to question merrily:
"Where are you going?"
But next some far more serious thing to say:
I could not answer, could not look away.

Oh, that hard, round, and so distracting eye:
Little mirror of all sky!—
And then the after-song another tree
Held, and sent radiating back on me.

If no man had invented human word,
And a bird-song had been
The only way to utter what we mean,
What would we men have heard,
What understood, what seen,
Between the trills and pauses, in between
The singing and the silence of a bird?

CHILDREN OF LOVE

The holy boy
Went from his mother out in the cool of day
Over the sun-parched fields
And in among the olives shining green and shining gray.

There was no sound,
No smallest voice of any shivering stream.
Poor sinless little boy,
He desired to play, and to sing; he could only sigh and dream.

Suddenly came
Running along to him naked, with curly hair,
That rogue of the lovely world,
That other beautiful child whom the virgin Venus bare.

The holy boy
Gazed with those sad blue eyes that all men know.
Impudent Cupid stood
Panting, holding an arrow and pointing his bow.

("Will you not play?
Jesus, run to him, run to him, swift for our joy.
Is he not holy, like you?
Are you afraid of his arrows, O beautiful dreaming boy?")

And now they stand
Watching one another with timid gaze;
Youth has met youth in the wood,
But holiness will not change its melancholy ways.

Cupid at last
Draws his bow and softly lets fly a dart.
Smile for a moment, sad world!—
It has grazed the white skin and drawn blood from the sorrowful heart.

Now for delight,
Cupid tosses his locks and goes wantonly near;
But the child that was born to the cross
Has let fall on his cheek, for the sadness of life a compassionate tear.

Marvelous dream!
Cupid has offered his arrows for Jesus to try;
He has offered his bow for the game,
But Jesus went weeping away, and left him there wondering why.

STRANGE MEETINGS

If Suddenly a Clod of Earth

If suddenly a clod of earth should rise,
And walk about, and breathe, and speak, and love,
How one would tremble, and in what surprise
Gasp: "Can *you* move"?

I see men walking and I always feel:
"Earth! How have you done this? What can you be?"
I can't learn how to know men, or conceal
How strange they are to me.

A Flower Is Looking

A flower is looking through the ground,
Blinking at the April weather;
Now a child has seen the flower:
Now they go and play together.

Now it seems the flower will speak,
And will call the child its brother—
But, oh strange forgetfulness!—
They don't recognize each other.

SOLITUDE

When you have tidied all things for the night,
And while your thoughts are fading to their sleep,
You'll pause a moment in the late firelight,
Too sorrowful to weep.

The large and gentle furniture has stood
In sympathetic silence all the day
With that old kindness of domestic wood;
Nevertheless the haunted room will say:
"Someone must be away."

The little dog rolls over half awake,
Stretches his paws, yawns, looking up at you,
Wags his tail very slightly for your sake,
That you may feel he is unhappy too.

A distant engine whistles, or the floor
Creaks, or the wandering night-wind bangs a door

Silence is scattered like a broken glass.
The minutes prick their ears and run about,
Then one by one subside again and pass
Sedately in, monotonously out.

You bend your head and wipe away a tear.
Solitude walks one heavy step more near.

MILK FOR THE CAT

When the tea is brought at five o'clock,
And all the neat curtains are drawn with care,
The little black cat with bright green eyes
Is suddenly purring there.

At first she pretends, having nothing to do,
She has come in merely to blink by the grate,
But, though tea may be late or the milk may be sour,
She is never late.

And presently her agate eyes
Take a soft large milky haze,
And her independent casual glance
Becomes a stiff hard gaze.

Then she stamps her claws or lifts her ears
Or twists her tail and begins to stir,
Till suddenly all her little body becomes
One breathing trembling purr.

The children eat and wriggle and laugh;
The two old ladies stroke their silk:
But the cat is grown small and thin with desire,
Transformed to a creeping lust for milk.

The white saucer like some full moon descends
At last from the clouds of the table above;
She sighs and dreams and thrills and glows,
Transfigured with love.

She nestles over the shining rim,
Buries her chin in the creamy sea;
Her tail hangs loose; each drowsy paw
Is doubled under each bending knee.

A long dim ecstasy holds her life;
Her world is an infinite shapeless white,
Till her tongue has curled the last holy drop,
Then she sinks back into the night,

Draws and dips her body to heap
Her sleepy nerves in the great arm-chair,
Lies defeated and buried deep
Three or four hours unconscious there.

DOG

O little friend, your nose is ready; you sniff,
Asking for that expected walk,
(Your nostrils full of the happy rabbit-whiff)
And almost talk.

And so the moment becomes a moving force;
Coats glide down from their pegs in the humble dark;
You scamper the stairs,
Your body informed with the scent and the track and the mark
Of stoats and weasels, moles and badgers and hares.

We are going *Out*. You know the pitch of the word,
Probing the tone of thought as it comes through fog
And reaches by devious means (half-smelt, half-heard)
The four-legged brain of a walk-ecstatic dog.

Out through the garden your head is already low.
You are going your walk, you know,
And your limbs will draw
Joy from the earth through the touch of your padded paw.

Now, sending a look to us behind,
Who follow slowly the track of your lovely play,
You fetch our bodies forward away from mind
Into the light and fun of your useless day.

Thus, for your walk, we took ourselves, and went
Out by the hedge, and tree, to the open ground.
You ran, in delightful strata of wafted scent,
Over the hill without seeing the view;
Beauty is hinted through primitive smells to you:
And that ultimate Beauty you track is but rarely found.

*

Home . . . and further joy will be waiting there:
Supper full of the lovely taste of bone,
You lift up your nose again, and sniff, and stare
For the rapture known
Of the quick wild gorge of food, then the still lie-down;
While your people will talk above you in the light
Of candles, and your dreams will merge and drown
Into the bed-delicious hours of night.

MAN CARRYING BALE

The tough hand closes gently on the load;
  Out of the mind a voice
Calls "Lift!" and the arms, remembering well their work,
  Lengthen and pause for help.
Then a slow ripple flows along the body,
While all the muscles call to one another:
  "Lift!" and the bulging bale
  Floats like a butterfly in June.

So moved the earliest carrier of bales,
  And the same watchful sun
Glowed through his body feeding it with light.
  So will the last one move,
And halt, and dip his head, and lay his load
Down, and the muscles will relax and tremble . . .
  Earth, you designed your man
Beautiful both in labor and repose.

THE NIGHTINGALE NEAR THE HOUSE

Here is the soundless cypress on the lawn:
It listens, listens. Taller trees beyond
Listen. The moon at the unruffled pond
    Stares. And you sing, you sing.

That star-enchanted song falls through the air
From lawn to lawn down terraces of sound,
Darts in white arrows on the shadowed ground;
    And all the night you sing.

My dreams are flowers to which you are a bee
As all night long I listen, and my brain
Receives your song; then loses it again
    In moonlight on the lawn.

Now is your voice a marble high and white,
Then like a mist on fields of paradise,
Now is a raging fire, then is like ice,
    Then breaks, and it is dawn.

CITY-STORM

The heavy sounds are over-sweet
That droop above the hooded street,
At any moment ripe to fall and lie,
And when the Wind will swagger up the town
They'll bend a moment, then will fly
All clattering down.

Troupes come and go of urchin breeze:
They flick your face or smack the trees,
Then round the corner spin and leap
With whistling cries,
Rake their rubbish in a heap
And throw it in your eyes.

(Much preparation of the earth and air
Is needed everywhere
Before that first large drop of rain can fall.)

Smells of the Sea, or inland Grass,
Come staring through the town and pass.
Brilliant old Memories drive in state
Along the way, but cannot wait;
And many a large unusual bird
Hovers across the sky, half-heard.

But listen. It is He;
At last he comes:
Gigantic tyrant panting through the street,
Slamming the windows of our little homes,

Banging the doors, knocking the chimneys down.
Oh, his loud tramp: how scornfully he can meet
Great citizens, and lash them with his sleet!
Everything will be altered in our town.
He'll wipe the film of habit clean away,
While he remains,
His cloak is over everything we do,
And the whole town complains:—

A somber scroll;
An inner room.
A crystal bowl:
Waters of gloom.
Oh, the darkened house—
Into silence creep!
The world is cold.
All people weep.

THE HURRIER

O furrowed plaintive face,
No time for peace?
Your grim appointment will not wait?
No, our great earthly clock
Ticks through your spine, and locomotion wags
An angry tail.
Quick, do not miss the toiling trailing tram.
Hurry, or you are lost, for anywhere
Hunger may lurk and leer.
You may have been elected, mid so many,
To be his prey,
Even today.
On horned imagination drive your limbs.
It will need your whole life to be at peace:
Then all appointments cease.
But now you neither have the time for death,
Nor time conveniently to draw your breath.

W. W. Gibson

W(ilfrid) W(ilson) Gibson was born in 1880 at Hexham, Northumberland, and, by his fiftieth year, was the author of some twenty-two books of poems and five volumes of poetic plays and dialogues. The first five or six of these were pseudo-Tennysonian, imitative in manner and sentimental in tone. Their titles give the key: *Urlyn the Harper* (1902), *The Queen's Vigil* (1902), *The Golden Helm* (1903), *The Nets of Love* (1905).

With *Daily Bread* (1910), *Fires* (1912), and *Borderlands* (1914) Gibson executed a complete right-about-face and, with dramatic brevity, wrote a series of poems mirroring the dreams, pursuits, and fears of common humanity. *Thoroughfares* (1914) marks an advance in technique and power. In *Livelihood* (1917) Gibson seems to be theatricalizing and merely exploiting his working-people, yet several of his later lyrics recapture the quality of such poems as "The Old Man," "The Stone" and "The Machine." *Hill-Tracks* (1918) attempts to hold (as Edward Thomas actually did hold) the beauty of village-names through the glamor of the English countryside. *Neighbors* (1920) again takes up the strain of a somewhat too conscious poeticizing of the casual. *Islands* (1932) and *Fuel* (1934) prolong the attempt.

Gibson's later work suffers from his facility; a thinning out of power, even of feeling, is evident in *Krindlesyke* (1922), *Kestrel Edge* (1924) and *I Heard a Sailor* (1925). The best of Gibson is in the first *Collected Poems* (1923), which was followed by other collections, including a volume of plays, *Within Four Walls* (1950).

PRELUDE

As one, at midnight, wakened by the call
Of golden-plovers in their seaward flight,
Who lies and listens, as the clear notes fall
Through tingling silence of the frosty night—
Who lies and listens, till the last note fails,
And then, in fancy, faring with the flock
Far over slumbering hills and dreaming dales,
Soon hears the surges break on reef and rock;
And, hearkening, till all sense of self is drowned
Within the mightier music of the deep,
No more remembers the sweet piping sound
That startled him from dull, undreaming sleep;
So I, first waking from oblivion, heard,
With heart that kindled to the call of song,
The voice of young life, fluting like a bird,
And echoed that light lilting; till, ere long,
Lured onward by that happy, singing-flight,
I caught the stormy summons of the sea,
And dared the restless deeps that, day and night,
Surge with the life-song of humanity.

THE STONE

"And will you cut a stone for him,
To set above his head?
And will you cut a stone for him—
A stone for him?" she said.

Three days before, a splintered rock
Had struck her lover dead—
Had struck him in the quarry dead,
Where, careless of the warning call,
He loitered, while the shot was fired—
A lively stripling, brave and tall,
And sure of all his heart desired . . .
A flash, a shock,
A rumbling fall . . .
And, broken 'neath the broken rock,
A lifeless heap, with face of clay;
And still as any stone he lay,
With eyes that saw the end of all.

I went to break the news to her;
And I could hear my own heart beat
With dread of what my lips might say
But, some poor fool had sped before;
And flinging wide her father's door,
Had blurted out the news to her,
Had struck her lover dead for her,
Had struck the girl's heart dead in her,
Had struck life lifeless, at a word,
And dropped it at her feet:
Then hurried on his witless way,
Scarce knowing she had heard.

And when I came, she stood alone,
A woman turned to stone:
And, though no word at all she said,
I knew that all was known.
Because her heart was dead,
She did not sigh nor moan,
His mother wept:
She could not weep,
Her lover slept:
She could not weep.
Three days, three nights,
She did not stir:
Three days, three nights,
Were one to her,
Who never closed her eyes
From sunset to sunrise,
From dawn to evenfall:
Her tearless, staring eyes,
That seeing naught, saw all.

The fourth night when I came from work,
I found her at my door.

"And will you cut a stone for him?"
She said: and spoke no more:
But followed me, as I went in,
And sank upon a chair;
And fixed her gray eyes on my face,
With still, unseeing stare.
And, as she waited patiently,
I could not bear to feel
Those still, gray eyes that followed me,
Those eyes that plucked the heart from me,
Those eyes that sucked the breath from me
And curdled the warm blood in me,
Those eyes that cut me to the bone,
And pierced my marrow like cold steel.

And so I rose, and sought a stone;
And cut it, smooth and square:
And, as I worked, she sat and watched,
Beside me, in her chair.
Night after night, by candlelight,
I cut her lover's name:
Night after night, so still and white,
And like a ghost she came;
And sat beside me in her chair;
And watched with eyes aflame.

She eyed each stroke;
And hardly stirred:
She never spoke
A single word:
And not a sound or murmur broke
The quiet, save the mallet-stroke.

With still eyes ever on my hands,
With eyes that seemed to burn my hands,
My wincing, overwearied hands,
She watched, with bloodless lips apart,
And silent, indrawn breath:
And every stroke my chisel cut,
Death cut still deeper in her heart:
The two of us were chiseling,
Together, I and death.

And when at length the job was done,
And I had laid the mallet by,
As if, at last, her peace were won,
She breathed his name; and, with a sigh,
Passed slowly through the open door:
And never crossed my threshold more.

Next night I labored late, alone,
To cut her name upon the stone.

SIGHT

By the lamplit stall I loitered, feasting my eyes
On colors ripe and rich for the heart's desire—
Tomatoes, redder than Krakatoa's fire,
Oranges like old sunsets over Tyre,
And apples golden-green as the glades of Paradise.

And as I lingered, lost in divine delight,
My heart thanked God for the goodly gift of sight
And all youth's lively senses keen and quick . . .
When suddenly, behind me in the night,
I heard the tapping of a blind man's stick.

THE WHITE DUST

I felt no tremor and I caught no sounds;
But a fresh crack scored my ceiling: white dust dropped,
Sprinkling my polished table . . .
Underground,
Fathoms beneath my comfortable room,
In the pit's dripping gloom,
A new drift's rock-roof, insecurely propped,
Had settled; and, in settling, crushed just then

The life out of six men:
Six hearts had stopped . . .

But I, unguessing, looked up fretfully
At the fresh crack, and rose impatiently
To wipe the dust from my mahogany.

Alfred Noyes

Alfred Noyes was born at Staffordshire, September 16, 1880, one of the few contemporary poets who have been fortunate enough to write a kind of poetry that is not only readable but extraordinarily saleable.

His first book, *The Loom of Years* (1902), was published when he was only 22 years old, and *Poems* (1904) emphasized the promise of this first publication. Swinburne, grown old and living in retirement, was so struck with Noyes's talent that he had the young poet out to read to him. Unfortunately, Noyes never developed his gifts as deeply as his admirers expected. His poetry, extremely straightforward and rhythmical, degenerated too often into sentimentalities and cheap tirades; the later work attempted to express programs and profundities far beyond Noyes's limited power.

What is most appealing about his best verse is its ease and heartiness; this singer's gift lies in the almost personal bond established between the poet and his public. It may be said that many people have such a good time reading his vivacious lines because Noyes had such a good time writing them. Rhyme in a thumping rhythm seems to be not merely his trade but his morning exercise. Noyes's own relish quickens the glees and catches like *Forty Singing Seamen* (1907), the lusty choruses in *Tales of the Mermaid Tavern* (1913), the seemingly inspired nonsense of the earlier *Forest of Wild Thyme* (1905).

The least popular work of Noyes is, as a unified product, his most remarkable performance. It is an epic in twelve books of blank verse, *Drake* (1908), a pageant of the sea and England's drama upon it. It is a spirited echo of the maritime Elizabethans, a vivid orchestral work interspersed with lyric passages and brisk songs. The companion volume, an attempted reconstruction of the literary phase of the same period, is less successful; but these *Tales of the Mermaid Tavern* (which introduce Shakespeare, Marlowe, Drayton, Raleigh, Ben Jonson, and other immortals) are colorful, if somewhat too insistently rollicking and smoothly lilting.

Noyes's eight volumes were assembled in 1913 and published in two books of *Collected Poems*. The third volume of his rapidly accumulating *Collected Poems* appeared in 1920, the fourth in 1927. In 1922 Noyes began *The Torch-Bearers,* "An Epic Trilogy," a sort of outline of man's accomplishment rendered in verse.

In his early sixties Noyes visited America on a transcontinental tour and remained in California until he was seventy, when he returned to England. Besides his poetry he had written several prose works, including *Aspects of Poetry* and an autobiography, *Two Worlds for Memory* (1953). He died June 28, 1958.

Although most of his smooth-running rhymes seemed doomed to rush to an early death—are, in fact, already extinct—Noyes will remain a poet pleasant to read because of his "Sherwood," the lilt of "The Barrel-Organ," the galloping "The Highwayman" and a handful of other ballads.

SHERWOOD

Sherwood in the twilight, is Robin Hood awake?
Gray and ghostly shadows are gliding through the brake;
Shadows of the dappled deer, dreaming of the morn,
Dreaming of a shadowy man that winds a shadowy horn.

Robin Hood is here again: all his merry thieves
Hear a ghostly bugle-note shivering through the leaves,
Calling as he used to call, faint and far away,
In Sherwood, in Sherwood, about the break of day.

Merry, merry England has kissed the lips of June;
All the wings of fairyland were here beneath the moon;
Like a flight of rose-leaves fluttering in a mist
Of opal and ruby and pearl and amethyst.

Merry, merry England is waking as of old,
With eyes of blither hazel and hair of brighter gold:
For Robin Hood is here again beneath the bursting spray
In Sherwood, in Sherwood, about the break of day.

Love is in the greenwood building him a house
Of wild rose and hawthorn and honeysuckle boughs;
Love is in the greenwood: dawn is in the skies;
And Marian is waiting with a glory in her eyes.

Hark! The dazzled laverock climbs the golden steep:
Marian is waiting: is Robin Hood asleep?
Round the fairy grass-rings frolic elf and fay,
In Sherwood, in Sherwood, about the break of day.

Oberon, Oberon, rake away the gold,
Rake away the red leaves, roll away the mold,
Rake away the gold leaves, roll away the red,
And wake Will Scarlet from his leafy forest bed.

Friar Tuck and Little John are riding down together
With quarter-staff and drinking-can and gray goose-feather;
The dead are coming back again; the years are rolled away
In Sherwood, in Sherwood, about the break of day.

Softly over Sherwood the south wind blows;
All the heart of England hid in every rose
Hears across the greenwood the sunny whisper leap,
Sherwood in the red dawn, is Robin Hood asleep?

Hark, the voice of England wakes him as of old
And, shattering the silence with a cry of brighter gold,
Bugles in the greenwood echo from the steep,
Sherwood in the red dawn, is Robin Hood asleep?

Where the deer are gliding down the shadowy glen
All across the glades of fern he calls his merry men;
Doublets of the Lincoln green glancing through the May,
In Sherwood, in Sherwood, about the break of day;

Calls them and they answer: from aisles of oak and ash
Rings the *Follow! Follow!* and the boughs begin to crash;
The ferns begin to flutter and the flowers begin to fly;
And through the crimson dawning the robber band goes by.

Robin! Robin! Robin! All his merry thieves
Answer as the bugle-note shivers through the leaves:
Calling as he used to call, faint and far away,
In Sherwood, in Sherwood, about the break of day.

THE BARREL-ORGAN

There's a barrel-organ caroling across a golden street
  In the City as the sun sinks low;
And the music's not immortal; but the world has made it sweet
  And fulfilled it with the sunset glow;
And it pulses through the pleasures of the City and the pain
  That surround the singing organ like a large eternal light;
And they've given it a glory and a part to play again
  In the Symphony that rules the day and night.
And now it's marching onward through the realms of old romance,
  And trolling out a fond familiar tune,
And now it's roaring cannon down to fight the King of France,
  And now it's prattling softly to the moon.
And all around the organ there's a sea without a shore
  Of human joys and wonders and regrets;
To remember and to recompense the music evermore
  For what the cold machiney forgets . . .

Yes; as the music changes,
  Like a prismatic glass,
It takes the light and ranges
  Through all the moods that pass:
Dissects the common carnival
  Of passions and regrets,
And gives the world a glimpse of all
  The colors it forgets.

And there *La Traviata* sighs
  Another sadder song;
And there *Il Trovatore* cries
  A tale of deeper wrong;

And bolder knights to battle go
  With sword and shield and lance,
Than ever here on earth below
  Have whirled into—a dance!—

Go down to Kew in lilac-time, in lilac-time, in lilac-time;
  Go down to Kew in lilac-time (it isn't far from London!)
And you shall wander hand in hand with Love in summer's wonderland;
  Go down to Kew in lilac-time (it isn't far from London!)

The cherry-trees are seas of bloom and soft perfume and sweet perfume,
  The cherry-trees are seas of bloom (and oh, so near to London!)
And there they say, when dawn is high and all the world's a blaze of sky
  The cuckoo, though he's very shy, will sing a song for London.

The nightingale is rather rare and yet they say you'll hear him there
  At Kew, at Kew in lilac-time (and oh, so near to London!)
The linnet and the throstle, too, and after dark the long halloo
  And golden-eyed *tu-whit, tu-whoo* of owls that ogle London.

For Noah hardly knew a bird of any kind that isn't heard
  At Kew, at Kew in lilac-time (and oh, so near to London!)
And when the rose begins to pout and all the chestnut spires are out
  You'll hear the rest without a doubt, all chorusing for London:—

Come down to Kew in lilac-time, in lilac-time, in lilac-time;
  Come down to Kew in lilac-time (it isn't far from London!)
And you shall wander hand in hand with Love in summer's wonderland;
  Come down to Kew in lilac-time (it isn't far from London!)

And then the troubadour begins to thrill the golden street,
  In the City as the sun sinks low;
And in all the gaudy busses there are scores of weary feet
Marking time, sweet time, with a dull mechanic beat,
And a thousand hearts are plunging to a love they'll never meet,
Through the meadows of the sunset, through the poppies and the wheat,
  In the land where the dead dreams go.

Verdi, Verdi, when you wrote *Il Trovatore* did you dream
  Of the City when the sun sinks low,
Of the organ and the monkey and the many-colored stream
On the Picadilly pavement, of the myriad eyes that seem
To be litten for a moment with a wild Italian gleam
As *A che la morte* parodies the world's eternal theme
  And pulses with the sunset-glow?

There's a thief, perhaps, that listens with a face of frozen stone
  In the City as the sun sinks low;
There's a portly man of business with a balance of his own,
There's a clerk and there's a butcher of a soft reposeful tone,
And they're all of them returning to the heavens they have known:
They are crammed and jammed in busses and—they're each of them alone
  In the land where the dead dreams go.

There's a laborer that listens to the voices of the dead
  In the City as the sun sinks low;
And his hand begins to tremble and his face is rather red
As he sees a loafer watching him and—there he turns his head
And stares into the sunset where his April love is fled,
For he hears her softly singing and his lonely soul is led
  Through the land where the dead dreams go . . .

There's a barrel-organ caroling across a golden street
  In the City as the sun sinks low;
Though the music's only Verdi there's a world to make it sweet
Just as yonder yellow sunset where the earth and heaven meet
Mellows all the sooty City! Hark, a hundred thousand feet
Are marching on to glory through the poppies and the wheat
  In the land where the dead dreams go.

So it's Jeremiah, Jeremiah,
  What have you to say
When you meet the garland girls
  Tripping on their way?

All around my gala hat
  I wear a wreath of roses
(A long and lonely year it is
  I've waited for the May!)
If anyone should ask you,
  The reason why I wear it is—
My own love, my true love, is coming home today.

And it's buy a bunch of violets for the lady
  (*It's lilac-time in London; it's lilac-time in London!*)
Buy a bunch of violets for the lady;
  While the sky burns blue above:

On the other side the street you'll find it shady
  (*It's lilac time in London; it's lilac-time in London!*)
But buy a bunch of violets for the lady,
  And tell her she's your own true love.

There's a barrel-organ caroling across a golden street
  In the City as the sun sinks glittering and slow;
And the music's not immortal; but the world has made it sweet
And enriched it with the harmonies that make a song complete
In the deeper heavens of music where the night and morning meet,
  As it dies into the sunset glow;
And it pulses through the pleasures of the City and the pain
  That surround the singing organ like a large eternal light,
And they've given it a glory and a part to play again
  In the Symphony that rules the day and night.

And there, as the music changes,
  The song runs round again;
Once more it turns and ranges
  Through all its joy and pain:
Dissects the common carnival
  Of passions and regrets;
And the wheeling world remembers all
  The wheeling song forgets.

Once more *La Traviata* sighs
  Another sadder song:
Once more *Il Trovatore* cries
  A tale of deeper wrong;
Once more the knights to battle go
  With sword and shield and lance
Till once, once more, the shattered foe
  Has whirled into—a dance!

Come down to Kew in lilac-time, in lilac-time, in lilac-time;
  Come down to Kew in lilac-time (it isn't far from London!)
And you shall wander hand in hand with Love in summer's wonderland,
  Come down to Kew in lilac-time (it isn't far from London!)

EPILOGUE

(from "The Flower of Old Japan")

Carol, every violet has
Heaven for a looking-glass!

Every little valley lies
Under many-clouded skies;
Every little cottage stands
Girt about with boundless lands.
Every little glimmering pond
Claims the mighty shores beyond—
Shores no seaman ever hailed,
Seas no ship has ever sailed.

All the shores when day is done
Fade into the setting sun,
So the story tries to teach
More than can be told in speech.

Beauty is a fading flower,
Truth is but a wizard's tower,
Where a solemn death-bell tolls,
And a forest round it rolls.
We have come by curious ways
To the light that holds the days;
We have sought in haunts of fear
For that all-enfolding sphere:
And lo! it was not far, but near.
We have found, O foolish-fond,
The shore that has no shore beyond.
Deep in every heart it lies
With its untranscended skies;
For what heaven should bend above
Hearts that own the heaven of love?

Carol, Carol, we have come
Back to heaven, back to home.

Padraic Colum

Padraic Columm was born at Longford, Ireland (in the same county as Oliver Goldsmith), December 8, 1881, and was educated at the local schools. At twenty he was a member of the group that created the Irish National Theatre.

Colum began as a dramatist with *Broken Soil* (1904), *The Land* (1905), *Thomas Muskerry* (1910), and this early dramatic influence has colored much of his work; in fact, his best poetry is in the form of dramatic lyrics. *Wild Earth,* his most quoted collection of verse, first appeared in 1909, and an amplified edition of it was published in America in 1916. Colum himself had come to America (where he has lived ever since) shortly before that date; his *Dramatic Poems* appeared in 1922. *Creatures* (1927), utterly different in theme from its predecessors, is held together by the same gift of condensation. Though Colum's animals are less obviously divine than his gods, his treatment of them is no less devotional. He combines an innocence of vision with wisdom of experience. *Old Pastures* (1930) and *Flower Pieces* (1939) are sensitive and ingratiating.

As a recorder, Colum has been equally successful as an autobiographer, a folklorist, and a popular adapter of myths and legends for young people. In 1953 he was awarded the Gregory Medal by the Irish Academy of Letters.

THE PLOWER

Sunset and silence! A man: around him earth savage, earth broken;
Beside him two horses—a plow!

Earth savage, earth broken, the brutes, the dawn man there in the sunset,
And the Plow that is twin to the Sword, that is founder of cities!

"Brute-tamer, plow-maker, earth-breaker! Can'st hear?
"There are age between us.
"Is it praying you are as you stand there alone in the sunset?

"Surely our sky-born gods can be naught to you, earth-child and earth-master?
"Surely your thoughts are of Pan, or of Wotan, or Dana?

"Yet, why give thought to the gods? Has Pan led your brutes where they stumble?
"Has Dana numbed pain of the child-bed, or Wotan put hands to your plow?

"What matter your foolish reply! O man, standing lone and bowed earthward,
"Your task is a day near its close. Give thanks to the night-giving God."

*

Slowly the darkness falls, the broken lands blend with the savage;
The brute-tamer stands by the brutes, a head's breadth only above them.

A head's breadth? Aye, but therein is hell's depth, and the height up to heaven,
And the thrones of the gods and their halls, their chariots, purples, and splendors.

AN OLD WOMAN OF THE ROADS

O, to have a little house!
To own the hearth and stool and all!
The heaped-up sods upon the fire,
The pile of turf against the wall!

To have a clock with weights and chains
And pendulum swinging up and down!
A dresser filled with shining delph,
Speckled and white and blue and brown!

I could be busy all the day
Clearing and sweeping hearth and floor,
And fixing on their shelf again
My white and blue and speckled store!

I could be quiet there at night
Beside the fire and by myself,
Sure of a bed and loth to leave
The ticking clock and the shining delph!

Och! but I'm weary of mist and dark,
And roads where there's never a house nor bush,
And tired I am of bog and road,
And the crying wind and the lonesome hush!

And I am praying to God on high,
And I am praying Him night and day,
For a little house—a house of my own—
Out of the wind's and the rain's way.

INTERIOR

The little moths are creeping
Across the cottage pane;
On the floor the chickens gather,
And they make talk and complain.

And she sits by the fire
Who has reared so many men;
Her voice is low like the chickens'
With the things she says again.

"The sons that come back do be restless,
They search for the thing to say;
Then they take thought like the swallows,
And the morrow brings them away.

"In the old, old days, upon Innish,
The fields were lucky and bright,
And if you lay down you'd be covered
By the grass of one soft night."

She speaks and the chickens gather,
And they make talk and complain,
While the little moths are creeping
Across the cotttage pane.

A DROVER

To Meath of the pastures,
From wet hills by the sea,
Through Leitrim and Longford,
Go my cattle and me.

I hear in the darkness
Their slipping and breathing—
I name them the by-ways
They're to pass without heeding;

Then the wet, winding roads,
Brown bogs with black water;
And my thoughts on white ships
And the King o' Spain's daughter.

Oh! farmer, strong farmer!
You can spend at the fair;
But your face you must turn
To your crops and your care.

And soldiers, red soldiers!
You've seen many lands;
But you walk two by two,
And by captain's commands.

Oh! the smell of the beasts,
The wet wind in the morn;
And the proud and hard earth
Never broken for corn;

And the crowds at the fair,
The herds loosened and blind,
Loud words and dark faces
And the wild blood behind.

(Oh! strong men, with your best
I would strive breast to breast,
I could quiet your herds
With my words, with my words.)

I will bring you my kine,
Where there's grass to the knee;
But you'll think of scant croppings
Harsh with salt of the sea.

WILD ASS

The wild ass lounges, legs struck out
In vagrom unconcern:
The tombs of Achaemenian kings
Are for those hooves to spurn.

And all of rugged Tartary
Lies with him on the ground.
The Tartary that knows no awe
That has nor ban nor bound.

The wild horse from the herd is plucked
To bear a saddle's weight;
The boar is one keeps covert, and
The wolf runs with a mate.

But he's the solitary of space,
Curbless and unbeguiled;
The only being that bears a heart
Not recreant to the wild.

Joseph Campbell

(SEOSAMH MacCATHMHAOIL)

Joseph Campbell was born in Belfast in 1881, and was not only a poet but an artist; he made all the illustrations for *The Rushlight* (1906), a volume of his own poems. Writing under the Gaelic form of his name, he published half a dozen books of verse, the most striking of which is *The Mountainy Singer* (1909).

He went to America, where, for a time, he was instructor at Fordham University, and died July 13, 1944.

I AM THE MOUNTAINY SINGER

I am the mountainy singer—
The voice of the peasant's dream,
The cry of the wind on the wooded hill,
The leap of the fish in the stream.

Quiet and love I sing—
The cairn on the mountain crest,
The *cailin* in her lover's arms,
The child at its mother's breast.

Beauty and peace I sing—
The fire on the open hearth,
The *cailleach* spinning at her wheel,
The plow in the broken earth.

Travail and pain I sing—
The bride on the childing bed,
The dark man laboring at his rhymes,
The ewe in the lambing shed.

Sorrow and death I sing—
The canker come on the corn,
The fisher lost in the mountain loch,
The cry at the mouth of morn.

No other life I sing,
For I am sprung of the stock
That broke the hilly land for bread,
And built the nest in the rock!

THE OLD WOMAN

As a white candle
  In a holy place,
So is the beauty
  Of an aged face.

As the spent radiance
  Of the winter sun,
So is a woman
  With her travail done,

Her brood gone from her,
  And her thoughts as still
As the waters
  Under a ruined mill.

Lascelles Abercrombie

Lascelles Abercrombie was born in 1881, at Ashton-upon-Mersey, near Manchester. He was educated at Malcolm College and Manchester University. After that, he engaged in a variety of professions; he taught literature at the University in Liverpool and in London. He succumbed to a long illness in 1938.

Like Masefield, Abercrombie gained his reputation rapidly. Unknown until 1909, upon the publication of *Interludes and Poems,* he was recognized as one of the true metaphysical poets of his period. *Emblems of Love* (1912), the ripest collection of his dialogues, justified the enthusiasm of his admirers.

Many of Abercrombie's poems, the best of which are too long to quote, are founded on scriptural themes, but his blank verse is biblical neither in mood nor in manner. It is the undercurrent rather than the surface of his verse which moves with a strong religious conviction. Abercrombie's images are daring and brilliant; his lines, sometimes too closely packed, glow with an intensity that is spiritual and yet recognizably human.

As a dramatist, Abercrombie had achieved a series of literary but scarcely popular successes with *Deborah* (1914), *Four Short Plays* (1921), and *Phoenix* (1923), brilliantly written though not eminently actable pieces. His knotted, almost tortured, style presents many difficulties to the performers as well as to audiences; but, once the speech is mastered, a swift intellectuality and a dramatic sense are disclosed beneath the obvious eloquence.

It is only the superficially dense style which keeps Abercrombie an unpopular, almost an unread, poet. Actually his diction, though thickened, is extraordinarily flexible; his characters, if overburdened with analysis, are vividly imagined; and, as Edward Thomas wrote, "the march or leap or stagger or hesitation of the syllables correspond to varying emotions with thrilling delicacy."

It seems a pity that the poet who conceived the ecstatic action of *The Sale of St. Thomas* (1911), the racing vigor of "Witchcraft: New Style," and the brilliant couplets of "Epilogue," should interest so few readers. Lacking a responsive following, Abercrombie turned almost entirely to prose. During his illness he wrote no less than six volumes about prosody and the technique of verse; *The Theory of Poetry* (1924) is one of the most illuminating books on the subject.

SONG

(from "Judith")

Balkis was in her marble town,
And shadow over the world came down.
Whiteness of walls, towers and piers,
That all day dazzled eyes to tears,
Turned from being white-golden flame,
And like the deep-sea blue became.
Balkis into her garden went;
Her spirit was in discontent
Like a torch in restless air.
Joylessly she wandered there,
And saw her city's azure white
Lying under the great night,
Beautiful as the memory
Of a worshiping world would be
In the mind of a god, in the hour
When he must kill his outward power;
And, coming to a pool where trees
Grew in double greeneries,
Saw herself, as she went by
The water, walking beautifully,
And saw the stars shine in the glance
Of her eyes, and her own fair countenance
Passing, pale and wonderful,
Across the night that filled the pool.
And cruel was the grief that played
With the queen's spirit; and she said:
"What do I here, reigning alone?
For to be unloved is to be alone.
There is no man in all my land
Dare my longing understand;
The whole folk like a peasant bows
Lest its look should meet my brows
And be harmed by this beauty of mine.
I burn their brains as I were sign
Of God's beautiful anger sent
To master them with punishment
Of beauty that must pour distress
On hearts grown dark with ugliness.
But it is I am the punisht one.
Is there no man, is there none,
In whom my beauty will but move
The lust of a delighted love;
In whom some spirit of God so thrives
That we may wed our lonely lives?
Is there no man, is there none?"—
She said, "I will go to Solomon."

EPILOGUE

What shall we do for Love these days?
How shall we make an altar-blaze
To smite the horny eyes of men
With the renown of our Heaven,
And to the unbelievers prove
Our service to our dear god, Love?
What torches shall we lift above
The crowd that pushes through the mire,
To amaze the dark heads with strange fire?
I should think I were much to blame,
If never I held some fragrant flame
Above the noises of the world,
And openly 'mid men's hurrying stares,
Worshipt before the sacred fears
That are like flashing curtains furl'd
Across the presence of our lord Love.
Nay, would that I could fill the gaze
Of the whole earth with some great praise
Made in a marvel for men's eyes,
Some tower of glittering masonries,
Therein such a spirit flourishing
Men should see what my heart can sing:
All that Love hath done to me
Built into stone, a visible glee;
Marble carried to gleaming height
As moved aloft by inward delight;
Not as with toil of chisels hewn,
But seeming poised in a mighty tune.

For of all those who have been known
To lodge with our kind host, the sun,
I envy one for just one thing:
In Cordova of the Moors
There dwelt a passion-minded King,
Who set great bands of marble-hewers
To fashion his heart's thanksgiving
In a tall palace, shapen so
All the wondering world might know
The joy he had of his Moorish lass.
His love, that brighter and larger was
Than the starry places, into firm stone
He sent, as if the stone were glass
Fired and into beauty blown.
Solemn and invented gravely
In its bulk the fabric stood,
Even as Love, that trusteth bravely
In its own exceeding good
To be better than the waste
Of time's devices; grandly spaced,
Seriously the fabric stood.
But over it all a pleasure went
Of carven delicate ornament,
Wreathing up like ravishment,
Mentioning in sculptures twined
The blitheness Love hath in his mind;
And like delighted senses were
The windows, and the columns there
Made the following sight to ache
As the heart that did them make.
Well I can see that shining song
Flowering there, the upward throng
Of porches, pillars and windowed walls,
Spires like piercing panpipe calls,
Up to the roof's snow-cloudy flight;
All glancing in the Spanish light
White as water of arctic tides,
Save an amber dazzle on sunny sides.
You had said, the radiant sheen
Of that palace might have been
A young god's fantasy, ere he came
His serious worlds and suns to frame;
Such an immortal passion
Quiver'd among the slim hewn stone.
And in the nights it seemed a jar
Cut in the substance of a star,
Wherein a wine, that will be poured
Some time for feasting Heaven, was stored
But within this fretted shell,
The wonder of Love made visible,
The King a private gentle mood
There placed, of pleasant quietude.
For right amidst there was a court,
Where always muskèd silences
Listened to water and to trees;
And herbage of all fragrant sort,—
Lavender, lad's love, rosemary,
Basil, tansy, centaury,—
Was the grass of that orchard, hid
Love's amazements all amid.
Jarring the air with rumor cool,
Small fountains played into a pool
With sound as soft as the barley's hiss
When its beard just sprouting is;
Whence a young stream, that trod on moss
Prettily rippled the court across.
And in the pool's clear idleness,
Moving like dreams through happiness,
Shoals of small bright fishes were;
In and out weed-thickets bent
Perch and carp, and sauntering went

With mounching jaws and eyes a-stare;
Or on a lotus leaf would crawl,
A brinded loach to bask and sprawl,
Tasting the warm sun ere it dipt
Into the water; but quick as fear
Back his shining brown head slipt
To crouch on the gravel of his lair,
Where the cooled sunbeams broke in wrack,
Spilt shatter'd gold about his back.
So within that green-veiled air,
Within that white-walled quiet, where
Innocent water thought aloud,—
Childish prattle that must make
The wise sunlight with laughter shake
On the leafage overbowed,—
Often the King and his love-lass
Let the delicious hours pass.
All the outer world could see
Graved and sawn amazingly
Their love's delighted riotise,
Fixt in marble for all men's eyes;
But only these twain could abide
In the cool peace that withinside
Thrilling desire and passion dwelt;
They only knew the still meaning spelt
By Love's flaming script, which is
God's word written in ecstasies.
And where is now that palace gone,
All the magical skill'd stone,
All the dreaming towers wrought
By Love as if no more than thought
The unresisting marble was?
How could such a wonder pass?
Ah, it was but built in vain
Against the stupid horns of Rome,
That pusht down into the common loam
The loveliness that shone in Spain.
But we have raised it up again!
A loftier palace, fairer far,
Is ours, and one that fears no war.
Safe in marvelous walls we are;
Wondering sense like builded fires,
High amazement of desires,
Delight and certainty of love,
Closing around, roofing above
Our unapproacht and perfect hour
Within the splendors of love's power.

WOMAN'S BEAUTY

(from "Vashti")

What thing shall be held up to woman's beauty?
Where are the bounds of it? Yea, what is all
The world, but an awning scaffolded amid
The waste perilous Eternity, to lodge
This Heaven-wander'd princess, woman's beauty?
The East and West kneel down to thee, the North
And South; and all for thee their shoulders bear
The load of fourfold space. As yellow morn
Runs on the slippery waves of the spread sea,
Thy feet are on the griefs and joys of men
That shine to be thy causey. Out of tears
Indeed, and blitheness, murder and lust and love,
Whatever has been passionate in clay,
Thy flesh was tempered. Behold in thy body
The yearnings of all men measured and told,
Insatiate endless agonies of desire
Given thy flesh, the meaning of thy shape!
What beauty is there, but thou makest it?
How is earth good to look on, woods and fields,
The season's garden, and the courageous hills,
All this green raft of earth moored in the seas?
The manner of the sun to ride the air,

The stars God has imagined for the night?
What's this behind them that we cannot near,
Secret still on the point of being blabbed,
The ghost in the world that flies from being named
Where do they get their beauty from, all these?
They do but glaze a lantern lit for man,
And woman's beauty is the flame therein.

WITCHCRAFT: NEW STYLE

The sun drew off at last his piercing fires.
Over the stale warm air, dull as a pond
And moveless in the gray quieted street,
Blue magic of a summer evening glowed.
The sky, that had been dazzling stone all day,
Hollowed in smooth hard brightness, now dissolved
To infinite soft depth, and smoldered down
Low as the roofs, dark burning blue, and soared
Clear to that winking drop of liquid silver,
The first exquisite star. Now the half-light
Tidied away the dusty litter parching
Among the cobbles, veiled in the color of distance
Shabby slates and brickwork moldering, turned
The hunchback houses into patient things
Resting; and golden windows now began.

A little brisk gray slattern of a woman,
Pattering along in her loose-heeled clogs,
Pusht the brass-barred door of a public-house;
The spring went hard against her; hand and knee
Shoved their weak best. As the door poised ajar,
Hullabaloo of talking men burst out,
A pouring babble of inflamed palaver,
And overriding it and shouted down
High words, jeering or downright, broken like
Crests that leap and stumble in rushing water.
Just as the door went wide and she stept in,
"She cannot do it!" one was bawling out:
A glaring hulk of flesh with a bull's voice.
He fingered with his neckerchief, and stretcht
His throat to ease the anger of dispute,
Then spat to put a full stop to the matter.
The little woman waited, with one hand
Propping the door, and smiled at the loud man.
They saw her then; and the sight was enough
To gag the speech of every drinker there:
The din fell down like something chopt off short.
Blank they all wheeled towards her, with their mouths
Still gaping as though full of voiceless words.
She let the door slam to; and all at ease,

Amused, her smile wrinkling about her eyes,
Went forward; they made room for her quick enough.
Her chin just topt the counter; she gave in
Her bottle to the potboy, tuckt it back,
Full of bright tawny ale, under her arm,
Rapt down the coppers on the planisht zinc,
And turned: and no word spoken all the while.
The first voice, in that silent crowd, was hers,
Her light snickering laugh, as she stood there
Pausing, scanning the sawdust at her feet.
Then she switcht round and faced the positive man
Whose strong "She cannot do it!" all still felt
Huskily shouting in their guilty ears.
"She can't, eh? She can't do it?"—Then she'd heard!
The man, inside his ruddy insolent flesh,
Had hoped she did not hear. His barrel chest
Gave a slight cringe, as though the glint of her eyes
Prickt him. But he stood up to her awkwardly bold,
One elbow on the counter, gripping his mug
Like a man holding on to a post for safety.

The Man You can't do what's not nature: nobody can.
The Woman And louts like you have nature in your pocket?
The Man I don't say that —
The Woman If you kept saying naught,
No one would guess the fool you are.
Second Man Almost
My very words!
The Woman O you're the knowing man!
The spark among the cinders!
First Man You can't fetch
A free man back, unless he wants to come.
The Woman Nay, I'll be bound he doesn't want to come!
Third Man And he won't come: he told me flat he wouldn't.
The Woman Are you there too?
Third Man And if he does come back
It will be devilry brought him.
The Woman I shall bring him;—
Tonight.
First Man How will he come?
The Woman Running: unless
He's broke his leg, and then he'll have to come
Crawling. But he will come.
First Man How do you know
What he may choose to do, three countries off?
The Woman He choose?
Third Man You haven't got him on a lead.
The Woman Haven't I though!
Second Man That's right: it's what I said.
The Woman Aye, there are brains in your family.

First Man You have
Some sort of pull on him, to draw him home?
The Woman You may say that: I have hold of his mind.
And I can slack it off or fetch it taut,
And make him dance a score of miles away
An answer to the least twangling thrum
I play on it. He thought he lurkt at last
Safely; and all the while, what has he been?
An eel on the end of a night-line; and it's time
I hauled him in. You'll see, tonight I'll land him.
Third Man Bragging's a light job.
The Woman You daren't let me take
Your eyes in mine!—Haul, did I say? no need:
I give his mind a twitch, and up he comes
Tumbling home to me. Whatever work he's at,
He drops the thing he holds like redhot iron
And runs—runs till he falls down like a beast
Pole-axt, and grunts for breath; then up and on,
No matter does he know the road or not:
The strain I put on his mind will keep him going
Right as a homing-pigeon.
First Man Devilry
I call it.
The Woman And you're welcome.
Second Man But the law
Should have a say here.
The Woman What, isn't he mine,
My own? There's naught but what I please about it.
Third Man Why did you let him go?
The Woman To fetch him back!
For I enjoy this, mind. There's many a one
Would think to see me, There goes misery!
There's a queer starveling for you!—and I do
A thing that makes me like a saint in glory,
The life of me the sound of a great tune
Your flesh could never hear: I can send power
Delighting out of me! O, the mere thought
Has made my blood go smarting in my veins,
Such a flame glowing along it!—And all the same
I'll pay him out for sidling off from me.
But I'll have supper first.

When she was gone,
Their talk could scarcely raise itself again
Above a grumble. But at last a cry
Sharp-pitcht came startling in from the street: at once
Their moody talk exploded into flare
Of swearing hubbub, like gunpowder dropt
On embers; mugs were clapt down, out they bolted
Rowdily jostling, eager for the event.
All down the street the folk thronged out of doors,

But left a narrow track clear in the middle;
And there a man came running, a tall man
Running desperately and slowly, pounding
Like a machine, so evenly, so blindly;
And regularly his trotting body wagged.
Only one foot clattered upon the stones;
The other padded in his dogged stride:
The boot was gone, the sock hung frayed in shreds
About his ankle, the foot was blood and earth;
And never a limp, not the least flinch, to tell
The wounded pulp hit stone at every step.
His clothes were tattered and his rent skin showed,
Harrowed with thorns. His face was pale as putty,
Thrown far back; clots of drooping spittle foamed
On his mustache, and his hair hung in tails,
Mired with sweat; and sightless in their sockets
His eyeballs turned up white, as dull as pebbles.
Evenly and doggedly he trotted,
And as he went he moaned. Then out of sight
Round a corner he swerved, and out of hearing.
—"The law should have a say to that, by God!"

EPITAPH

Sir, you should notice me: I am the Man;
I am Good Fortune: I am satisfied.
All I desired, more than I could desire,
I have: everything has gone right with me.
Life was a hiding-place that played me false;
I croucht ashamed, and still was seen and scorned:
But now I am not seen. I was a fool,
And now I know what wisdom dare not know:
For I know Nothing. I was a slave, and now
I have ungoverned freedom and the wealth
That cannot be conceived: for I have Nothing.
I lookt for beauty and I longed for rest,
And now I have perfection: nay, I am
Perfection: I am Nothing, I am dead.

James Stephens

James Stephens was born in Dublin in February, 1882. His youth was difficult, his livelihood precarious. Stephens was "discovered" in an office and saved from clerical slavery by George Russell ("Æ"). Always a poet, many of Stephen's most poetic moments are in his highly colored prose. Yet, although the finest of his novels, *The Crock of Gold* (1912), contains more wild fantasy and quaint imagery than his verse, his *Insurrections* (1909) and *The Hill of Vision* (1912) reveal a rebellious spirit that is at once hotly ironic and coolly whimsical. *Green Branches* (1916) and *Reincarnations* (1918)—the latter being free adaptations from the Gaelic—are further persuasive volumes of his verse.

Collected Poems (1926) discloses two strongly differentiated personalities. There is the familiar and well-beloved Irish gamin, intimate with goats and gods, the playboy of the roads, deferential to rabbits and lesser folk, impudent to the universe. There is, also, the less popular but more sizeable poet, the thoughtful author of "The Crest Jewel," "In Waste Places," "The Main-Deep" with its surging rhythm held in a few syllables, and "A Prelude and a Song" which moves with the gentle solemnity of a river. Traces of Blake are in the later Stephens; the poet, discarding his light grotesquerie, becomes the seer. A less amusing singer is the result, but a more impassioned one. In youth Stephens delighted in gay mischiefs, pranking with unnatural phenomena; in maturity he is concerned with nothing less than elemental truths.

Both personalities combine in the prose fiction for which Stephens is famous. *Deirdre* (1923) and *In the Land of Youth* (1924) continue the re-creations from the Irish folk- and fairy-tales. *Hunger* (1918), originally published under the pseudonym "James Esse," was incorporated in the somber collection of short stories *Etched in Moonlight* (1928) which, curiously enough, was poorly received in England but an enormous success in America. An edition of his *Irish Fairy Tales* was arranged for children.

Strict Joy (1931) is a small book containing a dozen new poems, yet its very range is characteristic. Stephens lightly runs the scale from badinage to mysticism and seldom strikes an uncertain note, never a false one.

Kings and the Moon (1938) is another deceptive little volume. It is so simply written as to seem banal, so unaffected in thought as to appear sentimental. But the simplicity is attained by severe restraint, by clear perception instead of poetic diction, by the refusal to inflate an emotion or pad a line.

Stephens's final characteristic is his delightful blend of incongruities—he successfully mingles the bizarre and the charming, the buoyant and the profound. It is sometimes difficult to separate the elfin from the human in Stephens—Fred B. Millett has characterized Stephens' spirit as "that of a sensitive and uncannily observant gnome"—but Stephens charms by the very uncertainty, by the tricks of his imagination and the sudden warmth of his sympathy. Stephens died December 26, 1950.

EVENING

The drowsy sun went slowly to his rest
Gathering all his dusty gold again
Into one place:
He did not leave a trace
Upon the sky except one distant stain,
Scarce to be seen, upon the quiet west:
So evening came, and darkness, and the sound
Of moving feet upon the whispering ground.

Like timid girls the shades went pacing down
The spreading slopes apparelled soberly
In vestments grey;
And far away
The last red color faded to a brown,
So faint, so far, the eye could scarcely see:
And then the skirts of evening swung upon
That distant little light, and it was gone.

The bee sped home, the beetle's wing of horn
Went booming by, the darkness every side
Gathered around
On sky and air and ground;
And all the pliant trees sang far and wide
In cadenced lift of leaves a song of morn:
And then the moon's white circle, faint and thin,
Looked steady on the earth—*there is no sin.*

THE LAKE

He could see the little lake
Cuddled on a mountain's arm,
And the rushes were a-shake,
On the margin of the lake.

And the gloom of evening threw
On the surface of the lake,
Just a shadow on the blue
Where the night came creeping through.

There was silence all around,
Not a whisper stirred the lake,
And the trees made not a sound
Standing silent in the ground.

Then a moon of beauty swept
One slim finger on the lake,
And the glory of it crept
Past the lilies where they slept,

And just where a lily flung
Its broad flag upon the lake
Was a dead face pale and young
And the wet hair spread and swung;

And the moon beamed mild and dim
On that dead face in the lake,
Then it grew fierce, wide and grim,
And a mad moon glared at Him.

THE SHELL

And then I pressed the shell
Close to my ear
And listened well,
And straightway like a bell
Came low and clear
The slow, sad murmur of the distant seas,
Whipped by an icy breeze
Upon a shore
Wind-swept and desolate.
It was a sunless strand that never bore
The footprint of a man,
Nor felt the weight
Since time began
Of any human quality or stir
Save what the dreary winds and waves incur.
And in the hush of waters was the sound
Of pebbles rolling round,
For ever rolling with a hollow sound.
And bubbling sea-weeds as the waters go
Swish to and fro
Their long, cold tentacles of slimy gray.
There was no day,
Nor felt the weight
Setting the stars alight
To wonder at the moon:
Was twilight only and the frightened croon,
Smitten to whimpers, of the dreary wind
And waves that journeyed blind—
And then I loosed my ear . . . O, it was sweet
To hear a cart go jolting down the street.

WHAT THOMAS AN BUILE SAID IN A PUB

I saw God. Do you doubt it?
  Do you dare to doubt it?
I saw the Almighty Man. His hand
Was resting on a mountain, and
He looked upon the World and all about it:
I saw Him plainer than you see me now,
  You mustn't doubt it.

He was not satisfied;
  His look was all dissatisfied.
His beard swung on a wind far out of sight
Behind the world's curve, and there was light
Most fearful from His forehead, and He sighed,
"That star went always wrong, and from the start
  I was dissatisfied."

He lifted up His hand—
  I say He heaved a dreadful hand
Over the spinning Earth. Then I said, "Stay,
You must not strike it, God; I'm in the way;
And I will never move from where I stand."
He said, "Dear child, I feared that you were dead,"
  And stayed His hand.

TO THE FOUR COURTS, PLEASE

The driver rubbed at his nettly chin
With a huge, loose forefinger, crooked and black,
And his wobbly, violet lips sucked in,
And puffed out again and hung down slack:
One fang shone through his lop-sided smile,
In his little pouched eye flickered years of guile.

And the horse, poor beast, it was ribbed and forked,
And its ears hung down, and its eyes were old,
And its knees were knuckly, and as we talked
It swung the stiff neck that could scarcely hold
Its big, skinny head up—then I stepped in,
And the driver climbed to his seat with a grin.

God help the horse and the driver too,
And the people and beasts who have never a friend,
For the driver easily might have been you,
And the horse be me by a different end.
And nobody knows how their days will cease,
And the poor, when they're old, have little of peace.

LITTLE THINGS

Little things that run and quail
And die in silence and despair;

Little things that fight and fail
And fall on earth and sea and air;

All trapped and frightened little things
The mouse, the coney, hear our prayer.

As we forgive those done to us,
The lamb, the linnet, and the hare,

Forgive us all our trespasses,
Little creatures everywhere.

THE RED-HAIRED MAN'S WIFE

I have taken that vow—
  And you were my friend
But yesterday—now
  All that's at an end,
And you are my husband, and claim me, and I must depend.

Yesterday I was free,
  Now you, as I stand
Walk over to me
  And take hold of my hand.
You look at my lips, your eyes are too bold, your smile is too bland.

My old name is lost,
  My distinction of race:
Now the line has been crossed,
  Must I step to your pace?
Must I walk as you list, and obey and smile up in your face?

All the white and the red
  Of my cheeks you have won;
All the hair of my head,
  And my feet, tho' they run,
Are yours, and you own me and end me just as I begun.

Must I bow when you speak,
  Be silent and hear,
Inclining my cheek
  And incredulous ear
To your voice, and command, and behest, hold your lightest wish dear?

I am woman, but still
  Am alive, and can feel
Every intimate thrill
  That is woe or is weal.
I, aloof, and divided, apart, standing far, can I kneel?

If not, I shall know,
  I shall surely find out,
And your world will throw
  In disaster and rout;
I am woman and glory and beauty, I mystery, terror, and doubt.

I am separate still,
  I am I and not you:
And my mind and my will,
  As in secret they grew,
Still are secret, unreached and untouched and not subject to you.

HATE

My enemy came nigh,
And I
Stared fiercely in his face.
My lips went writhing back in a grimace,
And stern I watched him with a narrow eye.
Then, as I turned away, my enemy,
That bitter heart and savage, said to me:
"Some day, when this is past,
When all the arrows that we have are cast,
We may ask one another why we hate,
And fail to find a story to relate.
It may seem to us then a mystery
That we could hate each other."
Thus said he,
And did not turn away,
Waiting to hear what I might have to say.
But I fled quickly, fearing if I stayed
I might have kissed him as I would a maid.

THE WATCHER

A rose for a young head,
A ring for a bride,
Joy for the homestead
Clean and wide—
Who's that waiting
In the rain outside?

A heart for an old friend,
A hand for the new:
Love can to earth lend
Heaven's hue—
Who's that standing
In the silver dew?

A smile for the parting,
A tear as they go,
God's sweethearting
Ends just so—
Who's that watching
Where the black winds blow?

He who is waiting
In the rain outside,
He who is standing
Where the dew drops wide,
He who is watching
In the wind must ride
(Tho' the pale hands cling)
With the rose
And the ring
And the bride,
Must ride
With the red of the rose,
And the gold of the ring,
And the lips and the hair of the bride.

RIGHTEOUS ANGER

The lanky hank of a she in the inn over there
Nearly killed me for asking the loan of a glass of beer:
May the devil grip the whey-faced slut by the hair,
And beat bad manners out of her skin for a year.

That parboiled imp, with the hardest jaw you will see
On virtue's path, and a voice that would rasp the dead,
Came roaring and raging the minute she looked at me,
And threw me out of the house on the back of my head!

If I asked her master he'd give me a cask a day;
But she with the beer at hand, not a gill would arrange!
May she marry a ghost and bear him a kitten and may
The High King of Glory permit her to get the mange.

ODELL

My mind is sad and weary thinking how
The griffins of the Gael went over the sea

From noble Eiré, and are fighting now
In France and Flanders and in Germany.

If they, 'mid whom I sported without dread,
Were home I would not mind what foe might do,
Or fear tax-man Odell would seize my bed
To pay the hearth-rate that is overdue.

I pray to Him who, in the haughty hour
Of Babel, threw confusion on each tongue,
That I may see our princes back in power,
And see Odell, the tax-collector, hung.

BLUE BLOOD

(*After O'Bruaidar*)

We thought at first, this man is a king for sure,
Or the branch of a mighty and ancient and famous lineage—
That silly, sulky, illiterate, black-avised boor
Who was hatched by foreign vulgarity under a hedge.

The good men of Clare were drinking his health in a flood,
And gazing with me in awe of the princely lad,
And asking each other from what bluest blueness of blood
His daddy was squeezed, and the pa of the da of his dad?

We waited there, gaping and wondering, anxiously,
Until he'd stop eating and let the glad tidings out,
And the slack-jawed booby proved to the hilt that he
Was lout, son of lout, by old lout, and was da to a lout!

THE MAIN-DEEP

The long rólling,
Steady-póuring,
Deep-trenchéd
Green billow:

The wide-topped,
Unbróken,
Green-glacid,
Slow-sliding.

Cold-flushing,
On—on—on—
Chill-rushing,
Hush-hushing,

Hush—hushing. . . .

IN WASTE PLACES

As a naked man I go
Through the desert, sore afraid;
Holding high my head, although
I'm as frightened as a maid.

The lion crouches there! I saw
In barren rocks his amber eye!
He parts the cactus with his paw!
He stares at me as I go by!

He would pad upon my trace
If he thought I was afraid!
If he knew my hardy face
Veils the terrors of a maid.

He rises in the night-time, and
He stretches forth! He snuffs the air!

He roars! He leaps along the sand!
He creeps! He watches everywhere!

His burning eyes, his eyes of bale
Through the darkness I can see!
He lashes fiercely with his tail!
He makes again to spring at me!

I am the lion, and his lair!
I am the fear that frightens me!
I am the desert of despair!
And the night of agony!

Night or day, whate'er befall,
I must walk that desert land,
Until I dare my fear and call
The lion out to lick my hand.

GOOD AND BAD

Good and bad and right and wrong,
Wave the silly words away:
This is wisdom to be strong,
This is virtue to be gay:
Let us sing and dance until
We shall know the final art,
How to banish good and ill
With the laughter of the heart.

THE OUTCAST

Shy and timid, Gloom to me
Said, I am lost! How shall I go?
There is no place for Misery,
Welcome for Woe!

And to him,
Desolate and fey,
My stricken heart
Found nought to say.

But soon: Be thou my Joy, I said:
Give me your hand, rest here your head:
Come to my home, and eat my bread,
And rest thee from annoy.

For I shall give thee all of mine,
Until my all be sealéd thine,
And thou shalt be, in little time,
A Child of Joy.

Now, on my heart, as on a throne,
Gloom, as heavy as a stone,
Sits, and I go dark till he
Is Joy, and gives Joy back to me.

THE CREST JEWEL

I

The leaf will wrinkle to decay
And crumble into dust away!

The rose, the lily, grow to eld,
And are, and are no more, beheld!

Nothing will stay! For, as the eye
Rests upon an object nigh,

It is not there to look upon!
It is mysteriously gone!

And, in its place, another thing
Apes its shape and fashioning!

II

All that the sun will breathe today
The moon will lip and wear away

Tonight. And all will re-begin
Tomorrow as the dawn comes in.

Is no beginning, middle-trend
Or argument to that or end.

No cause and no effect, and no
Reason why it should be so.

Or why it might be otherwise
To other minds or other eyes.

III

The soul can dream itself to be
Adrift upon an endless sea

Of day and night. The soul can seem
To be all things that it can dream!

Yet needs but look within to find
That which is steady in the wind,

That which the fire does not appal,
Which good and ill mourn not at all

Which does not seek, or lack, or try.
And was not born, and cannot die!

IV

It has been writ in wisdom old—
This is the last word to be told:

—There is no dissolution! No
Creation! There are none in woe!

There is no teacher, teaching, taught!
Are none who long for, lack for aught!

Are none who pine for freedom! None
Are liberated under sun!

—And this is absolutely true
In Him who dreams in me and you.

James Joyce

James Augustine Aloysius Joyce was born February 2, 1882, in Dublin. Educated for the priesthood, he attended Jesuit schools in Ireland for thirteen years. At twenty he revolted, wrote a blasphemous broadside, left his country and repudiated his countrymen, "the most belated race in Europe."

From that time Joyce's life (according to Herbert Gorman, Joyce's official biographer) became "a constant struggle against terrific odds, prejudices, mob smugness, poverty, and physical disability." His work was censored, officially banned, and even burned; his books, forbidden by several governments, were illicitly published all over the world, and Joyce received no royalties from the pirated publications. He studied medicine in Paris; almost became a professional singer; taught languages in Trieste and Switzerland; wandered about the Continent until he finally settled in Paris. Illness and overwork necessitated ten eye operations in twenty years; before he was forty Joyce was practically blind. Writing was a painful effort for him; a few lines at a time scrawled on a large sheet of paper was all he could manage.

Joyce's literary début was quiet and undistinguished: *Chamber Music* (1907), a small volume of pseudo-Elizabethan verse in the traditional lyric manner. His next book, *Dubliners* (1914), marked the beginning of the artist's twofold struggle for recognition and for the right to pursue his own methods—methods which, depending upon the point of view, were lauded as pioneering or attacked as mere arrogance.

In his early thirties Joyce definitely broke with tradition in *A Portrait of the Artist as a Young Man* (1916), a welter of characters and theories, a kaleidoscope of the weird and the commonplace. Its central character became a chief figure in Joyce's *Ulysses* (1922), banned for many years from the United States. *Ulysses,* an autobiographical extension of reality, is one of the strangest novels ever written and one of the most extraordinary works of the age. It became a storm-center. It was reviled as the work of an obscene madman and praised as the utterance of an unqualifiedly great genius. With all its complexities, *Ulysses* is crystal-clear compared to *Finnegan's Wake* (1939). *Finnegan's Wake* seems to be a collision between the language of speech and the language of literature, a colossal series of telescopic phrases, vast figures which dissolve into allusions, and a constant elaboration of half-intelligible puns.

The enormous labor demanded by his cryptic work was too much for Joyce. He succumbed in a losing fight against blindness, illness, and poverty; he died in Zurich, Switzerland, January 13, 1941, a few weeks before his fifty-ninth birthday. Richard Ellmann's *James Joyce* (1959) is the most penetrating biography.

Pomes Penyeach (1927) is delicate and genuinely lyrical, strangely reminiscent of the seventeenth century singers. Like the early *Chamber Music,* the verse is conventional in theme, orthodox in treatment, harmonically simple, and the very antithesis of everything for which Joyce is celebrated.

STRINGS IN THE EARTH

Strings in the earth and air
  Make music sweet;
Strings by the river where
  The willows meet.

There's music along the river
  For Love wanders there,
Pale flowers on his mantle,
  Dark leaves on his hair.

All softly playing,
  With head to the music bent,
And fingers straying
  Upon an instrument.

I HEAR AN ARMY

I hear an army charging upon the land,
  And the thunder of horses plunging, foam about their knees:
Arrogant, in black armor, behind them stand,
  Disdaining the reins, with fluttering whips, the charioteers.

They cry unto the night their battle-name:
  I moan in sleep when I hear afar their whirling laughter.
They cleave the gloom of dreams, a blinding flame,
  Clanging, clanging upon the heart as upon an anvil.

They come shaking in triumph their long, green hair:
  They come out of the sea and run shouting by the shore.
My heart, have you no wisdom thus to despair?
  My love, my love, my love, why have you left me alone?

O SWEETHEART, HEAR YOU

O sweetheart, hear you
 Your lover's tale;
A man shall have sorrow
 When friends him fail.

For he shall know then
 Friends be untrue
And a little ashes
 Their words come to.

But one unto him
 Will softly move
And softly woo him
 In ways of love.

His hand is under
 Her smooth round breast;
So he who has sorrow
 Shall have rest.

ALL DAY I HEAR

All day I hear the noise of waters
 Making moan,
Sad as the sea-bird is when, going
 Forth alone,
He hears the winds cry to the waters'
 Monotone.

The gray winds, the cold winds are blowing
 Where I go.
I hear the noise of many waters
 Far below.
All day, all night, I hear them flowing
 To and fro.

SONG

O, it was out by Donnycarney,
 When the bat flew from tree to tree,
My love and I did walk together,
 And sweet were the words she said to me.

Along with us the summer wind
 Went murmuring—O, happily!—
But softer than the breath of summer
 Was the kiss she gave to me.

ON THE BEACH AT FONTANA

Wind whines and whines the shingle,
The crazy pierstakes groan;
A senile sea numbers each single
Slimesilvered stone.

From whining wind and colder
Gray sea I wrap him warm
And touch his trembling fineboned shoulder
And boyish arm.

Around us fear, descending
Darkness of fear above
And in my heart how deep unending
Ache of love!

FLOOD

Goldbrown upon the sated flood
The rockvine clusters lift and sway,
Vast wings above the lambent waters brood
Of sullen day.

A waste of waters ruthlessly
Sways and uplifts its weedy mane
Where brooding day stares down upon the sea
In dull disdain.

Uplift and sway, O golden vine,
Your clustered fruits to love's full flood,
Lambent and vast and ruthless as in thine
Incertitude!

James Elroy Flecker

Another remarkable poet whose early death was a blow to English literature was James Elroy Flecker. Born in London, November 5, 1884, he studied at Trinity College, Oxford, specialized in Oriental languages at Cambridge, and went to Constantinople in the Consular Service in 1910. The fact that the remainder of his life was spent in the East has a direct bearing on Flecker's work: his play *Hassan,* one of the most powerful and brilliantly colored modern dramas, is the definite reflection of his adopted Orientalism.

Possibly due to low vitality, Flecker found little to interest him but a reaction against realism in verse, a delight in verbal craftsmanship, and a passion for technical perfection—especially the deliberate technique of the French Parnassians, whom he worshiped. Flecker was opposed to any art that was emotional or that "taught" anything. "The poet's business," he declared, "is not to save the soul of man, but to make it worth saving." Flecker's desire to be objective rather than passionate was scarcely consistent with his actual creation, even though he maintained that "the Parnassians raised the technique of their art to a height which enabled them to express the subtlest ideas in powerful and simple verse." Technique and manner were his abstract gods.

The advent of the war began to make Flecker's verse more personal and romantic. The tuberculosis that finally killed him at Davos Platz, Switzerland, January 3, 1915, forced him from an Olympian disinterest to a deep concern with life and death. He passionately denied that he was weary of living "as the pallid poets are," and he was attempting higher flights of song when his singing ceased altogether.

Flecker's two notable volumes are *The Golden Journey to Samarkand* (1913) and *The Old Ships* (1915). *Collected Poems,* with an autobiographical introduction and notes by J. C. Squire, was published in 1917 and drew fresh attention to Flecker's half-classical, half-romantic, and always vivid style.

THE OLD SHIPS

I have seen old ships sail like swans asleep
Beyond the village which men still call Tyre,
With leaden age o'ercargoed, dipping deep
For Famagusta and the hidden sun
That rings black Cyprus with a lake of fire;
And all those ships were certainly so old—
Who knows how oft with squat and noisy gun,
Questing brown slaves or Syrian oranges,
The pirate Genoese
Hell-raked them till they rolled
Blood, water, fruit and corpses up the hold.
But now through friendly seas they softly run,
Painted the mid-sea blue or shore-sea green,
Still patterned with the vine and grapes in gold.

But I have seen,
Pointing her shapely shadows from the dawn
An image tumbled on a rose-swept bay,
A drowsy ship of some yet older day;
And, wonder's breath indrawn,
Thought I—who knows—who knows—but in that same
(Fished up beyond Aeaea, patched up new
—Stern painted brighter blue—)
That talkative, bald-headed seaman came
(Twelve patient comrades sweating at the oar)
From Troy's doom-crimson shore,
And with great lies about his wooden horse
Set the crew laughing, and forgot his course.

It was so old a ship—who knows, who knows?
—And yet so beautiful, I watched in vain
To see the mast burst open with a rose,
And the whole deck put on its leaves again.

STILLNESS

When the words rustle no more,
  And the last work's done,
When the bolt lies deep in the door,

And Fire, our Sun,
Falls on the dark-laned meadows of the floor;

When from the clock's last chime to the next chime
Silence beats his drum,
And Space with gaunt gray eyes and her brother Time
Wheeling and whispering come,
She with the mold of form and he with the loom of rhyme:

Then twittering out in the night my thought-birds flee,
I am emptied of all my dreams:
I only hear Earth turning, only see
Ether's long bankless streams,
And only know I should drown if you
Laid not your hand on me.

THE WAR SONG OF THE SARACENS

We are they who come faster than fate: we are they who ride early or late:
We storm at your ivory gate: Pale Kings of the Sunset, beware!
Not on silk nor in samet we lie, not in curtained solemnity die
Among women who chatter and cry, and children who mumble a prayer.
But we sleep by the ropes of the camp, and we rise with a shout, and we tramp
With the sun or the moon for a lamp, and the spray of the wind in our hair.

From the lands, where the elephants are, to the forts of Merou and Balghar,
Our steel we have brought and our star to shine on the ruins of Ruhm.
We have marched from the Indus to Spain, and, by God, we will go there again;
We have stood on the shore of the plain where the Waters of Destiny boom.
A mart of destruction we made at Jalúla where men were afraid,
For death was a difficult trade, and the sword was a broker of doom;

And the Spear was a Desert Physician who cured not a few of ambition.
And drave not a few to perdition with medicine bitter and strong;
And the shield was a grief to the fool and as bright as a desolate pool,
And as straight as the rock of Stamboul when their cavalry thundered along:
For the coward was drowned with the brave when our battle sheered up like a wave,
And the dead to the desert we gave, and the glory to God in our song.

TENEBRIS INTERLUCENTEM

A linnet who had lost her way
Sang on a blackened bough in Hell,
Till all the ghosts remembered well
The trees, the wind, the golden day.

At last they knew that they had died
When they heard music in that land,
And someone there stole forth a hand
To draw a brother to his side.

TO A POET A THOUSAND YEARS HENCE

I who am dead a thousand years,
And wrote this sweet archaic song,
Send you my words for messengers
The way I shall not pass along.

I care not if you bridge the seas,
Or ride secure the cruel sky,
Or build consummate palaces
Of metal or of masonry.

But have you wine and music still,
And statues and a bright-eyed love,
And foolish thoughts of good and ill,
And prayers to them who sit above?

How shall we conquer? Like a wind
That falls at eve our fancies blow,
And old Maeonides the blind
Said it three thousand years ago.

O friend unseen, unborn, unknown,
Student of our sweet English tongue,
Read out my words at night, alone:
I was a poet, I was young.

Since I can never see your face,
And never shake you by the hand,
I send my soul through time and space
To greet you. You will understand.

THE TOWN WITHOUT A MARKET

There lies afar behind a western hill
The Town without a Market, white and still;
For six feet long and not a third as high
Are those small habitations. There stood I,
Waiting to hear the citizens beneath
Murmur and sigh and speak through tongueless teeth.
When all the world lay burning in the sun
I heard their voices speak to me. Said one:
"Bright lights I loved and colors, I who find
That death is darkness, and has struck me blind."
Another cried: "I used to sing and play,
But here the world is silent, day by day."
And one: "On earth I could not see or hear,
But with my fingers touched what I was near,
And knew things round and soft, and brass from gold,
And dipped my hand in water, to feel cold,
And thought the grave would cure me, and was glad

When the time came to lose what joy I had."
Soon all the voices of a hundred dead
Shouted in wrath together. Someone said,
"I care not, but the girl was sweet to kiss
At evening in the meadows." "Hard it is,"
Another cried, "to hear no hunting horn.
Ah me! the horse, the hounds, and the great gray morn
When I rode out a-hunting." And one sighed,
"I did not see my son before I died."
A boy said, "I was strong and swift to run:
Now they have tied my feet; what have I done?"
A man, "But it was good to arm and fight
And storm their cities in the dead of night."
An old man said, "I read my books all day,
But death has taken all my books away."
And one, "The popes and prophets did not well
To cheat poor dead men with false hopes of hell.
Better the whips of fire that hiss and rend
Than painless void proceeding to no end."
I smiled to hear them restless, I who sought
Peace. For I had not loved, I had not fought,
And books are vanities, and manly strength
A gathered flower. God grants us peace at length!
I heard no more, and turned to leave their town
Before the chill came, and the sun went down.
Then rose a whisper, and I seemed to know
A timorous man, buried long years ago.
"On Earth I used to shape the Thing that seems.
Master of all men, give me back my dreams.
Give me the world that never failed me then,
The hills I made and peopled with tall men,
The palace that I built and called my home,
My cities which could break the pride of Rome,
The three queens hidden in the sacred tree,
And those white cloudy folk who sang to me,
O death, why hast thou covered me so deep?
I was thy sister's child, the friend of Sleep."

Then said my heart, Death takes and cannot give.
Dark with no dream is hateful: let me live!

THE BALLAD OF HAMPSTEAD HEATH

From Heaven's Gate to Hampstead Heath
  Young Bacchus and his crew
Came tumbling down, and o'er the town
  Their bursting trumpets blew.

The silver night was wildly bright,
  And madly shone the moon
To hear a song so clear and strong,
  With such a lovely tune.

From London's houses, huts and flats,
  Came busmen, snobs, and Earls,
And ugly men in bowler hats
  With charming little girls.

Sir Moses came with eyes of flame,
  Judd, who is like a bloater,
The brave Lord Mayor in coach and pair,
  King Edward, in his motor.

Far in a rosy mist withdrawn
 The God and all his crew,
Silenus pulled by nymphs, a faun,
 A satyr drenched in dew,

Smiled as they wept those shining tears
 Only Immortals know,
Whose feet are set among the stars,
 Above the shifting snow.

And one spake out into the night,
 Before they left for ever,
"Rejoice, rejoice!" and his great voice
 Rolled like a splendid river.

He spake in Greek, which Britons speak
 Seldom, and circumspectly;
But Mr. Judd, that man of mud,
 Translated it correctly.

And when they heard that happy word,
 Policemen leapt and ambled:
The busmen pranced, the maidens danced,
 The men in bowlers gambolled.

A wistful Echo stayed behind
 To join the mortal dances,
But Mr. Judd, with words unkind,
 Rejected her advances,

And passing down through London Town
 She stopped, for all was lonely,
Attracted by a big brass plate
 Inscribed: FOR MEMBERS ONLY.

And so she went to Parliament,
 But those ungainly men
Woke up from sleep, and turned about,
 And fell asleep again.

Anna Wickham

Anna Wickham was born in Wimbledon, Surrey, in 1884. She went to Australia at six, returned when she was twenty-one, studied for Opera in Paris with De Reszke and suddenly, after a few years of marriage, became a poet. In a burst of creative energy she wrote nine hundred poems in four years.

Her first two books (*The Contemplative Quarry,* 1915, and *The Man with a Hammer,* 1916) were republished in America in one volume, *The Contemplative Quarry* (1921). This was followed by *The Little Old House* (1922). Another volume, *The Noiseless Propeller,* was prepared, but its publication was postponed. The most casual reading of Anna Wickham's work reveals the strength of her candor. The poems could scarcely be put in the category of "charming" verse; they are astringent and sometimes harsh, gnarled frequently by their own violences of mood. But there is no disputing their incisiveness and integrity. Mrs. Wickham's lines present the picture of woman struggling between dreams and domesticity; they are acutely sensitive, restless, analytical. The very tone of her poetry reflects the disturbed music and the nervous protests of her age.

Sometimes her verse tends toward introverted self-questioning, but usually it is as just in phrase as it is fearless in thought. Much of her poetry is a poetry of the senses, and in this she seems kin to D. H. Lawrence. But where Lawrence, lost and suffering in the "mazes of the female mystery," is sexually tormented, Anna Wickham, unhampered in her sensuality, delights even in her torments. She turns upon men for maintaining a traditional attitude, not to the real women of today, but to creatures half-historical, half-illusory; she berates women for fostering this tendency, thus weakening men and enchaining themselves.

We, vital women, are no more content
Bound, first to passion, then to sentiment.
Of you, the masters, slaves in our poor eyes
Who most are moved by women's tricks and lies,
We ask our freedom. In good sooth,
We only ask to know and speak the truth!

Yet Mrs. Wickham does more than "only ask to know and speak the truth." Her angers and revulsions cannot choke the lyric impulse. Time and again she makes songs that are sweet without being sentimental, almost perfect in their simple cadences, shrewd yet lightly persuasive.

For the most part she is torn between being the instrument of love and love itself; making, with a wry determination, an unhappy compromise between the conflicting claims of modernity and maternity. She is rarely objective; even such dramatic projections as "Meditation at Kew" and the acrid humor of "Nervous Prostration" are too bitter to be impersonal. Out of all her poems, the plangent as well as the powerful, rises this cry which is also an apologia:

Let it be something for my song,
If it is sometimes swift and strong.

"Self-Analysis," "Divorce," and "The Affinity" are this remarkable and unappreciated poet *in petto*. Divided between her desire for mastery and being mastered, for perfection and her distrust of it, she typifies the woman who has repudiated order but is frustrated in lawlessness; even her domesticity, which she celebrates, is, if not self-condemning, self-contradicting.

Although Mrs. Wickham has written longer poems, her terse, pungently flavored lyrics are most characteristic of her. She is a psychologist by intention, but a psychologist who has not forgotten how to sing. At her worst she offers an interesting exhibit of the age; at her best she displays a genius for the firm epithet and quick-thrusting phrase—and an unforgettable power of emotion.

CREATRIX

Let us thank Almighty God
For the woman with the rod.
Who was ever and is now
Strong, essential as the plow.
She shall goad and she shall drive,
So to keep man's soul alive.
Amoris with her scented dress
Beckons, in pretty wantonness;
But the wife drives, nor can man tell
What hands so urge, what powers compel.

SONG

I was so chill, and overworn, and sad,
To be a lady was the only joy I had.
I walked the street as silent as a mouse,
Buying fine clothes, and fittings for the house.

But since I saw my love
I wear a simple dress,
And happily I move
Forgetting weariness.

SELF-ANALYSIS

The tumult of my fretted mind
Gives me expression of a kind;

But it is faulty, harsh, not plain—
My work has the incompetence of pain.

I am consumed with a slow fire,
For righteousness is my desire;
Towards that good goal I cannot whip my will,
I am a tired horse that jibs upon a hill.

I desire Virtue, though I love her not—
I have no faith in her when she is got:
I fear that she will bind and make me slave
And send me songless to the sullen grave.

I am like a man who fears to take a wife,
And frets his soul with wantons all his life.
With rich, unholy foods I stuff my maw;
When I am sick, then I believe in law.

I fear the whiteness of straight ways—
I think there is no color in unsullied days.
My silly sins I take for my heart's ease,
And know my beauty in the end disease.

Of old there were great heroes, strong in fight,
Who, tense and sinless, kept a fire alight:
God of our hope, in their great name,
Give me the straight and ordered flame!

SEHNSUCHT

Because of body's hunger are we born,
And by contriving hunger are we fed;
Because of hunger is our work well done,
As so are songs well sung, and things well said.
Desire and longing are the whips of God—
God save us all from death when we are fed.

WEAPONS

Up the crag
In the screaming wind,
Naked and bleeding
I fought blind.

Then at dawn
On the snowy height
I seized a spear
By the eastern light.

On I trudged
In the eye of the sun,
Past the cromlech
I found a gun.

Then I strayed
In the cities of men,
In the house of my Love
I found a pen!

THE LAST ROUND

Clasp you the God within yourself
And hold it fast;
After all combats shall ye come
To this good fight at last.

God is a mighty wrestler
He battles in the night;
Not till the end shall it be known
What foe you fight.

When God in you is overthrown
He'll show a light
And claim the victor for his own
And crown the fight.

TO A CRUCIFIX

O courteous Christ—Kind guest, most gracious host,
Which of these ugly things had pained you most
That silly priests repeat your words for gain
Or in your house hang symbols of your pain?

How had you withered at the servile breath
Spent in the praises of your common death,
Scorning these claims to honor and to pride
For such a death as multitudes have died.

Not in the cross was such indignity
As these acclaiming Christian ages see,
When you who lived for cure and for relief
Are most remembered for your wounds and grief.

FRIEND CATO

When the master sits at ease
He joys in generalities;
In aphorisms concerning all things human,
But most of all concerning woman.
Saying, "Women are this or that.
Woman is round, or high, or square, or flat."

Sir, a shepherd knows his sheep apart,
And mothers know young babes by heart.
To taste no little shade of difference
Is sign of undiscerning sense.
Cato, in pity, hear our just demur,
Man to be critic, must be connoisseur.

THE SONG-MAKER

I would live for a day and a night,
In the rigorous land where everything's right.
Then I would sit and make a song,
In the leisurely land where everything's wrong.

DEDICATION OF THE COOK

If any ask why there's no great She-Poet,
Let him come live with me, and he will know it:
If I'd indite an ode or mend a sonnet,
I must go choose a dish or tie a bonnet;

For she who serves in forced virginity
Since I am wedded will not have me free;
And those new flowers my garden is so rich in
Must die for clammy odors of my kitchen.

Yet had I chosen Dian's barrenness
I'm not full woman, and I can't be less,
So could I state no certain truth for life,
Can I survive and be my good man's wife?

Yes! I will make the servant's cause my own
That she in pity leave me hours alone
So I will tend her mind and feed her wit
That she in time have her own joy of it;
And count it pride that not a sonnet's spoiled
Lacking her choice betwixt the baked and boiled.
So those young flowers my garden is so rich in
Will blossom from the ashes of my kitchen!

MEDITATION AT KEW

Alas! for all the pretty women who marry dull men,
Go into the suburbs and never come out again,
Who lose their pretty faces, and dim their pretty eyes,
Because no one has skill or courage to organize.

What do these pretty women suffer when they marry?
They bear a boy who is like Uncle Harry,
A girl, who is like Aunt Eliza, and not new,
These old, dull races must breed true.

I would enclose a common in the sun,
And let the young wives out to laugh and run;
I would steal their dull clothes and go away,
And leave the pretty naked things to play.

Then I would make a contract with hard Fate
That they see all the men in the world and choose a mate,
And I would summon all the pipers in the town
That they dance with Love at a feast, and dance him down.

From the gay unions of choice
We'd have a race of splendid beauty, and of thrilling voice.
The World whips frank, gay love with rods,
But frankly, gayly shall we get the gods.

THE TIRED WOMAN

O my Lover, blind me,
Take your cords and bind me,
Then drive me through a silent land
With the compelling of your open hand!

There is too much of sound, too much for sight,
In thundrous lightnings of this night,
There is too much of freedom for my feet,
Bruised by the stones of this disordered street.

I know that there is sweetest rest for me,
In silent fields, and in captivity.
O Lover! drive me through a stilly land
With the compelling of your open hand.

DIVORCE

A voice from the dark is calling me.
In the close house I nurse a fire.
Out in the dark, cold winds rush free,
To the rock heights of my desire.
I smother in the house in the valley below,
Let me out to the night, let me go, let me go!

Spirits that ride the sweeping blast,
Frozen in rigid tenderness,
Wait! For I leave the fire at last,
My little-love's warm loneliness.
I smother in the house in the valley below,
Let me out in the night, let me go, let me go!

High on the hills are beating drums,
Clear from a line of marching men
To the rock's edge the hero comes.
He calls me, and he calls again.
On the hill there is fighting, victory, or quick death,
In the house is the fire, which I fan with sick breath
I smother in the house in the valley below,
Let me out in the dark, let me go, let me go!

AFTER ANNUNCIATION

Rest, little Guest.
Beneath my breast.
Feed, sweet Seed,
At your need.

I took Love for my lord
And this is my reward,
My body is good earth,
That you, dear Plant, have birth.

THE CHERRY-BLOSSOM WAND

I will pluck from my tree a cherry-blosom wand,
And carry it in my merciless hand,

So I will drive you, so bewitch your eyes,
With a beautiful thing that can never grow wise.

Light are the petals that fall from the bough,
And lighter the love that I offer you now;
In a spring day shall the tale be told
Of the beautiful things that will never grow old.

The blossoms shall fall in the night wind,
And I will leave you so, to be kind:
Eternal in beauty are short-lived flowers,
Eternal in beauty, these exquisite hours.

I will pluck from my tree a cherry-blossom wand,
And carry it in my merciless hand,
So I will drive you, so bewitch your eyes,
With a beautiful thing that shall never grow wise.

SOUL'S LIBERTY

He who has lost soul's liberty
Concerns himself for ever with his property,
As, when the folk have lost both dance and song,
Women clean useless pots the whole day long.

Thank God for war and fire
To burn the silly objects of desire,
That from the ruin of a church thrown down
We see God clear and high above the town.

TO MEN

(*Variation on Ella Wheeler Wilcox, after a poem of the same name*)

Sirs—though we fail you—let us live;
Be just, have pity, and forgive.
Think how poor Mother Eve was brought
To being as God's afterthought.

God had a vast expanse of clay
To fashion Adam's primal day;
Yet was the craftsman's limit shown
His image could not live alone.

Yet God supports eternal life
Without the comfort of a wife;
So it was proved e'er we began
God had miscalculated man.

And of his fault, he took a part
Formed woman's brain and woman's heart
Of Imperfection—vainly planned—
To love, to serve, to understand.

How can you wonder, if we stray
Through coward night and sloven day
When power in us can but reflect
God's wifelessness and man's defect.

Had lonely God when earth was new
Some blest remembrances of two,
He had not made one half of life
A shambles and a hell-stung strife.

*

Do you remember, O my Dear,
The seventh night of our first year,
The night, when my first son was given
With ecstasy to tutor Heaven—

Had God loved thus, all Hell were blind
And famine, lust and murder kind.
Come, my co-adjutor, beloved smith,
Raise, thou thy hammer—break the myth.

There is no marvel of creation
Exists beyond our full relation—
Yet God shall strengthen from his sins
To breed us new and breed us twins.

Thou bungling artificer, yet
Thou shalt be artist and beget
And on the form of Chaos lie
To wash the earth and raise the sky.

Not equal I, but counterpart
And in relation is my heart
Perfect with man's—as with his mind—
Mine is all strong to loose and bind.

Come then, my husband, here and rest
On my so well-remolded breast.
At morning we'll go out and see
How well God works for you and me.

THE SINGER

If I had peace to sit and sing,
Then I could make a lovely thing;
But I am stung with goads and whips,
So I build songs like iron ships.

Let it be something for my song,
If it is sometimes swift and strong.

ENVOI

God, thou great symmetry,
Who put a biting lust in me
From whence my sorrows spring,
For all the frittered days
That I have spent in shapeless ways,
Give me one perfect thing.

D. H. Lawrence

D(avid) H(erbert) Lawrence was born September 17, 1885, in the colliery town of Eastwood, a drab hamlet on the border between Derbyshire and Nottinghamshire. The son of workers, his novels return again and again to the rural and industrial backgrounds of his boyhood. Lawrence obtained a scholarship at the Nottingham High School and at sixteen became a pupil-teacher. After a short appointment in a London school, he abandoned teaching for literature. He traveled considerably in search of health and, during his last fifteen years, lived in Italy, New Mexico, and Southern France.

Even in his mid-twenties—in *The White Peacock* (1909), *Love Poems and Others* (1913) and, first of all, in *Sons and Lovers* (1913)—Lawrence pronounced the strain with which he was to be so closely identified. The two volumes of *Collected Poems* (1929) are autobiographically candid, completely characterizing. No one in his generation pursued the cry of sex so passionately, so painfully as D. H. Lawrence; and no one was more confused by it. A magnificently equipped craftsman, a writer *pur sang,* his gamut never extended. His novels, with two unimportant exceptions and, more explicitly, his poems are concerned with little else than the dark fire, the broken body, the struggle, death and resurrection of crucified flesh, the recurring cycle of fulfillment and frustration. This is Lawrence's theme, a theme which he varied with great skill, but one which he could neither leave nor fully control. It is not merely his passion, it is his obsession.

This is as far as Lawrence goes. And he could go no farther except in that limbo where sex and love are desperately confused. He could not separate his spirit from his loins; he was, at the same time, mentally detached and emotionally victimized.

His agony grew sharper, his solution vaguer. This, it seems, was the core of Lawrence's *malaise*. There is something about his excitation which is uncomfortably flagellant; his sudden heats and swift revulsions are too neurotic to evoke more than pity; hysteria, in many of the poems, is subdued but not silenced.

But there is something here beyond the sex-fearful, sex-fascinated being; something beyond the self-worshiping, self-deluded artist, and that is Lawrence's intensity. Whatever its faults, the pitch and register of his work is poetry. Impotence itself has power in his propulsive verse. A poet of sensibilities which are refined to the point of being always wounded, a recorder of kaleidoscopic images and sensory nuances, Lawrence at forty-four had made a permanent if painful contribution to literature. There are passages in his novels—especially in *The Rainbow* (1915) and *Women in Love* (1921)—that have the accent and the sweep of poetry; these are poems that fasten on the mind and will not be shaken off. It is rather a curious commentary that his objective or "fictional" poems are among his best. Nothing that he has written, none of his verse is more surely projected than the dramatic lyrics in dialect: "A Youth Mowing," "Violets," "Whether or Not," that remarkable sequence which a ruder Browning might have fathered and which is a completely rounded tale, a poignantly condensed novel.

Lawrence is more the enmeshed self, less the detached poet in "A Young Wife," "Love on the Farm," "Wedding Morn," and the irritated fragments in *Pansies* (1929). Here speaks "the hot blood's blindfold art," chaotically, characteristically, but always eloquently.

After a struggle of many years, Lawrence succumbed to tuberculosis. His wish that he be taken to New Mexico, either to die or to recuperate, could not be granted and he died March 2, 1930, at Vence, France. Immediately thereafter reappraisals set in: Lawrence was subjected to new examinations as poet, prophet, and pamphleteer. No less than four "intimate" biographers, including his wife, attempted the almost impossible task of presenting Lawrence as he seemed to the world and himself—and succeeded only in presenting him as he appeared to Mabel Dodge Luhan, Middleton Murry, Catherine Carswell, and Freda Lawrence. Horace Gregory was more critical in his study of Lawrence's symbols, estimating the man in relation to his work in *Pilgrim of the Apocalypse*. Lawrence's early stories were collected with a Memoir by David Garnett; posthumous and partly finished stories were issued for several years after his death. *Last Poems,* a volume of some three hundred pages with an introduction by Richard Aldington, appeared in 1933. The book consists of the greater part of two large manuscripts found among Lawrence's papers. It ranges from the sharp, snarling, and often trivial pensées, which Lawrence liked to call "Pansies," to long premonitory poems on death, poems which voice a new dignity.

Few writers had roused more violent and controversial issues; four of his books had been suppressed, a show of his paintings (an art to which Lawrence turned in his forties) was raided. Though he was unusually fecund, opposition kindled a bitter flame in him and his creative passion turned to propaganda. *Fantasia of the Unconscious* is a fantastic variation on Jung; *Studies in Classic American Literature* is a queerly proportioned but provocative plea for the recognition of a native spirit; *Pornography and Obscenity* (1929) is a tract, an argument for the appreciation of the realities as against the hypocrisies of sexual morality.

But his polemical writing is, after all, the least of his work. In the best of his novels and poems he achieved a style that was dynamic, inflamed, savagely honest. A conscientious barbarian, he was, as Stuart Sherman wrote, "a revolutionist in favor of an individualistic, aristocratic barbarianism." He seldom wrote badly. True, his preoccupation was sex (he was described as "the novelist of the over- and the under-sexed"); he dealt almost entirely with the intensification or the perversion of the sexual instinct. But his deeper obsession, the "inner theme," was the possession and maintenance of masculine power and the understanding of men's and women's basic relations with each other. He clarified, though he did not altogether resolve, the complexities in two essays published in *We Need One Another* (1933). Here Lawrence pleaded for a relinquishing of the over-inflated ego and a realization of the sexes' spiritual dependence—"the great flow of the relationship goes on, undying, and this is the flow of living sex, the relation that lasts a lifetime, and of which sex-desire is only one vivid, most vivid, manifestation."

This conviction was fully expressed only toward the end of Lawrence's life; most of his writing lacks such clarity. One homily was apparent in all his works: The world has gone stale, feebly promiscuous, prettily fetid. Small spurts of lust instead of a long passion; talk instead of acts. The world has ceased to be masculine. Its discontent, like its nervous art, its soft-rotten culture, its middle-class *malaise,* is all the outcome of womanishness. Women, pretending to need us, have used us up; women have destroyed us with merciless softness. All we cherish has become effeminized, vitiated with the white poison of their approval and the black venom of their jealousy. Suffering from a "mind-perverted, will-perverted, ego-perverted love," the world will be happy only when man—overcivilized man—regains the free power and security which are the well-spring of emotional vitality. The defect in thinking is obvious. It is not "maleness" which troubles the artist but his consciousness of it. It is this lack of peace which Lawrence instinctively resented and which kept him enslaved to his narrow freedom. Coming up from that lower English world "where the good form and restraint of the public school tradition was a gag to be spat out once the speaker gained the strength of self-confidence," Lawrence, rising by self-improvement, could never resist improving others. In this he was, beneath his libertarian manner, the Puritan. "He came up," said Henry S. Canby, "when the bourgeois Victorian morality was losing its vigor, and he preached his new gospel of virility just as the Methodists preached revivalism to the Angelicans." His methods were extravagant, often exacerbated, but they were vitally his own. He had, above all, the faculty of making the reader revalue his own standards. Whatever status as an artist the future may assign him, there can be no question that he was a force.

A YOUTH MOWING

There are four men mowing down by the Isar;
I can hear the swish of the scythe-strokes, four
Sharp breaths taken; yea, and I
Am sorry for what's in store.

The first man out of the four that's mowing
Is mine, I claim him once and for all;
Though it's sorry I am, on his young feet, knowing
None of the trouble he's led to stall.

As he sees me bring the dinner, he lifts
His head as proud as a deer that looks
Shoulder-deep out of the corn; and wipes
His scythe-blade bright, unhooks

The scythe-stone and over the stubble to me.
Lad, thou hast gotten a child in me,
Laddie, a man thou'lt ha'e to be,
Yea, though I'm sorry for thee.

LIGHTNING

I felt the lurch and halt of her heart
  Next my breast, where my own heart was beating;
And I laughed to feel it plunge and bound,
And strange in my blood-swept ears was the sound
  Of the words I kept repeating,
Repeating with tightened arms, and the hot blood's blind-fold art.

Her breath flew warm against my neck,
  Warm as a flame in the close night air;
And the sense of her clinging flesh was sweet
Where her arms and my neck's blood-surge could meet.
  Holding her thus, did I care
That the black night hid her from me, blotted out every speck?

I leaned me forward to find her lips,
  And claim her utterly in a kiss,
When the lightning flew across her face,
And I saw her for the flaring space
  Of a second, afraid of the clips
Of my arms, inert with dread, wilted in fear of my kiss.

A moment, like a wavering spark,
  Her face lay there before my breast,
Pale love lost in a snow of fear,
And guarded by a glittering tear,
  And lips apart with dumb cries;
A moment, and she was taken again in the merciful dark.

I heard the thunder, and felt the rain,
  And my arms fell loose, and I was dumb.
Almost I hated her, she was so good,
Hated myself, and the place, and my blood,
  Which burned with rage, as I bade her come
Home, away home, ere the lightning floated forth again.

SUSPENSE

The wind comes from the north
Blowing little flocks of birds
Like spray across the town,
And a train roaring forth
Rushes stampeding down
South, with flying curds
Of steam, from the darkening north.

Whither I turn and set
Like a needle steadfastly,
Waiting ever to get
The news that she is free;
But ever fixed, as yet,
To the lode of her agony.

A YOUNG WIFE

The pain of loving you
Is almost more than I can bear.

I walk in fear of you.
The darkness starts up where
You stand, and the night comes through
Your eyes when you look at me.

Ah, never before did I see
The shadows that live in the sun!

Now every tall glad tree
Turns round its back to the sun
And looks down on the ground, to see
The shadow it used to shun.

At the foot of each glowing thing
A night lies looking up.

Oh, and I want to sing
And dance, but I can't lift up
My eyes from the shadows: dark
They lie spilt round the cup.

What is it?—Hark
The faint fine seethe in the air!

Like the seething sound in a shell!
It is death still seething where
The wild-flower shakes its bell
And the skylark twinkles blue—

The pain of loving you
Is almost more than I can bear.

CHERRY ROBBERS

Under the long dark boughs, like jewels red
  In the hair of an Eastern girl
Hangs strings of crimson cherries, as if had bled
  Blood-drops beneath each curl.

Under the glistening cherries, with folded wings
  Three dead birds lie:
Pale-breasted throstles and a blackbird, robberlings
  Stained with red dye.

Against the haystack a girl stands laughing at me,
  Cherries hung round her ears.
Offers me her scarlet fruit: I will see
  If she has any tears.

A WINTER'S TALE

Yesterday the fields were only gray with scattered snow,
And now the longest grass leaves hardly emerge;
Yet her deep footsteps mark the snow, and go
On toward the pines at the hill's white verge.

I cannot see her, since the mist's pale scarf
Obscures the dark wood and the dull orange sky;
But she's waiting, I know, impatient and cold, half
Sobs struggling into her frosty sigh.

Why does she come so promptly, when she must know
She's only the nearer to the inevitable farewell?
The hill is steep, on the snow my steps are slow—
Why does she come, when she knows what I have to tell?

LOVE ON THE FARM

What large, dark hands are those at the window
Grasping in the golden light
Which weaves its way through the evening wind
  At my heart's delight?

Ah, only the leaves! But in the west
I see a redness suddenly come
Into the evening's anxious breast—
  'Tis the wound of love goes home!

The woodbine creeps abroad
Calling low to her lover:
  The sun-lit flirt who all the day
  Has poised above her lips in play
  And stolen kisses, shallow and gay
  Of pollen, now has gone away—
    She wooes the moth with her sweet, low word;
And when above her his moth-wings hover
Then her bright breast she will uncover
And yield her honey-drop to her lover.

Into the yellow, evening glow
Saunters a man from the farm below;
Leans, and looks in at the low-built shed
Where the swallow has hung her marriage bed.
  The bird lies warm against the wall.
  She glances quick her startled eyes
  Towards him, then she turns away
  Her small head, making warm display
  Of red upon the throat. Her terrors sway
  Her out of the nest's warm, busy ball,
  Whose plaintive cry is heard as she flies
  In one blue stoop from out the sties
  Into the twilight's empty hall.

Oh, water-hen, beside the rushes,
Hide your quaintly scarlet blushes,
Still your quick tail, lie still as dead,
Till the distance folds over his ominous tread!

The rabbit presses back her ears,
Turns back her liquid, anguished eyes
And crouches low; then with wild spring
Spurts from the terror of his oncoming;
To be choked back, the wire ring
Her frantic effort throttling:
  Piteous brown ball of quivering fears!
Ah, soon in his large, hard hands she dies,
And swings all loose from the swing of his walk!
Yet calm and kindly are his eyes
And ready to open in brown surprise
Should I not answer to his talk
Or should he my tears surmise.

I hear his hand on the latch, and rise from my chair
Watching the door open; he flashes bare
His strong teeth in a smile, and flashes his eyes
In a smile like triumph upon me; then careless-wise
He flings the rabbit soft on the table board
And comes toward me: he! the uplifted sword
Of his hand against my bosom! and oh, the broad
Blade of his glance that asks me to applaud
His coming! With his hand he turns my face to him
And caresses me with his fingers that still smell grim
Of rabbit's fur! God, I am caught in a snare!
I know not what fine wire is round my throat;
I only know I let him finger there
My pulse of life, and let him nose like a stoat
Who sniffs with joy before he drinks the blood.

And down his mouth comes to my mouth! and down
His bright dark eyes come over me, like a hood
Upon my mind! his lips meet mine, and a flood
Of sweet fire sweeps across me, so I drown
Against him, die, and find death good.

PIANO

Softly, in the dusk, a woman is singing to me;
Taking me back down the vista of years, till I see
A child sitting under the piano, in the boom of the tingling strings
And pressing the small, poised feet of a mother who smiles as she sings.

In spite of myself, the insidious mastery of song
Betrays me back, till the heart of me weeps to belong
To the old Sunday evenings at home, with winter outside
And hymns in the cozy parlor, the tinkling piano our guide.

So now it is vain for the singer to burst into clamor
With the great black piano appassionato. The glamour
Of childish days is upon me, my manhood is cast
Down in the flood of remembrance, I weep like a child for the past.

GREEN

The dawn was apple-green,
  The sky was green wine held up in the sun,
The moon was a golden petal between.

She opened her eyes, and green
They shone, clear like flowers undone
For the first time, now for the first time seen.

A WHITE BLOSSOM

A tiny moon as small and white as a single jasmine flower
Leans all alone above my window, on night's wintry bower,
Liquid as lime-tree blossom, soft as brilliant water or rain
She shines, the first white love of my youth, passionless and in vain.

WEDDING MORN

The morning breaks like a pomegranate
  In a shining crack of red;
Ah, when tomorrow the dawn comes late
  Whitening across the bed
It will find me at the marriage gate
  And waiting while light is shed
On him who is sleeping satiate
  With a sunk, unconscious head.

And when the dawn comes creeping in,
  Cautiously I shall raise
Myself to watch the daylight win
  On my first of days,
As it shows him sleeping a sleep he got
  With me, as under my gaze
He grows distinct, and I see his hot
  Face freed of the wavering blaze.

Then I shall know which image of God
  My man is made toward;
And I shall see my sleeping rod
  Or my life's reward;
And I shall count the stamp and worth
  Of the man I've accepted as mine,
Shall see an image of heaven or of earth
  On his minted metal shine.

Oh, and I long to see him sleep
  In my power utterly;
So I shall know what I have to keep. . . .
  I long to see
My love, that spinning coin, laid still
  And plain at the side of me
For me to reckon—for surely he will
  Be wealth of life to me.

And then he will be mine, he will lie
  Revealed to me;
Patent and open beneath my eye
  He will sleep of me;
He will lie negligent, resign
  His truth to me, and I
Shall watch the dawn light up for me
  This fate of mine.

And as I watch the wan light shine
  On his sleep that is filled of me,
On his brow where the curved wisps clot and twine
  Carelessly,
On his lips where the light breaths come and go
  Unconsciously,
On his limbs in sleep at last laid low
  Helplessly,
I shall weep, oh, I shall weep, I know
  For joy or for misery.

WHETHER OR NOT

I

Dunna thee tell me it's his'n, mother,
  Dunna thee, dunna thee!
—Oh, ay, he'll come an' tell thee his-sèn,
  Wench, wunna he?

Tha doesna mean ter say ter me, mother,
  He's gone wi' that—
—My gel, owt'll do for a man i' th' dark;
  Tha's got it flat!

But 'er's old, mother, 'er's twenty year
  Older nor him—
—Ay, an' yaller as a crowflower; an' yet i' th' dark
  Er'd do for Tim.

Tha niver believes it, does ter, mother?
  It's somebody's lies.
—Ax 'im thy-sèn, wench; a widder's lodger!
  It's no surprise.

II

A widow o' forty-five
Wi' a bitter, dirty skin,
To ha' 'ticed a lad o' twenty-five,
An' 'im to 'ave been took in!

A widow o' forty-five
As 'as sludged like a horse all 'er life
Till 'er's tough as whit-leather, to slive[1]
Atween a lad an' 'is wife!

A widow o' forty-five!
A glum old otchel, wi' long
Witch teeth, an' 'er hawk-eyes, as I've
Mistrusted all along!

An' me as 'as kept my-sèn
Shut like a daisy bud,
Clean an' new an' nice, so's when
He wed he'd ha'e summat good!

An' 'im as nice an' fresh
As any man i' th' force,
To ha' gone an' given his clean young flesh
To a woman that coarse!

III

You're stout to brave this snow, Miss Stainwright,
  Are you makin' Brinsley way?
—I'm off up th' line to Underwood
  Wi' a dress as is wanted today.

[1] To slive = to slip, to interfere.

Oh, are you goin' to Underwood?
'Appen then you've 'eered!
—What's that as 'appen I've 'eered on, Missis?
Speak up, you nedn't be feared.

Why, your young man an' Widow Naylor,
'Er as 'e lodges wi'!
They say he's got 'er wi' childt; but there—
It's nothing to do wi' me!

Though if it's true, they'll turn 'im out
O' th' p'lice force, without fail;
An' if it's *not* true, you may back your life
They'll listen to *her* tale.

—Well, I'm believin' no tale, Missis,
I'm seein' for my-sèn.
An' when I know for sure, Missis,
I'll talk *then*.

IV

Nay, robin red-breast, tha needna
Sit noddin' thy head at me!
My breast's as red as thine, I reckon,
Flayed red, if tha could but see.

Nay, yo' blessed pee-whips,
Yo' needna scraight[1] at me!
I'm scraightin' my-sèn but arena goin'
Ter let iv'rybody see.

Tha *art* smock-raveled, bunny,
Larropin' neck an' crop
I' th' snow! but I's warrant thee
I'm further ower th' top.

V

Now sithee theer at th' reelroad crossin'
Warmin' 'is-sèn at the stool o' fire
Under the tank as fills th' ingines,
If there isn't my dearly-beloved liar!

My constable, wi' 'is buttoned breast
As stout as the truth, my Sirs! an' 'is face
As bold as a robin! It's much he cares
For this nice old shame an' disgrace.

Oh, but 'e drops 'is flag when 'e sees me!
Yi, an' 'is face goes white! Oh, yes,
Tha can stare at me wi' thy fierce blue eyes;
Tha won't stare me out, I guess.

[1] Scraight = cry.

VI

Whativer brings thee out so far
  In a' this depth o' snow?
—I'm takin' 'ome a weddin'-dress,
  If yer mun know.

Why, is there a weddin' at Underwood
  As tha ne'd trudge up 'ere?
—It's Wider Naylor's weddin'-dress,
  'Er'll be wantin' it, I 'ear.

'Er doesna want no weddin'-dress—
  —Why—? but what dost mean?
—Doesn't ter know what I mean, Timmy?
  Yi, tha must ha' bin 'ard ter wean!

Tha'rt a good-un at suckin'-in yet, Timmy!
  But tell me, isn't it true
As 'er'll be wantin' my weddin'-dress
  In a wik or two?

—Tha's no 'casions ter ha'e me on,
  Lizzie; what's done is done.
—*Done,* I should think so! An' might I ask
  When tha begun?

It's thee as 'as done it, as much as me,
  So there, an' I tell thee flat.
—Me gotten a childt ter thy landlady?
  —Tha's gotten thy answer pat.

As tha allus 'ast; but let me tell thee
  Hasna ter sent me whoam, when I
Was a'most burstin' mad o' my-sèn,
  An' walkin' in agony?

After I'd kissed thee at night, Lizzie,
  An' tha's laid against me, an' melted
Into me, melted right into me, Lizzie,
  Till I was verily swelted.

An' if my landlady seed me like it,
  An' if 'er clawkin' eyes
Went through me as the light went out,
  Is it any cause for surprise?

—No cause for surprise at all, my lad;
  After kissin' an cuddlin' wi' me, tha could
Turn thy mouth on a woman like that!
  I hope it did thee good.

—Ay, it did; but afterwards
  I could ha' killed 'er.
—Afterwards! how many times afterwards
  Could ter ha' killed 'er?

Say no more, Liz, dunna thee;
  'Er's as good as thee.
—Then I'll say good-by to thee, Timothy;
  Take 'er i'stead o' me.

I'll ta'e thy word good-by, Liz,
  Though I shonna marry 'er.
Nor 'er nor nub'dy.—It is
  Very brave of you, Sir!

—T' childt maun ta'e its luck, it mun,
  An' 'er maun ta'e *'er* luck.
F'r I tell yer I h'arena marryin' none
  On yer; yo'n got what yer took!

—That's spoken like a man, Timmy,
  That's spoken like a man!
" 'E up an' fired 'is pistol,
  An' then away 'e ran!"

I damn well shanna marry 'er,
  Nor yo', so chew it no more!
I'll chuck the flamin' lot o' you—
  —Yer nedn't 'ave swore!

VII

There's 'is collar round th' candlestick,
An' there's the dark-blue tie I bought 'im!
An' these is the woman's kids 'es's so fond on,
An' 'ere comes the cat as caught 'im!

I dunno wheer 'is eyes was—a gret
Round-shouldered hag! My Sirs, to think
Of 'im stoopin' to 'er! You'd wonder 'e could
Throw 'imself down *that* sink!

I expect yer know who I am, Mrs. Naylor?
  Who y'are? yis, you're Lizzie Stainwright.
An' 'appen you'd guess then what I've come for?
  —'Appen I mightn't, 'appen I might.

Yer knowed as I was courtin' Tim Merfin?
  —Yis, I knowed 'e wor courtin' thee.
An' yet yer've bin carryin' on wi' 'im!
  —Ay, an' 'im wi' me.

Well, now yer've got ter pay for it.
  —If I han, what's that ter thee?
'E isn't goin' ter marry yer.
  —Tha wants 'im thy-sèn, I see.

It 'asn't nothin' to do with me.
  —Then what art colleyfoglin' for?
I'm not 'avin' your orts an' slarts.
  Which on us said you wor?

But I want you to know 'e's not *marryin'* you.
  —Tha wants 'im thy-sèn too bad.
Though I'll see as 'e pays you, an' does what's right.
  —Tha'rt for doin' a lot wi' t' lad!

VIII

To think I should 'ave ter 'affle an' caffle
  Wi' a woman, an' name 'er a price
For lettin' me marry the lad as I thought
  Ter marry wi' cabs an' rice!

But we'll go unbeknown ter th' registrar,
  An' give *'er* the money there is;
For I won't be beholden to such as 'er,
  I won't, or my name's not Liz.

IX

Ta'e off thy duty stripes, Tim,
  An' come in 'ere wi' me;
Ta'e off thy p'liceman's helmet
  An' look at me.

I wish tha hadna done it, Tim,
  I do, an' that I do!
For whenever I look thee i' th' face, I s'll see
  Her face too.

I wish I could wesh 'er off'n thee;
  'Appen I can, if I try.
But tha'll ha'e ter promise ter be true ter me
  Till I die. . . .

X

Twenty pounds o' thy own tha hast, an' fifty pound ha'e I;
Thine shall go ter pay the woman, an' wi' my bit we'll buy
All as we s'll want for furniture when tha leaves this place;
An' we'll be married at th' registrar—now lift thy face.

Lift thy face an' look at me, man! canna ter look at me?
Sorry I am for this business, an' sorry if ever I've driven thee
To do such a thing; though it's a poor tale, it is, that I'm bound to say,
Afore I can ta'e thee I've got a widder o' forty-five ter pay!

Dunna thee think but what I've loved thee; I've loved thee too well.
An' 'deed an' I wish as this tale o' thine wor niver my tale to tell!
Deed an' I wish I c'd 'a' stood at th' altar wi' thee an' bin proud o' thee!
That I could 'a' bin first woman ter thee, as th'art first man ter me!

But we maun ma'e the best on't. So now rouse up an' look at me.
Look up an' say tha'rt sorry tha did it; say tha'rt sorry for me.
They'll turn thee out o' th' force, I doubt me; if they do, we can see
If my father can get thee a job on t'bank. Say tha'rt sorry, Timmy!

XI

Ay, I'm sorry, I'm sorry,
  But what o' that!
Ay, I'm sorry! Tha needa worry
  Nor fret thy fat.

I'm sorry for thee, I'm sorry f'r 'er,
  I'm sorry f'r us a'.
But what then? Tha wants me, does ter
  After a'?

Ah'n put my-sèn i' th' wrong, Liz,
  An' 'er as well.
An' tha'rt that right, tha knows; 'tis
  Other folks in hell.

Tha *art* so sure tha'rt right, Liz!
  That damned sure!
But 'ark thee 'ere, that widder woman
  's less graspin', if 'er's poor.

What 'er gen, 'er gen me
  Beout a thought.
'Er gen me summat; I shanna
  Say it wor nought.

I'm sorry for th' trouble, ay
  As comes on us a'.
But sorry for what I had? why
  I'm not, that's a'.

As for marryin', I shanna marry
  Neither on yer.
Ah've 'ad a' as I can carry
  From you an' from 'er.

So I s'll go an' leave yer,
  Both on yer,
I don't like yer, Liz, I want ter
  Get away from yer.

An' I don't really like 'er neither,
  Even though I've 'ad
More from 'er than from you; but either
  Of yer's too much for this lad.

Let me go! what's good o' talkin'?
  Let's a' ha' done.
Talk about love o' women!
  Ter me it's no fun.

I s'll say good-by, Liz, to yer,
  Yer too much i' th' right for me.
An wi' 'er somehow it isn't right.
  So good-by, an' let's let be!

AWARE

Slowly the moon is rising out of the ruddy haze,
Divesting herself of her golden shift, and so
Emerging white and exquisite; and I in amaze
See in the sky before me, a woman I did not know
I loved, but there she goes, and her beauty hurts my heart;
I follow her down the night, begging her not to depart.

KISSES IN THE TRAIN

I saw the midlands
  Revolve through her hair;
The fields of autumn
  Stretching bare,
And sheep on the pasture
  Tossed back in a scare.

And still as ever
  The world went round,
My mouth on her pulsing
  Neck was found,
And my breast to her beating
  Breast was bound.

But my heart at the center
  Of all, in a swound
Was still as a pivot,
  As all the ground
On its prowling orbit
  Shifted round.

And still in my nostrils
  The scent of her flesh,
And still my wet mouth
  Sought her afresh;
And still one pulse
  Through the world did thresh.

And the world all whirling
  Around in joy
Like the dance of a dervish
  Did destroy
My sense—and my reason
  Spun like a toy.

But firm at the center
  My heart was found;
Her own to my perfect
  Heart-beat bound,
Like a magnet's keeper
  Closing the round.

SPRING MORNING

Ah, through the open door
Is there an almond tree
Aflame with blossom!
    —Let us fight no more.

Among the pink and blue
Of the sky and the almond flowers
A sparrow flutters.
—We have come through.

It is really spring!—See
When he thinks himself alone
How he bullies the flowers.
—You and me

How happy we'll be!—See him,
He clouts the tufts of flowers
In his impudence.
—But, did you dream

It would be so bitter? Never mind
It is finished, the spring is here.
And we're going to be summer-happy
And summer-kind.

We have died, we have slain and been slain
We are not our old selves any more.
I feel new and eager
To start again.

It is gorgeous to live and forget.
And to feel quite new.
See the bird in the flowers?—he's making
A rare to-do!

He thinks the whole blue sky
Is much less than the bit of blue egg
He's got in his nest—we'll be happy
You and I, I and you.

With nothing to fight any more—
In each other, at least.
See, how gorgeous the world is
Outside the door!

TREES IN THE GARDEN

Ah in the thunder air
how still the trees are!

And the lime-tree, lovely and tall, every leaf silent
hardly looses even a last breath of perfume.

And the ghostly, creamy colored little tree of leaves
white, ivory white among the rambling greens,
how evanescent, variegated elder, she hesitates on the green grass
as if, in another moment, she would disappear
with all her grace of foam!

And the larch that is only a column, it goes up too tall to see:
and the balsam-pines that are blue with the gray-blue blueness of things from the sea,
and the young copper beech, its leaves red-rosy at the ends
how still they are together, they stand so still
in the thunder air, all strangers to one another
as the green grass glows upwards, strangers in the garden.

MORNING WORK

A gang of labourers on the piled wet timber
That shines blood-red beside the railway siding
Seem to be making out of the blue of the morning
Something faery and fine, the shuttles sliding,
The red-gold spools of their hands and faces shuttling
Hither and thither across the morn's crystalline frame
Of blue: trolls at the cave of ringing cerulean mining,
And laughing with work, living their work like a game.

SHIP OF DEATH

I sing of autumn and the falling fruit
and the long journey towards oblivion.

The apples falling like great drops of dew
to bruise themselves an exit from themselves.

Have you built your ship of death, oh, have you?
Build then your ship of death, for you will need it!

Can man his own quietus make
with a bare bodkin?

With daggers, bodkins, bullets, man can make
a bruise or break of exit for his life
but is that a quietus, oh tell me, is it quietus?

Quietus is the goal of the long journey
the longest journey towards oblivion.

Slips out the soul, invisible one, wrapped still
in the white shirt of the mind's experiences
and folded in the dark-red, unseen
mantle of the body's still mortal memories.

Frightened and alone, the soul slips out of the house
or is pushed out
to find himself on the crowded, arid margins of existence.

Oh, it is not so easy, I tell you it is not so easy
to set softly forth on the longest journey, the longest journey.

It is easy to be pushed out of the silvery city of the body
through any breach in the wall,
thrust out onto the grey grey beaches of shadow
the long marginal stretches of existence, crowded with lost souls
that intervene between our tower and the shaking sea of the beyond.

Oh build your ship of death, oh build it in time
and build it lovingly, and put it between the hands of your soul.

Once outside the gate of the walled silvery life of days
once outside, upon the grey marsh beaches, where lost souls moan
in millions, unable to depart
having no boat to launch upon the shaken, soundless
deepest and longest of seas,
once outside the gate
what will you do, if you have no ship of the soul?

Oh pity the dead that are dead, but cannot take
the journey, still they moan and beat
against the silvery adamant walls of this our exclusive existence.

They moan and beat, they gnash, they rage
they fall upon the new outcoming souls with rage
and they send arrows of anger, bullets and bombs of frustration
over the adamant walls of this, our by-no-means impregnable existence.

Pity, oh pity the poor dead that are only ousted from life
and crowd there on the grey mud beaches of the margins
gaunt and horrible
waiting, waiting till at last the ancient boatman with the common barge
shall take them abroad, towards the great goal of oblivion.

Pity the poor gaunt dead that cannot die
into the distance with receding oars
but must roam like outcast dogs on the margins of life,
and think of them, and with the soul's deep sigh
waft nearer to them the bark of delivery.

But for myself, but for my soul, dear soul
let me build a little ship with oars and food
and little dishes, and all accoutrements
dainty and ready for the departing soul.

And put it between the hands of the trembling soul.
So that when the hour comes, and the last door closes behind him
he shall slip down the shores invisible
between the half-visible hordes
to where the furthest and the longest sea
touches the margins of our life's existence
with wincing unwilling waves.

And launching there his little ship,
wrapped in the dark-red mantle of the body's memories
the little, slender soul sits swiftly down, and takes the oars
and draws away, away, away, towards the dark depths
fathomless deep ahead, far, far from the grey shores
that fringe with shadow all this world's existence.

Over the sea, over the farthest sea
on the longest journey
past the jutting rocks of shadow
past the lurking, octopus arms of agonised memory
past the strange whirlpools of remembered greed
through the dead weed of a life-time's falsity,
slow, slow my soul, in his little ship
on the most soundless of all seas
taking the longest journey

Pulling the long oars of a life-time's courage,
drinking the confident water from the little jug
and eating the brave bread of a wholesome knowledge
row, little soul, row on
on the longest journey, towards the greatest goal

Neither straight nor crooked, neither here nor there
but shadows folded on deeper shadows
and deeper, to a core of sheer oblivion
like the convolutions of shadow-shell
or deeper, like the foldings and involvings of a womb.

Drift on, drift on, my soul, towards the most pure
most dark oblivion.
And at the penultimate porches, the dark-red mantle
of the body's memories slips and is absorbed
into the shell-like, womb-like convoluted shadow.

And round the great final bend of unbroken dark
the skirt of the spirit's experience has melted away
the oars have gone from the boat, and the little dishes
gone, gone, and the boat dissolves like pearl
as the soul at last slips perfect into the goal, the core
of sheer oblivion and of utter peace,
the womb of silence in the living night.

Ah peace, ah lovely peace, most lovely lapsing
of this my soul into the plasm of peace.

Oh lovely last, last lapse of death, into pure oblivion
at the end of the longest journey
peace, complete peace!
But can it be that also it is procreation?

Oh build your ship of death
oh, build it!
Oh, nothing matters but the longest journey.

Humbert Wolfe

Humbert Wolfe was born at Milan in Italy, January 5, 1885. As he himself declared, he "lost no time in crossing to Bradford in the West Riding of Yorkshire, which town he reached during the same year and remained there till he left it for Oxford some 18 years later. Wrote sporadic and increasingly unsatisfactory verse from the age of 16 till his appointment to the British Civil Service in 1909."

Before he was fifty Wolfe had published a score of books, all, with two exceptions, in verse. Their chief quality is neither the satire which Wolfe used so incisively nor the grace of which he was somewhat too fond, but a confusion of the two. The surface characteristics are modern, but modern only in certain tricks of typography and employment of "suspended" rhymes. There is, above all, a fancy that delights to improvise on major themes which somehow slide into minor cadences. It is this contradiction which marks even the most definite of his volumes, an indetermination from which Wolfe was unable to escape. It is as if the "pale musicianer" of whom he speaks had composed a robust theme—and arranged it as a pretty duet for dulcimer and *viola d'amore.*

Wolfe's two best volumes are the early *Kensington Gardens* (1924) and the larger *Requiem* (1927). In the first, the fantasies enchant with their delicacy. The squirrel "like a small gray coffee-pot," the half-metal tulip "clean as a lady, cool as glass," the city financier with his "table-land of shiny hat," the "flushed example" of the rose with her "dazzling inch of scent"—all these are seen and communicated in such a way that the reader enjoys the mingling of recognition and surprise. *Requiem* is the most reflective of all Wolfe's work and the nearest to a synthesis. This symphonic and almost fugual creation retains Wolfe's exactitude of epithet embodied in a graver music than he usually employed.

Homage to Meleager (1930) and *Others Abide* (1927) display Wolfe as the translator of many epigrams from the Greek, a task for which he was eminently capable. *X at Oberammergau* (1935) again attempts to construct a major poem upon minor effects. The theme is timely: the conflict between personal good and universal evil. The design is large: the Gospel narrative and a Passion Play translated to the present scene. Unfortunately Wolfe's treatment fails to meet the demands of his subject.

It was evident that Wolfe was overworked. He had been one of the most responsible and hard-pressed Civil Servants. He was made a Commander of the Order of the British Empire in 1918 and a Companion of the Bath in 1925. The Second World War added more burdens than he could bear. He died of a heart attack on his fifty-fifth birthday, January 5, 1940.

In his lifetime Wolfe was underpraised for the tart dissonances and light fancies which were natural to him, overpraised for the symphonic elaborations which were scarcely his forte. He made the mistake of going in for fragility on a large scale; he tried to build cosmic allegories on every whimsicality. He will, however, outlive many louder poets by virtue of his frail-spun, faintly acid lyrics.

THE GRAY SQUIRREL

Like a small gray
coffee-pot,
sits the squirrel.
He is not

all he should be,
kills by dozens
trees, and eats
his red-brown cousins.

The keeper, on the
other hand
, who shot him, is
a Christian, and

loves his enemies,
which shows
the squirrel was not
one of those.

GREEN CANDLES

"There's someone at the door," said gold candlestick:
"Let her in quick, let her in quick!"
"There is a small hand groping at the handle.
Why don't you turn it?" asked green candle.

"Don't go, don't go," said the Heppelwhite chair,
"Lest you find a strange lady there."
"Yes, stay where you are," whispered the white wall:
"There is nobody there at all."

"I know her little foot," gray carpet said:
"Who but I should know her light tread?"
"She shall come in," answered the open door,
"And not," said the room, "go out any more."

TULIP

Clean as a lady,
cool as glass,
fresh without fragrance
the tulip was.

The craftsman, who carved her
of metal, prayed:
"Live, oh thou lovely!"
Half metal she stayed.

LOVE IS A KEEPER OF SWANS

Love is a keeper of swans!
Helen! amid what dark wherries
are you steering the silver boat,
that for all the love of Paris,
and his lips against your throat,
passed out of Troy with windless vans?

And, fairest of Italians,
where do you glimmer, Beatrice?
What light of heaven stains your wings
with gold that were all fleur de lys?
And do you hear when Dante sings?
"Love is a keeper of swans."

Love is a keeper of swans.
Have you left the barren plain,
and stormed a gold-eagle's eyrie?
Queen-swan of the eagle strain,
what mountain has you, Mary?
And is its name, as ever, still romance?

And you, bright cynet of immortal Hans,
you need not join your sisters yet.
You have all time. Why should you hasten?
What though the lake with reeds be set,
one reed is murmuring, oh, listen!
"Love is a keeper of swans."

MAN

The feathers in a fan
are not so frail as man;
the green embossèd leaf
than man is no more brief.
His life is not so loud
as the passing of a cloud;
his death is quieter
than harebells when they stir.
The years that have no form
and substance are as warm,
and space has hardly less
supreme an emptiness.
And yet man being frail
does on himself prevail,

and with a single thought
can bring the world to naught,
as being brief he still
bends to his fleeting will
all time and makes of it
the shadow of his wit.
Soundles in life and death
although he vanisheth,
the echo of a song
makes all the stars a gong.
Cold, void, and yet the grim
darkness is hot with him,
and space is but the span
of the long love of man.

THE WATERS OF LIFE

When, hardly moving, you decorate night's hush
with the slim pencil of your grace, retrieving
the clean flat stroke of some old Grecian brush
that painted dancers fair beyond believing;

when, leaning back the harvest of your hair
under the moon with beauty as still as hers,
your body's wonder writes upon the air
the perfect cadence of consummate verse,

I think, if this upon the air be shaken,
brief as a falling blossom, it can but be
that Time records, by beauty overtaken,
in one gold instant, immortality,

and that the patterns you weave upon the night
have such swift passion, such essential heat,
that all the painter sees, the poet can write,
are but pale shadows of your dancing feet.

THIS IS NOT DEATH

Lay aside phrases; speak as in the night
a child in terror might.
Confess that you are lonely, that you heard
some foot or hand that stirred,
that, holding your own breath, you almost hear
the midnight breath of Fear,
that tearless, soundless in your heart you pray:
"God! give me back the day!"
Yes! God can give it back, but not the one
that you have dreamed upon.
The black will turn to gray, the gray to blue
distance, but not for you,
and not for you the cheerful voice of men
will warm the heart again.
Nor will your friends or enemies intrude
upon that solitude
where only shadows drift and cross and pass,
seen sideways in your glass.

Make not complaint. For neither prayer nor tear
has its old power here.
This is not silence rounded by the deep
deliverance of sleep,
but by the empty spaces where the will
to wake again is still.
You chose, and you abide the choice, apart,
saying to your own heart:
"Beat if you must, though softly," to the brain:
"Must you imagine pain?"
And last of all say to the sobbing breath:
"No, fool, this is not death."

ILIAD

False dreams, all false,
mad heart, were yours.
The word, and nought else,
in time endures.
Not you long after,
perished and mute,
will last, but the defter
viol and lute.
Sweetly they'll trouble
the listeners
with the cold dropped pebble
of painless verse.
Not you will be offered,
but the poet's false pain.
You have loved and suffered,
mad heart, in vain.
What love doth Helen
or Paris have
where they lie still in
a nameless grave?
Her beauty's a wraith,
and the boy Paris
muffles in death
his mouth's cold cherries.
Yes! these are less,
that were love's summer,
than one gold phrase
of old blind Homer.
Not Helen's wonder
nor Paris stirs,
but the bright, untender
hexameters.
And thus, all passion
is nothing made,
but a star to flash in
an Iliad.
Mad heart, you were wrong!
No love of yours,
but only what's sung,
when love's over, endures.

Frances Cornford

Frances (Darwin) Cornford, daughter of Sir Francis Darwin, the third son of Charles Darwin, was born in 1886 at Cambridge. She married Francis Macdonald Cornford, Fellow and Lecturer of Trinty College, Cambridge, in 1909.

Her first volume, *Poems* (1910), though unaffected, showed little trace of individuality. With *Spring Morning* (1915) a much more distinct personality expressed itself. Hers is a firmly realized, clean-edged verse, with a clarity of utterance which is also found in the more suggestive *Autumn Midnight* (1923). Her later verse in *Different Days* (1928) is no less spontaneous than the simple "A Wasted Day," the acute and onomatopoetic "The Watch," and the delightfully teasing triolet "To a Fat Lady Seen from the Train." It is, however, more measured; gravity has been added without the loss of charm. Whether grave or mocking Mrs. Cornford's tone maintains a quiet distinction.

In *Mountains and Molehills* (1935), with distinctive woodcuts by Gwen Raverat, Mrs. Cornford continues to write of the English countryside with a quaint difference, of thoughts in a night nursery, of a back view particular yet universal, of Cambridge autumns, of madmen and fairies—a seemingly heterogeneous set of variations on traditional themes. A modest but distinctive *Collected Poems* was published in 1954.

THE COUNTRY BEDROOM

My room's a square and candle-lighted boat,
In the surrounding depths of night afloat.
My windows are the portholes, and the seas
The sound of rain on the dark apple-trees.

Sea-monster-like beneath, an old horse blows
A snort of darkness from his sleeping nose,
Below, among drowned daisies. Far off, hark!
Far off, one owl amidst the waves of dark.

TO A FAT LADY SEEN FROM THE TRAIN

O why do you walk through the fields in gloves,
  Missing so much and so much?
O fat white woman whom nobody loves,
Why do you walk through the fields in gloves,
When the grass is soft as the breast of doves
  And shivering sweet to the touch?
O why do you walk through the fields in gloves,
  Missing so much and so much?

THE WATCH

I wakened on my hot, hard bed;
Upon the pillow lay my head;
Beneath the pillow I could hear
My little watch was ticking clear.
I thought the throbbing of it went
Like my continual discontent;
I thought it said in every tick:
I am so sick, so sick, so sick:
O death, come quick, come quick, come quick,
Come quick, come quick, come quick, come quick. . . .

A WASTED DAY

I spoiled the day;
  Hotly, in haste

All the calm hours
  I gashed and defaced.

Let me forget,
  Let me embark
—Sleep for my boat—
  And sail through the dark.

Till a new day
  Heaven shall send,
Whole as an apple,
  Kind as a friend.

AT NIGHT

My brain is like the ravaged shores—the sand
Torn cruelly by footsteps from the land.
O hushing waves; O profound sea of sleep,
Send your curved ripples surely-lapping. Creep,
Pour on the scarrèd surface of my brain;
With your vast pity, wash it smooth again.

THE UNBESEECHABLE

(*To be set to music*)

"Time stands still
  With gazing on her face,"
Sang Dowland to his lute,
  Full of courtly grace.

Now that his musician's face
  And her face are dust,
Still I cry, Stand still:
  Still cry I must.

Stand still, Time,
  Hold, hold your pace;
Stiller stand than the smile
  On Pharaoh's face.

Stiller than December's frost
  That takes the heart with wonder,
Or the pause that comes between
  Lightning and thunder.

Time, stand still,
  Hush now your tread,
Stiller, stiller than a room
  Where lies the sheeted dead.

Where, though it's busy noon,
  Naught comes or goes;
Where the tree of endless peace
  To the ceiling grows.

O Time, Time—
  Stark and full of pain
Why drag me into space,
  A dog upon a chain?

I who would float with you,
  A ship sailing white,
Who cannot tell which power is hers
  And which the wind's delight.

So my refreshèd soul
  Time would adore,
If for one moment's breath
  Time were no more.

But, with Dowland's broken lute
  And his forgotten rhyme,
Still I cry, Stand still,
  Stand still, Time.

THE HILLS

Out of the complicated house, come I
To walk beneath the sky.
Here mud and stones and turf, here everything
Is mutely comforting.
Now hung upon the twigs and thorns appear
A host of lovely rain-drops cold and clear.
And on the bank
Or deep in brambly hedges dank
The small birds nip about, and say:
"Brothers, the Spring is not so far away!"
The hills like mother-giantesses old
Lie in the cold,
And with a complete patience, let
The cows come cropping on their bosoms wet,
And even tolerate that such as I
Should wander by
With paltry leathern heel which cannot harm
Their bodies' calm;
And, with a heart they cannot know, to bless
The enormous power of their peacefulness.

Siegfried Sassoon

☙ Siegfried (Loraine) Sassoon was born September 8, 1886. He was educated at Marlborough and Clare College, Cambridge, and, during the War, was a captain in the Royal Welsh Fusiliers. He fought in France and Palestine; he won the Military Cross for bringing in wounded on the battlefield.

Sassoon's literary development seems as contradictory as it is curious. Descended from Persian Jews on his father's side, from a traditional English country family on his mother's, Sassoon's boyhood was spent alternating between fox and rhyme hunting. He was divided between a love of rugged activity and a fondness for pale, Dowsonesque lyrics. Several volumes ranging from parody to the verge of preciosity were issued anonymously and privately printed. The earliest book, *Poems* (1906), was published in Sassoon's twentieth year and is, according to its author, "mostly weak imitations of Tennyson, Swinburne, and Rossetti." A sense of their unreality drove him to larger work, *The Daffodil Murderer* (1913), a poem which, beginning as a burlesque of Masefield, ended in serious self-expression.

By this time the poet had chaffed himself out of his juvenile admirations for Stephen Phillips and the Pre-Raphaelites, and strong feeling demanded a powerful expression. The war compelled it. With *The Old Huntsman* (1917) Sassoon came into his own idiom, taking his place immediately as "one of England's most brilliant rising stars." The first poem, a pseudo-Masefieldian monologue, was followed by a series of war poems, undisguised in their reality and bitterness. Every line of these quivering stanzas bore the mark of a sensitive and outraged nature; there was scarcely a phrase that did not protest against the "glorification" and false glamor of war.

Counter-Attack appeared in 1918. In this volume, Sassoon turned from ordered loveliness to the gigantic brutality of war. At heart a lyric idealist, the bloody years intensified and twisted his tenderness till what was subborn and satiric in him forced its way to the top. In *Counter-Attack* Sassoon found his angry outlet. Most of these poems are choked with passion; many of them are torn out, roots and all, from the very core of an intense conviction. They rush on, not so much because of the poet's art but almost in spite of it. A suave utterance, a neatly-joined structure would be out of place and even inexcusable in such verses as the title-poem, "The Rear-Guard," "Base Details," "Does It Matter?"—verses that are composed of love and indignation. "Let no one ever," Robert Nichols in his preface quotes Sassoon as saying, "from henceforth say one word in any way countenancing war. It is dangerous even to speak of how here and there the individual may gain some hardship of soul by it. For war is hell, and those who institute it are criminals. Were there even anything to say for it, it should not be said; for its spiritual disasters far outweigh any of its advantages. . . ." Nichols adds his approval to these sentences, saying, "For myself, this is the truth. War does not ennoble, it degrades."

Early in 1920, Sassoon visited America. At the same time, he brought out his *Picture Show* (1920), a vigorous answer to those who feared that Sassoon had "written himself out" or had begun to burn away in his own fire. Had Rupert

Brooke lived, he might have written many of these lacerated but somehow exalted lines. "The Dug-Out" and "Everyone Sang" are splendid examples of how much poignance and (in the latter) winged joy can be held in less than a dozen lines. Sassoon's three volumes are the most vital and unsparing records of the war we have had. They synthesize in poetry what Barbusse's *Under Fire* and Remarque's *All Quiet on the Western Front* spread out in panoramic prose or Sheriff's *Journey's End* compacted in his stripped tragedy.

Recreations, a privately distributed volume, printed at Christmas, 1923, for his friends, shows Sassoon in a more playfully intellectual vein. Another, even more strictly limited publication, *Lingual Exercises for Advanced Vocabularians,* was issued in 1925. Most of the contents of the two volumes appeared in *Satirical Poems* (1926). Less direct than his deeper notes, these poems display another interesting though not so compelling aspect of Sassoon's genius. *Poems of Pinchbeck Lyre* (1931), issued anonymously, is a revival of Sassoon's talent for parody; this small but bitter collection is a set of diabolical burlesques of Humbert Wolfe.

The Heart's Journey (1928) and *Vigils* (1935) represent a further maturing. They seem the work of another poet, but it is the essential Sassoon. Here is the distillation of the post-war years, of silence and sorrow, of long conflict and final unity. Here are the visionary ideals of youth sharpened and purified through pain; here is bitter knowledge saved from bitterness by the spirit of faith; here, in short, Sassoon's Songs of Innocence are mingled with his Songs of Experience. This spiritual autobiography reveals the old fire, but a fire subdued. It has dignity, a gentle ecstasy which places it in the line of great religious poetry. With almost monosyllabic simplicity of word and music, Sassoon shares the power of the mystic; he achieves a sense of identification with all things—be they inanimate objects like a lamp or a book, intangible concepts like music, or his fellowmen, living or dead—fusing every element in a rapt and universal love.

Memoirs of a Fox-Hunting Man (1928), first published anonymously, was awarded the two most coveted literary prizes in England: the Hawthornden Prize and the James Tait Black Memorial Prize in 1929. *Memoirs of an Infantry Officer,* its sequel, appeared in 1930.

Sherston's Progress (1936) and *The Old Century and Seven More Years* (1938) are further explorations in autobiography. *Rhymed Ruminations* (1941) was followed by a comprehensive *Collected Poems* (1949). *The Path to Peace* (1961) marks Sassoon's conversion to the Roman Catholic Church in his seventy-first year.

DREAMERS

Soldiers are citizens of death's gray land,
  Drawing no dividend from time's tomorrows.
In the great hour of destiny they stand,
  Each with his feuds, and jealousies, and sorrows.
Soldiers are sworn to action; they must win
  Some flaming, fatal climax with their lives.
Soldiers are dreamers; when the guns begin
  They think of firelit homes, clean beds, and wives.

I see them in foul dug-outs, gnawed by rats,
  And in the ruined trenches, lashed with rain,

Dreaming of things they did with balls and bats,
  And mocked by hopeless longing to regain
Bank-holidays, and picture shows, and spats,
  And going to the office in the train.

THE REAR-GUARD

Groping along the tunnel, step by step,
He winked his prying torch with patching glare
From side to side, and sniffed the unwholesome air.

Tins, boxes, bottles, shapes too vague to know,
A mirror smashed, the mattress from a bed;
And he, exploring fifty feet below
The rosy gloom of battle overhead.
Tripping, he grabbed the wall; saw someone lie
Humped at his feet, half-hidden by a rug,
And stooped to give the sleeper's arm a tug.
"I'm looking for headquarters." No reply.
"God blast your neck!" (For days he'd had no sleep.)
"Get up and guide me through this stinking place."
Savage, he kicked a soft, unanswering heap,
And flashed his beam across the livid face
Terribly glaring up, whose eyes yet wore
Agony dying hard ten days before;
And fists of fingers clutched a blackening wound.
Alone he staggered on until he found
Dawn's ghost that filtered down a shafted stair
To the dazed, muttering creatures underground
Who hear the boom of shells in muffled sound.
At last, with sweat of horror in his hair,
He climbed through darkness to the twilight air,
Unloading hell behind him step by step.

BASE DETAILS

If I were fierce and bald and short of breath,
  I'd live with scarlet Majors at the Base,
And speed glum heroes up the line to death.
  You'd see me with my puffy petulant face,
Guzzling and gulping in the best hotel,
  Reading the Roll of Honor. "Poor young chap,"
I'd say—"I used to know his father well.
  Yes, we've lost heavily in this last scrap."
And when the war is done and youth stone dead,
I'd toddle safely home and die—in bed.

ATTACK

At dawn the ridge emerges massed and dun
In the wild purple of the glowering sun

Smoldering through spouts of drifting smoke that shroud
The menacing scarred slope; and, one by one,
Tanks creep and topple forward to the wire.
The barrage roars and lifts. Then, clumsily bowed
With bombs and guns and shovels and battle-gear,
Men jostle and climb to meet the bristling fire.
Lines of gray, muttering faces, masked with fear,
They leave their trenches, going over the top,
While time ticks blank and busy on their wrists,
And hope, with furtive eyes and grappling fists,
Flounders in mud. O Jesu, make it stop!

COUNTER-ATTACK

We'd gained our first objective hours before
While dawn broke like a face with blinking eyes,
Pallid, unshaved and thirsty, blind with smoke.
Things seemed all right at first. We held their line,
With bombers posted, Lewis guns well placed,
And clink of shovels deepening the shallow trench.
The place was rotten with dead; green clumsy legs
High-booted, sprawled and groveled along the saps;
And trunks, face downward in the sucking mud,
Wallowed like trodden sand-bags, loosely filled;
And naked, sodden buttocks, mats of hair,
Bulged, clotted heads, slept in the plastering slime.
And then the rain began—the jolly old rain!

A yawning soldier knelt against the bank,
Staring across the morning blear with fog;
He wondered when the Allemands would get busy;
And then, of course, they started with five-nines
Traversing, sure as fate, and never a dud.
Mute in the clamor of shells he watched them burst
Spouting dark earth and wire with gusts from hell,
While posturing giants dissolved in drifts of smoke.
He crouched and flinched, dizzy with galloping fear,
Sick for escape,—loathing the strangled horror
And butchered, frantic gestures of the dead.

An officer came blundering down the trench:
"Stand-to and man the fire-step!" On he went. . . .
Gasping and bawling, "Fire-step . . . counter-attack!"
Then the haze lifted. Bombing on the right
Down the old sap: machine guns on the left;
And stumbling figures looming out in front.
"O Christ, they're coming at us!" Bullets spat,
And he remembered his rifle . . . rapid fire . . .
And started blazing wildly . . . then a bang
Crumpled and spun him sideways, knocked him out
To grunt and wriggle: none heeded him: he choked

And fought the flapping veils of smothering gloom,
Lost in a blurred confusion of yells and groans . . .
Down, and down, and down, he sank and drowned,
Bleeding to death. The counter-attack had failed.

DOES IT MATTER?

Does it matter?—losing your legs? . . .
For people will always be kind,
And you need not show that you mind
When the others come in after hunting
To gobble their muffins and eggs.

Does it matter?—losing your sight? . . .
There's such splendid work for the blind;
And people will always be kind,
As you sit on the terrace remembering
And turning your face to the light.

Do they matter?—those dreams from the pit? . . .
You can drink and forget and be glad,
And people won't say that you're mad;
For they'll know that you've fought for your country,
And no one will worry a bit.

THE DUG-OUT

Why do you lie with your legs ungainly huddled,
And one arm bent across your sullen, cold,
Exhausted face? It hurts my heart to watch you,
Deep-shadowed from the candle's guttering gold;
And you wonder why I shake you by the shoulder;
Drowsy, you mumble and sigh and turn your head. . . .
You are too young to fall asleep for ever;
And when you sleep you remind me of the dead.

INVOCATION

Come down from heaven to meet me when my breath
Chokes, and through drumming shafts of stifling death
I stumble toward escape, to find the door
Opening on morn where I may breathe once more
Clear cock-crow airs across some valley dim
With whispering trees. While dawn along the rim
Of night's horizon flows in lakes of fire,
Come down from heaven's bright hill, my song's desire.

Belov'd and faithful, teach my soul to wake
In glades deep-ranked with flowers that gleam and shake

And flock your paths with wonder. In your gaze
Show me the vanquished vigil of my days.
Mute in that golden silence hung with green,
Come down from heaven and bring me in your eyes
Remembrance of all beauty that has been,
And stillness from the pools of Paradise.

AFTERMATH

Have you forgotten yet? . . .
For the world's events have rumbled on since those gagged days,
Like traffic checked a while at the crossing of city ways:
And the haunted gap in your mind has filled with thoughts that flow
Like clouds in the lit heavens of life; and you're a man reprieved to go,
Taking your peaceful share of Time, with joy to spare.
But the past is just the same,—and War's a bloody game. . . .
Have you forgotten yet? . . .
Look down, and swear by the slain of the War that you'll never forget.

Do you remember the dark months you held the sector at Mametz,—
The nights you watched and wired and dug and piled sand-bags on parapets?
Do you remember the rats; and the stench
Of corpses rotting in front of the front-line trench,—
And dawn coming, dirty-white, and chill with a hopeless rain?
Do you ever stop and ask, "Is it all going to happen again?"

Do you remember that hour of din before the attack,—
And the anger, the blind compassion that seized and shook you then
As you peered at the doomed and haggard faces of your men?
Do you remember the stretcher-cases lurching back
With dying eyes and lolling heads, those ashen-gray
Masks of the lads who once were keen and kind and gay?

Have you forgotten yet? . . .
Look up, and swear by the slain of the War that you'll never forget!

EVERYONE SANG

Everyone suddenly burst out singing;
And I was filled with such delight
As prisoned birds must find in freedom
Winging wildly across the white
Orchards and dark green fields; on; on;
and out of sight.

Everyone's voice was suddenly lifted,
And beauty came like the setting sun.
My heart was shaken with tears, and horror
Drifted away. . . . O, but everyone

Was a bird; and the song was wordless; the
singing will never be done.

FALLING ASLEEP

Voices moving about in the quiet house:
Thud of feet and a muffled shutting of doors:
Everyone yawning. Only the clocks are alert.

Out in the night there's autumn-smelling gloom
Crowded with whispering trees; across the park
A hollow cry of hounds like lonely bells:
And I know that the clouds are moving across the moon;
The low, red, rising moon. Now herons call
And wrangle by their pool; and hooting owls
Sail from the wood above pale stooks of oats.

Waiting for sleep, I drift from thoughts like these;
And where today was dream-like, build my dreams.
Music . . . there was a bright white room below,
And someone singing a song about a soldier,
One hour, two hours ago: and soon the song
Will be *"last night"*: but now the beauty swings
Across my brain, ghost of remembered chords
Which still can make such radiance in my dream
That I can watch the marching of my soldiers,
And count their faces; faces; sunlit faces.

Falling asleep . . . the herons, and the hounds. . . .
September in the darkness; and the world
I've known; all fading past me into peace.

THE WISDOM OF THE WORLD

The wisdom of the world is this; to say, *"There is
No other wisdom but to gulp what time can give"* . . .
To guard no inward vision winged with mysteries;
To hear no voices haunt the hurrying hours we live;
To keep no faith with ghostly friends; never to know
Vigils of sorrow crowned when loveless passions fade . . .
From wisdom such as this to find my gloom I go,
Companioned by those powers who keep me unafraid.

EVERYMAN

The weariness of life that has no will
To climb the steepening hill:
The sickness of the soul for sleep, and to be still.

And then once more the impassioned pygmy fist
Clenched cloudward and defiant;

The pride that would prevail, the doomed protagonist,
Grappling the ghostly giant.

Victim and venturer, turn by turn; and then
Set free to be again
Companion in repose with those who once were men.

CONCLUSION

An image dance of change
Throngs my dim-sighted flesh,
To music's air-built mesh
Move thoughts forever strange.
I am so woven of sense
And subtlety uncharted
That I must vanish hence
Blind-souled and twilight-hearted.

Soon death the hooded lover
Shall touch my house of clay,
And life-lit eyes discover
That in the warbling gray
I have been early waking,
And while the dawn was breaking
Have stolen afield to find
That secrecy which quivers
Beyond the skies and rivers
And cities of the mind.

Till then my thought shall strive
That living I may not lose
The wonder of being alive,
Nor Time's least gift refuse.
For, though the end be night,
This wonder and this white
Astonishment of sight
Make hours of magic shine;
And heaven's a blaze and bloom
Of transience and divine
Inheritance of doom.

PREHISTORIC BURIALS

These barrows of the century-darkened dead,—
Memorials of oblivion, these turfed tombs
Of muttering ancestries whose fires, once red,
Now burn for me beyond mysterious glooms,
I pass them, day by day, while daylight fills
My sense of sight on these time-haunted hills.

Could I but see those burials that began
Whole History,—flint and bronze and iron beginnings,—
When under the wide Wiltshire sky, crude man
Warred with his world and augured our world-winnings!
Could I but enter that unholpen brain,
Cabined and comfortless and insecure,
Ruling some settlement on Salisbury Plain
And offering blood to blind primeval powers,—
Dim Caliban whose doom was to endure
Earth's ignorant nullity made strange with flowers.

LIMITATIONS

If you could crowd them into forty lines!
Yes; you can do it once you get a start:
All that you want is waiting in your head,
For long ago you've learnt it off by heart.

Begin: your mind's the room where you have slept,
(Don't pause for rhymes), till twilight woke you early.
The window stands wide-open, as it stood
When tree-tops loomed enchanted for a child
Hearing the dawn's first thrushes through the wood
Warbling (you know the words) serene and wild.

You've said it all before: you dreamed of Death,
A dim Apollo in the bird-voiced breeze
That drifts across the morning veiled with showers,
While golden weather shines among dark trees.

You've got your limitations; let them sing,
And all your life will waken with a cry:
Why should you halt when rapture's on the wing
And you've no limit but the cloud-flocked sky? . . .

But some chap shouts, "Here, stop it; that's been done!"
As God might holloa to the rising sun,
And then relent, because the glorying rays
Remind Him of green-glinting Eden days,
And Adam's trustful eyes as he looks up
From carving eagles on his beechwood cup.

Young Adam knew his job; he could condense
Life to an eagle from the unknown immense. . . .
Go on, whoever you are, your lines can be
A whisper in the music from the weirs
Of song that plunge and tumble toward the sea
That is the uncharted mercy of our tears.

*

I told you it was easy! . . . Words are fools
Who follow blindly, once they get a lead.
But thoughts are kingfishers that haunt the pools
Of quiet; seldom-seen: and all you need
Is just that flash of joy above your dream.
So, when those forty platitudes are done,
You'll hear a bird-note calling from the stream
That wandered through your childhood; and the sun
Will strike old flaming wonder from the waters. . . .
And there'll be forty lines not yet begun.

GRANDEUR OF GHOSTS

When I have heard small talk about great men
I climb to bed; light my two candles; then
Consider what was said; and put aside
What Such-a-one remarked and Someone-else replied.

They have spoken lightly of my deathless friends,
(Lamps for my gloom, hands guiding where I stumble,)
Quoting, for shallow conversational ends,
What Shelley shrilled, what Blake once wildly muttered. . . .

How can they use such names and not be humble?
I have sat silent; angry at what they uttered.
The dead bequeathed them life; the dead have said
What these can only memorize and mumble.

ALONE

"When I'm alone"—the words tripped off his tongue
As though to be alone were nothing strange.
"When I was young," he said; *"when I was young. . . ."*

I thought of age, and loneliness, and change.
I thought how strange we grow when we're alone,
And how unlike the selves that meet and talk,
And blow the candles out, and say good night.
Alone. . . . The word is life endured and known.
It is the stillness where our spirits walk
And all but inmost faith is overthrown.

PRESENCES PERFECTED

I looked on that prophetic land
Where, manifested by their powers,
Presences perfected stand
Whom night and day no more command
With shine and shadow of earthly hours.

I saw them. Numberless they stood
Half-way toward heaven, that men might mark
The grandeur of their ghostlihood
Burning divinely on the dark.

Names had they none. Through spirit alone
They triumphed, the makers of mankind,
Whose robes like flames were round them blown
By winds which raved from the unknown
Erebus of earth's ancestral mind.

ELECTED SILENCE

Where voices vanish into dream,
  I have discovered, from the pride
Of temporal trophydoms, this theme,
  That silence is the ultimate guide.

Allow me now much musing-space
  To shape my secrecies alone:
Allow me life apart, whose heart
  Translates instinctive tragi-tone.

How solitude can hear! O see
  How stillness unreluctant stands
Enharmonized with cloud and tree . . .
  O earth and heaven not made with hands!

Rupert Brooke

Possibly the most famous of the younger Georgians, Rupert Brooke was born at Rugby, August 3, 1887, where his father was assistant master at the school. As a youth, Brooke was fastidious, finicky in dress, but keenly interested in athletics; he played cricket, football, and tennis, and swam as well as most professionals. He was six feet tall, his finely molded head topped with a crown of loose hair of lively brown: "a golden young Apollo," said Edward Thomas. Another friend wrote, "To look at, he was part of the youth of the world." His beauty encouraged a naturally romantic disposition; his poems are a blend of delight in the splendor of actuality and disillusion in a loveliness that dies. The shadow of John Donne lies over many of his early and more than a few of his later pages, while the accent of Housman (*vide* "The Chilterns") prompts the conversational tone which Brooke adopted, extended, and popularized.

At first Brooke affected a tired sophistication not uncommon to the young poet of the times. However, the bored cynicisms, the fashionable ennuis were purged, when after several years of travel (he had been to Germany, Italy and Honolulu) the War came, turning Brooke away from

"A world grown old and cold and weary . . .
And half men, and their dirty songs and dreary,
And all the little emptiness of love."

Brooke enlisted with a relief that was like a rebirth; he sought new energy in the struggle "where the worst friend and enemy is but Death." After seeing service in Belgium, 1914, he spent the following winter in a training-camp in Dorsetshire and sailed with the British Mediterranean Expeditionary Force in February, 1915, to take part in the unfortunate Dardanelles Campaign.

Brooke never reached his destination. He died of blood-poison at Skyros in the Aegean, April 23, 1915. His early death was one of England's great literary losses; Lascelles Abercrombie, W. W. Gibson (with both of whom he had been associated on the quarterly, *New Numbers*), Walter De la Mare, Winston Spencer Churchill, and a host of others united to pay tribute to the most brilliant and passionate of the younger poets.

Brooke's sonnet-sequence, *1914* (from which "The Soldier" is taken), appeared with prophetic irony, a few weeks before his death. It contains the accents of immortality. "The Old Vicarage, Grantchester," "Heaven" and "Fish" are characteristic of the lighter and more playful side of Brooke's temperament. The metaphysician, not yet free of Donne, speaks in the mingled fancy and philosophy of "Dining-Room Tea," in several of the sonnets, and "Second Best." Both phases are combined in "The Great Lover," of which Abercrombie has written, "It is life he loves, and not in any abstract sense, but all the infinite little familiar details of life, remembered and catalogued with delightful zest."

Brooke published only two volumes during his lifetime. After his death, both volumes, with several posthumous poems, were issued as *Collected Poems of Rupert Brooke,* with a Memoir, in 1915. With a few exceptions, when Brooke yielded to the merely clever, his poetry is alert with the sparkle of his personality. It is the self-aware, self-examining mind that rules his emotions; his verse is a triumph of the intellectual imagination. "The theme of his poetry," says Walter De la Mare, "is the life of the mind, the senses, the feelings—life here and now. . . . His world stands out sharp and distinct, like the towers and pinnacles of a city under the light of a sunny sky." Brooke's delight was not in the shadows of revery and meditation, but in the swift play of ideas, in energetic action and reaction.

Thus Brooke was as thorough in his inconsistencies as in his sincerities. Impulse was his god—and his goad. He worshipped glamor and turned from it in revulsion, in a kind of sea- and beauty-sickness; he celebrated (in "Dust") the immortality of love and (in "Kindliness" and the sonnet already quoted) ridiculed its empty impermanence; turned from the intellect to sheer imagination—and abandoned fantasy for an ordered philosophy. His later work indicates that Brooke had tired of shifting extremes. It is impossible to predict what integration might have come with maturity. He was dead at twenty-seven.

THE GREAT LOVER

I have been so great a lover: filled my days
So proudly with the splendor of Love's praise,
The pain, the calm, and the astonishment,
Desire illimitable, and still content,
And all dear names men use, to cheat despair,
For the perplexed and viewless streams that bear
Our hearts at random down the dark of life.
Now, ere the unthinking silence on that strife
Steals down, I would cheat drowsy Death so far,
My night shall be remembered for a star
That outshone all the suns of all men's days.
Shall I not crown them with immortal praise
Whom I have loved, who have given me, dared with me
High secrets, and in darkness knelt to see
The inenarrable godhead of delight?
Love is a flame:—we have beaconed the world's night.
A city:—and we have built it, these and I.
An emperor:—we have taught the world to die.
So, for their sakes I loved, ere I go hence,
And the high cause of Love's magnificence,

And to keep loyalties young, I'll write those names
Golden for ever, eagles, crying flames,
And set them as a banner, that men may know,
To dare the generations, burn, and blow
Out on the wind of Time, shining and streaming. . . .

These I have loved:
White plates and cups, clean-gleaming,
Ringed with blue lines; and feathery, faëry dust;
Wet roofs, beneath the lamp-light; the strong crust
Of friendly bread; and many-tasting food;
Rainbows; and the blue bitter smoke of wood;
And radiant raindrops couching in cool flowers;
And flowers themselves, that sway through sunny hours;
Dreaming of moths that drink them under the moon;
Then, the cool kindliness of sheets, that soon
Smooth away trouble; and the rough male kiss
Of blankets; grainy wood; live hair that is
Shining and free; blue-massing clouds; the keen
Unpassioned beauty of a great machine;
The benison of hot water; furs to touch;
The good smell of old clothes; and other such—
The comfortable smell of friendly fingers,
Hair's fragrance, and the musty reek that lingers
About dead leaves and last year's ferns. . . .
Dear names,
And thousand others throng to me! Royal flames;
Sweet water's dimpling laugh from tap or spring;
Holes in the ground; and voices that do sing:
Voices in laughter, too; and body's pain,
Soon turned to peace; and the deep-panting train;
Firm sands; the little dulling edge of foam
That browns and dwindles as the wave goes home;
And washen stones, gay for an hour; the cold
Graveness of iron; moist black earthen mold;
Sleep; and high places; footprints in the dew;
And oaks; and brown horse-chestnuts, glossy-new;
And new-peeled sticks; and shining pools on grass;—
All these have been my loves. And these shall pass,
Whatever passes not, in the great hour,
Nor all my passion, all my prayers, have power
To hold them with me through the gate of Death.
They'll play deserter, turn with the traitor breath,
Break the high bond we made, and sell Love's trust
And sacramental covenant to the dust.
—Oh, never a doubt but, somewhere, I shall wake,
And give what's left of love again, and make
New friends now strangers. . . .
But the best I've known
Stays here, and changes, breaks, grows old, is blown

About the winds of the world, and fades from brains
Of living men, and dies.
Nothing remains.
O dear my loves, O faithless, once again
This one last gift I give: that after men
Shall know, and later lovers, far-removed
Praise you, "All these were lovely"; say, "He loved."

THE CHILTERNS

Your hands, my dear, adorable,
Your lips of tenderness
—Oh, I've loved you faithfully and well,
Three years, or a bit less.
It wasn't a success.

Thank God, that's done! and I'll take the road,
Quit of my youth and you,
The Roman road to Wendover
By Tring and Lilley Hoo,
As a free man may do.

For youth goes over, the joys that fly,
The tears that follow fast;
And the dirtiest things we do must lie
Forgotten at the last;
Even love goes past.

What's left behind I shall not find,
The splendor and the pain;
The splash of sun, the shouting wind,
And the brave sting of rain,
I may not meet again.

But the years, that take the best away,
Give something in the end;
And a better friend than love have they,
For none to mar or mend,
That have themselves to friend.

I shall desire and I shall find
The best of my desires;
The autumn road, the mellow wind
That soothes the darkening shires.
And laughter, and inn-fires.

White mist about the black hedgerows,
The slumbering Midland plain,
The silence where the clover grows,
And the dead leaves in the lane,
Certainly, these remain.

And I shall find some girl perhaps,
And a better one than you,
With eyes as wise, but kindlier,
And lips as soft, but true.
And I daresay she will do.

THE HILL

Breathless, we flung us on the windy hill,
Laughed in the sun, and kissed the lovely grass.
You said, "Through glory and ecstasy we pass;
Wind, sun, and earth remain, the birds sing still,
When we are old, are old. . . ." And when we die
All's over that is ours; and life burns on
Through other lovers, other lips," said I,
"Heart of my heart, our heaven is now, is won!"
"We are Earth's best, that learnt her lesson here.
Life is our cry. We have kept the faith!" we said;
"We shall go down with unreluctant tread
Rose-crowned into the darkness! . . ." Proud we were,
And laughed, that had such brave true things to say.
And then you suddenly cried, and turned away.

DUST

When the white flame in us is gone,
  And we that lost the world's delight
Stiffen in darkness, left alone
  To crumble in our separate night;

When your swift hair is quiet in death,
  And through the lips corruption thrust
Has stilled the labor of my breath—
  When we are dust, when we are dust!—

Not dead, not undesirous yet,
  Still sentient, still unsatisfied,
We'll ride the air, and shine and flit,
  Around the places where we died,

And dance as dust before the sun,
  And light of foot, and unconfined,
Hurry from road to road, and run
  About the errands of the wind.

And every mote, on earth or air,
  Will speed and gleam down later days,
And like a secret pilgrim fare
  By eager and invisible ways,

Nor ever rest, nor ever lie,
  Till, beyond thinking, out of view,
One mote of all the dust that's I
  Shall meet one atom that was you.

Then in some garden hushed from wind,
  Warm in a sunset's afterglow,
The lovers in the flowers will find
  A sweet and strange unquiet grow

Upon the peace; and, past desiring,
  So high a beauty in the air,
And such a light, and such a quiring,
  And such a radiant ecstasy there,

They'll know not if it's fire, or dew,
  Or out of earth, or in the height,
Singing, or flame, or scent, or hue,
  Or two that pass, in light, to light,

Out of the garden higher, higher . . .
  But in the instant they shall learn
The shattering fury of our fire,
  And the weak passionless hearts will burn

And faint in that amazing glow,
  Until the darkness close above;
And they will know—poor fools, they'll know!—
  One moment, what it is to love.

SONNET

Oh! Death will find me, long before I tire
  Of watching you; and swing me suddenly
Into the shade and loneliness and mire
  Of the last land! There, waiting patiently,

One day, I think, I'll feel a cool wind blowing,
  See a slow light across the Stygian tide,
And hear the Dead about me stir, unknowing,
  And tremble. And I shall know that you have died,

And watch you, a broad-browed and smiling dream,
  Pass, light as ever, through the lightless host,
Quietly ponder, start, and sway, and gleam—
  Most individual and bewildering ghost!—

And turn, and toss your brown delightful head
Amusedly, among the ancient Dead.

THE SOLDIER

If I should die, think only this of me;
That there's some corner of a foreign field
That is for ever England. There shall be
In that rich earth a richer dust concealed;
A dust whom England bore, shaped, made aware,
Gave, once, her flowers to love, her ways to roam,
A body of England's breathing English air,
Washed by the rivers, blest by suns of home.

And think, this heart, all evil shed away,
A pulse in the eternal mind, no less
Gives somewhere back the thoughts by England given;
Her sights and sounds; dreams happy as her day;
And laughter, learnt of friends; and gentleness,
In hearts at peace, under an English heaven.

HEAVEN

Fish (fly-replete, in depth of June
Dawdling away their wat'ry noon)
Ponder deep wisdom, dark or clear,
Each secret fishy hope or fear.
Fish say, they have their Stream and Pond;
But is there anything Beyond?
This life cannot be All, they swear,
For how unpleasant, if it were!
One may not doubt that, somehow, good
Shall come of Water and of Mud;
And, sure, the reverent eye must see
A Purpose in Liquidity.
We darkly know, by Faith we cry,
The future is not Wholly Dry.
Mud unto Mud!—Death eddies near—
Not here the appointed End, not here!
But somewhere, beyond Space and Time,
Is wetter water, slimier slime!
And there (they trust) there swimmeth One
Who swam ere rivers were begun,
Immense, of fishy form and mind,
Squamous, omnipotent and kind;
And under that Almighty Fin
The littlest fish may enter in.
Oh! never fly conceals a hook,
Fish say, in the Eternal Brook,
But more than mundane weeds are there,
And mud, celestially fair;
Fat caterpillars drift around,
And Paradisal grubs are found;
Unfading moths, immortal flies,
And the worm that never dies.
And in that Heaven of all their wish,
There shall be no more land, say fish.

SECOND BEST

Here in the dark, O heart;
Alone with the enduring Earth, and Night,
And Silence, and the warm strange smell of clovers;
Clear-visioned, though it break you; far apart
From the dead best, the dear and old delight;
Throw down your dreams of immortality,
O faithful, O foolish lover!
Here's peace for you, and surety; here the one
Wisdom—the truth!—"All day the good glad sun
Showers love and labor on you, wine and song;
The greenwood laughs, the wind blows, all day long

Till night." And night ends all things.
Then shall be
No lamp relumed in heaven, no voices crying,
Or changing lights, or dreams and forms that hover!
(And, heart, for all your sighing,
That gladness and those tears, are over, over. . . .)

And has the truth brought no new hope at all,
Heart, that you're weeping yet for Paradise?
Do they still whisper, the old weary cries?
" 'Mid youth and song, feasting and carnival,
Through laughter, through the roses, as of old
Comes Death, on shadowy and relentless feet,
Death, unappeasable by prayer or gold;
Death is the end, the end!"
Proud, then, clear-eyed and laughing, go to greet
Death as a friend!

Exile of immortality, strongly wise,
Strain through the dark with undesirous eyes
To what may lie beyond it. Sets your star,
O heart, for ever! Yet, behind the night,
Waits for the great unborn, somewhere afar,
Some white tremendous daybreak. And the light,
Returning, shall give back the golden hours,
Ocean a windless level, Earth a lawn
Spacious and full of sunlit dancing-places,
And laughter, and music, and among the flowers,
The gay child-hearts of men, and the child-faces,
O heart, in the great dawn!

THE BUSY HEART

Now that we've done our best and worst, and parted,
I would fill my mind with thoughts that will not rend.
(O heart, I do not dare go empty-hearted)
I'll think of Love in books, Love without end;
Women with child, content; and old men sleeping;
And wet strong plowlands, scarred for certain grain;
And babes that weep, and so forget their weeping;
And the young heavens, forgetful after rain;
And evening hush, broken by homing wings;
And Song's nobility, and Wisdom holy,
That live, we dead. I would think of a thousand things,
Lovely and durable, and taste them slowly,
One after one, like tasting a sweet food.
I have need to busy my heart with quietude.

DINING-ROOM TEA

When you were there, and you, and you,
Happiness crowned the night; I too,
Laughing and looking, one of all,
I watched the quivering lamplight fall
On plate and flowers and pouring tea
And cup and cloth; and they and we
Flung all the dancing moments by
With jest and glitter. Lip and eye
Flashed on the glory, shone and cried,
Improvident, unmemoried;
And fitfully, and like a flame
The light of laughter went and came.
Proud in their careless transcience moved
The changing faces that I loved.

Till suddenly, and otherwhence,
I looked upon your innocence.
For lifted clear and still and strange
From the dark woven flow of change
Under a vast and starless sky
I saw the immortal moment lie.
One instant I, an instant, knew
As God knows all. And it and you,
I, above Time, oh, blind! could see
In witless immortality.

I saw the marble cup; the tea,
Hung on the air, an amber stream;
I saw the fire's unglittering gleam,
The painted flame, the frozen smoke.
No more the flooding lamplight broke
On flying eyes and lips and hair;
But lay, but slept unbroken there,
On stiller flesh, and body breathless,
And lips and laughter stayed and deathless,
And words on which no silence grew.
Light was more alive than you.

For suddenly, and otherwhence,
I looked on your magnificence.
I saw the stillness and the light,
And you, august, immortal, white,
Holy and strange; and every glint
Posture and jest and thought and tint
Freed from the mask of transiency,
Triumphant in eternity,
Immote, immortal.
Dazed at length
Human eyes grew, mortal strength
Wearied; and Time began to creep.
Change closed about me like a sleep.
Light glinted on the eyes I loved.
The cup was filled. The bodies moved.
The drifting petal came to ground.
The laughter chimed its perfect round,
The broken syllable was ended.
And I, so certain and so friended,
How could I cloud, or how distress,
The heaven of your unconsciousness?
Or shake at Time's sufficient spell,
Stammering of lights unutterable?
The eternal holiness of you,
The timeless end, you never knew,
The peace that lay, the light that shone.
You never knew that I had gone
A million miles away, and stayed
A million years. The laughter played
Unbroken round me; and the jest
Flashed on. And we that knew the best
Down wonderful hours grew happier yet.
I sang at heart, and talked, and ate,
And lived from laugh to laugh, I too,
When you were there, and you, and you.

THE OLD VICARAGE, GRANTCHESTER

(Café des Westens, Berlin. May, 1912)

Just now the lilac is in bloom,
All before my little room;
And in my flower-beds, I think,
Smile the carnation and the pink;
And down the borders, well I know,
The poppy and the pansy blow . . .
Oh! there the chestnuts, summer through,
Beside the river make for you
A tunnel of green gloom, and sleep
Deeply above; and green and deep
The stream mysterious glides beneath,
Green as a dream and deep as death.
—Oh, damn! I know it! and I know
How the May fields all golden show,
And when the day is young and sweet,
Glide gloriously the bare feet
That run to bathe . . .
Du lieber Gott!
Here am I, sweating, sick, and hot,

And there the shadowed waters fresh
Leap up to embrace the naked flesh.
Temperamentvoll German Jews
Drink beer around;—and *there* the dews
Are soft beneath a morn of gold.
Here tulips bloom as they are told;
Unkempt about those hedges blows
An English unofficial rose;
And there the unregulated sun
Slopes down to rest when day is done,
And wakes a vague unpunctual star,
A slippered Hesper; and there are
Meads towards Haslingfield and Coton
Where *das Betreten's* not *verboten.*

εἴθε γενοίμην . . . would I were
In Grantchester, in Grantchester!—
Some, it may be, can get in touch
With Nature there, or Earth, or such.
And clever modern men have seen
A Faun a-peeping through the green,
And felt the Classics were not dead,
To glimpse a Naiad's reedy head,
Or hear the Goat-foot piping low; . . .
But these are things I do not know.
I only know that you may lie
Day long and watch the Cambridge sky,
And, flower-lulled in sleepy grass,
Hear the cool lapse of hours pass,
Until the centuries blend and blur
In Grantchester, in Grantchester. . . .
Still in the dawnlit waters cool
His ghostly Lordship swims his pool,
And tries the strokes, essays the tricks,
Long learnt on Hellespont, or Styx.
Dan Chaucer hears his river still
Chatter beneath a phantom mill.
Tennyson notes, with studious eye,
How Cambridge waters hurry by . . .
And in that garden, black and white,
Creep whispers through the grass all night;
And spectral dance, before the dawn,
A hundred vicars down the lawn;
Curates, long dust, will come and go
On lissom, clerical, printless toe;
And oft between the boughs is seen
The sly shade of a Rural Dean . . .
Till, at a shiver in the skies,
Vanishing with Satanic cries,
The prim ecclesiastical rout
Leaves but a startled sleeper-out,
Gray heavens, the first bird's drowsy calls,
The falling house that never falls.

God! I will pack, and take a train,
And get me to England once again!
For England's the one land, I know,
Where men with Splendid Hearts may go;
And Cambridgeshire, of all England,
The shire for Men who Understand;
And of *that* district I prefer
The lovely hamlet Grantchester.
For Cambridge people rarely smile,
Being urban, squat, and packed with guile;
And Royston men in the far South
Are black and fierce and strange of mouth;
At Over they fling oaths at one,
And worse than oaths at Trumpington,
And Ditton girls are mean and dirty,
And there's none in Harston under thirty,
And folks in Shelford and those parts
Have twisted lips and twisted hearts,
And Barton men make Cockney rhymes,
And Coton's full of nameless crimes,
And things are done you'd not believe
At Madingley on Christmas Eve.
Strong men have run for miles and miles,
When one from Cherry Hinton smiles,
Strong men have blanched, and shot their wives,
Rather than send them to St. Ives;
Strong men have cried like babes, bydam,
To hear what happened in Babraham.
But Grantchester! ah, Grantchester!
There's peace and holy quiet there,
Great clouds along pacific skies,
And men and women with straight eyes,
Lithe children lovelier than a dream,
A bosky wood, a slumb'rous stream,
And little kindly winds that creep
Round twilight corners, half asleep.
In Grantchester their skins are white;
They bathe by day, they bathe by night;
The women there do all they ought;
The men observe the Rules of Thought;
They love the Good; they worship Truth;
They laugh uproariously in youth;
(And when they get to feeling old,
They up and shoot themselves, I'm told) . . .

Ah God! to see the branches stir
Across the moon at Grantchester!

To smell the thrilling-sweet and rotten
Unforgettable, unforgotten
River-smell, and hear the breeze
Sobbing in the little trees.
Say, do the elm-clumps greatly stand
Still guardians of that holy land?
The chestnuts shade, in reverend dream,
The yet unacademic stream?
Is dawn a secret shy and cold
Anadyomene, silver-gold?
And sunset still a golden sea
From Haslingfield to Madingley?
And after, ere the night is born,
Do hares come out about the corn?
Oh, is the water sweet and cool,
Gentle and brown, above the pool?
And laughs the immortal river still
Under the mill, under the mill?
Say, is there Beauty yet to find?
And Certainty? And Quiet kind?
Deep meadows yet, for to forget
The lies, and truths, and pain? . . . oh! yet
Stands the Church clock at ten to three?
And is there honey still for tea?

Edith Sitwell

Edith Sitwell, daughter of Sir George and Lady Ida Sitwell, granddaughter of the Earl of Landesborough, was born at Scarborough, Yorkshire, in 1887. She was educated, as she puts it, "in secrecy" and in 1914 came to London, where she has lived ever since. A portrait of her, painted by Alvaro Guevara, hangs in the Tate Gallery. In her forties she occupied herself with prose, with a life of Pope, a history of Bath, and a critical anthology.

In 1916, she began the editing of *Wheels,* a determinedly modern anthology which outraged most of the conservative critics. Her own poems provided an even greater series of shocks. After a mild and undistinguished début—*The Mother and Other Poems* (1915)—Miss Sitwell published, in a succession so speedy as to seem little less than rapid-fire, *Clown's Houses* (1918), *The Wooden Pegasus* (1920), *Façade* (1922), *Bucolic Comedies* (1923).

In these volumes—particularly in the last two—Miss Sitwell limits her gamut; but, within her range, there is no poet quite like her. Her favorite instrument seems to be the xylophone, and it is amazing what effects she produces from its restricted timbre. Miss Sitwell is a virtuoso in the communication of a half-wooden, half-glassy tone which is seldom without brilliance. It has been objected that Miss Sitwell's poetry is artificial, and this may be true. But the criticism is not as devastating as it seems, for hers is obviously, and purposefully, an artificial world. It is a curious, semi-mechanical heaven and earth over which her keen eye ranges, a landscape in which Miss Sitwell sees, as none before her has seen, skies of paper, seas of wool, the "reynard-colored sun," the world "like a bare egg laid by the feathered air," the "coltish wind nuzzling the hand," trees "hissing like green geese," "barley-sugar children,"—she even hears Silence "like a slow-leaking tap." If Miss Sitwell's is nothing but a clock-work, conjuring-trick sort of poetry—and it is often more than that—there has rarely been so brilliant an exhibition of verbal legerdemain.

But, it must be reiterated, Miss Sitwell is more than an adroit juggler of startling phrases. Purely as a craftsman in nonsense, she has written some of the most delectable nonsense verses of the age; her grotesque nursery rhymes are, in their own genre, as memorable as De la Mare's. The secret of her serious poetry is scarcely more difficult to capture. After an initial bewilderment (due chieflly to the galloping pace) the wit of her comments, her strange associations, and the romanticism of an essentially feminine mind disclose themselves beneath the glitter.

Beginning with *The Sleeping Beauty* (1924) Miss Sitwell began to alter her bright idiom. Here, as in the succeeding *Troy Park* (1925) and *Rustic Elegies* (1927), she achieves an intensity which her other work, for all its felicities, never expressed. She delights to juxtapose actualities and impossibilities, shifting suddenly from patent absurdity to piercing sympathy. She is Donne one moment, Lewis Carroll the next. To apply the term "mystic" to her will surprise only those who have never cared to see through the glassy surface of her verse. To such readers, Miss Sitwell will remain the artificer of a *papier-mâché* universe, where grass is shrill, fire furry, where the creaking air, combed seas, and spangled emotions are equally automatic and heartless.

In the later volumes her occupation with the human drama is more apparent. Man's hunger for beauty is no longer a pitiful joke in a vegetable existence, but an insatiate passion. The pictures become autobiographical; "Colonel Fantock" reveals the poet in her simplest mood, and those who know her brothers Osbert and Sacheverell will have no difficulty identifying "Dagobert" and "Peregrine."

Gold Coast Customs and Other Poems (1930) repeats the pattern which Miss Sitwell's work has formed: a combination of contempt and nostalgia. The Swiftian scorn is for a fatuous world she refuses to join, and the nostalgia is for the quiet, aristocratic world left in childhood. *Collected Poems* (1930), more clearly than any single volume, emphasizes Miss Sitwell's alternation of wayward metaphysics and methodical madness. The poet reveals herself as a grown-up child, absurd, wise and determinedly innocent, who insists on translation of all objects in terms of her characters. Thus, in "Aubade," Miss Sitwell pictures the world as seen through the mind of a half-dreaming, half-doltish kitchen maid. Jane's sad bucolic stupidity colors the country morning. Coming down with her "cockscomb ragged hair" to light the fire, she feels each drop of rain hardening into a "dull blunt wooden stalactite"; she faces weeding in "eternities" of kitchen-garden where the flowers "cluck" (since most of them are cockscombs) and mock at her; even the flames remind her of the carrots and turnips which she is continually cleaning and cooking, and her own spirits hang limp as the "milk's weak mind."

Street Song (1942) and *The Song of the Cold* (1948) present a further departure. Were it not for the incorporation of some of the early verses in the latter volume, the reader would find it hard to believe that the new and old poems were composed by the same author. The poems written during and after the war discard the marionettes and macabre jingles for disturbing symbols and deeply human values. In "Still Falls the Rain" Miss Sitwell, writing from bombed London, uses two lines from the end of Marlowe's *Doctor Faustus* to dramatize the conflict between the world of legend and the world of nightmare reality. In "Dirge for the New Sunrise" and other later poems she exchanges the stylized opulence and kaleidoscopic images of her surrealist nursery tunes for an utterance which is solemn, incantatory, and sometimes too determinedly oracular.

Gardeners and Astronomers: New Poems (1953) was followed by an enlarged *Collected Poems* (1957), which appeared in the same year that she was named Dame of the Grand Cross of the Order of the British Empire by Queen Elizabeth II.

Besides her poetry, Miss Sitwell has written criticism, fiction, history—as depicted in the nostalgic *Bath* (1932)—and several volumes of biography, the most characteristic of which are *Alexander Pope* (1930) and *The English Eccentrics* (1933).

INTERLUDE

Amid this hot green glowing gloom
A word falls with a raindrop's boom.

Like baskets of ripe fruit in air
The bird-songs seem, suspended where

Those goldfinches—the ripe warm lights
Peck slyly at them—take quick flights.

My feet are feathered like a bird
Among the shadows scarcely heard;

I bring you branches green with dew
And fruits that you may crown anew

Your whirring waspish-gilded hair
Amid this cornucopia—

Until your warm lips bear the stains
And bird-blood leap within your veins.

AUBADE

Jane, Jane,
Tall as a crane,
The morning light creaks down again.

Comb your cockscomb-ragged hair;
Jane, Jane, come down the stair.

Each dull blunt wooden stalactite
Of rain creaks, hardened by the light,

Sounding like an overtone
From some lonely world unknown.

But the creaking empty light
Will never harden into sight,

Will never penetrate your brain
With overtones like the blunt rain.

The light would show (if it could harden)
Eternities of kitchen-garden,

Cockscomb flowers that none will pluck,
And wooden flowers that 'gin to cluck.

In the kitchen you must light
Flames as staring, red and white

As carrots or as turnips, shining
Where the cold dawn light lies whining.

Cockscomb hair on the cold wind
Hangs limp, turns the milk's weak mind. . . .

Jane, Jane,
Tall as a crane,
The morning light creaks down again!

SIR BEELZEBUB

WHEN
Sir
Beelzebub called for his syllabub in the hotel in Hell
Where Proserpine first fell,
Blue as the gendarmerie were the waves of the sea,

(Rocking and shocking the bar-maid).

Nobody comes to give him his rum but the
Rim of the sky hippopotamus-glum
Enhances the chances to bless with a benison
Alfred Lord Tennyson crossing the bar laid
With cold vegetation from pale deputations
Of temperance workers (all signed in Memoriam)
Hoping with glory to trip up the Laureate's feet,

(Moving in classical meters). . . .

Like Balaclava, the lava came down from the
Roof, and the sea's blue wooden gendarmerie
Took them in charge while Beelzebub roared for his rum.

. . . None of them come!

THE KING OF CHINA'S DAUGHTER

The King of China's daughter,
She never would love me
Though I hung my cap and bells upon
Her nutmeg tree.
For oranges and lemons,
The stars in bright blue air,
(I stole them long ago, my dear)
Were dangling there.
The Moon did give me silver pence,
The Sun did give me gold,

And both together softly blew
And made my porridge cold;
But the King of China's daughter
Pretended not to see,
When I hung my cap and bells upon
Her nutmeg tree.

SOLO FOR EAR-TRUMPET

The carriage brushes through the bright
Leaves (violent jets from life to light).
Strong polished speed is plunging, heaves
Between the showers of bright hot leaves.
The window-glasses glaze our faces
And jar them to the very basis,—
But they could never put a polish
Upon my manners, or abolish
My most distinct disinclination
For calling on a rich relation!
In her house,—bulwark built between
The life man lives and visions seen,—
The sunlight hiccups white as chalk,
Grown drunk with emptiness of talk,
And silence hisses like a snake,
Invertebrate and rattling ache. . . .

Till suddenly, Eternity
Drowns all the houses like a sea,
And down the street the Trump of Doom
Blares,—barely shakes this drawing-room
Where raw-edged shadows sting forlorn
As dank dark nettles. Down the horn
Of her ear-trumpet I convey
The news that: "It is Judgment Day!"
"Speaker louder; I don't catch, my dear."
I roared: *"It is the Trump we hear!"*
"The *What?*"—"The TRUMP!" . . .
"I shall complain—
Those boy-scouts practicing again!"

GARDENER JANUS CATCHES A NAIAD

Baskets of ripe fruit in air
The bird-songs seem suspended where

Between the hairy leaves trills dew
All tasting of fresh green anew.

Ma'am, I've heard your laughter flare
Through your waspish-gilded hair:

Feathered masks,
Pots of peas,—
Janus asks
Nought of these,
Creaking water
Brightly stripèd
Now I've caught her—
Shrieking biped.
Flute sounds jump
And turn together,
Changing clumps
Of glassy feather.
In among the
Pots of peas
Naiad changes—
Quick as these.

SPINNING SONG

The miller's daughter
Combs her hair,
Like flocks of dove
As soft as vair. . . .

Oh, how those soft flocks flutter down
Over the empty grassy town.

Like a queen in a crown
Of gold light, she
Sits 'neath the shadows'
Flickering tree—

Till the old dame went the way she came,
Playing bobcherry with a candle-flame.

Now Min the cat
With her white velvet gloves
Watches where sat
The mouse with her loves—

(Old and malicious Mrs. Grundy
Whose washing day is from Monday to Monday.)

"Not a crum," said Min,
"To a mouse I'll be giving.
For a mouse must spin
To earn her living."

So poor Mrs. Mouse and her three cross Aunts
Nibble snow that rustles like gold wheat plants.

And the miller's daughter
Combs her locks,
Like running water
Those dove-soft flocks;

And her mouth is sweet as a honey flower cold
But her heart is heavy as bags of gold.

The shadow-mice said
We will line with down
From those doves, our bed
And our slippers and gown,

For everything comes to the shadows at last
If the spinning-wheel Time move slow or fast."

PANOPE

How lovely are the tombs of the dead nymphs
On the heroic shore—the glittering plinths
Of jacynth . . . hyacinthine waves profound
Sigh of the beauty out of sight and sound

And many a golden foot that pressed the sand—
Panope walking like the pomp of waves
With plumaged helmet near the fountain caves
The panoply of suns on distant strand—

Is only now an arena for the worm,
Her golden flesh lies in the dust's frail storm

And beauty water-bright for long is laid
Deep in the empire of eternal shade—

Only the sighing waves know now the plinth
Of those deep tombs that were of hyacinth.

But still the echoes of that helmeted bright hair
Are like the pomp of tropic suns, the blare
That from the inaccessible horizon runs—
The eternal music of heroic suns
When their strong youth comes freshened from deep seas—
And the first music heard among the trees.

COLONEL FANTOCK

Thus spoke the lady underneath the tree:
I was a member of a family
Whose legend was of hunting—(all the rare
And unattainable brightness of the air)—
A race whose fabled skill in falconry
Was used on the small song-birds and a winged
And blinded Destiny. . . . I think that only
Winged ones know the highest eyrie is so lonely.

There in a land austere and elegant
The castle seemed an arabesque in music;
We moved in an hallucination born
Of silence, which like music gave us lotus
To ear, perfuming lips and our long eyelids
As we trailed over the sad summer grass
Or sat beneath a smooth and mournful tree.

And Time passed, suavely, imperceptibly.

But Dagobert and Peregrine and I
Were children then; we walked like shy gazelles
Among the music of thin flower-bells.
And life still held some promise,—never ask
Of what,—but life seemed less a stranger then
Than ever after in this cold existence.
I always was a little outside life,—
And so the things we touch could comfort me,
I loved the shy dreams we could hear and see—
For I was like one dead, like a small ghost,
A little cold air wandering and lost.

All day within the straw-roofed arabesque
Of the towered castle and the sleepy gardens wandered
We; those delicate paladins, the waves
Told us fantastic legends that we pondered.
And the soft leaves were breasted like a dove,
Crooning old mournful tales of untrue love.

When night came sounding like the growth of trees,
My great-grandmother bent to say good night,
And the enchanted moonlight seemed transformed
Into the silvery tinkling of an old

And gentle music-box that played a tune
Of Circean enchantments and far seas.
Her voice was lulling like the splash of these
When she had given me her good night kiss
There, in her lengthened shadow, I saw this
Old military ghost with mayfly whiskers,—
Poor harmless creature, blown by the cold wind,
Boasting of unseen, unreal victories
To a harsh unbelieving world unkind,—
For all the battles that this warrior fought
Were with cold poverty and helpless age—
His spoils were shelters from the winter's rage.
And so forever through his braggart voice,
Through all that martial trumpet's sound, his soul
Wept a little sound, so pitiful,
Knowing that he is outside life for ever
With no one that will warm or comfort him. . . .
He is not even dead, but Death's buffoon
On a bare stage, a shrunken pantaloon.—
His military banner never fell,
Nor his account of victories, the stories
Of old apocryphal misfortunes, glories
Which comforted his heart in later life
When he was the Napoleon of the schoolroom
And all the victories he gained were over
Little boys who would not learn to spell.

All day within the sweet and ancient gardens
He had my childish self for audience—
Whose body flat and strange, whose pale straight hair
Made me appear as though I had been drowned—
(We all have the remote air of a legend)—
And Dagobert my brother whose large strength,
Great body and grave beauty still reflect
The Angevin dead kings from whom we spring;
And sweet as the young tender winds that stir
In thickets where the earliest flower-bells sing
Upon the boughs, was his just character;
And Peregrine the youngest with a naïve
Shy grace like a faun's, whose slant eyes seemed
The warm green light beneath eternal boughs.
His hair was like the fronds of feathers, life
In him was changing ever, springing fresh
As the dark songs of birds . . . the furry warmth
And purring sound of fires was in his voice
Which never failed to warm and comfort me.

And there were haunted summers in Troy Park
When all the stillness budded into leaves;
We listened like Ophelia drowned in blond
And fluid hair, beneath stag-antlered trees;

Then in the ancient park the country-pleasant
Shadows fell as brown as any pheasant,
And Colonel Fantock seemed like one of these.
Sometimes for comfort in the castle kitchen
He drowsed, where with a sweet and velvet lip
The snapdragons within the fire
Of their red summer never tire.
And Colonel Fantock liked our company.
For us he wandered over each old lie,
Changing the flowering hawthorn full of bees
Into the silver helm of Hercules,
For us defended Troy from the top stair
Outside the nursery, when the calm full moon
Was like the sound within the growth of trees.
But then came one cruel day in deepest June
When pink flowers seemed a sweet Mozartian tune,
And Colonel Fantock pondered o'er a book.
A gay voice like a honeysuckle nook,—
So sweet,—said, "It is Colonel Fantock's age
Which makes him babble." . . . Blown by winter's rage
The poor old man then knew his creeping fate,
The darkening shadow that would take his sight
And hearing; and he thought of his saved pence
Which scarce would rent a grave . . . that youthful voice
Was a dark bell which ever clanged "Too late"—
A creeping shadow that would steal from him
Even the little boys who would not spell—
His only prisoners. . . . On that June day
Cold Death had taken his first citadel.

STILL FALLS THE RAIN

The Raids, 1940. Night and Dawn

Still falls the Rain—
Dark as the world of man, black as our loss—
Blind as the nineteen hundred and forty nails
Upon the cross.

Still falls the Rain
With a sound like the pulse of the heart that is changed to the hammer-beat
In the Potter's Field, and the sound of the impious feet

On the Tomb:
Still falls the Rain
In the Field of Blood where the small hopes breed and the human brain
Nurtures its greed, that worm with the brow of Cain.

Still falls the Rain
At the feet of the Starved Man hung upon the Cross.

Christ that each day, each night, nails there, have mercy on us—
On Dives and on Lazarus:
Under the rain the sore and the gold are as one.

Still falls the Rain—
Still falls the blood from the Starved Man's wounded Side:
He bears in His Heart all wounds,—those of the light that died,
The last faint spark
In the self-murdered heart, the wounds of the sad uncomprehending dark,

The wounds of the baited bear,—
The blind and weeping bear whom the keepers beat
On his helpless flesh . . . the tears of the hunted hare.

Still falls the Rain—
Then—O Ile leape up to my God: who pulles me doune—
See, see where Christ's blood streames in the firmament:
It flows from the Brow we nailed upon the tree
Deep to the dying, to the thirsting heart
That holds the fires of the world,—dark-smirched with pain
As Caesar's laurel crown.

Then sounds the voice of One who like the heart of man
Was once a child who among beasts has lain—
"Still do I love, still shed my innocent light, my Blood, for thee."

SONG

Now that Fate is dead and gone
And that Madness reigns alone,
Still the Furies shake the fires
Of their torches in the street
Of my blood. . . . And still they stand
In the city's street that tires
Of the tread of Man.

Three old rag-pickers are they—
Clothed with grandeur by the light
As a queen, but blind as Doom
Fumbling for the rag of Man
In an empty room.

Now they take the place of Fate
In whom the flames of Madness ran
Since her lidless eyes were cursed
With the world-expunging sight
Of the heart of Man.

How simple was the time of Cain
Before the latter Man-made Rain
Washed away all loss and gain
And the talk of right and wrong—
Murdered now and gone!

And the Ghost of Man is red
From the sweep of the world's blood . . .
In this late equality
Would you know the Ghost of Man
From the Ghost of the Flea?

But still the fires of the great Spring
In the desolate fields proclaim
Eternity . . . those wild fires shout
Of Christ the New Song.

Run those fires from field to field;
I walk alone and ghostly
Burning with Eternity's
Fires, and quench the Furies' song
In flame that never tires.

DIRGE FOR THE NEW SUNRISE

(Fifteen minutes past eight o'clock, on the morning of Monday, the 6th of August, 1945.)

Bound to my heart as Ixion to the wheel,
Nailed to my heart as the thief upon the cross,
I hang between our Christ and the gap where the world was lost

And watch the phantom Sun in Famine Street—
The ghost of the heart of Man . . . red Cain,
And the more murderous brain
Of Man, still redder Nero that conceived the death
Of his mother Earth, and tore
Her womb, to know the place where he was conceived.

But no eyes grieved—
For none were left for tears:
They were blinded as the years
Since Christ was born. Mother or Murderer, you have given or taken life—
Now all is one!

There was a morning when the holy Light
Was young. . . . The beautiful First Creature came
To our water-springs, and thought us without blame.

Our hearts seemed safe in our breasts and sang to the Light—
The marrow in the bone
We dreamed was safe . . . the blood in the veins, the sap in the tree
Were springs of Deity.

But I saw the little Ant-men as they ran
Carrying the world's weight of the world's filth
And the filth in the heart of Man—
Compressed till those lusts and greeds had a greater heat than that of the Sun.

And the ray from the heat came soundless, shook the sky
As if in search for food, and squeezed the stems
Of all that grows on the earth till they were dry.
—And drank the marrow of the bone:
The eyes that saw, the lips that kissed, are gone,
Or black as thunder lie and grin at the murdered Sun.

The living blind and seeing dead together lie
As if in love . . . There was no more hating them—
And no more love: Gone is the heart of Man.

Edwin Muir

Edwin Muir was born May 15, 1887, in Deerness on the mainland of Orkney. His father was a farmer who could not fit into the industrial pattern, and Edwin, youngest of a family of six, entered a law office when he was fourteen. He clerked in various positions until he was thirty-one, at which time he became an assistant editor on the *New Age* and married Willa Anderson, with whom he collaborated on translations of modern German authors.

Muir spent much time abroad. He wandered through Italy, Austria, and Czechoslovakia, was director of the British Institute in Prague and in Rome, lectured at Harvard, became Warden of Newbattle Abbey College, and lived the last thirty years of his life in Scotland. He died at seventy-one, January 4, 1959.

Writing in the traditional manner, Muir originated no new techniques, yet his extremely varied writings—novels, biographies, essays, travel books, and a rich autobiography, *The Story and the Fable* (1940)—disclose a mind which is original without straining for originality, a mind engaged on a quest for "the drowned original of the soul." In *World Within World,* Stephen Spender, recounting meetings with Muir, remarks, "On each occasion I was struck by the integrity of purpose in his life and work . . . a purpose which converted a life of shifting jobs into a spiritual pilgrimage."

It is this sense of "a spiritual pilgrimage" which makes Muir's *Collected Poems* (1960) so dreamlike and, at the same time, so vividly graphic. "The Labyrinth" is both a retelling of a favorite myth and a powerful evocation of the winding course of Muir's own life; "In Love for Long," "The Good Man in Hell," "The Combat" and "The Animals" are not only deep and sometimes enigmatical explorations, but also extraordinary contrasts in moods and symbols. "The Horses" is a poem which must excite the most casual reader with its prophetic terror and beauty.

This is a poetry which combines grace and wisdom with the greatest naturalness. Never having been fashionable, it cannot go out of fashion and, in its quiet authority, seems certain to survive.

THE GOOD MAN IN HELL

If a good man were ever housed in Hell
   By needful error of the qualities,
Perhaps to prove the rule or shame the devil,
   Or speak the truth only a stranger sees,

Would he, surrendering quick to obvious hate,
   Fill half eternity with cries and tears,
Or watch beside Hell's little wicket gate
   In patience for the first ten thousand years,

Feeling the curse climb slowly to his throat
   That, uttered, dooms him to rescindless ill,

Forcing his praying tongue to run by rote,
  Eternity entire before him still?

Would he at last, grown faithful in his station,
  Kindle a little hope in hopeless Hell,
And sow among the damned doubts of damnation,
  Since here someone could live and could live well?

One doubt of evil would bring down such a grace,
  Open such a gate, all Eden could enter in,
Hell be a place like any other place,
  And love and hate and life and death begin.

IN LOVE FOR LONG

I've been in love for long
With what I cannot tell
And will contrive a song
For the intangible
That has no mould or shape,
From which there's no escape.

It is not even a name,
Yet it is all constancy;
Tried or untried, the same,
It cannot part from me;
A breath, yet as still
As the established hill.

It is not any thing,
And yet all being is;
Being, being, being,
Its burden and its bliss.
How can I ever prove
What it is I love?

This happy happy love
Is sieged with crying sorrows,
Crushed beneath and above
Between to-days and morrows;
A little paradise
Held in the world's vice.

And there it is content
And careless as a child,
And in imprisonment
Flourishes sweet and wild;
In wrong, beyond wrong,
All the world's day long.

This love a moment known
For what I do not know
And in a moment gone
Is like the happy doe
That keeps its perfect laws
Between the tiger's paws
And vindicates its cause.

THE LABYRINTH

Since I emerged that day from the labyrinth,
Dazed with the tall and echoing passages,
The swift recoils, so many I almost feared
I'd meet myself returning at some smooth corner,
Myself or my ghost, for all there was unreal
After the straw ceased rustling and the bull
Lay dead upon the straw and I remained,
Blood-splashed, if dead or alive I could not tell
In the twilight nothingness (I might have been
A spirit seeking his body through the roads
Of intricate Hades)—ever since I came out
To the world, the still fields swift with flowers, the trees

All bright with blossom, the little green hills, the sea,
The sky and all in movement under it,
Shepherds and flocks and birds and the young and old,
(I stared in wonder at the young and the old,
For in the maze time had not been with me;
I had strayed, it seemed, past sun and season and change,
Past rest and motion, for I could not tell
At last if I moved or stayed; the maze itself
Revolved around me on its hidden axis
And swept me smoothly to its enemy,
The lovely world)—since I came out that day,
There have been times when I have heard my footsteps
Still echoing in the maze, and all the roads
That run through the noisy world, deceiving streets
That meet and part and meet, and rooms that open
Into each other—and never a final room—
Stairways and corridors and antechambers
That vacantly wait for some great audience,
The smooth sea-tracks that open and close again,
Tracks undiscoverable, indecipherable,
Paths on the earth and tunnels underground,
And bird-tracks in the air—all seemed a part
Of the great labyrinth. And then I'd stumble
In sudden blindness, hasten, almost run,
As if the maze itself were after me
And soon must catch me up. But taking thought,
I'd tell myself, 'You need not hurry. This
Is the firm good earth. All roads lie free before you.'
But my bad spirit would sneer, 'No, do not hurry.
No need to hurry. Haste and delay are equal
In this one world, for there's no exit, none,
No place to come to, and you'll end where you are,
Deep in the centre of the endless maze.'

I could not live if this were not illusion.
It is a world, perhaps; but there's another.
For once in a dream or trance I saw the gods
Each sitting on the top of his mountain-isle,
While down below the little ships sailed by,
Toy multitudes swarmed in the harbours, shepherds drove
Their tiny flocks to the pastures, marriage feasts
Went on below, small birthdays and holidays,
Ploughing and harvesting and life and death,
And all permissible, all acceptable,
Clear and secure as in a limpid dream.
But they, the gods, as large and bright as clouds,
Conversed across the sounds in tranquil voices
High in the sky above the untroubled sea;
And their eternal dialogue was peace
Where all these things were woven; and this our life
Was as a chord deep in that dialogue,

As easy utterance of harmonious words,
Spontaneous syllables bodying forth a world.

That was the real world; I have touched it once,
And now shall know it always. But the lie,
The maze, the wild-wood waste of falsehood, roads
That run and run and never reach an end,
Embowered in error—I'd be prisoned there
But that my soul has birdwings to fly free.

Oh these deceits are strong almost as life.
Last night I dreamt I was in the labyrinth,
And woke far on. I did not know the place.

THE COMBAT

It was not meant for human eyes,
That combat on the shabby patch
Of clods and trampled turf that lies
Somewhere beneath the sodden skies
For eye of toad or adder to catch.

And having seen it I accuse
The crested animal in his pride,
Arrayed in all the royal hues
Which hide the claws he well can use
To tear the heart out of the side.

Body of leopard, eagle's head
And whetted beak, and lion's mane,
And frost-grey hedge of feathers spread
Behind—he seemed of all things bred.
I shall not see his like again.

As for his enemy, there came in
A soft round beast as brown as clay;
All rent and patched his wretched skin;
A battered bag he might have been,
Some old used thing to throw away.

Yet he awaited face to face
The furious beast and the swift attack.
Soon over and done. That was no place
Or time for chivalry or for grace.
The fury had him on his back.

And two small paws like hands flew out
To right and left as the trees stood by.
One would have said beyond a doubt
This was the very end of the bout,
But that the creature would not die.

For ere the death-stroke he was gone,
Writhed, whirled, huddled into his den,
Safe somehow there. The fight was done,
And he had lost who had all but won.
But oh his deadly fury then.

A while the place lay blank, forlorn,
Drowsing as in relief from pain.
The cricket chirped, the grating thorn
Stirred, and a little sound was born.
The champions took their posts again.

And all began. The stealthy paw
Slashed out and in. Could nothing save
These rags and tatters from the claw?
Nothing. And yet I never saw
A beast so helpless and so brave.

And now, while the trees stand watching, still
The unequal battle rages there.
The killing beast that cannot kill
Swells and swells in his fury till
You'd almost think it was despair.

THE ANIMALS

They do not live in the world,
Are not in time and space.
From birth to death hurled
No word do they have, not one
To plant a foot upon,
Were never in any place.

For with names the world was called
Out of the empty air,
With names was built and walled,
Line and circle and square,
Dust and emerald;

Snatched from deceiving death
By the articulate breath.

But these have never trod
Twice the familiar track,
Never never turned back
Into the memoried day.
All is new and near
In the unchanging Here
Of the fifth great day of God,
That shall remain the same,
Never shall pass away.

On the sixth day we came.

THE HORSES

Barely a twelvemonth after
The seven days war that put the world to sleep,
Late in the evening the strange horses came.
By then we had made our covenant with silence,
But in the first few days it was so still
We listened to our breathing and were afraid.
On the second day
The radios failed; we turned the knobs; no answer.
On the third day a warship passed us, heading north,
Dead bodies piled on the deck. On the sixth day
A plane plunged over us into the sea. Thereafter
Nothing. The radios dumb;
And still they stand in corners of our kitchens,
And stand, perhaps, turned on, in a million rooms
All over the world. But now if they should speak,
If on a sudden they should speak again,
If on the stroke of noon a voice should speak,
We would not listen, we would not let it bring
That old bad world that swallowed its children quick
At one great gulp. We would not have it again.
Sometimes we think of the nations lying asleep,
Curled blindly in impenetrable sorrow,
And then the thought confounds us with its strangeness.
The tractors lie about our fields; at evening
They look like dank sea-monsters couched and waiting.
We leave them where they are and let them rust:
'They'll moulder away and be like other loam'.
We make our oxen drag our rusty ploughs,
Long laid aside. We have gone back
Far past our fathers' land.
And then, that evening
Late in the summer the strange horses came.
We heard a distant tapping on the road,
A deepening drumming; it stopped, went on again
And at the corner changed to hollow thunder.
We saw the heads
Like a wild wave charging and were afraid.
We had sold our horses in our fathers' time
To buy new tractors. Now they were strange to us
As fabulous steeds set on an ancient shield
Or illustrations in a book of knights.
We did not dare go near them. Yet they waited,

Stubborn and shy, as if they had been sent
By an old command to find our whereabouts
And that long-lost archaic companionship.
In the first moment we had never a thought
That they were creatures to be owned and used.
Among them were some half-a-dozen colts
Dropped in some wilderness of the broken world,
Yet new as if they had come from their own Eden.
Since then they have pulled our ploughs and borne our loads,
But that free servitude still can pierce our hearts.
Our life is changed; their coming our beginning.

W. J. Turner

Walter James (Redfern) Turner was born in Melbourne, Australia, in 1889. He was educated at Scotch College, Melbourne, and, at seventeen, made the long journey to Europe. He studied in Germany and, shortly afterward, came to England, where, except for intervals of travel, he lived until his death in 1946.

His activities have been numerous. He was literary editor of *The Daily Herald,* dramatic critic of *The London Mercury,* and musical critic for three English weeklies. In the last rôle, his essays have been collected in three volumes, the first being *Music and Life* (1921). Later Turner made a reputation as an incisive dramatist with the imaginative *The Man Who Ate the Popomack* (1922) and the satiric *Smaragda's Lover* (1924).

But it is as a poet that Turner first attracted and still challenges attention. *The Hunter and other Poems* (1916) contains other matter besides the whimsical "Romance," which has been much quoted. *The Dark Fire* (1918) suggests if it does not sound depths; repressed passion adds a somber note to the fancies. Turner's subsequent volumes, *Paris and Helen* (1921), *In Time Like Glass* (1921) and *Landscape of Cytherea* (1923), suffer from an overproductive and uncritical ease, but many of the individual poems are on a level with the author's successful work. A dramatic poem, *The Seven Days of the Sun* (1925), was followed by the simpler, more persuasive *New Poems* (1928). A critical study of Beethoven was published in 1927.

Pursuit of Psyche (1931) and *Jack and Jill* (1934) came as a surprise to all except Turner's insistent admirers. *Jack and Jill* has a freshness of idea and a technical proficiency which command instant attention. *Pursuit of Psyche,* Turner's most ambitious project, concerns (as the title suggests) the search for the spirit through the varying forms of human desire. The ten cantos suffer from the lack of a fiery imagination which should unify the whole—the poem has organization without integration—but its parts are admirable. There are reminders of Abercrombie's *Emblems of Love* not only in the philosophy but in the phrasing. Beauty fills

This common function of all living things
With a pure value, vivid as the pact
The rosebush makes with summer, or the wings
The dove makes with the wind, or water when ice is still.

But Turner is, at the same time, more abstract and more lyrical than Abercrombie. The shorter poems are particularly convincing, and such pieces as "Talking with Soldiers," "The Music of a Tree," and "The Lion" pronounce an imagination altogether his own, an imagination which has not been sufficiently praised.

Blow for Balloons (1935), Turner's first novel, is a mixture of naïve egotism, penetration, poetry, and general literary sans-culottisme—a headlong fantasy, the best part of which is the author's account of his boyhood in Australia. Turner's music criticism, acute and authoritative, is at its best in *Berlioz* (1934) and *Mozart* (1938).

ROMANCE

When I was but thirteen or so
  I went into a golden land,
Chimborazo, Cotopaxi
  Took me by the hand.

My father died, my brother too,
  They passed like fleeting dreams,
I stood where Popocatapetl
  In the sunlight gleams.

I dimly heard the master's voice
  And boys far-off at play,—
Chimborazo, Cotopaxi
  Had stolen me away.

I walked in a great golden dream
  To and fro from school—
Shining Popocatapetl
  The dusty streets did rule.

I walked home with a gold dark boy
  And never a word I'd say,
Chimborazo, Cotopaxi
  Had taken my speech away.

I gazed entranced upon his face
  Fairer than any flower—
O shining Popocatapetl,
  It was thy magic hour:

The houses, people, traffic seemed
  Thin fading dreams by day;
Chimborazo, Cotopaxi
  They had stolen my soul away!

SONG

Lovely hill-torrents are
  At cold winterfall;
Among the earth's silence, they
  Stonily call.

Gone Autumn's pageantry;
  Through woods all bare
With strange, locked voices
  Shining they stare!

THE ROBBER

The Trees were taller than the night,
  And through my window square,
Earth-stupefied, great oranges
  Drowsed in the leaf-carved air.

Into that tree-top crowded dream
  A white arm stretched, and soon
Those green-gold oranges were plucked,
  Were sucked pale by the Moon.

And white and still that robber lay
  On the frail boughs asleep,
Eating the solid substance through
  In silence clear and deep.

Suddenly he went, and then
  The wood was dark as death:
Come back, O robber; robber, come;
  These gray trees are but breath:

These gray trees are but breath, the Night
  Is a wind-walled, dream-filled Hall!
But on the mirror of the air
  The wood wreathed dark and tall.

No movement and no sound there was
  Within that silent House.
Behind a cloud, the Robber laughed
  In a mad white carouse.

TALKING WITH SOLDIERS

The mind of the people is like mud,
From which arise strange and beautiful things,
But mud is none the less mud,
Though it bear orchids and prophesying Kings,
Dreams, trees, and water's bright babblings.

It has found form and color and light,
The cold glimmer of the ice-wrapped Poles:
It has called a far-off glow: Arcturus,
And some pale weeds: lilies of the valley.

It has imagined Virgil, Helen and Cassandra,
The sack of Troy, and the weeping for Hector—
Rearing stark up 'mid all this beauty
In the thick, dull neck of Ajax.

There is a dark Pine in Lapland,
And the great, figured Horn of the Reindeer
Moving soundlessly across the snow,
Is its twin brother, double-dreamed,
In the mind of a far-off people.

It is strange that a little mud
Should echo with sounds, syllables, and letters,
Should rise up and call a mountain Popocatapetl,
And a green-leafed wood Oleander.

These are the ghosts of invisible things;
There is no Lapland, no Helen and no Hector,
And the Reindeer is a darkening of the brain,
And Oleander is but oleander.

Mary Magdalena and the vine Lachryma Christi
Were like ghosts up the ghost of Vesuvius,
As I sat and drank wine with the soldiers,
As I sat in the Inn on the mountain,
Watching the shadows in my mind.

The mind of the people is like mud:
Where are the imperishable things,
The ghosts that flicker in the brain—
Silent women, orchids, and prophesying Kings,
Dreams, trees, and water's bright babblings!

THE LION

Strange spirit with inky hair,
Tail tufted stiff in rage,
I saw with sudden stare
Leap on the printed page.

The stillness of its roar
  From midnight deserts torn
Clove silence to the core
  Like the blare of a great horn.

I saw the sudden sky;
  Cities in crumbling sand;
The stars fall wheeling by;
  The lion roaring stand:

The stars fall wheeling by,
  Their silent, silver stain
Cold on his glittering eye,
  Cold on his carven mane.

The full-orbed Moon shone down,
  The silence was so loud,
From jaws wide-open thrown
  His voice hung like a cloud.

Earth shrank to blackest air;
  That spirit stiff in rage
Into some midnight lair
  Leapt from the printed page.

THE MUSIC OF A TREE

Once, walking home, I passed beneath a Tree,
It filled the dark like stone statuary,
  It was so quiet and still,
  Its thick green leaves a hill
Of strange and faint earth-branching melody:

Over a wall it hung its leaf-starred wood,
And as I lonely there beneath it stood,
  In that sky-hollow street
  Where rang no human feet,
Sweet music flowed and filled me with its flood;

And all my weariness then fell away,
The houses were more lovely than by day;
  The Moon and that old Tree
  Sang there, and secretly,
With throbbing heart, tip-toe I stole away.

IN TIME LIKE GLASS

In Time like glass the stars are set,
And seeming-fluttering butterflies
Are fixed fast in Time's glass net
With mountains and with maids' bright eyes.

Above the cold Cordilleras hung
The winged eagle and the Moon:
The gold, snow-throated orchid sprung
From gloom where peers the dark baboon:

The Himalayas' white, rapt brows;
The jewel-eyed bear that threads their caves;
The lush plains' lowing herds of cows;
That Shadow entering human graves:

All these like stars in Time are set,
They vanish but can never pass;
The Sun that with them fades is yet
Fast-fixed as they in Time like glass.

INDIA

They hunt, the velvet tigers in the jungle,
The spotted jungle full of shapeless patches—
Sometimes they're leaves, sometimes they're hanging flowers,
Sometimes they're hot gold patches of the sun:
They hunt, the velvet tigers in the jungle!

What do they hunt by glimmering pools of water,
By the round silver Moon, the Pool of Heaven?—
In the striped grass, amid the barkless trees—
The stars scattered like eyes of beasts above them!

What do they hunt, their hot breath scorching insects?
Insects that blunder blindly in the way,
Vividly fluttering—they also are hunting,
Are glittering with a tiny ecstasy!

The grass is flaming and the trees are growing,
The very mud is gurgling in the pools,
Green toads are watching, crimson parrots flying,
Two pairs of eyes meet one another glowing—
They hunt, the velvet tigers in the jungle.

SILENCE

It was a bright day and all the trees were still
In the deep valley, and the dim Sun glowed;
The clay in hard-baked fire along the hill
Leapt through dark trunks to apples green and gold,
Smooth, hard and cold, they shone like lamps of stone.

They were bright bubbles bursting from the trees,
Swollen and still among the dark green boughs;
On their bright skins the shadows of the leaves
Seemed the faint ghosts of summers long since gone,
Faint ghosts of ghosts, the dreams of ghostly eyes.

There was no sound between those breathless hills.
Only the dim Sun hung there, nothing moved;
The thronged, massed, crowded multitude of leaves
Hung like dumb tongues that loll and gasp for air:
The grass was thick and still between the trees.

There were big apples lying on the ground,
Shining, quite still, as though they had been stunned
By some great violent spirit stalking through,
Leaving a deep and supernatural calm
Round a dead beetle upturned in a furrow.

A valley filled with dark, quiet, leaf-thick trees,
Loaded with green, cold, faintly shining suns;
And in the sky a great dim burning disc!—
Madness it is to watch these twisted trunks
And to see nothing move and hear no sound.

Let's make a noise, Hey! . . . Hey! . . . Hullo!
Hullo!

THE SUN

The sun has come, I know,
For yesterday I stood
Beside it in the wood—
But O how pale, how softly did it glow.
I stooped to warm my hands
Before its rain-washed gold;
But it was pebble-cold,
Startled to find itself in these dark lands.

Isaac Rosenberg

Isaac Rosenberg was born at Bristol on November 25, 1890. At the age of seven his parents brought him to London; at fourteen he was compelled to leave school and work for his living. Later some friends interested themselves in the boy who had begun to show great talent as a writer and draftsman, and made it possible for the young Jew from the East End to attend the Slade School. After three years of art schooling, during which Rosenberg won prizes, ill health forced him to leave England. In 1914, he went to South Africa, to a married sister in Capetown. It was there that he definitely decided to become a poet. He attempted to support himself by writing and lecturing, but his efforts were without success and, in less than a year, he was back in London. War had broken out. Sick and unhappy, Rosenberg enlisted in 1915. Early in 1916, he was sent to France, totally unfitted for military life. Nevertheless, his endurance was amazing; he hated war with all the force of his keen mind and disabled body, but he never whined. He was killed in action on April 1, 1918.

As a poet, Rosenberg is greater in promise than achievement. Most of the privately printed *Night and Day* (1912), although published at the age of twenty-two, was written in his 'teens. Even the succeeding *Youth* (1915) suffers from verbal awkwardness; a fear of falling into weak writing led him to complicate his images until they are, for the most part, turgid and overburdened. But in *Moses* (1916), and in the posthumous war-poems, the passionate young poet speaks in his own half-savage voice. Here and there a passage suggests Abercrombie, who Rosenberg admired greatly; but the images are so fiercely fresh, the accent so personal, that there is no mistaking the strength and originality of Rosenberg's gift.

Rosenberg's three small books, as well as a quantity of uncollected verse including an unfinished play, were published in one volume, *Poems,* in 1922, edited by Gordon Bottomley and introduced by Lawrence Binyon. An enlarged *Collected Works of Issac Rosenberg* (1937) includes his prose, letters, some drawings, and many poems never before published. In the foreword Siegfried Sassoon recognized in Rosenberg a fusion of English and Hebrew culture. "Behind all his poetry there is a racial quality—biblical and prophetic. His experiments were a strenuous effort for impassioned expression; his imagination had a sinewy and muscular aliveness. Often he saw things in terms of sculpture, but he did not carve or chisel; he *modelled* words with fierce energy and aspiration, finding ecstasy in form, dreaming in grandeurs of superb light and deep shadow. . . . Watching him working with words, I find him a poet of movement. Words which express movement are often used by him and are essential to his natural utterance."

EXPRESSION

Call—call—and bruise the air:
Shatter dumb space!
Yea! We will fling this passion
    everywhere;
Leaving no place

For the superb and grave
Magnificent throng,
The pregnant queens of quietness
    that brave
And edge our song

Of wonder at the light
(Our life-leased home),
Of greeting to our housemates.
    And in might
Our song shall roam

Life's heart, a blossoming fire
Blown bright by thought,
While gleams and fades the infinite
    desire,
Phantasmed naught.

Can this be caught and caged?
Wings can be clipt
Of eagles, the sun's gaudy measure
    gauged,
But no sense dipt

In the mystery of sense.
The troubled throng
Of words break out like smothered
    fire through dense
And smouldering wrong.

CHAGRIN

Caught still as Absalom,
Surely the air hangs
From the swayless cloud-boughs,
Like hair of Absalom
Caught and hanging still.

From the imagined weight
Of spaces in a sky
Of mute chagrin, my thoughts
Hang like branch-clung hair

To trunks of silence swung,
With the choked soul weighing down
Into thick emptiness.
Christ! end this hanging death,
For endlessness hangs therefrom.

Invisibly—branches break
From invisible trees—
The cloud-woods where we rush,
Our eyes holding so much,
Which we must ride dim ages round
Ere the hands (we dream) can touch,
We ride, we ride, before the morning
The secret roots of the sun to tread,
And suddenly
We are lifted of all we know
And hang from implacable boughs.

BREAK OF DAY IN THE TRENCHES

The darkness crumbles away—
It is the same old druid Time as ever.
Only a live thing leaps my hand—
A queer sardonic rat—
As I pull the parapet's poppy
To stick behind my ear.
Droll rat, they would shoot you if they knew
Your cosmopolitan sympathies.
Now you have touched this English hand
You will do the same to a German—
Soon, no doubt, if it be your pleasure
To cross the sleeping green between.
It seems you inwardly grin as you pass
Strong eyes, fine limbs, haughty athletes
Less chanced than you for life,
Bonds to the whims of murder,
Sprawled in the bowels of the earth,
The torn fields of France.
What do you see in our eyes
At the shrieking iron and flame
Hurled through still heavens?
What quaver—what heart aghast?
Poppies whose roots are in man's veins
Drop, and are ever dropping;
But mine in my ear is safe,
Just a little white with the dust.

ON RECEIVING NEWS OF THE WAR

Snow is a strange white word.
No ice or frost
Has asked of bud or bird
For Winter's cost.

Yet ice and frost and snow
From earth to sky
This Summer land doth know.
No man knows why.

In all men's hearts it is.
Some spirit old
Hath turned with malign kiss
Our lives to mould.

Red fangs have torn His face.
God's blood is shed.

He mourns from His lone place
His children dead.

O! ancient crimson curse!
Corrode, consume.
Give back this universe
Its pristine bloom.

I AM THE BLOOD

I am the blood
Streaming the veins of sweet-
ness; sharp and sweet,
Beauty has pricked the live
veins of my soul
And sucked all being in.

I am the air
Prowling the room of beauty,
climbing her soft
Walls of surmise, her ceilings
that close in.
She breathes me as her breath.

I am the death
Whose monument is beauty,
and forever,
Although I lie unshrouded
in life's tomb,
She is my cenotaph.

THE ONE LOST

I mingle with your bones;
You steal in subtle noose
This lighted dust Jehovah loans
And now I lose.

What will the Lender say
When I shall not be found,
Safe-sheltered at the Judgment Day,
Being in you bound?

He'll hunt through wards of Heaven,
Call to uncoffined earth,
"Where is this soul, unjudged, not given
Dole for good's dearth?"

And I, lying so safe
Within you, hearing all,
To have cheated God shall laugh,
Freed by your thrall.

THE JEW

Moses, from whose loins I sprung,
Lit by a lamp in his blood
Ten immutable rules, a moon
For mutable lampless men.

The blond, the bronze, the ruddy,
With the same heaving blood,
Keep tide to the moon of Moses.
Then why do they sneer at me?

THE DEAD HEROES

Flame out, you glorious skies,
Welcome our brave;
Kiss their exultant eyes;
Give what they gave.

Flash, mailèd seraphim,
Your burning spears;
New days to outflame their dim
Heroic years.

Thrills their baptismal tread
The bright proud air;
The embattled plumes outpread
Burn upwards there.

Flame out, flame out, O Song!
Star, ring to star!
Strong as our hurt is strong,
Our children are.

Their blood is England's heart;
By their dead hands,
It is their noble part
That England stands.

England—Time gave them thee;
They gave back this
To win Eternity
And claim God's kiss.

Richard Aldington

Richard Aldington was born in England in 1892, and educated at Dover College and London University. His first poems were published in England in 1909; *Images Old and New* appeared in 1915. Aldington and "H. D." (the chief American Imagist) were conceded to be two of the foremost Imagist poets; their sensitive and clean-cut lines put to shame their scores of imitators. Both appeared, with four others, under Amy Lowell's ægis in the three issues of *Some Imagist Poets,* published from 1915 to 1917.

Aldington's *War and Love* (1918) is somewhere more regular in pattern; the poems in this latter volume are less consciously programmatic but more searching. Recently, Aldington, in common with most of the *vers libristes,* has been writing in regular rhythms and fixed forms. *Images of Desire* (1919) was followed by *Exile and Other Poems* (1923) which contains whole sections of surprisingly archaic, pseudo-Elizabethan songs. *A Fool i' the Forest* (1925) is a return to Aldington's earlier manner with the addition of foreign dissonances. Though the influence of Eliot is obvious, this phantasmagoria is in many ways Aldington's most important work. Juxtaposing classic calm with the incongruities of a mechanical civilization, Aldington projects an agony unrelated to either ancient or modern backgrounds. This agony was amplified in Aldington's first novel, *Death of a Hero* (1929), a novel dealing with three generations, beginning in the snug little England of the Victorian Nineties; a work kaleidoscopic in effect and, as might be imagined, rich in musical variety. *Roads to Glory* (1931), *All Men Are Enemies* (1933), and *Women Must Work* (1934) are his decreasingly important books of prose. His *Collected Poems* was published in 1928. He died in France, July 28, 1962.

Critics differ concerning Aldington's position as a poet; none disputes his eminence as a translator. Among his many translations (of which more than twenty were published prior to 1929) are *The Poems of Anyte of Tegea, The Poems of Meleager,* Cyrano de Bergerac's *Voyages to the Moon and the Sun.* His autobiography, *Life for Life's Sake* (1941) is a lively record of the literary movements and influences from 1912 to 1940. His *Collected Poems* appeared in 1949; his biography of Wellington (1946) was awarded the Tait Black Memorial Prize.

IMAGES

I

Like a gondola of green scented fruits
Drifting along the dank canals of Venice,
You, O exquisite one,
Have entered into my desolate city.

II

The blue smoke leaps
Like swirling clouds of birds vanishing.
So my love leaps forth toward you,
Vanishes and is renewed.

III

A rose-yellow moon in a pale sky
When the sunset is faint vermilion
In the mist among the tree-boughs
Art thou to me, my beloved.

IV

A young beech tree on the edge of the forest
Stands still in the evening,

Yet shudders through all its leaves in the light air
And seems to fear the stars—
So are you still and so tremble.

V

The red deer are high on the mountain,
They are beyond the last pine trees.
And my desires have run with them.

VI

The flower which the wind has shaken
Is soon filled again with rain;
So does my heart fill slowly with tears,
O Foam-Driver, Wind-of-the-Vineyards,
Until you return.

THE FAUN SEES SNOW FOR THE FIRST TIME

Zeus,
Brazen-thunder-hurler,
Cloud-whirler, son-of-Kronos,
Send vengeance on these Oreads
Who strew
White frozen flecks of mist and cloud

Over the brown trees and the tufted grass
Of the meadows, where the stream
Runs black through shining banks
Of bluish white.

Zeus,
Are the halls of heaven broken up
That you flake down upon me
Feather-strips of marble?

Dis and Styx!
When I stamp my hoof
The frozen-cloud specks jam into the cleft
So that I reel upon two slippery points. . . .

Fool, to stand here cursing
When I might be running!

AT THE BRITISH MUSEUM

I turn the page and read:
"I dream of silent verses where the rhyme
Glides noiseless as an oar."

The heavy musty air, the black desks.
The bent heads and rustling noises
In the great dome
Vanish . . .
And
The sun hangs in the cobalt-blue sky,
The boat drifts over the lake shallows,
The fishes skim like umber shadows through undulating weeds,
The oleanders drop their rosy petals on the lawns,
And the swallows dive and swirl and whistle
About the cleft battlements of Can Grande's castle. . . .

EVENING

The chimneys, rank on rank,
Cut the clear sky;
The moon,
With a rag of gauze about her loins,
Poses among them, an awkward Venus—

And here am I looking wantonly at her
Over the kitchen sink.

VICARIOUS ATONEMENT

This is an old and very cruel god. . . .

We will endure;
We will try not to wince
When he crushes and rends us.

If indeed it is for your sakes,
If we perish or moan in torture,
Or stagger under sordid burdens
That you may live—
Then we can endure.

If our wasted blood
Makes bright the page
Of poets yet to be;
If this our tortured life
Save from destruction's nails
Gold words of a Greek long dead;
Then we can endure,
Then hope,
Then watch the sun rise
Without utter bitterness.

But, O thou old and very cruel god,
Take if thou canst this bitter cup from us.

POSSESSION

I must possess you utterly
And utterly must you possess me;
So even if that dreamer's tale
Of heaven and hell be true
There shall be two spirits rived together
Either in whatever peace be heaven
Or in the icy whirlwind that is hell
For those who loved each other more than God—
So that the other spirits shall cry out:
"Ah! Look how the ancient love yet holds to them
That these two ghosts are never driven apart
But kiss with shadowy kisses and still take
Joy from the mingling of their misty limbs!"

AFTER TWO YEARS

She is all so slight
And tender and white
  As a May morning.
She walks without hood
At dusk. It is good
  To hear her sing.

It is God's will
That I shall love her still
  As he loves Mary,
And night and day
I will go forth to pray
  That she love me.

She is as gold
Lovely, and far more cold.
  Do thou pray with me,
For if I win grace
To kiss twice her face
  God has done well to me.

Osbert Sitwell

Osbert Sitwell (brother of Sacheverell and Edith Sitwell) was born in London, December 6, 1892, was educated at Eton, and became an officer in the Grenadier Guards, with whom he served in France for various periods from 1914 to 1917. After contesting the 1918 election at Scarborough in the Liberal interests, he devoted himself to literature.

His first contributions appeared in *Wheels* (an annual anthology of a few of the younger radical writers, edited by his sister) and disclosed an ironic touch. That impression was strengthened by *Argonaut and Juggernaut* (1920), where Sitwell's cleverness and satire are intensified if not fused. *Out of the Flame* (1923) reenforces this judgment. It is in two parts; a contrast, not a combination. There is the world of ideal beauty which the poet loves and the world of idle luxury which rouses his critical spleen and satirical hate.

After 1923 this author distinguished himself in prose, registering a deep impression with the short stories in *Triple Fugue* (1924) and the novel *Before the Bombardment* (1926). Sharing the nostalgia of his sister, Edith, he also returns to his childhood for much of the material in *England Reclaimed: A Book of Eclogues* (1927). Satire is still here, but it is satire softened with sympathy. If he laughs at such rustic figures as Mr. Goodbeare and Moping Fred, he smiles with Mr. and Mrs. Nutch, the gamekeepers, gardeners and the homely gentles of the countryside. The author aims at "recording a broad panorama, essentially English, but which seems now, by force of circumstance, to be slipping away into the past." *The Collected Poems and Satires of Osbert Sitwell* (1931) contrasts stylized witticsms with ingratiating period pieces.

Penny Foolish (1935) assembles Sitwell's enthusiasms and irritations—English public school, games, and war being among the latter, and the telephone among the former. His reminiscences ran to four autobiographical volumes—*Laughter in the Next Room; Great Morning; The Scarlet Tree; Left Hand, Right Hand!*—and were followed by the family memoirs of *Noble Essences* (1950).

FOUNTAINS

Proud fountains, wave your plumes,
Spread out your phoenix-wing,
Let the tired trees rejoice
Beneath your blossoming
(Tired trees, you whisper low).

High up, high up, above
These green and drooping sails,
A fluttering young wind
Hovers and dives, but fails
To steal a foaming feather.

Sail, like a crystal ship,
Above your sea of glass;
Then, with your quickening touch,
Transmute the things that pass
(Come down, cool wind, come down).

All humble things proclaim,
Within your magic net,
Their kinship to the Gods.
More strange and lovely yet
All lovely things become.

Dead, sculptured stone assumes
The life, from which it came;
The kingfisher is now
A moving tongue of flame,
A blue, live tongue of flame—

While birds, less proud of wing,
Crouch, in wind-ruffled shade,
Hide shyly, then pour out
Their jealous serenade;
. . . Close now your golden wings!

ELEGY FOR MR. GOODBEARE

Do you remember Mr. Goodbeare, the carpenter,
Godfearing and bearded Mr. Goodbeare,
Who worked all day
At his carpenter's tray,
Do you remember Mr. Goodbeare?
Mr. Goodbeare, that Golconda of gleaming fable,
Lived, thin-ground between orchard and stable,
Pressed thus close against Alfred, his rival—
Mr. Goodbeare, who had never been away.

Do you remember Mr. Goodbeare,
Mr. Goodbeare, who never touched a cup?
Do you remember Mr. Goodbeare,
Who remembered a lot?
  Mr. Goodbeare could remember
    When things were properly kept up:
  Mr. Goodbeare could remember
    The christening and the coming-of-age:
  Mr. Goodbeare could remember
    The entire and roasted ox:
  Mr. Goodbeare could remember
    When the horses filled the stable,
  And the port-wine-colored gentry rode after the tawny fox:
  Mr. Goodbeare could remember
    The old lady in her eagle rage,
      Which knew no bounds:
  Mr. Goodbeare could remember
    When the escaped and hungering tiger
  Flickered lithe and fierce through Foxton Wood,
  When old Sir Nigel took his red-tongued, clamoring hounds,
  And hunted it then and there,
    As a Gentleman Should.

Do you remember Mr. Goodbeare,
Mr. Goodbeare who never forgot?
Do you remember Mr. Goodbeare,
That wrinkled and golden apricot,

Dear, bearded, godfearing Mr. Goodbeare
Who remembered remembering such a lot?

Oh, do you remember, do you remember,
As I remember and deplore,
That day in drear and far-away December
When dear, godfearing, bearded Mr. Goodbeare
Could remember
No more?

ON THE COAST OF COROMANDEL

On the coast of Coromandel
Dance they to the tunes of Handel;
Chorally, that coral coast
Correlates the bone to ghost,
Till word and limb and note seem one,
Blending, binding act to tone.

All day long they point the sandal
On the coast of Coromandel.
Lemon-yellow legs all bare
Pirouette to peruqued air
From the first green shoots of morn,
Cool as northern hunting-horn,
Till the nightly tropic wind
With its rough-tongued, grating rind
Shatters the frail spires of spice.
Imaged in the lawns of rice
(Mirror-flat and mirror green
Is that lovely water's sheen)
Saraband and rigadoon
Dance they through the purring noon,
While the lacquered waves expand
Golden dragons on the sand—
Dragons that must, steaming, die
From the hot sun's agony—
When elephants, of royal blood,
Plod to bed through lilied mud,
Then evening, sweet as any mango,
Bids them do a gay fandango,
Minuet, jig or gavotte.
How they hate the turkey-trot,
The nautch-dance and the highland fling,
Just as they will never sing
Any music save by Handel
On the coast of Coromandel!

Hugh MacDiarmid

Hugh MacDiarmid (whose real name is Christopher Murray Grieve) was born in Scotland in 1892. From the beginning it was evident that he was a radical in politics and an experimenter in poetry. His volumes, from *Penny Wheep* to *Stony Limits and Other Poems* (1934) are as uneven as they are Communistic. Much of these are written in MacDiarmid's own particular Scots, but even his straight English is a confusion of satire and sentimentality, rough humor and metaphysical refinements, rugged strength and lyric clarity.

A selection of MacDiarmid's poetry was published in the United States in 1946. Entitled *Speaking for Scotland,* it proved that MacDiarmid was Scotland's most considerable modern poet. "He has effected, almost single-handed, a literary revolution," wrote David Daiches; "he has destroyed one Scottish tradition and founded another." In 1941 he edited a *Golden Treasury of Scottish Poetry;* two years later he published his autobiography, *Lucky Poet.*

WITH A LIFTING OF THE HEAD

Scotland, when it is given to me
As it will be
To sing the immortal song
The crown of all my long
Travail with thee,
I know in that high hour
I'll have, and use, the power
Sublime contempt to blend
With its ecstatic end—
As who, in love's embrace,
Forgetfully may frame
Above the poor slut's face
Another woman's name.

PARLEY OF BEASTS

Auld Noah was at hame wi' them a',
The lion and the lamb,
Pair by pair they entered the Ark,
And he took them as they cam'.

If twa a' ilka beist there is
Into this room s'ud come,
Wad I could welcome them like him,
And no' stand gowpin' dumb!

Be chief wi' them and they wi' me
And a' wi' ane anither,

As Noah and his couples were
There in the Ark thegither.

It's fain I'd mell wi' tiger and tit,
Wi' elephant and eel,
But noo-a'days e'en wi' ain's sel
At hame it's hard to feel.

CATTLE SHOW

I shall go among red faces and virile voices,
See stylish sheep, with fine heads and well-wooled,
And great bulls mellow to the touch,
Brood mares of marvellous approach, and geldings
With sharp and flinty bones and silken hair.

And through th' enclosure draped in red and gold
I shall pass on to spheres more vivid yet
Where countesses' coque feathers gleam and glow
And, swathed in silks, the painted ladies are
Whose laughter plays like summer lightning there.

TO A SEA EAGLE

I used to walk on solid gr'und
Till it fell awa' frae my feet
And, left in the void, I'd instantly
To get accustomed wi't.

Watchin' your prood flight noo I feel
As a man may dae wi' a bairn,
For withoot ony show at a'
In deeper abysses I'm farin'.

Aye, withoot ony show at a',
Save whiles a song I may sing
Gets in resonance wi' the sun
And ootshines't like a turnin' wing.

ON THE OXFORD BOOK OF VICTORIAN VERSE

Most poets to a muse that is stone-deaf cry.
This English poetry that they vaunt so high,
What is it except for two or three men
Whose best work is beyond all but a few men's ken?

Stupidity will not accept the fact, and so
Cheek by jowl with Shakespeare and Milton must go
Even in famous anthologies the incredibly small,
A Domett, Toke Lynch, and Wathen Mark Call.

A horde no man is the better for reading,
A horde no man is the worse for not heeding,
Create with these the notion that poetry's less rare
Than it is; that there's something for most men there.

Something—but what? Poetry's not written for men
And lies always beyond all but all men's ken
—Only fools—countless fools—are deceived by the claims
Of a Menella Bute Smedley and most other names.

So when this book is revised for reissue
Let us have you included lest somebody should miss you.
Here with your peers—Spoof, Dubb, and Blong,
Smiffkins, Pimple, and Jingle. *Oh Lord! how long?*

THE SKELETON OF THE FUTURE

(At Lenin's Tomb)

Red granite and black diorite, with the blue
Of the labradorite crystals gleaming like precious stones
In the light reflected from the snow; and behind them
The eternal lightning of Lenin's bones.

Wilfred Owen

Wilfred Owen's biography is pitifully brief. He was born at Oswestry on the 18th of March, 1893, was educated at the Birkenhead Institute, matriculated at London University in 1910, obtained a private tutorship in 1913 near Bordeaux and remained there for two years. In 1915, in spite of delicate health, he joined the Artist's Rifles, served in France from 1916 to June, 1917, when he was invalided home. Fourteen months later, he returned to the Western Front, was awarded the Military Cross for gallantry in October, and was killed while trying to get his men across the Sambre Canal—with tragic irony—a week before the armistice, on November 4, 1918.

Owen's name was unknown to the world until his friend Siegfried Sassoon unearthed the contents of his posthumous volume, *Poems* (1920). It was evident at once that here was one of the most important contributions to the literature of the War, expressed by a poet whose courage was surpassed only by his integrity of mind and nobility of soul. The restrained passion as well as the pitiful outcries in Owen's poetry have a spiritual kinship with Sassoon's stark verses. They reflect that second stage of the War, when the glib patter wears thin and the easy patriotics have a sardonic sound in the dug-outs and trenches. "He never," writes Sassoon, "wrote his poems (as so many war poets did) to make the effect of a personal gesture. He pitied others; he did not pity himself."

In a scrap which serves as an unfinished preface, Owen wrote, "This book is not about heroes. English poetry is not yet fit to speak of them. Nor is it about deeds or lands, nor anything about glory, honor or dominion. . . .

except War.
Above all, this book is not concerned with Poetry,
The subject of it is War, and the pity of War.
The Poetry is in the pity."

"Strange Meeting," "Miners," and the poignant "Futility" illustrate, beneath their emotional content, Owen's great fondness for assonance. He was continually experimenting with devices to enrich or take the place of rhyme, testing alliterative consonants as substitutes for the prepared and often monotonous matching of vowels. Almost half of his volume is a record of such unique and surprisingly successful experiments. But it is the nobility, the profound sympathy, compassionate without ever becoming maudlin, that gives Owen's verse a place among the authentic poetry of his day. "Dulce et Decorum Est" is obviously a reaction against the "glory" of war; but it is bigger than its subject, something far beyond a protest, surpassing its program.

It is difficult to choose among Owen's few but compelling poems. "Apologia pro Poemate Meo," "Greater Love," "Anthem for Doomed Youth" and the rhymed suspensions already mentioned will live beyond the tragic events during which they were created. They influenced the post-war poets (*vide* C. Day Lewis' *A Hope for Poetry*) in theme as well as technique; time has already found a place for them.

A new and enlarged edition entitled *The Poems of Wilfred Owen* was published in 1931 with an introduction by Edmund Blunden. This complete collection included many poems hitherto unprinted, notably "The Unreturning," "Arms and the Boy"—both full of Owen's peculiar broken music—and "From My Diary," in which Owen added initial consonantal dissonances (Blunden calls them "pararhymes") to the usual end-rhymes. They emphasize that Owen's death at twenty-five was one of modern poetry's greatest losses.

FUTILITY

Move him into the sun—
Gently its touch awoke him once,
At home, whispering of fields unsown.
Always it woke him, even in France.
Until this morning and this snow.
If anything might rouse him now
The kind old sun will know.

Think how it wakes the seeds—
Woke, once, the clay of a cold star.
Are limbs so dear-achieved, are sides
Full-nerved,—still warm,—too hard to stir?
Was it for this the clay grew tall?
—Oh, what made fatuous sunbeams toil
To break earth's sleep at all?

APOLOGIA PRO POEMATE MEO

I, too, saw God through mud—
The mud that cracked on cheeks when wretches smiled.
War brought more glory to their eyes than blood,
And gave their laughs more glee than shakes a child.

Merry it was to laugh there—
Where death becomes absurd and life absurder.
For power was on us as we slashed bones bare
Not to feel sickness or remorse of murder.

I, too, have dropped off fear—
Behind the barrage, dead as my platoon,
And sailed my spirit surging, light and clear,
Past the entanglement where hopes lay strewn;

And witnessed exultation—
Faces that used to curse me, scowl for scowl,
Shine and lift up with passion of oblation,
Seraphic for an hour, though they were foul.

I have made fellowships—
Untold of happy lovers in old song.
For love is not the binding of fair lips
With the soft silk of eyes that look and long,

By joy, whose ribbon slips,—
But wound with war's hard wire whose stakes are strong;
Bound with the bandage of the arm that drips;
Knit in the welding of the rifle-thong.

I have perceived much beauty
In the hoarse oaths that kept our courage straight;
Heard music in the silentness of duty;
Found peace where shell-storms spouted reddest spate.

Nevertheless, except you share
With them in hell the sorrowful dark of hell,
Whose world is but the trembling of a flare,
And heaven but as the highway for a shell,

You shall not hear their mirth:
You shall not come to think them well content
By any jest of mine. These men are worth
Your tears: You are not worth their merriment.

ANTHEM FOR DOOMED YOUTH

What passing-bells for these who die as cattle?
Only the monstrous anger of the guns.
Only the stuttering rifles' rapid rattle

Can patter out their hasty orisons.
No mockeries for them; no prayers nor bells,
Nor any voice of mourning save the choirs,—
The shrill, demented choirs of wailing shells;
And bugles calling for them from sad shires.

What candles may be held to speed them all?
Not in the hands of boys, but in their eyes
Shall shine the holy glimmers of good-bys.
The pallor of girls' brows shall be their pall;
Their flowers the tenderness of silent minds,
And each slow dusk a drawing-down of blinds.

DULCE ET DECORUM EST

Bent double, like old beggars under sacks,
Knock-kneed, coughing like hags, we cursed through sludge,
Till on the haunting flares we turned our backs,
And towards our distant rest began to trudge.
Men marched asleep. Many had lost their boots,
But limped on, blood-shod. All went lame, all blind;
Drunk with fatigue; deaf even to the hoots
Of gas-shells dropping softly behind.

Gas! Gas! Quick, boys!—An ecstasy of fumbling,
Fitting the clumsy helmets just in time,
But someone still was yelling out and stumbling
And flound'ring like a man in fire or lime.
Dim through the misty panes and thick green light,
As under a green sea, I saw him drowning.

In all my dreams before my helpless sight
He plunges at me, guttering, choking, drowning.

If in some smothering dreams, you too could pace
Behind the wagon that we flung him in,
And watch the white eyes wilting in his face,
His hanging face, like a devil's sick of sin,
If you could hear, at every jolt, the blood
Come gargling from the froth-corrupted lungs
Bitten as the cud
Of vile, incurable sores on innocent tongues,—
My friend, you would not tell with such high zest
To children ardent for some desperate glory,
The old lie: *Dulce et decorum est*
Pro patria mori.[1]

FROM MY DIARY, JULY 1914

Leaves
  Murmuring by myriads in the shimmering trees.

[1] "It is sweet and dignified to die for one's country."

Lives
  Wakening with wonder in the Pyrenees.
Birds
  Cheerily chirping in the early day.
Bards
  Singing of summer scything thro' the hay.
Bees
  Shaking the heavy dews from bloom and frond.
Boys
  Bursting the surface of the ebony pond.
Flashes
  Of swimmers carving thro' the sparkling cold.
Fleshes
  Gleaming with wetness to the morning gold.
A mead
  Bordered about with warbling water brooks.
A maid
  Laughing the love-laugh with me; proud of looks.
The heat
  Throbbing between the upland and the peak.
Her heart
  Quivering with passion to my pressed cheek.
Braiding
  Of floating flames across the mountain brow.
Brooding
  Of stillness; and a sighing of the bough.
Stirs
  Of leaflets in the gloom; soft petal-showers;
Stars
  Expanding with the starr'd nocturnal flowers.

THE UNRETURNING

Suddenly night crushed out the day and hurled
Her remnants over cloud-peaks, thunder-walled.
Then fell a stillness such as harks appalled
When far-gone dead return upon the world.

There watched I for the Dead; but no ghost woke.
Each one whom Life exiled I named and called.
But they were all too far, or dumbed, or thralled;
And never one fared back to me or spoke.

Then peered the indefinite unshapen dawn
With vacant gloaming, sad as half-lit minds,
The weak-limned hour when sick men's sighs are drained.
And while I wondered on their being withdrawn,
Gagged by the smothering wing which none unbinds,
I dreaded even a heaven with doors so chained.

GREATER LOVE

Red lips are not so red
As the stained stones kissed by the English dead.
Kindness of wooed and wooer
Seems shame to their love pure.
O Love, your eyes lose lure
When I behold eyes blinded in my stead!

Your slender attitude
Trembles not exquisite like limbs knife-skewed,
Rolling and rolling there
Where God seems not to care;
Till the fierce love they bear
Cramps them in death's extreme decrepitude.

Your voice sings not so soft,—
Though even as wind murmuring through raftered loft,—
Your dear voice is not clear,
Gentle, and evening clear,
As theirs whom none now hear
Now earth has stopped their piteous mouths that coughed.

Heart, you were never hot,
Nor large, nor full like hearts made great with shot;
And though your hand be pale,
Paler are all which trail
Your cross through flame and hail:
Weep, you may weep, for you may touch them not.

MINERS

There was a whispering in my hearth,
A sigh of the coal,
Grown wistful of a former earth
It might recall.

I listened for a tale of leaves
And smothered ferns,
Proud forests, and the low sly lives
Before the fawns.

My fire might show steam-phantoms simmer
From Time's old caldron,
Before the birds made nests in summer,
Or men had children.

But the coals were murmuring of their mine.
And moans down there,
Of boys that slept wry sleep, and men
Writhing for air.

I saw white bones in the cinder-shard,
Bones without number.
For many hearts with coal are charred,
And few remember.

I thought of all that worked dark pits
Of war, and died
Digging the rock where Death reputes
Peace lies indeed:

Comforted years will sit soft-chaired,
In rooms of amber,
The years will stretch their hands, well cheered
By our life's ember;

The centuries will burn rich loads
With which we groaned,
Whose warmth shall lull their dreamy lids,
While songs are crooned;
But they will not dream of us poor lads
Lost in the ground.

ARMS AND THE BOY

Let the boy try along this bayonet-blade
How cold steel is, and keen with hunger of blood;
Blue with all malice, like a madman's flash;
And thinly drawn with famishing for flesh.

Lend him to stroke these blind, blunt bullet-heads
Which long to nuzzle in the heart of lads,
Or give him cartridges of fine zinc teeth,
Sharp with the sharpness of grief and death.

For his teeth seem for laughing round an apple.
There lurk no claws behind his fingers supple;
And god will grow no talons at his heels,
Nor antlers through the thickness of his curls.

STRANGE MEETING

It seemed that out of the battle I escaped
Down some profound dull tunnel, long since scooped
Through granites which Titanic wars had groined.
Yet also there encumbered sleepers groaned,
Too fast in thought or death to be bestirred.
Then, as I probed them, one sprang up, and stared
With piteous recognition in fixed eyes,
Lifting distressful hands as if to bless.
And by his smile, I knew that sullen hall;
By his dead smile I knew I stood in Hell.
With a thousand fears that vision's face was grained;
Yet no blood reached there from the upper ground,
And no guns thumped, or down the flues made moan.
"Strange, friend," I said, "here is no cause to mourn."
"None," said the other, "save the undone years,
The hopelessness. Whatever hope is yours,
Was my life also; I went hunting wild
After the wildest beauty in the world,
Which lies not calm in eyes, or braided hair,
But mocks the steady running of the hour,
And if it grieves, grieves richlier than here.
For by my glee might many men have laughed,
And of my weeping something has been left,
Which must die now. I mean the truth untold,
The pity of war, the pity war distilled.
Now men will go content with what we spoiled,
Or, discontent, boil bloody, and be spilled.
They will be swift with swiftness of the tigress,
None will break ranks, though nations trek from progress.
Courage was mine, and I had mystery,
Wisdom was mine, and I had mastery;
To miss the march of this retreating world

Into vain citadels that are not walled.
Then when much blood had clogged their chariot-wheels
I would go up and wash them from sweet wells,
Even with truths that lie too deep for taint.
I would have poured my spirit without stint
But not through wounds; not on the cess of war.
Foreheads of men have bled where no wounds were.
I am the enemy you killed, my friend.
I knew you in this death; for so you frowned
Yesterday through me as you jabbed and killed.
I parried; but my hands were loath and cold.
Let us sleep now. . . ."

THE SEND-OFF

Down the close, darkening lanes they sang their way
To the siding-shed,
And lined the train with faces grimly gay.
Their breasts were stuck all white with wreath and spray
As men's are, dead.

Dull porters watched them, and a casual tramp
Stood staring hard,
Sorry to miss them from the upland camp.
Then, unmoved, signals nodded, and a lamp
Winked to the guard.

So secretly, like wrongs hushed-up, they went.
They were not ours:
We never heard to which front these were sent.
Nor there if they yet mock what women meant
Who gave them flowers.

Shall they return to beatings of great bells
In wild trainloads?
A few, a few, too few for drums and yells,
May creep back, silent, to still village wells
Up half-known roads.

THE SHOW

My soul looked down from a vague height with Death,
As unremembering how I rose or why,
And saw a sad land, weak with sweats of dearth,
Gray, cratered like the moon with hollow woe,
And fitted with great pocks and scabs of plagues.

Across its beard, that horror of harsh wire,
There moved thin caterpillars, slowly uncoiled.
It seemed they pushed themselves to be as plugs
Of ditches, where they writhed and shrivelled, killed.

By them had slimy paths been trailed and scraped
Round myriad warts that might be little hills.
From gloom's last dregs these long-strung creatures crept,
And vanished out of dawn down hidden holes.

(And smell came up from those foul openings
As out of mouths, or deep wounds deepening.)

On dithering feet upgathered, more and more,
Brown strings towards strings of gray, with bristling spines,
All migrants from green fields, intent on mire.
Those that were gray, of more abundant spawns,
Ramped on the rest and ate them and were eaten.
I saw their bitten backs curve, loop, and straighten,
I watched those agonies curl, lift, and flatten.

Whereat, in terror what that sight might mean,
I reeled and shivered earthward like a feather.
And Death fell with me, like a deepening moan.
And He, picking a manner of worm, which half had hid
Its bruises in the earth, but crawled no further,
Showed me its feet, the feet of many men,
And the fresh-severed head of it, my head.

Sylvia Townsend Warner

Sylvia Townsend Warner was born December 1893 at Harrow on the Hill, Middlesex, where her father was a schoolmaster. From 1916 to 1926 she worked on the preparation of the critical edition of *Tudor Church Music,* a vast and learned compilation in ten volumes, of which she was one of four editors. Research work in the music of the fifteenth and sixteenth centuries was not only her occupation but her preoccupation, and it was not until 1922 that she started writing as a by-product.

Although she first attracted wide attention with the fanciful *Lolly Willowes: or The Loving Huntsman,* which was the first "book-of-the-month" in America in 1926, her literary début was made with a volume of verse, *The Espalier* (1925). There followed two more books of prose, quaintly misnamed novels by the publishers: *Mr. Fortune's Maggot* (1927) and *The True Heart* (1929). Three years after her first volume, her second book of poems appeared, *Time Importuned* (1928).

Although her work seems to fall into two categories, it actually forms a unified expression. The poems, objective, sharply characterized, compact with drama, are condensed stories; the novels are poetry from beginning to end. *Lolly Willowes* is a fantasy which alternates between the unshamedly tender and the lightly terrible. *Mr. Fortune's Maggot* adds compassionate understanding to extravaganza; fantasy turns here to philosophy whose motto implies surrender instead of possession in love. The title-story of *The Salutation* (1932) is a sequel to *Mr. Fortune's Maggot,* exquisite in style, tragic in effect. *The True Heart* is the simplest and the deepest of her larger works. Seemingly an idyll of Victorian England, it is really one of the oldest love stories, the classic tale of Psyche and Eros retold. Although no critic seems to have noted the fact, Miss Warner has supplied sufficient hints; "Sukey" is obviously an Anglicized Psyche; the mad Love, Eros, is the witless "Eric"; Venus is less than half-disguised as "Mrs. Seaborn."

Thus all of Miss Warner's work is a paradoxical union of subtlety and simplicity, with no sense of strain between these opposites. Each quality is equally characteristic of this author; if the mode tends toward increasing simplicity, it is as though the subtle brain were being counseled if not always controlled by the simple —and the true—heart.

The element which holds these contraries in so nice a balance is the rightness, the so-to-speak connoisseurship of Miss Warner's taste. She can be utterly exquisite when elegance dictates the mood; her coarseness is no less in place when theme and measure demand rudeness. Thus *Time Importuned* has the same sparse imagery and no little of the earth smell of which *The Espalier* is redolent, but the rustic note is not so broad; the rough country humor which underlines her bucolic comedies turns to rustic elegies without effort or affectation. "Nelly Trim," a poem which touches the ballad with nothing short of magnificence, finds its complement in "The Rival"; the neat incisiveness of "The Alarum" is matched by the bittersweetness of "Song."

Craftsmen will be quick to detect Miss Warner's innovations. She is particularly resourceful in her use of the unrhymed line; she is as adroit in her mingling of assonantal and dissonantal rhyme as Wilfred Owen and Humbert Wolfe. But it is unwise to place too much emphasis on technique. Each reader will discover a different quality on which to lay stress: the poet's marked accent; or her half-modern, half-archaic blend of naïvéte and erudition; or the low-pitched but tart tone of voice, like a feminine Thomas Hardy.

Opus 7 (1931) is, in spite of its unimaginative title, a highly imaginative tale in precise couplets of one Rebecca Random who, with her "green thumb," has a way with flowers, but who has no love for them except as a means of supplying herself with gin. It is both a delicate and a diabolic long poem, realistic and revenant, musing and epigrammatic. It is as though the ghost of Pope had seized Miss Warner's pen and, allowing her to control her own fancy, had added a series of commentaries to prove that the proper student of mankind was woman. *Whether a Dove or Seagull* (1933) contains more than a hundred poems, half of which are by Miss Warner and half by her friend Valentine Ackland. The authors believed that by issuing their separate work under one cover the element of contrast would add to the pleasure of the reader; by withholding their signatures from the poems they attained the freshness as well as the provocation of anonymity. The book contains some of Miss Warner's finest poems.

In her forties Miss Warner grew more prolific without losing her discriminating touch. *More Joy in Heaven* (1935) and *A Garland of Straw* (1943) are collections of short stories; *The Cat's Cradle Book* (1940) contains subtle and mischievous fables; *Summer Will Show* (1936), *The Corner That Held Them* (1948) and *The Flint Anchor* (1954) are highly imaginative novels.

Greatly gifted, Miss Warner just misses greatness. Ironic, critical, compassionate, her mind rules her heart a fraction too well. But, although she rarely gives herself to a self-forgetting, world-forsaking ecstasy, Miss Warner is one who combines raillery and tragedy, light airs and grave implications.

FOUR EPITAPHS

John Bird, a laborer, lies here,
Who served the earth for sixty year
With spade and mattock, drill and plow;
But never found it kind till now.

*

I, an unwedded wandering dame,
For quiet into the country came:
Here, hailed it; but did not foretell
I'd stay so long and rest so well.

*

I, Richard Kent, beneath these stones,
Sheltered my old and trembling bones;
But my best manhood, quick and brave,
Lies buried in another grave.

*

Her grieving parents cradled here
Ann Monk, a gracious child and dear.
Lord, let this epitaph suffice:
Early to Bed and Early to Rise.

COUNTRY THOUGHT

Idbury bells are ringing
And Westcote has just begun,
And down in the valley
Ring the bells of Bledington.

To hear all the church-bells
Ring-ringing together,
Chiming so pleasantly
As if nothing were the matter.

The notion might come
To some religious thinker,
That The Lord God Almighty
Is a traveling tinker,

Who travels through England
From north to south,
And sits him at the roadside
With a pipe in his mouth,

A-tinkling and a-tinkering
To mend up the souls
That week-day wickedness
Has worn into holes.

And yet there is not
One tinker, but Three—
One at Westcote, One at Bledington
And One at Idbury.

NELLY TRIM

"Like men riding,
The mist from the sea
Drives down the valley
And baffles me."
"Enter, traveler,
Whoever you be."

By lamplight confronted
He staggered and peered;
Like a wet bramble
Was his beard.
"Sit down, stranger,
You look a-feared."

Shudders rent him
To the bone,
The wet ran off him
And speckled the stone.
"Dost bide here alone, maid?"
"Yes, alone."

As he sat down
In the chimney-nook
Over his shoulder
He cast a look,
As if the night
Were pursuing; she took

A handful of brash
To mend the fire,
He eyed her close
As the flame shot higher;
He spoke—and the cattle
Moved in the byre.

"Though you should heap
Your fire with wood,
'Twouldn't warm me
Nor do no good,
Unless you first warm me
As a maiden should."

With looks unwavering,
With breath unstirred,
She took off her clothes
Without a word,
And stood up naked
And white as a curd.

He breathed her to him
With famished sighs,
Against her bosom
He sheltered his eyes,
And warmed his hands
Between her thighs.

Strangely assembled
In the quiet room,
Alone alight
Amidst leagues of gloom,
So brave a bride,
So sad a groom;

And strange love-traffic
Between these two;
Nor mean, nor shamefaced—
As though they'd do
Something more solemn
Than they knew:

As though by this greeting
Which chance had willed
'Twixt him so silent
And her so stilled,
Some pledge or compact
Were fulfilled,

Made for all time
In times unknown,
'Twixt man and woman
Standing alone
In mirk night
By a tall stone.

His wayfaring terrors
All cast aside,
Brave now the bridegroom
Quitted the bride;
As he came, departing—
Undenied.

But once from darkness
Turned back his sight
To where in the doorway
She held a light:
"Good-by to you, maiden."
"Stranger, good night."

Long time has this woman
Been bedded alone.
The house where she slept
Lies stone on stone:
She'd not know her ash-tree,
So warped has it grown.

But yet this story
Is told of her
As a memorial;
And some aver
She'd comfort thus any
Poor traveler.

A wanton, you say—
Yet where's the spouse,
However true
To her marriage-vows,
To whom the lot
Of the earth-born allows

More than this?—
To comfort the care
Of a stranger, bound
She knows not where,
And afraid of the dark,
As his fathers were.

THE ALARUM

With its rat's tooth the clock
Gnaws away delight.
Piece by piece, piece by piece
It will gnaw away tonight,

Till the coiled spring released
Rouses me with a hiss
To a day, to another night
Less happy than this.

And yet my own hands wound it
To keep watch while I slept;
For though they be with sorrow
Appointments must be kept.

AFTER HE HAD GONE

After he had gone the wind rose,
Buffeting the house and rumbling in the chimney,
And I thought: It will roar against him like a lion
As onward he goes.

Seven miles before him, all told—
Chilled will be the lips I kissed so warm at parting,
Kissed in vain; for he's forth into the wind, and kisses
Won't keep out the cold.

Closer should I have kissed, fondlier prayed:
Pleasant is the room in the wakeful firelight,
And within is the bed, arrayed with peace and safety.
Would he had stayed!

ELIZABETH

"Elizabeth the Beloved"—
So much says the stone
That is all with weather defaced,
With moss overgrown.

But if to husband or child,
Brother or sire, most dear
Is past deciphering;
This only is clear:

That once she was beloved,
Was Elizabeth,
And is now beloved no longer,
If it be not of Death.

TRIUMPH OF SENSIBILITY

"Tiger, strolling at my side,
Why have you unbound the zone
Of your individual pride?
Why so meek did you come sneaking
After me as I walked alone?

"Since the goat and since the deer
Wait the shattering death you wield
In a constancy of fear,
By your stripes, my strange disciple,
Am I also to be healed?"

"Woman, it was your tender heart
Did my bloody heart compel.
Master-mistress of my art,
Past my wit of wrath your pity,
Ruthless and inexorable.

"I hunt flesh by fallible sense;
You a more exquisite prey pursue
With a finer prescience,
And lap up another's unhappiness:
Woman, let me learn of you."

SAD GREEN

The glass falls lower,
And lowers the wet sky,
And by a fire sit I
Hearing the lawn-mower

Nearing and waning—
Howbeit out of tune
The essential voice of June,
Patient and uncomplaining;

For though by frost and thunder
Summer be overthrown,
The grass plat must be mown
And the daisies kept under.

SONG

She has left me, my pretty,
Like a fleeting of apple-blows
She has left her loving husband.
And who she has gone to
The Lord only knows.

She has left me, my pretty,
A needle in a shirt,
Her pink flannelette bedgown,
And a pair of pattens
Caked over with dirt.

I care not for the pattens,
Let 'em lie in the mold;
But the pretty pink bedgown
Will comfort my lumbago
When midnights are cold;

And the shirt I will wear it,
And the needle may bide.
Let it prick, let it rankle,
Let my flesh remember
How she lay against my side!

SONG FROM THE BRIDE OF SMITHFIELD

A thousand guileless sheep have bled,
A thousand bullocks knelt in fear,
To daub my Henry's cheek with red
And round the curl above his ear.

And wounded calves hung up to drip
Have in slow sweats distilled for him
To dew that polishes his lip,
The inward balm that oils each limb.

In vain I spread my maiden arts,
In vain for Henry's love I pine.
He is too skilled in bleeding hearts
To turn this way and pity mine.

THE RIVAL

The farmer's wife looked out of the dairy:
She saw her husband in the yard;
She said: "A woman's life is hard,
The chimney smokes, the churn's contrary."
  She said:
"I of all women am the most ill-starred.

"Five sons I've borne and seven daughters,
And the last of them is on my knee.
Finer children you could not see.
Twelve times I've put my neck in the halter:
  You'd think
So much might knit my husband's love to me.

"But no! Though I should serve him double
He keeps another love outdoors,
Who thieves his strength, who drains his stores,
Who haunts his mind with fret and trouble;
  I pray
God's curse may light on such expensive whores.

"I am grown old before my season,
Weather and care have worn me down;
Each year delves deeper in my frown,
I've lost my shape and for good reason:
  But she
Yearly puts on young looks like an Easter gown.

"And year by year she has betrayed him
With blight and mildew, rain and drought,
Smut, scab, and murrain, all the rout;
But he forgets the tricks she's played him
  When first
The fields give a good smell and the leaves put out.

"Aye, come the Spring, and the gulls keening,
Over her strumpet lap he'll ride,
Watching those wasteful fields and wide,
Where the darkened tilth will soon be greening,
  With looks
Fond and severe, as looks the groom on bride."

KILLING NO MURDER

You, master of delays,
Need no artillery but days
One after one
Loosed off in blank against hope's garrison;
No art,
Save doing nothing, to undo a heart.

MODO AND ALCIPHRON

In the Lybian desert I
Saw a hermit's carcass lie,
And a melancholy fiend
Over the battered bosom leaned.

Black as a widow dead for love,
Motionless he drooped above;
Only his tail from side to side
Switched the sand with narrow stride.

"Grievest thou, imp, to see thy spoil
Lie thus quenched on burning soil?
Rinsed the brain, and the loin's lust
Safely reconciled with dust?

"Or perchance thy mournful hide
Dreads how well the lash will chide
When Pope Satan makes thee skip
For a negligent stewardship?"

With a sullen silence he
Raised his head, and looked at me,
Looked me through, and looked away,
Not for all that I could say

Looked again. Quoth I, I've matched
Patience with yours; and so I watched
The slow, sun-swollen daytime through
To mark what this strange fiend would do

Cramped and cold I woke from sleep
To hear the fiend begin to weep.
Twinkling in starlight the tears ran
Along his beard, and he began:

"Dead is the holy Alciphron!
Modo's occupation's gone.
All my pretty joys are sped,
Gentle Alciphron is dead!

"Never was there saint so mild
And so easily beguiled;
'Twas pure pleasure to torment
Anything so innocent.

"Danced I, gleaming in a dress
Of nimble maiden nakedness,
His prompt heart with hastening beat
Drummed the measure for my feet,

"And his glances whipped me round,
Till toppling in a dizzy swound
With long recovery I would twine
About him like the conjugal vine,

"While my forked and flickering tongue,
Constant as summer lightning, hung
On the scant flesh that wrapped his bones,
Till sighs long-husbanded, chuckling groans,

"Vouched for the pleasures he endured;
By thorns such pleasures must be cured,
And when most thick the thin blood fell
I knew that I had pleased him well.

"Then at other times I'd sit
Praising his spiritual wit,
Assuring him how deftly he
Could comprehend the Trinity,

"Flesh Christ, with never a trespassing glide
To error on this or t'other side,
Show how original sin doth breed
Inherent in the genital seed,

"And every tinkling sophist quell,
Who questions that the troops of hell
Pester the saint upon his knees,
Actual and numerous as his fleas.

"But most of all 'twas my delight
To cajole him from the elected night
Wherewith the christian cowls his sense
From the allurement and offense

"Of a lost planet. I would be
Damnation singing from a tree
With voice more wildly ravishing
For being damned, or in a spring

"With chill adulteries surprise
Him parched; often I thieved his eyes
To love me in lizard, or in braid
Of sun begetting from a shade

"A spawn of dancing babies—all
Accursed as their original.
In many a salad I laid a snare
Of joy that he on such poor fare

"Fared well, or else on wafts of thyme
Into the warded brain would climb
Unchallenged, or tweaked him by the nose
With the remembrance of a rose.

"Thus did we wrestle, and never chaste
Turtles did rarer dalliance taste,
Thus mixed our opposites, as true
As plighted dock and nettle do,

'Thus to all time example gave
Of the mutual comfort saint should have
With devil, devil with saint, and thus
I clean forgot how envious

"In his unmated splendor sits
He, the Tyrant—"
                As oak splits
Before the ax, and falls with loud
Indignant groan, so groaned, so bowed,

The fiend, and lay in silence long;
But once or twice against the throng
Of stars raised up a blackening fist;
Then mourned, as mourning from a mist:

"Alas, how faithless man can be
To a friend's eternity!
Into untiring malice doomed,
Virtue as long-breathed I presumed;

"With never a care save which art next
To ply I looked on time unvexed,
Nor, in this plenty of sand, did doubt
The tale of his was running out.

"So Alciphron grew old, though I
Knew it not. This gew-gawed sky
Its virgin hood of gray had on,
And light was scarce, when Alciphron

"Awoke, and laid his hand on me,
And stared east. *Haec dies,* said he,
Quam fecit Dominus. I too
Looked east, and saw a path run through

"The kindling cloud. It bruised my gaze
To meet the intolerable blaze,
The ostentatious Rose, the blare
And uproar of light which threatened there;

"But Alciphron beheld and smiled,
Crowing for pleasure like a child
Who views its promised sugarplum:
Then, with a crash which has left dumb

"All thunder since, about us came
A simpering angel in a flame,
Who seized upon redemption's prey,
And bore him, like a child, away.

"Thus, O woe, I'm left alone
With this unanswering flesh and bone.
All my pretty joys are sped,
Gentle Alciphron is dead!

"Nothing is left me of my joy
But this contemptuous broken toy.
Modo's occupation's gone,
Dead is the holy Alciphron!"

THE ABSENCE

How happy I can be with my love away!
No care comes all day;
Like a dapple of clouds the hours pass by,
Time stares from the sky
But does not see me where I lie in the hay,
So still do I lie.

Like points of dew the stars well in the skies;
Taller the trees rise.
Dis-shadowed, unselved, I wander slow,
My thoughts flow and flow,
But whither tending I know not, nor need surmise,
So softly I go,

Till to my quiet bed I must undress—
Then I say, Alas!
That he whom, too anxious or too gay,
I torment all day
Can never know me in my harmlessness
While he is away.

BUILDING IN STONE

God is still glorified—
To him the wakeful arch holds up in prayer,
Nightly dumb glass keeps vigil to declare
His East, and Eastertide;

The constant pavement lays
Its flatness for his feet, each pier acquaints
Neighbor, him housed; time-thumbed, forgotten saints
Do not forget to praise;

All parcels of the whole,
Each hidden, each revealed, each thrust and stress,
Antiphonally interlocked, confess
Him, stay, and him, control.

Whether upon the fens
Anchored, with all her canvas and all her shrouds,
Ely signal him to willows and clouds
And cattle, or whether Wren's

Unperturbed dome, above
The city roaring with mechanic throat
And climbing in layer on layer of Babel, float
Like an escaping dove,

Or whether in countryside
Stationed all humble and holy churches keep
Faith with the faith of those who lie asleep,
God is still glorified;

Since by the steadfastness
Of his most mute creation man conjures
—Man, so soon hushed—the silence which endures
To bear in mind, and bless.

THE GREEN VALLEY

Here in the green scooped valley I walk to and fro
In all my journeyings I have not seen
A place so tranquil, so green;
And yet I think I have seen it long ago,
The grassy slopes, and the cart-track winding, so.

O now I remember it well, now all is plain,
Why twitched my memory like a dowser's rod
At waters hidden under sod.
When I was a child they told me of Charlemagne,
Of Gan the traitor, and Roland outmatched and slain.

Weeping for Roland then, I scooped in my spirit

A scant green Roncesvalles, a holy ground,
Which here in Dorset I've found:
But finding, I knew it not. The years disinherit
Their children. The horn is blown, but I do not hear it.

Charles Hamilton Sorley

Charles Hamilton Sorley, who promised great things, was born at Old Aberdeen in May, 1895. Son of Professor Sorley of Cambridge, he studied at Marlborough College and University College, Oxford. He was finishing his studies abroad and was on a walking-tour along the banks of the Moselle when war came. Sorley returned home to receive an immediate commission in the 7th Battalion of the Suffolk Regiment. In August, 1915, at the age of twenty, he was made a captain. On October 13, 1915, he was killed in action near Hulluch.

Jingoism, violent propaganda, falsely patriotic slogans could not obscure his piercing vision. "There is no such thing as a just war," he wrote. "What we are doing is casting out Satan by Satan." At nineteen, while he was training at Shorncliffe, he dared to write, "England—I am sick of the sound of the word. In training to fight for England, I am training to fight for that deliberate hypocrisy, that terrible middle-class sloth of outlook and appalling 'imaginative indolence' that has marked us out from generation to generation. . . . Indeed I think that after the War all brave men will renounce their country and confess that they are strangers and pilgrims on the earth." Such electrifying sentences, as well as his independent appreciations of Masefield, Richard Jefferies, and Thomas Hardy, are to be found in the posthumous *Letters of Charles Sorley* (1919). These letters perform the same service to Sorley the poet as the letters of Keats perform in rounding out that greater poet who also died at the beginning of manhood.

Sorley left but one book, *Marlborough and Other Poems,* a posthumous collection, edited by his father, published in 1916. The verse contained in it is sometimes rough but never rude. Although he admired Masefield, loveliness rather than liveliness was his aim. Restraint, tolerance, and a dignity unusual for a boy of twenty distinguish his verse. There is scarcely a line in Sorley's work which does not breathe the spirit of compelling exaltation.

Whether it blows with breezy youth in "The Song of the Ungirt Runners" or burns with steady ardor in the sonnets, his poetry is, in the fullest sense, radiant. What Sorley might have accomplished is apparent though indefinable. He died before he was twenty-one.

TWO SONNETS

I

Saints have adored the lofty soul of you.
Poets have whitened at your high renown.
We stand among the many millions who
Do hourly wait to pass your pathway down.

You, so familiar, once were strange: we tried
To live as of your presence unaware.
But now in every road on every side
We see your straight and steadfast signpost there.

I think it like that signpost in my land
Hoary and tall, which pointed me to go
Upward, into the hills, on the right hand,
Where the mists swim and the winds shriek and blow,
A homeless land and friendless, but a land
I did not know and that I wished to know.

II

Such, such is Death: no triumph: no defeat:
Only an empty pail, a slate rubbed clean,
A merciful putting away of what has been.

And this we know: Death is not Life effete,
Life crushed, the broken pail. We who have seen
So marvelous things know well the end not yet.
Victor and vanquished are a-one in death:
Coward and brave: friend, foe. Ghosts do not say,
"Come, what was your record when you drew breath?"
But a big blot has hid each yesterday
So poor, so manifestly incomplete.
And your bright Promise, withered long and sped,
Is touched; stirs, rises, opens and grows sweet
And blossoms and is you, when you are dead.

THE SONG OF THE UNGIRT RUNNERS

We swing ungirded hips,
And lightened are our eyes,
The rain is on our lips,
We do not run for prize.
We know not whom we trust
Nor whitherward we fare,
But we run because we must
  Through the great wide air.

The waters of the seas
Are troubled as by storm.
The tempest strips the trees
And does not leave them warm.
Does the tearing tempest pause?
Do the tree tops ask it why?
So we run without a cause
  'Neath the big bare sky.

The rain is on our lips,
We do not run for prize.

But the storm the water whips
And the wave howls to the skies.
The winds arise and strike it
And scatter it like sand,
And we run because we like it
  Through the broad bright land.

TO GERMANY

You are blind like us. Your hurt no man designed,
And no man claimed the conquest of your land.
But gropers both, through fields of thought confined,
We stumble and we do not understand.
You only saw your future bigly planned,
And we the tapering paths of our own mind,
And in each other's dearest ways we stand,
And hiss and hate. And the blind fight the blind.

When it is peace, then we may view again
With new-won eyes each other's truer form
And wonder. Grown more loving-kind and warm
We'll grasp firm hands and laugh at the old pain,
When it is peace. But until peace, the storm,
The darkness and the thunder and the rain.

ROOKS

There where the rusty iron lies,
  The rooks are cawing all the day.
Perhaps no man, until he dies,
  Will understand them, what they say.

The evening makes the sky like clay.
  The slow wind waits for night to rise.
The world is half content. But they

Still trouble all the trees with cries,
  That know, and cannot put away,
The yearning to the soul that flies
  From day to night, from night to day.

ALL THE HILLS AND VALES

All the hills and vales along
Earth is bursting into song,
And the singers are the chaps
Who are going to die perhaps.
    O sing, marching men,
    Till the valleys ring again.

Give your gladness to earth's keeping,
So be glad, when you are sleeping.

Cast away regret and rue,
Think what you are marching to.
Little live, great pass.
Jesus Christ and Barabbas
Were found the same day.
This died, that went his way.
So sing with joyful breath.
For why, you are going to death.
Teeming earth will surely store
All the gladness that you pour.

Earth that never doubts nor fears,
Earth that knows of death, not tears,
Earth that bore with joyful ease
Hemlock for Socrates,
Earth that blossomed and was glad
'Neath the cross that Christ had,
Shall rejoice and blossom too
When the bullet reaches you.
Wherefore, men marching
On the road to death, sing!
Pour your gladness on earth's head,
So be merry, so be dead.

From the hills and valleys earth
Shouts back the sound of mirth,
Tramp of feet and lilt of song
Ringing all the road along.
Ringing, swinging, glad song-throwing,
Earth will echo still when foot
Lies numb and voice mute.
On, marching men, on
To the gates of death with song.
Sow your gladness for earth's reaping,
So you may be glad, though sleeping.
Strew your gladness on earth's bed,
So be merry, so be dead.

Robert Graves

Robert (Ranke) Graves, son of the Irish poet and song-writer Alfred Percival Graves, was born July 26, 1895. He was educated at Charterhouse and Oxford, after which he joined the British Expeditionary Force and served three times in France, in the same regiment as Siegfried Sassoon. His activities were as numerous as incongruous. He won a prize at the Olympic games, lost his capital as an unsuccessful shopkeeper, was the biographer of Colonel T. E. Lawrence, and taught literature in Cairo.

Graves was one of the writers who, roused by the War and giving himself to his country, refused to glorify warfare or chant new hymns of hate. Like Sassoon, Graves reacted against the storm of fury and blood-lust, but, fortified by a lighter and more whimsical spirit, where Sassoon is violent, Graves is volatile; where Sassoon grew bitter, Graves was almost blithe in his irony.

An easy gaiety rises from *Fairies and Fusiliers* (1917), a surprising and healing humor that is warmly individual. In *Country Sentiment* (1919) Graves turns to a more rustic simplicity. But a buoyant fancy ripples beneath the most archaic of his ballads and a quaintly original turn of mind saves them from their own echoes.

With *Country Sentiment,* Graves, so one was ready to believe, had established his characteristics. His gift was charming rather than startling, playful and lightly *macabre* rather than profound; qualities, which, while not those of a great poet, were distinctly those of an enjoyable one. The young poet seemed happy in his combinations (and mutations) of two traditionally English forms: the ballad and the Mother Goose rhyme. "A Frosty Night," "Star-Talk," "True Johnny," "It's a Queer Time," "Neglectful Edward," "I Wonder What It Feels Like to Be Drowned?" are some of the measures written out of a surplus and careless fertility, with little effort, scarcely with thought, and with one eye winking at the Nursery.

In his thirties, temporarily putting aside the direct lyric impulse, Graves threw himself into controversies. He issued broadsides from his home in Majorca. He began to probe and analyze the ways, means, and results of the creative process—his own as well as others'. No less than seven volumes were devoted to interpretation and technique; *On English Poetry* (1922), *The Meaning of Dreams* (1924), *Poetic Unreason* (1925), *Contemporary Techniques of Poetry* (1925), *Another Future of Poetry* (1926), *A Survey of Modernist Poetry,* the last in collaboration with Laura Riding (1928). His volumes of verse during this period reflect changing preoccupations. *The Pier Glass* (1921), *Whipperginny* (1923), *Mock Beggar Hall* (1924), *Welchman's Hose* (1925), *The Marmosite's Miscellany,* issued by "John Doyle" (1925), turn from fancy to philosophy, from Skelton to Freud.

Much of this intellectual turmoil is reflected in *Good-Bye to All That* (1929) and *But It Still Goes On* (1930), two autobiographies which poignantly, ironically, and not always successfully wave farewell to Graves' youth. Without bravado and with surprisingly little bitterness the poet describes the sordid side of war, the drudgery of trench life and the abuses of officialdom, but his pages are intensified with a hatred of injustice in all its forms.

After forty, Graves gave himself energetically to reappraisals of history, legend, and myth. *I, Claudius* (1934) and *Claudius the God* (1935) were followed by the searching prose of *Wife to Mr. Milton* (1943), *Hercules, My Shipmate* (1945), the controversial *King Jesus* (1946), the erudite *The White Goddess* (1948) which T. S. Eliot hailed as "a prodigious, monstrous, stupefying, indescribable book," and *Watch the Northwind Rise* (1949), a witty fantasy of a future utopia run by witchcraft. The poet was always apparent in all these books as well as in *Poems: 1938-1945* and *Collected Poems: 1914-1947*—volumes which increased his stature.

At sixty-five Graves was the prolific author of some twenty-five books of poems, a dozen novels, and more than two dozen miscellaneous volumes: biographies, essays, short stories, adaptations, interpretations, criticisms, causeries and mischievous retellings of *The Greek Myths* (1955). Upon the publication of a new *Collected Poems; 1959* his place was assured. It was an isolated place. "Not only has he never been a member of a school or followed any prevailing fashion," wrote J. M. Cohen in his book-length study, *Robert Graves* (1960), "but even in his generation he stands alone, too young to have experienced the impact of Continental symbolism and not young enough to have been affected by the social stress which determined the initial poetic course of Auden and his group." "Having written poetry for forty-five years and been for the greater part of that time not exactly neglected but often regarded as peripheral," reported Walter Allen in a *London Letter,* "he is suddenly recognized by the younger poets as *the* living English poet."

Although Graves truculently derided the obscurantists (see *The Crowning Privilege,* delivered as lectures during his tenure at Oxford), his own poetry is not always easy to comprehend. For example "To Juan at the Winter Solstice" is one of his more magical poems; but in order to appreciate its cryptic lines the reader must have an acquaintance with mythology, the many-titled queen-goddesses, the kings who must die and be reborn at the winter solstice, the basic legends which have a central meaning—"there is one story and one story only"—and an understanding of *The White Goddess* which maintains that the leading theme of poetry is the relations, often tragic, of men and women.

The belated salvos were unaccompanied by the usual murmurs of dissent. It was generally agreed that Graves had an obstinate integrity and an innate ability to capture and communicate the essence of poetry. "He is helplessly original," declared Richard Wilbur when introducing Graves at the American Academy of Arts and Letters. "His poems issue directly from a self-trusting and inimitable sensibility . . . They are 'occasional'—that is, however handsomely made, they have the air of being spontaneous answers to actual experience."

NEGLECTFUL EDWARD

Nancy

Edward, back from the Indian Sea,
"What have you brought for Nancy?"

Edward

"A rope of pearls and a gold earring,
And a bird of the East that will not sing.
A carven tooth, a box with a key—"

Nancy

"God be praised you are back," says she,
"Have you nothing more for your Nancy?"

Edward

"Long as I sailed the Indian Sea
I gathered all for your fancy:
Toys and silk and jewels I bring,

And a bird of the East that will not sing:
What more can you want, dear girl, from me?"

Nancy

"God be praised you are back," said she,
"Have you nothing better for Nancy?"

Edward

"Safe and home from the Indian Sea,
And nothing to take your fancy?"

Nancy

"You can keep your pearls and your gold earring,
And your bird of the East that will not sing,
But, Ned, have you nothing more for me
Than heathenish gew-gaw toys?" says she,
"Have you nothing better for Nancy?"

IT'S A QUEER TIME

It's hard to know if you're alive or dead
When steel and fire go roaring through your head.
One moment you'll be crouching at your gun
Traversing, mowing heaps down half in fun:
The next, you choke and clutch at your right breast—
No time to think—leave all—and off you go . . .
To Treasure Island where the Spice winds blow,
To lovely groves of mango, quince and lime—
Breathe no good-by, but ho, for the Red West!
It's a queer time.

You're charging madly at them yelling "Fag!"
When somehow something gives and your feet drag.
You fall and strike your head; yet feel no pain
And find . . . you're digging tunnels through the hay
In the Big Barn, 'cause it's a rainy day.
Oh, springy hay, and lovely beams to climb!
You're back in the old sailor suit again.
It's a queer time.

Or you'll be dozing safe in your dug-out—
A great roar—the trench shakes and falls about—
You're struggling, gasping, struggling, then . . . *hullo!*
Elsie comes tripping gayly down the trench,
Hanky to nose—that lyddite makes a stench—
Getting her pinafore all over grime.
Funny! because she died ten years ago!
It's a queer time.

The trouble is, things happen much too quick;
Up jump the Boches, rifles thump and click.

You stagger, and the whole scene fades away:
Even good Christians don't like passing straight
From Tipperary or their Hymn of Hate
To Alleluiah-chanting, and the chime
Of golden harps . . . and . . . I'm not well today . . .
It's a queer time.

A PINCH OF SALT

When a dream is born in you
With a sudden clamorous pain,
When you know the dream is true
And lovely, with no flaw nor stain,
O then, be careful, or with sudden clutch
You'll hurt the delicate thing you prize so much.

Dreams are like a bird that mocks,
Flirting the feathers of his tail.
When you seize at the salt box,
Over the hedge you'll see him sail.
Old birds are neither caught with salt nor chaff:
They watch you from the apple bough and laugh.

Poet, never chase the dream.
Laugh yourself, and turn away.
Mask your hunger; let it seem
Small matter if he come or stay;
But when he nestles in your hand at last,
Close up your fingers tight and hold him fast.

STAR-TALK

"Are you awake, Gemelli,
This frosty night?"
"We'll be awake till réveillé,
Which is Sunrise," say the Gemelli,
"It's no good trying to go to sleep:
If there's wine to be got we'll drink it deep,
But sleep is gone tonight,
But sleep is gone tonight."

"Are you cold too, poor Pleiads,
This frosty night?"
"Yes, and so are the Hyads:
See us cuddle and hug," say the Pleiads,
"All six in a ring: it keeps us warm:
We huddle together like birds in a storm:
It's bitter weather tonight,
It's bitter weather tonight."

"What do you hunt, Orion,
  This starry night?"
"The Ram, the Bull and the Lion,
And the Great Bear," says Orion,
"With my starry quiver and beautiful belt
I am trying to find a good thick pelt
  To warm my shoulders tonight,
  To warm my shoulders tonight."

"Did you hear that, Great She-bear,
  This frosty night?"
"Yes, he's talking of stripping *me* bare
Of my own big fur," says the She-bear,
"I'm afraid of the man and his terrible arrow:
The thought of it chills my bones to the marrow,
  And the frost so cruel tonight!
  And the frost so cruel tonight!"

"How is your trade, Aquarius,
  This frosty night?"
"Complaints is many and various
And my feet are cold," says Aquarius,
"There's Venus objects to Dolphin-scales,
And Mars to Crab-spawn found in my pails,
  And the pump has frozen tonight,
  And the pump has frozen tonight."

I WONDER WHAT IT FEELS LIKE TO BE DROWNED?

Look at my knees,
That island rising from the steamy seas!
The candle's a tall lightship; my two hands
Are boats and barges anchored to the sands,
With mighty cliffs all round;
They're full of wine and riches from far lands. . . .
I wonder what it feels like to be drowned?

I can make caves,
By lifting up the island and huge waves
And storms, and then with head and ears well under
Blow bubbles with a monstrous roar like thunder,
A bull-of-Bashan sound.
The seas run high and the boats split asunder . . .
I wonder what it feels like to be drowned?

The thin soap slips
And slithers like a shark under the ships.
My toes are on the soap-dish—that's the effect
Of my huge storms; an iron steamer's wrecked.

The soap slides round and round;
He's biting the old sailors, I expect. . . .
I wonder what it feels like to be drowned?

ESCAPE

(*August 6, 1916. Officer Previously Reported Died of Wounds, Now Reported Wounded: Graves, Capt. R., Royal Welch Fusiliers*)

. . . But I *was* dead, an hour or more:
I woke when I'd already passed the door
That Cerberus guards and half-way down the road
To Lethe, as an old Greek sign-post showed.
Above me, on my stretcher swinging by,
I saw new stars in the sub-terrene sky,
A Cross, a Rose in Bloom, a Cage with Bars,
And a barbed Arrow feathered with fine stars.
I felt the vapors of forgetfulness
Float in my nostrils: Oh, may Heaven bless
Dear Lady Proserpine, who saw me wake
And, stooping over me, for Henna's sake
Cleared my poor buzzing head and sent me back
Breathless, with leaping heart along the track.
After me roared and clattered angry hosts
Of demons, heroes, and policemen ghosts.
"Life, life! I can't be dead, I won't be dead:
Damned if I'll die for anyone," I said . . .
Cerberus stands and grins above me now,
Wearing three heads, lion and lynx and sow.
"Quick, a revolver! but my Webley's gone,
Stolen . . . no bombs . . . no knife . . . (the crowd swarms on,
Bellows, hurls stones) . . . not even a honeyed sop . . .
Nothing . . . Good Cerberus . . . Good dog . . . But stop!
Stay! . . . A great luminous thought . . . I do believe
There's still some morphia that I bought on leave."
Then swiftly Cerberus' wide mouths I cram
With Army biscuit smeared with Tickler's jam;
And Sleep lurks in the luscious plum and apple.
He crunches, swallows, stiffens, seems to grapple
With the all-powerful poppy . . . then a snore,
A crash; the beast blocks up the corridor
With monstrous hairy carcase, red and dun—
Too late: for I've sped through.
O Life! O Sun!

THE TRAVELER'S CURSE AFTER MISDIRECTION

(*from the Welsh*)

May they wander stage by stage
Of the same vain pilgrimage,
Stumbling on, age after age,
Night and day, mile after mile,
At each and every step, a stile;
At each and every stile, withal,
May they catch their feet and fall;
At each and every fall they take,

May a bone within them break;
And may the bones that break within
Not be, for variation's sake,
Now rib, now thigh, now arm, now shin,
But always, without fail, THE NECK.

SONG: ONE HARD LOOK

Small gnats that fly
In hot July
And lodge in sleeping ears,
Can rouse therein
A trumpet's din
With Day of Judgment fears.

Small mice at night
Can wake more fright
Than lions at midday.
A straw will crack
The camel's back;
There is no easier way.

One smile relieves
A heart that grieves
Though deadly sad it be,
And one hard look
Can close the book
That lovers love to see.

A FROSTY NIGHT

Mother

Alice, dear, what ails you,
  Dazed and white and shaken?
Has the chill night numbed you?
  Is it fright you have taken?

Alice

Mother, I am very well,
  I felt never better,
Mother, do not hold me so,
  Let me write my letter.

Mother

Sweet, my dear, what ails you?

Alice

  No, but I am well;
The night was cold and frosty,
  There's no more to tell.

Mother

Aye, the night was frosty,
  Coldly gaped the moon,
Yet the birds seemed twittering
  Through green boughs of June.

Soft and thick the snow lay,
  Stars danced in the sky.
Not all the lambs of May-day
  Skip so bold and high.

Your feet were dancing, Alice,
  Seemed to dance on air,
You looked a ghost or angel
  In the starlight there.

Your eyes were frosted starlight,
  Your heart fire and snow.
Who was it said, "I love you"?

Alice

  Mother, let me go!

IN THE WILDERNESS

Christ of His gentleness
Thirsting and hungering,
Walked in the wilderness;
Soft words of grace He spoke
Unto lost desert-folk
That listened wondering.
He heard the bitterns call
From ruined palace-wall,
Answered them brotherly.
He held communion
With the she-pelican
Of lonely piety.
Basilisk, cockatrice,
Flocked to his homilies,
With mail of dread device,
With monstrous barbèd slings,
With eager dragon-eyes;
Great bats on leathern wings
And poor blind broken things,
Foul in their miseries.
And ever with Him went,
Of all His wanderings
Comrade, with ragged coat,
Gaunt ribs—poor innocent—

Bleeding foot, burning throat,
The guileless old scapegoat;
For forty nights and days
Followed in Jesus' ways,
Sure guard behind Him kept,
Tears like a lover wept.

A FORCED MUSIC

Of Love he sang, full hearted one,
But when the song was done,
The King demanded more,
Aye, and commanded more.
The boy found nothing for encore,
Words, melodies—none,
Ashamed the song's glad rise and plaintive fall
Had so charmed King and Queen and all.

He sang the same verse once again
But urging less Love's pain.
With altered time and key
He showed variety,
Seemed to refresh the harmony
Of his only strain,
So still the glad rise and the plaintive fall
Could charm the King, the Queen and all.

He of his song then wearying ceased,
But was not yet released:
The Queen's request was "More,"
And her behest was "More."
He played of random notes some score,
Then suddenly let his twangling harp down fall
And fled in tears from King and Queen and all.

LOST LOVE

His eyes are quickened so with grief,
He can watch a grass or leaf
Every instant grow; he can
Clearly through a flint wall see,
Or watch the startled spirit flee
From the throat of a dead man:
Across two counties he can hear,
And catch your words before you speak;
The woodlouse or the maggot's weak
Clamor rings in his sad ear;
And noise so slight it would surpass
Credence:—drinking sound of grass,
Worm-talk, clashing jaws of moth
Chumbling tiny holes in cloth:
The groan of ants who undertake
Gigantic loads for honor's sake,
Their sinews creak, their breath comes thin:
Whir of spiders when they spin,

And minute, whispering, mumbling sighs
Of idle grubs and flies.
This man is quickened so with grief,
He wanders god-like or like thief
Inside and out, below, above,
Without relief seeking lost love.

TO BRING THE DEAD TO LIFE

To bring the dead to life
Is no great magic.
Few are wholly dead:
Blow on a dead man's embers
And a live flame will start.

Let his forgotten griefs be now,
And now his withered hopes;
Subdue your pen to his handwriting
Until it proves as natural
To sign his name as yours.

Limp as he limped,
Swear by the oaths he swore;
If he wore black, affect the same;
If he had gouty fingers,
Be yours gouty too.

Assemble tokens intimate of him—
A seal, a cloak, a pen:
Around these elements then build
A home familiar to
The greedy revenant.

So grant him life, but reckon
That the grave which housed him
May not be empty now:
You in his spotted garments
Shall yourself lie wrapped.

TO JUAN AT THE WINTER SOLSTICE

There is one story and one story only
That will prove worth your telling,
Whether as learned bard or gifted child;
To it all lines or lesser gauds belong
That startle with their shining
Such common stories as they stray into.

Is it of trees you tell, their months and virtues,
Or strange beasts that beset you,
Of birds that croak at you the Triple will?

Or of the Zodiac and how slow it turns
Below the Boreal Crown,
Prison of all true kings that ever reigned?

Water to water, ark again to ark,
From woman back to woman:
So each new victim treads unfalteringly
The never altered circuit of his fate,
Bringing twelve peers as witness
Both to his starry rise and starry fall.

Or is it of the Virgin's silver beauty,
All fish below the thighs?
She in her left hand bears a leafy quince;
When with her right she crooks a finger, smiling,
How may the King hold back?
Royally then he barters life for love.

Or of the undying snake from chaos hatched,
Whose coils contain the ocean,
Into whose chops with naked sword he springs,
Then in black water, tangled by the reeds,
Battles three days and nights,
To be spewed up beside her scalloped shore?

Much snow is falling, winds roar hollowly,
The owl hoots from the elder,
Fear in your heart cries to the loving-cup:
Sorrow to sorrow as the sparks fly upward.
The log groans and confesses:
There is one story and one story only.

Dwell on her graciousness, dwell on her smilling,
Do not forget what flowers
The great boar trampled down in ivy time.
Her brow was creamy as the crested wave,
Her sea-blue eyes were wild
But nothing promised that is not performed.

THE WHITE GODDESS

All saints revile her, and all sober men
Ruled by the God Apollo's golden mean—
In scorn of which we sailed to find her
In distant regions likeliest to hold her
Whom we desired above all things to know,
Sister of the mirage and echo.

It was a virtue not to stay,
To go our headstrong and heroic way
Seeking her out at the volcano's head,

Among pack ice, or where the track had faded
Beyond the cavern of the seven sleepers:
Whose broad high brow was white as any leper's,
Whose eyes were blue, with rowan-berry lips,
With hair curled honey-coloured to white hips.

Green sap of Spring in the young wood a-stir
Will celebrate the Mountain Mother,
And every song-bird shout awhile for her;
But we are gifted, even in November
Rawest of seasons, with so huge a sense
Of her nakedly worn magnificence
We forget cruelty and past betrayal,
Heedless of where the next bright bolt may fall.

CRY FAUGH!

Caria and Philistia considered
Only pre-marital adventures wise;
The bourgeois French argue contrariwise.

Socrates and Plato burked the issue
(Namely, how man-and-woman love should be)
With homosexual ideology.

Apocalyptic Israelites, foretelling
The Imminent End, called only for a chaste
Sodality: all dead below the waist.

Curious, various, amoral, moral—
Confess, what elegant square or lumpish hamlet
Lives free from nymphological disquiet?

'Yet males and females of the lower species
Contrive to eliminate the sexual problem,'
Scientists ponder: 'Why not learn from them?'

Cry faugh! on science, ethics, metaphysics,
On antonyms of sacred and profane—
Come walk with me, love, in a golden rain

Past toppling colonnades of glory,
The moon alive on each uptilted face:
Proud remnants of a visionary race.

L. A. G. Strong

Leonard Alfred George Strong was born on March 8, 1896, in the parish of Plympton, in Devon. "One of his parents," Strong informed the editor some years ago, "is Irish, the other is half English and half Irish, so that he is fairly entitled to describe himself as a mongrel. He spent his childhood partly on Southern Dartmoor and partly on the borders between Dublin and Wicklow. From a preparatory school at Plymouth, he went with a scholarship to Brighton College, and thence, five years later, won an open Classical Scholarship at Wadham College, Oxford. Illness interrupting his career, he finally graduated in 1920 and taught at Summer Fields, a famous preparatory school near Oxford. Delicate health has confined him to a spectator's part in his favorite sports. Swimming is the only form of violent exercise he has been able to keep up—perhaps because, as legend has it, one of his ancestors, Teig Riarch O'Dowda, King of Connaught, captured and married a mermaid, thereby endowing his descendants with a taste for the sea!"

In 1930 Strong left Oxford and full-time teaching and came down to London and set up shop as a writer. He had behind him the considerable English success of his novel *Dewer Rides* (1929). A complete literary man, Strong's first American reputation came through his poetry. *Dublin Days* (1921), *Selected Poems* (1931), and *Call to the Swans* (1936) were all well received. A prolific novelist and short story writer, Strong worked more surely in the short story. *Travellers* (1945), a short story collection, received the James Tait Black Memorial Prize. Two works of nonfiction are especially noteworthy: *The Sacred River* (1949), one of the sounder books on James Joyce, and *The Writer's Trade* (1953), a professional's account of a beguiling and problematic profession. Strong, who died in 1958, had a virtuosity which would seem peculiar to the English literary life. There was little to which he could not turn his hand. Not only was he poet, novelist, and critic, a writer of detective stories, a BBC radio and television script writer as well as a broadcaster, a teacher of "verse-speaking" in a London drama school, but also he was a director of the distinguished London publishing firm of Metheun.

OLD DAN'L

Out of his cottage to the sun
Bent double comes old Dan'l,
His chest all over cotton wool,
His back all over flannel.

"Winter will finish him," they've said
Each winter now for ten:
But come the first warm day of Spring
Old Dan'l's out again.

ZEKE

Gnarly and bent and deaf's a pos',
Pore old Ezekiel Purvis
Goeth crippin' slowly up the 'ill
To the Commoonion Survis.

And tappy, tappy up the haisle
Goeth stick and brassy ferule:
And Passen[1] 'ath to stoopy down
An' 'oller in ees yerole.

[1] Parson.

AN OLD WOMAN, OUTSIDE THE ABBEY THEATER

In this Theayter they has plays
On us, and high-up people comes
And pays to see things playin' here
They'd run like hell from in the slums.

RUFUS PRAYS

In the darkening church
Where but a few had stayed
At the Litany Desk
The idiot knelt and prayed.

Rufus, stunted, uncouth,
The one son of his mother.
"Eh, I'd sooner 'ave Rufie,"
She said, "than many another:

" 'E's useful about the 'ouse,
And so gentle as 'e can be.
An' 'e gets up early o' mornin's
And makes me a cup o' tea."

The formal evensong
Had passed over his head:
He sucked his thumb, and squinted,
And dreamed, instead.

Now while the organ boomed
To the few who still were there,
At the Litany Desk
The idiot made his prayer:

"Gawd bless Mother,
'N make Rufie a good lad:
Take Rufie to Heaven
'N forgive him when 'e's bad.

" 'N early mornin's in Heaven
'E'll make mother's tea,
'N a cup for the Lord Jesus
'N a cup for Thee."

THE MAD WOMAN OF PUNNET'S TOWN

A-swell within her billowed skirts
Like a great ship with sails unfurled,
The mad woman goes gallantly
Upon the ridges of her world.

With eagle nose and wisps of gray
She strides upon the westward hills,
Swings her umbrella joyously
And waves it to the waving mills.

Talking and chuckling as she goes
Indifferent both to sun and rain,
With all that merry company:
The singing children of her brain.

LOWERY COT

This is the house where Jesse White
Run staring in one misty night,
And said he seed the Holy Ghost
Out to Lowery finger-post.

Said It rised up like a cloud
Muttering to Itself out loud,
And stood tremendous on the hill
While all the breathing world was still.

They put en shivering to bed,
And in three days the man was dead.
Gert solemn visions such as they
Be overstrong for mortal clay.

THE DOOR

One in the boat cried out
Pointing to land,
For the sun leaped clear of the mist
And a rainbow spanned
With one vast arch the mountain, the trees, and the sand.

The mountain stood like a huge
Ghost in a cloud;
The startled trees were caught
In a wavering crowd;
And the four in their glittering oilskins cried aloud

As that pure and soaring arch
More marvelous grew,
And the sandhills stared beneath it
Wild and new,
And down the unearthly beaches lamenting flew

Gull upon gull distraught
Blown through that Door,
Handful on handful flung
High over the shore.
Such desperate beauty they never had seen before.

MARCH EVENING

This pool, the quiet sky,
Is rippled with a chime.
Night gathers, and the cry

Of lambs in the far fold
Comes to us as we climb:
The moorland air is cold.

Ghost-pale the grass, and bare
The bowlder-scattered crest.
A frightened rabbit starts—
With quickening eyes and hearts
We turn about, and stare
Into the open west.

The Cornish hills lie small,
So huge the sky has grown.
We can look down on all
Western and southern ground,
And see the Eddystone,
Pricking the seaward pall,
Wink over Plymouth Sound.

Below us, dim and deep,
Mist-hidden, murmuring,
The valley winds away:
Beneath its shadow Spring
Lies light asleep
In dreams of coming day,
With cuckoos on the wing
And steep banks blossoming.

Again the quiet sky
Is troubled with a chime
That spreads in rings of sound.
We sigh, and think, What rhyme
That man has ever bound
Can hold a sigh?

Edmund Blunden

Edmund (C.) Blunden was born in 1896, and educated at Queen's College, Oxford. During the War he served as lieutenant in the Royal Sussex Regiment. His bucolic poems were a direct revulsion from his experiences as a soldier. In 1916 he published three small volumes of pastorals which appeared as one book, *The Wagoner and other Poems,* in 1920. In the same year, he edited, with Alan Porter, *The Poems of John Clare,* most of the verses being deciphered from a mass of old manuscript. Two years later, he published *The Shepherd* (1922), which was awarded the Hawthornden Prize for that year. He was Professor of English Literature at Tokyo University from 1924 to 1927.

The most casual glance at his volumes discloses that Blunden's use of the pastoral note is not, as it is with some of his contemporaries, a mere literary device. Here, the verse is gnarled and twisted as the bent trees of which he loves to write; there is rude country air in his lines and even the words have the smell of apple orchards. It has been objected that Blunden depends too often on unusual and obsolescent terms, but—as Robert Bridges wrote in a pamphlet on *The Dialectical Words in Blunden's Poems* (1921)—"his poetry cannot be imagined without them, and the strength and beauty of the effects must be estimated in his successes and not in his failures."

Blunden's subsequent poetry is milder; a softness but not a flabbiness of texture clothes *To Nature* (1923), *Masks of Time* (1925) and *Retreat* (1928). These verses, lacking the earthy flavor of the early poems, lose the spiciness that dialect confers, but they retain the contemplative quality of Blunden's mind and a dignity which inheres both in the tradition and in the man. *Near and Far* (1929), on the other hand, is composed of pretty trifles which did Blunden's reputation no good. The contents, betraying a monotonous solemnity, are, as Peter Quennell remarked, "a drowsy methodical grinding out of familiar tunes."

In spite of his attainments, Blunden remained known to only a small circle until 1929. In that year he published his large prose work, *Undertones of War,* which was received with instant enthusiasm in Europe and America and took its place among such vivid anti-militaristic documents as Remarque's *All Quiet on the Western Front,* Zweig's *The Case of Sergeant Grischa,* Hemingway's *A Farewell to Arms,* and E. E. Cummings' *The Enormous Room.*

The Poems of Edmund Blunden (1932) collects all the poetry written by Blunden between 1914 and 1930. Nature and war are the chief themes and, though one sometimes wishes for more abandon, no reader can be deaf to the admirable diction and the grave music. *Poems: 1930-1940* and *Shells by a Stream* (1945) reflect the author's gentle clarity but suffer from an obsession with vanished innocence. Blunden is also the author of books on Hardy and Shelley.

(The definitions appended to the poems are by Robert Bridges.)

THE POOR MAN'S PIG

Already fallen plum-bloom stars the green
  And apple-boughs as knarred[1] as old toads' backs
Wear their small roses ere a rose is seen;
  The building-thrush watches old Job who stacks

The bright-peeled osiers on the sunny fence,
  The pent sow grunts to hear him stumping by,
And tries to push the bolt and scamper thence,
  But her ringed snout still keeps her to the sty.

Then out he lets her run; away she snorts
  In bundling gallop for the cottage door,
With hungry hubbub begging crusts and orts.[2]
  Then like a whirlwind bumping round once more;
Nuzzling the dog, making the pullets run,
  And sulky as a child when her play's done.

A COUNTRY GOD

When groping farms are lanterned up
  And stolchy[3] plowlands hid in grief,
And glimmering byroads catch the drop
  That weeps from sprawling twig and leaf,
And heavy-hearted spins the wind
  Among the tattered flags of Mirth,—
Then who but I flit to and fro,
With shuddering speech, with mope and mow,
  And glass the eyes of earth?

[1] *Knarred,* a word meaning "wrinkled," is a country-cousin to our "gnarled."
[2] *Orts* are fragments or scraps of refuse.
[3] *Stolchy* is such an excellent onomatopoetic word that it scarcely needs explanation. But there is an old English verb *stolch:* "to tread down in wet land or mud."

Then haunt I by some moaning brook
  Where lank and snaky brambles swim,
Or where the hill pines swartly look
  I whirry[1] through the dark and hymn
A dull-voiced dirge and threnody,
  An echo of the sad world's drone
That now appals the friendly stars—
O wail for blind brave youth, whose wars
  Turn happiness to stone.

How rang the cavern-shades of old
  To my melodious pipes, and then
My bright-haired bergomask patrolled
  Each lawn and plot for laughter's din:
Never a sower flung broadcast,
  No hedger brished[2] nor scythesman swung,
Nor maiden trod the purpling press,
But I was by to guard and bless
  And for their solace sung.

But now the sower's hand is writhed
  In livid death, the bright rhythm stolen,
The gold grain flatted and unscythed,
  The boards in the vineyard, gnarled and sullen,
Havocking the grapes; and the pouncing wind
  Spins the spattered leaves of the glen
In a mockery dance, death's hue-and-cry;
With all my murmurous pipes flung by
  And summer not to come again.

THE BARN

Rain-sunken roof, grown green and thin
For sparrows' nests and starlings' nests;
Disheveled eaves; unwieldy doors,
Cracked rusty pump, and oaken floors,
And idly-penciled names and jests
  Upon the posts within.

The light pales at the spider's lust,
The wind tangs[3] through the shattered pane:
An empty hop-poke spreads across
The gaping frame to mend the loss
And keeps out sun as well as rain,
  Mildewed with clammy dust.

The smell of apples stored in hay
And homely cattle-cake is there.
Use and disuse have come to terms,
The walls are hollowed out by worms,
But men's feet keep the mid-floor bare
  And free from worse decay.

All merry noise of hens astir
Or sparrows squabbling on the roof
Comes to the barn's broad open door;
You hear upon the stable floor
Old hungry Dapple strike his hoof,
  And the blue fan-tail's whir.

The barn is old, and very old,
But not a place of spectral fear.
Cobwebs and dust and speckling sun
Come to old buildings every one.
Long since they made their dwelling here,
  And here you may behold

[1] *Whirry* is another sound-word, not to be confused with "worry." It means "to fly rapidly with noise"—a combination of "whir" and "hurry."

[2] *Brished* is country dialect for "brush"—principally used in connection with trimming trees and hedges.

[3] *Tangs*—an old term (differing from our word meaning "taste") denoting a barb or a sting. Blunden uses it here as a verb.

Nothing but simple wane and change;
Your tread will wake no ghost, your voice
Will fall on silence undeterred.
No phantom wailing will be heard,
Only the farm's blithe cheerful noise;
The barn is old, not strange.

EASTERN TEMPEST

This flying angel's torrent cry
Will hurl the mountains through the sky!
A wind like fifty winds at once
Through the bedragoned kingdom runs,
And hissing rain slants icy stings
At many a wretch afield who clings
His cloak of straw, with glistening spines
Like a prodigious porcupine's.
The reptile grasses by his path
Wind sleek as unction from that Wrath
Which with its glassy claw uproots
The broad-leaved *kiri,* flays and loots
Torn and sprung sinews, leaves for dead
The young crops with the shining head,
While blotched blunt melons darkly dot
The slaughtered swathes like cannon-shot.
The lotus in the pond upheaves
Its sacred, slow, appealing leaves,
And many a bush with wrestling jerk
Defies the demon's murderous work—
Yet nature stares white-lipped, to read
In Chance's eye what desperate deed?
A kinder god discerns, replies,
And stills the land's storm-shouts to sighs;
The clouds in massy folds apart
Disclose the day's bright bleeding heart,
Huge plumes and scarves black-tossing wide
As if a Kubla Khan had died!
From flame to flame the vision glows,
Till all the pools of heaven unclose
The lotus-light, the hue, the balm
Of wisdom infinitely calm.

THE MIDNIGHT SKATERS

The hop-poles stand in cones,
The icy pond lurks under,
The pole-tops touch the star-gods' thrones
And sound the gulfs of wonder,
But not the tallest there, 'tis said,
Could fathom to this pond's black bed.

Then is not Death at watch
Within those secret waters?
What wants he but to catch
Earth's heedless sons and daughters?
With but a crystal parapet
Between, he has his engines set.

Then on, blood shouts, on, on,
Twirl, wheel and whip above him,
Dance on this ball-floor thin and wan,
Use him as though you love him;
Court him, elude him, reel and pass,
And let him hate you through the glass.

THE RECOVERY

From the dark mood's control
I free this man; there's light still in the West.
The most virtuous, chaste, melodious soul
Never was better blest.

Here medicine for the mind
Lies in a gilded shade; this feather stirs
And my faith lives; the touch of this tree's Rind,—
And temperate sense recurs.

No longer the loud pursuit
Of self-made clamors dulls the ear; here dwell
Twilight societies, twig, fungus, root,
Soundless, and speaking well.

Beneath the accustomed dome
Of this chance-planted, many-centuried tree
The snake-marked earthy multitudes are come
To breathe their hour like me.

The leaf comes curling down,
Another and another, gleam on gleam;
Above, celestial leafage glistens on,
Borne by time's blue stream.

The meadow- stream will serve
For my refreshment; that high glory yields
Imaginings that slay; the safe paths curve
Through unexalted fields

Like these, where now no more
My early angels walk and call and fly,
But the mouse stays his nibbling, to explore
My eye with his bright eye.

Sacheverell Sitwell

Sacheverell Sitwell, brother of Edith and Osbert Sitwell, was born in 1897 at Scarborough and educated at Eton. As soon as he was of military age, he joined the Grenadier Guards as second lieutenant. After the War he attended Balliol College, Oxford, for a short time, but came to London before completing his courses, confining his activities to literature.

From the first, his poetry was experimental, but even the early *The People's Palace* contained his gesture. *The Hundred and One Harlequins* (1922) and *The Thirteenth Caesar* (1924) are less dependent on influences, although the accents of such dissimilar poets as Vachel Lindsay and T. S. Eliot arise from his pages. Here the youngest of the Sitwells displays a lively imagination, a delight in toying with the subject as well as distorting it, a glittering, if sometimes too self-conscious, cleverness.

His more recent work shows him milder in manner and idiom. Less distinctive than his strepitant sister and brother, he seems to be developing a more traditional vein. His larger efforts would seem to dispute this; "Canons of Giant Art" and "Doctor Donne and Gargantua" are exercises in the approved modern manner. But they are not the poet. Try as he will with all the resources of the brain, his art is not in them. His art (and for that manner his heart) finds its response in unaffected song, a group of twenty-five lyrics being the core of *The Cyder Feast* (1927). Apart from a dissonance or two, an inverted image, a strained or dislocated adjective, these horticultural verses might have been written in the eighteenth century.

It is curious to note how the more modern "modernists" turn their eyes not to formless futurism, but to a precise past. Thus we find T. S. Eliot rediscovering Dryden and Lancelot Andrewes, Humbert Wolfe looting the Greek Anthology, Edith Sitwell turning from Gertrude Stein and Dr. Steiner to pen an introduction to the didactic rhymes of Jane Taylor. And here, in *The Cyder Feast,* in the midst of the "alchemy of dank leaves," one finds the youngest Sitwell writing "Four Variations upon William Browne of Tavistock," "Variations on a Theme by Robert Herrick," "Variation upon a Couplet of Alexander Pope," "An Adaption from John Milton." Moreover most of the poems not adapted or "varied" betray accents of a period that is scarcely Sitwellian. "Tulip Tree" and "Kingcups" are two examples among many. *Canons of Giant Art* (1933) continues the classical "heroic" strain.

The eruption of a kind of architectural fancy is natural in one who has established himself as an authority on the genesis of the rococo, notably in *Southern Baroque Art* (1924), *German Baroque Art* (1927), and *The Gothick North* (1929). *Selected Poems* (1948) was introduced with a proud preface by Osbert Sitwell.

FOUNTAINS

This night is pure and clear as thrice refinèd silver.
Silence, the cape of Death, lies heavy
Round the bare shoulders of the hills.
Faint throbs and murmurs

At moments growing to a mutter, then subsiding,
Fill the night with mystery and panic.
The honey-tongued arguings of fountains
Stir the air with flutes and gentle voices.

The graven fountain-masks suffer and weep—
Curved with a smile, the poor mouths
Clutch at a half-remembered song
Striving to forget the agony of ever laughing,—
Laughing while they hear the secrets
Echoed from the depths of Earth beneath them.

This half-remembered song—
This flow of sad-restrainèd laughter
Jars with the jets of youthful water
Springing from the twisted masks,
For this is but the birth of water;
And singing joyfully
It springs upon the world
And wanders ceaselessly
Along its jeweled valleys to the sea,
Rattling like rolls of drums
The shells and pebbles down its bed.

The endless argument of water ceases,
A few drops fall heavily, splashing on the marble:
A Sultan with his treasures
Seeking to gain the goodwill of his love,
Pouring before her chains of crackling pearls
And weeping heavy jealous tears
Because she will not heed him.

THE RED-GOLD RAIN

(*Orange Tree by Day*)

Sun and rain at work together
Ripened this for summer weather;
Sun gave it color tawny red
And rain its life as though it bled;
In the long days full of fire
Its fruit will cool us when we tire.
Against the house-wall does it grow
With smooth stem like a fountain's flow,
Dark are its leaves, a colder shade
Than ever rock or mountain made;
When the wind plays soft they sing,
For here the birds' songs never ring,
Quite still the fruit that in a golden shower
Will fall one day to flood this tower.

"PSITTACHUS EOIS IMITATRIX ALES AB INDIS"—*Ovid*

The parrot's voice snaps out—
No good to contradict—
What he says he'll say again:
Dry facts, like biscuits,—

His voice and vivid colors
Of his breast and wings
Are immemorably old;
Old dowagers dressed in crimpèd satin
Boxed in their rooms
Like specimens beneath a glass
Inviolate—and never changing,
Their memory of emotions dead:
The ardor of their summers

Sprayed like camphor
On their silken parasols
Intissued in a cupboard.

Reflective, but with never a new thought
The parrot sways upon his ivory perch—
Then gravely turns a somersault
Through rings nailed in the roof—
Much as the sun performs his antics
As he climbs the aerial bridge
We only see
Through crystal prisms in a falling rain.

TULIP TREE

Whose candles light the tulip tree?
What is this subtle alchemy,
That builds an altar in one night
And touches the green boughs with light?
Look at the shaped leaves below
And see the scissor-marks they show,
As if a tailor had cut fine
The marking of their every line!

These are no leaves of prudery
Hiding what all eyes should see;
No Adam and no Eve lie hid
Below this leafy coverlid:
The long limbs of that flower-hid girl
Would need no leaves to twist and curl,
The markings of that leaf-hid boy
Want no flowers to mar and cloy.

And so these cut leaves and their lights
Live only for the tulip-rites
At this altar of bright fires
Sweet-scented lest their ardor tires;
Leaf, and flower, and scent are all
Alive for this lit interval:
Between two winters are they born
To make great summer seem forlorn.

KINGCUPS

When poetry walked the live, spring wood
Hid, ghostlike, in the leaves' green hood
She came to a slant fence of sun,
Whose golden timbers, one by one,
Trod into a marsh's toils
And here she stayed her flowery spoils;
But pitying the marshes' plight
She shook her lap and wide and bright
Great kingcups to that waste she threw
Where nothing lived and nothing grew;
Now, where poetry passed, there stays
The light of suns, the fire of days,
And these cups for kings to hold
Make summer with their wide-eyed gold.

THE RIVER GOD

Leap out, chill water, over reeds and brakes,
Flash bright your sword
Out of my hand that never shakes,
Your voice rings louder than my whispered word,
For my song is but a murmur down the wind and water
No louder than the leaves that make my chequered shade,
Cooling the bank on which I'm laid.
My urn I move not, lest the blade may break,
Its round lip no more dropping water,
When this, my river, at its source will die
And sinking through the sand will bare each daughter,
Born of this glassy world, though now they lie
On the green bank high above that falling flood,
And wait like snow for sun or rain to move them.
I could not help them, were my stream to stop,
Until it springs again from out my urn,
But now it floods the pool and wells up high,
Sparkling like the sun's gold eye,

While from this plenitude it flows away
And hides those nymphs again below its glass.
Heaped on the hills, till with the sun they flow,
Safe runs the river now made sure with snow,
Snow, as those nymphs cool, as white my locks,
Which, while they also fall, tell time like clocks.

FROM "AGAMEMNON'S TOMB"

One by one, as harvesters, all heavy laden,
The bees sought their corridor into the dome
With honey of the asphodel, the flower of death,
Or thyme, rain-sodden, and more sweet for that;
Here was their honeycomb, high in the roof,
I heard sweet summer from their drumming wings,
Though it wept and rained and was the time of tears;
They made low music, they murmured in the tomb,
As droning nuns through all a shuttered noon,
Who prayed in this place of death, and knew it not.

How sweet such death, with honey from the flowers,
A little air, a little light, and drone of wings,
To long monotony, to prison of the tomb!
But he did not know it. His bones, picked clean,
Were any other bones. The trick is in our mind:
They love not a bed, nor raiment for their bones,
They are happy on cold stone or in the aching water,
And neither care, nor care not, they are only dead.
It once was Agamemnon, and we think him happy:
O false, false hope! How empty his happiness,
All for a fine cavern and the hum of bees.

Ruth Pitter

Ruth Pitter was born in Ilford, a village in the Essex forest, November 7, 1897. Daughter of a schoolteacher, she was educated at Coborn School, Bow, London. There (to continue her informal autobiographical note) she learned to cook "and got a certain amount of natural science, and a faint but indelible smear of Latin. Matriculated, and as war came when I was nearly through my Intermediate Arts year, and I had no predilections as regards a career, I went to the War Office and worked for nearly two years at 25 shillings a week." The first World War over, Miss Pitter learned woodwork and painting, went into business, and made a specialty of hand-painted trays. The second World War bombed her shop out of existence.

Ruth Pitter wrote verse at the age of five and published her first book in her twenty-third year. She never had a large popular success, although she was continually acclaimed by her fellow poets. *A Trophy of Arms* (1936) was prefaced by

James Stephens; *A Mad Lady's Garland* (1935) carried two introductions, one by Hilaire Belloc and the other by the poet laureate John Masefield. Beset by increasing difficulties and an ungenial mental climate, Miss Pitter steadfastly refused to dramatize her conflicts. Calm, even dream-like, the surface of her poetry is deceptive. The texture is smooth and graceful; the idiom is quietly conventional; the statements are seemingly casual. But the craftsmanship is unusually disciplined, and the tone is unmistakably the tone of a high order of poetry.

The Spirit Watches (1940) indicates a firm control of fluid material as well as constant growth. The fanciful soliloquies have changed to intense meditations, the mocking parodies have turned into earnest wit. Miss Pitter is that rare thing: a mystic with a sense of humor, an initiate whose revelations are immediate, eager, and seldom arcane. *The Ermine* (1953) received the Heinemann Foundation Award, and in 1955 Miss Pitter was awarded the Queen's Gold Medal for Poetry.

THE TASK

Reverse the flight of Lucifer,
Hurl back to heaven the fallen star;
Recall Eve's fate, establish her
Again where the first glories are:
Again where Eden's rivers are.

Thrust back contention, merge in one
Warring dualities, make free
Night of the moon, day of the sun;
End the old war of land and sea,
Saying, There shall be no more sea.

With love of love now make an end;
Let male and female strive no more;
Let good and bad their quarrel mend
And with an equal voice adore;
The lion with the lamb adore.

Bow softly saint, rise humble sin,
Fall from your throne, creep from your den:
The king, the kingdom is within,
That is for evermore, amen:
Was dead and is alive. Amen.

THE COFFIN-WORM

The Worm unto his love: lo, here's fresh store;
Want irks us less as men are pinched the more.
Why dost thou lag? thou pitiest the man?
Fall to, the while I teach thee what I can.
Men in their lives full solitary be:
We are their last and kindest company.
Lo, where care's claws have been! those marks are grim;
Go, gentle Love, erase the scar from him.
Hapless perchance in love (most men are so),
Our quaint felicity he could not know:
We and our generation shall sow love
Throughout that frame he was not master of;
Flatter his wishful beauties; in his ear
Whisper he is at last beloved here;
Sing him (and in no false and siren strain)
We will not leave him while a shred remain
On his sweet bones. Then shall our labor cease,
And the imperishable part find peace,
Even from love. Meanwhile how blest he lies,
Love in his heart, his empty hands, his eyes.

THE UNICORN

Hate me or love, I care not, as I pass
To those hid citadels
Where in the depth of my enchanted glass
The changeless image dwells;
To where for ever blooms the nameless tree;
For ever, alone and fair,
The lovely Unicorn beside the sea
Is laid, and slumbers there.

Give or withhold, all's nothing, as I go
On to those glimmering grounds
Where falling secretly and quiet as snow
The silent music sounds;
Where earth is withered away before the
eyes,
And heaven hangs in the air,
For in the oak the bird of paradise
Alights, and triumphs there.

Slay me or spare, it matters now: I fly
Ever, for ever rest
Alone and with a host: in the void sky
There do I build my nest:
I lay my beams from star to star, and make
My house where all is bare;
Hate, slay, withhold, I rear it for thy sake
And thou art with me there.

THE ETERNAL IMAGE

Her angel looked upon God's face
As eagles gaze upon the sun,
Fair in the everlasting place.

And saw that everything is one
And moveless, in the eternal light:
Never completed, not begun.

She on the earth, with steadfast sight,
Stood like an image of the Muse
Amid the falling veils of night:

Her feet were silvered in the dews,
Dew fell upon her darkling tree,
And washed the plain with whitish hues.

Standing so still, what does she see?
She sees the changeless creature shine
Apparelled in eternity:

She knows the constancy divine;
The whole of life sees harvested,
And frozen into crystalline

And final form, the quick, the dead,
All that has ever seemed to change,
Possess at once the pale and red:

All that from birth to death may range
Newborn and dead she sees, nor says
The vision to be sad or strange.

How may this serve her mortal ways?
Truly it cannot buy her bread
Nor ease the labor of her days:

But calm her waking, quiet her bed.
For she has seen the perfect round
That binds the infant to the dead,

And one by one draws underground
All men; and still, and one by one,
Into the air the living bound,

Never completed, not begun.
With burning hair, with moveless grace,
As eagles gaze against the sun

Her angel looks upon God's face.

TIME'S FOOL

Time's fool, but not heaven's: yet hope not for any return.
The rabbit-eaten dry branch and the halfpenny candle
Are lost with the other treasure: the sooty kettle
Thrown away, become redbreast's home in the hedge, where the nettle
Shoots up, and bad bindweed wreathes rust-fretted handle.
Under that broken thing no more shall the dry branch burn.

Poor comfort all comfort: once what the mouse had spared
Was enough, was delight, there where the heart was at home;
The hard cankered apple holed by the wasp and the bird,
The damp bed, with the beetle's tap in the headboard heard,
The dim bit of mirror, three inches of comb:
Dear enough, when with youth and with fancy shared.

I knew that the roots were creeping under the floor,
That the toad was safe in his hole, the poor cat by the fire,
The starling snug in the roof, each slept in his place:
The lily in splendor, the vine in her grace,
The fox in the forest, all had their desire,
As then I had mine, in the place that was happy and poor.

THE SWAN BATHING

Now to be clean he must abandon himself
To that fair yielding element whose lord he is.
There where she is strongest, in mid-current,
Facing the stream, he half sinks, who knows how?
His armed head, his prow wave-worthy, he dips under:
The meeting streams glide rearward, fill the hollow
Of the proud wings; then as if fainting he falls sidelong,
Prone, without shame, reveals the shiplike belly,
Tumbling reversed, with limp black paddles waving,
And down, gliding abandoned, helplessly wallows,
The head and neck, wrecked mast and pennon, trailing.

It is enough: satisfied he rears himself,
Sorts with swift movement his disordered tackle,
Rises, again the master: and so seated
Riding, he spreads his wings and flogs the water
Lest she should triumph; in a storm of weeping
And a great halo of her tears transfigured,
With spreading circles of his force he smites her,
Till remote tremblings heave her rushy verges
And all her lesser lives are rocked with rumour.

Now they are reconciled; with half-raised pinion
And backward-leaning head pensively sailing,

With silver furrow the reflected evening
Parting, he softly goes; and one cold feather
Drifts, and is taken gently by the rushes:
By him forgotten, and by her remembered.

Richard Hughes

Richard Hughes was born in 1900 of a Welsh family settled in England. Educated at Charterhouse School and Oriel College, Oxford, his first play, *The Sisters' Tragedy,* was produced in London in 1922 while Hughes was still an undergraduate. In the same year, his first volume of poems, *Gypsy-Night,* appeared and before he graduated he was poetry-critic to the London *Saturday Westminster* and contributor to leading periodicals. He traveled extensively in Europe, North Africa, and America, often on foot, and has, he confesses, "a slight amateur knowledge of Balkan revolutions and seamanship."

Hughes began his career as a poet although his reputation was made by two dramas. The first of these has been mentioned; the other, composed in his twenties, was a comedy praised by Shaw and selected with works of Chekhov and Pirandello as "one of the three most important productions in London in seven years."

Gypsy-Night (1922) marked the début of a poet with acute sensibility, a precocious apprehension emphasized by the short stories in *A Moment of Time* (1925). After a silence of three years, Hughes published his first full-length novel, *The Innocent Voyage* (1929), published in England as *A High Wind in Jamaica.* This tale is an accomplishment in an untried genre. Upon a basis of traditional melodrama, including pirates and kidnaping, Hughes has constructed a story wholly unexpected, an unromantic romance, where the psychological reënforces the fantastic and where the union of cut-throats and children is convincing, delicate and, at the same time, horrible. Modern writing has produced several techniques for dealing fancifully with the commonplace; Hughes has developed a realistic way of handling the extraordinary.

This gift of familiarizing the unusual is of paramount service to his poetry. Chekhov counseled writers to cease being insincere about the moon and say what they really felt about a rain-puddle. But, Hughes implies, one can also be faithful to subject and self, when writing about the moon, or the mad immortal unicorn, or the elephant-swallowing roc, or inditing meditative and ecstatic odes to vision, or transfixing the windlike passing of Time. Such subjects brighten the pages of *Confessio Juvenis* (1926) which, as its title indicates, collects Hughes' early work. But if it is a poet's eye which rolls toward these strangenesses, it is his mind which carries them off in a fine frenzy.

Besides three privately printed volumes, Hughes is the author of some seven books. His collected *Plays* were issued in 1928 and his edition of John Skelton's poems appeared in 1924. *In Hazard* (1938) emphasizes his gift for fantastic fiction.

INVOCATION TO THE MUSE

Fair maiden, fair maiden,
  Come spin for me:
Come spin till you're laden
  Though hard it may be.

'Tis an honor and glory
  To be a king's maid,
Though (I'll not tell a story)
  You won't be well paid.
Aetat. 6

TRAMP

(The Bath Road, June)

When a brass sun staggers above the sky,
When feet cleave to boots, and the tongue's dry,
And sharp dust goads the rolling eye
Come thoughts of wine and dancing thoughts of girls:
They shiver their white arms, and the head whirls,
And noon light is hid in their dark curls;
Then noon feet stumble, and head swims,
Till out shines the sun, and the thought dims;
And death, for blood, runs in the weak limbs.

To fall on flints in the shade of tall nettles
Gives easy sleep as a bed of rose petals,
And dust drifting from the highway
As light a coverlet as down may.
The myriad feet of many-sized flies
May not open those tired eyes.

But the first wind of night
Twitches the coverlet away quite:
The first wind and large first rain,
Flickers the dry pulse to life again,
Flickers the lids burning on the eyes:
Come sudden flashes of the slipping skies:
Hunger, oldest visionary,
Hides a devil in a tree,
Hints a glory in the clouds,
Fills the crooked air with crowds
Of ivory sightless demons singing—
Eyes start: straightens back:
Limbs stagger and crack:
But brain flies, brain soars
Up, where the Sky roars
Upon the backs of cherubim:
Brain rockets up to Him.

Body gives another twist
To the slack waist-band;
In agony clenches fist
Till the nails bite the hand.
Body floats light as air,
With rain in its sparse hair.

Brain returns; and he would tell
The things he has seen well:

But Body will not stir his lips:
So Mind and Body come to grips
And deadly each hates the other
As his treacherous blood-brother.

Yet no sight, no sound shows
How the struggle goes.

I sink at last faint in the wet gutter;
So many words to speak that the tongue cannot utter.

LOVER'S REPLY TO GOOD ADVICE

Could you bid an acorn
When in earth it heaves
On Time's backward wing be borne
To forgotten leaves:
Could you quiet Noah's flood
To an essence rare,
Or bid the roaring wind
Confine in his lair:

Could round the iron shell
When the spark was in it
Hold gun-powder so well
That it never split:
Had you reins for the sun,
And curb and spur,
Held you God in a net
So He might not stir:

Then might you take this thing,
Then strangle it, kill:
By weighing, considering,
Conform it to will:
As man denied his Christ
Deny it, mock, betray—
But being Seed, Wind, God,
It bears all away.

ON TIME

Unhurried as a snake I saw Time glide
Out of the shape of his material frame:
I, who am part of Time's material name,
Saw that unhurried serpent quietly slide
Through a straight crack in his material side
Between a prince and a stone: flicker, and presently coil,
A small bright worm about a stalk of fennel;
While light stood still as spar, and smell
Spread like a fan, sound hung festooned, and toil
Rose balanced and patterned like a storied palace
Whose wild tons grapple in immovable grace;
While laughter sat on a rustic seat with tears
And watched the corn-sheaves lean across the plow:
Ah! then what wind across the nodding years!
What ecstasies upon the bough
Sang, like a fountain to its peers:
And in the meadows what deep-rooted men
Flowered their lovely faces in the grass,
Where death, like a butterfly of dark-colored glass,
Flitted and sipped, and sipped again!

BURIAL OF THE SPIRIT OF A YOUNG POET

Dead hangs the fruit on that tall tree:
The lark in my cold hand is dead.
What meats his funeral stars decree
By their own light I've spread:
The bearded fog among the leaves
Too sad to move, excludes the air:
No bursting seed this stiff soil heaves,
Nor ever will again, when we have laid him there.

Then come, ye silent wheels of fire,
Ye birds among the tulip-trees,
And let your brilliancy conspire
In rings of visual threnodies:
And thou, heart-breaking nightingale
Who phoenix-like forever burnst
In thine own voice, oh Philomel
Let not thy tuneful flame now fail,
But burn in it this spirit pale
Which once was grand, but now to naught, to nothing-naught returns.

Roy Campbell

Roy Campbell was born October 2, 1901, in Durban, South Africa. A tempestuous figure, he was an editor discharged for his opinions, a professional steer-thrower and bull-fighter, a soldier under Franco, a Free-thinker who became a Fascist and, subsequently, a Roman Catholic. He died in an automobile smashup in Portugal, April 24, 1957.

The Flaming Terrapin appeared in 1922. It was at once apparent that a poet of unusual vitality had come out of the Colonies. Campbell had chosen a huge theme and he had sufficient vigor to cope with it. The poem is a broad allegory: The ark of Noah plunges through terror and tempest carrying with it all of humanity. Unlike the Biblical vessel, this ark does not merely float; it is pulled along, swept to its goal by a tremendous saurian, blood brother to Leviathan, a Flaming Terrapin, which is the symbol of the all-suffering, all-surviving power of persistence. It is this monster, the life-force, which brings the ark to a richer Ararat.

So much for the theme. The reader, however, is scarcely aware of the philosophic content, for the lines sweep him on at such a pace that he is conscious of little except the momentum of the verse, the bright concatenation of figures, and a general sense of exuberance. The headlong speed may be accounted a vice, but Campbell's poetic vices and virtues are inseparable. Both proceed from prodigality; epithet and emotion rush forward in continual and creative excitement.

The Wayzgoose (1928) is a more local and less arousing work. Satirizing conditions in South Africa, it limits not only Campbell's audience but his own spirit, for this poet needs amplitude for his effects. The subsequent poetry is in the early, gustier vein with a new control. "Tristan Da Cunha" and "The Palm" display less alacrity and violence than *The Flaming Terrapin,* but contain much of its lavish energy. "The Palm" is particularly successful in its combinations of assonance and interior rhyming. In addition, the new poems have a condensed power which dignifies the sometimes too crashing effects in *Adamastor* (1930), the satirical "Charlotade," *The Georgiad* (1931), and *Flowering Reeds* (1933). They still suffer from the poet's uncertainty; undecided whether to be a satirist or a poet in the grand manner, Campbell fell back upon sonority and his own dynamic energy.

THE ZEBRAS

From the dark woods that breathe of fallen showers,
Harnessed with level rays in golden reins,
The zebras draw the dawn across the plains
Wading knee-deep among the scarlet flowers.
The sunlight, zithering their flanks with fire,
Flashes between the shadows as they pass
Barred with electric tremors through the grass
Like wind along the gold strings of a lyre.

Into the flushed air snorting rosy plumes
That smolder round their feet in drifting fumes,

With dove-like voices call the distant fillies,
While round the herds the stallion wheels his flight,
Engine of beauty volted with delight,
To roll his mare among the trampled lilies.

TRISTAN DA CUNHA

Snore in the foam: the night is vast and blind,
The blanket of the mist around your shoulders,
Sleep your old sleep of rock, snore in the wind,
Snore in the spray! The storm your slumber lulls,
His wings are folded on your nest of bowlders
As on their eggs the gray wings of your gulls.

No more as when, ten thousand years ago,
You hissed a giant cinder from the ocean—
Around your rocks you furl the shawling snow,
Half sunk in your own darkness, vast and grim,
And round you on the deep with surly motion
Pivot your league-long shadow as you swim.

Why should you haunt me thus but that I know
My surly heart is in your own displayed,
Round whom such wastes in endless circuit flow,
Whose hours in such a gloomy compass run
A dial with its league-long arm of shade
Slowly revolving to the moon and sun.

My heart has sunk, like your gray fissured crags,
By its own strength o'ertoppled and betrayed:
I too have burned the wind with fiery flags,
Who now am but a roost for empty words—
An island of the sea whose only trade
Is in the voyages of its wandering birds.

Did you not, when your strength became your pyre,
Deposed and tumbled from your flaming tower,
Awake in gloom from whence you sank in fire
To find Antaeus-like, more vastly grown,
A throne in your own darkness, and a power
Sheathed in the very coldness of your stone?

Your strength is that you have no hope or fear,
You march before the world without a crown:
The nations call you back, you do not hear:
The cities of the earth grow gray behind you,
You will be there when their great flames go down
And still the morning in the van will find you.

You march before the continents: you scout
In front of all the earth: alone you scale
The masthead of the world, a lorn look-out,

Waving the snowy flutter of your spray
And gazing back in infinite farewell
To suns that sink, and shores that fade away.

From your gray tower what long regrets you fling
To where, along the low horizon burning,
The great swan-breasted seraphs soar and sing,
And suns go down, and trailing splendors dwindle,
And sails on lonely errands unreturning,
Glow with a gold no sunrise can rekindle.

Turn to the Night, these flames are not for you
Whose steeple for the thunder swings its bells:
Gray Memnon, to the tempest only true,
Turn to the night, turn to the shadowing foam,
And let your voice, the saddest of farewells,
With sullen curfew toll the gray wings home.

The wind your mournful syren haunts the gloom:
The rocks, spray-clouded, are your signal-guns
Whose stony niter, puffed with flying spume
Rolls forth in grim salute your broadside hollow,
Over the gorgeous burials of suns,
To sound the tocsin of the storms that follow.

Plunge forward; like a ship to battle hurled,
Slip the long cables of the failing light,
The level rays that moor you to the world:
Sheathed in your armor of eternal frost,
Plunge forward, in the thunder of the fight
To lose yourself as I would fain be lost.

Exiled, like you, and severed from my race
By the cold ocean of my own disdain,
Do I not freeze in such a wintry space,
Do I not travel through a storm as vast
And rise at times, victorious from the main,
To fly the sunrise at my shattered mast?

Your path is but a desert where you reap
Only the bitter knowledge of your soul,
You fish with nets of seaweed in the deep
As fruitlessly as I with nets of rhyme,
Yet forth you stride: yourself the way, the goal,
The surges are your strides, your path is time.

Hurled by what aim to what tremendous range!
A missile from the great sling of the past
Your passage leaves its track of death and change
And ruin on the world: you fly beyond,
Leaping the current of the ages vast
As lightly as a pebble skims a pond.

The years are undulations in your flight
Whose awful motion we can only guess:
Too swift for sense, too terrible for sight,
We only know how fast behind you darken
Our days like lonely beacons of distress:
We know that you stride on and will not hearken.

Now in the eastern sky the fairest planet
Pierces the dying wave with dangled spear,
And in the whirring hollows of your granite
That vaster Sea, to which you are a shell,
Sighs with a ghostly rumor like the drear
Moan of the nightwind in a hollow cell.

We shall not meet again: over the wave
Our ways divide, and yours is straight and endless—
But mine is short and crooked to the grave:
Yet what of these dark crowds, amid whose flow
I battle like a rock, aloof and friendless—
Are not their generations, vague and endless,
The waves, the strides, the feet on which I go?

FROM "THE FLAMING TERRAPIN"

Part I

Maternal Earth stirs redly from beneath
Her blue sea-blanket and her quilt of sky,
A giant Anadyomene from the sheath
And chrysalis of darkness; till we spy
Her vast barbaric haunches, furred with trees,
Stretched on the continents, and see her hair
Combed in a surf of fire along the breeze
To curl about the dim sierras, where
Faint snow-peaks catch the sun's far-swiveled beams:
And, tinder to his rays, the mountain-streams
Kindle, and volleying with a thunder-stroke
Out of their roaring gullies, burst in smoke
To shred themselves as fine as women's hair,
And hoop gay rainbows on the sunlit air.
Winnowed by radiant eagles, in whose quills
Sing the swift gales, and on whose waving plumes
Flashing sunbeams ignite—the towering hills
Yearn to the sun, rending the misty fumes
That clogged their peaks, and from each glistening spire
Fling to the winds their rosy fleece of fire.
Far out to sea the gales with savage sweep
Churning the water, waken drowsy fins
Huge fishes to propel from monstrous sleep,
That spout their pride as the red day begins,
"We are the great volcanoes of the deep!"

Now up from the intense creative Earth
Spring her strong sons: the thunder of their mirth
Vibrates upon the shining rocks and spills
In floods of rolling music on the hills.
Action and flesh cohere in one clean fusion
Of force with form: the very ethers breed
Wild harmonies of song: the frailest reed
Holds shackled thunder in its heart's seclusion.
And every stone that lines my lonely way,
Sad tongueless nightingale without a wing,
Seems on the point of rising up to sing
And donning scarlet for its dusty gray!

How often have I lost this fervent mood,
And gone down dingy thoroughfares to brood
On evils like my own from day to day;
"Life is a dusty corridor," I say,
"Shut at both ends." But far across the plain,
Old Ocean growls and tosses his gray mane,
Pawing the rocks in all his old unrest
Or lifting lazily on some white crest
His pale foam-feathers for the moon to burn—
Then to my veins I feel new sap return,
Strength tightens up my sinews long grown dull,
And in the old charred crater of the skull
Light strikes the slow somnambulistic mind
And sweeps her forth to ride the rushing wind,
And stamping on the hill-tops high in air,
To shake the golden bonfire of her hair.

This sudden strength that catches up men's souls
And rears them up like giants in the sky,
Giving them fins where the dark ocean rolls,
And wings of eagles when the whirlwinds fly,
Stands visible to me in its true self
(No spiritual essence of wing'd elf
Like Ariel on the empty winds to spin).
I see him as a mighty Terrapin,
Rafting whole islands on his stormy back,
Built of strong metals molten from the black
Roots of the inmost earth: a great machine,
Thoughtless and fearless, governing the clean
System of active things: the winds and currents
Are his primeval thoughts: the raging torrents
Are moods of his, and men who do great deeds
Are but the germs his awful fancy breeds.

For when the winds have ceased their ghostly speech
And the long waves roll moaning from the beach,
The Flaming Terrapin that towed the Ark
Rears up his hump of thunder on the dark,

And like a mountain, seamed with rocky scars,
Crinkles white rings, as from its ancient sleep
Into a foam of life he wakes the Deep.
His was the crest that from the angry sky
Tore down the hail: he made the bowlders fly
Like balls of paper, splintered icebergs, hurled
Lassoes of dismal smoke around the world,
And like a bunch of crisp and crackling straws,
Coughed the sharp lightning from his craggy jaws.
His was the eye that blinked beyond the hill
After the fury of the flood was done,
And breaching from the bottom, cold and still,
Leviathan reared up to greet the Sun.
Perched on the stars around him in the air,
White angels rinsed the moonlight from their hair,
And the drowned trees into new flowers unfurled
As it sank dreaming down upon the world.
As he rolled by, all evil things grew dim.
The Devil, who had scoffed, now slunk from him
And sat in Hell, dejected and alone,
Rasping starved teeth against an old dry bone.

Before the coral reared its sculptured fern
Or the pale shellfish, swinging in the waves
With pointed steeples, had begun to turn
The rocks to shadowy cities—from dark caves
The mixed and drowsy poisons of the sea
Mixed their corrosive strength with horny stones,
And coaxed new substances from them to be
The ponderous material of his bones.
The waves by slow erosion did their part
Shaping his heavy bonework from the mass,
And in that pillared temple grew a heart
That branched with mighty veins, through which to pass
His blood, that, filtering the tangled mesh,
Built walls of gristle, clogged each hollow gap
With concrete vigor, till through bone and flesh
Flowed the great currents of electric sap.
While thunder clanging from the cloudy rack
With elemental hammers fierce and red,
Tempered the heavy target of his back,
And forged the brazen anvil of his head.

Freed from the age-long agonies of birth
This living galleon oars himself along
And roars his triumph over all the earth
Until the sullen hills burst into song.
His beauty makes a summer through the land,
And where he crawls upon the solid ground,
Gigantic flowers, exploding from the sand,
Spread fans of blinding color all around.

His voice has roused the amorphous mud to life—
Dust thinks: and tired of spinning in the wind,
Stands up to be a man and feel the strife
Of brute-thoughts in the jungle of his mind.
Bellerophon, the primal cowboy, first
Heard that wild summons on the stillness burst,
As, from the dusty mesa leaping free,
He slewed his white-winged broncho out to sea,
And shaking loose his flaming coils of hair,
Shot whistling up the smooth blue roads of air:
As he rose up, the moon with slanted ray
Ruled for those rapid hoofs a shining way,
And streaming from their caves, the sirens came
Riding on seals to follow him: the flame
Of their moon-tinseled limbs had flushed the dim
Green depths, and as when winds in Autumn skim
Gold acres, rustling plume with fiery plume,
Their long hair flickered skyward in the gloom,
Tossed to the savage rhythms of their tune.
Till, far across the world, the rising moon
Heard, ghost-like, in the embered evening sky
Their singing fade into a husky sigh,
And splashed with stars and dashed with stinging spray
The dandy of the prairies rode away!

That voice on Samson's mighty sinews rang
As on a harp's tense chords: each fiber sang
In all his being: rippling their strings of fire,
His nerves and muscles, like a wondrous lyre,
Vibrated to that sound; and through his brain
Proud thoughts came surging in a georgeous train.
He rose to action, slew the grumbling bear,
Hauled forth the flustered lion from its lair
And swung him yelping skyward by the tail:
Tigers he mauled, with tooth and ripping nail
Rending their straps of fire, and from his track
Slithering like quicksilver, pouring their black
And liquid coils before his pounding feet,
He drove the livid mambas of deceit.
Oppression, like a starved hyena, sneaked
From his loud steps: Tyranny, vulture-beaked,
Rose clapping iron wings, and in a cloud
Of smoke and terror, wove its own dark shroud,
As he strode by and in his tossing hair,
Rippled with sunshine, sang the morning air.

Like a great bell clanged in the winds of Time,
Linking the names of heroes chime by chime
That voice rolled on, and as it filled the night
Strong men rose up, thrilled with the huge delight

Of their own energy. Upon the snows
Of Ararat gigantic Noah rose,
Stiffened for fierce exertion, like the thong
That strings a bow before its arrow strong
Sings on the wind; and from his great fists hurled
Red thunderbolts to purify the world.

THE PALM

Blistered and dry was the desert I trod
When out of the sky with the step of a god,
Victory-vanned with her feathers out-fanned,
The palm tree alighting my journey delayed
And spread me, inviting, her carpet of shade.
Vain were evasions, though urgent my quest,
And there as the guests of her lovely persuasions
To lie in the shade of her branches was best.
Like a fountain she played, spilling plume over plume in
A golden cascade for the winds to illumine,
Ascending in brilliance and falling in shade,
And spurning the ground with a tiptoe resilience
Danced to the sound of the music she made.
Her voice intervened on my shadowed seclusion
Like the whispered intrusion of seraph or fiend,
In its tone was the hiss of the serpent's wise tongue,
But soft as the kiss of a lover it stung—
"Unstrung is your lute? For despair are you silent?
Am I not an island in oceans as mute?
Around me the thorns of the desert take root;
Though I spring from the rock of a region accurst,
Yet fair is the daughter of hunger and thirst
Who sings like the water the valleys have nursed,
And rings her blue shadow as deep and as cool
As the heavens of azure that sleep on a pool.
And you, who so soon by the toil were undone,
Could you guess through what horrors my beauty had won
Ere I crested the noon as the bride of the sun?
The roots are my anchor struck fast in the hill,
The higher I hanker, the deeper they drill,
Through the red mortar their claws interlock
To ferret the water through warrens of rock.
Each inch of my glory was wrenched with a groan,
Corroded with fire from the base of my throne
And drawn like a wire from the heart of a stone:
Though I soar in the height with a shape of delight
Uplifting my stem like the string of a kite,
Yet still must each grade of my climbing be told
And still from the summit my measure I hold,
Sounding the azure with plummet of gold,
Partaking the strain of the heavenward pride
That soars me away from the earth I deride.

Though my stem be a rein that would tether me down
And fasten a chain on the height of my crown,
Yet through its tense nerve do I measure my might,
The strain of its curb is the strength of my flight:
And when by the hate of the hurricane blown
It doubles its forces with fibers that groan,
Exulting I ride in the tower of my pride
To feel that the strength of the blast is my own. . . .
Rest under my branches, breathe deep of my balm
From the hushed avalanches of fragrance and calm,
For suave is the silence that poises the palm.

The wings of the egrets are silken and fine,
But hushed with the secrets of Eden are mine:
Your spirit that grieves like the wind in my leaves
Shall be robbed of its care by those whispering thieves
To study my patience and hear, the day long,
The soft foliations of sand into song—
For bitter and cold though it rasp to my root,
Each atom of gold is the chance of a fruit,
The sap is the music, the stem is the flute,
And the leaves are the wings of the seraph I shape
Who dances, who springs in a golden escape,
Out of the dust and the drought of the plain,
To sing with the silver hosannahs of rain."

AUTUMN

I love to see, when leaves depart,
The clear anatomy arrive,
Winter, the paragon of art,
That kills all forms of life and feeling
Save what is pure and will survive.

Already now the clanging chains
Of geese are harnessed to the moon:
Stripped are the great sun-clouding planes:
And the dark pines, their own revealing,
Let in the needles of the noon.

Strained by the gale the olives whiten
Like hoary wrestlers bent with toil
And, with the vines, their branches lighten
To brim our vats where summer lingers
In the red froth and sun-gold oil.

Soon on our hearth's reviving pyre
Their rotted stems will crumble up:
And like a ruby, panting fire,
The grape will redden on your fingers
Through the lit crystal of the cup.

ON SOME SOUTH AFRICAN NOVELISTS

You praise the firm restraint with which they write—
  I'm with you there, of course.
They use the snaffle and the curb all right;
  But where's the bloody horse?

TOLEDO

July, 1936

Toledo, when I saw you die
And heard the roof of Carmel crash,
A spread-winged phoenix from its ash
The Cross remained against the sky!
With horns of flame and haggard eye
The mountain vomited with blood,
A thousand corpses down the flood
Were rolled gesticulating by.
And high above the roaring shells
I heard the silence of your bells
Who've left those broken stones behind
Above the years to make your home
And burn, with Athens and with Rome,
A sacred city of the mind.

FROM "THE GEORGIAD"

Hail, Mediocrity, beneath whose spell
Lion and fox as loving neighbors dwell:
For it is sweet with modesty to swell
When one has not a ghost of pride to quell.
Puffed up with modesty, the ambitious toad
May safely swell, and fear not to explode,
Until, ballooned with emptiness, he rise
To dwarf the ox he envies for his size.

THE SERF

His naked skin clothed in the torrid mist
That puffs in smoke around the patient hooves,
The ploughman drives, a slow somnambulist,
And through the green his crimson furrow grooves.
His heart, more deeply than he wounds the plain,
Long by the rasping share of insult torn,
Red clod, to which the war-cry once was rain
And tribal spears the fatal sheaves of corn,
Lies fallow now. But as the turf divides
I see in the slow progress of his strides
Over the toppled clods and falling flowers,
The timeless, surly patience of the serf
That moves the nearest to the naked earth
And ploughs down palaces, and thrones, and towers.

C. Day Lewis

C. (Cecil) Day Lewis was born April 27, 1904, at Ballintubber, Queens County, Ireland. He was educated at Sherbourne School and Wadham College, Oxford, where he became affiliated with Stephen Spender, W. H. Auden, and others of the post-war group. He taught at the Junior School of Cheltenham College and wrote with increasing rapidity and purpose.

There were two early publications (*Beechen Vigils* and *Country Comets*) which were derivative and received little attention. *Transitional Poem* (1929) is Day Lewis' first serious bid for notice. The early influences are not altogether discarded, but it is immediately evident that a new and indubitably lyric voice is being sounded. This is "nature poetry," but nature poetry sharply differentiated from the philosophic-meditative manner of Wordsworth and the tired detachment of the Georgians. Day Lewis is no mere onlooker, he is a passionate participant; there is courage as well as color in his lines, and even the awkward passages are redeemed by a challenging vision.

That vision is amplified, sometimes distorted, and finally explicated in *From Feathers to Iron* (1931) and *The Magnetic Mountain* (1933), both of which, with *Transitional Poem,* were assembled in *Poems 1929-1933,* published in America in 1935. Since the three young English poets were printed almost simultaneously in this country, Day Lewis was continually linked with Spender and Auden in the public press. Actually the so-called "triumvirate" was composed of three different types of poet. Auden is satirical, experimental, and often (except to those who understand his private parables) incomprehensible; Spender is rhapsodic, sometimes sentimental, and usually forthright; Lewis is almost continuously lyrical and candid. Although he, too, plays with internal rhyme and concealed assonance, he is less concerned than Auden with craftsmanship; although he shares Spender's political convictions, he does not lose himself, as Spender sometimes does, in emotion. Yet if he is the most dependable he is the least original of the three. He has not yet outgrown his influences; one does not have to read closely to recognize the accents of Gerard Manley Hopkins, Wilfred Owen, T. S. Eliot, most of all W. H. Auden, to all of whom C. Day Lewis pays credit. There are even moments (as in the poem "You'll be leaving soon and it's up to you boys") which sound strangely like Robert W. Service and Rudyard Kipling's "If" turned upside down. It should also be said that his social sentiments have little to do with the final effect of his poetry; it is, poetically speaking, unimportant that an author has chosen communism for his faith rather than a more popular conservatism. He knows that in the end a poet is measured by his poetry, not by his policies; that, although Southey was an ardent believer in the French Revolution, Southey means nothing to us, and readers of the *Ode on the Intimations of Immortality* do not care when or why Wordsworth ceased to be a liberal. But Day Lewis also knows that a poet must have a creed; and a belief in the dignity and possible brotherhood of man is certainly no more to be deplored than a belief in the sacredness of the Georgian Squirearchy and its incorporated nightingales. As a matter of record, the best of his poems are the least protesting ones.

Lewis continually fluctuates between a tradition which he distrusts, but in which he is quite at home, and a conviction which his mind applauds but his imagination has not yet fully accepted. From the conflict no less than half a dozen serene, illuminating, and indignant lyrics are born, lyrics which will find their way into even the most cautious anthologies. It is his certainties, coming after a generation of negativism, which matter, not his arbitrary symbols of "kestrel," "airman," and "magnetic mountain" (for imagination, poet, and the co-operative commonwealth). It is not the fighting figures and stretched metaphors, straining under the demands of their author, but the athletic belief, the alert spirit, which breaks through to music spontaneous and bitter-sweet.

A Time to Dance (1935) emphasizes this, although the title poem is something of a disappointment. It is ambitiously "symphonic," but it ends in a jumble of crude parodies, awkward as humor, ineffective as satire. Nevertheless, it apostrophizes the spirit—

For those who had the power,
Unhesitating whether to kill or cure:
Those who were not afraid
To dam the estuary or start the forest fire:
Whose hearts were filled
With enthusiasm as with a constant wind.

Short Is the Time (1944) and *Poems: 1933-1947* are often enthusiastic, sometimes exact, and occasionally electric—electricity being one of Lewis's favorite symbols. Lewis is always deft; his technique is almost as resourceful as Auden's, he employs the rhetorical flourish as roundly as Spender. The later poems extend his scope; they range all the way from mere exuberance to introspective autobiography. The lyrics are especially rewarding. If they frequently substitute energy for intensity, they are not without moral purpose and verbal power.

An unusually prolific author, Lewis has also written several serious novels, a penetrating book-length essay, *A Hope for Poetry* (1934), various textbooks and studies for young people, translations of Virgil's *Aeneid* and *Georgics,* part of an autobiography, *The Buried Day* (1960), and, under the pseudonym of Nicholas Blake, some sixteen skilfully plotted novels of crime and detection with such alluring titles as "A Penknife in My Heart," "The Widow's Cruise," "Malice in Wonderland," and "The Corpse in the Snowman."

NEARING AGAIN THE LEGENDARY ISLE

Nearing again the legendary isle
Where sirens sang and marines were skinned,
We wonder now what was there to beguile
That such stout fellows left their bones behind.

Those chorus-girls are surely past their prime,
Voices grow shrill and paint is wearing thin,
Lips that sealed up the sense from gnawing time
Now beg the favor with a graveyard grin.

We have no flesh to spare and they can't bite,
Hunger and sweat have stripped us to the bone;
A skeleton crew we toil upon the tide
And mock the theme-song meant to lure us on:

No need to stop the ears, avert the eyes
From purple rhetoric of evening skies.

REST FROM LOVING AND BE LIVING

Rest from loving and be living.
Fallen is fallen past retrieving
The unique flyer dawn's dove
Arrowing down feathered with fire.

Cease denying, begin knowing.
Comes peace this way, here comes renewing
With dower of bird and bud, knocks
Loud on winter wall on death's door.

Here's no meaning but of morning.
Naught soon of night but stars remaining,
Sink lower, fade, as dark womb
Recedes creation will step clear.

NOW SHE IS LIKE THE WHITE TREE-ROSE

Now she is like the white tree-rose
That takes a blessing from the sun:
Summer has filled her veins with light,
And her warm heart is washed with noon.

Or as a poplar, ceaselessly
Gives a soft answer to the wind:
Cool on the light her leaves lie sleeping,
Folding a column of sweet sound.

Powder the stars. Forbid the night
To wear those brilliants for a brooch
So soon, dark death, you may close down
The mines that made this beauty rich.

Her thoughts are pleiads, stooping low
O'er glades where nightingale has flown:
And like the luminous night around her
She has at heart a certain dawn.

DO NOT EXPECT AGAIN A PHOENIX HOUR

Do not expects again a phoenix hour,
The triple-towered sky, and dove complaining,
Sudden the rain of gold and heart's first ease
Tranced under trees by the eldritch light of sundown.

By a blazed trail our joy will be returning:
One burning hour throws light a thousand ways,
And hot blood stays into familiar gestures.
The best years wait, the body's plenitude.

Consider then, my lover, this is the end
Of the lark's ascending, the hawk's unearthly hover:
Spring season is over soon and first heatwave;
Grave-browed with cloud ponders the huge horizon.

Draw up the dew. Swell with pacific violence.
Take shape in silence. Grow as the clouds grew,
Beautiful brood the cornlands, and you are heavy;
Leafy the boughs—they also hide big fruit.

CHIEFLY TO MIND APPEARS

Chiefly to mind appears
That hour on Silverhowe
When evening's lid hung low
And the sky was about our ears.
Buoyed between fear and love
We watched in eastward form
The armadas of the storm
And sail superbly above;
So near, they'd split and founder
On the least jag of sense,
One false spark fire the immense
Broadside the confounding thunder.
They pass, give not a salvo,
And in their rainy wash
We hear the horizons crash
With monitors of woe.

Only at highest power
Can love and fear become
Their equilibrium,
And in that eminent hour
A virtue is made plain
Of passionate cleavage
Like the hills' cutting edge
When the sun sets to rain.
This is the single mind,
This is the star-solved equation
Of life with life's negation:
A deathless cell designed
To demonstrate death's act,
Which, the more surely it moves
To earth's influence, but proves
Itself the more intact.

TEMPT ME NO MORE

Tempt me no more; for I
Have known the lightning's hour,
The poet's inward pride,
The certainty of power.

Bayonets are closing round.
I shrink; yet I must wring
A living from despair
And out of steel a song

Though song, though breath be short,
I'll share not the disgrace
Of those that ran away
Or never left the base.

Comrades, my tongue can speak
No comfortable words;
Calls to a forlorn hope
Give work and not rewards.

Oh keep the sickle sharp
And follow still the plow:
Others may reap, though some
See not the winter through.

Father who endest all,
Pity our broken sleep;
For we lie down with tears
And waken but to weep.

And if our blood alone
Will melt this iron earth,
Take it. It is well spent
Easing a savior's birth.

THE CONFLICT

I sang as one
Who on a tilting deck sings
To keep their courage up, though the wave hangs
That shall cut off their sun.

As storm-cocks sing,
Flinging their natural answer in the wind's teeth,
And care not if it is waste of breath
Or birth-carol of spring.

As ocean-flyer clings
To height, to the last drop of spirit driving on
While yet ahead is land to be won
And work for wings.

Singing I was at peace,
Above the clouds, outside the ring:
For sorrow finds a swift release in song
And pride its poise.

Yet living here,
As one between two massing powers I live
Whom neutrality cannot save
Nor occupation cheer.

None such shall be left alive:
The innocent wing is soon shot down,
And private stars fade in the blood-red dawn
Where two worlds strive.

The red advance of life
Contracts pride, calls out the common blood,
Beats song into a single blade,
Makes a depth-charge of grief.

Move then with new desires,
For where we used to build and love
Is no man's land, and only ghosts can live
Between two fires.

WHEN THEY HAVE LOST

When they have lost the little that they looked for,
The poor allotment of ease, custom, fame:
When the consuming star their fathers worked for
Has guttered into death, a fatuous flame:
When love's a cripple, faith a bed-time story,
Hope eats her heart out and peace walks on knives,
And suffering men cry an end to this sorry
World of whose children want alone still thrives:
Then shall the mounting stages of oppression
Like mazed and makeshift scaffolding torn down
Reveal his unexampled, best creation—
The shape of man's necessity full-grown.
Built from their bone, I see a power-house stand
To warm men's hearts again and light the land.

NEWSREEL

Enter the dream-house, brothers and sisters, leaving
Your debts asleep, your history at the door:
This is the home for heroes, and this loving
Darkness a fur you can afford.

Fish in their tank electrically heated
Nose without envy the glass wall: for them
Clerk, spy, nurse, killer, prince, the great and the defeated,
Move in a mute day-dream.

Bathed in this common source, you gape incurious
At what your active hours have willed—
Sleep-walking on that silver wall, the furious
Sick shapes and pregnant fancies of your world.

There is the mayor opening the oyster season:
A society wedding: the autumn hats look well:
An old crock's race, and a politician
In fishing-waders to prove that all is well.

Oh, look at the warplanes! Screaming hysteric treble
In the long power-dive, like gannets they fall steep.
But what are they to trouble—
These silver shadows to trouble your watery, womb-deep sleep?

See the big guns, rising, groping, erected
To plant death in your world's soft womb,
Fire-bud, smoke-blossom, iron seed projected—
Are these exotics? They will grow nearer home:

Grow nearer home—and out of the dream-house stumbling
One night into a strangling air and the flung
Rags of children and thunder of stone niagaras tumbling,
You'll know you slept too long.

Peter Quennell

Peter Quennell was born March 5, 1905, in Kent. He was educated at Berkhamstead Grammar School and at Balliol College, Oxford, where he spent two years, and where he was co-editor of *Oxford Poetry*. He made "the customary pilgrimages" to Greece and the Balkans, and since 1927 has lived in London.

Poems (1926) appeared before Quennell was twenty-one years old, four of the poems being "very early"—"Procne," for example, having been written at the age of sixteen. Quennell's verse is wholly unlike that of his living compatriots, although American readers will detect a similarity to the verbal elegances of Wallace Stevens. It is as near the abstract as verse can come and still depend on words. Here language flowers of itself, feeding automatically on its own air; image suggests image, and associations grow freely on seemingly unrelated suggestions. In "The Divers" and "Leviathan," among others, the poetry wanders far from common experience or recognizable emotions or, for that matter, its own subject. But it is never less than poetry. Although the figures flowing into each other have the uncertain, fluid outlines of dream pictures, the musical progression is clear.

It is as music, first of all, that Quennell's poetry succeeds. His accomplishment is the greater since, without the aid of rhyme or definite rhythm, he achieves melodies intangible but more original than lightly summoned tunes. The actors in his verse are vague, the happenings remote and unreal, yet the intent is never false, and the effect is a set of nicely adjusted modulations and strange harmonics. It is, in essence, a poetry of shock, but shock without eccentricity, smoothed and almost without surprise.

As an essayist, Quennell has developed slowly but with increasing surety. His *Baudelaire and the Symbolists* (1930) contains five essays outlining the stream which sprang from Baudelaire and which swayed not only French literature but determined in no inconsiderable degree the course of English poetry during and after the Eighteen Nineties. *Sympathy* (1933) assembles his imaginative short stories.

Quennell made his most successful bid for popularity as biographer. Readers and reviewers united to praise the wit and vitality of his *Byron: The Years of Fame* (1935), the still more vivid *Byron in Italy* (1941), and *Four Portraits* (1945).

PROCNE

So she became a bird and bird-like danced
On a long sloe-bough, treading the silver blossom
With a bird's lovely feet,
And shaken blossoms fell into the hands
Of sunlight, and he held them for a moment
And let them drop.
And in the autumn Procne came again
And leapt upon the crooked sloe-bough singing
And the dark berries winked like earth-dimmed beads,
As the branch swung beneath her dancing feet.

THE DIVERS

Ah, look,
How sucking their last sweetness from the air
These divers run upon the pale sea verge;
An evening air so smooth my hand could round
And grope a circle of the hollow sky
Without a harshness or impediment.

Look now,
How they run cowering and each unknots
A rag, a girdle twisted on his loins,
Stands naked, quivered in the cool of night.

As boldest lovers will tire presently,
When dawn dries up a radiance on the limbs,
And lapse to common sleep,
To the deep tumult of habitual dreams,
Each sighing, with loosened limbs, as if regretfully,
Gives up his body to the foamless surge.

Water combs out his body, and he sinks
Beyond all form and sound.
Only the blood frets on,
Grown fearful, in a shallow dissonance.

Water strains on his hair and drums upon his flank,
Consumes his curious track
And straight or sinuous path
Dissolves as swift, impermanent as light.

Still his strange purpose drives him, like a beam,
Like the suspended shaft of cavern-piercing sun;
And, hardier still,
With wavering hands, divides the massive gloom,—
A vast caress through which he penetrates,
Or obscure death withdrawing
Veil upon veil,
Discovering new darkness and profounder terror.

"Consider you your loss,
For now what strength of foot or hand
Can take you by the narrow way you came
Through the clear darkness up again and up.
Watch a procession of the living days,
Where dawn and evening melt so soft together
As wine in water, or milk shed in water,
Filming and clouding into even dullness."

"Who weeps me now with pulse of noisy tears,
Who strikes the breast?
If I regret among the flowing weed,
My regret is
Not vocal, cannot pierce to hidden day,
Momentary, soon quenched, like a strangled flame."

LEVIATHAN

(Second Section)

A music met Leviathan returning,
While the still troubled waters of his passage
Danct every island like a lily head.
Through all the shadowed throats of the wide forest
His unnumbered monster children rode to greet him
On horses winged and dappled over like flowers.

Now huddled waves had lulled their bursting foam
And slight clouds laid their breasts upon the sea;
The sullen winds, head downward from the sky,
Solicited his movement on their viols.

And the palm trees, heat weary,
Chafing smooth limbs within a rinded shell,
Spoke of his coming with soft acclamation,
Like watchers long grown tired, languid and sorry:

"Look, how he comes"—as faint as whispering deer—
"What storm and state he brings." Then louder voices,
The unchaste turtles crying out with pleasure,
And badgers from the earth
Sprawled upon the rocks with animal laughter.

"The Cretan bull ferrying across the sea
Bore home no richer load;
In the reed forest of Eurotas' bank
That quivering swan, clapping strong wings together,
With harsh, sweet voice called out no keener marriage."

Then shrill response, as seeming from the air,
Invoking joy, summoning desire:

"Hither desires,
Coming as thick and hot as the press and hurry of blood
Striking the apse of the brain,
Ranging abroad, carrying your torches high,
Running as light and remote as a scattered cast of pearls."

Then antic spirits from the tulip trees:
"We must have tumblers like a wheel of fire.

We must have dancers moving their suave hands:
The tumblers strung backward like a hoop
Until they thrust vermilioned cheeks between their knees.
And the intricacy
Of sweet involving gayety,
And wine to warm our innocence,
Music to sooth the prickled sense,
Sounding like water or like ringing glass."

The mitered Queen of Heaven stirred on her broad, low throne,
Setting the lattice just so much ajar
That wandering airs from earth should cool the room,
Peered down on more-than-Leda and smoothed her wrinkled snood,
Crying to her Father-Spouse—"Dear Lord, how sweet she looks."
The clumsy hierarchies,
Wearied by their continual task of praise,
Rested wide heifer eyes upon her fallen lids.
Islanded in stars,
Even the keen Intelligences turned away
From the mathematic splendor of the spheres' incessant rolling chime.

Himself, the Father moved,
Traditional and vast,
Remembering fresher years,
Might have inclined his steeply pinnacled head,
But his more zealous son,
As neat as Thammuz, with smooth, pallid cheeks,
Sensing an evil, shut the casement fast.

*

But I, remembering Atlantis, wept,
Remembering her paths and unswept flowers,
Clean beaches, patterned by a light sea wrack,
And the ruined halcyon nests that came on shore.

Tears, in their freedom, cloud the eyes,
Drowsing the sense.
Honey and poppy equally mixed together,
They cannot drug away or curtain off with sleep
Such pitiless disharmony of shapes.

Patrick Kavanagh

Patrick Kavanagh, whom many consider the best Irish poet since Yeats, was born in 1905 in County Monaghan, Ireland. His schooling was brief. Educated at the National Elementary School until fourteen, he suffered from poverty and illness for a long time. He worked as a shoemaker (his father's trade) and as a small farmer until his mid-thirties, starved on free lance journalism through the Second World War, had cancer of the lung and recovered in his fiftieth year when the lung was removed. Among his other tribulations was a long lawsuit which he won in the end. Established as a writer, he became a lecturer at University College in Dublin, Joyce's university.

Besides his verse, Kavanagh is the author of *The Green Fool,* which he belittled as a "lying stage Irish autobiography," and *Tarry Flynn,* "a truthful work of fiction," which can be considered as his own story. It is, however, Kavanagh's poetry rather than his prose which gives him essential distinction. *A Soul for Sale* (1953) contains "Father Mat," "The Great Hunger," and other poems that display an original mind which, candid in expression, plays with humor and irony. *Come Dance with Kitty Strobling and Other Poems* (1960) is a richer and more rounded collection. Exuberant with a love for all the complexity and casualness of the actual world—"Nothing whatever is by love debarred"—he answers himself in "Question to Life":

> So be reposed and praise, praise praise
> The way it happened and the way it is.

Sometimes the spirit—"I will have love, have love / From anything"—recalls Hopkins', but Kavanagh has his own quiet, half-wild, half-whimsical voice. It is explicit in such poems as "The Self-Slaved," "Canal Bank Walk," "The One," "Question to Life," "Intimate Parnassus," and "Miss Universe," with its concluding high mockery:

> There are no recriminations in Heaven. O the sensual throb
> Of the explosive body, the tumultuous thighs!
> Adown a summer lane comes Miss Universe,
> She whom no lecher's art can rob,
> Though she is not a virgin who was wise.

No one can fail to detect the individual diction under what the London *Times Literary Supplement* characterized as "the mask of ease and diffidence, the digressive offhand manner, the poet murmuring to himself."

THE SELF-SLAVED

Me I will throw away.
Me sufficient for the day
The sticky self that clings
Adhesions on the wings.

To love and adventure,
To go on the grand tour
A man must be free
From self-necessity.

See over there
A created splendour
Made by one individual
From things residual
With all the various
Qualities hilarious
Of what
Hitherto was not:

A November mood
As by one man understood;
Familiar, an old custom
Leaves falling, a white frosting
Bringing a sanguine dream
A new beginning with an old theme.

Throw away thy sloth
Self, carry off my wrath
With its self-righteous
Satirising blotches.
No self, no self-exposure
The weakness of the proser
But undefeatable
By means of the beatable.

I will have love, have love
From anything made of
And a life with a shapely form
With gaiety and charm
And capable of receiving
With grace the grace of living
And wild moments too
Self when freed from you.
Prometheus calls me on.
Prometheus calls me: Son,
We'll both go off together
In this delightful weather.

CANAL BANK WALK

Leafy-with-love banks and the green waters of the canal
Pouring redemption for me, that I do
The will of God, wallow in the habitual, the banal,
Grow with nature again as before I grew.
The bright stick trapped, the breeze adding a third
Party to the couple kissing on an old seat,
And a bird gathering materials for the nest for the Word
Eloquently new and abandoned to its delirious beat.
O unworn world enrapture me, encapture me in a web
Of fabulous grass and eternal voices by a beech,
Feed the gaping need of my senses, give me ad lib
To pray unselfconsciously with overflowing speech
For this soul needs to be honoured with a new dress woven
From green and blue things and arguments that cannot be proven.

QUESTION TO LIFE

Surely you would not ask me to have known
Only the passion of primrose banks in May
Which are merely a point of departure for the play
And yearning poignancy when on their own.
Yet when all is said and done a considerable
Portion of living is found in inanimate
Nature, and a man need not feel miserable
If fate should have decided on this plan of it.
Then there is always the passing gift of affection
Tossed from the windows of high charity

In the office girl and civil servant section
And these are no despisable commodity.
So be reposed and praise, praise praise
The way it happened and the way it is.

THE ONE

Green, blue, yellow and red—
God is down in the swamps and marshes
Sensational as April and almost incredible the flowering of our catharsis.
A humble scene in a backward place
Where no one important ever looked
The raving flowers looked up in the face
Of the One and the Endless, the Mind that has baulked
The profoundest of mortals. A primrose, a violet,
A violent wild iris—but mostly anonymous performers
Yet an important occasion as the Muse at her toilet
Prepared to inform the local farmers
That beautiful, beautiful, beautiful God
Was breathing His love by a cut-away bog.

INTIMATE PARNASSUS

Men are what they are, and what they do
Is their own business. If they praise
The gods or jeer at them, the gods can not
Be moved, involved or hurt. Serenely
The citizens of Parnassus look on
As Homer tells us, and never laugh
When any mortal has joined the party.
What happens in the small towns—
Hate, love, envy—is not
The concern of the gods. The poet poor,
Or pushed around, or to be hanged, retains
His full reality; and his authority
Is bogus if the sonorous beat is broken
By disturbances in human hearts—his own
Is detached, experimental, subject matter
For ironic analysis, even for pity
As for some stranger's private problem.
It is not cold on the mountain, human women
Fall like ripe fruit while mere men
Are climbing out on dangerous branches
Of banking, insurance and shops; going
To the theatre; becoming
Acquainted with actors; unhappily
Pretending to a knowledge of art.
Poet, you have reason to be sympathetic—

Count them the beautiful unbroken
And then forget them
As things aside from the main purpose
Which is to be
Passive, observing with a steady eye.

William Empson

William Empson was born September 27, 1906, in Yorkshire and was educated at Winchester and Magdalene College, Cambridge. His first book—a book of criticism—*Seven Types of Ambiguity,* was published when he was twenty-four, after which he went to Tokyo and remained there three years as professor in English Literature. He returned to the East in 1937 to teach English literature, arrived at the start of a war, and spent two years with the refugee university at Changsha. Back in England, he joined the British Broadcasting Company, edited foreign broadcasts, and supervised programs in Chinese. After lecturing in the United States at the Kenyon Summer School, he was appointed professor of English literature at Sheffield University in 1953.

Seven Types of Ambiguity is a germinal book. Largely responsible for "The New Criticism," it explores not only the various possible meanings of a poem but the the multiple suggestions of individual words. It is, said Stanley Edgar Hyman, "the most elaborate and probably the finest close reading of poetry ever put down, the fantastic, wonderful, and almost endless spinning out of the implications and linguistic possibilities." On many writers its influence was excellent. It emphasized a studied approach instead of a vague wandering about the subject; it stressed the serious use of scientific as well as classical references rather than worn-out allusions and empty abstractions. On others, however, Empson's influence was harmful. He tended to place too great a value on erudition, on style instead of substance, on manner instead of content. *Seven Types of Ambiguity* was followed by *Some Versions of Pastoral* (1935) and *The Structure of Complex Words* (1951).

Empson's poetry has the same tone as his prose, intellectual and complex. *Collected Poems* (1935, 1940, corrected and amplified in 1955) is an involved and often witty display of virtuosity. The verse succeeds in spite of its almost total lack of music; Empson's tone-deaf ear permits him to commit such cacophonies as "soon boil fool's pots," "Law makes long spokes of the short stakes," and "Your spun farm's root still on that axis dwells." Many of the supplementary Notes (there are twenty-seven pages of them) point out—and gratuitously explain—Empson's double meanings and "ambiguous" puns. But if Empson is a riddling scholar he is also a valuable as well as an amusing instructor. He concludes one of his Notes by saying: "I suppose the reason I tried to defend my clotted kind of poetry was that I felt it was going a bit too far."

"Clotted" much of his poetry undoubtedly is, but it is never without discipline. "This Last Pain" is thickly philosophical but it has an intensity of feeling as well as organization; "Rolling the Lawn" is a half-metaphysical, half-playful sonnet;

"Homage to the British Museum" is a summation of incongruities; "Just a Smack at Auden" is a brilliantly rhymed parody of that poet's earlier tone and pyrotechnical mannerisms; "Missing Dates" is a paradox of form and feeling, a set of loose implications held within the tight confines of a villanelle, one of the strictest of old verse patterns. Even when Empson's poetry is most knotted (or "clotted") it is subtly concentrated, a concentration in which the reader must participate.

THIS LAST PAIN

This last pain for the damned the Fathers found:
"They knew the bliss with which they were not crowned."
Such, but on earth, let me foretell,
Is all, of heaven or of hell.

Man, as the prying housemaid of the soul,
May know her happiness by eye to hole:
He's safe; the key is lost; he knows
Door will not open, nor hole close.

"What is conceivable can happen too,"
Said Wittgenstein, who had not dreamt of you;
But wisely; if we worked it long
We should forget where it was wrong.

Those thorns are crowns which, woven into knots,
Crackle under and soon boil fools' pots;
And no man's watching, wise and long,
Would ever stare them into song.

Thorns burn to a consistent ash, like man;
A splendid cleanser for the frying-pan:
And those who leap from pan to fire
Should this brave opposite admire.

All those large dreams by which men long live well
Are magic-lanterned on the smoke of hell;
This then is real, I have implied,
A painted, small, transparent slide.

These the inventive can hand-paint at leisure,
Or most emporia would stock our measure;
And feasting in their dappled shade
We should forget how they were made.

Feign then what's by a decent tact believed
And act that state is only so conceived,
And build an edifice of form
For house where phantoms may keep warm.

Imagine, then, by miracle, with me,
(Ambiguous gifts, as what gods give must be)
What could not possibly be there,
And learn a style from a despair.

ROLLING THE LAWN

You can't beat English lawns. Our final hope
Is flat despair. Each morning therefore ere
I greet the office, through the weekday air,
Holding the Holy Roller at the slope
(The English fetish, not the Texas Pope)
Hither and thither on my toes with care
I roll ours flatter and flatter. Long, in prayer,
I grub for daisies at whose roots I grope.
Roll not the abdominal wall; the walls of
  Troy
Lead, since a plumb-line ordered, could
  destroy.
Roll rather, where no mole dare sap, the
  lawn,
And ne'er his tumuli shall tomb your brawn.
World, roll yourself; and bear your roller,
  soul,
As martyrs gridirons, when God calls the roll.

HOMAGE TO THE BRITISH MUSEUM

There is a Supreme God in the ethnological section;
A hollow toad shape, faced with a blank shield.
He needs his belly to include the Pantheon,
Which is inserted through a hole behind.
At the navel, at the points formally stressed, at the organs of sense,
Lice glue themselves, dolls, local deities,
His smooth wood creeps with all the creeds of the world.

Attending there let us absorb the cultures of nations
And dissolve into our judgement all their codes.
Then, being clogged with a natural hesitation
(People are continually asking one the way out),
Let us stand here and admit that we have no road.
Being everything, let us admit that is to be something,
Or give ourselves the benefit of the doubt;
Let us offer our pinch of dust all to this God,
And grant his reign over the entire building.

JUST A SMACK AT AUDEN

Waiting for the end, boys, waiting for the end.
What is there to be or do?
What's become of me or you?
Are we kind or are we true?
Sitting two and two, boys, waiting for the end.

Shall I build a tower, boys, knowing it will rend
Crack upon the hour, boys, waiting for the end?
Shall I pluck a flower, boys, shall I save or spend?
All turns sour, boys, waiting for the end.

Shall I send a wire, boys? Where is there to send?
All are under fire, boys, waiting for the end.
Shall I turn a sire, boys? Shall I choose a friend?
The fat is in the pyre, boys, waiting for the end.

Shall I make it clear, boys, for all to apprehend,
Those that will not hear, boys, waiting for the end,
Knowing it is near, boys, trying to pretend,
Sitting in cold fear, boys, waiting for the end?

Shall we send a cable, boys, accurately penned,
Knowing we are able, boys, waiting for the end,
Via the Tower of Babel, boys? Christ will not ascend.
He's hiding in his stable, boys, waiting for the end.

Shall we blow a bubble, boys, glittering to distend,
Hiding from our trouble, boys, waiting for the end?
When you build on rubble, boys, Nature will append
Double and re-double, boys, waiting for the end.

Shall we make a tale, boys, that things are sure to mend,
Playing bluff and hale, boys, waiting for the end?
It will be born stale, boys, stinking to offend,
Dying ere it fail, boys, waiting for the end.

Shall we go all wild, boys, waste and make them lend,
Playing at the child, boys, waiting for the end?
It has all been filed, boys, history has a trend,
Each of us enisled, boys, waiting for the end.

What was said by Marx, boys, what did he perpend?
No good being sparks, boys, waiting for the end.
Treason of the clerks, boys, curtains that descend,
Lights becoming darks, boys, waiting for the end.

Waiting for the end, boys, waiting for the end.
Not a chance of blend, boys, things have got to tend.
Think of those who vend, boys, think of how we wend,
Waiting for the end, boys, waiting for the end.

MISSING DATES

Slowly the poison the whole blood stream fills.
It is not the effort nor the failure tires.
The waste remains, the waste remains and kills.

It is not your system or clear sight that mills
Down small to the consequence a life requires;
Slowly the poison the whole blood stream fills.

They bled an old dog dry yet the exchange rills
Of young dog blood gave but a month's desires
The waste remains, the waste remains and kills.

It is the Chinese tombs and the slag hills
Usurp the soil, and not the soil retires.
Slowly the poison the whole blood stream fills.

Not to have fire is to be a skin that shrills.
The complete fire is death. From partial fires
The waste remains, the waste remains and kills.

It is the poems you have lost, the ills
From missing dates, at which the heart expires.
Slowly the poison the whole blood stream fills.
The waste remains, the waste remains and kills.

John Betjeman

John Betjeman, born in London in 1906, was educated at Marlborough and Oxford, where he was a contemporary of MacNeice and Auden. Earning his living as a teacher and journalist, he became an authority on English architecture, quaint villages, and unimportant but, to him, endearing places. *Mount Zion* (1933), *Continual Dew* (1937), *Old Bats in New Belfries* (1940), *Old Lights for New Chancels* (1945) are the titles of some of his volumes of verse; *Ghastly Good Taste* (1933), *Cornwall Shell Guide* (1936), *English, Scottish, and Welsh Landscape* (1944), *Berkshire* (1949), *Shell Guide to Shropshire* (1951) are some of his books of prose. Auden characterized his writing as "slick but not streamlined"; the phrase was adopted as the title of a selection of his poems (*Slick but Not Streamlined*) which appeared in 1947, and Auden supplied the introduction.

Nothing Betjeman had published before his fifty-second year prepared the public for the overwhelming success of his *Collected Poems* (1958). It sold a thousand copies a day for months, went into edition after edition, and won several awards, including the Duff Cooper Memorial Prize, which was presented to him by Princess Margaret. It appealed to all classes of readers, partly because of its mixture of wry cleverness and sentiment, partly because of its devotional and nostalgic tone, but chiefly because it was English to the core; it was merely accepted, pleasantly reviewed, but not vociferously acclaimed in America. Betjeman was hailed as a lyrical satirist, but he objected to the term. "I have," he wrote, "tried to catch the atmosphere of places and times in different parts of England and Eire. But when I do so I am not being satirical but topographical . . . I love suburbs and gas-lights and Pont Street and Gothic Revival churches and mineral railways, provincial towns and garden cities. They are, many of them, part of my background."

Only a lover of the ordinary and the seemingly prosaic could make poems with such titles as "Sudden Illness at the Bus Stop," "An Archaeological Picnic," "Invasion Exercise at the Poultry Farm," "Indoor Games Near Newbury," "Business Girls," "Monody on the Death of Aldersgate Station," "A Liverish Journey First Class," or address an athletic Olympic girl with a pseudo-love poem which ends ruefully:

> And when the match is over, I
> Would flop beside you, hear you sigh;
> And then, with what supreme caress,
> You'll tuck me up into my press.
> Fair tigress of the tennis courts,
> So short in sleeve and strong in shorts,
> Little, alas, to you I mean,
> For I am bald and old and green.

Humor and even hilarity are here—this footnote, for example: "The names in the last lines of these stanzas [T. S. Eliot, Edith Sitwell, Thomas Hardy, etc.] are put in not out of malice or satire but merely for their euphony." However, it is chiefly Betjeman's charm, a wistful piety, a tenderness for things past and present things overlooked, which has made him the celebrant of the commonplace and slightly outmoded, the unofficial laureate of the middle-class, the inglorious and often mute.

Summoned by Bells (1960) is Betjeman's partial biography which appeared in his mid-fifties. Written in blank verse, it is a sustained narrative of his bourgeois background, his unhappiness at the school where he was bullied, his lack of interest in the family manufacturing firm, his solace in nature and his escape via books, church architecture, and High Church religion. A few months after the publication of the book, Betjeman was awarded the Queen's Gold Medal for Poetry.

THE COTTAGE HOSPITAL

At the end of a long-walled garden
    in a red provincial town,
A brick path led to a mulberry—
    scanty grass at its feet.
I lay under blackening branches
    where the mulberry leaves hung down
Sheltering ruby fruit globes
    from a Sunday-tea-time heat.
Apple and plum espaliers
    basked upon bricks of brown;
The air was swimming with insects,
    and children played in the street.

Out of this bright intentness
    into the mulberry shade
Musca domestica (housefly)
    swung from the August light
Slap into slithery rigging
    by the waiting spider made
Which spun the lithe elastic
    till the fly was shrouded tight.
Down came the hairy talons
    and horrible poison blade
And none of the garden noticed
    that fizzing, hopeless fight.

Say in what Cottage Hospital
    whose pale green walls resound
With the tap upon polished parquet
    of inflexible nurses' feet
Shall I myself be lying
    when they range the screens around?
And say shall I groan in dying,
    as I twist the sweaty sheet?
Or gasp for breath uncrying,
    as I feel my senses drown'd
While the air is swimming with insects
    and children play in the street?

SLOUGH

Come, friendly bombs, and fall on Slough
It isn't fit for humans now,
There isn't grass to graze a cow
    Swarm over, Death!

Come, bombs, and blow to smithereens
Those air-conditioned, bright canteens,
Tinned fruit, tinned meat, tinned milk, tinned beans
    Tinned minds, tinned breath.

Mess up the mess they call a town—
A house for ninety-seven down
And once a week a half-a-crown
    For twenty years,

And get that man with double chin
Who'll always cheat and always win,
Who washes his repulsive skin
    In women's tears,

And smash his desk of polished oak
And smash his hands so used to stroke
And stop his boring dirty joke
    And make him yell.

But spare the bald young clerks who add
The profits of the stinking cad;
It's not their fault that they are mad,
    They've tasted Hell.

It's not their fault they do not know
The birdsong from the radio,
It's not their fault they often go
    To Maidenhead

And talk of sports and makes of cars
In various bogus Tudor bars
And daren't look up and see the stars
    But belch instead.

In labour-saving homes, with care
Their wives frizz out peroxide hair
And dry it in synthetic air
    And paint their nails.

Come, friendly bombs, and fall on Slough
To get it ready for the plough.
The cabbages are coming now:
    The earth exhales.

REMORSE

The lungs draw in the air and rattle it out again;
The eyes revolve in their sockets and upwards stare;
No more worry and waiting and troublesome doubt again—
She whom I loved and left is no longer there.

The nurse puts down her knitting and walks across to her,
With quick professional eye she surveys the dead.
Just one patient the less and little the loss to her,
Distantly tender she settles the shrunken head.

Protestant claims and Catholic, the wrong and the right of them,
Unimportant they seem in the face of death—
But my neglect and unkindness—to lose the sight of them
I would listen even again to that labouring breath.

INEVITABLE

First there was putting hot-water bottles to it,
Then there was seeing what an osteopath could do,
Then trying drugs to coax the thing and woo it,
Then came the time when he knew that he was through.

Now in his hospital bed I see him lying
Limp on the pillows like a cast-off Teddy bear.
Is he too ill to know that he is dying?
And, if he does know, does he really care?

Grey looks the ward with November's overcasting
But his large eyes seem to see beyond the day;
Speech becomes sacred near silence everlasting
Oh if I *must* speak, have I words to say?

In the past weeks we had talked about Variety,
Vesta Victoria, Lew Lake and Wilkie Bard,
Horse-buses, hansoms, crimes in High Society—
Although we knew his death was near, we fought against it hard.

THE ARREST OF OSCAR WILDE AT THE CADOGAN HOTEL

He sipped at a weak hock and seltzer
As he gazed at the London skies
Through the Nottingham lace of the curtains
Or was it his bees-winged eyes?

To the right and before him Pont Street
Did tower in her new built red,
As hard as the morning gaslight
That shone on his unmade bed,

"I want some more hock in my seltzer,
 And Robbie, please give me your hand—
Is this the end or beginning?
 How can I understand?

"So you've brought me the latest *Yellow Book*:
 And Buchan has got in it now:
Approval of what is approved of
 Is as false as a well-kept vow.

"More hock, Robbie—where is the seltzer?
 Dear boy, pull again at the bell!
They are all little better than *cretins,*
 Though this *is* the Cadogan Hotel.

"One astrakhan coat is at Willis's—
 Another one's at the Savoy:
Do fetch my morocco portmanteau,
 And bring them on later, dear boy."

A thump, and a murmur of voices—
 ("Oh why must they make such a din?")
As the door of the bedroom swung open
 And TWO PLAIN CLOTHES POLICEMEN came in:

"Mr. Woilde, we 'ave come for tew take yew
 Where felons and criminals dwell:
We must ask yew tew leave with us quoietly
 For this *is* the Cadogan Hotel."

He rose, and he put down *The Yellow Book*.
 He staggered—and, terrible-eyed,
He brushed past the palms on the staircase
 And was helped to a hansom outside.

Louis MacNeice

Louis MacNeice was born September 12, 1907, in the North of Ireland. His family, however, came from the West of Ireland, so he is not to be designated an Orangeman. He was at Oxford, Merton College, from 1926 to 1930, when he married and moved to Birmingham, after which he lectured in Greek in London.

His first volume, *Blind Fireworks* (1929), is more than an exhibit of the usual juvenilia, but the author dismisses it with the assurance that none of it will survive. The influence of Edith Sitwell (obvious in "Cradle Song") is here, but an alert mind is fashioning an idiom of its own. In the succeeding *Poems* published in 1935, the imaginative power is apparent. Like his immediate contemporaries, MacNeice prefers to spice the piquant half-rhyme with the traditional full vowel; like Auden and Spender, he uses the strictly contemporary scene. Like them, also, he adapts, turns, and generally "heightens" the ordinary speech of the day. It is in such poems as "Sunday Morning," "Morning Sun" and "Birmingham" that MacNeice, in common with a few others, points to a revival of vitality, a reliance on contemporary life, however complicated and difficult it may be.

Poems: 1925-1940 is an odd mingling of the delicate lyrics which MacNeice wrote as a youth and the semi-jazz approximations which he composed in his thirties. In the later poems he often relies on a casual style and complacent finalities; he overuses the offhand tone and carries the natural order of words to the pitch of banality. The ideas suffer; the style becomes a loose set of statements dropped haphazardly into verse. This is, as Edwin Muir wrote in *The Present Age,* "the poetry of a man who will never go farther than he feels he can legitimately go, and who is never swept off his feet." *Springboard* (1945) and *Holes in the Sky* (1948) employ flat statement and the plodding manner to the point of weariness. Nevertheless, when MacNeice is not dispirited, he can sharpen his idiom and shoot a phrase which rankles but lodges firmly in the mind.

Besides his poetry, MacNeice wrote *Out of the Picture* (1937), a play in verse which is fantastic and satirical; collaborated with W. H. Auden in *Letters from Iceland* (1937); issued a sensible, if not inspired, examination of *Modern Poetry* (1938); and published a searching and highly readable summary of *The Poetry of W. B. Yeats* (1941).

THE BRITISH MUSEUM READING ROOM

Under the hive-like dome the stooping haunted readers
Go up and down the alleys, tap the cells of knowledge—
    Honey and wax, the accumulation of years—
Some on commission, some for the love of learning,
Some because they have nothing better to do
Or because they hope these walls of books will deaden
    The drumming of the demon in their ears.

Cranks, hacks, poverty-stricken scholars,
In pince-nez, period hats or romantic beards
    And cherishing their hobby or their doom.
Some are too much alive and some are asleep
Hanging like bats in a world of inverted values,
Folded up in themselves in a world which is safe and silent:
    This is the British Museum Reading Room.

Out on the steps in the sun the pigeons are courting,
Puffing their ruffs and sweeping their tails or taking
    A sun-bath at their ease
And under the totem poles—the ancient terror—
Between the enormous fluted Ionic columns
There seeps from heavily jowled or hawk-like foreign faces
    The guttural sorrow of the refugees.

AND LOVE HUNG STILL

And love hung still as crystal over the bed
  And filled the corners of the enormous room;
The boom of dawn that left her sleeping, showing
  The flowers mirrored in the mahogany table.

O my love, if only I were able
  To protract this hour of quiet after passion,
Not ration happiness but keep this door for ever
  Closed on the world, its own world closed within it.

But dawn's waves trouble with the bubbling minute,
  The names of books come clear upon their shelves,
The reason delves for duty and you will wake
  With a start and go on living on your own.

The first train passes and the windows groan,
  Voices will hector and your voice become
A drum in tune with theirs, which all last night
  Like sap that fingered through a hungry tree
Asserted our one night's identity.

CRADLE SONG

The clock's untiring fingers wind the wool of darkness
And we all lie alone, having long outgrown our cradles
(Sleep, sleep, Miriam)
And the flames like faded ladies always unheeded simper
And all is troubledness.

Soft the wool, dark the wool
Is gathered slowly, wholly up
Into a ball, all of it.

And yet in the back of the mind, lulled all else,
There is something unsleeping, un-tamperable-with,
Something that whines and scampers
And like the ladies in the grate will not sleep nor forget itself,
Clawing at the wool like a kitten.

The clock's fingers wind, wind the wool of Lethe,
(Sleep, sleep, Miriam)
It glides across the floor drawn by hidden fingers

And the beast droops his head
And the fire droops its flounces
And winks a final ogle out of the fading embers
But no one pays attention;

This is too much, the flames say, insulted,
We who were once the world's beauties and now
No one pays attention
No one remembers us.

Sleep, sleep, Miriam.
And as for this animal of yours
He must be cradled also.
That he may not unravel this handiwork of forgetfulness.
That he may not philander with the flames before they die.

The world like a cradle rises and falls
On a wave of confetti and funerals
And sordor and stinks and stupid faces
And the deity making bored grimaces.

Oh what a muddle he has made of the wool,
(God will tomorrow have his hands full),
You must muzzle your beast, you must fasten him
For the whole of life—the interim.

Through the interim we pass
Everyone under an alias
Till they gather the strands of us together
And wind us up for ever and ever.

SUNDAY MORNING

Down the road someone is practicing scales,
The notes like little fishes vanish with a wink of tails,
Man's heart expands to tinker with his car
For this is Sunday morning, Fate's great bazaar,
Regard these means as ends, concentrate on this Now,
And you may grow to music or drive beyond Hindhead anyhow,
Take corners on two wheels until you go so fast
That you can clutch a fringe or two of the windy past,
That you can abstract this day and make it to the week of time
A small eternity, a sonnet self-contained in rhyme.

But listen, up the road, something gulps, the church spire
Opens its eight bells out, skulls' mouths which will not tire
To tell how there is no music or movement which secures
Escape from the weekday time. Which deadens and endures.

MUSEUMS

Museums offer us, running from among the buses,
A centrally heated refuge, parquet floors and sarcophaguses,
Into whose tall fake porches we hurry without a sound

Like a beetle under a brick that lies, useless, on the ground.
Warmed and cajoled by the silence the cowed cypher revives,
Mirrors himself in the cases of pots, paces himself by marble lives,
Makes believe it was he that was the glory that was Rome,
Soft on his cheek the nimbus of other people's martyrdom,
And then returns to the street, his mind an arena where sprawls
Any number of consumptive Keatses and dying Gauls.

MORNING SUN

Shuttles of trains going north, going south, drawing threads of blue
The shining of the lines of trams like swords
Thousands of posters asserting a monopoly of the good, the beautiful, the true
Crowds of people all in the vocative, you and you,
The haze of the morning shot with words.

Yellow sun comes white off the wet streets but bright
Chromium yellows in the gay sun's light
Filleted sun streaks the purple mist,
Everything is kissed and reticulated with sun
Scooped-up and cupped in the open fronts of shops
And bouncing on the traffic which never stops.

And the street fountain blown across the square
Rainbow-trellises the air and sunlight blazons
The red butcher's and scrolls of fish on marble slabs
Whistled bars of music crossing silver sprays
And horns of cars, touché, touché, rapiers' retort, a moving cage,
A turning page of shine and sound, the day's maze.

But when the sun goes out, the streets go cold, the hanging meat
And tiers of fish are colorless and merely dead
And the hoots of cars neurotically repeat and the tiptoed feet
Of women hurry and falter whose faces are dead
And I see in the air but not belonging there
The blown gray powder of the fountain gray as the ash
That forming on a cigarette covers the red.

BIRMINGHAM

Smoke from the train-gulf hid by hoardings blunders upward, the brakes of cars
Pipe as the policeman pivoting round raises his flat hand, bars
With his figure of a monolith Pharaoh the queue of fidgety machines
(Chromium dogs on the bonnet, faces behind the triplex screens)
Behind him the streets run away between the proud glass of shops
Cubical scent-bottles artificial legs arctic foxes and electric mops
But beyond this center the slumward vista thins like a diagram:
There, unvisited, are Vulcan's forges who doesn't care a tinker's damn.

Splayed outwards through the suburbs houses, houses for rest
Seducingly rigged by the builder, half-timbered houses with lips pressed

So tightly and eyes staring at the traffic through bleary haws
And only a six-inch grip of the racing earth in their concrete claws;
In these houses men as in a dream pursue the Platonic Forms
With wireless and cairn terriers and gadgets approximating to the fickle norms
And endeavor to find God and score one over the neighbor
By climbing tentatively upward on jerry-built beauty and sweated labor.

The lunch hour: the shops empty, shopgirls' faces relax
Diaphanous as green glass empty as old almanacs
As incoherent with ticketed gewgaws tiered behind their heads
As the Burne-Jones windows in St. Philip's broken by crawling leads
Insipid color, patches of emotion, Saturday thrills—
(This theater is sprayed with "June")—the gutter take our old playbills,
Next week-end it is likely in the heart's funfair we shall pull
Strong enough on the handle to get back our money; or at any rate it is possible.

On shining lines the trams like vast sarcophagi move
Into the sky, plum after sunset, merging to duck's egg, barred with mauve
Zeppelin clouds, and pentecost-like the cars' headlights bud
Out from sideroads and the traffic signals, crême-de-menthe or bull's blood,
Tell one to stop, the engine gently breathing, or to go on
To where like black pipes of organs in the frayed and fading zone
Of the West the factory chimneys on sullen sentry will all night wait
To call, in the harsh morning, sleep-stupid faces through the daily gate.

NUTS IN MAY

May come up with bird-din
And May come up with sun-dint,
May come up with water-wheels
  And May come up with iris.

In the sun-peppered meadow the shepherds are old,
Their flutes are broken and their tales are told,
And their ears are deaf when the guns unfold
The new philosophy over the wold.

May come up with pollen of death,
May come up with cordite,
May come up with a chinagraph
  And May come up with a stopwatch.

In the high court of heaven Their tail-feathers shine
With cowspit and bullspit and spirits of wine
They know no pity, being divine,
And They give no quarter to thine or mine.

May come up with Very lights,
May come up with duty,
May come up with a bouncing cheque,
  An acid-drop and a bandage.

Yes, angels are frigid and shepherds are dumb,
There is no holy water when the enemy come,
The trees are askew and the skies are a-hum
And you have to keep mum and go to it and die for your life and keep mum.

May come up with fiddle-bows,
May come up with blossom,
May come up the same again,
  The same again but different.

W. H. Auden

W(ystan) H(ugh) Auden was born in York, February 21, 1907. He was educated at Gresham's School, Holt, and Christ Church, Oxford. From 1930 to 1935 he taught school at Malvern. He was with the G. P. O. Film Unit from 1935 to 1936. In 1939 he came to America and took out citizenship papers.

By the time Auden was thirty he had already been the center of several controversies; an English magazine had brought out a special Auden number; an entire movement seems to have stemmed from his energy and versatility. At thirty-three he had written and compiled four books of poetry, three plays, a collection of prose fiction, two books of travel, and two anthologies. *Poems* (1930) and *The Orators* (1932) were published, together with the supplementary *Dance of Death,* in a one-volume American edition severely entitled *Poems* (1934). Printed in this country simultaneously with Stephen Spender, Auden was continually reviewed with Spender, and when it was learned that both poets had in common an Oxford education, poetic influences, and radical political policies, critics coupled them as though they were two parts of one poet, dangerous but distinguished Siamese twins. No understanding reader could have confused or coupled the two. Spender is a romantic and, in spite of a modern vocabulary, traditional poet; Auden is a satirical and restlessly experimental writer. But contrasts are as misleading as comparisons, and Spender's work is considered separately on page 468. Auden has entirely different claims upon the reader.

The outstanding feature of Auden's poetry is its combination of variety and originality. When Auden uses traditional forms, he imposes a new pattern upon them, from archaic ballads to street-corner "blues." No contemporary poet has a greater natural command of language; he makes rhetoric out of banal jargon, and summons eloquence without raising his voice. Even in the difficult long poems, parts break through which require no key or comment. "Paid on Both Sides" is typical; it is a thirty-page play (its author calls it a "charade") which has a collapsing civilization for its background and which, in its confusion of purpose and effects, baffles intelligences higher than the average. Yet every individual scene is dynamic; the sense of shock is communicated with a horror that is immediately comprehended.

It has been said with some justice that Auden's philosophy is self-divided. He is merciless in his mockery of "the old gang," yet he is not convincingly on the "other side." He speaks for those who are bullied into war and exploited in peace, but he is not really one of them. Nevertheless, Auden somehow manages to unite opposites, to combine the latest findings in science with the oldest dreams and visions. He reconciles incongruities with breathtaking daring and clothes abstractions in flesh and blood.

With *On This Island* (1937) Auden simplified his effects and clarified his idiom. He did not discard eloquence, but he frequently spoke in "plain" terms and easy measures, imitated popular songs, composed ballads reminiscent of folk tunes, and put purposely crude rhymes to "coarse" themes. The lines were more tightly organized, the form was strictly shaped. Auden somehow combined the fastidious scholar and the man-of-the-people. In *Another Time* (1940) the poetry alternates between nobility and rowdiness; cabaret songs, tender lyrics and tricky rhymes occur between poems as brilliant as "Law, say the gardeners, is the sun" and as uplifting as "In Memory of W. B. Yeats." In the midst of intricate experiments, there are love poems of the sharpest sensitivity. Auden is perhaps the only modern poet who can really express himself in a villanelle or a sestina—he uses the latter form to remarkable effect in the "Journal of an Airman" and in "Hearing of harvests rotting in the valleys."

The Double Man (1941) makes it more apparent than ever that Auden is the most provocative as well as the most unpredictable poet of his generation. In a poem of some seventeen hundred lines Auden speaks as the poet who has become the multiple man: the bravura performer and the careful craftsman, the lively iconoclast and the studious wit. *The Double Man* was immediately hailed as a phenomenon, a landmark, a Return to Order. The most experimental of contemporary poets had gone to school to Pope, and the result of his exercise in discipline seemed to be a turning-point for the 1940's, the long-awaited reply to the Wastelanders.

For the Time Being (1944) and the *Collected Poetry of W. H. Auden* (1945) defined an epoch; a book of critical essays acknowledged Auden's importance by its very title: *Auden and After*. Auden broke through the barriers between light verse and oratory, between high spirits and high seriousness. *For the Time Being* contains two long poems: "The Sea and the Mirror," which is an extraordinary commentary on Shakespeare's *The Tempest,* learned and illuminating; and the title poem, a Christmas cantata which, in its mixture of classic and colloquial speech, is a profound paradox. Auden's early work, like Eliot's, was written mainly out of revulsion. Disgust of a sick world overcame pity; fierce satire and coarse mockery ran the gamut from bitterness to burlesque; the tone was desperate and morose. An atmosphere of foreboding, of imminent catastrophe, hung over the work, an "immeasurable neurotic dread."

By the time he was forty Auden was recognized as the most influential poet after Eliot. It was observed that there was a geographical as well as a poetical justice in the fact. Auden, born in England, made his home in America; Eliot, born in Missouri, exchanged his American birthright for English citizenship. Like Eliot, Auden progressed from cynicism to mysticism, from a bewildered distrust of civilization to a doggedly religious hope for it. Going beyond Eliot,

Auden substituted exuberance for depression; to compressed constraint he added openness, flexibility, and an easy mastery of charm.

In the later and more solemn work, emphasized in the *Collected Poetry,* Auden did not relinquish his intransigence or his provocative wit. Those who complained of his preoccupation with metaphysics failed to see that Auden's attempts to find a fixed faith enlarged his gamut and altered a self-centered concern. Poems to Freud, Matthew Arnold, and Henry James, Yeats and Voltaire, Ernst Toller and Edward Lear speak for his catholicity as well as his convictions. That Auden has never lost his personal and pungent humor is proved again and again, notably by the brilliantly turned "Under Which Lyre," a Phi Beta Kappa poem ironically subtitled "A Reactionary Tract for the Times."

The Age of Anxiety (1947), which received the Pulitzer Prize in 1948, is another long stride in Auden's progress. Tcehnically it is a prime example of his virtuosity; using the language of the 1940's, it employs the severely stressed poetic form of the Anglo-Saxons, the tough, triply alliterative line of *Beowulf.* But the idiom is as modern as it is characteristic: a purposeful blend of casual horror and baleful *vers de société*—the patter which sometimes makes Auden seem the Freudians' Noel Coward—and the effect is that of a contemporary Purgatory. In this metropolitan baroque "eclogue," which opens in a New York bar, four people reenact the seven ages and seven stages of man, from a morass of reminiscence through the deserts of disillusion, including a dirge lamenting the lost leader (the "lost dad," the vanished God), to the final frustration which compels a hope of other values.

Thus Auden establishes himself as a protean poet, a capricious artist delighting in straight-face frivolities and a probing spirit torn between agnosticism and blind belief, a superb rhetorician rich in learning and a lover of extravagant oddities, a dramatic lyricist and a natural dialectician—in short, a poet who is equally adept at sheer fooling and pure enchantment.

In addition to the Pulitzer Prize, Auden received the King's Poetry Medal in 1937 and the Award of Merit Medal of the National Academy of Arts and Letters in 1945. Versatile enough in his own right, Auden has had to resort to collaborators in order to keep pace with his own energetic career. With John Garrett he compiled an anthology, *The Poet's Tongue* (1935); with Louis MacNeice he composed *Letters from Iceland* (1937); with Christopher Isherwood he wrote two plays, *The Dog Beneath the Skin* (1935), a satire, and *On the Frontier* (1938), a melodrama, and *Journey to a War* (1939), an account of a trip through war-torn China. The best analyses of Auden's varying sensibility appear in Stephen Spender's *The Destructive Element* (1935), David Daiches' *Poetry and the Modern World* (1940), and Francis Scarfe's *Auden and After* (1943).

Between his mid-forties and early fifties Auden completed three new volumes of varied and wide-ranging poetry: *Nones* (1951), *The Shield of Achilles* (1955), and *Homage to Clio* (1960). He was elected Professor of Poetry at Oxford in 1956.

CHORUS FROM A PLAY

Doom is dark and deeper than any sea-dingle:
Upon what man it fall
In spring, day-wishing flowers appearing,
Avalanche sliding, white snow from rock-face,
That he should leave his house;
No cloud-soft hands can hold him, restraint by women,
But ever that man goes
By place-keepers, by forest trees,
A stranger to strangers over undried sea,
Houses for fishes, suffocating water;
Or lonely on fell as chat,
By pot-holed becks
A bird stone-haunting, an unquiet bird.

There head falls forward, fatigued at evening,
And dreams of home:
Waving from window, spread of welcome,
Kissing of wife under single sheet;
But waking sees
Bird-flocks nameless to him, through doorway voices
Of new men making another love.

Save him from hostile capture
From sudden tiger's spring at corner:
Protect his house,
His anxious house where days are counted
Fom thunderbolt protect,
From gradual ruin spreading like a stain:
Converting number from vague to certain
Bring joy, bring day of his returning,
Lucky with day approaching, with leaning dawn.

WHO'S WHO

A shilling life will give you all the facts:
How Father beat him, how he ran away,
What were the struggles of his youth, what acts
Made him the greatest figure of his day:
Of how he fought, fished, hunted, worked all night;
Though giddy, climbed new mountains; named a sea:
Some of the last researches even write
Love made him weep his pints like you and me.

With all his honors on, he sighed for one
Who, say astonished critics, lived at home;
Did little jobs about the house with skill
And nothing else; could whistle; would sit still
Or potter round the garden; answered some
Of his long marvellous letters, but kept none.

ODE; TO MY PUPILS

Though aware of our rank and alert to obey orders,
Watching with binoculars the movement of the grass for an ambush,
The pistol cocked, the code-word committed to memory;
        The youngest drummer
Knows all the peace-time stories like the oldest soldier,
        Though frontier-conscious,

About the tall white gods who landed from their open boat,
Skilled in the working of copper, appointing our feast-days,
Before the islands were submerged, when the weather was calm,
        The maned lion common,
An open wishing-well in every garden;
        When love came easy.

Perfectly certain, all of us, but not from the records,
Not from the unshaven agent who returned to the camp;
The pillar dug from the desert recorded only
        The sack of a city,
The agent clutching his side collapsed at our feet,
        "Sorry! They got me!"

Yes, they were living here once but do not now,
Yes, they are living still but do not here;
Lying awake after Lights Out a recruit may speak up:
        "Who told you all this?"
The tent-talk pauses a little till a veteran answers
        "Go to sleep, Sonny!"

Turning over he closes his eyes, and then in a moment
Sees the sun at midnight bright over cornfield and pasture,
Our hope. . . . Someone jostles him, fumbling for boots,
        Time to change guard:
Boy, the quarrel was before your time, the aggressor
        No one you know.

Your childish moments of awareness were all of our world,
At five you sprang, already a tiger in the garden,
At night your mother taught you to pray for our Daddy
        Far away fighting,
One morning you fell off a horse and your brother mocked you:
        "Just like a girl!"

You've got their names to live up to and questions won't help,
You've a very full program, first aid, gunnery, tactics,
The technique to master of raids and hand-to-hand fighting;
        Are you in training?
Are you taking care of yourself? are you sure of passing
        The endurance test?

Now we're due to parade on the square in front of the Cathedral,
When the bishop has blessed us, to file in after the choir-boys,
To stand with the wine-dark conquerors in the roped-off pews,
        Shout ourselves hoarse:
"They ran like hares: we have broken them up like fire-wood;
        They fought against God."

While in a great rift in the limestone miles away
At the same hour they gather, tethering their horses beside them;
A scarecrow prophet from a bowlder foresees our judgment,
        Their oppressors howling;
And the bitter psalm is caught by the gale from the rocks:
        "How long shall they flourish?"

What have we all been doing to have made from Fear
That laconic war-bitten captain addressing them now?
"Heart and head shall be keener, mood the more
        As our might lessens":
To have caused their shout "We will fight till we lie down beside
        The Lord we have loved."

There's Wrath who has learnt every trick of guerilla war-fare,
The shamming dead, the night-raid, the feinted retreat;
Envy their brilliant pamphleteer, to lying
        As husband true,
Expert Impersonator and linguist, proud of his power
        To hoodwink sentries.

Gluttony living alone, austerer than us,
Big, simple Greed, Acedia famed with them all
For her stamina, keeping the outposts, and somewhere Lust
        With his sapper's skill,
Muttering to his fuses in a tunnel "Could I meet here with Love,
        I would hug her to death."

There are faces there for which for a very long time
We've been on the look-out, though often at home we imagined,
Catching sight of a back or hearing a voice through a doorway,
        We had found them at last;
Put our arms round their necks and looked in their eyes and discovered
        We were unlucky.

And some of them, surely, we seem to have seen before:
Why, that girl who rode off on her bicycle one fine summer evening
And never returned, she's there; and the banker we'd noticed
        Worried for weeks;
Till he failed to arrive one morning and his room was empty,
        Gone with a suitcase.

They speak of things done on the frontier we were never told,
The hidden path to their squat Pictish tower

They will never reveal though kept without sleep, for their code is
"Death to the squealer":
They are brave, yes, though our newspapers mention their bravery
In inverted commas.

But careful; back to our lines; it is unsafe there,
Passports are issued no longer; that area is closed;
There's no fire in the waiting-room now at the climbers' Junction,
And all this year
Work has been stopped on the power-house; the wind whistles under
The half-built culverts.

Do you think that because you have heard that on Christmas Eve
In a quiet sector they walked about on the skyline,
Exchanged cigarettes, both learning the words for "I love you"
In either language:
You can stroll across for a smoke and a chat any evening?
Try it and see.

That rifle-sight you're designing; is it ready yet?
You're holding us up; the office is getting impatient;
The square munition-works out on the old allotments
Needs stricter watching;
If you see any loiterers there you may shoot without warning,
We must stop that leakage.

All leave is cancelled tonight; we must say good-by.
We entrain at once for the North; we shall see in the morning
The headlands we're doomed to attack; snow down to the tide-line:
Though the bunting signals
"Indoors before it's too late; cut peat for your fires,"
We shall lie out there.

THE STRINGS' EXCITEMENT

The strings' excitement, the applauding drum
Are but the initiating ceremony
That out of cloud the ancestral face may come.

And never hear their subaltern mockery,
Graphiti-writers, moss-grown with whimsies,
Loquacious when the watercourse is dry.

It is your face I see, and morning's praise
Of you is ghost's approval of the choice,
Filtered through roots of the effacing grass.

Fear, taking me aside, would give advice
"To conquer her, the visible enemy,
It is enough to turn away the eyes."

Yet there's no peace in this assaulted city
But speeches at the corners, hope for news,
Outside the watchfires of a stronger army.

And all emotions to expression came,
Recovering the archaic imagery:
This longing for assurance takes the form

Of a hawk's vertical stooping from the sky;
These tears, salt for a disobedient dream,
The lunatic agitation of the sea;

While this despair with hardened eyeballs cries
"A Golden Age, a Silver . . . rather this,
Massive and taciturn years, the Age of Ice."

THIS LUNAR BEAUTY

This lunar beauty
Has no history
Is complete and early;
If beauty later
Bear any feature
It had a lover
And is another.

This like a dream
Keeps other time
And daytime is
The loss of this;
For time is inches
And the heart's changes
Where ghost has haunted
Lost and wanted.

But this was never
A ghost's endeavor
Nor finished this,
Was ghost at ease;
And till it pass
Love shall not near
The sweetness here
Nor sorrow take
His endless look.

ALWAYS THE FOLLOWING WIND

Voice:

Always the following wind of history
Of others' wisdom makes a buoyant air
Till we come suddenly on pockets where
Is nothing loud but us; where voices seem
Abrupt, untrained, competing with no lie
Our fathers shouted once. They taught us war,
To scamper after darlings, to climb hills,
To emigrate from weakness, find ourselves
The easy conquerors of empty bays:
But never told us this, left each to learn,
Hear something of that soon-arriving day
When to gaze longer and delighted on
A face or idea be impossible.
Could I have been some simpleton that lived
Before disaster sent his runners here;
Younger than worms, worms have too much to bear.
Yes, mineral were best: could I but see
These woods, these fields of green, this lively world
Sterile as moon.

Chorus:

The Spring unsettles sleeping partnerships,
Foundries improve their casting process, shops
Open a further wing on credit till
The winter. In summer boys grow tall
With running races on the froth-wet sand,
War is declared there, here a treaty signed;
Here a scum breaks up like a bomb, there troops
Deploy like birds. But proudest into traps
Have fallen. These gears which ran in oil for week
By week, needing no look, now will not work;
Those manors mortgaged twice to pay for love
Go to another.

O how shall man live
Whose thought is born, child of one farcical night,
To find him old? The body warm but not
By choice, he dreams of folk in dancing bunches,
Of tart wine spilt on home-made benches,
Where learns, one drawn apart, a secret will
Restore the dead; but comes thence to a wall.
Outside on frozen soil lie armies killed
Who seem familiar, but they are cold.
Now the most solid wish he tries to keep
His hands show through; he never will look up,
Say "I am good." On him misfortune falls
More than enough. Better where no one feels,
The out-of-sight, buried too deep for shafts.

CHORUS

(*from "Paid on Both Sides"*)

To throw away the key and walk away
Not abrupt exile, the neighbors asking why,
But following a line with left and right
An altered gradient at another rate
Learns more than maps upon the whitewashed wall
The hand put up to ask; and makes us well
Without confession of the ill. All pasts
Are single old past now, although some posts
Are forwarded, held looking on a new view;
The future shall fulfill a surer vow
Not smiling at queen over the glass rim
Nor making gunpowder in the top room,
Not swooping at the surface still like gulls
But with prolonged drowning shall develop gills.

But there are still to tempt; areas not seen
Because of blizzards or an erring sign
Whose guessed-at wonders would be worth alleging,
And lies about the cost of a night's lodging.
Travelers may sleep at inns but not attach,
They sleep one night together, not asked to touch;
Receive no normal welcome, not the pressed lip,
Children to lift, not the assuaging lap.
Crossing the pass descend the growing stream
Too tired to hear except the pulses' strum,
Reach villages to ask for a bed in
Rock shutting out the sky, the old life done.

BALLAD

O what is that sound which so thrills the ear
Down in the valley drumming, drumming?

Only the scarlet soldiers, dear,
  The soldiers coming.

O what is that light I see flashing so clear
  Over the distance brightly, brightly?
Only the sun on their weapons, dear,
  As they step lightly.

O what are they doing with all that gear;
  What are they doing this morning, this morning?
Only the usual maneuvers, dear,
  Or perhaps a warning.

O why have they left the road down there;
  Why are they suddenly wheeling, wheeling?
Perhaps a change in the orders, dear;
  Why are you kneeling?

O haven't they stopped for the doctor's care;
  Haven't they reined their horses, their horses?
Why, they are none of them wounded, dear.
  None of these forces.

O is it the parson they want, with white hair;
  Is it the parson, is it, is it?
No, they are passing his gateway, dear,
  Without a visit.

O it must be the farmer who lives so near,
  It must be the farmer, so cunning, cunning;
They have passed the farm already, dear,
  And now they are running.

O where are you going? stay with me here.
  Were the vows you swore me deceiving, deceiving?
No, I promised to love you, my dear,
  But I must be leaving.

O it's broken the lock and splintered the door,
  O it's the gate where they're turning, turning;
Their feet are heavy on the floor
  And their eyes are burning.

VILLANELLE

Time can say nothing but I told you so,
Time only knows the price we have to pay;
If I could tell you, I would let you know.

If we should weep when clowns put on their show,
If we should stumble when musicians play,
Time can say nothing but I told you so.

There are no fortunes to be told, although
Because I love you more than I can say,
If I could tell you, I would let you know.

The winds must come from somewhere when they blow,
There must be reasons why the leaves decay;
Time can say nothing but I told you so.

Perhaps the roses really want to grow,
The vision seriously intends to stay;
If I could tell you, I would let you know.

Suppose the lions all get up and go,
And all the brooks and soldiers run away?
Time can say nothing but I told you so;
If I could tell you, I would let you know.

"LOOK, STRANGER"

Look, stranger, at this island now
The leaping light for your delight discovers,
Stand stable here
And silent be,
That through the channels of the ear
May wander like a river
The swaying sound of the sea.

Here at the small field's ending pause
Where the chalk wall falls to the foam, and its tall ledges.
Oppose the pluck
And knock of the tide,
And the shingle scrambles after the sucking surf, and the gull lodges
A moment on its sheer side.

Far off like floating seeds the ships
Diverge on urgent voluntary errands;
And the full view
Indeed may enter
And move in memory as now these clouds do,
That pass the harbor mirror
And all the summer through the water saunter.

HEARING OF HARVESTS ROTTING IN THE VALLEYS

Hearing of harvests rotting in the valleys,
Seeing at end of street the barren mountains,
Round corners coming suddenly on water,
Knowing them shipwrecked who were launched for islands,
We honor founders of these starving cities,
Whose honor is the image of our sorrow.

Which cannot see its likeness in their sorrow
That brought them desperate to the brink of valleys;
Dreaming of evening walks through learned cities,

They reined their violent horses on the mountains,
Those fields like ships to castaways on islands,
Visions of green to them that craved for water.

They built by rivers and at night the water
Running past windows comforted their sorrow;
Each in his little bed conceived of islands
Where every day was dancing in the valleys,
And all the year trees blossomed on the mountains,
Where love was innocent, being far from cities.

But dawn came back and they were still in cities;
No marvelous creature rose up from the water,
There was still gold and silver in the mountains,
And hunger was a more immediate sorrow;
Although to moping villagers in valleys
Some waving pilgrims were describing islands.

"The gods," they promised, "visit us from islands,
Are stalking head-up, lovely through the cities;
Now is the time to leave your wretched valleys
And sail with them across the lime-green water;
Sitting at their white sides, forget their sorrow,
The shadow cast across your lives by mountains."

So many, doubtful, perished in the mountains
Climbing up crags to get a view of islands;
So many, fearful, took with them their sorrow
Which stayed them when they reached unhappy cities;
So many, careless, dived and drowned in water;
So many, wretched, would not leave their valleys.

It is the sorrow; shall it melt? Ah, water
Would gush, flush, green these mountains and these valleys
And we rebuild our cities, not dream of islands.

LAW, SAY THE GARDENERS, IS THE SUN

Law, say the gardeners, is the sun,
Law is the one
All gardeners obey
Tomorrow, yesterday, today.

Law is the wisdom of the old
The impotent grandfathers shrilly scold;
The grandchildren put out a treble tongue,
Law is the senses of the young.

Law, says the priest with a priestly look,
Expounding to an unpriestly people,
Law is the words in my priestly book,
Law is my pulpit and my steeple.

Law, says the judge as he looks down his nose,
Speaking clearly and most severely,
Law is as I've told you before,
Law is as you know I suppose,
Law is but let me explain it once more,
Law is The Law.

Yet law-abiding scholars write;
Law is neither wrong nor right,
Law is only crimes
Punished by places and by times,
Law is the clothes men wear
Anytime, anywhere,
Law is Good-morning and Good-night.

Others say, Law is our Fate;
Others say, Law is our State;
Others say, others say
Law is no more,
Law is gone away.

And always the loud angry crowd
Very angry and very loud
Law is We,
And always the soft idiot softly Me.

If we, dear, know we know no more
Than they about the law,

If I no more than you
Know what we should and should not do
Except that all agree
Gladly or miserably
That the law is
And that all know this,
If therefore thinking it absurd
To identify Law with some other word,
Unlike so many men
I cannot say Law is again,
No more than they can we suppress
The universal wish to guess
Or slip out of our own position
Into an unconcerned condition.

Although I can at least confine
Your vanity and mine
To stating timidly
A timid similarity,
We shall boast anyway:
Like love I say.

Like love we dont know where or why
Like love we cant compel or fly
Like love we often weep
Like love we seldom keep.

LAY YOUR SLEEPING HEAD, MY LOVE

Lay your sleeping head, my love,
Human on my faithless arm;
Time and fevers burn away
Individual beauty from
Thoughtful children, and the grave
Proves the child ephemeral:
But in my arms till break of day
Let the living creature lie,
Mortal, guilty, but to me
The entirely beautiful.

Soul and body have no bounds:
To lovers as they lie upon
Her tolerant enchanted slope
In their ordinary swoon,
Grave the vision Venus sends
Of supernatural sympathy,
Universal love and hope;
While an abstract insight wakes
Among the glaciers and the rocks
The hermit's sensual ecstasy.

Certainty, fidelity
On the stroke of midnight pass
Like vibrations of a bell,
And fashionable madmen raise
Their pedantic boring cry:
Every farthing of the cost,
All the dreaded cards foretell,
Shall be paid, but from this night
Not a whisper, not a thought,
Not a kiss nor look be lost.

Beauty, midnight, vision dies:
Let the winds of dawn that blow
Softly round your dreaming head
Such a day of sweetness show
Eye and knocking heart may bless,
Find the mortal world enough;
Noons of dryness see you fed
By the involuntary powers,
Nights of insult let you pass
Watched by every human love.

IN MEMORY OF W. B. YEATS

I

He disappeared in the dead of winter:
The brooks were frozen, the airports almost deserted,
And snow disfigured the public statues;
The mercury sank in the mouth of the dying day.
O all the instruments agree
The day of his death was a dark cold day.

Far from his illness
The wolves ran on through the everygreen forests,
The peasant river was untempted by the fashionable quays;

By mourning tongues
The death of the poet was kept from his poems.

But for him it was his last afternoon as himself,
An afternoon of nurses and rumors;
The provinces of his body revolted,
The squares of his mind were empty,
Silence invaded the suburbs,
The current of his feeling failed: he became his admirers.

Now he is scattered among a hundred cities
And wholly given over to unfamiliar affections;
To find his happiness in another kind of wood
And be punished under a foreign code of conscience.
The words of a dead man
Are modified in the guts of the living.

But in the importance and noise of tomorrow
When the brokers are roaring like beasts on the floor of the Bourse,
And the poor have the sufferings to which they are fairly accustomed,
And each in the cell of himself is almost convinced of his freedom;
A few thousand will think of this day
As one thinks of a day when one did something slightly unusual.

O all the instruments agree
The day of his death was a dark cold day.

2

You were silly like us: your gift survived it all;
The parish of rich women, physical decay,
Yourself; mad Ireland hurt you into poetry.
Now Ireland has her madness and her weather still,
For poetry makes nothing happen: it survives
In the valley of its saying where executives
Would never want to tamper; it flows south
From ranches of isolation and the busy griefs,
Raw towns that we believe and die in; it survives,
A way of happening, a mouth.

Earth, receive an honored guest;
William Yeats is laid to rest:
Let the Irish vessel lie
Emptied of its poetry.

Time that is intolerant
Of the brave and innocent,
And indifferent in a week
To a beautiful physique,

Worships language and forgives
Everyone by whom it lives;

Pardons cowardice, conceit,
Lays its honors at their feet.

Time that with this strange excuse
Pardoned Kipling and his views,
And will pardon Paul Claudel,
Pardons him for writing well.

In the nightmare of the dark
All the dogs of Europe bark,
And the living nations wait,
Each sequestered in its hate;

Intellectual disgrace
Stares from every human face,
And the seas of pity lie
Locked and frozen in each eye.

Follow, poet, follow right
To the bottom of the night,
With your unconstraining voice
Still persuade us to rejoice;

With the farming of a verse
Make a vineyard of the curse,
Sing of human unsuccess
In a rapture of distress;

In the deserts of the heart
Let the healing fountain start,
In the prison of his days
Teach the free man how to praise.

SEPTEMBER 1, 1939

I sit in one of the dives
On Fifty-Second Street
Uncertain and afraid
As the clever hopes expire
Of a low dishonest decade:
Waves of anger and fear
Circulate over the bright
And darkened lands of the earth,
Obsessing our private lives;
The unmentionable odour of death
Offends the September night.

Accurate scholarship can
Unearth the whole offence
From Luther until now
That has driven a culture mad,
Find what occurred at Linz,
What huge imago made
A psychopathic god:
I am the public know
What all schoolchildren learn,
Those to whom evil is done
Do evil in return.

Exiled Thucydides knew
All that a speech can say
About Democracy,
And what dictators do,
The elderly rubbish they talk
To an apathetic grave;
Analysed all in his book,
The enlightenment driven away,
The habit-forming pain,
Mismanagement and grief:
We must suffer them all again.

Into this neutral air
Where blind skyscrapers use
Their full height to proclaim
The strength of Collective Man,
Each language pours its vain
Competitive excuse:
But who can live for long
In an euphoric dream;
Out of the mirror they stare,
Imperialism's face
And the international wrong.

Faces along the bar
Cling to their average day:
The lights must never go out,
The music must always play,
All the conventions conspire
To make this fort assume
The furniture of home;
Lest we should see where we are,
Lost in a haunted wood,
Children afraid of the night
Who have never been happy or good.

The windiest militant trash
Important Persons shout
Is not so crude as our wish:
What mad Nijinsky wrote
About Diaghilev
Is true of the normal heart;
For the error bred in the bone
Of each woman and each man
Craves what it cannot have,
Not universal love
But to be loved alone.

From the conservative dark
Into the ethical life
The dense commuters come,
Repeating their morning vow;
"I *will* be true to the wife,
I'll concentrate more on my work,"
And helpless governors wake
To resume their compulsory game:
Who can release them now,
Who can reach the deaf,
Who can speak for the dumb?

All I have is a voice
To undo the folded lie,
The romantic lie in the brain
Of the sensual man-in-the-street
And the lie of Authority
Whose buildings grope the sky:
There is no such thing as the State
And no one exists alone;
Hunger allows no choice
To the citizen or the police;
We must love one another or die.

Defenceless under the night
Our world in stupor lies;
Yet, dotted everywhere,
Ironic points of light
Flash out wherever the Just
Exchange their messages:
May I, composed like them
Of Eros and of dust,
Beleaguered by the same
Negation and despair,
Show an affirming flame.

MUNDUS ET INFANS

Kicking his mother until she let go of his soul
Has given him a healthy appetite: clearly, her rôle
    In the New Order must be
To supply and deliver his raw materials free;
    Should there be any shortage
She will be held responsible; she also promises
To show him all such attention as befits his age.
    Having dictated peace,

With one fist clenched behind his head, heel drawn up to thigh,
The cocky little ogre dozes off, ready,
    Though, to take on the rest
Of the world at the drop of a hat or the mildest
    Nudge of the impossible,
Resolved, cost what it may, to seize supreme power, and
Sworn to resist tyranny to the death with all
    Forces at his command.

A pantheist not a solipsist, he cooperates
With a universe of large and noisy feeling states,
    Without troubling to place
Them anywhere special; for, to his eyes, Funny face
    Or Elephant as yet
Mean nothing. His distinction between Me and Us
Is a matter of taste; his seasons are Dry and Wet;
    He thinks as his mouth does.

Still, his loud iniquity is still what only the
Greatest of saints become—someone who does not lie:
    He because he cannot
Stop the vivid present to think; they by having got
    Past reflection into
A passionate obedience in time. We have our Boy-
Meets-Girl era of mirrors and muddle to work through
    Without rest, without joy.

Therefore we love him because his judgments are so
Frankly subjective that his abuse carries no
    Personal sting. We should
Never dare offer our helplessness as a good
    Bargain, without at least
Promising to overcome a misfortune we blame
History or Banks or the Weather for; but this beast
    Dares to exist without shame.

Let him praise his Creator with the top of his voice,
Then, and the motions of his bowels; let us rejoice
    That he lets us hope, for
He may never become a fashionable or
    Important personage.
However bad he may be, he has not yet gone mad;
Whoever we are now, we were no worse at his age:
    So of course we ought to be glad

When he bawls the house down. Has he not a perfect right
To remind us at any moment how we quite
    Rightly expect each other
To go upstairs or for a walk if we must cry over
    Spilt milk, such as our wish
That since, apparently, we shall never be above
Either or both, we had never learned to distinguish
    Between hunger and love?

SONG: AS I WALKED OUT ONE EVENING

As I walked out one evening,
  Walking down Bristol Street,
The crowds upon the pavement
  Were fields of harvest wheat.

And down by the brimming river
  I heard a lover sing
Under an arch of the railway:
  "Love has no ending.

I'll love you, dear, I'll love you
  Till China and Africa meet
And the river jumps over the mountain
  And the salmon sing in the street.

I'll love you till the ocean
  Is folded and hung up to dry
And the seven stars go squawking
  Like geese about the sky.

The years shall run like rabbits
  For in my arms I hold
The Flower of the Ages
  And the first love of the World."

But all the clocks in the city
  Began to whirr and chime:
"O let not Time deceive you,
  You cannot conquer Time.

In the burrows of the Nightmare
  Where Justice naked is,
Time watches from the shadow
  And coughs when you would kiss.

In headaches and in worry
  Vaguely life leaks away,
And Time will have his fancy
  To-morrow or to-day.

Into many a green valley
  Drifts the appalling snow;
Time breaks the threaded dances
  And the diver's brilliant bow.

O plunge your hands in water,
  Plunge them in up to the wrist;
Stare, stare in the basin
  And wonder what you've missed.

The glacier knocks in the cupboard,
  The desert sighs in the bed,
And the crack in the tea-cup opens
  A lane to the land of the dead.

Where the beggars raffle the banknotes
  And the Giant is enchanting to Jack,
And the Lily-white Boy is a Roarer
  And Jill goes down on her back.

O look, look in the mirror,
  O look in your distress;
Life remains a blessing
  Although you cannot bless.

O stand, stand at the window
  As the tears scald and start;
You shall love your crooked neighbour
  With your crooked heart."

It was late, late in the evening,
  The lovers they were gone;
The clocks had ceased their chiming
  And the deep river ran on.

SONG: FISH IN THE UNRUFFLED LAKES

Fish in the unruffled lake
The swarming colors wear,
Swans in the winter air
A white perfection have,
And the great lion walks
Through his innocent grove;
Lion, fish, and swan
Act, and are gone
Upon Time's toppling wave.

We till shadowed days are done,
We must weep and sing
Duty's conscious wrong,
The Devil in the clock,

The Goodness carefully worn
For atonement or for luck;
We must lose our loves;
On each beast and bird that moves
Turn an envious look.

Sighs for folly said and done
Twist our narrow days;
But I must bless, I must praise
That you, my swan, who have
All gifts that to the swan
Impulsive Nature gave,
The majesty and pride,
Last night should add
Your voluntary love.

SONG: STOP ALL THE CLOCKS

Stop all the clocks, cut off the telephone,
Prevent the dog from barking with a juicy bone,
Silence the pianos and with muffled drum
Bring out the coffin, let the mourners come.

Let aeroplanes circle moaning overhead
Scribbling on the sky the message He Is Dead,
Put crêpe bows round the white necks of the public doves,
Let the traffic policemen wear black cotton gloves.

He was my North, my South, my East and West,
My working week and my Sunday rest,
My noon, my midnight, my talk, my song;
I thought that love would last for ever: I was wrong.

The stars are not wanted now; put out every one:
Pack up the moon and dismantle the sun;
Pour away the ocean and sweep up the woods:
For nothing now can ever come to any good.

UNDER WHICH LYRE

A Reactionary Tract for the Times

Ares at last has quit the field,
The bloodstains on the bushes yield
To seeping showers.
And in their convalescent state
The fractured towns associate
With summer flowers.

Encamped upon the college plain
Raw veterans already train
As freshman forces;
Instructors with sarcastic tongue
Shepherd the battle-weary young
Through basic courses.

Among bewildering appliances
For mastering the arts and sciences
They stroll or run,
And nerves that never flinched at slaughter
Are shot to pieces by the shorter
Poems of Donne.

Professors back from secret missions
Resume their proper eruditions,
Though some regret it;
They liked their dictaphones a lot,
They met some big wheels and do not
Let you forget it.

But Zeus' inscrutable decree
Permits the will to disagree
To be pandemic,
Ordains that vaudeville shall preach,
And every commencement speech
Be a polemic.

Let Ares doze, that other war
Is instantly declared once more
'Twixt those who follow
Precocious Hermes all the way
And those who without qualms obey
Pompous Apollo.

Brutal like all Olympic games,
Though fought with smiles and Christian names
And less dramatic,
This dialectic strife between
The civil gods is just as mean,
And more fanatic.

What high immortals do in mirth
Is life and death on Middle Earth;
Their a-historic
Antipathy forever gripes
All ages and somatic types:
The sophomoric

Who face the future's darkest hints
With giggles or with prairie squints
As stout as Cortez,
And those who like myself turn pale
As we approach with ragged sail
The fattening forties.

The sons of Hermes love to play,
And only do their best when they
Are told they oughtn't;
Apollo's children never shrink
From boring jobs but have to think
Their work important.

Related by antithesis,
A compromise between them is
Impossible;
Respect perhaps, but friendship never:
Falstaff the fool confronts forever
The prig Prince Hal.

So, standing here, surrounded by
The eyes of Miltons and the high
Foreheads of Shaws,
A Hermes man, I call on you,
Phi-Beta-Kappa brethren, to
Defend his cause.

If he would leave the self alone,
Apollo's welcome to the throne,
Fasces and falcons;
He loves to rule, has always done it:
The earth would soon, did Hermes run it,
Be like the Balkans.

But, jealous of our god of dreams,
His common sense in secret schemes
To rule the heart;
Unable to invent the lyre,
Creates with simulated fire
Official art.

And when he occupies a college,
Truth is replaced by Useful Knowledge;
He pays particular
Attention to Commercial Thought,
Public Relations, Hygiene, Sport,
In his curricula.

Athletic, extrovert and crude,
For him, to work in solitude
Is the offense,
The goal a populous Nirvana:
His shield bears this device: *Mens sana*
Qui mal y pense.

Today his arms, we must confess,
From Right to Left have met success,
His banners wave
From Yale to Princeton, and the news
From Broadway to the Book Reviews
Is very grave.

His radio Homers all day long
In over-Whitmanated song
That does not scan,
With adjectives laid end to end,
Extol the doughnut and commend
The Common Man.

His too each homely lyric thing
On sport or spousal love or spring
Or dogs or dusters,
Invented by some courthouse bard
For recitation by the yard
In filibusters.

To him ascend the prize orations
And sets of fugal variations
On some folk ballad,
While dietitians sacrifice
A glass of prune juice or a nice
Marshmallow salad.

Charged with his compound of sensational
Sex plus some undenominational
Religious matter,
Enormous novels by co-eds
Rain down on our defenseless heads
Till our teeth chatter.

In fake Hermetic uniforms
Behind our battle-line, in swarms
That keep alighting,
His existentialists declare
That they are in complete despair,
Yet go on writing.

No matter. He shall be defied.
We have the ladies on our side.
What though his threat
To organize us grow more critical?
Zeus willing, we, the unpolitical
Shall best him yet.

Lone scholars, sniping from the walls
Of learned periodicals,
Our facts defend,
Our intellectual marines,
Landing in Little Magazines,
Capture a trend.

By night our student Underground
At cocktail parties whisper round
From ear to ear;
Fat figures in the public eye
Collapse next morning, ambushed by
Some witty sneer.

In our morale must lie our strength:
So, that we may behold at length
Routed Apollo's
Battalions melt away like fog,
Keep well the Hermetic Decalogue,
Which runs as follows:

Thou shalt not do as the dean pleases,
Thou shalt not write thy doctor's thesis
On education,
Thou shalt not worship projects nor
Shalt thou or thine bow down before
Administration.

Thou shalt not answer questionnaires
Or quizzes upon World Affairs,
Nor with compliance
Take any test. Thou shalt not sit
With statisticians nor commit
A social science.

Thou shalt not be on friendly terms
With guys in advertising firms,
Nor speak with such
As read the Bible for its prose,
Nor, above all, make love to those
Who wash too much.

Thou shalt not live within thy means
Nor on plain water and raw greens.
If thou must choose
Between the chances, choose the odd;
Read the *New Yorker;* trust in God;
And take short views.

AFTER CHRISTMAS

(From "For the Time Being")

Well, so that is that. Now we must dismantle the tree,
Putting the decorations back into their cardboard boxes—
Some have got broken—and carrying them up to the attic.
The holly and the mistletoe must be taken down and burnt,
And the children got ready for school. There are enough
Left-overs to do, warmed-up, for the rest of the week—
Not that we have much appetite, having drunk such a lot,
Stayed up so late, attempted—quite unsuccessfully—
To love all of our relatives, and in general
Grossly overestimated our powers. Once again
As in previous years we have seen the actual Vision and failed
To do more than entertain it as an agreeable
Possibility, once again we have sent Him away,
Begging though to remain His disobedient servant,
The promising child who cannot keep His word for long.
The Christmas Feast is already a fading memory,

And already the mind begins to be vaguely aware
Of an unpleasant whiff of apprehension at the thought
Of Lent and Good Friday which cannot, after all, now
Be very far off. But, for the time being, here we all are,
Back in the moderate Aristotelian city
Of darning and the Eight-Fifteen, where Euclid's geometry
And Newton's mechanics would account for our experience,
And the kitchen table exists because I scrub it.
It seems to have shrunk during the holidays. The streets
Are much narrower than we remembered; we had forgotten
The office was as depressing as this. To those who have seen
The Child, however dimly, however incredulously,
The Time Being is, in a sense, the most trying time of all.
For the innocent children who whispered so excitedly
Outside the locked door where they knew the presents to be
Grew up when it opened. Now, recollecting that moment
We can repress the joy, but the guilt remains conscious;
Remembering the stable where for once in our lives
Everything became a You and nothing was an It.
And craving the sensation but ignoring the cause,
We look round for something, no matter what, to inhibit
Our self-reflection, and the obvious thing for that purpose
Would be some great suffering. So, once we have met the Son,
We are tempted ever after to pray to the Father;
"Lead us into temptation and evil for our sake."
They will come, all right, don't worry; probably in a form
That we do not expect, and certainly with a force
More dreadful than we can imagine. In the meantime
There are bills to be paid, machines to keep in repair,
Irregular verbs to learn, the Time Being to redeem
From insignificance. The happy morning is over,
The night of agony still to come; the time is noon:
When the Spirit must practise his scales of rejoicing
Without even a hostile audience, and the Soul endure
A silence that is neither for nor against her faith
That God's Will will be done, that, in spite of her prayers,
God will cheat no one, not even the world of its triumph.

Stephen Spender

Stephen Spender was born near London February 28, 1909, of mixed German, Jewish and English origins; his mother was Violet Schuster, his father was Harold Spender, the well-known journalist. As a child he was especially interested in painting; at seventeen he supported himself by printing chemists' labels on his own press. At nineteen he attended University College, Oxford, but found university training alien to his temperament, and did not then complete his courses. After traveling abroad he returned to Oxford, and went down from University in 1931.

In his eighteenth year Spender himself set up and printed a paper-bound pamphlet of verse, *Nine Experiments* (1928), which is now unprocurable. Immature though much of it is, an individuality already declares itself. *Twenty Poems* (1930), printed while Spender was still an undergraduate, emphasizes his fecundity; it sounds, tentatively but distinctly, the note of passion so recognizable in the later verse. An imagination, and a fiery one, is at play in such early poems as "A Whim of Time," "Farewell in a Dream," "Winter Landscape," and "Epilogue."

Poems, published in England in 1933, reveals a complete poet. Maturity is suggested and a revolutionary fervor which caused the critics to compare Spender to Shelley. Some of the reviewers demurred at the unconcealed communism throughout, but the lyrical impulse was so great that Spender was hailed as one of the most significant voices of his day. Spender's subject matter is arresting—sometimes too arresting, for it directs too much attention on externals and leads to controversy about that which matters least in poetry. Spender himself is a little too conscious, even too belligerent, about his properties. Riding in a train, watching the world hasten away "like the quick spool of a film," he sees the grass, the cottage by the lake, the familiar symbols, "vivid but unreal."

> Real were iron lines, and, smashing the grass
> The cars in which we ride, and real our compelled time:
> Painted on enamel beneath the moving glass
> Unreal were cows, the wave-winged storks, the lime:
> These burned in a clear world from which we pass
> Like *rose* and *love* in a forgotten rhyme.

Oftener than not, Spender brings machinery over into poetry, accomplishing a fusion of modern imagery and traditional magic. He does not merely state the superficial aspects of the machine age, he assimilates and re-creates the daily symbols of his environment. As early as 1928, while a remnant of the Georgians were still invoking literary laverocks, lonely lambs, and dependable nightingales, Spender was writing, "Come let us praise the gasworks." A few years later, the same accent expressed itself in simple, transparent delight:

> More beautiful and soft than any moth
> With burring furred antennae feeling its huge path
> Through dusk, the air-liner with shut-off engines
> Glides over suburbs and the sleeves set trailing tall
> To point the wind. Gently, broadly, she falls,
> Scarcely disturbing charted currents of air.

Spender is not always as direct as this. Inclined to sentimentality he overcompensates by forcing himself to the other extreme; distrusting the appearance of his simplicities he disguises them in strained metaphors and involved images. The result is a blurring of vision and an ambiguity of communication. Too often the reader has to guess at the meaning of a line which begins clearly enough but ends in a verbal fog. There is, however, no uncertainty about Spender's emotion. The emotion is clear, warm, compelling. It is serious and straightforward, especially in such poems as "The Express," "What I Expected," reaching a powerful climax in "The Prisoners," "The Funeral" and the moving "An Elementary Classroom."

It is not Spender's choice of opinions which makes his work exciting; it is the integrity of his aim accompanied by charged and highly suggestive phrases, the thrust of his vision. The old images have gone down with the bombed buildings, as he tells us in "Not Palaces"; they are part of "beauty's filtered dusts." All our faculties must cooperate to appreciate the new values—the eye, that quickly darting, delicately wandering gazelle; the ear, which "suspends on a chord the spirit drinking timelessness"; touch, that intensifies all senses.

Vienna (1935) is Spender's least successful effort. *The Still Centre* (1939) is a return to Spender's power, an exploration of "the human conditions," personal in method, universal in implication. It was combined with new poems and republished as *Ruins and Visions* in 1942. A new note, resolute and increasingly confessional, is apparent here and in *Poems of Dedication* (1947) and *The Edge of Being* (1949). The limitations are obvious: the heavily burdened and sometimes inchoate line, the total lack of humor, the frequent failure of the baffled brain to win the approval of the badgered heart. But there is always the desperate sincerity, the intense voice of something dearly held and deeply felt. It is the voice that speaks up for "the palpable and obvious love of man," an utterance which, achieving the high level of the lines beginning "I think continually of those who were truly great," is exalted and often noble.

In addition to his poetry, Spender has been prolific in criticism, fiction, and drama. *Trial of a Judge* (1938) is a tragedy of the Nazi terror, a telescoping of the real and the incredible. *The Burning Cactus* (1936) is a volume of short stories, slightly reminiscent of D. H. Lawrence in its hurt sensibility. *The Destructive Element* (1935) is a critical appraisal of a civilization at once creative and corrupt, and a justification of his theory that "Poetry does not state truth; it states the condition within which something felt is true." An unusually candid autobiography, *World Within World* (1951), was followed by a winnowed *Collected Poems* (1955).

FAREWELL IN A DREAM

Now shout into my dream. These trumpets snored
Less golden by my side, when you were there . . .
It is no reason now to think me coward
That, being insulted by a gamekeeper,
I hung my head, or looked into the air:
Thrusting between the peaks without a word,
Buttressed against the winds, or like a sword,
Then you were undisputed conqueror.

But dragged into this nightmare symphony
Of drum and tempest surging in my head,
Faced by these symbols of reality
You showed as one most pitifully naked.
I hailed your earth. Salute my Hades too.
Since we must part, let's part as heroes do.

STATISTICS

Lady, you think too much of speeds,
  Pulleys and cranes swing in your mind;
  The Woolworth Tower has made you blind
To Egypt and the pyramids.

Too much impressed by motor-cars
  You have a false historic sense.
  But I, perplexed at God's expense
Of electricity on stars,

From Brighton pier shall weigh the seas,
  And count the sands along the shore:
  Despise all moderns, thinking more
Of Shakespeare and Praxiteles.

A WHIM OF TIME

A whim of time, the general arbiter,
Proclaims the love instead of death of friends.
Under the domed sky and athletic sun
The three stand naked, the new, bronzed German,
The young communist and myself, being English.
Yet to unwind the traveled sphere ten years
And two take arms, spring to a ghostly posture:
Or else roll on the thing a further ten
And the poor clerk with world-offended eyes
Builds with red hands his heaven; makes our bones
A necessary scaffolding to peace.

Now I suppose that the once-envious dead
Have learnt a strict philosophy of clay
After these centuries, to haunt us no longer
In the churchyard, or at the end of the lane,
Or howling at the edge of the city
Beyond the last bean-rows, near the new factory.
Our fathers enemies, yet lives no feud
Of prompting Hamlet on the kitchen stair,
There falls no shade across our blank of peace
Being together struck across the path
Or taper finger threatening solitude.

Our father's misery, the dead man's mercy,
The cynic's mystery, weaves a philosophy—
That history of man traced purely from dust
Is lipping skulls on the revolving rim
Or posture of slavery with the granite head bowed:
These, risen a moment, joined or separate,
Fall heavily, then are always separate.
A stratum scarce reckoned by geologers,
Sod lifted, turned, slapped back again with spade.

EPILOGUE

Time is a thing
That does not pass through boredom and the wishing,
But must be fought with, rushed at, over-awed,
And threatened with a sword:

For that prodigious voyager, the Mind,
Another self doth find
At each hour's stage, and riven, hewn and wrought
Cannot foretell its port.

Let heart be done, shut close the whining eyes,
And work, or drink, or sleep, till life defies
Minute, month, hour and day
Which are harrowed, and beaten, and scared away.

DISCOVERED IN MID-OCEAN

He will watch the hawk with an indifferent eye
Or pitifully;
Nor on those eagles that so feared him, now
Will strain his brow;
Weapons men use, stone, sling, and strong-thewed bow
He will not know.

This aristocrat, superb of all instinct,
With death close linked
Had paced the enormous cloud, almost had won
War on the sun;
Till now like Icarus mid-ocean-drowned,
Hands, wings, are found. . . .

WHAT I EXPECTED

What I expected was
Thunder, fighting,
Long struggles with men
And climbing.
After continual straining
I should grow strong;
Then the rocks would shake
And I should rest long.

What I had not foreseen
Was the gradual day
Weakening the will
Leaking the brightness away,
The lack of good to touch
The fading of body and soul
Like smoke before wind
Corrupt, unsubstantial.

The wearing of Time,
And the watching of cripples pass
With limbs shaped like questions
In their odd twist,
The pulverous grief
Melting the bones with pity,
The sick falling from earth—
These, I could not foresee.

For I had expected always
Some brightness to hold in trust,
Some final innocence
To save from dust;
That, hanging solid,
Would dangle through all
Like the created poem
Or the dazzling crystal.

THE PRISONERS

Far, far the least of all, in want,
Are these,
The prisoners
Turned massive with their vaults and dark with dark.

They raise no hands, which rest upon their knees,
But lean their solid eyes against the night,
Dimly they feel
Only the furniture they use in cells.

Their time is almost Death. The silted flow
Of years on years
Is marked by dawns
As faint as cracks on mud-flats of despair.

My pity moves amongst them like a breeze
On walls of stone
Fretting for summer leaves, or like a tune
On ears of stone.

Then, when I raise my hands to strike,
It is too late,
There are no chains that fall
Nor visionary liquid door
Melted with anger.

When have their lives been free from walls and dark
And airs that choke?
And where less prisoner to let my anger
Like a sun strike?

If I could follow them from room to womb
To plant some hope
Through the black silk of the big-bellied gown
There would I win.

No, no, no,
It is too late for anger,
Nothing prevails
But pity for the grief they cannot feel.

WINTER LANDSCAPE

Come home with white gulls waving across gray
Fields. Evening. A daffodil West.
Somewhere in clefts of rock the birds hide, breast to breast.

I warm with fire. Curtain shrouds dying day.
Alone. By the glowing ember
I shut out the bleak-tombed evenings of November.

And breast to breast, those swans. Sheep huddle and press
Close. Each to each. Oh,
Is there no herd of men like beasts where man may go?

Come home at last; come, end of loneliness.
Sea. Evening. Daffodil West.
And our thin dying souls against Eternity pressed.

THE FUNERAL

Death is another milestone on their way.
With laughter on their lips and with winds blowing round them
They record simply
How this one excelled all others in making driving-belts.

This is festivity, it is the time of statistics
When they record what one unit contributed:
They are glad as they lay him back in the earth
And thank him for what he gave them.

They walk home remembering the straining red flags,
And with pennons of song still fluttering through their blood
They speak of the world-state
With its towns like brain-centers and its pulsing arteries.

They think how one life hums, revolves and toils,
One cog in a golden and singing hive:
Like spark from fire, its task happily achieved,
It falls away quietly.

No more are they haunted by the individual grief
Nor the crocodile tears of European genius,
The decline of a culture
Mourned by scholars who dream of the ghosts of Greek boys.

THE EXPRESS

After the first powerful plain manifesto
The black statement of pistons, without more fuss
But gliding like a queen, she leaves the station.
Without bowing and with restrained unconcern
She passes the houses which humbly crowd outside,
The gasworks and at last the heavy page
Of death, printed by gravestones in the cemetery.
Beyond the town there lies the open country
Where, gathering speed, she acquires mystery,
The luminous self-possession of ships on ocean.
It is now she begins to sing—at first quite low
Then loud, and at last with a jazzy madness—
The song of her whistle screaming at curves,
Of deafening tunnels, brakes, innumerable bolts.

And always light, aerial, underneath
Goes the elate meter of her wheels.
Steaming through metal landscape on her lines
She plunges new eras of wild happiness
Where speed throws up strange shapes, broad curves
And parallels clean like the steel of guns.
At last, further than Edinburgh or Rome,
Beyond the crest of the world, she reaches night
Where only a low streamline brightness
Of phosphorus on the tossing hills is white.
Ah, like a comet through flames she moves entranced
Wrapt in her music no bird song, no, nor bough
Breaking with honey buds, shall ever equal.

THE LANDSCAPE NEAR AN AERODROME

More beautiful and soft than any moth
With burring furred antennae feeling its huge path
Through dusk, the air-liner with shut-off engines
Glides over suburbs and the sleeves set trailing tall
To point the wind. Gently, broadly, she falls,
Scarcely disturbing charted currents of air.

Lulled by descent, the travelers across sea
And across feminine land indulging its easy limbs
In miles of softness, now let their eyes trained by watching
Penetrate through dusk the outskirts of this town
Here where industry shows a fraying edge.
Here they may see what is being done.

Beyond the winking masthead light
And the landing-ground, they observe the outposts
Of work: chimneys like lank black fingers
Or figures frightening and mad: and squat buildings
With their strange air behind trees, like women's faces
Shattered by grief. Here where few houses
Moan with faint light behind their blinds
They remark the unhomely sense of complaint, like a dog
Shut out and shivering at the foreign moon.

In the last sweep of love, they pass over fields
Behind the aerodrome, where boys play all day
Hacking dead grass: whose cries, like wild birds,
Settle upon the nearest roofs
But soon are hid under the loud city.

Then, as they land, they hear the tolling bell
Reaching across the landscape of hysteria
To where, larger than all the charcoaled batteries
And imaged towers against that dying sky,
Religion stands, the church blocking the sun.

AN ELEMENTARY SCHOOL CLASSROOM IN A SLUM

Far far from gusty waves, these children's faces.
Like rootless weeds the torn hair round their paleness.
The tall girl with her weighed-down head. The paper-
seeming boy with rat's eyes. The stunted unlucky heir
Of twisted bones, reciting a father's gnarled disease,
His lesson from his desk. At back of the dim class
One unnoted, mild and young: his eyes live in a dream
Of squirrels' game, in tree room, other than this.

On sour cream walls, donations. Shakespeare's head
Cloudless at dawn, civilized dome riding all cities.
Belled, flowery, Tyrolese valley. Open-handed map
Awarding the world its world. And yet, for these
Children, these windows, not this world, are world,
Where all their future's painted with a fog,
A narrow street sealed in with a lead sky,
Far far from rivers, capes, and stars of words.

Surely Shakespeare is wicked, the map a bad example
With ships and sun and love tempting them to steal—
For lives that slyly turn in their cramped holes
From fog to endless night? On their slag heap, these children
Wear skins peeped through by bones, and spectacles of steel
With mended glass, like bottle bits in slag.
Tyrol is wicked; map's promising a fable:
All of their time and space are foggy slum,
So blot their maps with slums as big as doom.

Unless, governor, teacher, inspector, visitor,
This map becomes their window and these windows
That open on their lives like crouching tombs
Break, O break open, till they break the town
And show the children to the fields and all their world
Azure on their sands, to let their tongues
Run naked into books, the white and green leaves open
The history theirs whose language is the sun.

MASK

The face of the landscape is a mask
Of bone and iron lines where time
Has plowed its character.
I look and look to read a sign,
Through errors of light and eyes of water
Beneath the land's will, of a fear
And the memory of a struggle,
As man behind his mask still wears a child.

NOT PALACES

Not palaces, an era's crown
Where the mind dreams, intrigues, rests;
The architectural gold-leaved flower
From people ordered like a single mind,
I build. This only what I tell:
It is too late for rare accumulation,
For family pride, for beauty's filtered dusts;
I say, stamping the words with emphasis,
Drink from here energy and only energy,
As from the electric charge of a battery,
To will this time's change.
Eye, gazelle, delicate wanderer,
Drinker of horizon's fluid line;
Ear that suspends on a chord
The spirit drinking timelessness;
Touch, love—all senses—
Leave your gardens, your singing feasts,
Your dreams of suns circling before our sun,
Of heaven after our world.
Instead, watch images of flashing brass
That strike the outward sense, the polished will,
Flag of our purpose which the wind engraves.
No spirit seek here rest. But this: No man
Shall hunger; Man shall spend equally.
Our goal which we compel: Man shall be man.

The program of the antique Satan
Bristling with guns on the indented page,
With battleship towering from hilly waves:
For what? Drive of a running purpose,
Destroying all but its age-long exploiters.
Our program like this, yet opposite:
Death to the killers, bringing light to life.

I THINK CONTINUALLY OF THOSE

I think continually of those who were truly great.
Who, from the womb, remembered the soul's history
Through corridors of light where the hours are suns,
Endless and singing. Whose lovely ambition
Was that their lips, still touched with fire,
Should tell of the spirit clothed from head to foot in song.
And who hoarded from the spring branches
The desires falling across their bodies like blossoms.

What is precious is never to forget
The delight of the blood drawn from ageless springs
Breaking through rocks in worlds before our earth;

Never to deny its pleasure in the simple morning light,
Nor its grave evening demand for love;
Never to allow gradually the traffic to smother
With noise and fog the flowering of the spirit.

Near the snow, near the sun, in the highest fields
See how these names are fêted by the waving grass,
And by the streamers of white cloud,
And whispers of wind in the listening sky;
The names of those who in their lives fought for life,
Who wore at their hearts the fire's center.
Born of the sun they traveled a short while towards the sun,
And left the vivid air signed with their honor.

SONNET: "YOU WERE BORN; MUST DIE"

You were born; must die; were loved; must love;
Born naked; were clothed; still naked walk
Under your clothes. Under your skin you move
Naked; naked under acts and talk.
  The miles and hours upon you feed.
They eat your eyes out with their distance
They eat your heart out with devouring need
They eat your death out with lost significance.
  There is one fate beneath those ignorances
Those flesh and bone parcels in which you're split
O thing of skin and words hanging on breath:
Harlequin skeleton, it
Strums on your gut such songs and merry dances
Of love, of loneliness, of life being death.

JUDAS ISCARIOT

The eyes of twenty centuries
Pursue me along corridors to where
I am painted at their ends on many walls.
  Ever-revolving futures recognize
This red hair and red beard, where I am seated
Within the dark cave of the feast of light.
  Out of my heart-shaped shadow I stretch my hand
Across the white table into the dish
But not to dip the bread. It is as though
The cloth on each side of one dove-bright face
Spread dazzling wings on which the apostles ride
Uplifting them into the vision
Where their eyes watch themselves enthroned
  My russet hand across the dish
Plucks enviously against one feather
  —But still the rushing wings spurn me below!

    Saint Sebastian of wickedness
I stand: all eyes legitimate arrows piercing through

The darkness of my wickedness. They recognize
My halo hammered from thirty silver pieces
And the hemp rope around my neck
Soft as that spirit's hanging arms
When on my cheek he answered with the kiss
Which cuts for ever—
My strange stigmata,
All love and hate, all fire and ice!

But who betrayed whom? O you,
Whose light gaze forms the azure corridor
Through which those other pouring eyes
Arrow into me—answer! Who
Betrayed whom? Who had foreseen
All, from the first? Who read
In his mind's light from the first day
That the kingdom of heaven on earth must always
Reiterate the garden of Eden,
And each day's revolution be betrayed
Within man's heart each day?
Who wrapped
The whispering serpent round the tree
And hung between the leaves the glittering purse
And trapped the fangs with God-appointed poison?
Who knew
I must betray the truth, and made the lie
Betray its truth in me?

Those hypocrite eyes which aimed at you
Now aim at me. And yet, beyond this world
We are alone, eternal opposites,
Each turning on his pole of truth, your pole
Invisible light, and mine
Becoming what man is. We stare
Across two thousand years, and heaven, and hell,
Into each other's gaze.

THOUGHTS DURING AN AIR RAID

Of course, the entire effort is to put myself
Outside the ordinary range
Of what are called statistics. A hundred are killed
In the outer suburbs. Well, well, I carry on.
So long as the great "I" is propped upon
This girdered bed which seems more like a hearse,
In the hotel bedroom with flowering wallpaper
Which rings in wreathes above, I can ignore
The pressure of those names under my fingers
Heavy and black as I rustle the paper,
The wireless wail in the lounge margin.
Yet, supposing that a bomb should dive
Its nose right through this bed, with me upon it?

The thought is obscene. Still, there are many
To whom my death would only be a name,
One figure in a column. The essential is
That all the "I"s should remain separate
Propped up under flowers, and no one suffer
For his neighbour. Then horror is postponed
For everyone until it settles on him
And drags him to that incommunicable grief
Which is all mystery or nothing.

WINTER AND SUMMER

Within my head, aches the perpetual winter
Of this violent time, where pleasures freeze.
My inner eye anticipates for ever
Looking through naked trees and running wheels
Onto a blank transparent sky
Leading to nothing; as though, through iron aims,
It was stared back at by the filmy surface
Of a lid covering its own despair.
Thus, when the summer breaks upon my face
With the outward shock of a green wave
Crested with leaves and creamy foam of flowers,
I think the luxurious lazy meadows
Are a deceiving canvas covering
With a balmy paint of leafy billows,
The furious volleys of charioteering power
Behind the sun, racing to destroy.
  When under light lawns, heavy in their soil,
I hear the groaning of the wasted lives
Of those who revolve unreflecting wheels,
  Alas, I prove that I am right,
For if my shadowed mind affirmed the light
It would return to those green, foolish years
When to live seemed to stand knee-deep in flowers:
There, winter was an indoor accident,
Where, with head pressed against the glass, I watched
The garden, falsified by snow,
Waiting to melt, and become real again.

W. R. Rodgers

W. R. Rodgers, an Ulsterman, was born in Belfast, Ireland, in 1909. During some twelve years he was an Irish country parson; subsequently he was connected with the British Broadcasting Corporation. His first book *Awake! And Other Wartime Poems,* was published in 1940, but the entire edition was destroyed in an enemy bombing raid. The book was reset and republished in 1942.

The prime quality of Rodgers's verse is its forthrightness. His is an energetic, free-speaking utterance which is honest and winning, vigorous to the point of occasional nonchalant noisiness. His liveliness is accompanied (and sometimes impeded) by a love of alliteration and assonance: "Now all our hurries that hung up on hooks," "whirling and wheeling and whorling," "juts and jets jumpily," etc. His breathless pace and hearty overemphasis recall Hopkins, especially in such lines as these from "Snow":

And soon the knock and hiss of cistern ceased as
Gradually with inklings and wrinkling strings
Of ice the thickening cold anchored the skin
And slow core of water, gluing and glossing
All leaks, niggling or great, naked or guarded.

But, in *New British Poets,* Kenneth Rexroth maintains that Rodgers's "labial, sibilant, and nasal music is a kind of counter-Hopkins. . . . The quality I associate most clearly with his work is a rugged, protestant magnanimity, courteous and polished enough superficially, but with, still underneath, a certain masculine gaucherie. The comparison that springs to mind is Andrew Marvell." In a review in *The Nation,* another poet, George Barker, concluded: "He has the gift of gab that in the long run makes Swinburne a greater poet than George Meredith; he has a green thumb for the verb with a nerve running along it; and he has simple but passionate convictions about the state of things generally." *Europa and the Bull* (1952) is, like his other work, uneven but stimulating.

Rodgers was elected to the Irish Academy of Letters in 1951.

THE RAIDER

There, wrapped in his own roars, the lone airman
Swims like a mote through the thousands of eyes
That look up at him ironing out the skies,
Frocked and fanged by fire, by nagging fingers
Of guns jagged and jogged, with shell-bursts tasselled.

Does ever the airman's eye, speeding on
To grim conclusion, alight and loiter
Curiously on the country below?
Or does his gaze easily dissolve
Upon the moving surfaces, and flow
Evenly away like rain on rivers?

Or, roaring back over our armoured rims
Does his mind take in only the bloom and boom
Of bomb beneath him, noting how neatly
It mopped up a map-point town or snouted out
This tip or else that tap-root of resistance?

Yet, pity him too, that navigator
Who now in archipelago of steel
Nears that place where, hooked upon barbed air, he'll
Halt, hang hump-backed, and look into his crater.

SING, BROTHERS, SING!

In cinemas we sought
The syrupy event,
In morning paper bought
Our cozy sentiment.

We eyed shop-windows packed
With leisure gun and rod
For the fastidious act
Of poking fun like God.

Each evening to amuse,
The radio-cage unveiled,
To speak the shocking news
The parrot never failed,

Its insulated tones
Reporting perfectly
Alarming war-zones,
The usual perfidy.

The bright and mirror voice
Reviewed the scrimmages,
Deleting heat and noise
From all its images.

Each evening it drew
A round-robin applause,
For it confirmed anew
Our own and Nature's laws.

At our back-door we failed to hear
War's dust-bin chariot drawing near.

WHITE CHRISTMAS

Punctually at Christmas the soft plush
Of sentiment snows down, enbosoms all
The sharp and pointed shapes of venom, shawls
The hills and hides the shocking holes of this
Uneven world of want and wealth, cushions
With cosy wish like cotton-wool the cool
Arm's-length interstices of caste and class,
And into obese folds subtracts from sight
All truculent acts, bleeding the world white.

Punctually that glib pair, Peace and Goodwill,
Emerges royally to take the air,
Collect the bows, assimilate the smiles,
Of waiting men. It is a genial time;

Angels, like stalactites, descend from heaven;
Bishops distribute their own weight in words,
Congratulate the poor on Christlike lack;
And the member for the constituency
Feeds the five thousand, and has plenty back.

Punctually, to-night, in old stone circles
Of set reunion, families stiffly sit
And listen: this is the night and this the happy time
When the tinned milk of human kindness is
Upheld and holed by radio-appeal:
Hushed are hurrying heels on hard roads,
And every parlour's a pink pond of light
To the cold and travelling man going by
In the dark, without a bark or a bite.

But punctually to-morrow you will see
All this silent and dissembling world
Of stilted sentiment suddenly melt
Into mush and watery welter of words
Beneath the warm and moving traffic of
Feet and actual fact. Over the stark plain
The stilted mill-chimneys once again spread
Their sackcloth and ashes, a flowing mane
Of repentance for the false day that's fled.

NEITHER HERE NOR THERE

In that land all Is and nothing's Ought;
No owners or notices, only birds;
No walls anywhere, only lean wire of words
Worming brokenly out from eaten thought;
No oats growing, only ankle-lace grass
Easing and not resenting the feet that pass;
No enormous beasts, only names of them;
No bones made, bans laid, or bones expected,
No contracts, entails, hereditaments,
Anything at all that might tie or hem.

In that land all's lackadaisical;
No lakes of coddled spawn, and no locked ponds
Of settled purpose, no netted fishes;
But only inkling streams and running fronds,
Fritillaried with dreams, weedy with wishes;
Nor arrogant talk is heard, haggling phrase,
But undertones, and hesitance, and haze;
On clear days mountains of meaning are seen
Humped high on the horizon; no one goes
To con their meaning, no one cares or knows.
In that land all's flat, indifferent; there
Is neither springing house nor hanging tent,

No aims are entertained, and nothing is meant,
For there are no ends and no trends, no roads,
Only follow your nose to anywhere.
No one is born there, no one stays or dies,
For it is a timeless land, it lies
Between the act and the attrition, it
Marks off bound from rebound, make from break, tit
From tat, also to-day from to-morrow.
No Cause there comes to term, but each departs
Elsewhere to whelp its deeds, expel its darts;
There are no homecomings, of course, no good-byes
In that land, neither yearning nor scorning,
Though at night there is the smell of morning.

Kathleen Raine

Kathleen J. Raine was born in 1909, daughter of a schoolmaster, and was educated at Girton College, Cambridge, where, later, she taught. She married the poet and professor, Charles Madge, by whom she had two children, but the marriage was dissolved.

Regarding her own work with critical detachment, Kathleen Raine did not publish a volume until she was in her mid-thirties, when *Stone and Flower* appeared in 1943. Three other books preceded her *Collected Poems* (1956), all of them disclosing a spontaneous lyric voice with a scrupulous examination of the sensibilities and the subconscious impulses which drive them. Nature and its impact on human nature are her constant preoccupation; hers is a severe seventeenth century mind confronting the confusion of the twentieth century.

"Love," she wrote in an introduction to her *Collected Poems,* "is important only in Plato's sense in so far as it gives wings to the imagination—whatever in love is personal and not imaginative matters not at all . . . The ever-recurring forms of nature mirror eternal reality; the never-recurring productions of human history reflect only fallen man."

Kathleen Raine is also the author of studies of Blake, Coleridge, and *Aspects of English Literature*. An American publication of her *Selected Poems* appeared in a limited printing in 1952.

QUESTION AND ANSWER

That which is, being the only answer
The question is its measure. Ask the flower
And the question unfolds in eloquent petals about the centre;
Ask fire, and the rose bursts into flame and terror.

Ask water, and the streams flow and dew falls;
Shell's minute spiral wisdom forms in pools.

Earth answers fields and gardens and the grave; birds rise
Into the singing air that opens boundless skies.

Womb knows the eternal union and its child,
Heart the blood-sacrifice of the wounded god.
Death charts the terrible negative infinity,
And with the sun rises perpetual day.

THE PYTHONESS

I am that serpent-haunted cave
Whose navel breeds the fates of men.
All wisdom issues from a hole in the earth:
The gods form in my darkness, and dissolve again.

From my blind womb all kingdoms come,
And from my grave seven sleepers prophesy.
No babe unborn but wakens to my dream,
No lover but at last entombed in me shall lie.

I am that feared and longed-for burning place
Where man and phoenix are consumed away,
And from my low polluted bed arise
New sons, new suns, new skies.

AIR

Element that utters doves, angels and cleft flames,
The bees of Helicon and the cloudy houses,
Impulse of music and the world's equipoise,

Dancer that never wearies of the dance
That prints in the blown dust eternal wisdom
Or carves its abstract sculpture in the snow,
The wind unhindered passes beyond its trace.

But from a high fell on a summer day
Sometimes below you may see the air like water,
The dazzle of the light upon its waves,
The flow unbroken to the end of the world.

The bird of god descends between two moments
Like silence into music, opening a way through time.

LOVE POEM

Yours is the face that the earth turns to me,
Continuous beyond its human features lie
The mountain forms that rest against the sky.
With your eyes, the reflecting rainbow, the sun's light

Sees me; forest and flowers, bird and beast
Know and hold me forever in the world's thought,
Creation's deep untroubled retrospect.

When your hand touches mine, it is the earth
That takes me—the deep grass,
And rocks and rivers; the green graves,
And children still unborn, and ancestors,
In love passed down from hand to hand from God.
Your love comes from the creation of the world,
From those paternal fingers, streaming through the clouds
That break with light the surface of the sea.

Here, where I trace your body with my hand,
Love's presence has no end;
For these, your arms that hold me, are the world's.
In us, the continents, clouds and oceans meet
Our arbitrary selves, extensive with the night,
Lost, in the heart's worship, and the body's sleep.

F. T. Prince

Frank Templeton Prince was born in 1912 at Kimberley, South Africa, and was educated in his native country and at Balliol College, Oxford. After serving as a captain in the Intelligence Corps during the Second World War he became a lecturer at the University of Southampton.

A fastidious scholar, Prince rejected most of his early *Poems* (1938) when he published *Soldiers Bathing and Other Poems* (1954), retaining only a few of the lyrics. The title-poem of his second volume elicited high praise from poets of every school; Stephen Spender considered it magnificent, and others called attention to its eloquent imagery. "Mr. Prince," wrote a reviewer in the London *Times Literary Supplement,* "has admirably extended the poetic conventions of our time to express without fear his own enthusiasm." "The Babiaantje," a poem in an entirely different key, is a colorful reflection of Prince's youthful background.

SOLDIERS BATHING

The sea at evening moves across the sand.
Under a reddening sky I watch the freedom of a band
Of soldiers who belong to me. Stripped bare
For bathing in the sea, they shout and run in the warm air;
Their flesh, worn by the trade of war, revives
And my mind towards the meaning of it strives.

All's pathos now. The body that was gross,
Rank, ravening, disgusting in the act or in repose,

All fever, filth and sweat, its bestial strength
And bestial decay, by pain and labor grows at length
Fragile and luminous. "Poor bare forked animal,"
Conscious of his desires and needs and flesh that rise and fall,
Stands in the soft air, tasting after toil
The sweetness of his nakedness: letting the sea-waves coil
Their frothy tongues about his feet, forgets
His hatred of the war, its terrible pressure that begets
A machinery of death and slavery,
Each being a slave and making slaves of others, finds that he
Remembers lovely freedom in a game,
Mocking himself, and comically mimics fear and shame.

He plays with death and animality.
And, reading in the shadows of his pallid flesh, I see
The idea of Michelangelo's cartoon
Of soldiers bathing, breaking off before they were half done
At some sortie of the enemy, an episode
Of the Pisan wars with Florence. I remember how he showed
Their muscular limbs that clamber from the water
And heads that turn across the shoulder, eager for the slaughter,
Forgetful of their bodies that are bare
And hot to buckle on and use the weapons lying there.
—And I think too of the theme another found
When, shadowing men's bodies on a sinister red ground,
Another Florentine, Pollaiuolo,
Painted a naked battle: warriors, straddled, hacked the foe,
Dug their bare toes into the soil and slew
The brother-naked man who lay between their feet and drew
His lips back from his teeth in a grimace.

They were Italians who knew war's sorrow and disgrace
And showed the thing suspended, stripped: a theme
Born out of the experience of war's horrible extreme
Beneath a sky where even the air flows
With *lachrimae Christi*. For that rage, that bitterness, those blows
That hatred of the slain, what could it be
But indirectly or directly a commentary
On the Crucifixion? And the picture burns
With indignation and pity and despair by turns,
Because it is the obverse of the scene
Where Christ hangs murdered, stripped, upon the Cross.
    I mean,
That is the explanation of its rage.

And we too have our bitterness and pity that engage
Blood, spirit in this war. But night begins,
Night of the mind: who nowadays is conscious of our sins?
Though every human deed concerns our blood,
And even we must know what nobody has understood,
That some great love is over all we do,
And that is what has driven us to this fury, for so few

Can suffer all the terror of that love:
The terror of that love has set us spinning in this groove
Greased with our blood.
These dry themselves and dress,
Combing their hair, forget the fear and shame of nakedness.
Because to love is frightening, we prefer
The freedom of our crimes. Yet, as I drink the dusky air,
I feel a strange delight that fills me full,
Strange gratitude, as if evil itself were beautiful,
And kiss the wound in thought, while in the west
I watch a streak of red that might have issued from Christ's breast.

THE BABIAANTJE

Hither, where tangled thickets of the acacia
Wreathed with a golden powder, sigh
And when the boughs grow dark, the hoopoe
Doubles his bell-like cry,
Spreading his bright striped wings and brown crest
Under a softening spring sky,—
I have returned because I cannot rest,
And would not die.

Here it was as a boy that, I remember,
I wandered ceaselessly, and knew
Sweetness of spring was in the bird's cry,
And in the hidden dew
The unbelievably keen perfume
Of the Babiaantje, a pale blue
Wild hyacinth that between narrow grey leaves
On the ground grew.

The flower will be breathing there now, should I wish
To search the grass beneath those trees,
And having found it, should go down
To snuff it, on my knees.
But now, although the crested hoopoe
Calls like a bell, how barren these
Rough ways and dusty woodlands look to one
Who has lost youth's peace!

Lawrence Durrell

Lawrence Durrell was born of Irish parentage, in the town of Jullundur in the Himalayas, February 27, 1912. He went to Indian schools until he was ten, at which time he was brought to St. Edmund's School in Canterbury, England. One of four children, while still young he was brought by his mother to the Mediterranean island of Corfu. In his forties he said that it tired him merely to think of all the journeys he had taken as a Foreign Service press officer, a British Council lecturer, and a private individual. "Backwards and forwards across the Balkans, round about among the islands of Greece . . . Egypt . . . Rhodes . . . Belgrade . . . the Argentine pampas."

Before he became a sensationally successful novelist, Durrell kept himself alive by being not only a journalist and a quasi-diplomat but also a lecturer, an instructor, a rent-collector, and a pianist in a nightclub. He bought himself a house in Cyprus, won the confidence of the natives by speaking Greek without a foreign accent, and taught English in the local gymnasium until the revolutionary situation elevated him to the status of a senior government official.

Energetically creative, in his late forties Durrell was the author of some twenty volumes ranging from poetry to the panoramic *Alexandria Quartet* (1957-1960), a major work of fiction; from the witty exposures of diplomatic procedure, *Esprit de Corps,* to a penetrating commentary of the crisis in Cyprus, *Bitter Lemons* (1958), an account which is both farcical and tragical; from the controversial novel, *The Black Book* (1938), with its implicit tribute to Henry Miller, to a translation of Royidis' scandalous *Pope Joan* (1961). For about twenty years, until he wrote the tetralogy which made him both famous and wealthy, Durrell had been making no more than a hundred pounds on each book and was seriously considering getting a job as a laborer or a sheepherder in the south of France, to which country he had emigrated.

Durrell's achievements in prose, feats of an ingenious but apparently effortless style, have obscured his accomplishment as a poet. Yet *Collected Poems* (1960) show many of the virtues if not the virtuosity of his prose. "Swans," "A Water-Colour of Venice," "In Arcadia," and "Visitations" are expressions of one who has been characterized as a poet who happened to stumble into prose. Most of his poems, when they are not downright mocking or bawdy, evoke not only the mood of a place but also the measure of a man, discriminating, meditative, sometimes mordant but always acutely responsive to the scene and its multiple suggestions.

> Something is incomplete here,
> Something in the story is unfinished,
> A tale with no beginning,
> The fragment of a voice that interrupts,
> Like this unbroken coast,
> Like this half-drawn landscape,
> Like this broken torso of a poem.

Alternating simple and complex, sometimes plain and sometimes flashing with imagery, Durrell achieves continual sensuousness and, in the midst of confusion, an allusive elegance, a final serenity.

SWANS

Fraudulent perhaps in that they gave
No sense of muscle but a swollen languor
Though moved by webs: yet idly, idly

As soap-bubbles drift from a clay-pipe
They mowed the lake in tapestry,

Passing in regal exhaustion by us,
King, queen and cygnets, one by one,
Did one dare to remember other swans
In anecdotes of Gauguin or of Rabelais?
Some became bolsters for the Greeks,
Some rubber Lohengrins provided comedy.

The flapping of the wings excited Leda.
The procession is over and what is now
Alarming is more the mirror split
From end to end by the harsh clap
Of the wooden beaks, than the empty space
Which follows them about,
Stained by their whiteness when they pass.

We sit like drunkards and inhale the swans.

VISITATIONS

Left like an unknown's breath on mirrors,
The enchanters, the persuaders
Whom the seasons swallow up,
Only leave us ash in saucers,
Or to mice the last invaders
Open cupboard-doors or else
Lipstick-marks upon a cup.

Fingerprint the crook of time,
Ask him what he means by it,
Eyes and thoughts and lovely bodies,
David's singing, Daphne's wit
Like Eve's apple undigested
Rot within us bit by bit.

Experience in a humour ends,
Wrapped in its own dark metaphor,
And divining winter breaks:
Now one by one the Hungers creep
Up from the orchards of the mind
Here to trouble and confuse
Old men's after-dinner sleep.

IN ARCADIA

By divination came the Dorians,
Under a punishment composed an arch.
They invented this valley, they taught
The rock to flow with odourless water.

Fire and a brute art came among them.

Rain fell, tasting of the sky.
Trees grew, composing a grammar.
The river, the river you see was brought down
By force of prayer upon this fertile floor.

Now small skills: the fingers laid upon
The nostrils of flutes, the speech of women
Whose tutors were the birds; who singing
Now civilized their children with the kiss.

Lastly, the tripod sentenced them.

Ash closed on the surviving sons.
The brown bee memorized here, rehearsed
Migration from an inherited habit.
All travellers recorded an empty zone.

Between rocks 'O death', the survivors.
O world of bushes eaten like a moon,
Kissed by the awkward patience of the ant.
Within a concave blue and void of space.

Something died out by this river: but it seems
Less than a nightingale ago.

A WATER-COLOUR OF VENICE

Zarian was saying: Florence is youth,
And after it Ravenna, age,
Then Venice, second-childhood.

The pools of burning stone where time
And water, the old siege-masters,
Have run their saps beneath
A thousand saddle-bridges,
Puffed up by marble griffins drinking,

And all set free to float on loops
Of her canals like great intestines
Now snapped off like a berg to float,
Where now, like others, you have come alone,
To trap your sunset in a yellow glass,
And watch the silversmith at work
Chasing the famous salver of the bay . . .

Here sense dissolves, combines to print only
These bitten choirs of stone on water,
To the rumble of old cloth bells,
The cadging of confetti pigeons,
A boatman singing from his long black coffin . . .

To all that has been said before
You can add nothing, only that here,
Thick as a brushstroke sleep has laid
Its fleecy unconcern on every visage,

At the bottom of every soul a spoonful of sleep.

George Barker

George Barker was born February 26, 1913, in Loughton, Essex, attended school in Chelsea and the Regent Street Polytechnic, but had to leave at fourteen to go to work. He struggled to make a living at all sorts of work, including that of a garage mechanic, and was, at one time, so poor that he slept in parks with newspapers wrapped around him for warmth.

His first book, *Alanna Autumnal,* a novel, was published before he was twenty; *Thirty Preliminary Poems* appeared in the same year. At twenty-four he published *Calamiterror,* which, with its portmanteau Joyceian title, is a long, complex, apocalyptic poem. A year after *Lament and Triumph,* Barker achieved his first American publication with *Selected Poems* (1941). At twenty-six he taught English literature in Japan.

Barker's poetry is passionate, prolix, and often determinedly irrational. The pace is headlong, the pitch is high. Dudley Fitts, praising Barker's ingenuities ("I prefer the least controlled resonances of Mr. Barker to the sterile piddling of so many of the younger poets"), criticized his overquaint archness, his too surprising distortions, and "the violent hurling together of unpredictable images whose symbolic value seems often hopelessly private." In Barker, as in Dylan Thomas, there is great freedom of emotion matched by a freely flowing inventiveness. This emotional drive sometimes includes and sometimes ignores conventional standards of expression. Separating feeling from thinking, Barker and Thomas often lose themselves in a richly sensual but obscure rhetoric. Both poets delight in a loosely rolling language which, when they are not mastering the words, allows the words to master them. At their best, they are not only daring but distinguished. Barker's originality is not factitious; accomplishing desperate ascents he is willing to risk a plunge into absurdity. The juxtaposition of the sublime and the banal, of surging syllables and pounding energy, are apparent in *Sacred and Secular Elegies* (1943) and *Love Poems* (1947).

The heavy clusters of words, thick patches of sound used like impressionistic colors, are refined and clarified in the later work. The tone of the *Love Poems* is not only quieter but purer than anything Barker has written. Without losing its ability to communicate excitement, Barker's poetry has grown increasingly direct, tender, and deeply moving. *A Vision of Beasts and Gods* appeared in 1954.

"MY JOY, MY JOCKEY, MY GABRIEL"

(*First Cycle of Love Poems: V*)

My joy, my jockey, my Gabriel
Who bares his horns above my sleep
Is sleeping now. And I shall keep him
In valley and on pinnacle
And marvellous in my tabernacle.

My peace is where his shoulder holds
My clouds among his skies of face;
His plenty is my peace, my peace:
And like a serpent by a boulder
His shade I rest in glory coiled.

Time will divide us and the sea
Wring its sad hands all day between;
The autumn bring a change of scene.
But always and for ever he
At night will sleep and keep by me.

"O TENDER UNDER HER RIGHT BREAST"

(*Second Cycle of Love Poems: II*)

O tender under her right breast
Sleep at the waterfall
My daughter, my daughter, and be at rest
As I at her left shall.

At night the pigeon in the eaves
Leaves open its bright eye;
Nor will the Seven Sisters cease
To watch you where you lie.

The pine like a father over your bed
Will bend down from above
To lay in duty at your head
The candles of its love.

And in their mothering embrace,
Sleep on the Rockies' bosom;
The Okanogan Valley shall grace
Canada round your cradle.

The silver spoon and the one-eyed man,
The rabbit's foot and the clover,
Be at your bed from morning till
As now, the day is over.

"SHUT THE SEVEN SEAS AGAINST US"

(*Third Cycle of Love Poems: II*)

Shut the Seven Seas against us,
Close the five continents,
Set sepulchred the North Star
In a forsaken tense;
Lay every Sun and System
For ever away in bed,—
Nevertheless that day shall come
That resurects the dead.

When sleepless the wakes, weeping,
Mourn life on every leaf,
And the Moon covers her eye over
Rather than see our grief;
When in their dreams the liars and
The loveless regret life,—
The dove that stirs in every storm
Shall arrive bright with olive.

Step, Primavera, from your bed,
Dazzling with existence;
Put the Sun and the Moon and the Systems
right;
Hang heaven on circumstance:
Lean from all windows like waterfalls,
Look, Love on us below:—
And so from their somnolence in sense
All things shall rise to you.

"SATAN IS ON YOUR TONGUE"

(*Secular Elegy: III*)

Satan is on your tongue, sweet singer, with
Your eye on the income and the encomium,
Angels rhapsodize for and from their faith.
And in the studios of chromium
Lucifer seduces Orpheus with a myth.

But the principle of evil is not autonomous.
Like the liberty horse with a plume at a circus
Under the whipmaster it steps proud in its circles.
When I let slip an instant the whip of the will
All hell's scot-free with fire at the nostril.

Thus if the crux and judgment never is
Left to our own to do with as we will,
But the decision, like a master key, lies
Entirely in the higher hands that holds all—
How can we be as innocent as this?

Everything that is profound loves the mask,
Said the Dionysian who never wore one.
Thus our damnation and our condemnation,
Wiser than Nietzsche, never taking a risk,
Wears the face of a necessary satisfaction.

Not, Love, when we kiss do the archangels weep
For we are naked then wherever we are
Like tigers in the night. But in our sleep
The masks go down and the beast is bare:
It is not Love but double damnation there.

Marooned on the islands of pride, lonely
And mad on the pyramids of achievement,
Disillusioned in cathedrals of doxology,
The sad man senses this continual bereavement:
God has just died, and now there is only

Us. The gold bull with its horns of finances
Over the sensual mountains goes gallivanting
In glory: all night and all day it dances
Absurd and happy because nothing is wanting.
The sad man hides his grief in his five senses.

Boy with the marvellous silver fish at thigh,
Whom two hundred million could call Little Father
Spawning all Russia in a night, go gather
Kisses and rosebuds under the German sky:
Tomorrow they'll find the mess of blood and the feather.

"O GOLDEN FLEECE"

(*Secular Elegy: VI*)

O Golden Fleece she is where she lies tonight
Trammelled in her sheets like midsummer on a bed,
Kisses like moths flitter over her bright
Mouth, and as she turns her head,
All space moves over to give her beauty room.

Where her hand, like a bird on the branches of her arm,
Droops its wings over the bedside as she sleeps,
There the air perpetually stays warm
Since, nested, her hand rested there. And she keeps
Under her green thumb life like a growing poem.

My nine-tiered tigress in the cage of sex
I feed with meat that you tear from my side
Crowning your nine months with the paradox:
The love that kisses with a homicide
In robes of red generation resurrects.

The bride who rides the hymeneal waterfall
Spawning all possibles in her pools of surplus,
Whom the train rapes going into a tunnel,
The imperial multiplicator nothing can nonplus:
My mother Nature is the origin of it all.

At Pharoah's Feast and in the family cupboard,
Gay corpse, bright skeleton, and the fly in amber,
She sits with her laws like antlers from her forehead
Enmeshing everyone, with flowers and thunder
Adorning the head that destiny never worried.

VERSES FOR A FIRST BIRTHDAY

Hang at my hand as I write now
My small one whom the dogs follow,
That, nuzzled in my stomach, dance
Like sea-lions with her innocence.

The roaring forties in the bed
Beat up disaster on her head,
And on the wall the calendar
Always enumerated War.

Thunder in the teacup and
Prognostications in the sand
Menaced her amusements with
The abracadabra of death.

She who kisses prettier than
Two breezes meeting round a fan
What shall she hold in her arms
But the catastrophes like lambs?

And when, among the temporal
Ruins of her landscape, shall
The giddygoat and Cupid chase
All but Disney from the place?

On the rag of a single summer
She dried all the tears of the future;
When the Winter made her grieve
The vernal equinox was up her sleeve

Happily the unhappy shall lie down
By her, and bounty be her own
Bubble. The hitherto inconsolable
Find solace at her first syllable.

The dove, in its code of coos,
Will carry abroad her good news:
That it was Love, and not
Law kept the ark afloat.

For the desire, and the daughter,
And the dog chasing its tail,
Renew all things in Nature,
And Nature renews it all.

Dylan Thomas

Dylan Thomas was born October 27, 1914, in Swansea, Wales, and was briefly educated at the local grammar school. A reporter for a year on the *South Wales Evening Post,* he became a reader and script-writer for radio and accepted other odd jobs and assignments. His vivid *Portrait of the Artist as a Young Dog* (1940) is largely autobiographical. At the age of twenty Thomas published his first volume, *18 Poems* (1934). Most of the poems in that volume and in *25 Poems* (1936), together with several from *The Map of Love* (1939), and eleven short stories were published in *The World I Breathe* (1939). *New Poems* appeared in 1943; *The Selected Writings of Dylan Thomas,* with an interpretive introduction by John L. Sweeney, in 1946.

At first glance Thomas's poems seem not only obscure but barbaric. The lines appear to be full of wild eldritch noises, with words, screams and shouts flung out in spectacular abandon. Upon re-reading, however, it is apparent that Thomas's poems, far from being disorganized, are curiously disciplined. The order imposed upon them does not stem from the strictures of traditional form but from a logic of emotion. The images blossom freely and profusely—there are obvious overtones of Hopkins and Hart Crane—but they are controlled by key phrases, central associations, and dominant ideas. Writing out of his own background and beliefs, Thomas plunges boldly into a new and dynamic language, a fierce vigor of speech remarkable even in a time of frantic experiment. Thomas is, as Stephen Spender wrote, "a poet obsessed with words, a linguistic genius, and with a mind filled with echoes of his Welsh Nonconformist religious upbringing and of childhood experiences which made a deep impression on him. His poems have a bardic primitive quality, and at the same time there is superimposed on this an awareness of the discoveries of modern psychology. But, above all, he impresses by his rich use of words and by his ability to write in free yet compelling meters."

Sensational and tempestuous, Thomas's poems are packed with brilliance, confusing in design but convincing in impact. They are composed of nightmare violence, sexual symbols, images of pain and the agonies of birth. Thomas identifies himself with the elemental powers of nature—"the force that through the green fuse drives the flower drives my green age; that blasts the roots of trees is my destroyer." The poet, irrepressibly spontaneous, becomes his own myth. "The more subjective a poem, the clearer the narrative line," wrote Thomas, and the remark is particularly true of his own poetry. It includes the "simple terrestrial gladness" (Peter Viereck's phrase) of "Fern Hill," that bright and joyful picture of summer on a Welsh farm, and the poignant evocation of "The Hunchback in the Park." Although profuse in imagery, "In Memory of Ann Jones" is one of Thomas's most luxuriant and yet one of his clearest poems. The gathering pictures of the burial, the feast, the home, and the spirit of the woman are logically and emotionally united. In *Auden and After* Francis Scarfe calls attention to the concentration of effects: "The typical furniture of her room, which appears early in the poem ('In a room with a stuffed fox and a stale fern') serves as a dominant tied image, reappearing brilliantly at the end to drive home the idea that her love might even bring the dead to life. . . . The poem is, in the poet's words, 'a monstrous thing blindly magnified out of praise.' "

Rhetoric is used so lavishly, allusiveness employed with such prodigality, that much of Thomas's verse seems to borrow the technique of surrealism. Actually Thomas has little kinship with the surrealists; he is desperately concerned with the frenzy of life, the struggle to be born and the agonized desire for peace, including the final peace of death. Even when the words seem to hurtle into incomprehensibility, the feeling emerges, almost explodes, from the poem. It communicates its thought darkly or jubilantly, but always powerfully, even before the full meaning of the poem is evident.

Beginning in his mid-thirties Thomas made several visits to the United States. His recitals of half-declaimed, half-chanted poetry were sensationally successful. Everywhere he went Thomas was acclaimed, adulated, and ruined. He drank too much, often having beer and brandy for breakfast. He alternately took his mission seriously and made fun of himself as well as his audiences by saying he was at work on such lectures as "A Bard's Eye View of New York by a Dollar-Mad Nightingale" and "A Typical Day in My Welsh Bog." He described himself as "old, small, dark, intelligent, and darting-doting-dotting-eyed, balding and toothlessing." He said he wanted to write only "poems of God's world by a man who doesn't believe in God"; at another time he declared: "My words are written for the love of man and the praise of God—and I'd be a damned fool if they weren't." During his third visit, he drank more recklessly than ever; his thirty-ninth birthday celebration in New York was followed by a complete collapse. Taken to the hospital, it was discovered that he was afflicted with encephalopathy, a virulent disease of the brain, and he died on November 9, 1953.

Thomas's death brought forth a spate of biographies, memoirs, tributes, and documented exposures of his excesses. Especially provocative are John Malcolm Brinnin's *Dylan Thomas in America* (1955), Caitlin Thomas's account of herself and her huband, *Leftover Life to Kill* (1957), and Henry Treece's revised *Dylan Thomas: Dog Among the Fairies* (1958).

Thomas's *Collected Poems,* appearing a year before his death, was followed by various posthumous books: *Quite Early One Morning* (1954), stories, sketches, and essays; *Under Milk Wood* (1954), a play which had been broadcast and in which he had taken part; *Adventures in the Skin Trade and Other Stories* (1955) and *A Prospect of the Sea* (1958), articles and vignettes from his notebooks. All of these are alive with Thomas's word-play, his love of alliterative sentences, Hopkins-like compound words, Joyceian fused puns, and, most of all, an exuberance which, in the best of his poetry, sometimes attains exaltation.

WHEN ALL MY FIVE AND COUNTRY SENSES SEE

When all my five and country senses see,
The fingers will forget green thumbs and mark
How, through the halfmoon's vegetable eye,
Husk of young stars and handful zodiac,
Love in the frost is pared and wintered by,
The whispering ears will watch love drummed away

Down breeze and shell to a discordant beach,
And, lashed to syllables, the lynx tongue cry
That her fond wounds are mended bitterly.
My nostrils see her breath burn like a bush.

My one and noble heart has witnesses
In all love's countries, that will grope awake;
And when blind sleep drops on the spying senses,
The heart is sensual, though five eyes break.

LIGHT BREAKS WHERE NO SUN SHINES

Light breaks where no sun shines;
Where no sea runs, the waters of the heart
Push in their tides;
And, broken ghosts with glowworms in their heads,
The things of light
File through the flesh where no flesh decks the bones.

A candle in the thighs
Warms youth and seed and burns the seeds of age;
Where no seed stirs,
The fruit of man unwrinkles in the stars,
Bright as a fig;
Where no wax is, the candle shows its hairs.

Dawn breaks behind the eyes;
From poles of skull and toe the windy blood
Slides like a sea;
Nor fenced, nor staked, the gushers of the sky
Spout to the rod
Divining in a smile the oil of tears.

Night in the sockets rounds,
Like some pitch moon, the limit of the globes;
Day lights the bone;
Where no cold is, the skinning gales unpin
The winter's robes;
The film of spring is hanging from the lids.

Light breaks on secret lots,
On tips of thought where thoughts smell in the rain;
When logics die,
The secret of the soil grows through the eye,
And blood jumps in the sun;
Above the waste allotments the dawn halts.

THE HAND THAT SIGNED THE PAPER FELLED A CITY

The hand that signed the paper felled a city;
Five sovereign fingers taxed the breath,
Doubled the globe of dead and halved a country;
These five kings did a king to death.

The mighty hand leads to a sloping shoulder,
The finger joints are cramped with chalk;
A goose's quill has put an end to murder
That put an end to talk.

The hand that signed the treaty bred a fever,
And famine grew, and locusts came;
Great is the hand that holds dominion over
Man by a scribbled name.

The five kings count the dead but do not soften
The crusted wound nor pat the brow;
A hand rules pity as a hand rules heaven;
Hands have no tears to flow.

THE FORCE THAT THROUGH THE GREEN FUSE DRIVES

The force that through the green fuse drives the flower
Drives my green age; that blasts the roots of trees
Is my destroyer.
And I am dumb to tell the crooked rose
My youth is bent by the same wintry fever.

The force that drives the water through the rocks
Drives my red blood; that dries the mouthing streams
Turns mine to wax.
And I am dumb to mouth unto my veins
How at the mountain spring the same mouth sucks.

The hand that whirls the water in the pool
Stirs the quicksand; that ropes the blowing wind
Hauls my shroud sail.
And I am dumb to tell the hanging man
How of my clay is made the hangman's lime.

The lips of time leech to the fountain head;
Love drips and gathers, but the fallen blood
Shall calm her sores.
And I am dumb to tell a weather's wind
How time has ticked a heaven round the stars.

And I am dumb to tell the lover's tomb
How at my sheet goes the same crooked worm.

THE HUNCHBACK IN THE PARK

The hunchback in the park
A solitary mister
Propped between trees and water
From the opening of the garden lock
That let the trees and water enter
Until the Sunday sombre bell at dark,

Eating bread from a newspaper
Drinking water from the chained cup
That the children filled with gravel
In the fountain basin where I sailed my ship
Slept at night in a dog kennel
But nobody chained him up.

Like the park birds he came early
Like the water he sat down
And Mister they called hey Mister
The truant boys from the town
Running when he had heard them clearly
On out of sound

Past lake and rockery
Laughing when he shook his paper
Hunchbacked in mockery
Through the loud zoo of the willow groves
Dodging the park keeper
With his stick that picked up leaves.

And the old dog sleeper
Alone between nurses and swans
While the boys among willows
Made the tiger jump out of their eyes
To roar on the rockery stones
And the groves were blue with sailors

Made all day until bell time
A woman figure without fault
Straight as a young elm
Straight and tall from his crooked bones
That she might stand in the night
After the lock and chains

All night in the unmade park
After the railings and shrubberies
The birds the grass the trees the lake
Had followed the hunchback
And the wild boys innocent as strawberries
To his kennel in the dark.

AND DEATH SHALL HAVE NO DOMINION

And death shall have no dominion.
Dead men naked they shall be one
With the man in the wind and the west
  moon;
When their bones are picked clean and the
  clean bones gone,
They shall have stars at elbow and foot;
Though they go mad they shall be sane,
Though they sink through the sea they shall
  rise again;
Though lovers be lost love shall not;
And death shall have no dominion.

And death shall have no dominion.
Under the windings of the sea
They lying long shall not die windily;
Twisting on racks when sinews give way,
Strapped to a wheel, yet they shall not break;
Faith in their hands shall snap in two,
And the unicorn evils run them through;
Split all ends up they shan't crack;
And death shall have no dominion.

And death shall have no dominion.
No more may gulls cry at their ears
Or waves break loud on the seashores;
Where blew a flower may a flower no more
Lift its head to the blows of the rain;
Though they be mad and dead as nails,
Heads of the characters hammer through
  daisies;
Break in the sun till the sun breaks down,
And death shall have no dominion.

ESPECIALLY WHEN THE OCTOBER WIND

Especially when the October wind
With frosty fingers punishes my hair,
Caught by the crabbing sun I walk on fire
And cast a shadow crab upon the land,
By the sea's side, hearing the noise of birds,
Hearing the raven cough in winter sticks,
My busy heart who shudders as she talks
Sheds the syllabic blood and drains her
  words.
Shut, too, in a tower of words, I mark
On the horizon walking like the trees

The wordy shapes of women, and the rows
Of the star-gestured children in the park.
Some let me make you of the vowelled beeches,
Some of the oaken voices, from the roots
Of many a thorny shire tell you notes,
Some let me make you of the water's speeches.

Behind a pot of ferns the wagging clock
Tells me the hour's word, the neural meaning
Flies on the shafted disc, declaims the morning
And tells the windy weather in the cock.
Some let me make you of the meadow's signs;
The signal grass that tells me all I know
Breaks with the wormy winter through the eye.
Some let me tell you of the raven's sins.

Especially when the October wind
(Some let me make you of autumnal spells,
The spider-tongued, and the loud hill of Wales)
With fist of turnips punishes the land,
Some let me make you of the heartless words.
The heart is drained that, spelling in the scurry
Of chemic blood, warned of the coming fury.
By the sea's side hear the dark-vowelled birds.

IN MEMORY OF ANN JONES

After the funeral, mule praises, brays,
Windshake of sailshaped ears, muffle-toed tap
Tap happily of one peg in the thick
Grave's foot, blinds down the lids, the teeth in black,
The spittled eyes, the salt ponds in the sleeves,
Morning smack of thc spadc that wakes up sleep,
Shakes a desolate boy who slits his throat
In the dark of the coffin and shed dry leaves,
That breaks one bone to light with a judgment clout
After the feast of tear-stuffed time and thistles
In a room with a stuffed fox and a stale fern,
I stand, for this memorial's sake, alone
In the snivelling hours with dead, humped Ann
Whose hooded, fountain heart once fell in puddles
Round the parched worlds of Wales and drowned each sun
(Though this for her is a monstrous image blindly
Magnified out of praise; her death was a still drop;
She would not have me sinking in the holy
Flood of her heart's fame; she would lie dumb and deep
And need no druid of her broken body).
But I, Ann's bard on a raised hearth, call all
The seas to service that her wood-tongued virtue
Babble like a bellbuoy over the hymning heads,
Bow down the walls of the ferned and foxy woods
That her love sing and swing through a brown chapel,
Bless her bent spirit with four, crossing birds.
Her flesh was meek as milk, but this skyward statue
With the wild breast and blessed and giant skull
Is carved from her in a room with a wet window
In a fiercely mourning house in a crooked year.
I know her scrubbed and sour humble hands

Lie with religion in their cramp, her threadbare
Whisper in a damp word, her wits drilled hollow,
Her fist of a face died clenched on a round pain;
And sculptured Ann is seventy years of stone.
These cloud-sopped, marble hands, this monumental
Argument of the hewn voice, gesture and psalm
Storm me forever over her grave until
The stuffed lung of the fox twitch and cry Love
And the strutting fern lay seeds on the black sill.

FERN HILL

Now as I was young and easy under the apple boughs
About the lilting house and happy as the grass was green,
  The night above the dingle starry,
    Time let me hail and climb
  Golden in the heydays of his eyes,
And honored among wagons I was prince of the apple towns
And once below a time I lordly had the trees and leaves
    Trail with daisies and barley
  Down the rivers of the windfall light.

And as I was green and carefree, famous among the barns
About the happy yard and singing as the farm was home,
  In the sun that is young once only,
    Time let me play and be
  Golden in the mercy of his means,
And green and golden I was huntsman and herdsman, the calves
Sang to my horn, the foxes on the hills barked clear and cold,
    And the sabbath rang slowly
  In the pebbles of the holy streams.

All the sun long it was running, it was lovely, the hay-
Fields high as the house, the tunes from the chimneys, it was air
  And playing, lovely and watery
    And fire green as grass.
  And nightly under the simple stars
As I rode to sleep the owls were bearing the farm away,
All the moon long I heard, blessed among stables, the nightjars
  Flying with the ricks, and horses
    Flashing into the dark

And then to awake, and the farm, like a wanderer white
With the dew, come back, the cock on his shoulder: it was all
  Shining, it was Adam and maiden,
    The sky gathered again
  And the sun grew round that very day.
So it must have been after the birth of the simple light
In the first, spinning place, the spellbound horses walking warm
  Out of the whinnying green stable
    On to the fields of praise.

And honored among foxes and pheasants by the gay house
Under the new-made clouds and happy as the heart was long
    In the sun born over and over,
        I ran my heedless ways,
    My wishes raced through the house-high hay
And nothing I cared, at my sky blue trades, that time allows
In all his tuneful turning so few and such morning songs
    Before the children green and golden
        Follow him out of grace.

Nothing I cared, in the lamb white days, that time would take me
Up to the swallow-thronged loft by the shadow of my hand,
    In the moon that is always rising,
        Nor that riding to sleep
    I should hear him fly with the high fields
And wake to the farm forever fled from the childless land.
Oh as I was young and easy in the mercy of his means,
        Time held me green and dying
    Though I sang in my chains like the sea.

A REFUSAL TO MOURN THE DEATH, BY FIRE, OF A CHILD IN LONDON

Never until the mankind making
Bird beast and flower
Fathering and all humbling darkness
Tells with silence the last light breaking
And the still hour
Is come of the sea tumbling in harness

And I must enter again the round
Zion of the water bead
And the synagogue of the ear of corn
Shall I let pray the shadow of a sound
Or sow my salt seed
In the least valley of sackcloth to mourn

The majesty and burning of the child's death.
I shall not murder
The mankind of her going with a grave truth
Nor blaspheme down the stations of the breath
With any further
Elegy of innocence and youth.

Deep with the first dead lies London's daughter,
Robed in the long friends,
The grains beyond age, the dark veins of her mother,
Secret by the unmourning water
Of the riding Thames.
After the first death, there is no other.

DO NOT GO GENTLE INTO THAT GOOD NIGHT

Do not go gentle into that good night,
Old age should burn and rave at close of day;
Rage, rage against the dying of the light.

Though wise men at their end know dark is right,
Because their words had forked no lightning they
Do not go gentle into that good night.

Good men, the last wave by, crying how bright
Their frail deeds might have danced in a green bay,
Rage, rage against the dying of the light.

Wild men who caught and sang the sun in flight,
And learn, too late, they grieved it on its way,
Do not go gentle into that good night.

Grave men, near death, who see with blinding sight
Blind eyes could blaze like meteors and be gay,
Rage, rage against the dying of the light.

And you, my father, there on the sad height,
Curse, bless, me now with your fierce tears, I pray.
Do not go gentle into that good night.
Rage, rage against the dying of the light.

Norman Nicholson

Norman Nicholson was born January 8, 1914, in the small mining town of Millom, Cumberland, one of the loveliest counties in England, and his verse (to quote Kenneth Rexroth) "has the same peace, care, and mystical stillness that Wordworth sought, and sometimes found, in the same region." Son of a well-known tradesman in the town, Nicholson actively took part in the everyday life of the people. He was connected with the music festivals, the church work, the cricket club, and the youth movement; he lectured for the Workers' Educational Association. "All this is very different from the life of the literary world," he writes, "with which I have dealings only by correspondence. My home is at the mouth of the Duddon—Wordsworth's favorite river. Thus we have almost on top of one another the sea, industry, and the finest scenery in England."

Nicholson catches some of that juxtaposition in his poetry. The Wordsworthian bucolic note is there, but it is sharpened by a critical observation, hardened by an awareness of man's inhumanity to earth. Nicholson's first book of poems, *Five Rivers* (1945), owes its title to the five little rivers which flow from the western mountains of the English Lake District into the Irish Sea. The volume is almost wholly lyrical in tone, lucid and personal. But it never depends on mere fluidity and the reiterations of the stereotypes dear to the nature-lover's handbook. Nicholson's is genuine worship—"the Word shall shine on rock and beast and tree." Two other volumes of poetry, *Rock Face* (1948) and *The Pot Geranium* (1954), emphasize Nicholson's penetrating observation and vigorous imagination.

Five Rivers which won the first Royal Society of Literature Award, was preceded by *An Anthology of Religious Verse* (1942) and *Man and Literature* (1943). It was followed by *The Fire of the Lord* (1946), a novel concerned with the primitive feeling of awe and veneration for land breaking out in an urban population through a half-mad evangelist, and *The Old Man of the Mountains* (1946), a play in which the prophet Elijah is placed in modern Cumberland.

ROCKFERNS

On quarry walls the spleenwort spreads
Its green zipfasteners and black threads,
And pinches tight its unfurled purses
In every crevice with the cresses,
As if a blast of dynamite
Had spattered it upon the slate
That where the bluestone spine was broken
Spores might penetrate and quicken.
For in the fractures of the rock
Roots dig further than a pick,
As, though the sinews may not feel it,
The worm probes deeper than the bullet.
When this pen is dropped, my hand
May thrust up in a buckler frond,
And then my crushed and calcined bones
Prove better soil than arid stones.
Why need I fear the bursting bomb
Or whatsoever death shall come,
If brains and bowels be cast forth
Splintered to spleenwort on the earth?
And if a subtler part may cruise
Twice round the sun and Betelgeuse,
My soul shall detonate on high
And plant itself in cracks of sky.

THE BLACKBERRY

Between the railway and the mine,
Brambles are in fruit again.
   Their little nigger fists they clench,
   And hold the branches in a clinch.
Waggons of ore are shunted past,
And spray the berries with red dust,
   Which dulls the bright mahogany
But when the housewife, wind-and-rain,
Rubs the berry spick and span,
   Compound it gleams like a fly's eye,
   And every ball reflects the sky.
There the world's repeated like

Coupons in a ration book;
  There the tall curved chimneys spread
  Purple smoke on purple cloud.
Grant us to know that hours rushed by
Are photographed upon God's eye;
  That life and leaf are both preserved
  In gelatine of Jesus' blood.
And grant to us the sense to feel
The large condensed within the small;
  Wash clear our eyes that we may see
  The sky within the blackberry.

MICHAELMAS

Like a hound with nose to the trail
The 'bus follows the road;
The road leaps up the hill.
In the valley the railway line is carved like a groove in the wood,
The little towns smoke in the hollows;
The slagbanks are grey beneath the brown, bludgeoning fell.

This is the day the air has eyes,
And the Devil falls like hail
From the bright and thundering skies,
And soaks into soil and rock,
And the bad blood rises in nettle and dock,
And toadstools burst like boils between the toes of the trees.

The war that began in heaven still goes on.
Thorn trees twist like spears,
The owl haunts the grain,
The coursed rabbit weeps icicles of tears;
But the feathers of the clouds foretell
St. Michael's victory in the purged and praising rain.

Henry Reed

Henry Reed was born in 1914 in Birmingham, and educated there at schools and the University. Graduated M. A., he served in the Army and the Foreign Office, became a journalist and broadcaster—much of his verse was contained in plays for radio. One of these, *The Streets of Pompeii,* was awarded the Premio della Radio Italiana in 1953, and was subsequently broadcast in Canada and the United States. Besides his original writings, Reed has made notable translations from the French and Italian, in particular works by Pirandello, Betti and Montherlant.

A Map of Verona (1947) is a book in five sections, one of which, "Ishmael," consists of lyric interludes that were part of a radio version of *Moby Dick,* and which were extended into a full length work. A precisionist, Reed is equally at ease in compact lyrics and a flexible blank verse, in philosophical contemplation and styptic burlesque, as in "Chard Whitlow," a dry parody of Eliot's semi-arid, semi-sententious manner. The broad mockery of "Naming of Parts" (from a section ironically entitled "Lessons of the War") is sharply in contrast with the quiet tension of "Sailor's Harbor" and the straightforward but poignant narrative style of "The Auction Sale." Whatever the mood or subject matter, the style is distinctive, delicate but sure.

NAMING OF PARTS

Today we have naming of parts. Yesterday,
We had daily cleaning. And tomorrow morning,
We shall have what to do after firing. But today,
Today we have naming of parts. Japonica
Glistens like coral in all of the neighbouring gardens,
    And today we have naming of parts.

This is the lower sling swivel. And this
Is the upper sling swivel, whose use you will see,
When you are given your slings. And this is the piling swivel,
Which in your case you have not got. The branches
Hold in the gardens their silent, eloquent gestures,
    Which in our case we have not got.

This is the safety-catch, which is always released
With an easy flick of the thumb. And please do not let me
See anyone using his finger. You can do it quite easy
If you have any strength in your thumb. The blossoms
Are fragile and motionless, never letting anyone see
    Any of them using their finger.

And this you can see is the bolt. The purpose of this
Is to open the breech, as you see. We can slide it
Rapidly backwards and forwards; we call this
Easing the spring. And rapidly backwards and forwards
The early bees are assaulting and fumbling the flowers:
    They call it easing the Spring.

They call it easing the Spring. It is perfectly easy
If you have any strength in your thumb: like the bolt,
And the breech, and the cocking-piece, and the point of balance,
Which in our case we have not got; and the almond-blossom
Silent in all of the gardens and the bees going backwards and forwards,
    For today we have naming of parts.

SAILOR'S HARBOR

My thoughts, like sailors becalmed in Cape Town harbor,
Await your return, like a favorable wind, or like
New tackle for the voyage, without which it is useless starting.

We watch the sea daily, finish our daily tasks
By ten in the morning, and with the day to waste,
Wander through the suburbs, with quiet thoughts of the brothels,
And sometimes thoughts of the churches.

In the eating-houses we always contrive to get near to
The window, where we can keep an eye on the life-
Bearing sea. Suddenly a wind might blow, and we must not miss
First sight of the waves as they darken with promise for us.
We have been here too long. We know the quays,
And the streets near the quays, more than should ever be necessary.
When can we go on our way?

Certain we are of this, that when the wind comes,
It may be deceptive and sweet and finally blow
To shipwreck and ruin between here and the next port of call.
At all times we think of this. At last we have come to know
The marine charts can safely assure us of less and less
As we go farther south. So we cannot go out on the boulevards
Or climb Table Mountain,

Though if we had certainty, here there might be delight.
But all that is world in itself, the mountain, the streets,
The sand-dunes outside the town, we shyly and sadly return from.
They are too much to bear. And our curiosity
Lies alone in the over-scrubbed decks and the polished brasses
(For we have to look trim in the port) and in
The high-piled ambiguous cargo.

CHARD WHITLOW

(Mr. Eliot's Sunday Evening Postscript)

As we get older we do not get any younger.
Seasons return, and today I am fifty-five,
And this time last year I was fifty-four,
And this time next year I shall be sixty-two.
And I cannot say I should like (to speak for myself)
To see my time over again—if you can call it time:
Fidgeting uneasily under a draughty stair,
Or counting sleepless nights in the crowded Tube.

There are certain precautions—though none of them very reliable—
Against the blast from bombs and the flying splinter,
But not against the blast from heaven, *vento dei venti,*
The wind within a wind unable to speak for wind;
And the frigid burnings of purgatory will not be touched
By any emollient.
I think you will find this put,
Better than I could ever hope to express it,
In the words of Kharma: "It is, we believe,
Idle to hope that the simple stirrup-pump
Will extinguish hell."

Oh, listeners,
And you especially who have turned off the wireless,
And sit in Stoke or Basingstoke listening appreciatively to the silence,
(Which is also the silence of hell) pray not for your selves but your souls.

And pray for me also under the draughty stair.
As we get older we do not get any younger.

And pray for Kharma under the holy mountain.

THE AUCTION SALE

Within the great grey flapping tent
The damp crowd stood or stamped about;
And some came in, and some went out
To drink the moist November air;
None fainted, though a few looked spent
And eyed some empty unbought chair.
It was getting on. And all had meant
Not to go home with empty hands
But full of gain, at little cost,
Of mirror, vase, or vinaigrette.
Yet often, after certain sales,
Some looked relieved that they had lost,
Others, at having won, upset.
Two men from London sat apart,
Both from the rest and each from each,
One man in grey and one in brown.
And each ignored the other's face,
And both ignored the endless stream
Of bed and bedside cabinet,
Gazing intent upon the floor,
And they were strangers in that place.

Two other men, competing now,
Locals, whom everybody knew,
In shillings genially strove
For some small thing in ormolu.
Neither was eager; one looked down
Blankly at eighty-four, and then
Rallied again at eighty-eight,
And took it off at four pounds ten.
The loser grimly shook his fist,
But friendly, there was nothing meant.
Little gained was little missed,
And there was smiling in the tent.

The auctioneer paused to drink,
And wiped his lips and looked about,
Engaged in whispered colloquy
The clerk, who frowned and seemed to think,
And murmured: "Why not do it next?"
The auctioneer, though full of doubt,
Unacquiescent, rather vexed,
At last agreed, and at his sign
Two ministrants came softly forth
And lifted in an ashen shroud
Something extremely carefully packed,
Which might have been some sort of frame,
And was a picture-frame in fact.
They steadied it gently and with care,
And held it covered, standing there.

The auctioneer again looked round
And smiled uneasily at friends,
And said: "Well, friends, I have to say
Something I have not said to-day:
There's a reserve upon this number.
It is a picture which though unsigned
Is thought to be of the superior kind,
So I am sure you gentlemen will not mind
If I tell you at once before we start
That what I have been asked to say
Is, as I have said, to say:
There's a reserve upon this number."
There was a rustle in that place,
And some awoke as though from slumber.
Anxious disturbance fluttered there;
And as if summoned to begin,
Those who had stepped outside for air
Retrieved themselves and stepped back in.

The ministrants, two local boys,
Experienced in this sort of work,
And careful not to make too much noise,
Reached forward to unhook the shroud
Which slowly opening fell away
And on the public gaze released
The prospect of a great gold frame
That through the reluctant leaden air
Flashed a mature unsullied grace
Into the faces of the crowd.
And there was silence in that place.

Effulgent in the Paduan air,
Ardent to yield the Venus lay
Naked upon the sunwarmed earth.
Bronze and bright and crisp her hair,
By the right hand of Mars caressed,
Who sunk beside her on his knee,
His mouth towards her mouth inclined,
His left hand near her silken breast.
Flowers about them sprang and twined,
Accomplished Cupids leaped and sported,
And three, with dimpled arms enlaced
And brimming gaze of stifled mirth,
Looked wisely on at Mars's nape,
While others played with horns and pikes,
Or smaller objects of like shape.

And there was silence in the tent.
They gazed in silence; silently
The wind dropped down, no longer shook
The flapping sides and gaping holes.
And some moved back, and others went
Closer, to get a better look.

In ritual, amorous delay,
Venus deposed her sheltering hand
Where her bright belly's aureate day
Melted to dusk about her groin;
And, as from words that Mars had said
Into that hidden, subtle ear,
She turned away her shining head.

The auctioneer cleared his throat,
And said: "I am sure I'm right in feeling
You will not feel it at all unfair
For what when all is said and done
Is a work of very artistic painting
And not to be classed with common lumber
And anyway extremely rare,
You will not feel it at all unfair
If I mention again before proceeding,
There's a reserve on this number."
Someone was heard to say with meaning:
"What, did I hear him say *reserve*?"
(Meaning, of course, a different meaning.)
This was a man from Sturminster,
Renowned for a quiet sense of fun,
And there was laughter in that place,
Though, not, of course, from everyone.

A calm and gentle mile away,
Among the trees a river ran
Boated with blue and scarlet sails;
A towered auburn city stood
Beyond them on the burnished heights,
And afar off and over all
The azure day for mile on mile
Unrolled towards the Dolomites.

The auctioneer said:
"I very much fear I have to say
I'm afraid we cannot look all day.
The reserve is seven hundred pounds.
Will anyone offer me seven fifty?
Seven thirty? Twenty-five?
Thank you, sir. Seven twenty-five."
It was the man in brown who nodded,
Soon to be joined by him in grey.
The bidding started quietly.
No one from locally joined in.
Left to the men from London way,
The auctioneer took proper pride,
And knew the proper way to guide
By pause, by silence, and by tapping,
The bidding towards a proper price.
And each of the two with unmoved face
Would nod and pause and nod and wait.
And there was tension in that place.

And still within the Paduan field,
The silent summer scene stood by,
The sails, the hill-tops, and the sky,
And the bright warmth of Venus' glance
That had for centuries caught the eye
Of whosoever looked that way,
And now caught theirs, on this far day.

Two people only did not look.
They were the men so calmly nodding,
Intently staring at the floor;
Though one of them, the one in brown,
Would sometimes slowly lift his gaze
And stare up towards the canvas roof,
Whereat a few men standing near
Inquiring eyes would also raise
To try to see what he was seeing.
The bidding mounted steadily
With silent nod or murmured yes
And passed the fifteen hundred mark,
And well beyond, and far beyond,
A nodding strife without success,
Till suddenly, with one soft word,
Something unusual occurred.

The auctioneer had asked politely,
With querying look and quiet smile:

"Come then, may I saw two thousand?"
There was the customary pause,
When suddenly with one soft word,
Another voice was strangely heard
To join in, saying plainly: "Yes."
Not their voices, but a third.
Everyone turned in some surprise
To look, and see, and recognise
A young man who some time ago
Had taken a farm out Stalbridge way,
A very pleasant young man, but quiet,
Though always a friendly word to say,
Though no one in the dealing line,
But quiet and rather unsuccessful,
And often seen about the place
At outings or on market-day,
And very polite and inoffensive,
And quiet, as anyone would tell you,
But not from round here in any case.

The auctioneer, in some surprise,
Said: "Please, sir, did I hear you say
Yes to two thousand? Is that bid?
Twenty hundred am I bid?"
The two were silent, and the third,
The young man, answered plainly: "Yes.
Yes. Two thousand. Yes, I did."
Meaning that he had said that word.
"Ah, yes. Yes, thank you, sir," concurred
The auctioneer, surprised, but glad
To know that he had rightly heard,
And added: "Well, then, I may proceed.
I am bid two thousand for this picture.
Any advance upon that sum?
Any advance upon two thousand?
May I say two thousand twenty?
Twenty? Thirty? Thank you, sir.
May I say forty? Thank you, sir.
Fifty? You, sir? Thank you, sir."

And now instead of two, the three
Competed in the bargaining.
There was amazement in that place,
But still it gave, as someone said,
A sort of interest to the thing.
The young man nodded with the others,
And it was seen his nice young face,
Had lost its flush and now was white,
And those who stood quite near to him
Said (later, of course, they did not speak
While the bidding was going on)
That on his brow were beads of sweat,
Which as he nodded in acceptance
Would, one or two, fall down his cheek.

And in the tightening atmosphere
Naked upon the sunwarmed earth
Pauses were made and eyebrows raised,
Answered at last by further nods,
Ardent to yield the nods resumed
Venus upon the sunwarmed nods
Abandoned Cupids danced and nodded
His mouth towards her bid four thousand
Four thousand, any advance upon,
And still beyond four thousand fifty
Unrolled towards the nodding *sun.*
But it was seen, and very quickly,
That after four thousand twenty-five,
The man from over Stalbridge way
Did not respond, and from that point
He kept his silent gaze averted,
To show he would not speak again.
And it was seen his sweating face,
Which had been white, was glowing red,
And had a look almost of pain.

Oh hand of Venus, hand of Mars,
Oh ardent mouth, oh burnished height,
Oh blue and scarlet gentle sails,
Oh Cupids smiling in the dance,
Oh unforgotten, living glance,
Oh river, hill and flowering plain,
Oh ever-living dying light.

And had a look almost of pain.
The rest was quickly done. The bids
Advanced at slowly slackening pace
Up to four thousand sixty-five.
And at this point the man in grey
Declined his gaze upon the floor
And kept it there, as though to say
That he would bid no more that day
It was quite clear he had not won,
This man in grey, though anyone
Practised to read the human face
Might on his losing mouth descry
What could no doubt be termed a smile.
While on the face of him in brown
A like expertness might discern
Something that could be termed a frown.

There was a little faint applause.

The auctioneer sighed with joy,
The customary formalities

Were quickly over, and the strangers
Nodding a brief good-bye departed.
Venus and Mars were carefully veiled.
The auctioneer went on and proffered
Cupboard, table, chair and tray.
Bids of a modest kind were offered,
The traffic of a normal day.
A little later it was seen
The young man too had slipped away.
Which was, of course, to be expected.
Possibly there was nothing else
There at the sale to take his fancy.
Or possibly he even might
Be feeling ashamed at intervening,
Though possibly not, for after all,
He had certainly been within his right.

At all events, an hour later,
Along the Stalbridge Road a child
Saw the young man and told her mother,
Though not in fact till some days after,
That she had seen him in the dusk,
Not walking on the road at all,
But striding beneath the sodden trees;
And as she neared she saw that he
Had no covering on his head,
And did not seem to see her pass,
But went on, through the soaking grass,
Crying: that was what she said.

Bitterly, she later added.

Crying bitterly, she said.

John Manifold

☙ John Manifold was born in 1915, in Melbourne, Australia. Ranked as the first important Australian poet, Manifold modestly insists that there are at least four of his predecessors who merit the honor, but have not enjoyed much publicity overseas. "Down under," he writes, "we send soldiers and wool abroad, but keep poets and wine at home." After attending Geelong Grammar School, Manifold sailed from Australia to attend Jesus College, Cambridge. He stayed in England, working as a schoolmaster and a journalist, and went to Europe as translator for a German publisher. During the war he served in the Queen's Regiment, was commissioned into the Intelligence Corps in December, 1940, and was a captain in the Army of the Rhine. "The war," he said, "has confirmed more of my beliefs than it has destroyed. I still think that the human race is on the average rather likable, that nationality is no more important than class or occupation in making people likable or not, that authority is bad for the soul and responsibility good for it, and that once a thing has become official it's dead and damned."

Manifold's range is immediately apparent in *Selected Verse* (1946), from the macabre ballad of "The Griesly Wife" to the social consciousness of "Night Piece" and the tightness of his realistic sonnets. Manifold is both militant and lyrical; his position as poet is suggested by "A Hat in the Ring," with its satirically clinched couplets; of which the following are typical:

Verse is the chain of words in which to bind
The things we wish most often brought to mind.
Think of an ore new-fossicked, sparse, and crude,
Stamped out and minted it will buy your food,
Cajole a mistress, soften the police,
Raise a revolt or win ignoble peace,
Corrupt or strengthen, sunder or rejoin;
Words are the quartz, but poetry's the coin.

Whether narartive or lyric, his is the poetry of action. It is interesting to compare his sonnet, "The Sirens," with C. Day Lewis's "Nearing Again the Legendary Isle" on page 421.

THE GRIESLY WIFE

"Lie still, my newly married wife,
Lie easy as you can.
You're young and ill accustomed yet
To sleeping with a man."

The snow lay thick, the moon was full
And shone across the floor.
The young wife went with never a word
Barefooted to the door.

He up and followed sure and fast,
The moon shone clear and white.
But before his coat was on his back
His wife was out of sight.

He trod the trail wherever it turned
By many a mound and scree,
And still the barefoot track led on,
And an angry man was he.

He followed fast, he followed slow,
And still he called her name,
But only the dingoes[1] of the hills
Yowled back at him again.

His hair stood up along his neck,
His angry mind was gone,
For the track of the two bare feet gave out
And a four-foot track went on.

Her nightgown lay upon the snow
As it might upon the sheet,
But the track that led from where it lay
Was never of human feet.

His heart turned over in his chest,
He looked from side to side,
And he thought more of his gumwood fire
Than he did of his griesly[2] bride.

And first he started walking back
And then begun to run,
And his quarry wheeled at the end of her track
And hunted him in turn.

Oh, long the fire may burn for him
And open stand the door,
And long the bed may wait empty:
He'll not be back any more.

NIGHT PIECE

Three men came talking up the road
And still "tomorrow" was the word.

The night was clear with the lamp's glitter.
The first man spoke and his voice was bitter:

"Tomorrow like another day
I draw the dole and rust away."

The second one said scared and low,
"Tomorrow I may have to go."

And the two spoke never another word
But drew together and looked at the third.

[1] Dingoes: wild dogs.
[2] Griesly: uncanny

And the third man said, "If tomorrow exists,
It's a day of streets like rivers of fists,

"It's the end of crawling, the end of doles,
And men are treated as human souls."

I stood in the doorway and heard these things
As the three came past with the step of kings.

DEFENSIVE POSITION

Cupping her chin and lying there, the Bren[1]
Watches us make her bed the way a queen
Might watch her slaves. The eyes of a machine,
Like those of certain women, now and then

Put an unsettling influence on men,
Making them suddenly feel how they are seen:
Full of too many purposes, hung between
Impulse and impulse like a child of ten.

The careless challenge, issued so offhanded,
Seems like to go unanswered by default—
A strong position, small but not commanded
By other heights, compels direct assault.

The gunner twitches, and unreprimanded
Eases two tensions, running home the bolt.

THE SIRENS

Odysseus heard the sirens; they were singing
Music by Wolf and Weinberger and Morley
About a region where the swans go winging,
Vines are in color, girls are growing surely
Into nubility, and pylons bringing
Leisure and power to farms that live securely
Without a landlord. Still, his eyes were stinging
With salt and sea-blink, and the ropes hurt sorely.

Odysseus saw the sirens; they were charming,
Blonde, with snub breasts and little neat posteriors,
But could not take his mind off the alarming
Weather report, his mutineers in irons,
The radio failing: it was bloody serious.
In twenty minutes he forgot the sirens.

Judith Wright

Judith Wright was born in 1915 near Armidale, New South Wales, Australia. Descended from a pioneer family, she was in the countryside most of her girlhood and received her education by correspondence and from a local school before she attended Sydney University. She supported herself as a stenographer, private secretary, statistician, and agriculturist; at Tamoborine, in southern Queensland, she specialized in fowls.

[1] Bren: a portable machine-gun

Her work has had a characteristic quality ever since her first book, *The Moving Image* (1946), a personal texture accentuated in *Woman to Man* (1949, reprinted in 1955) and *The Two Fires* (1955). She has been praised for "the richness and vitality of her images" and for her "marriage of passion and reason." The best of the poems in *The Two Fires* are a paradox of loveliness and terror; they are set against the menace of the bomb, the threat of destruction to a world begun in fire and seemingly doomed to die in it. They combine, moreover, a love of natural beauty with a dexterous wit. This is a poetry which is both spontaneous and controlled, often powerful and sometimes deeply moving.

Besides her creative work, Judith Wright edited *The Oxford Book of Australian Verse.*

THE TWO FIRES

Among green shades and flowering ghosts, the remembrances of love,
inventions of the holy unwearying seed,
bright falling fountains made of time, that bore
through time the holy seed that knew no time—
I tell you, ghosts in the ghosts of summer days,
you are dead as though you never had been.
For time has caught on fire, and you too burn:
leaf, stem, branch, calyx and the bright corolla
are now the insubstantial wavering fire
in which love dies: the final pyre
of the beloved, the bridegroom and the bride.
These two we have denied.

In the beginning was the fire;
Out of the death of fire, rock and the waters;
and out of water and rock, the single spark, the divine truth.
Far, far below, the millions of rock-years divide
to make a place for those who were born and died
to build the house that held the bridegroom and the bride.
Those two, who reigned in passion in the flower,
whom still the hollow seasons celebrate,
no ritual now can recreate.
Whirled separate in the man-created fire
their cycles end, with the cycle of the holy seed;
the cycle from the first to the last fire.
These too time can divide;
these too have died.

And walking here among the dying centuries—
the centuries of moss, of fern, of cycad,
of the towering tree—the centuries of the flower—
I pause where water falls from the face of the rock.

My father rock, do you forget the kingdom of the fire?
The aeons grind you into bread—
into the soil that feeds the living and transforms the dead;

and have we eaten in the heart of the yellow wheat
the sullen unforgetting seed of fire?

And now, set free by the climate of man's hate,
that seed sets time ablaze.
The leaves of fallen years, the forest of living days,
have caught like matchwood. Look, the whole world burns.
The ancient kingdom of the fire returns.
And the world, that flower that housed the bridegroom and the bride,
burns on the breast of night.
The world's denied.

AT COOLOOLAH

The blue crane fishing in Cooloolah's twilight
has fished there longer than our centuries.
He is the certain heir of lake and evening,
and he will wear their colour till he dies,

but I'm a stranger, come of a conquering people.
I cannot share his calm, who watch his lake,
being unloved by all my eyes delight in,
and made uneasy, for an old murder's sake.

Those dark-skinned people who once named Cooloolah
knew that no land is lost or won by wars,
for earth is spirit: the invader's feet will tangle
in nets there and his blood be thinned by fears.

Riding at noon and ninety years ago,
my grandfather was beckoned by a ghost—
a black accoutred warrior armed for fighting,
who sank into bare plain, as now into time past.

White shores of sand, plumed reed and paperbark,
clear heavenly levels frequented by crane and swan—
I know that we are justified only by love,
but oppressed by arrogant guilt, have room for none.

And walking on clean sand among the prints
of bird and animal, I am challenged by a driftwood spear
thrust from the water; and, like my grandfather,
must quiet a heart accused by its own fear.

. . . AND MR. FERRITT

But now Mr Ferritt
with his troublesome nose,
with his shaven chin
and his voice like a grief
that grates in dark corners,
moves in his house
and scrapes his dry skin
and sees it is morning.

O day, you sly thief,
now what have you taken
of all the small things

I tie on my life?
The radio serial
whines in the kitchen,
caught in a box,
and cannot get out.
The finch in his cage,
the border of phlox
as straight as a string
drawn up in my garden,
the potted geranium,
all are there.
But day from his cranium
twitches one hair;
and never again
will a hair grow there.
—O day, you sly thief,
how you pluck at my life,
frets Mr Ferritt;
but there, he must bear it.

Outside the fence
the wattle-tree grows.
It tosses; it shines;
it speaks its one word.
Beware, beware!
Mr Ferritt has heard.
—What are axes for?
What are fences for?
Who planted that wattle-tree
right at my door?
God only knows.
All over the garden
its dust is shaken.
No wonder I sneeze
as soon as I waken.

O world, you sly thief;
my youth you have taken,
and what have you given
who promised me heaven,
but a nagging wife
and a chronic catarrh,
and a blonde on the pictures
as far as a star?
And wild and gold
as a film-star's hair
that tree stands there,
blocking the view
from my twenty-perch block.
What are axes for,
what are fences for
but to keep this tree
away from my door?

And down came the tree.
But poor Mr Ferritt
still has hay-fever.
Nothing will cure it.

Alun Lewis

Alun Lewis was born July 1, 1915, in Wales, and taught in a Welsh secondary school. In 1942, during the Second World War, he was sent to India. Two years later, he was killed in Lower Burma, March 15, 1944.

Raiders' Dawn (1942), Lewis's first book of poems, appeared in the same year as a collection of his short stories, *The Last Inspection*. His second book of poetry, *Ha! Ha! Among the Trumpets* (1945) was published shortly after his death with the title he had chosen, "a sardonic title," he said "from *Job* 39." It carried an appreciative foreword by Robert Graves which quoted some of Lewis's characteristic correspondence. A posthumous book of letters and hitherto unpublished stories, *In the Green Tree* (1949), is a tragic commentary on his life and early death.

Lewis's poetry is often marred by a compulsion to register immediate impressions without sufficient consideration or imagination. But it is not without dignity and the power of simple but penetrating statements.

THE UNKNOWN SOLDIER

Everything has lasted till today.
He stares upon it like a velvet king.
Velasquez might have made this flaccid mask,
The silence round the languid mouth,
The weak and glassy eyes, the crumpled brow.
All things are out-distanced now.

All days are heaped in wrath upon today.
The senses sleep except one crazy spark
That leaps the lesion slashed between his eyes
And cries—not for a fertile century,
Nor for the secular ransom of the soul—
But for a sip of water from my flask.
What is the soul to him?
He has outlasted everything.

Joy's deceitful liturgy has ceased.
Tomorrow and tomorrow have no place
Among the seas of rain, the seas of peace
That are the elements of this poor face.
The mean humiliating self no more
Has access to him, nor the friends
Whose sensual persuasions first began
The brittle scattering that this day ends.
On pander, lord and jester slams the door.
An impotent in his kingdom the grey king
No longer clings to that which dies.

He has abandoned everything.
Velasquez, close those doglike dolorous eyes.

TO A COMRADE IN ARMS

Red fool, my laughing comrade,
Hiding your woman's love
And your man's madness,
Patrolling farther than nowhere
To gain what is nearer than here,
Your face will grow grey as Christ's garments
With the dust of ditches and trenches,
So endlessly faring.

Red fool, my laughing comrade,
Hiding your mystic symbols
Of bread broken for eating
And palm-leaves strewn for welcome,
What foe will you make your peace with
This summer that is more cruel
Than the ancient God of the Hebrews?

When bees swarm in your nostrils
And honey drips from the sockets
Of eyes that to-day are frantic
With love that is frustrate,

What vow shall we vow who love you
For the self you did not value?

Alex Comfort

Alex Comfort was born in London February 10, 1920, and was educated at Highgate School and Trinity College, Cambridge. His first volume, *A Wreath for the Living* (1942), appeared when he was twenty-two; five more books were published while he was still in his mid-twenties. Nevertheless, Comfort considers his literary output secondary to his real career, which is that of a practicing physician, a researcher, and lecturer in physiology at London Hospital.

A collection of poems, *The Song of Lazarus* (1945) was published in the same year as *The Power House,* a challenging novel of great strength, to which was added another novel, *On This Side Nothing* (1949), and three plays. Comfort's poetry is part of "the new romanticism," a movement which runs counter to the consciously intellectual manner cultivated by Eliot, extended by Auden, and incorporated by their imitators. Rebelling against the canons of the cerebralists, Comfort evolves his own personal philosophy. It centers, as Kenneth Rexroth has written, about "the personality at war with death—physical death, or the mechanization of the State, and all the other institutions of irresponsibility and spiritual sloth." The resulting work is a largeness of conception and a lyric poetry which richly express its author's pacifism and his sensuous enjoyment of life.

FEAR OF THE EARTH

In these cold evenings, when the rain
streams, and the leaves stand closer shuffling feet
the woods grow perilous. They are hungry, the trees,
eavesdropping, sending long shoots to tap the pane.

I can hear you, root, under my hearthstone moving;
white finger, longer since yesterday, nearer
the marrow. In these evenings
the earth leans closer: stones quietly jostle.

I can hear you, under my foot bending
your strange finger. I have heard
cold fruits of my flesh plotted, soft globes swaying—
have known of my skin a leaf foreshadowed.

The captive roses jostle under the hedge.
The celandine is innocent. Underneath
her finger fumbles eyeholes. Every petal
speaks man not hardy nor perennial.

The trees grow perilous. The patient dandelion
should not remain at large in our terrible garden.

EPITAPH

One whom I knew, a student and a poet,
makes his way shorewards tonight out of the sea
blown to a houseless coast near Bettystown
where along sleeping miles the sea is laying
printless meadows of sand, and beyond them to seaward
endless untrodden fields louder than corn. These nets
follow the long beaches. Tonight a guest
noses his way to shore. They wait for him
where the sand meets the grass—and one unmarried holds
her spine's long intricate necklace for his shoulders
pillows his broken face, his for another's
for she died waiting. He will learn much
of roots and the way of sand and the small stones,
and that the shoreward dead are friends to all
at whose heels yell the clock-faced citizens.
So like a ship the dead man comes to shore.

NOTES FOR MY SON

(*From "The Song of Lazarus": VI*)

Remember when you hear them beginning to say Freedom
Look carefully—see who it is that they want you to butcher.

Remember, when you say that the old trick would not have
fooled you for a moment,
That every time it is the trick which seems new.

Remember that you will have to put in irons
Your better nature, if it will desert to them.

Remember, remember their faces—watch them carefully:
For every step you take is on somebody's body

And every cherry you plant for them is a gibbet,
And every furrow you turn for them is a grave.

Remember, the smell of burning will not sicken you
If they persuade you that it will thaw the world

Beware. The blood of a child does not smell so bitter
If you have shed it with a high moral purpose.

So that because the woodcutter disobeyed
they will not burn her today or any day

So that for lack of a joiner's obedience
The crucifixion will not now take place

So that when they come to sell you their bloody corruption
You will gather the spit of your chest
And plant it in their faces.

SONG FOR THE HEROES

I wonder sometimes if the soldiers lying
Under the soil, wrapped in their coats like beggars
sleeping under an arch, their hands filled with leaves
could take vengeance for once on the men who sent them,
coming back like beggars, seeing the homes and fields
that their obedience lost to them, the men of all countries

whether they would have anything to say
as ghosts at frosty windows to sons or brothers
other than this—"Obedience is death."
If you are willing to die, then choose obedience.

"We who are here now, men of all nations,
our hands are full of twigs, stones on our eyes,
half-afraid of what we have done (but that is forgotten

a short wild dream, when we were other men
not ourselves—but now we are ourselves again
tradesmen, farmers, students—it is we who are telling you)

you must choose carefully, for your life, and not only your life
will depend on it, in years or days, between believing
like us, that by obedience you could help or profit

the land, the fields, the people; and saying "Death is obedience."

"Because we know now that every cause is just
and time does not discriminate between the aggressor
and the dead child, the Regrettable Necessity

And the foul atrocity—the grass is objective
And turns all citizens into green mounds—
we have had time, as soldiers always have time,

resting before Plataea or Dunkirk or Albuhera
to think about obedience—though we will still spring up
at the whistle; it is too late to withdraw—that someone must pay
for all this, and it will be the people.

"We have nothing to tell you but this: to choose carefully
and if you must still obey, we are ready,
your fathers, grandfathers, great-grandfathers, to find you

a place at our dry table, to greet you as soldiers
with a dry nod, and sit, elbow to elbow
silently for always under the sky of soil:

but know you are choosing. When they begin to appeal
to your better nature, your righteous indignation,
your pity for men like yourselves, stand still,

look down and see the lice upon your hide.

"It may be that you, or else your children, at last
will put down your hand and crush them. But if not
remember that we are waiting, good men as you,

not fools, but men who knew the price of obeying,
the lice for what they were, the Cause for a fraud,
hoped for no good and cherished no illusions;

and we will see your mounds spring up in clusters
beside our own, and welcome you with a nod,
crucified like us all, all fellow-ghosts together,
not fooled by the swine, but going with open eyes.

"You have only to speak once—they will melt like smoke,
you have only to meet their eyes—they will go
howling like devils into bottomless death

but if you choose to obey, we shall not blame you
for every lesson is new. We will make room for you
in this cold hall, where every cause is just.

Perhaps you will go with us to frosty windows
putting the same choice as the years go round
eavesdropping when the Gadarenes call our children

or sit debating—when will they disobey?

wrapped in our coats against the impartial cold."
All this I think the buried men would say
clutching their white ribs and their rusted helmets

nationless bones, under the still ground.

Sidney Keyes

Sidney Keyes was born May 27, 1922, in Dartford, Kent. His mother died of peritonitis a few weeks after her son was born, and his father, who had been in war service in India, entrusted the boy to his grandparents. His grandfather, a farmer who had become a famous miller, dominated the child who was sickly and so Keyes did not attend school until he was nine. At sixteen he began to write poems that were unusually perceptive. He was drawn to such visionaries as

Blake, Yeats, Hölderlin, and Rilke, but he was also attracted to the macabre suggestions of Donne, Webster, Beddoes, Rouault, and Klee.

At nineteen he prepared a volume of poems and gave it a title, *The Iron Laurel,* but as the manuscript was about to go to press, Keyes persuaded the publisher to postpone issuing the book. A few months later he entered the Army. He was in Africa less than two weeks when, during the Tunisian campaign he was sent forward with a dawn patrol. He was taken prisoner and died, according to the report, "of unknown causes" on April 29, 1943.

Like Charles Hamilton Sorley, another poet-victim of war who also died before he was twenty-one, Keyes had no use for the glib patriotics of wartime propaganda. "How can we account for the fact that a whole nation has gone stark mad with love of death?" he said in a letter. "The contemporary German attitude to death appears to be one of hopeless infatuation, mixed with fear and repulsion . . . Perhaps their task is to explore death, just as it has been that of the Jews to explore pain, and of the French (perhaps) to explore the possibilities of pleasure, whether of the intellect or the senses . . . It remains for someone to make an art of love, a much harder task."

It is the exploration of love which directs Keyes's lyrical impulses. Such poems as "Neutrality," "William Yeats in Limbo," and "The Gardener" are both intellectual and emotional. They share, as Harold Nicolson wrote, "with others of his age a dark resentment at the denial of opportunity; but with him resentment is no mere mood of irritation; it has about it a solemn tone of fate. It is not, therefore, his amazing poetic skill only which differentiates Sidney Keyes from so many of his contemporaries, but above all his grave acceptance of the tragedy to which his youth was destined."

NEUTRALITY

Here not the flags, the rhythmic
Feet of returning legions; nor at household shrines
The small tears' offering, the postcards
Treasured for years, nor the names cut in brass.
Here not the lowered voices.
Not the drum.

Only at suppertime, rain slanting
Among our orchards, printing its coded
But peaceful messages across our pavements.
Only the cryptic swift performing
His ordered evolutions through our sky.
Only the growing.

And in the night, the secret voices
Of summer, the progression
Of hours without suspense, without surprise.
Only the moon beholds us, even the hunting owl
May watch us without malice.
Without envy.

We are no cowards, we are pictures
Of ordinary people, as you once were.
Blame not nor pity us; we are the people
Who laugh in dreams before the ramping boar
Appears, before the loved one's death.
We are your hope.

THE GARDENER

If you will come on such a day
As this, between the pink and yellow lines
Of parrot-tulips, I will be your lover.
My boots flash as they beat the silly gravel.
O come, this is your day.

Were you to lay your hand like a veined leaf
Upon my square-cut hand, I would caress
The shape of it, and that would be enough.
I note the greenfly working on the rose.
Time slips between my fingers like a leaf.

Do you resemble the silent pale-eyed angels
That follow children? Is your face a flower?
The lovers and the beggars leave the park—
And still you will not come. The gates are closing.

O it is terrible to dream of angels.

GREENWICH OBSERVATORY

This onion-dome holds all intricacies
Of intellect and star-struck wisdom; so
Like Coleridge's head with multitudinous
Passages riddled, full of strange instruments
Unbalanced by a touch, this organism
From wires and dials spins introverted life.
It never looks, squat on its concrete shoulders,
Down at the river's swarming life, nor sees
Cranes' groping insect-like activity
Nor slow procession of funnels past the docks.
Turning its inner wheels, absorbed in problems
Of space and time, it never hears
Birds singing in the park or children's laughter
Alive, but in another way, it broods
On this its Highgate, hypnotized
In lunar reverie and calculation.
Yet night awakes it; blind lids open
Leaden to look upon the moon:
A single goggling telescopic eye
Enfolds the spheric wonder of the sky.

WILLIAM YEATS IN LIMBO

Where folds the central lotus
Flesh and soul could never seek?
Under what black-scar'd mountain
May Pallas with Adonis meet?

Spirit-bodies' loveliness
Cannot expiate my pain:
How should I learn wisdom
Being old and profane?

My thoughts have swarmed like bees
In an old ruined tower:
How should I go to drive them out
Lacking joy and power?

How could I learn youth again,
With figured symbols weaving
Truth so easily, now I
Am old and unbelieving?

By what chicanery of time
May sword and sheath be separated?
Silent be the singer who thinks of me
And how I was defeated.

EARLY SPRING

Now that the young buds are tipped with a falling sun—
Each twig a candle, a martyr, St. Julian's branched stag—
And the shadows are walking the cobbled square like soldiers
With their long legs creaking and their pointed hands
Reaching the railings and fingering the stones
Of what expended, unprojected graves:
The soil's a flirt, the lion Time is tamed,
And pain like a cat will come home to share your room.

Philip Larkin

⁂ Philip Larkin was born August 9, 1922, in Coventry, Warwickshire. He was educated at King Henry School in Coventry and St. John's College, Oxford. After leaving Oxford he presided over a small independent public library in Shropshire for nearly three years, then went as librarian to the University of Leicester, then to the Queen's University of Belfast, and then to the University of Hull. When asked why he chose to be a librarian, he replied, "A librarian is what you are when you have failed to do all the things you do want to do and have succeeded in avoiding all the things you don't want to do."

Before he was convinced that he was meant to be a poet he was sure that he was a novelist. Two novels, *Jill* (1946) and *A Girl in Winter* (1947), promised more than his first book of poems, *The North Ship* (1945). *A Girl in Winter* is an extraordinary evocation of sensibility and atmosphere, of unhappiness and tenderness, embodied in a language that is both plain and poetic. The combination of plainness and poetic subtlety marks the poetry in *The Less Deceived* (1955). Colloquial and, at first glance, commonplace, Larkin's verse is completely convincing; it is, wrote Walter Allen, "unemphatic, as unrhetorical as it is possible for poetry to be and yet remain poetry . . . It is unillusioned, skeptical, resolutely determined to claim nothing for itself that it has not experienced at its own nerve-ends."

Using the most unpretentions means, Larkin somehow distills the essence of the ordinary scene and the trivial moment while, at the same time, he suggests the importance of the inconsequential. He has the gift, rare in his times, of clarity, and a way of making things and events appear both "irrelevant and beautiful." The tone is casual and the touch is deceptively light, but the import is serious, immediate, and effectively communicated.

COMING

On longer evenings,
Light, chill and yellow,
Bathes the serene
Foreheads of houses.
A thrush sings,
Laurel-surrounded
In the deep bare garden,
Its fresh-peeled voice
Astonishing the brickwork.
It will be spring soon,
It will be spring soon—
And I, whose childhood
Is a forgotten boredom,
Feel like a child
Who comes on a scene
Of adult reconciling,
And can understand nothing
But the unusual laughter,
And starts to be happy.

NEXT, PLEASE

Always too eager for the future, we
Pick up bad habits of expectancy.
Something is always approaching; every day
Till then we say,

Watching from a bluff the tiny, clear,
Sparkling armada of promises draw near.
How slow they are! And how much time they waste,
Refusing to make haste!

Yet still they leave us holding wretched stalks
Of disappointment, for, though nothing balks
Each big approach, leaning with brasswork prinked,
Each rope distinct,

Flagged, and the figurehead with golden tits
Arching our way, it never anchors; it's
No sooner present than it turns to past.
Right to the last

We think each one will heave to and unload
All good into our lives, all we are owed
For waiting so devoutly and so long.
But we are wrong:

Only one ship is seeking us, a black-
Sailed unfamiliar, towing at her back
A huge and birdless silence. In her wake
No waters breed or break.

NO ROAD

Since we agreed to let the road between us
Fall to disuse,
And bricked our gates up, planted trees to screen us,
And turned all time's eroding agents loose,
Silence, and space, and strangers—our neglect
Has not had much effect.

Leaves drift unswept, perhaps; grass creeps unmown;
No other change.
So clear it stands, so little overgrown,
Walking that way tonight would not seem strange,
And still would be allowed. A little longer,
And time will be the stronger,

Drafting a world where no such road will run
From you to me;
To watch that world come up like a cold sun,
Rewarding others, is my liberty.
Not to prevent it is my will's fulfilment.
Willing it, my ailment.

SPRING

Green-shadowed people sit, or walk in rings,
Their children finger the awakened grass,
Calmly a cloud stands, calmly a bird sings,
And, flashing like a dangled looking-glass,
Sun lights the balls that bounce, the dogs that bark,
The branch-arrested mist of leaf, and me,
Threading my pursed-up way across the park,
An indigestible sterility.

Spring, of all seasons most gratuitous,
Is fold of untaught flower, is race of water,
Is earth's most multiple, excited daughter;

And those she has least use for see her best,
Their paths grown craven and circuitous,
Their visions mountain-clear, their needs immodest.

ARRIVALS, DEPARTURES

This town has docks where channel boats come sidling;
Tame water lanes, tall sheds, the traveller sees
(His bag of samples knocking at his knees),
And hears, still under slackened engines gliding,
His advent blurted to the morning shore.

And we, barely recalled from sleep there, sense
Arrivals lowing in a doleful distance—
Horny dilemmas at the gate once more.
Come and choose wrong, they cry, *come and choose wrong;*
And so we rise. At night again they sound,

Calling the traveller now, the outward bound:
O not for long, they cry, *O not for long—*

And we are nudged from comfort, never knowing
How safely we may disregard their blowing,
Or if, this night, happiness too is going.

CHURCH GOING

Once I am sure there's nothing going on
I step inside, letting the door thud shut.
Another church: matting, seats, and stone,
And little books; sprawlings of flowers, cut
For Sunday, brownish now; some brass and stuff
Up at the holy end; the small neat organ;
And a tense, musty, unignorable silence,
Brewed God knows how long. Hatless, I take off
My cycle-clips in awkward reverence,

Move forward, run my hand around the font.
From where I stand, the roof looks almost new—
Cleaned, or restored? Someone would know: I don't.
Mounting the lectern, I peruse a few
Hectoring large-scale verses, and pronounce
'Here endeth' much more loudly than I'd meant.
The echoes snigger briefly. Back at the door
I sign the book, donate an Irish sixpence,
Reflect the place was not worth stopping for.

Yet stop I did: in fact I often do,
And always end much at a loss like this,
Wondering what to look for; wondering, too,
When churches fall completely out of use
What we shall turn them into, if we shall keep
A few cathedrals chronically on show,
Their parchment, plate and pyx in locked cases,
And let the rest rent-free to rain and sheep.
Shall we avoid them as unlucky places?

Or, after dark, will dubious women come
To make their children touch a particular stone;
Pick simples for a cancer; or on some
Advised night see walking a dead one?
Power of some sort or other will go on
In games, in riddles, seemingly at random;
But superstition, like belief, must die,
And what remains when disbelief has gone?
Grass, weedy pavement, brambles, buttress, sky,

A shape less recognisable each week,
A purpose more obscure. I wonder who
Will be the last, the very last, to seek
This place for what it was; one of the crew
That tap and jot and know what rood-lofts were?

Some ruin-bibber, randy for antique,
Or Christmas-addict, counting on a whiff
Of gown-and-bands and organ-pipes and myrrh?
Or will he be my representative,

Bored, uninformed, knowing the ghostly silt
Dispersed, yet tending to this cross of ground
Through suburb scrub because it held unspilt
So long and equably what since is found
Only in separation—marriage, and birth,
And death, and thoughts of these—for whom was built
This special shell? For, though I've no idea
What this accoutred frowsty barn is worth,
It pleases me to stand in silence here;

A serious house on serious earth it is,
In whose blent air all our compulsions meet,
Are recognised, and robed as destinies.
And that much never can be obsolete,
Since someone will forever be surprising
A hunger in himself to be more serious,
And gravitating with it to this ground,
Which, he once heard, was proper to grow wise in,
If only that so many dead lie round.

Charles Tomlinson

Charles Tomlinson was born in 1927 in Staffordshire and attended Queen's College, Cambridge. After living in London and Northern Italy, he came to Somerset and taught at Bristol University. His first volume, *The Necklace,* was published in 1955, his second, *Seeing Is Believing,* in 1958.

Concerning his aims Tomlinson wrote: "The hardness of crystals, the facets of cut glass, but also the shifting of light, the energizing weather which is a result of the combination of sun and frost—these are the images for a certain mental climate, components for the moral landscape of my poetry in general." Such a description pronounces the limitations of Tomlinson's poetry which tends to be more visual than emotional or "moral." Praised by Richard Wilbur for its "kinetic imagination" as "the freshest, most exhilarating book of poems to come out of England in years," *Seeing Is Believing* owes something to Wilbur and more to another American poet, Wallace Stevens.

Tomlinson's world is a special one, one in which he seems to be a spectator rather than a participator. The craftsmanship is dazzling; the designs are clean, smooth, and highly polished; the results are cool, elegant, and eclectic. There is, however, an intellectual searching beneath the surface texture, and if the phrasing sometimes tends to be precious, it is never without the air of distinction and the charm of surprise.

THE CRANE

That insect, without antennae, over its
Cotton-spool lip, letting
An almost invisible tenuity
Of steel cable, drop
Some seventy feet, with the
Grappling hook hidden also
Behind a dense foreground
Among which it is fumbling, and
Over which, mantis-like
It is begging or threatening, gracile
From a clear sky—that paternal
Constructive insect, without antennae,
Would seem to assure us that
"The future is safe, because
It is in my hands." And we do not
Doubt this veracity, we can only
Fear it—as many of us
As pause here to remark
Such silent solicitude
For lifting intangible weights
Into real walls.

THE JAM TRAP

Wings filmed, the threads of knowledge thicken
Corded with mire. Bodies immerse
Slackly in sweetness. Sweetness is not satisfaction
Nor was the elation of the pursuit
The measure of its end. Aromas and inclinations
Delectable essences, and now
The inextricable gesture, sounds
Which communicate nothing, their sole speech
A scurrying murmur, each to himself his own
Monotone burden of discouragement. Preferring
The fed flock that, scattered, re-forms
Massed into echelon above copious fields,
The sky, their chosen element, has abandoned them.

IN DEFENSE OF METAPHYSICS

Place is the focus. What is the language
Of stones? I do not mean
As emblems of patience, philosophers' hopes
Or as the astrological tangents
One may assemble, draw out subjectively
From a lapidary inertia. Only we
Are inert. Stones act, like pictures, by remaining
Always the same, unmoving, waiting on presence
Unpredictable in absence, inhuman
In a human dependence, a physical
Point of contact, for a movement not physical
And on a track of force, the milestone
Between two infinities. Stones are like deaths.
They uncover limits.

Index of Authors and Titles

The names of authors and the page references to the sections devoted to their work are shown in italics. Titles of poems are shown in roman.

D
E 5
F 6
G 7
H 8
I 9
J 0
K 1